Fundamentals of Organizational Behavior

W9-APJ-009

2 EDITION

Andrew J. DuBrin

Professor of Management
College of Business
Rochester Institute of Technology

SOUTH-WESTERN

THOMSON LEARNING

Australia · Canada · Mexico · Singapore · Spain · United Kingdom · United States

Fundamentals of Organizational Behavior, 2e
By Andrew J. DuBrin

Vice President/Publisher: Jack W. Calhoun
Executive Editor: John Szilagyi
Developmental Editor: Judith O'Neill
Marketing Manager: Rob Bloom
Marketing Coordinator: Shannon O'Callaghan
Production Manager: Sharon L. Smith
Production Editor: Starratt E. Alexander
Manufacturing Coordinator: Sandee Milewski
Internal Design: Ann Small, A Small Design Studio, Cincinnati
Cover Design: Rik Moore
Cover Illustration: Rob Colvin, Artville, LLC
Photo Manager: Cary Benbow
Production House and Compositor: Navta Associates, Inc.
Printer: Courier Kendallville, Inc.

Printed in the United States of America
1 2 3 4 5 04 03 02 01

For more information contact South-Western College Publishing,
5101 Madison Road, Cincinnati, Ohio, 45227 or find us on the Internet at
http://www.swcollege.com

For permission to use material from this text or product, contact us by
• telephone: 1-800-730-2214
• fax: 1-800-730-2215
• web: http://www.thomsonrights.com

Library of Congress Cataloging-in-Publication Data
DuBrin, Andrew J.
    Fundamentals of organizational behavior : an applied approach/
  Andrew J. DuBrin.—2nd ed.
      p. cm.
  Includes bibliographical references and index.
  ISBN 0-324-02281-6 (alk. paper)
  1. Organizational behavior. I. Title.

HD58.7.D8 2002
158.7—dc21   00-053823

Welcome to the second and slightly expanded edition of *Fundamentals of Organizational Behavior*. This book is designed for courses in organizational behavior and management that focus on the application of organizational behavior knowledge to achieve enhanced productivity, quality, and satisfaction in the workplace. In short, organizational behavior is about human behavior on the job, and, as such, knowledge of organizational behavior, clearly, is an important repository for any manager to draw on. Yet the same information that can propel a manager to excel can also assist individual organizational contributors in becoming more adaptive and effective. Nonmanagerial professionals, technology workers, sales representatives, and service providers of all stripes surely benefit from the insight and analysis that organizational behavior conveys just as surely as do managers and prospective managers. All are welcome under its umbrella. Ever wonder about the tactical and strategic decisions that managers make in beating back the skeptics or in competing in a down market? The study of organizational behavior can provide you with a window into those decisions and the actions that result therefrom.

Organizational behavior, because of its key contributions in driving workforce productivity, is a standard part of the curriculum in schools and colleges of business, management, and public administration. As a result, there is a proliferation of research and writing in the field. To present just an overview of this vast amount of information, many introductory texts are lengthy indeed, easily spilling over onto 800 or more pages. To soften the impact of such encyclopedic approaches to the study of organizational behavior, many of these texts also lavishly layer figures and photographs onto their extended narratives, but *Fundamentals of Organizational Behavior* takes an altogether different tack. It takes a briefer, more focused, and more applied approach to learning about the field. Instead of trying to dazzle with a baffling array of concepts, research findings, theories, and news clippings, this text judiciously concentrates on only the most useful ideas. It blends clear and thoughtful exposition of traditional topics, such as motivation, with topics of more recent origin, such as partnering, self-managing teams, knowledge management, and diversity. And although each chapter packs in a lot of information, it is information that always cuts to the chase, so to speak. We also assure you that it is practical, ready-to-use information that you can put into action as soon as you leave the classroom.

To achieve a more concise text, we were very selective about what to include in each chapter. Our major strategy was to omit elaborate theories and findings that are no longer the subject of active research, practice, or training programs. However, we did not permit a concern with brevity to strip the text down to a sterile outline devoid of human interest, examples, and useful applications.

The size and scope of the book are well suited to college courses that supplement a core textbook with journal articles, major projects, speciality texts, or other instructional media. The comprehensiveness of *Fundamentals of Organizational Behavior*, combined with its brevity, make it suitable for organizational training programs about human behavior in the workplace as well. The student who masters this text will not only acquire an overview of and appreciation for organizational behavior research, literature, theory, and opinion but, additionally, will develop a feel for managing and influencing others through the application of systematic knowledge about human behavior.

THE FEATURES

In addition to summarizing and synthesizing relevant information about each organizational behavior topic and providing concrete examples of its theories in action, *Fundamentals of Organizational Behavior* incorporates many useful features to make the material more accessible, collaborative, and incisive as each chapter unfolds. It also works hard to be technologically relevant. Internet addresses are integrated into every chapter, at the end of opening vignettes, as part of Organizational Behavior in Action boxes and Case Problems, and in a new end-of-chapter problem set, Organizational Behavior On-line.

- *Learning Objectives* introduce the major themes of each chapter and provide a framework for study.
- *Definitions* of boldfaced key terms are highlighted in the text and are reinforced at the end of each chapter and in an end-of-book glossary.
- *Opening Vignettes* explore real organizational issues, highlighting the stake all types of organizations have in using human capital well. Each vignette concludes by asking and answering the "so what" question, ensuring that *Fundamentals of Organizational Behavior* addresses the usefulness of organizational behavior ideas, not just the ideas themselves.
- *Organizational Behavior in Action* boxes isolate the actions of managers and professionals in dealing effectively with the human aspects of management, making visible the connection between theory and practice.
- *Self-Assessments* and *Skill-Development Exercises* support self-directed learning while driving the connections between research, theory, and practice down to the personal level. They not only provide a point of departure for students in understanding and valuing their own individual attitudes and behaviors but also serve to create an ongoing dialogue as each assessment and exercise can be returned to many times over the course of a semester.
- *Implications for Managerial Practice* boxes, located near the end of each chapter, set off several smart suggestions for applying organizational behavior information in a managerial context.
- End-of-chapter *Summaries of Key Points* integrate all key topics and concepts into several cogent paragraphs and link them with the chapter's stated learning objectives.
- *Key Terms and Phrases* provide a useful review of each chapter's terminology.
- End-of-chapter *Discussion Questions and Activities* are suitable for individual or group analysis.

- *Organizational Behavior On-line* combines "To Do" exercises and "To Bookmark" resources.
- End-of-chapter *Case Problems* illustrate major themes of the chapter and are again suitable for individual or group analysis. Case Problems are uniquely designed to complement this text and include relevant follow-up discussion questions and links to related Web sites.
- A brief list of *Suggested Readings* points the reader to more in-depth information on chapter topics and provides ideas for research papers.

THE FRAMEWORK

Fundamentals of Organizational Behavior is a blend of description, skill development, insight, and prescription. Divided into four parts, it moves from the micro to the macro, beginning with a brief introduction to the discipline. It then moves to an exploration of the individual, to a discussion of groups and intergroup dynamics, to an examination of organizational systems.

As just noted, Part 1 provides an introduction to organizational behavior. Chapter 1 focuses on the nature and scope of organizational behavior and provides the foundation for what is to come.

Part 2 includes six chapters that deal with the individual in the organization. Chapter 2 describes fundamental aspects of understanding individuals in terms of individual differences, diversity, ability, and personality. Chapter 3 describes individuals from the standpoint of learning, perception, attitudes, values, and ethics. Chapter 4 is about individual decision making and creativity. Chapter 5 presents basic concepts of motivation and Chapter 6 discusses techniques for enhancing motivation. Chapter 7 describes the nature and management of conflict and stress.

Part 3, about groups and intergroup relations, contains four chapters. Chapter 8 is about interpersonal communications, and Chapter 9 covers group dynamics and teamwork. Chapter 10 deals with leadership, a cornerstone topic in organizational behavior and management. Chapter 11 extends the study of leadership by describing power, politics, and influence.

Part 4, about the organizational system and the global environment, contains four chapters covering macro issues in organizational behavior. Chapter 12 deals with organizational structure and design. Chapter 13 is about organizational culture and change. Chapter 14 covers a contemporary topic of major importance: organizational learning and knowledge management. Chapter 15 covers cultural diversity and international organizational behavior.

THE FACTS—The Second Edition, New and Enhanced

The second edition expands and thoroughly updates the first edition, with particular attention paid to refueling many first-edition features. Longer end-of-chapter case problems, longer boxed inserts on organizational behavior in action, more self-assessments, and more emphasis on career management enrich this edition. Other general changes include the timely integration of technology throughout, a brief Internet exercise for each chapter, useful URLs to bookmark now and mine later, more insights and analysis on cultural diversity, and more narrative written specifically around the exhibits (or figures). About 85 percent of the case problems, lead-in case vignettes, and boxed inserts about organizational behavior in action are new. Major additions and new or enhanced topical coverage are listed here, chapter by chapter:

Chapter 1: Meta-analysis; productivity advantages of concentrating on people.

Chapter 2: Self-esteem and productivity; multiple intelligences; risk taking and thrill seeking.

Chapter 3: Comparison of value stereotypes of Baby Boomers, Generation X, and Generation Y.

Chapter 4: The influence of procrastination on decision making.

Chapter 5: Learning goal orientation versus performance goal orientation.

Chapter 6: Motivation through recognition and stock options.

Chapter 7: Recent U.S. Supreme Court rulings on sexual harassment; personal dispositions as contributors to conflict; an approach to conflict resolution labeled confront, contain, and connect.

Chapter 8: E-mail etiquette; communication problems created by presentation technology; power-oriented linguistic style.

Chapter 9: The take-charge leadership role within a group.

Chapter 10: Emotional intelligence and leadership; the leader's role in managing polarities; the situational leadership model; 360-degree feedback for improving leadership effectiveness.

Chapter 11: Signs of empowerment versus disempowerment; flattery as an influence tactic.

Chapter 12: Social network analysis; organigraph organizational charts; hybrid organization structure; outsourcing.

Chapter 13: Transition from tight job descriptions to flexible work roles; managing change for oneself.

Chapter 14: An entirely new chapter on organizational learning and knowledge management; includes the 4I framework.

Chapter 15: Cultural diversity considerably expanded; role of mentoring in facilitating the career progress of minorities; importance of respect in cross-cultural relations with issues underpinning the new economy, with more coverage of diversity, e-business, information technology, knowledge management, and the push for building leaner and more adaptive global organizations.

THE RESOURCES

Fundamentals of Organizational Behavior is accompanied by the following comprehensive instructional and learning support materials:

Experiencing OB

- *Experiencing Organizational Behavior,* by R. Dennis Middlemist, of Colorado State University. Optional access to this award-winning collection of Web-based modules on organizational behavior principles is available only on-line at http://www.experiencingob.com. Designed to reinforce key ideas and theories through a combination of text and animated models, *Experiencing Organizational Behavior* offers additional support right at your workstation. Lets you explore questions as they arise, order and organize what you have learned, and integrate new material with what you already know. Visit http://www. experiencingob.com for more information, including a free demo.

- An *Instructor's Manual with Test Bank* (ISBN 0-324-02282-4). Available in print or for download at http://dubrin.swcollege.com, this author-generated manual includes an exceptional array of instructional resources, all geared to offering instructors insights into how course content might be taught. Each chapter includes an outline along with key lecture notes; answers to end-of-chapter discussion questions and activities, usually in the form of a comment rather than an absolute; and notes about the self-assessments and skill-building exercises. An examination for each chapter is also included, with 25 multiple-choice questions, 25 true/false questions, and three or four essays. Appendix A contains suggestions for using Computer-Assisted Scenario Analysis (CASA). Especially designed to help students develop a contingency point of view, CASA is a user-friendly technique that can be used with any word-processing software. It allows the student to insert a new scenario into case problems and then answer questions based on the new scenario. CASA helps to develop an awareness of the contingency factor in making decisions. A briefer version of CASA was published in the October 1992 issue of the *Journal of Management Education*. Appendix B contains the answers to chapter exams. Transparency masters, which duplicate key figures from the text, are also rolled into the manual, as is integration of BusinessLink video cases.

- *PowerPoint™ Slides.* New to this edition! Over 250 slides to supplement course content are available for download at http://dubrin.swcollege.com. For use by students as note-taking guides and by instructors to enhance lectures, these full-color images were designed to help you get the most out of your experience with *Fundamentals of Organizational Behavior*.

- *ExamView Testing Software* (ISBN 0-324-11855-4). New to this edition! ExamView testing software contains all of the questions in the printed Test Bank. ExamView is an easy-to-use test-creation program compatible with Microsoft Windows. Instructors can add or edit questions, instructions, and answers. Instructors can also create and administer quizzes online, whether over the Internet, a local area network (LAN), or a wide area network (WAN).

- *BusinessLink Video* (ISBN 0-324-02285-9). A new library of five video case studies provides an excellent platform for classroom analysis of the experiences and challenges of a range of innovative businesses, including Yahoo!, Valassis Communications, and the W. B. Doner advertising agency, whose clients include Mazda, Blockbuster, and May Department Stores, among others.

- *CNN Video: Management and Organizations* (ISBN 0-324-13495-9). New to this edition! Features short segments from CNN's Headline News, CNNfn (the financial network), CNN Today, Movers with Jan Hopkins, and other programs to use as lecture launchers, discussion starters, or topical introductions.

ACKNOWLEDGMENTS

The final topical content and organization of this text were heavily influenced by the results of a survey of professors who expressed interest in using a shorter, more concise text. Instructors from 50 colleges provided their opinions on what subjects form the foundation of their courses. They also provided feedback on the types of pedagogical activities and features provide real value to the introductory organizational behavior course.

The comments of the survey respondents were enhanced by contributions from the following instructors who provided detailed reviews during development of this new edition:

David C. Baldridge—*University of Connecticut*
Talya N. Bauer—*Portland State University*
Regina M. O'Neill—*Suffolk University*

Mary Humphrys—*University of Toledo*
Marianne W. Lewis—*University of Cincinnati*
James Smas—*Kent State University*
Mary Anne Watson—*University of Tampa*
Lori K. Young—*Kent State University*

Thanks also to the staff at South-Western who worked with me to publish this new edition of *Fundamentals of Organizational Behavior:* executive editor John Szilagyi, developmental editor Judy O'Neill, marketing manager Rob Bloom, production editor Starratt Alexander, designer Rick Moore, and photo manager Cary Benbow.

My special thanks also go to Professors Douglas Benton of Colorado State University, Terri Scandura of the University of Miami, and Ann Welsh of the University of Cincinnati, who read the entire first-edition manuscript and made many valuable suggestions, that continue to inform my work.

Finally, writing without loved ones would be a lonely task. My thanks therefore go to my family: Drew, Douglas, Gizella, Melanie, Rosemary, and Clare. Thanks also to Carole, the woman in my life, for the happiness she brings me.

Andrew J. DuBrin

ABOUT THE AUTHOR

Andrew J. DuBrin is professor of management in the College of Business at the Rochester Institute of Technology, where he teaches courses and conducts research in management, organizational behavior, leadership, and career management. He has served the college as chairman of the management department and as team leader. He received his Ph.D. in industrial psychology from Michigan State University. His business experience is in human resource management and he consults with organizations and with individuals. His specialties include leadership and career management.

DuBrin is an established author of both textbooks and trade titles and also writes for professional journals, magazines, and newspapers. He has written textbooks on the principles of management [including *Essentials of Management*, now in its fifth edition for South-Western College Publishing], leadership, organizational behavior, industrial psychology, and human relations. His trade titles cover many current issues, including reengineering, team play, office politics, coping with adversity, and overcoming career self-sabotage.

Preface   iii

PART 1   Introduction to Organizational Behavior

1   The Nature and Scope of Organizational Behavior   1

PART 2   The Individual in the Organization

2   Individual Differences, Mental Ability, and Personality   19
3   Learning, Perception, Attitudes, Values, and Ethics   41
4   Individual Decision Making and Creativity   65
5   Foundation Concepts of Motivation   87
6   Motivational Methods and Programs   109
7   Conflict, Stress, and Well-Being   133

PART 3   Groups and Interpersonal Relations

8   Interpersonal Communication   159
9   Group Dynamics and Teamwork   183
10   Leadership in Organizations   207
11   Power, Politics, and Influence   237

PART 4   The Organizational System and the Global Environment

12   Organization Structure and Design   255
13   Organizational Culture and Change   277
14   The Learning Organization and Knowledge Management   305
15   Cultural Diversity and International Organizational Behavior   323

Glossary   347
Index   357

Contents

Preface iii

PART 1 Introduction to Organizational Behavior

1 The Nature and Scope of Organizational Behavior   1
The Meaning and Research Methods of Organizational Behavior .   2
How You Can Benefit from Studying Organizational Behavior . . .   4
A Brief History of Organizational Behavior   6
The Productivity Advantage of Focusing on People 10
Skill Development in Organizational Behavior 10
A Framework for Studying Organizational Behavior 12

PART 2 The Individual in the Organization

2 Individual Differences, Mental Ability, and Personality 19
Individual Differences 20
Demographic Diversity 22
Mental Ability 26
Personality Differences 30

3 Learning, Perception, Attitudes, Values, and Ethics 41
Learning 42
Perception 45
Attitudes 48
Values 50
Ethics 53

4 Individual Decision Making and Creativity 65
Types of Decisions 66
A Classical/Behavioral Decision-Making Model 67
Bounded Rationality and Influences on Decision Making 70
The Nature of Creativity 74
Enhancing and Improving Creativity 80

5 Foundation Concepts of Motivation 87
Need Theories of Motivation 88
Goal-Setting Theory 94
Reinforcement Theory 96
Expectancy Theory of Motivation 97
Equity Theory and Social Comparison 99
Social Learning Theory 100
Intrinsic Versus Extrinsic Motivation 101

6 Motivational Methods and Programs 109
Motivation through Job Design 110
Organizational Behavior Modification 117
Rules for the Application of OB Mod 119
Motivation through Recognition 121
Motivation through Financial Incentives 122
Choosing an Appropriate Motivational Model 126

7 Conflict, Stress, and Well-Being 133
Conflict in Organizations 134
Functional and Dysfunctional Consequences of Conflict 139
Work Stress 144
Organizational Approaches to Stress Management 150

PART 3 Groups and Interpersonal Relations

8 Interpersonal Communication 159
The Communication Process 160
Communication and Information Technology 161
Nonverbal Communication 165
Organizational Channels of Communication 166
Barriers to Interpersonal Communication 169
Overcoming Communication Barriers 171
Dealing with Gender Differences in Communication Style 173
The Power-Oriented Linguistic Style 176

9 Group Dynamics and Teamwork 183
Types of Groups and Teams 184
Stages of Group Development 189
Characteristics of Effective Work Groups 191
Group Problem Solving and Decision Making 195
Potential Problems within Groups 196
Building Teamwork 200

1 0 Leadership in Organizations 207
The Nature of Leadership 208
Leadership Traits and Characteristics 209
Contingency Theories of Leadership 216
Transformational and Charismatic Leadership 223
360-Degree Feedback for Improving Leadership Effectiveness . . . 227

Gender Differences in Leadership 228
Leadership Substitutes and Followership 229

1 1 Power, Politics, and Influence 237
The Meaning of Power, Politics, and Influence 238
Sources of Individual and Subunit Power 238
Empowerment of Group Members 240
Factors Contributing to and Examples of Political Behavior 242
Organizational Influence Tactics 248
The Control of Dysfunctional Politics and Ethical Considerations . 249

PART 4 The Organizational System and the Global Environment

1 2 Organizational Structure and Design 255
Foundation Concepts of Organizational Structure 256
The Bureaucratic Form of Organization 259
Key Modifications of the Bureaucratic Structure 265
Leading-Edge Organization Structures 268
Organigraphs: Drawing How Companies Really Work 270

1 3 Organization Culture and Change 277
Organizational Culture 278
General Considerations about Managing Change 282
Why People Resist Change 285
Downsizing and Restructuring as a Change Strategy 287
Organization Development as a Change Strategy 292
Managing Change Yourself 296

1 4 The Learning Organization and Knowledge Management 305
The Learning Organization 306
Building Blocks of a Learning Organization 309
Knowledge Management 313
Knowledge Management Strategies and Techniques 314
Methods for Sharing Information 316

1 5 Cultural Diversity and International Organizational Behavior 323
Cultural Diversity: Scope, Competitive Advantages, and
Success Factors 324
Cross-Cultural Values 328
Multicultural Managers and Organizations 333
Barriers to Good Cross-Cultural Relations 335
Cross-Cultural Processes 336
Diversity Training and Cultural Training 339

Glossary 347
Index 357

The Nature and Scope of Organizational Behavior

PHOTO: © HOWARD GREY/STONE

Addie Perkins Williamson, Erika Hayes, and Cheryl Henderson are psychologists specializing in organizational behavior. The group frequently receives the assignment of helping companies about to merge develop realistic expectations about the merger, just as they would help romantic partners anticipate some of the struggles they might encounter after they marry. The team of consultants encourages companies in the pre-merger stage to really learn about and understand each other and to make sure they have the same expectations about the merger.

In one consulting assignment, they worked with a large American corporation that bought a foreign travel agency. At first, the corporation was interested only in enhancing its economies of scale and had no desire to learn about the travel agency's business strategy. But during merger talks, officials at the agency convinced the corporation to absorb the agency's successful business practices, not just its personnel and equipment.

Henderson notes that, unfortunately, few executives take this step before entering a merger agreement. After the merger is under way, Williamson, Hayes, and Henderson encourage companies to address and resolve problems before they escalate out of control. For example, Hayes says that executives should immediately tell key employees that they're needed, to prevent those workers from resigning for fear of being laid off.

For more information about these organizational psychologists, visit the Center for Organizational and Leadership Effectiveness at http://www.c-o-l-e.com.

Source: Scott Sleek, "Some Corporate Mergers, Like Marriages, End Up on the Rocks: Psychologists' Corporate Counseling Eases the Way for Mergers and Acquisitions," *Monitor*, July 1998, p. 13.

OBJECTIVES

After reading and studying this chapter and doing the exercises, you should be able to

 Explain what organizational behavior means.

 Summarize the research methods of organizational behavior.

Identify the potential advantages of organizational behavior knowledge.

 Explain key events in the history of organizational behavior.

 Describe how focusing on the human element can contribute to organizational and managerial effectiveness.

 Understand how a person develops organizational behavior skills.

Chapter 1

SO WHAT? What do the comments made by these consultants tell us about how companies can use organizational behavior knowledge to help improve organizational effectiveness? When companies take seriously the advice about working out human problems in advance of a merger, they enhance the chances of that merger being successful. At the same time, they minimize the chances of wasted human effort, such as productive workers quitting out of fear of being downsized.

The purpose of this book is to present systematic knowledge about people and organizations that can be used to enhance individual and organizational effectiveness. Managers and potential managers are the most likely to apply this information. Yet the same information is important for other workers. Among them are professionals, sales representatives, customer service specialists, and technical specialists.

In the modern organization, workers at every level do some of the work that was formerly the preserve of managers. Team members, for example, are often expected to motivate and train each other. One reason organizations get by with fewer managers than previously is that workers themselves are now expected to manage themselves to some extent. Self-management of this type includes the team scheduling its own work and making recommendations for quality improvement.

In this chapter, we approach an introduction to organizational behavior from several perspectives. We will explain the meaning of the term, see why organizational behavior is useful, and take a brief glance at its history. After describing how to develop skills in organizational behavior, we present a framework for understanding the field. An important goal in studying organizational behavior is to be able to make sense of any organization in which you are placed. For example, you might be able to answer the question, "What is going on here from a human standpoint?"

THE MEANING AND RESEARCH METHODS OF ORGANIZATIONAL BEHAVIOR

Explain what organizational behavior means.

A starting point in understanding the potential contribution of organizational behavior is to know the meaning of the term. It is also important to be familiar with how information about organizational behavior is acquired.

The Meaning of Organizational Behavior

Organizational behavior is the study of human behavior in the workplace, the interaction between people and the organization, and the organization itself.[1] The major goals of organizational behavior are to explain, predict, and control behavior.

Explanation refers to describing the underlying reasons, or process by which, phenomena occur. For example, an understanding of leadership theory would explain why one person is a more effective leader than another. The same theory would help predict which people (such as those having charismatic qualities) are likely to be effective as leaders. Leadership theory could also be useful in controlling (or influencing) people. One leadership theory, for example, contends that to influence group members, the leader should help them remove barriers to goal attainment.

Data Collection and Research Methods in Organizational Behavior

To explain, predict, and control behavior, organizational behavior (OB) specialists must collect information systematically and conduct research. The purpose of collecting data is to conduct research.

Methods of Data Collection

Three frequently used methods of collecting data in organizational behavior are surveys, interviews, and direct observation of behavior. The *survey questionnaire* used by a specialist in organizational behavior is prepared rigorously. Before preparing a final questionnaire, a scientist collects relevant facts and generates hypotheses (educated guesses) about important issues to explore. The questionnaire is carefully designed to measure relevant issues about the topic under survey. Among the surveys included in this text is the Creative Personality Test in Chapter 4.

Research about human behavior in the workplace relies heavily upon the *interview* as a method of data collection. Even when a questionnaire is the primary method of data collection, it is probable that interviews were used to obtain ideas for survey questions. Interviews are also helpful in uncovering explanations about phenomena and furnishing leads for further inquiry. Another advantage of interviews is that a skilled interviewer can probe for additional information. One disadvantage of the interview method is that skilled interviewers are required.

Much information about organizational behavior is collected by observers placing themselves in the work environment. *Systematic observations* are then made about the phenomena under study. One concern about this method is that the people being observed may turn in atypical performances when they know they are being observed. A variation of systematic observation is *participant observation*. The observer becomes a member of the group about which he or she is collecting information. For example, to study stress experienced by customer service representatives, a researcher might work temporarily in a customer service center.

Researcher Methods

Four widely used research methods of organizational behavior are case studies, laboratory experiments, field experiments (or studies), and meta-analysis. Although *cases* are a popular teaching method, they are often looked upon critically as a method of conducting research. Case information is usually collected by an observer recording impressions in his or her mind or on a notepad. People have a tendency to attend to information specifically related to their own interests or needs. Despite this subjective element in the case method, cases provide a wealth of information that can be used to explain what is happening in a given situation.

An *experiment* is the most rigorous research method. The essence of conducting an experiment is making sure that the variable being modified (the independent variable) is influencing the results. The independent variable (such as a motivational technique) is thought to influence the dependent variable (such as productivity).

A major characteristic of the *laboratory experiment* is that the conditions are supposedly under the experimenter's control. A group of people might be brought into a room to study the effects of stress on problem-solving ability. The stressor the experiment introduces is an electronic beeping noise. In a field setting, assuming the experiment were permitted, the experimenter might be unaware of what other stressors the subjects were facing. A key concern about laboratory experiments is that their results might not be generalizable to the outside world.

Field experiments (or *studies*) attempt to apply the experimental method to real-life situations. Variables can be controlled more readily in the laboratory than in the field, but information obtained in the field is often more relevant. An example of a field experiment would be investigating the effect of giving employees more power on their ability to produce high-quality work. The independent variable would be empowerment, while the dependent variable would be quality of work.

A widely used approach to reaching conclusions about behavior is to combine the results of a large number of studies. A **meta-analysis** is a quantitative or statistical review of the literature on a particular subject, and is also an examination of a range of studies for the purpose of reaching a combined result or best estimate. A meta-analysis is therefore a review of studies, combining their quantitative information. You can also view meta-analysis as a quantitative review of the literature on a particular subject. For example, a researcher might want to combine the results of 100 different studies about the job performance consequences of stress before reaching a conclusion. Many of the research findings presented throughout this text are based on meta-analysis rather than the results of a single study.

Meta-analysis gives the impression of being scientific and reliable because so much information is assimilated, using sophisticated statistical tools. One might argue, however, that it is better to rely on one rigorous study than to include many poorly conducted studies. William R. Shadish, a specialist in the field, has commented, "Meta-analysis has been controversial since it first became popular in the late 1970s. People either love it or hate it."[2]

② HOW YOU CAN BENEFIT FROM STUDYING ORGANIZATIONAL BEHAVIOR

Summarize the research methods of organizational behavior.

Studying organizational behavior can enhance your effectiveness as a manager or professional. Yet, the benefits from studying organizational behavior are not as immediately apparent as those derived from the study of functional fields such as accounting, marketing, sales, purchasing, or information systems. Such fields constitute the *content* of managerial and professional work. Organizational behavior, in contrast, relates to the *process* of conducting such work. An exception may be seen with organizational behavior specialists whose content, or functional knowledge, is organizational behavior.

Visualize an information systems specialist who has extremely limited interpersonal skills such as communicating, motivating, and resolving conflict. She will have a difficult time applying her technical expertise to organizational problems. She will therefore flop in serving her internal customers because she fails to use effective interpersonal processes. In contrast, if the same information systems specialist had solid interpersonal skills, she could do a better job of serving her customers. (She would probably also hold on to her job longer.)

Studying and learning about organizational behavior offers four key advantages: (1) skill development, (2) personal growth, (3) enhancing organizational effectiveness, and (4) sharpening and refining common sense.

Skill Development

An essential requirement for entering into, surviving, and succeeding in the modern workplace is to have appropriate skills. A person needs both skills related to his or her discipline and generic skills such as problem solving and dealing with people. The study of organizational behavior contributes directly to these generic skills. Later in this chapter, we will provide details about how one develops skills related to organizational behavior.

Organizational behavior skills have gained in importance in the modern workplace. According to executive search consultant, Millington F. McCoy, continual rapid change in organizations has altered the mix of skills that top managers (as well as other managers) need. "Because organizations are less hierarchical, and more global, executives must be able to work effectively in teams that bring together diverse people, skills, and talents. That requires greater strength in the soft characteristics—not just a great résumé, but a cultural fit with my client organization. The brilliant person who lacks basic interpersonal skills can quickly become isolated—and therefore ineffective."[3]

The distinction between *soft* skills and *hard* skills is relevant for understanding the importance of skill development in organizational behavior. Soft skills generally refer to interpersonal skills such as motivating others, communicating, and adapting to people of different cultures. Hard skills generally refer to technical skills, such as information technology and job design. Some skills, such as those involved with decision making, appear to be a mixture of soft and hard components. To make good decisions you have to be creative and imaginative (perhaps a soft skill), yet you also have to weigh evidence carefully (most likely a hard skill).

Personal Growth through Insight into Human Behavior

As explained by Robert P. Vecchio, an important reason for studying organizational behavior is the personal fulfillment gained from understanding others.[4] Understanding fellow human beings can also lead to enhanced self-knowledge and self-insight. For example, while studying what motivates others, you may gain an understanding of what motivates you. Participating in the experiential exercises often included in a study of organizational behavior is another vehicle for personal growth. A case in point is the study of leadership in Chapter 10. You will be invited to take a self-quiz about readiness to assume a leadership role. Taking the test and reviewing the results will give you insight into the types of attitudes and behaviors you need to function as a leader.

Personal growth through understanding others and self-insight are meritorious in themselves, and they also have practical applications. Managerial and professional positions require sharp insights into others for such tasks as selecting people for jobs and assignments, communicating, and motivating. Sales representatives who can size up the needs of prospects and customers have a competitive advantage.

Enhancing Organizational Effectiveness

A major benefit from studying organizational behavior is that it provides information that can be applied to organizational problems. An important goal of organizational behavior is to improve **organizational effectiveness**, the extent to which an organization is productive and satisfies the demands of its interested parties. Each chapter of this text contains information that is applied directly or indirectly by many organizations. One visible example is the widespread use of teams in the workplace. Certainly organizational behavior specialists did not invent teams. We suspect even prehistoric people organized some of their hunting forays by teams. Nevertheless, the conclusions of OB researchers facilitated the shift to teams in organizations.

Over 40 years ago, organizational behavior specialists began to conduct formal research about the functioning of teams. A general finding of this research was that when team members are given substantial responsibility, they are happier and achieve higher productivity.[5] The accumulation of this knowledge strengthened and inspired attempts by many organizations to organize into teams.

The accompanying Organizational Behavior in Action illustrates how applying basic knowledge about human behavior in the workplace can enhance productivity and organizational effectiveness. Observe also how focusing on both hard skills and soft skills is important to achieve the desired results.

Understanding organizational behavior also improves organizational effectiveness because it uncovers factors that contribute to or hinder effective performance. Among these many factors are employee motivation, personality factors, and communication barriers. Furthermore, an advanced understanding of people is a major contributor to managerial success. This is especially true because so much of a manager's job involves accomplishing tasks through people.

Sharpening and Refining Common Sense

A manager commented after having read through several chapters of an organizational behavior text, "Why should I study this field? It's just common sense. My job involves dealing with people, and you can't learn that through a book." The sentiments expressed by this manager are shared by many other students of organizational behavior. However logical such an opinion might sound, common sense is not an adequate substitute for OB knowledge. Knowledge of organizational behavior sharpens and enlarges the domain for common sense. It markedly reduces the amount of time necessary to learn important behavior knowledge and skills, much as law school reduces the amount of time formerly spent in being a law apprentice.

You may know through common sense that giving recognition to people is generally an effective method of motivating them toward higher performance. By studying organizational behavior, you might learn that recognition should be given frequently but not always when somebody attains high performance. (You specifically learn about intermittent rewards in your study of motivation.) Formal knowledge thus enhances your effectiveness.

Organizational behavior knowledge also refines common sense by challenging you to reexamine generally accepted ideas that may be only partially true. One such idea is that inactivity is an effective way to reduce stress from a hectic schedule. In reality, some hard-driving people find inactivity more stressful than activity. For them, lying on a beach for a week might trigger intense chest pains. For these people, diversionary activity—such as doing yard work—is more relaxing than inactivity.

A BRIEF HISTORY OF ORGANIZATIONAL BEHAVIOR

Identify the potential advantages of organizational behavior knowledge.

The history of organizational behavior is rooted in the **behavioral approach to management**, or the belief that specific attention to workers' needs creates greater satisfaction and productivity. In contrast to the largely technical emphasis of scientific management, a common theme of the behavioral approach is the need to focus on people. Scientific management did not ignore people. For example, it heavily emphasized financial incentives to increase productivity. Yet the general thrust centered around performing work in a highly efficient manner.

Organizational Behavior *in Action*

G e t t i n g   T e l e w o r k e r s   o n   T r a c k

about one-half of all companies in the United States and Canada allow employees to telecommute through ongoing or pilot programs. But this work arrangement has not consistently delivered the results, such as reduced overhead costs and higher productivity, that many companies expected, according to the William Olsten Center for Workforce Strategies in Melville, New York. Steve Schilling, president of TeleCommute Solutions in Atlanta, Georgia, believes that employees need the right type of training to work successfully at home.

Even when employers do provide training, they often focus on the wrong aspects of telecommuting, says Schilling. The most common mistake is to "train on technology" but not to get into the basic–experience–type things or the coordination-type things. While telecommuters need to feel confident about operating the technology that will make their off-site experience successful, telecommuting experts agree that organizations need to focus training on more critical issues, such as communication. Another consultant, Charles Grantham, notes, "When you start to substitute e-mail and voice mail for face-to-face conversations, communication gets a little bit messier."

Schilling adds, "When you're implementing a telecommuting program, step one is to understand that there are a lot of issues at play beyond technology—and that the cultural, managerial and interpersonal implications of telecommuting are really much bigger than technology."

George Piskurich, an instructional designer, integrates four key issues into a training program to get at key human problems in telecommuting.

- How to set good objectives and measure productivity (deals with the problem of lack of face time).
- How to develop performance management skills (deals with the problem of absence from the workplace).

- How to enhance communication with people in the office (deals with creativity stemming from interaction with workmates).
- What to expect when you are a telecommuter (deals with unmet expectations, such as the home being a place to work without interruptions).

Another useful training technique is to provide presentations from employees who have already experienced telecommuting. Another trainer notes, "We've found that people talking through their experience, called *testimonial time*, is important. You can have all of the slick films and presentations you want, but what people want is to hear authentic voices."

Some telecommuting programs help prospective teleworkers deal with family, friends, and neighbors who think telecommuters are always available because they work from home. One such technique is to tactfully explain to family and friends that you have certain established office hours during which you should be interrupted only for emergencies.

Bernadette Fusaro, work/life manager at Merrill Lynch, agrees that training is the key to the success of its telecommuting program. She says, "The one thing that distinguishes our program and helps to make it successful is the training factor. It really helps to address issues beforehand and makes the flexible work arrangement so successful."

In case you were wondering: yes, telecommuters have carved out a large share of cyberspace. The World Environmental Organization maintains a list of top 100 telecommuting sites at http://www.100toptelecommuting.com/, where everything from telecommuting basics to telecommuting advocacy groups can be found.

Source: Lin Grensing-Pophal: "Training Employees to Telecommute: A Recipe for Success," *HR Magazine*, December 1998, pp. 76–82.

Organizational behavior is also heavily influenced by sociology in its study of group behavior, organization structure, diversity, and culture. The insights of cultural anthropologists also contribute to an understanding of organizational culture (the values and customs of a firm). In recent years, several companies have hired anthropologists to help them cultivate the right organizational culture. Organizational behavior also gains insights from political science toward understanding of the distribution of power in organizations.

Three key developments in the history of organizational behavior are the Hawthorne studies, the human relations movement, and the contingency approach to management and leadership.

The Hawthorne Studies

Many scholars pinpoint the Hawthorne studies as the true beginnings of the behavioral approach to management.[6] Without the insights gleaned from these studies, organizational behavior might not have emerged as a discipline. The purpose of the first study conducted at the Hawthorne plant of Western Electric (an AT&T subsidiary) was to determine the effect of changes in lighting on productivity. In this study, workers were divided into an experimental group and a control group. Lighting conditions for the experimental group varied in intensity from 24 to 46 to 70 footcandles. The lighting for the control group remained constant.

As expected, the experimental group's output increased with each increase in light intensity. But unexpectedly, the performance of the control group also changed. The production of the control group increased at about the same rate as that of the experimental group. Later, the lighting in the experimental group's work area was reduced. This group's output continued to increase, as did that of the control group. A decline in the productivity of the control group finally did occur, but only when the intensity of the light was roughly the same as moonlight. Clearly, the researchers reasoned, something other than illumination caused the changes in productivity.

The relay assembly test room produced similar results over a six-year period. In this case, relationships among rest, fatigue, and productivity were examined. First, normal productivity was established with no formal rest periods and a 48-hour week. Rest periods of varying length and frequency were then introduced. Productivity increased as the frequency and length of rest periods increased. Finally, the original conditions were reinstated. The return to the original conditions, however, did not result in the expected productivity drop. Instead, productivity remained at its usual high level.

One interpretation of these results was that the workers involved in the experiment enjoyed being the center of attention. Workers reacted positively because management cared about them. The phenomenon is referred to as the **Hawthorne effect**. It is the tendency of people to behave differently when they receive attention because they respond to the demands of the situation. In a research setting, this could mean that the people in an experimental group perform better simply because they are participating in an experiment. In a work setting, this could mean that employees perform better when they are part of any program—whether or not that program is valuable.

The Hawthorne studies also produced other findings that served as the foundation for the human relations movement. Although many of these findings may seem obvious today, documenting them reinforced what many managers believed to be true. Key findings included the following:

1. Economic incentives are less potent than generally believed in influencing workers to achieve high levels of output.
2. Dealing with human problems is complicated and challenging.
3. Leadership practices and work-group pressures profoundly influence employee satisfaction and performance.
4. Personal problems can strongly influence worker productivity.
5. Effective communication with workers is critical to managerial success.
6. Any factor influencing employee behavior is embedded in a social system. (For instance, to understand the impact of pay on performance, you have to understand the climate in the work group and the leadership style of the manager.)

Despite the contributions of the Hawthorne studies, they have been criticized as lacking scientific rigor. The most interesting criticism contends that the workers in the control group were receiving feedback on their performance. Simultaneously, they were being paid more as they produced more. The dual impact of feedback and differential rewards produced the surprising results—not the Hawthorne effect.[7]

The Human Relations Movement

The **human relations movement** was based on the belief that there is an important link among managerial practices, morale, and productivity. Workers bring various social needs to the job. In performing their jobs, workers typically become members of several work groups. Often these groups provide satisfaction of some of the workers' needs. Satisfied workers, it was argued, would be more productive workers. The challenge for managers was to recognize workers' needs and the powerful influence that work groups can have on individual and organizational productivity.

A second major theme of the human relations movement was a strong belief in workers' capabilities. Given the proper working environment, virtually all workers would be highly productive. Significant amounts of cooperation among workers and managers were critical to achieving high levels of productivity.

A cornerstone of the human relations movement is Douglas McGregor's analysis of the assumptions managers make about human nature.[8] Theory X is a set of traditional assumptions about people. Managers who hold these assumptions are pessimistic about workers' capabilities. They believe that people dislike work, seek to avoid responsibility, are not ambitious, and must be supervised closely. McGregor urged managers to challenge these assumptions about human nature because they may be untrue in most circumstances.

Theory Y is an alternative, and optimistic, set of assumptions. These assumptions include the idea that people do accept responsibility, can exercise self-control, have the capacity to innovate, and consider work to be as natural as rest or play. McGregor argued that these assumptions accurately describe human nature in far more situations than most managers believe. He therefore proposed that these assumptions should guide managerial practice.

The Contingency Approach

Beginning in the early 1960s, organizational behaviorists emphasized that it is difficult to find universal principles of managing people that can be applied in all situations. To make effective use of knowledge about human behavior, one must understand which factors in the situation are most influential.

The **contingency approach to management** emphasizes that there is no one best way to manage people or work. A method that leads to high productivity or morale in one situation may not achieve the same results in another. The contingency approach is derived from the study of leadership styles. Experienced managers and leaders know that not all workers respond identically to identical leadership initiatives. A recurring example is that well-motivated, competent team members require less supervision than those who are poorly motivated and less competent. In Chapter 10, we present more information about the contingency approach to leadership.

The strength of the contingency approach is that it encourages managers and professionals to examine individual and situational differences before deciding on a course of action. Its major problem is that it is often used as an excuse for not acquiring formal knowledge about organizational behavior and management. If management depends on the situation, why study organizational behavior or management? The answer, of course, is because a formal study of management helps a manager decide which factors are relevant in particular situations. In the leadership example just cited, relevant factors are the skills and motivation of the group members.

THE PRODUCTIVITY ADVANTAGE OF FOCUSING ON PEOPLE

Explain key events in the history of organizational behavior.

Substantial evidence has accumulated that emphasizing the human factor increases productivity and gives a firm a competitive advantage. Jeffrey Pfeffer examined the evidence from hundreds of studies about the influence of people-oriented management practices on economic performance. For example, a review of 131 field studies dealing with a change in management practices toward greater concern for people reported that economic improvements took place three-fourths of the time. Furthermore, a study of nearly 200 banks found that better human resource practices are associated with substantial differences in financial performance.[9]

Why does paying more attention to the human element improve business performance? One explanation Pfeffer offers is that people work harder. For example, when people have greater control over the work environment and when they are encouraged by peer pressure from teammates, effort increases. Even more of the advantage comes from people working smarter. People-oriented management practices enable workers to use their wisdom and to receive appropriate training. Another contributor to improved performance stems from eliminating positions that focus primarily on watching and controlling workers.

Much of organizational behavior deals with people-oriented management practices. Many of these practices will be described in later chapters. For now, examine Exhibit 1-1, which lists eight key managerial practices of successful organizations. Many of these practices will be covered directly or indirectly at various points in the text.

SKILL DEVELOPMENT IN ORGANIZATIONAL BEHAVIOR

Describe how focusing on the human element can contribute to organizational and managerial effectiveness.

Developing skills in organizational behavior means learning to work effectively with individuals, groups, and organizational forces.

The distinction between hard skills and soft skills mentioned previously is not necessarily the distinction between difficult and easy. Neither are hard skills better

1. **Employment security.** Workers are not in constant threat of being downsized or fired for flimsy reasons.
2. **High standards in selecting personnel.** The company attracts a large number of applicants and strives to find highly qualified candidates for all positions.
3. **Extensive use of self-managed teams and decentralized decision making.** Workers are organized into teams with the authority to make decisions, and managers throughout the company can make many decisions independently.
4. **Comparatively high compensation based on performance.** Paying employees better than the competition leads to success, as does paying employees based on their own performance or that of the department or company.
5. **Extensive employee training.** The most successful companies invest in training as a matter of faith because they believe that a well-trained workforce contributes to profits in the long run.
6. **Reduction of status differences between higher management and other employees.** Successful firms take steps to de-emphasize status differences among individuals and groups that make some people feel less valued. Examples include calling everyone an associate and decreasing differences in compensation among levels of workers.
7. **Information sharing among managers and other workers.** Sharing information about such matters as financial performance and company plans helps build trust among employees. Having ready access to useful information also helps many workers perform their jobs better.
8. **Promotion from within.** Loyalty is enhanced when employees believe that they have a shot at being promoted to good jobs within the company.

Sources: Jeffrey Pfeffer, *The Human Equation* (Boston, MA: Harvard Business School Press, 1998), pp. 64–98; Joanne Cole, "Interview with Jeffrey Pfeffer: Putting People First," *HRFOCUS*, April 1998, pp. 11–12; Pfeffer, "Producing Sustainable Competitive Advantage through the Effective Management of People," *Academy of Management Executive*, February 1995, pp. 64–65.

EXHIBIT 1-1

Key Managerial Practices of Successful Organizations

than soft skills or vice versa. A company president may have a difficult job, yet she uses mostly *soft* skills such as leading others and bringing about organizational change. In contrast, an entry-level financial analyst might use *hard* skills in preparing an analysis. His job, however, might be considered easier than the company president's.

Developing most organizational behavior skills is more complex than developing a structured skill such as conducting a physical inventory or arranging an e-mail address book. Nevertheless, you can develop organizational behavior skills by reading this text and doing the exercises. The text follows a general learning model:

1. Conceptual information and behavioral guidelines. Each chapter in this text presents research-based information about organizational behavior, including a section titled Implications for Managerial Practice.
2. Conceptual information demonstrated by examples and brief descriptions of organizational behavior in action, generally featuring managers and leaders.
3. Experiential exercises. The text provides an opportunity for practice and personalization through cases and self-assessment exercises. Self-quizzes are included because they are an effective method of helping you personalize the information. To personalize is to link conceptual information to yourself. For example, you will read about creative problem solving and also complete a quiz about creativity. Readers who look for opportunities to practice organizational behavior skills outside the classroom will acquire skills more quickly.
4. Feedback on skill utilization, or performance, from others. Feedback exercises appear at several places in the text. Implementing OB skills outside of the classroom will provide additional opportunities for feedback.

As you work through the text, keep the four-part learning model in mind. To help visualize this basic learning model, refer to Exhibit 1-2.

EXHIBIT 1-2

*A Model for Developing
Organizational Behavior
Skills*

*Organizational behavior
skills can be developed by
using a systematic approach.*

Learner Uses
1. Conceptual knowledge and behavior guidelines
2. Conceptual information and examples
3. Experiential exercises
4. Feedback on skill utilization

→ Skill Development in Organizational Behavior

12

A FRAMEWORK FOR STUDYING ORGANIZATIONAL BEHAVIOR

Understand how a person
develops organizational
behavior skills.

A challenge in studying organizational behavior is that it lacks the clear-cut boundaries of subjects like cell biology or French. Some writers in the field consider organizational behavior to be the entire practice of management. Others focus organizational behavior much more on the human element and its interplay with the total organization. Such is the orientation of this text. Exhibit 1-3 presents a basic framework for studying organizational behavior. The framework is simultaneously a listing of the contents of Chapters 2 through 15.

Proceeding from left to right, the foundation of organizational behavior is the study of individual behavior, presented in Chapters 2 though 7. No group or organization is so powerful that the qualities of individual members do not count. Visualize a famous athletic team with a winning history. Many fans contend that the spirit and tradition of the team, rather than individual capabilities, carry it through to victories against tough opponents. Yet if the team has a couple of poor recruiting years or loses a key coach, it may lose more frequently.

Key factors in understanding how individuals function include individual differences, mental ability and personality, learning, perception, attitudes, values, and ethics. It is also important to understand individual decision making, foundation concepts of motivation, motivational programs, conflict, stress, and well-being.

As suggested by the arrows in Exhibit 1-3, the various levels of study are interconnected. Understanding how individuals behave contributes to an understanding of groups and interpersonal relations that will be studied in Chapters 8 through 11. The topics include communication, group dynamics (how groups operate) and teamwork, and leadership. Although leadership relates directly to interpersonal relationships, top-level leaders are also concerned with influencing the entire organization. The study of power, politics, and influence is closely related to leadership.

The next level of analysis and study in organizational behavior is the organizational system and the global environment, as presented in Chapters 12 through 15. Components of the organizational and environmental level studied here are organizational structure and design, organizational culture and change, the learning organization and knowledge management, and international (or cross-cultural) organizational behavior. International organizational behavior could just as well have been studied before the other topics. Our position, however, is that everything else a person learns about organizational behavior contributes to an understanding of cross-cultural relations in organizations.

EXHIBIT
1-3

*A Framework for Studying
Organizational Behavior*

To better understand organizational behavior, recognize that behavior at the individual, group, organizational system, and global environment are all linked to one another.

13

The connecting arrows in Exhibit 1-3 emphasize the interrelatedness of processes and topics at the three levels. Motivation provides a clear example. A person's motivational level is dependent upon his or her individual makeup as well as work group influences and the organizational culture. Some work groups and organizational cultures rev up new members because of their highly charged atmospheres. The arrows also run in the other direction. Highly motivated workers, for example, improve work group performance, contribute to effective interpersonal relationships, and enhance the organizational culture.

IMPLICATIONS FOR MANAGERIAL PRACTICE

Each of the following chapters includes a brief section explaining how managers and professionals can use selected information to enhance managerial practice. Our first implication is the most comprehensive and perhaps the most important: Managers should raise their level of awareness about the availability of organizational behavior information. Before making decisions in dealing with people in a given situation, pause to search for systematic information about people and organizations. For example, if you need to resolve conflict, first review information about conflict resolution such as that presented in Chapter 7. The payoff could be improved handling of the conflict.

SUMMARY OF KEY POINTS

 Explain what organizational behavior means.
Organizational behavior is the study of human behavior in the workplace, the interaction between people and the organization, and the organization itself. Organizational behavior relates to the process, rather than the content, of managerial work.

 Summarize the research methods of organizational behavior.
Three frequently used methods of collecting data on organizational behavior are surveys (typically questionnaires), interviews, and direct observation of behavior. Four widely used research methods are case studies, laboratory experiments, field experiments, and meta-analysis. The essence of conducting an experiment is to make sure that the independent variable is influencing the results.

 Identify the potential advantages of organizational behavior knowledge.
Knowledge about organizational behavior offers four key advantages: skill development, personal growth, the enhancement of organizational effectiveness, and sharpening and refining common sense. Organizational behavior skills have gained in importance in the modern workplace, partly because of the prevalence of diverse teams.

 Explain key events in the history of organizational behavior.
The history of organizational behavior parallels the behavioral approach to management, which formally began with the Hawthorne studies. Among their major implications were that leadership practices and work-group pressures profoundly influence employee satisfaction and performance.

The human relations movement and the contingency approach to management are also key developments in the history of organizational behavior. The human relations movement was based on the belief that there is an important link among managerial practices, morale, and productivity. Theory X versus Theory Y (pessimistic versus optimistic assumptions about people) is a key aspect of the movement. The contingency approach emphasizes taking into account individual and situational differences in managing people.

 Describe how focusing on the human element can contribute to organizational and managerial effectiveness.
Substantial evidence has accumulated that emphasizing the human factor increases productivity and gives a firm a competitive advantage. The positive effects come from people working harder and smarter by having more control over their work environment and using their wisdom.

 Understand how a person develops organizational behavior skills.
Organizational behavior skills can be developed by following a general learning model that includes the use of conceptual knowledge and behavioral guidelines, experiential exercises, and feedback on skill utilization.

The framework for studying organizational behavior in the text emphasizes the interconnectedness of three levels of information: individuals, groups and interpersonal relations, and the organizational system and the global environment.

KEY TERMS AND PHRASES

Organizational Behavior, *2*
The study of human behavior in the workplace, the interaction between people and the organization, and the organization itself.

Meta-analysis, *4*
A quantitative or statistical review of the literature on a particular subject; an examination of a range of studies for the purpose of reaching a combined result or best estimate.

Organizational Effectiveness, *5*
The extent to which an organization is productive and satisfies the demands of its interested parties.

Behavioral Approach to Management, *6*
The belief that specific attention to the workers' needs creates greater satisfaction and productivity.

Hawthorne Effect, *8*
The tendency of people to behave differently when they receive attention because they respond to the demands of the situation.

Human Relations Movement, *9*
An approach to dealing with workers based on the belief that there is an important link among managerial practices, morale, and productivity.

14

Contingency Approach to Management, *10*

The viewpoint that there is no one best way to manage people or work but that the best way depends on certain situational factors.

DISCUSSION QUESTIONS AND ACTIVITIES

1. What contributions might organizational behavior knowledge make in the Internet age?

2. What does it means to say that organizational behavior relates to the *process* of a manager's job?

3. Give a possible explanation why meta-analysis is considered so important in evaluating prescription drugs.

4. **COLLABORATE** Work by yourself, or form a small brainstorming group, to furnish an example from physical science in which common sense proves to be untrue.

5. Have you ever worked for a manager who held Theory X assumptions about people? What was the impact of his or her assumptions on your motivation and satisfaction?

6. Review the key managerial practices of successful organizations summarized in Exhibit 1-1. Indicate which of these practices would be particularly important for you as an employee, and why they would be important.

7. How might a person obtain feedback on the effectiveness of his or her organizational behavior skills?

ORGANIZATIONAL BEHAVIOR ON-LINE

TO DO

Focusing on People Pays Dividends

The purpose of this exercise is to find some evidence that emphasizing the human element benefits a company, such as by increasing productivity, quality, or profits. Find evidence from Internet sources that can be located through free search engines in contrast to using databases paid for by libraries or companies. The difference is a subtle one. Library databases often point you to printed sources available in libraries such as the type of professional journals included in many of the references in this text. In other words, a library database brings the library to you. (However, the same database will sometimes locate unpublished and unprinted information.)

Use the Internet to find sources not already in print, such as unpublished research or comments by an executive or a consultant. In this way, you are developing the skills to find information through the Internet that is not available elsewhere. A good starting point is to use a search engine that searches other search engines such as http://www.google.com or http://www.webcrawler.com. Because this type of Internet search requires such a high skill level, you may want to work in teams, each trying several different search terms such as "payoff from a people orientation" or "return on human resources emphasis."

TO BOOKMARK

Organizational Behavior Research Methods
http://www.nsf.gov/home/sbe/start.htm

Historical Perspectives on Organizational Behavior
http://www.cba.neu.edu/~ewertheim/introd/history.htm

Interpersonal Skills
http://www.medknowlogy.com/skill.htm
http://www.smartbiz.com/

CASE PROBLEM: The Legendary Chainsaw Al Dunlap

In his prime, Albert J. (Al) Dunlap was a manager who was widely discussed and widely written about. He symbolized a business executive whose primary focus was to give shareholders a good return on their investment by taking actions that would elevate the value of company stock. Dunlap's supporters perceived him to be a shareholder champion and a decisive, hard-hitting executive. Dunlap's detractors perceived him as having a brutal, take-no-prisoners approach to management. His willingness to dismantle companies to improve their profitability earned him the nickname "Chainsaw Al." His slashing, aggressive management style contributed to his also being referred to as "Rambo in Pinstripes."

During an 18-month stint in 1994 to 1995 at Scott Paper, Dunlap laid off 35 percent of the workforce, paid down debt, refocused the firm, and then sold it to Kimberly-Clark Corporation. During his tenure, the stock price tripled. By exercising his stock options and receiving special grants, Dunlap earned $100 million. Dunlap had also engineered restructurings of American Can, Lily Tulip, and Crown Zellerbach.

When Dunlap joined Sunbeam in 1996, the board of directors gave him a three-year contract granting him 300,000 shares and an enormous 3.75 million stock options, one of the ten largest grants ever at the time. After the stock package was one month old, Dunlap had a paper profit of $73 million. His reaction to the substantial profit was that he was worth it.

On Dunlap's first day on the job at Sunbeam, he held a meeting with the top-management staff. The meeting turned into a tirade, with Dunlap tearing into the management group for several hours. Richard L. Boynton, president of the household-products division said, "It was like a dog barking at you for hours. He just yelled, ranted, and raved. He was condescending, belligerent, and disrespectful." During the meeting, Dunlap explained, "This is the best day of your life if you're good at what you do and willing to accept change. And it's the worst day of your life if you're not." Dunlap also explained that if he had been a Sunbeam shareholder he would have hung the former management. Dunlap explained to the executive group that "We've got too many people, too many products, too many facilities, and too many headquarters."

Dunlap began his restructuring by hiring an outside consultant to work out the hundreds of details of the vast payroll cuts and closing of facilities. The restructuring plan resulted in terminating one-half the company's 6,000 employees and 87 percent of its products. Company managers gathered evidence that the restructuring resulted in chaos. A shortage of experienced and talented people took place as a result of the drastic layoffs. With employees being fired every day, most departments and functions lacked the employees needed to get a normal day's work accomplished. Plants, needed to produce goods that retailers had ordered, were being closed.

The information systems groups were downsized so drastically that the company lacked backup computers while it upgraded its computer system. The computers were down for months, forcing Sunbeam bookkeepers to hand-write invoices to major customers such as Wal-Mart and Sears Roebuck. Sunbeam could no longer keep track of its orders and shipments, and customers were irate.

Director of human resources, James Wilson, knew that Dunlap had started a new era at Sunbeam. Dunlap's first expense report included a charge for a bulletproof vest. Later, Dunlap expensed a handgun for himself and hired a bodyguard who accompanied him everywhere he went.

After reducing the size of Sunbeam, Dunlap moved to rebuild and enlarge the company. In one day he spent $1.8 billion for three companies in the hopes that they would complement each other: Coleman Co., a manufacturer of camping gear; Signature Brands, which manufactures Mr. Coffee coffeemakers; and First Alert, a manufacturer of smoke detectors. All three firms were consolidated and run through the Sunbeam division of Cuisinart.

David Fannin, the general counsel at Sunbeam, was one of the executives who clashed with Dunlap. Similar to many of his colleagues, Fannin had frequently absorbed the full force of the chief executive's emotional outbursts.

Dunlap imposed seemingly unrealistic growth goals on the company, such as doubling revenues to $2 billion by 1999. When managers were unable to reach the targets Dunlap established, he became almost violent. In Dunlap's presence, knees trembled and stomachs churned. According

to company managers, Dunlap would throw papers or furniture, thump his hands on his desk, and shout so ferociously that a manager's hair would be blown back by the stream of air rushing from Dunlap's mouth. "Hair spray day" became a code expression among top managers, signifying that Dunlap was throwing tantrums that day. When Dunlap was particularly angry, he would scream just inches from his victims.

Managers were able to improve sales for a while, but the deteriorating condition of the company could no longer support sustained high sales. As Dunlap completed 23 months with Sunbeam, the board was ready to fire him. In one quarter, sales were $81 million below projection. A later analysis revealed that the true shortfall was closer to $200 million. Fannin told the board, "The day-to-day atmosphere at the company has really deteriorated. Al is no longer in touch with the business and what's going on at the company....Al isn't talking to people. He has cut himself off." Fannin also told the board that he could not work for Dunlap another day.

Further investigation of Sunbeam's financial condition revealed that the company was paying its bills, including meeting payroll, with revolving credit. Dunlap, who proclaimed himself the outstanding CEO in America, had driven a well-known company into the ground.

As word of poor company sales and internal chaos became widely known, the stock tumbled dramatically. The stock-price plunge contributed to the board firing Dunlap. In addition, overstatements of sales were uncovered, such as classifying inventory in the hands of distributors as completed sales. Many Sunbeam employees cheered his departure.

Dunlap makes big decisions with a minimum of input from others, partly because he is convinced of his own greatness. Dunlap is highly critical of others, including executives who do not follow his slash-and-burn style of management. When asked, "Are you a tough, hard-nosed guy?" Dunlap replied, "I'm a piece of cake. I do turnarounds. You have to be tough; otherwise you don't get it done—and I've had to get rid of a lot of people. I've always held the view that I'm not willing to sacrifice 100 percent of the people for 30 percent." Another statement Dunlap makes to defend his management style is "If you want a friend, buy a dog. I've got two."

Last seen, Dunlap was spending most of his time playing golf and giving lectures on leadership and management to business groups. In February 1998, the Boca Raton, Florida police department answered a telephone call from a golfer who alleged he had been assaulted with a metal golf ball retriever wielded by Al Dunlap. Apparently, the man had asked Dunlap to return a golf ball that the former CEO had retrieved out of the water.

Case Questions

1. In what ways might Al Dunlap have been neglectful of the human element as a leader?

2. What types of organizational behavior skills would have helped Al Dunlap in his executive career?

3. For what reasons was Dunlap hired into a series of high-level executive positions?

4. How would working for Dunlap help you develop your organizational behavior skills?

Sources: John A. Byrne, "Chainsaw," *Business Week*, October 18, 1999, pp. 128–149; Byrne, *Chainsaw: The Notorious Career of Al Dunlap in the Era of Profit-at-Any Price* (New York: HarperBusiness, 2000); Byrne, "How Al Dunlap Self-destructed: The Inside Story of What Drove Sunbeam's Board to Act," *Business Week*, July 6, 1998, pp. 58–65; Daniel Kadlec, "Is That You, Al? A Famous Cost Cutter Decides to Build Not Sell," *Time*, March 16, 1998, p. 44; Joseph Nocera, "Confessions of a Corporate Killer," *Fortune*, September 30, 1996, p. 200.

For more information on Al Dunlap, visit http://www.pbs.org/bottomline/html/dunlap/html, for a series of provocative and revealing interviews.

SUGGESTED READINGS

Christensen, Clayton M., and Overdorf, Michael. "Meeting the Challenge of Disruptive Change." *Harvard Business Review*, March–April 2000, pp. 66–76.

D'Aquanni, Tom, and Taylor, Gary. "Breaking the Political Stranglehold in the Executive Suite." *Management Review*, March 2000, pp. 42–45.

Guttman, Howard M. "Conflict at the Top." *Management Review*, November 1999, pp. 49–53.

Kotter, John P. *What Leaders Really Do*. Boston: Harvard Business School Publishing, 1999.

Richman, Wendy L., Kielser, Sara, Weisband, Suzanne, and Drasgow, Fritz. "A Meta-Analytic Study of Social Desirability Distortion in Computer-Administered Questionnaires, Traditional Questionnaires, and Interviews." *Journal of Applied Psychology*, October 1999, pp. 754–775.

Schwab, Donald P. *Research Methods for Organizational Behavior*. Mahwah, NJ: Lawrence Ehrlbaum Associates, 1999.

Silverman, Daniel. *The Neuro-Genetic Roots of Organizational Behavior*. Blue Summitt, PA: University Press of America, 1999.

Stone, Ann (ed.). *Peter Drucker on the Profession of Management*. Boston: Harvard Business School Publishing, 1998.

Wah, Louisa. "The Emotional Tightrope." *Management Review*, January 2000, pp. 38–43.

Wenger, Etienne C., and Snyder, William M. "Communities of Practice: The Organizational Frontier." *Harvard Business Review*, January–February 2000, pp. 139–145.

ENDNOTES

1. Gregory Morehead and Ricky W. Griffin, *Organizational Behavior: Managing People and Organizations*, 4th ed. (Boston: Houghton Mifflin, 1995), p. 3.

2. "Study Claims Problems with Meta-Analyses, but Psychologists Aren't Worried," *Monitor*, November 1997, p. 9.

3. David Stauffer, "With Today's Global Reach and Team Approach, Soft Skills are Crucial," *Marriott Executive Memo*, Number 8, 1997, p. 4.

4. Robert P. Vecchio, *Organizational Behavior: Core Concepts*, 4th ed. (Fort Worth, TX: The Dryden Press, 2000), pp. 5–6.

5. An example of such research is Rajiv D. Banker, Joy M. Field, Roger C. Schroeder, and Kingshuk K. Sinha, "Impact of Work Teams on Manufacturing Performance: A Longitudinal Field Study," *Academy of Management Journal*, August 1996, pp. 867–890.

6. E. J. Roethlisberger and W. J. Dickson, *Management and the Worker* (Cambridge, MA: Harvard University Press, 1939).

7. H. McIlvaine Parsons, "What Caused the Hawthorne Effect? A Scientific Detective Story," *Administration & Society* (November 1978), pp. 259–283.

8. Douglas McGregor, *The Human Side of Enterprise* (New York: McGraw-Hill, 1960), pp. 33–57.

9. Jeffrey Pfeffer, *The Human Equation* (Boston, MA: Harvard Business School Press, 1998), p. 59; Barry A. Macy and Hiroaki Izumi, "Organizational Change, Design, and Work Innovation: A Meta-Analysis of 131 North American Field Studies, 1961–1991," in W. A. Passmore and R. W. Woodman, eds. *Research in Organizational Change and Development*, Vol. 7 (Greenwich, CT: JAI Press, 1993), pp. 235–313.

Individual Differences, Mental Ability, and Personality

Jonathan Hoenig, 23, works in the investment field as an options trader. He explains, "I grew up outside Chicago and was always interested in the Board of Trade. I'd watch the floor locals and decided futures are the real game. All these buy-and-hold guys—futures traders eat them for lunch. My addiction—options and futures—is the nosebleed section of our Mount McKinley of money."

Pat Brown, 46, is a captain in the New York Fire Department. He looks at his work this way: "I was in the Marines in Vietnam, and fire fighting is like war. If a life is in there, you go in, you get 'em out—even when it's black and smoky, your body's burning up and you're fighting the natural urge to run. The F. D. N. Y. trains you to be aggressive and hypervigilant, not to take stupid risks. We don't do this for sport, for thrills or money. You're risking your life to save somebody. That's what makes this job special. We take risks for a greater good."

For more information on the physical rush associated with taking risks and seeking thrills, visit the X Games website at http://expn.go.com/. The quest for adventure, however, spans many arenas beyond extreme sports. What drives skateboarding champion Tony Hawk to attempt risky 720-degree rotations may also have impelled the mental stunts of Albert Einstein.

OBJECTIVES

After reading and studying this chapter and doing the exercises, you should be able to

1 Explain how individual differences influence the behavior of people in organizations.

2 Describe key factors contributing to demographic diversity.

3 Explain how mental ability relates to job performance.

4 Identify major personality variables that influence job performance.

5 Explain how emotional intelligence is an important part of organizational behavior.

Chapter 2

Source: Karl Taro Greenfeld, "Life on the Edge," *Time* (6 September, 1999): 32, 34. Used with permission of the publisher.

SO WHAT? The comments from the twenty-something options trader from Chicago and the middle-aged fire fighter from New York illustrate an important fact about organizational behavior: Understanding differences among employees can lead to substantial improvements in individual and organizational productivity. A high propensity for risk taking and thrill seeking is generally an asset in the supercharged business of options trading, where gambling that the price of pigs for human consumption will drop 20 percent within six months is an everyday phenomenon. Exceptions, to be sure, also exist. A few people with conservative slants toward risk taking could conceivably be successful in the hectic world of options and futures. Risk taking of a different kind—the willingness to put one's life in peril to save another—is, without a doubt, an asset in a fire fighter. Without such a high propensity to take risks, would a person be willing to enter a burning building?

The purpose of this chapter is to explain how individual differences affect performance. In addition, we describe key sources of individual differences: demographic diversity, mental ability, and personality. In Chapter 3, we will consider other sources of individual differences that influence behavior in organizations: learning, perception, values, and cultural influences. Although our focus in this chapter is on individual differences, we will also be describing principles of human behavior that apply to everyone. For example, everyone has different components to his or her intelligence. We all have some capacity to deal with numbers, words, and abstract reasoning.

INDIVIDUAL DIFFERENCES

Explain how individual differences influence the behavior of people in organizations.

People show substantial **individual differences,** or variations in how they respond to the same situation based on personal characteristics. An extroverted production planner might attempt to influence a plant superintendent by taking him to lunch and making an oral presentation of her ideas. In the same situation, an introverted planner might attempt to influence the superintendent by sending him an elaborate report. Understanding individual differences helps to explain human behavior, but environmental influences are also important.[1]

A basic proposition of psychology states that behavior is a function of the person interacting with his or her environment.[2] The equation reads $B = f(P \times E)$. B stands for behavior, P stands for the person, and E represents the environment. A key implication of this equation is that behavior is determined by the effects of the individual and the environment on each other. For example, a person's tendencies toward impatience might be triggered by working for a firm that requires many levels of approval on a decision. The same person working in a flatter organization (one that requires fewer layers of approval) might be more patient. Have you ever noticed that some environments, and some people, bring out your best traits? Or your worst traits?

Another way of understanding the impact of individual differences in the workplace is to say that these differences moderate how people respond to situations. Ninety-five percent of field sales representatives assigned laptop computers might access data about inventory as instructed. The five percent of the sales force who dislike high-tech devices (and prefer human contact) might telephone the warehouse about inventory status.

Individual differences affect most aspects of behavior on the job. Here we identify eight consequences of individual differences that have a major impact on managing people.

1. *People differ in productivity.* A comprehensive analysis of individual differences illustrates the magnitude of human variation in job performance. The researchers synthesized studies involving over 10,000 workers. They found that as jobs become more complex, individual differences have a bigger impact on work output.[3] An outstanding industrial sales representative might produce 100 times as much sales revenue as a mediocre one. In contrast, an outstanding production specialist might produce only twice as much as a mediocre one. (An industrial sales position is more complex than the job of production specialist. Industrial selling involves a variety of activities including persuading others, analyzing problems, and mining data via a computer.)

2. *People differ in ability and talent.* Factors such as motivation, self-confidence, a favorable appearance, and being politically astute are not sufficient for work accomplishment. People also need the right abilities and talents to perform the job well. Ability is a major source of individual differences that influences job performance. A study with over 5,000 workers documents the idea that ability also influences job satisfaction. Intelligence was found to be positively related to job satisfaction because more intelligent people tend to obtain better, more interesting, and more challenging jobs. However, intelligence is negatively related to job satisfaction as jobs become less complex.[4] (Smart people dislike routine jobs!)

3. *People vary in their propensity for achieving high-quality results.* Some people take naturally to striving for high quality because they are conscientious, have a good capacity for being precise, and take pride in their work. Workers who are less conscientious, less precise, and have little pride will have more difficulty achieving quality targets.

4. *People differ in how much they want to be empowered and involved.* A major thrust of the modern workplace is to grant workers more authority to make decisions by themselves and to involve them in suggesting improvements. Many workers welcome such empowerment and enrichment because they seek self-fulfillment on the job. However, many other workers are not looking for more responsibility and job involvement. They prefer jobs that require a minimum of mental involvement and responsibility.

5. *People differ in the style of leadership they prefer and need.* Many individuals prefer as much freedom as possible on the job and can function well under such leadership. Other individuals want to be supervised closely by their manager. People also vary with respect to the amount of supervision they require. In general, less-competent, less-motivated, and less-experienced workers need more supervision. One of the biggest headaches facing a manager is to supervise people who need close supervision yet resent it when it is administered.

6. *People differ in their need for contact with other people.* As a by-product of their personality traits and occupational interests, people vary widely in how much human contact they need to keep them satisfied. Some people can work alone all day and remain highly productive. Others become restless unless they are engaged in business or social conversation with another employee. Sometimes a business luncheon is scheduled more out of a manager's need for social contact than out of a need for discussing job problems.

7. *People differ in their amount of commitment and loyalty to the firm.* Some employees are so committed to their employers that they act as if they were part owners of the firm. As a consequence, committed and loyal employees are highly concerned about producing high-quality goods and services. And they maintain excellent records of attendance and punctuality, which helps reduce

the cost of doing business. At the other extreme, some employees feel little commitment or loyalty toward their employer. They feel no pangs of guilt when they produce scrap or when they miss work for trivial reasons.

8. *Workers vary in their level of self-esteem, which, in turn, influences their productivity and capacity to take on additional responsibilities.* People with high self-esteem believe that they can cope with the basic challenges of life (self-efficacy) and also that they are worthy of happiness (self-respect). According to Nathaniel Branden, people whose self-esteem is low and who are not confident of their thinking ability are likely to fear decision making, lack negotiation and interpersonal skills, and be reluctant or unable to change.[5] A group of economists found that self-esteem, as measured by a personality test, had a big impact on the wages of young workers. The researchers found that human capital—schooling, basic skills, and work experience—predictably had a significant impact on wages. Yet ten percent of this effect was really attributable to self-esteem, which highly correlated with human capital. It was also found that differences in productivity, as measured by comparative wages, related more to differences in self-esteem than to differences in human capital.[6]

The sampling of individual differences cited are usually attributed to a combination of genetic make-up and environmental influences. Some workers are more productive because they have inherited better problem-solving ability and have lived since childhood in environments that encourage the acquisition of knowledge and skills. Recent experimentation with mice has given more support to the position that genetics play a major role in determining mental ability. Neuroscientists created a supermouse by altering the DNA structure of its forebears in ways that changed the reactions between neurons deep within its cranium. (A supermouse, for example, navigates a maze to find food much more quickly than its ordinary cousins.) The scientists concluded, "Our results suggest that the genetic enhancement of mental and cognitive attributes such as intelligence and memory in mammals is feasible."[7] Many other personality traits, such as introversion, also are partially inherited.

Despite the importance of heredity, the environment, including the workplace, still plays a significant role in influencing job behavior. The manager must therefore strive to create a positive environment in which workers can perform toward their best.

DEMOGRAPHIC DIVERSITY

②

Describe key factors contributing to demographic diversity.

Workers vary widely with respect to background, or demographic characteristics, and these differences sometimes affect job performance and behavior. **Demographic diversity** is differences in background factors relating to the workforce that help shape worker attitudes and behavior. Key sources of demographic diversity include gender, age, race and ethnicity, and physical disability. As is well known, the U.S. workforce is becoming increasingly diverse. Understanding demographic differences among workers can help the manager both capitalize on diversity and avoid negative stereotyping. For example, some managers still hold the stereotype that single people are less conscientious than married people.

Sex and Gender Differences

A topic of intense debate and continuing interest is whether men and women differ in aspects of behavior related to job performance. (Sex differences refer to actual biological differences such as the average height of men versus women. Gender differences refer to differences in the perception of male and female roles.) The overall evidence suggests that there are few differences between men and women in such factors as ability and motivation that will affect their job performance.[8]

Despite the general finding of limited sex and gender differences, much has been written about the different styles and communication patterns of men and women. Chapter 8 presents more details about male-female differences in communication patterns. A major finding is that men more typically communicate to convey information or establish status. Men also tend to emphasize immediate goals and communicate to exchange facts and ideas. Women are more likely to communicate to establish rapport and solve problems.

Men are generally more aggressive than women and therefore less sensitive to the feelings of others. Women, according to this generalization, tend to be more courteous and polite. A study of sex differences in influence tactics supported this observation. Of the 15 influence tactics studied, only one showed a significant difference between the sexes: Women sent greeting cards to work associates more frequently.[9] Another gender difference, according to James Q. Wilson, is that men are more likely to value equity, whereas women value equality. *Equity* refers to people being treated fairly, such as getting the salary increase they deserve. *Equality* refers to people sharing equally, such as all people in a department receiving an identical salary increase.[10]

Even if many workplace differences between men and women have been observed, a review of the evidence about gender differences suggests that the similarities between men and women far outweigh the differences.[11] The accompanying Organizational Behavior in Action illustrates how a major industry is capitalizing on both the similarities and differences among men and women. The industry is overcoming the exclusionary aspects of gender stereotypes, yet accepting the fact that certain gender differences are worth exploiting.

Age and Experienced-Based Differences

Potential differences in productivity and job behavior based on age are beginning to receive considerable attention. According to demographic trends, around 2010 many baby boomers will retire. Because the next generation is smaller than its predecessor, workers with the skills and experience needed to fill positions left open by retiring boomers may be in short supply. A potential solution will be to encourage many people to keep working longer and to employ more older people in general.[12] In order for older people to gain prominence in the workforce, however, both subtle and overt forms of job discrimination must be reduced. The American Association of Retired Persons dispatched pairs of "testers," one 57 and one 32, to apply for 102 entry-level sales or management positions. Although they presented equal credentials, the older applicants received less favorable responses over 41 percent of the time.[13] Yet for the handful of people who have risen to the very top of their fields, such as major corporation executives or economists, age discrimination is less likely to take place.

The research evidence about job-related consequences of age is mixed. One study of 24,000 federal workers found that age was barely related to performance.

Organizational Behavior *in Action*

Building Gender Equality in the Construction Industry

From California to Connecticut, building contractors are desperately searching for women who are handy with a hammer and comfortable in a hard hat. With the economy booming and buildings going up rapidly, the construction industry faces a severe labor shortage. As a result, recruiters have been looking to hire women fresh out of high school and former homemakers returning to the workforce. They're even talking to grade-schoolers to tap the next generation of workers.

"The industry is just dying for people. We don't care what kind—man, woman, whatever. They just need to have skills," said Robert Moorhead, spokesperson for the National Center for Construction Education and Research in Gainesville, Florida. "The truth is, as an industry, we have an image problem: the notion that all construction workers are burly, unshaven men who like to lift large pieces of sheet metal and dig ditches."

"Contractors have a backlog. Some in the Pacific Northwest have had to turn away work," said Howard B. Stussman, editor-in-chief of *Engineering New-Record*, a trade publication. The industry has been losing 200,000 workers per year for the past 10 years, Stussman said. Fewer young people are entering the industry to replace their retiring elders, so the average age of a craft worker, such as an electrician or carpenter, has risen to 49, Moorhead said.

In its recruitment effort, the industry stresses that technology has eliminated many old questions about whether women have the upper body strength to handle the job. "A lot of the heavy lifting requirements have been made obsolete through machinery—through cranes, tractors, and other types of equipment. There are alternative methods to lifting materials. The person doesn't have to break their back," said Dennis Day, a spokesperson for the Associated General Contractors, a construction industry-group.

Nonetheless, women seem to be gravitating to positions where manual dexterity is at a premium: electrical and plumbing crafts, for instance. "Women make great tapers, plasterers, and spacklers because it's very methodical detail work," said Stephanie Collier, executive director of Alphas Development Group, Inc., a nonprofit economic development group. "It's like wallpapering, and women get into that. Men just want to get it done."

Arlene Berger, 47, a carpenter for 17 years in Waterford, Connecticut, finds the work highly rewarding. "There's a sense of accomplishment," she said. "I can drive all over and look at the work I've done."

Kimberly Salvatore, 42, is a mother of three and a site engineer for C. R. Klewin Northeast, a construction company in Norwich, Connecticut. She occasionally gets some ribbing about her long fingernails but doesn't feel that sexual harassment is a deterrent. "With some men, it's kind of a joke that we're here," she said. "You have to be pretty tough to last, but it's worth it."

Along with the growth in the construction industry, federal regulation is also feeding the demand for women. To get a share of lucrative federal business, contractors must show that women put in 6.9 percent of all hours on a project.

The National Association of Women in Construction maintains an encyclopedic site on topics of interest to women employed in the construction industry. Visit http://www. nawic.org for more information.

Source: Brigitte Greenberg, "Women Scale the Wall in Construction," Associated Press, February 26, 1999.

Not surprisingly, both age and experience predicted performance better for jobs requiring *higher* levels of complexity to master than for other jobs.[14]

A review of articles spanning 22 years studying the relationship between age and performance (involving almost 40,000 workers) found that age and job performance were generally unrelated. However, among workers in the 17- to 21-year-old category, the 21-year-olds tended to be more productive than the 17-year-olds.[15]

Even if being older and more experienced does not always contribute to job performance, older workers do have notable attributes. In contrast to younger workers, they have lower absenteeism, illness, and accident rates; higher job satisfaction; and more positive work values.[16]

Racial and Ethnic Differences

As the workforce becomes more diverse, it is worth exploring racial and ethnic differences possibly related to job performance and behavior. **Racioethnicity** is a current term referring to a variety of racial and ethnic differences. Racioethnic differences in job performance and behavior are more attributable to culture than to race or ethnic background itself. For example, it is part of the culture of European countries for workers to take long lunch breaks. An Italian manager working in an Italian subsidiary might take a two-hour lunch break, while her American counterpart takes a 45-minute break. The Italian manager's behavior reflects cultural values rather than the fact of being Italian. Chapter 15 presents more details about cross-cultural differences in job behavior.

Few studies have been conducted of the relationship between race and job performance. Nevertheless, a comparable number of white managers and African-American managers in three different companies were studied. Both groups of managers were comparable in terms of age, length of time with the employer, job function, and rank in the organization. It was found that African-American managers received slightly lower performance ratings than did white managers. The differences were found for both technical and interpersonal aspects of performance. African-American managers also reported having less job discretion and lower feelings of acceptance than did white managers. The researchers offered this explanation:

The results of the present study, with its demographically comparable sample of African Americans and whites, strengthen the conclusion that African Americans may be excluded from opportunities for power and integration within organizations and that such exclusion may be detrimental to their job performance.[17]

Disability Status

Another key source of diversity is whether a person is able-bodied or physically disabled. Mental disability is also gaining attention as a source of workforce diversity. The Americans with Disabilities Act (ADA) of 1991 has alerted managers to the importance of understanding how disabilities might affect job performance. The act is designed to protect people with disabilities from discrimination in employment, public accommodations, transportation, and telecommunications. The ADA defines **disability** as a physical or mental condition that substantially limits an individual's major life activities. According to the Equal Employment Opportunity Commission (EEOC), major life activities are learning, thinking, concentrating, interacting with others, caring for oneself, speaking, performing manual tasks, working, and sleeping. All of these activities can be considered job related. For example, sleep deprivation interferes with job performance.

The ADA requires companies with at least 25 employees to avoid hiring practices that discriminate against people with disabilities. If an employee can perform the essential functions of a job, the employee should be considered qualified. The person is qualified even is he or she must perform certain tasks differently than someone who is not disabled or must use equipment different from the equipment ordinarily used.

Making the appropriate accommodations increases the chances that a physically disabled person will perform as well as an able-bodied person. In general, employers have found the presence of a physical disability does not adversely affect job performance.[18] Also, recent U.S. Supreme Court rulings suggest that disabilities that can be compensated for feasibly do not interfere with job performance. In *Sutton v. United Air Lines*, twin women pilots who are nearsighted claimed that the airline violated the ADA by denying them jobs on that basis because their vision is correctable with glasses or contact lenses. The Court agreed that an individual cannot be considered "disabled" if her condition is correctable with assistive devices.[19]

As will be described in Chapter 15, demographic diversity will often give an organization a competitive advantage. Diversity also affects employee behavior and attitudes. A study of almost 1,600 insurance company employees found that an individual's demographic similarity to his or her work group influenced positively the individual's perception of group productivity and commitment to the work group. (The demographic characteristics studied were sex and racioethnicity.) Another key finding was that the greater the similarity between an individual's demographic characteristics and others in the work group, the more positive would be the individual's perceptions of advancement opportunities.[20] In short, job satisfaction tends to be higher for employees when others of similar demographic characteristics are present in the workplace.

MENTAL ABILITY

Explain how mental ability relates to job performance.

Mental ability, or intelligence, is a major source of individual differences that affect job performance and behavior. **Intelligence** is the capacity to acquire and apply knowledge, including solving problems. Abstract problems can best be solved by intelligent workers. A hundred years of consistent research findings indicate that intelligence, as measured by mental ability tests, is positively related to job performance.[21]

Few people seriously doubt that mental ability is related to job performance. Controversy does abound, however, about two aspects of intelligence. One is how accurately and fairly intelligence can be measured. It is argued, for example, that intelligence tests discriminate against environmentally disadvantaged people. Another controversial aspect is the relative influence of heredity and environment on intelligence. Some people believe that intelligence is mostly the product of genes, while others believe that upbringing is the key factor.

Hans J. Eysenck, a leading authority in the field of intelligence and personality, concluded that a large component of mental ability is inheritable. Evidence for the genetic contributor to scores in intelligence tests has been reinforced by the twin and adoption studies demonstrating that monozygotic twins (same zygote, or identical twins), whether reared apart or together, exhibit relatively high correlations in intelligence. In contrast, dyzgotic twins (different zygote, or fraternal twins), whether reared apart or together, have correlations that are substantially lower.[22]

The argument that environment is the major contributor to intelligence centers around evidence that if placed in an enriched environment, many people are able to elevate their intelligence test scores. Related to this argument is the fact that IQs have been steadily rising worldwide, with each successive generation having an average IQ higher than the previous one. Possible explanations for gains in mental ability (as measured by IQ tests) include better nutrition, more training in mental tasks, and more sophistication in taking tests. All of these reasons indicate that the environment heavily influences intelligence.[23] [If it is true that mental ability can be improved by a stimulating environment, giving employees ample opportunity to stretch themselves mentally will help them improve their intellectual skills.]

Here we describe several aspects of mental ability that have implications for organizational behavior: the components of intelligence, the triarchic theory of intelligence that features practical intelligence, and multiple intelligences.

Components of Intelligence

Intelligence consists of multiple components. A component of intelligence is much like a separate mental aptitude. A standard theory of intelligence explains that intelligence consists of a **g (general) factor** along with **s (special) factors** that contribute to problem-solving ability. Another way of describing g is that it represents a general cognitive factor that pervades almost all kinds of mental ability. Scores on tests of almost any type (such as math or creative ability) are influenced by g. High scores on g are associated with good scholastic performance. In the workplace, g is the best predictor of success in job training, job performance, occupational prestige, and accomplishment within occupations. Also, g is related to many social outcomes including early death due to vehicular accidents.[24] The g factor helps explain why some people perform so well in many different mental tasks—they have the *right stuff*.

Various researchers have identified different s factors contributing to overall mental aptitude. Exhibit 2-1 lists and defines seven factors that have been consistently noted. Being strong in any mental aptitude often leads to enjoyment of work associated with that aptitude. Conversely, enjoyment of an activity might lead to the development of an aptitude for that activity.

EXHIBIT 2-1

Special Factors Contributing to Overall Mental Aptitude

- **Verbal comprehension:** The ability to understand the meaning of words and their relationship to one another, and to comprehend written and spoken information.
- **Word fluency:** The ability to use words quickly and easily, without an emphasis on verbal comprehension.
- **Numerical:** The ability to handle numbers, engage in mathematical analysis, and do arithmetic calculations.
- **Spatial:** The ability to visualize forms in space and manipulate objects mentally, particularly in three dimensions.
- **Memory:** Having a good rote memory for symbols, words, and lists of numbers, along with other associations.
- **Perceptual speed:** The ability to perceive visual details, to pick out similarities and differences, and to perform tasks requiring visual perception.
- **Inductive reasoning:** The ability to discover a rule or principle and apply it in solving a problem, and to make judgments and decisions that are logically sound.

Source: These seven factors stem from the pioneering work of L. L. Thurstone, *Primary Mental Abilities*, Psychometric Monographs, 1 (1938).

The Triarchic Theory of Intelligence (Emphasis on Practical Intelligence)

Many people, including specialists in organizational behavior, are concerned that the traditional way of understanding intelligence inadequately describes mental ability. An unfortunate implication of intelligence testing is that intelligence as traditionally calculated is largely the ability to perform tasks related to scholastic work. Thus, a person who scored high on an intelligence test could follow a complicated instruction manual but not be street smart, such as being able to run a successful small business.

To overcome the limited idea that intelligence involves mostly the ability to solve abstract problems, the **triarchic theory of intelligence** has been proposed, presented in Exhibit 2-2. The theory holds that intelligence is composed of three different subtypes: analytical, creative, and practical. The *analytical* subtype is the traditional type of intelligence needed for solving difficult problems in abstract reasoning. Analytical intelligence is required to perform well in most school subjects. The *creative* subtype is the type of intelligence required for imagination and combining things in novel ways. The *practical* subtype is the type of intelligence required for adapting to your environment to suit your needs. Practical intelligence is a major contributor to being street smart.[25]

The idea of practical intelligence helps explain why a person who has a difficult time getting through school can still be a successful businessperson, politician, or visual artist. Practical intelligence incorporates the ideas of common sense, wisdom, and street smarts. One reservation about practical intelligence is the implication that people who are highly intelligent in the analytical sense are not practical thinkers. In truth, most executives and other high-level workers score quite well on tests of mental ability. These tests usually measure analytical intelligence.[26]

EXHIBIT 2-2

The Triarchic Theory of Intelligence

Three managers took a mental ability test as part of a career counseling program.

Analytical. Manager A scored well on mental ability tests and was good at both test taking and analytical thinking. He exemplifies the analytical aspect of intelligence and has excellent skills in budgeting.

Creative. Manager B had mediocre test scores, but she was a creative thinker and insightful in sizing up people and business situations. She exemplifies the creative aspect of intelligence and has achieved good success as a branch manager.

Practical. Manager C also had mediocre test scores, but he had street smarts and understood how to manipulate his environment in a variety of contexts. Before becoming a manager, he was an excellent sales representative.

Source: Based on information in Robert J. Trotter, "Three Heads Are Better than One," *Psychology Today*, August 1986, pp. 56–62; modified and updated with information from Robert J. Sternberg, book review in *Personnel Psychology*, Summer 1999, pp. 471–476.

An important implication for organizations about practical intelligence centers around problem-solving ability and age. Analytical intelligence may decline from early to late adulthood. However, the ability to solve problems of a practical nature is maintained or increased through late adulthood. As people become older, they compensate well for declining raw mental energy by focusing on things they do well. In job situations calling for wisdom, such as resolving conflicts, age and experience may be an advantage.

Multiple Intelligences

Another approach to understanding the diverse nature of mental ability is the theory of **multiple intelligences**, developed by Howard Gardner. According to Gardner's theory, people know and understand the world in distinctly different ways, or look at it through different lenses. Individuals possess the eight intelligences, or faculties, listed below, in varying degrees.

1. *Linguistic:* Enables people to communicate through language, including reading, writing, and speaking.
2. *Logical-mathematical:* Enables individuals to see relationships between objects and solve problems such as in calculus and statistics.
3. *Musical:* Gives people the capacity to create and understand meanings made out of sounds, and to enjoy different types of music.
4. *Spatial:* Enables people to perceive and manipulate images in their brain and to recreate them from memory, such as in making graphic designs.
5. *Bodily/kinesthetic:* Enables people to use their body and perceptual and motor systems in skilled ways such as dancing, playing sports, and expressing emotion through facial expressions.
6. *Intrapersonal:* Enables people to distinguish among their own feelings and acquiring accurate self-knowledge.
7. *Interpersonal:* Makes it possible for individuals to recognize and make distinctions among the feelings, motives, and intentions of others as in managing and parenting.
8. *Naturalist:* Enables individuals to differentiate among, classify, and utilize various features of the physical external environment.

Your profile of intelligences influences how you will best learn, and to which types of jobs you are best suited. Gardner believes that it is possible to develop these separate intelligences through concentrated effort. Another consideration is that any of these intelligences will fade if not used.[27] These separate types of intelligences might also be perceived as different talents or abilities. Having high general problem solving ability would therefore contribute to high standing on each one of the eight intelligences.

A concern about the theory of multiple intelligences is that it is not as well documented as theories of intelligence that emphasize general cognitive ability. Should evidence be collected to support the existence of multiple intelligences, the theory could be applied to improve productivity. Workers could be assigned positions that best fit their profile of intelligences. A person who was not strong in linguistic intelligence or logical-mathematical intelligence might have high enough interpersonal intelligence to be effective as a customer service representative.

PERSONALITY DIFFERENCES

Identify major personality
variables that influence job
performance.

Personality characteristics such as conscientiousness and extroversion contribute to success in many jobs. Most job failures are not attributed to a person's intelligence or technical competence but to personality characteristics. The subject of personality is therefore important in organizational behavior. Despite its importance, considerable controversy centers on the concept of personality. Among the areas of disagreement are whether personality can be accurately measured and whether it is influenced more by heredity or environment.

Personality refers to the persistent and enduring behavior patterns of an individual that are expressed in a wide variety of situations. Your personality is the combination of attributes, traits, and characteristics that makes you unique. Your walk, talk, appearance, speech, creativity, and traits all contribute to your personality. Personality can therefore be regarded as the core of who we are.[28]

We approach the topic of personality by first describing seven key personality traits related to job performance and behavior, including an example of relevant research. We then describe psychological types related to cognitive styles. Two experiential activities related to personality will also be presented.

Seven Major Personality Factors and Traits

E x p e r i e n c i n g   J O B

To reexamine the forces that
shape personality and test
your understanding of how
personality and test your
understanding of how
personality affects behavior,
visit South-Western's
animated concept and
activity site at _http://www._
experiencingob.com.
Exclusive review tools on
the topics of Personality &
Attitudes help you make
sense of it all. Free demo
available!

According to the Big Five personality theory, the basic structure of human personality is represented by five broad factors: extraversion, emotional stability, agreeableness, conscientiousness, and openness to experience. Although the Big Five approach to personality is well documented, other aspects of personality are still of merit. We therefore also present two other factors of particular significance to job behavior: self-monitoring of behavior, risk-taking, and thrill seeking. People develop all seven factors to different degrees, partially from being raised in a particular environment. For example, a person might have a natural tendency to be agreeable. Growing up in an environment in which agreeableness was encouraged would help the person become even more agreeable.

All seven factors have a substantial impact on job behavior and performance; some of this evidence is presented below. The interpretation and meaning of these factors provide useful information because they help you to pinpoint areas for personal development. Although these factors are partially inherited, most people can improve their development in them.

1. _Extraversion._ Traits associated with the extraversion factor include being social, gregarious, assertive, talkative, and active. An outgoing person is often described as extraverted, whereas a shy person is described as being introverted. Many successful leaders are extraverted, yet some effective leaders are introverted because they rely on other factors such as giving feedback and encouragement to others. (Note that _extraversion_ in everyday language is spelled _extroversion._)

2. _Emotional stability._ Positive traits associated with emotional stability include being calm, enthusiastic, and secure. The low-end traits include being anxious, depressed, angry, embarrassed, emotional, and worried. A person with low emotional stability is often referred to as _neurotic_ or _emotionally unstable._ (You be the psychologist. Evaluate the emotional stability of Al Dunlap, the executive featured in the case problem for Chapter 1.)

3. _Agreeableness._ An agreeable person is friendly and cooperative. Traits associated with the agreeableness factor include being courteous, flexible, trusting, good

natured, cooperative, forgiving, softhearted, and tolerant. Agreeableness is a plus for customer service positions, such as the greeters at Wal-Mart.

4. *Conscientiousness.* A variety of meanings have been attached to the conscientious factor, but it generally implies being dependable. Traits associated with conscientiousness include being careful, thorough, responsible, organized, and a good planner. Other related traits include being hardworking, achievement oriented, and persevering. Being superconscientious can lead to workaholism and perfectionism. Martha Stewart, the guru of home decoration, and also the head of a business empire, is extraordinarily conscientious about details. In describing Stewart's managerial skills, a business reporter noted: "For a woman who has spent her life pursuing both fame and perfection, stepping back won't be easy. Stories of her obsession with detail abound. At CBS, set builders still recall her wrath when she discovered that they failed to follow her specifications for cabinet hardware in her TV kitchen."[29]

5. *Openness to experience.* People who score high on openness to experience have well-developed intellects. Traits associated with this factor include being imaginative, cultured, curious, original, broad-minded, intelligent, and artistically sensitive. Many successful managers and professionals search printed information and the Internet for useful ideas. Also many top-level executives support the arts.

6. *Self-monitoring of behavior.* The self-monitoring trait refers to the process of observing and controlling how we appear to others. High self-monitors are pragmatic and are even chameleon-like actors in social groups. They often say what others want to hear. Low self-monitors avoid situations that require them to adopt different outer images. In this way, their outer behavior adheres to their inner values. Low self-monitoring can often lead to inflexibility. People who are skilled at office politics usually score high on the self-monitoring factor.

7. *Risk taking and thrill seeking.* Some people crave constant excitement on the job and are willing to risk their lives to achieve thrills. The willingness to take risks and pursue thrills is a personality trait that has grown in importance in the high-technology era. Many people work for employers, start businesses, and purchase stocks with uncertain futures. Both the search for giant payoffs and daily thrills motivate these individuals. A strong craving for thrills may have some positive consequences for the organization, including willingness to perform such dangerous feats as setting explosives, capping an oil well, controlling a radiation leak, and introducing a product in a highly competitive environment. However, extreme risk takers and thrill seekers can create such problems as being involved in a disproportionate number of vehicular accidents and making imprudent investments. You will recall two examples of high risk takers and thrill seekers presented at the outset of this chapter. Take the Self-Assessment that follows to measure your tendency toward risk taking.

Depending on the job, any one of the seven personality factors mentioned above can be important for good job performance. The most consistent finding is that conscientiousness is positively related to job performance for a variety of occupations. Furthermore, the combination of intelligence ("can do") with conscientiousness ("will do") is especially important for job performance. In a study of 91 sales representatives for an appliance manufacturer, the combination of intelligence and conscientiousness made accurate predictions of job success. Representatives who scored high on intelligence and conscientiousness tended to

SELF-ASSESSMENT

The Risk Taking Scale

Can you look at a person and tell whether he or she is a risk taker? "I've never been able to do it, and I've studied them for more than 30 years," says Frank Farley, a psychologist at Temple University. "You have to scratch the surface and get to know them." Still, there are many clues when you meet them: some risk takers have high energy levels and display impulsiveness. How can you size up your capacity for risk? Here's an informal quiz. Although some of the questions seem obvious, your final score reflects the range of risk that you are comfortable with, not just whether you like taking risks or not. Answer true or false:

		True	False
1.	I don't like my opinions being challenged.		☑
2.	I would rather be an accountant than a TV anchor.		☑
3.	I believe that I can control my destiny.	☑	
4.	I am a highly creative person.	☑	
5.	I like a lot of varied romantic partners.		☑
6.	I don't like trying exotic foods.		☑
7.	I would choose bonds over growth stocks.		☑
8.	Friends would call me a thrill seeker.		☑
9.	I like to challenge authority.		☑
10.	I prefer familiar things to new things.	☑	☑
11.	I'm known for my curiosity.		☑
12.	I would not like to be an entrepreneur.		☑
13.	I'd rather not travel abroad.	☑	☑
14.	I am easily bored.		☑
15.	I wouldn't like to be a stand-up comedian.	☑	
16.	I've never gotten speeding tickets.		☑
17.	I am extremely adventurous.		☑
18.	I need a lot of stimulation in my life.		☑
19.	I would rather work for a salary than a commission.	☑	
20.	Making my own decisions is very important to me.	☑	

Give yourself 1 point each time your answer agrees with the key. If you score 16–20, you are probably a high risk taker. 10–15: You're a moderate risk taker. 5–10: You are cautious. 0–5: You are a very low risk taker.

1)	F	6)	F	11)	T	16)	F
2)	F	7)	F	12)	F	17)	T
3)	T	8)	T	13)	F	18)	T
4)	T	9)	T	14)	T	19)	F
5)	T	10)	F	15)	F	20)	T

sell more appliances and receive better performance ratings from their supervisors. In a related study with the same sales representatives, extraversion was a good predictor of job performance.[30] In general, favorable results in using personality measures to predict job performance are more likely to occur when the job requirements are carefully analyzed. For example, agreeableness is more important for an airline reservations assistant than a Web designer.

Research has also documented the importance of personality factors for performance as a team member. George A. Neuman and Julie Wright studied 79 four-person, human resource work teams with respect to how general cognitive ability, job-specific skills, and personality traits were related to job performance. For individuals, agreeableness and conscientiousness predicted coworker ratings of team member performance even after cognitive ability and skills were taken into account. Measures were also taken of group cognitive ability, skills, and personality by using the lowest score for any individual as the team value. (A chain is only as strong as its weakest link.) For groups, both agreeableness and conscientiousness were useful predictors of work-team performance such as amount of work completed and supervisor ratings of team performance.[31]

Psychological Types and Cognitive Styles (Myers-Briggs)

Personality also influences a person's **cognitive style**, or the mental processes used to perceive and make judgments from information. A knowledge of these cognitive styles can help you relate better to people because you can better appreciate how they make decisions. According to the famous psychiatrist Carl Jung, how people gather and evaluate information determines their cognitive style. Jung's analysis became the basis for a widely used test of personality and cognitive style called the Myers-Briggs Type Indicator.[32]

Gathering Information

To solve problems, it is necessary to gather information. Two different styles of information gathering are sensation and intuitive. **Sensation-type individuals** prefer routine and order. They search for precise details when gathering information to solve a problem. They prefer to work with established facts rather than to search for new possibilities. **Intuitive-type individuals** prefer an overall perspective, or the big picture. Such people enjoy solving new problems. In addition, they dislike routine and would prefer to look for possibilities rather than work with facts.

When shopping for an automobile, a sensation-type individual would want to gather a large number of facts about such matters as miles or kilometers per gallon, provisions of the warranty, finance charges, and resale value. In contrast, the intuitive-type individual would be more concerned about the overall style of the car and how proud she or he would be as the owner.

Evaluating Information

The evaluation aspect of problem solving involves judging how to deal with information after it has been collected. Styles of information evaluation range from an emphasis on feeling to an emphasis on thinking. **Feeling-type individuals** have a need to conform and adapt to the wishes of others. Because of these tendencies, they try to avoid problems that might result in disagreements. **Thinking-type individuals** rely on reason and intellect to deal with problems. They downplay emotion in problem solving and decision making.

Assume that a team leader asks group managers their opinion on an idea for a new product. Feeling-type people in the group are likely to look for the good in the proposal and then express approval for the project. Thinking-type team members are likely to be more independent in their evaluation of the new product idea. As a result, they will express their opinion whether or not it is what the manager wants to hear. (Notice that feeling-type people are high self-monitors and thinking types are the opposite.)

The Four Cognitive Styles

The two dimensions of information gathering and evaluation are combined to produce a four-way classification of cognitive (or problem-solving) styles. Exhibit 2-3 lists the four styles and occupations well suited to them. The four styles are as follows:

- Sensation/Thinking
- Intuitive/Thinking
- Sensation/Feeling
- Intuitive/Feeling

If you take the Myers-Briggs Type Indicator, often available in career centers, you will be presented a diagnosis of your type. Or you can study the four types and make a judgment as to your cognitive style. Recognizing your cognitive style can help you identify work that you are likely to perform well. For example, a person of an intuitive/feeling type is likely to be skillful in resolving the complaints of customers and group members. The same person might not be well suited by temperament to the analytical work of managers.

The role plays in the Skill-Development Exercise that follows give you an opportunity to practice managing for individual differences in personality. Remember that a role player is an extemporaneous actor. Put yourself in the shoes of the character you play and visualize how he or she would act. Because you are given only the general idea of a script, use your imagination to fill in the details.

EXHIBIT 2-3

Four Problem-Solving Styles and Work Match-Up

Emotional Intelligence

Recent brain research has combined personality factors with practical intelligence, indicating that how effectively people use their emotions has a major impact on their success. The topmost layers of the brain govern componential intelligence,

Sensation/Thinking	Sensation/Feeling
Decisive, dependable, alert to details	Pragmatic, analytical, methodical, conscientious
Accounting, bookkeeping	Supervision
Computer programming	Selling
Manufacturing technology	Negotiating
Intuitive/Thinking	**Intuitive/Feeling**
Creative, progressive, perceptive	Colorful, people oriented, helpful
Design of systems	Customer service
Law, paralegal work	Business communications
Middle manager	Human resources

Source: John R. Schermerhorn, Jr., James G. Hunt, and Richard N. Osburn, *Managing Organizational Behavior*, 5th ed. (New York: John Wiley, 1994): 119.

SKILL-DEVELOPMENT EXERCISE

COLLABORATE

Personality Role Plays

Run each role play for about ten minutes. The people not involved in the role play will observe and then provide feedback when the role play is completed.

1. **The Extravert.** One student assumes the role of a successful outside sales representative who has just signed a $3 million order for the company. The elated sales rep returns to the office. Another student assumes the role of the sales manager. He or she decides that this is a splendid opportunity to build a good relationship with the triumphant sales rep.

2. **Open to Experience.** One student plays the role of an experienced worker in the department who is told to spend some time showing around a new co-op student. It appears that this worker is

open to experience. Another student plays the role of the co-op student, who is also open to experience and eager to be successful in this new position.

3. **Sensation and Intuitive Types.** One student plays the role of a sensation-type individual who is responsible for reviewing the company expense accounts. Another student plays the role of a manager in whose department many expense account abuses (such as lack of documentation and high expenses) have been uncovered. The person in charge of the accounts is visiting the manager in the latter's office to discuss this problem.

such as analytical problem solving. The innermost areas of the brain govern emotion, such as dealing with anger when being criticized by a customer.

Emotional intelligence refers to qualities such as understanding one's own feelings, empathy for others, and the regulation of emotion to enhance living. This type of intelligence has to do with the ability to connect with people and understand their emotions. A worker with high emotional intelligence would be able to engage in such behaviors as sizing up people, pleasing others, and influencing them. Based on research in dozens of companies, Daniel Goleman discovered that the most effective leaders are alike in one essential way: they all have a high degree of emotional intelligence. Without a high degree of emotional intelligence, a person can have excellent training, superior analytical skills, and loads of innovative suggestions. However, he or she will still not make a great leader. Five key factors included in emotional intelligence are as follows:[33]

1. *Self-awareness:* The ability to understand your moods, emotions, and needs as well as their impact on others. Self-awareness also includes using intuition to make decisions you can live with happily. (Managers with high self-awareness often seek feedback to see how well their actions are being received by others.)

2. *Self-regulation:* The ability to control impulsiveness, calm down anxiety, and react with appropriate anger to situations. The right degree of self-regulation helps prevent a person from throwing temper tantrums when activities do not go as planned. (A manager with high self-regulation would not suddenly decide to fire a group member just because of one difference of opinion.)

3. *Motivation:* A passion to work for reasons in addition to money or status, such as finding joy in the task itself. Also, drive, persistence, and optimism when faced with setbacks. (Resilience of this nature is important for leaders and managers because they are frequently called on to help a group work through trying circumstances such as a dramatic decline in business or damage to the company's reputation.)

4. *Empathy.* The ability to respond to the unspoken feelings of others. Also, the skill to respond to people according to their emotional reactions. (Empathy is important for managerial workers because if they empathize with people, they can better understand their positions on issues and how to communicate with and influence people.)
5. *Social skill.* Competency in managing relationships and building networks of support, and having positive relationships with people. (A manager with good social skills would develop good working relationships with customers, managers of other departments, and group members.)

Many training programs are designed to improve emotional intelligence, but the earlier that people develop skills in handling emotional reactions the better. This is true because the key to emotional intelligence lies in the way the brain is programmed in childhood. People learn most of their emotional habits when they are young, but can still learn to improve inappropriate responses later in life.[34]

Emotional intelligence underscores the importance of being practical minded and having effective interpersonal skills to succeed in organizational life. Many topics included in the study of organizational behavior, such as communication, conflict resolution, and power and politics, are components of emotional intelligence. The message is an old one: Both cognitive and noncognitive skills are required for success!

IMPLICATIONS FOR MANAGERIAL PRACTICE

A major implication of individual differences in personality and abilities is that these factors have a major impact on the selection, placement, job assignment, training, and development of employees. When faced with such decisions, the manager should seek answers to such questions as

- Is this employee intelligent enough to handle the job and deal with out-of-the-ordinary problems?
- Is this employee too intelligent for the assignment? Will he or she become bored quickly?

- Is this employee's personality suited to the assignment? For instance, is the employee conscientious enough? Is the employee open to new learning?

Many employees perform below standard not because they are not trying but because their abilities and personality traits are not suited to the job. For instance, an employee who prepares garbled reports may be doing so because of below-average verbal comprehension, not low motivation. Training programs and coaching can be useful in making up for deficits that appear on the surface to be motivational problems.

SUMMARY OF KEY POINTS

 Explain how individual differences influence the behavior of people in organizations.

Understanding individual differences helps to explain human behavior. Nevertheless, behavior is a function of the person interacting with the environment, as expressed by the equation $B = f(P \times E)$.

Individual differences impact on managing people because people differ in (1) productivity, (2) ability and talent, (3) propensity for achieving quality results, (4) desire for empowerment and involvement, (5) style of leadership preferred and needed, (6) need for people contact, (7) commitment and loyalty to the firm, and (8) self-esteem.

 Describe key factors contributing to demographic diversity.

Understanding demographic differences among workers can help the manager capitalize on diversity and avoid negative stereotyping. Key sources of demographic diversity include sex and gender, age, race and ethnicity, and physical disability.

 Explain how mental ability relates to job performance.

Mental ability, or intelligence, is one of the major sources of individual differences that affect job performance and behavior. Intelligence consists of many components. One perspective is that intelligence includes a general factor along with special factors that contribute to problem-solving ability. A related perspective is that intelligence consists of seven components including verbal comprehension and numerical.

To overcome the limited idea that intelligence involves mostly the ability to solve abstract problems, the triarchic theory of intelligence has been proposed. Its three component types of intelligence are analytical, creative, and practical (adapting to your environment to suit your needs).

Another approach to understanding the diverse nature of mental ability is the theory of multiple intelligences. According to this theory, people posses eight intelligences, or faculties: linguistic, logical-mathematical, musical, spatial, bodily/kinesthetic, intrapersonal, interpersonal, and naturalist.

37

 Identify major personality variables that influence job performance.

Personality is one of the major sources of individual differences. Seven major personality factors are extraversion, emotional stability, agreeableness, conscientiousness, openness to experience, self-monitoring of behavior, and risk taking and thrill seeking. Depending on the job, any one of these personality factors can be important for success.

Personality also influences a person's cognitive style, or the mental process used to perceive and make judgments from information. How people gather and evaluate information determines their cognitive style. Two different styles of gathering information are sensation and intuitive. Sensation-type individuals prefer routine and order. Intuitive-type people prefer an overall perspective and enjoy solving new problems. The two extreme styles of evaluating information are an emphasis on feeling and thinking. Feeling-type people are conformists and avoid disagreement, whereas thinking-type individuals rely on intellect more than emotion in problem solving.

 Explain how emotional intelligence is an important part of organizational behavior.

The concept of emotional intelligence helps explain how emotions and personality factors contribute to success. A worker with high emotional intelligence would be able to engage in such behaviors as sizing up people, pleasing others, and influencing them. The components of emotional intelligence are self-awareness, self-regulation, motivation (passion for work and resilience), empathy, and social skill.

KEY TERMS AND PHRASES

Individual differences, *20*
Variations in how people respond to the same situation based on personal characteristics.

Demographic diversity, *22*
Differences in background factors about the workforce that help shape worker attitudes and behavior.

Racioethnicity, *25*
A term referring to the variety of racial and ethnic differences.

Disability, *25*
A physical or mental condition that substantially limits an individual's major life activities.

Intelligence, *26*

The capacity to acquire and apply knowledge, including solving problems.

g (general) factor, *27*

A major component of intelligence that contributes to problem-solving ability.

s (special) factors, *27*

Components of intelligence that contribute to problem-solving ability.

Triarchic Theory of Intelligence, *28*

The theory that intelligence is composed of three different types of intelligence: componential, experiential, and contextual.

Multiple Intelligences, *29*

A theory that proposes that people know and understand the world in distinctly different ways according to the varying degrees to which they possess eight faculties: linguistic, logical-mathematical, musical, spatial, bodily/kinesthetic, intrapersonal, interpersonal, and naturalist.

Personality, *30*

The persistent and enduring behavior patterns of an individual that are expressed in a wide variety of situations.

Cognitive Style, *33*

The mental processes used to perceive and make judgments from information.

Sensation-type Individual, *33*

A type of person whose style of gathering information is based on a preference for routine and order.

Intuitive-type Individual, *33*

A type of person whose style of gathering information is based on a preference for the overall perspective, or the big picture.

Feeling-type Individual, *33*

A type of person who in evaluating information has the need to conform and adapt to others.

Thinking-type Individual, *33*

A type of person who in evaluating information relies on reason and intellect to deal with problems.

Emotional Intelligence, *35*

Qualities such as understanding one's own feelings, empathy for others, and the regulation of emotion to enhance living.

DISCUSSION QUESTIONS AND ACTIVITIES

1. Give an example from your own life of how B = f(P × E).
2. Ten years into the future, your classmates will show wide variations in terms of their career achievement. How might individual differences explain some of these differences in accomplishment?
3. Work together in a small discussion group to uncover several positive demographic stereotypes about workers. **COLLABORATE**
4. Suppose you or a family member required brain surgery. Would you be willing to be operated on by a neurosurgeon who claimed he or she was street smart although had below-average analytical intelligence? Explain your reasoning.
5. Which of the personality traits described in this chapter do you think are particularly important for a financial planner (one who gives paid financial advice to clients)? Explain.
6. Why does having high self-esteem contribute to being more productive and earning a higher income?
7. Refer back to the case about Al Dunlap presented in Chapter 1. Evaluate Dunlap in terms of the various aspects of emotional intelligence.

ORGANIZATIONAL BEHAVIOR ON-LINE

TO DO

Gaining Self-Insight

Yet another application of the Internet is to enhance your self-insight. Use the Internet to obtain a measure of your emotional intelligence. To test your emotional IQ, go to http://www.utne.com/cgi/bin/eq. Web sites do not last forever, so if this site is no longer in operation, search for another site that offers a measure "ell" of emotional intelligence. Another option: http://www.allhealth.com/onlinepsych/iq/olpgen.

Compare your score on the test of emotional IQ to your self-perception of your emotional intelligence.

TO BOOKMARK

On-line Tests and Quizzes

http://www.onlinepsych.com

http://www.queendom.com

Discrimination Laws

http://www.eeoc.gov/small/index.html

CASE PROBLEM: The Experienced Touch at Heritage Christian Home

Walk into Heritage Christian Home on Yorktown Road in Penfield, New York, and something seems a little older. It's not that the facilities are out of date or the methods of dealing with the developmentally disabled residents are antiquated, but these days there is a more mature feeling about the staff.

Faced with a tight labor market created by a national economy moving at a record pace, homes such as Heritage that serve the developmentally disabled are finding themselves employing an older workforce. A staff job that five years ago might have gone to a recent college graduate might be filled today by a retiree embarking on a second career.

David Loughborough, 65, started working for Heritage last month. "When you turn 65, there aren't a whole lot of people looking for you," Loughborough said. "But I just wasn't ready to retire."

Bonnie Senkala, 54, spent 30 years at Eastman Kodak Company before going to work part-time for Heritage, a place she "never even heard of" until a friend told her they were hiring. Employed since September, she says she feels right at home. "I feel like the residents relate to me, maybe because I'm the age of their parents," Senkala said.

Loughborough and Senkala work as resident counselors. They help residents with everything from cooking to laundry, cleaning to personal finance. Loughborough and Senkala say they never imagined working in a home for the developmentally disabled. A year ago Heritage wouldn't have expected to hire them.

"Typically three-quarters of our applicants were female, age 22 to 28," said Marisa Geitner, who oversees organizational development at Heritage's 32 homes in the area. Today, 140 of Heritage's 735 employees are over age 40. A year ago, the company employed only about half as many 40-somethings, said Rod Christian, Heritage's director of development. The tight labor market is only part of the reason, Christian said.

In the late 1990s, state officials launched New York State Cares, a campaign to whittle down the state's 10,000-person waiting list for admission to group homes. In response, many organizations have expanded rapidly, opening more than five homes a year. "There are just more people to hire," said Barbara Wale, chief operating officer for ARC of Monroe County. Wale says her organization is seeing increases in older applicants.

The staffing crunch is forcing service providers to buy more advertising. "We used to just put a classified ad in the paper and we'd get plenty of applications," Wale said. "Now we have to branch out." For the first time, Heritage has spent money on TV and radio ads. The company produced a 10-minute recruiting video shown on local cable access. ARC has also gone to the airwaves. ARC and Heritage managers have started conducting walk-in interviews in their offices.

Officials at Heritage are not distraught by the graying of their workforce. Christian calls it a plus. A more mature workforce brings stability and skills with it, he said. Many older workers also bring parenting skills, for which there are no substitutes, Christian said.

Loughborough thinks his experience rubs off on his often younger bosses. "I feel like I bridge a gap and can serve as an example for some of the people I'm working for," he said.

Case Questions

1. Is the administration at Heritage Christian Home practicing age discrimination by relying heavily on older people to fill their staffing requirements?

2. What does the story about Heritage illustrate about differences in job behavior related to demographic differences?

3. What hiring standards should Heritage and similar organizations establish when the general unemployment rate increases (when boom times are over)?

4. What recommendations can you make to homes for the developmentally disabled to improve their recruitment of resident counselors?

Source: David Tyler, "Mature Workers Find New Home: Providers of Care for the Developmentally Disabled Find Older People Fill Staff Needs," *Democrat and Chronicle* (Rochester, New York) 7 March 2000, by permission of the publisher.

For more information on Heritage Christian Home, Inc. and its recruitment strategies, visit its corporate web site at http://www.heritagechristianhome.org/.

SUGGESTED READINGS

Barrick, Murray R., Stewart, Greg L., Neubert, Mitchell J., and Mount, Michael K. "Relating Member Ability and Personality to Work-Team Processes and Team Effectiveness." *Journal of Applied Psychology*, June 1998, pp. 377–391.

Collins, Judith M., and Gleaves, David H. "Race, Job Applicants, and the Five-Factor-Model of Personality: Implications for Black Psychology, Industrial/Organizational Psychology, and the Five-Factor Theory." *Journal of Applied Psychology*, August 1998, pp. 331–334.

Eysenck, Hans. *Dimensions of Personality*. New Brunswick, NJ: Transaction, 1998.

Lyness, Karen S., and Thompson, Donna E. "Climbing the Corporate Ladder: Do Male and Female Executives Follow the Same Route?" *Journal of Applied Psychology*, February 2000, pp. 86–101.

Raymark, Patrick H., Schmit, Mark J., and Guion, Robert M. "Identifying Potentially Useful Personality Constructs For Employee Selection." *Personnel Psychology*, Autumn 1997, pp. 723–736.

Sackett, Paul R., Gruys, Melissa L., and Ellingson, Jill E. "Ability-Personality Interactions When Predicting Job Performance." *Journal of Applied Psychology*, August 1998, pp. 545–556.

Salgado, Jesús F. "The Five-Factor Model of Personality and Job Performance in the European Community." *Journal of Applied Psychology*, February 1997, pp. 30–43.

Schneider, Benjamin, Smith, D. Brent, Taylor, Sylvester, and Fleenor, John. "Personality and Organizations: A Test of the Homogeneity of Personality Hypothesis." *Journal of Applied Psychology*, June 1998, pp. 462–470.

Segal, Morley. *Points of Influence: A Guide to Using Personality Theory at Work.* San Francisco: Jossey-Bass, 1997.

Sunoo, Brenda Paik. "Blending a Successful Workforce." *Workforce*, March 2000, pp. 44–48.

Williams, John E., Satterwhite, Robert C., and Saiz, José. *The Importance of Psychological Traits: A Cross-Cultural Study.* New York: Plenum Press, 1998.

ENDNOTES

1. For a full explanation of individual differences and job behavior, see Kevin R. Murphy (ed.), *Individual Differences and Behavior in Organizations* (San Francisco: Jossey-Bass, 1996).

2. Kurt Lewin, *A Dynamic Theory of Personality* (New York: McGraw-Hill, 1935).

3. John E. Hunter, Frank L. Schmidt, and Michael E. Judiesch, "Individual Differences in Output Variability as a Function of Job Complexity," *Journal of Applied Psychology*, February 1990), pp. 28–42.

4. Yoav Ganzach, "Intelligence and Job Satisfaction," *The Academy of Management Journal*, October 1998, pp. 526–539.

5. Nathaniel Branden, *Self-Esteem at Work: How Confident People Make Powerful Companies* (San Francisco: Jossey-Bass, 1998).

6. "The Vital Role of Self-Esteem: It Boosts Productivity and Earnings," *Business Week*, February 2, 1998, p. 26.

7. Michael D. Lemonick, "Smart Genes?" *Time*, September 13, 1999, p. 54.

8. Gary N. Powell, "One More Time: Do Female and Male Managers Differ?" *Academy of Management Executive*, August 1990, p. 74; Daniel J. Canary and Kathryn Dindia, *Sex Differences and Similarities in Communication* (Mahwah, NJ: Erlbaum, 1998).

9. Andrew J. DuBrin, "Sex Differences in the Use and Effectiveness of Tactics of Impression Management," *Psychological Reports* 74 (1994), pp. 531–544.

10. James Q. Wilson, *The Moral Sense* (New York: The Free Press, 1993).

11. Daniel J. Canary and Tara M. Emmers-Sommer, *Sex and Gender Differences in Personal Relationships* (New York: Guilford Press, 1997).

12. Allison Kindelan, "Older Workers Can Alleviate Labor Shortages," *HR Magazine*, September 1998, p. 200.

13. George J. Church, "Unmasking Age Bias," *Time*, September 7, 1998, H4.

14. Bruce J. Avolio, David A. Waldman, and Michael A. McDaniel, "Age and Work Performance in Nonmanagerial Jobs: The Effects of Experience and Occupational Type," *Academy of Management Journal*, June 1990, pp. 407–422.

15. Glen M. McEvoy and Wayne F. Cascio, "Cumulative Evidence of the Relationship between Employee Age and Job Performance," *Journal of Applied Psychology*, February 1989, pp. 11–17.

16. Susan R. Rhodes, "Age-Related Differences in Work Attitudes and Behavior: A Review and Conceptual Analysis," *Psychological Bulletin*, March 1983, pp. 328–367.

17. Jeffrey H. Greenhaus, Saroj Parasuraman, and Wayne M. Wormely, "Effects of Race on Organizational Experiences, Job Performance Evaluations, and Career Outcomes," *Academy of Management Journal*, March 1990, p. 80.

18. John P. Fernandez, *Managing the Diverse Work Force* (Lexington, MA: Lexington Books, 1991).

19. Carole O'Blenes, "Legal Intelligence: ADA Lessons From The Front Lines," *Management Review*, September 1999, p. 60.

20. Christine M. Riordan and Lynn McFarlane Shore, "Demographic Diversity and Employee Attitudes: An Empirical Examination of Relational Demography Within Work Units," *Journal of Applied Psychology*, June 1997, pp. 342–358.

21. Orlando Behling, "Employee Selection: Will Intelligence and Conscientiousness Do the Job?" *Academy of Management Executive*, February 1998, p. 78.

22. Hans J. Eysenck, *Intelligence: A New Look* (New Brunswick, NJ: Transaction, 1998).

23. James R. Flynn, "The Discovery of IQ Gains Over Time," *American Psychologist*, January 1999, pp. 5–20.

24. Arthur R. Jensen, *The g Factor: The Science of Mental Ability* (Westport, CT: Praeger, 1998).

25. Robert J. Sternberg, *Beyond IQ: A Triarchic Theory of Human Intelligence* (New York: Cambridge University Press, 1995); Bridget Murray, "Sparking Interest in Psychology Class," *APA Monitor*, October 1996, p. 51.

26. Richard K. Wagner, "Intelligence, Training, and Employment," *American Psychologist*, October 1997, pp. 1059–1069.

27. Howard Gardner, *Leading Minds: An Anatomy of Leadership* (New York: Basic Books, 1996); Thalia Zepatos, "6 Other Ways to Judge IQ," *USA Weekend*, March 13–15, 1998, p. 18; http://www.funderstanding.com/multipleint.htm.

28. "From 'Character' to 'Personality'," *APA Monitor*, December 1999, p. 22.

29. "Martha's World," *Business Week*, January 17, 2000, p. 64.

30. These studies and similar ones are reviewed in Leonard D. Goodstein and Richard I. Lanyon, "Applications of Personality Assessment to the Workplace: A Review," *Journal of Business and Psychology*, Spring 1999, pp. 293–298.

31. George A. Neuman and Julie Wright, "Team Effectiveness: Beyond Skills and Cognitive Ability," *Journal of Applied Psychology*, June 1999, pp. 376–389.

32. The Myers-Briggs Type Indicator (MBTI) is published by the Consulting Psychological Press, Inc., Palo Alto, CA 94306.

33. Daniel Goleman, *Emotional Intelligence* (New York: Bantam, 1995); Goleman, *Working with Emotional Intelligence* (New York: Bantam, 1998); Seymour Epstein, *Constructive Thinking: The Key to Emotional Intelligence* (Westport, CT: Praeger, 1998); Anne Fisher, "Success Secret: A High Emotional IQ," *Fortune*, October 26, 1998, pp. 293–298.

34. Patrick A. McGuire, "Teach your Children Well—and Early, Goleman Says," *APA Monitor*, October 1998, p. 15.

Learning, Perception, Attitudes, Values, and Ethics

According to one career advisor, looking for a job in an Internet company can be an eye-opening experience, a glimpse into a corporate culture that works round the clock, basks in the eclectic, and thrives on a lack of structure. Because of that, the first thing to consider is whether an Internet start-up is even right for you.

"We're talking about highly motivated people who don't need to be told what to do," said David Kopp, founder of Winfire.com, a software firm based in Newport Beach, California. "When you have only 30 people at a company, every one of them has a major impact. You have to know it's not going to be just 40 hours a week."

The Internet world loves to weed out people early. So brush up on tenacity and cop an attitude. "It's really the idea people that make this industry happen," said Tricia Friedman, a vice president at Irvine, California-based www.com, which is building an Internet broadcast network. Friedman received 600 résumés in response to one Internet ad for an entry-level customer-service job. She invited only nine applicants to interview. "I really go by the mantra that you hire for attitude and train for skill."

To learn more about employment opportunities with the two dot.coms discussed in this vignette, visit http://www.winfire.com/company/careers.asp or http://www.com/who/jobs/.

PHOTO: © TERRY VINE/STONE

OBJECTIVES

After reading and studying this chapter and doing the exercises, you should be able to

1 Explain two learning processes relevant to organizational behavior.

2 Describe key aspects of the perceptual process, along with common perceptual problems.

3 Discuss the importance of attitudes to behavior in organizations.

4 Summarize why values are an important part of organizational behavior.

5 Apply the eight-step guide to ethical decision making when faced with an ethical dilemma.

Source: Kate Berry, "Attitude and Tenacity Help in Getting an Internet Job," Knight Ridder, November 15, 1999.

Chapter 3

SO WHAT? **Why do so many employers push so hard to get at the attitudes of candidates in their employment pools?** Intangible though they may be, attitudes and values have a major impact on productivity and turnover as every effective manager knows. In this chapter, we describe five aspects of individual functioning: learning, perception, attitudes, values, and ethics. Understanding these aspects of behavior helps managers deal more effectively with people. Understanding these aspects of behavior should also make job seekers realize that technical aptitude alone is not enough to survive in today's information-age economy.

LEARNING

Explain two learning processes relevant to organizational behavior.

Given that most organizations emphasize continuous learning, it is useful to understand how people learn. **Learning** is a relatively permanent change in behavior based on practice or experience. A person does not learn how to grow physically, digest food, hear sounds, or see light. These are innate, inborn patterns of behavior. But a person does learn how to conduct a performance appraisal, use a computer network to access information, or prepare a report. Unless learning takes place, few employees would be able to perform their jobs satisfactorily. Our concern here is with two methods of learning complex material: (1) modeling and shaping and (2) cognitive learning, including informal learning. In recognition of the fact that people learn in different ways, we will also discuss learning styles.

Modeling and Shaping

When you acquire a complicated skill such as coaching a team member, you experience much more than the acquisition of a few habits. You learn a large number of habits, and you learn how to put them together in a cohesive, smooth-flowing pattern. Two important processes that help in learning complicated skills are modeling and shaping.

Modeling (or imitation) occurs when you learn a skill by observing another person perform that skill. Many sales representatives acquire sales skills by observing a competent sales representative in action. Videocassettes are widely used to facilitate modeling of such skills as interviewing, resolving conflict, and conducting a meeting. Modeling often brings forth behaviors that people did not previously seem to have in their repertoire. To model effectively, one must carefully observe the demonstration and then attempt the new skill shortly thereafter. Although modeling is an effective learning method, the learner must have the proper capabilities and motivation.

Shaping is learning through the reinforcement or rewarding of small steps that build up to the final or desired behavior. It is another way in which complicated skills are learned. At each successful step of the way, the learner receives positive reinforcement. As the learner improves his or her ability to perform the task, more skill is required to receive the reward.

A clerical worker might be shaped into an inside sales representative (taking telephone and computer orders). He acquires a series of small skills beginning with learning the inventory system. He receives a series of rewards as he moves along the path from a support specialist to an inside sales representative who can understand and satisfy customer requirements. Among the forms of positive reinforcement he receives are approval for his new skills, pay increments, and the feeling of pride as new small skills are learned. Among the punishments he receives to assist learning are negative statements from customers when he fills an order incorrectly.

Cognitive Learning

Cognitive learning theory emphasizes that learning takes place in a complicated manner involving much more than acquiring habits and small skills. Learners also strive to learn, develop hunches, and have flashes of insight. Furthermore, they use many aspects of their personality (such as openness to experience) in acquiring knowledge. Suppose that a safety and health specialist discovers the cause underlying a mysterious rash on the skin of many employees. Cognitive learning theory would emphasize that the specialist may have reached the conclusion by acquiring bits of information that formed a cohesive pattern. The theory would also emphasize the goal orientation of the safety and health specialist, along with the person's reasoning and analytical skills. Dedication to the cause and problem-solving ability would also contribute to the learning.

Another type of learning in organizations that fits a cognitive theory explanation is **informal learning**, defined as any learning that occurs in which the learning process is not determined or designed by the organization.[1] The central premise of such learning is that employees acquire some important information outside of a formal learning situation. The employees capitalize upon a learning situation outside of a formal learning situation where the rewards stemming from the learning situation are not explicit.

Informal learning can be spontaneous such as receiving a suggestion on how to calculate the value of an American dollar in terms of a Eurodollar, and vice versa, while having lunch in a company cafeteria. Or, the company might organize the work to encourage such informal learning. The company might provide common areas such as an atrium or food and beverage lounges that encourage employee interaction. Sometimes these common work areas are furnished with white boards and markers to facilitate exchanging ideas.

Research conducted by the Center for Workforce Development indicated that up to 70 percent of learning takes place informally. Informal learning frequently does not have an expressed goal.[2] For example, informal learning might take place when a coworker shows a new employee how to use the company Intranet rather than through a classroom presentation. According to the study in question, informal learning can be divided into four types:

- *Practical skills:* Examples include job-specific skills and knowledge, and technical competence.
- *Intrapersonal skills:* Examples include problem-solving, critical thinking, boundaries for risk taking, and stress management.
- *Interpersonal skills:* Examples include peer-to-peer communications, presentations skills, and conflict resolution.
- *Cultural awareness:* Examples include professional awareness, professional advancement, social norms, understanding company goals, quality standards, and company expectations and priorities.

An important implication of informal learning for managers is that knowledgeable and well-motivated employees can help one another with learning. However, the manager must still be on guard against misinformed and poorly motivated employees creating negative learning. Classroom training is helpful in increasing the chances that the right type of learning takes place.

A factor influencing how much cognitive learning takes place is the orientation of the learner. A *mastery orientation* relates to a dedication to increasing one's competence on a task. These learners are eager to improve their ability on the tasks. For example, a person might want to learn how to make more effective oral presentations so he or she could better enjoy presenting at meetings. With a *performance orientation,* learners focus on how well they perform on a task and make comparisons with others. Learners with a performance orientation are keenly interested in displaying their ability to (or performing for) others. Evidence has been collected from college students that a mastery orientation is associated with greater effort and more complex learning strategies. (An example of a complex learning strategy would be paraphrasing and generating questions with answers.) In contrast, performance orientation is associated with less effort devoted to the task and less frequent use of complex learning strategies.[3]

Learning Styles

Another important concept in understanding learning is **learning style**, the fact that people learn best in different ways. An example of a learning style is that some people acquire new material best through passive learning. Such people quickly acquire information through studying texts, manuals, and magazine articles. They can juggle images in their mind as they read about abstract concepts such as supply and demand, cultural diversity, or customer service. Others learn best by doing rather than by studying—for example, learning about customer service by dealing with customers in many situations.

Another key dimension of learning styles is whether a person learns best by working alone or cooperatively, as in a study group. Learning by oneself allows for more intense concentration, and one can proceed at one's own pace. Learning in groups and through classroom discussion allows people to exchange viewpoints and perspectives. Considerable evidence has been accumulated that peer tutoring and cooperative learning are effective for acquiring knowledge.[4] Another advantage of cooperative learning is that it is more likely to lead to changes in behavior. Assume that a manager holds group discussions about the importance of achieving high quality. Employees participating in these group discussions are more likely to assertively pursue high quality on the job than those who only read about the topic.

Learning styles have been divided into four modes. According to this approach, effective learners rely on four different learning modes: concrete experience, reflective observation, abstract conceptualization, and active experimentation. To learn from *concrete experience,* people must involve themselves fully, openly, and without bias in new experience. To learn from *reflective observation,* people must reflect on and observe these experiences from several perspectives. *Abstract conceptualization* requires people to create concepts that integrate their observations into logically sound theories or explanations. Finally, the effective learner must be able to use these theories to make decisions and solve problems (*active experimentation*).[5]

Considerable practice would be required to develop such a four-barreled approach to learning. Yet the payoff would be substantial in terms of learning complex activities such as motivating people or developing business strategy.

A manager can apply the concept of learning styles by asking group members to reflect on how they learn best. When new work-related material has to be learned, group members can select the learning method that is most effective for them. Some group members might study manuals, while others would work in study groups. A more cautious approach to capitalizing on learning styles is to encourage learners to use more than one mode of learning. They should invest some time in individual study and also interact with others to enhance learning.

PERCEPTION

Most of us interpret what is going on in the world around us as we perceive it—not as it really is. This tendency is much more pronounced when interpreting meanings than when interpreting tangible physical phenomena. Five members of a team might give varying interpretations to receiving a four-percent salary increase for the upcoming year. Yet the same five people would share the same accurate perception that an office tower is being constructed across the street. **Perception** deals with the various ways in which people interpret things in the outside world and how they act on the basis of these perceptions.

Perceptions on the job are important. Many studies, for example, have investigated the consequence of employee job perceptions. The results show that employees who perceive their job to be challenging and interesting have high job satisfaction and motivation. In addition, these favorable perceptions lead to better job performance.[6] Our concern here is with two aspects of perception of most concern to managerial workers: (1) perceptual distortions and problems, and (2) how people attribute causes to events.

Describe key aspects of the perceptual process, along with common perceptual problems.

45

Perceptual Distortions and Problems

Under ideal circumstances, people perceive information as it is intended to be communicated or as it exists in reality. For example, it is hoped that a home office executive assigned to a task force at a company division will perceive the assignment as a compliment. Yet the executive given such an assignment may perceive it as a way of being eased out the door. As shown in Exhibit 3-1, both characteristics of the stimulus and people's perceptual processes can lead to perceptual distortions.

Characteristics of the Stimulus

As implied above, perceptual problems are most likely encountered when the stimulus or cue to be perceived affects the emotional status of the perceiver. If you have strong attitudes about the issue at stake, you are most likely to misperceive the event. The perception of a stimulus or an event depends on the emotions, needs, attitudes, and motives of a person. Imagine that an irate customer writes a letter to a CEO complaining about shabby service received when asking for a refund on a defective product. The CEO widely distributes this letter on E-mail. Among the possible perceptions of this event are the following:

Interpretation by customer service manager: "I'm really in trouble now. It's my job to ensure top-quality service throughout the organization. The CEO thinks I've messed up big time."

Interpretation by customer service specialist immediately involved with the case: "It's nice to have a laugh once in a while. One customer out of 2,000 I've dealt with last year is upset. The other 99.9 percent have no gripe, so why worry?"

Interpretation by merchandising manager: It's obvious the big boss is upset with the customer service group. I don't blame him. We get no complaints about the quality of merchandise. I hope those customer service reps can get their act together."

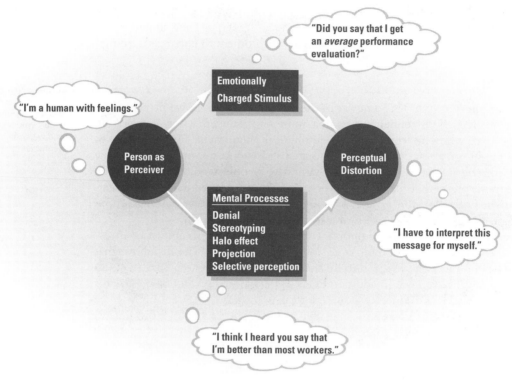

46

Contributors to Perceptual Distortions

Mental Processes of People

The devices people use to deal with sensory information play a major role in creating perceptual problems. The general purpose of these perceptual shortcuts is usually to make the reality less painful or disturbing. As such, these mental processes are types of defensive behavior.

Denial. If the sensory information is particularly painful to us, we often deny to ourselves and others that the information even exists. A purchasing agent was confronted by her manager with the fact that she was entertained so lavishly by a supplier that it was tantamount to a kickback. The purchasing agent replied that she thought the company was only concerned about sales incentives involving tangible goods or money. Yet the agent had been on a committee six months previously that formulated the new regulations on kickbacks. Another frequent form of denial in organizations is when managers ignore hints that they are falling out of favor and thus may soon lose their job. They lose advantage by not conducting a job search until they have been terminated.

The implication for the managerial worker is to stand ready for a message to be distorted if the issue is emotional. Be prepared to clarify and repeat messages and to solicit feedback to ensure that the message was received as intended. Chapter 8 deals at length with the topic of overcoming communication barriers.

Stereotyping. A common shortcut to the perceptual process is to evaluate an individual on the basis of our perception of the group or class to which he or she belongs. Stereotypes, reduce tension in an unusual way. Encountering a person who does not fit our stereotype of the people in the person's group can be painful to our ego. We lessen the discomfort by looking for behavior that conforms to the stereotype. Assume that you believe that Asian workers are meticulous (not an untrue stereotype). When you meet an Asian on the job, you might have a tendency to search for evidence of meticulousness.

Halo Effect. A tendency exists to color everything that we know about a person because of one recognizable favorable or unfavorable trait. When a company does not insist on the use of objective measures of performance, it is not uncommon for a supervisor to give favorable performance ratings to persons who dress well or smile frequently. The fine appearance or warm smile of these people has created a halo around them. Group members often create a positive halo about one member who is articulate and witty. Yet, in reality, the person's professional competence may be average.

Projection. Another shortcut in the perceptual process is to project our own faults onto others instead of making an objective appraisal of the situation. A manager might be asked to recommend a group member for a difficult troubleshooting assignment out of town. The manager might be hesitant, saying, "Most of the people in my group do not handle pressure well." In reality, handling pressure poorly is the manager's key weakness.

Selective Perception. People use this mechanism when they draw an unjustified conclusion from an unclear situation. A feedback letter from the manager might be interpreted as a letter of documentation to help the company build a case for firing the individual. Selective perception can have negative consequences when it leads to self-deception about potentially bad news.

Many workers have succumbed to heart attacks because they denied symptoms that their general knowledge and common sense told them were warnings of trouble. For example, one manager was at a company retreat. He suffered shooting pains in his left arm and left side of the chest. When a roommate at the retreat asked if he was ill, the manager claimed he was just having indigestion. He suffered a near-fatal heart attack the next morning.

What can managerial workers do with knowledge about perceptual distortions? If it appears that a work associate is making obvious use of a perceptual distortion, one should gently confront the person about the discrepancy in his or her thinking. In the heart attack situation, the roommate might have said, "Look, I claim no medical training, but I insist we get you to a doctor right away, just in case you are suffering from more than indigestion."

Attribution Theory

Another important aspect of perception is how people perceive the causes of behavior in themselves and others. **Attribution theory** is the process by which people ascribe causes to the behavior they perceive. People have a general tendency to attribute their achievements to good inner qualities, while they attribute failure to adverse factors within the environment. A manager thus would attribute increased productivity to his or her superior leadership skills but blame low productivity on poor support from the organization.

According to attribution theory, people attribute causes after gathering information about three dimensions of behavior: consensus, distinctiveness, and consistency.[7]

- *Consensus* relates to comparing a person's behavior with that of peers. High consensus exists when a person acts similarly to others in the group and low consensus when the person acts differently.
- *Distinctiveness* is a function of comparing a person's behavior on one task with that person's behavior on other tasks. High distinctiveness means that the person has performed the task in question quite differently from other tasks. Low distinctiveness refers to stable performance or quality from one task to another.

Experiencing OB

To dig deeper into the key components of attribution theory as well as interact with the idea that people often attribute causes of their own behaviors very differently from how they attribute the causes of the behaviors in others, visit South-Western's animated concept and activity site at *http://www.experiencingob. com.* Exclusive review tools on the topics of Perception & Attribution help you connect the dots. Free demo available!

47

- *Consistency* is determined by assessing whether a person's performance on a given task is consistent or not consistent over time.

Observe that consensus relates to other *people*, distinctiveness relates to other *tasks*, and consistency involves *time*. The combination of these factors leads to attribution of causes. People attribute behavior to external (or environmental) causes when they perceive high consensus, high distinctiveness, and low consistency. People attribute behavior to internal (or personal) factors when they perceive low consensus, low distinctiveness, and high consistency.

What might this approach to attribution theory mean in practice? A manager would attribute poor-quality work to external factors, such as poor equipment and resources, under these conditions: All workers are producing low-quality work (high consensus); the low quality occurs on only one of several tasks (high distinctiveness); and the low quality occurs during only one time period (low consistency). In contrast, the manager will attribute low quality to personal characteristics of the workers under these conditions: Only one person is performing poorly (low consensus); the low-quality work occurs for several tasks (low distinctiveness); and the low-quality work has persisted over time (high consistency).

Locus of Control

A logical extension of attribution theory is the concept of **locus of control**—the way in which people look at causation in their lives. Some people have an internal locus of control because they perceive their outcomes as controlled internally. As a result, they feel generally in control of their lives. Some people have an external locus of control because they perceive much of what happens to them as being controlled by circumstances.[8] People with an internal locus of control feel that they create their own opportunities in life, while those with an external locus attribute much of their success and failure to luck.

Workers with an internal locus of control are generally more mature, self-reliant, and responsible. In one study of 900 employees in a public utility, it was found that employees with an internal locus of control had higher levels of job satisfaction. Also, they were more attuned to a participative management style.[9]

Attribution theory, including locus of control, has another important implication for organizational behavior aside from those already mentioned. People search for causes of events and alter their behavior because of these perceptions. Managers should therefore invest time in explaining the causes of events to workers, to avoid misperceptions and counterproductive behavior.

ATTITUDES

Discuss the importance of attitudes to behavior in organizations.

"You've got an attitude," said the supervisor to the store associate, thus emphasizing the importance of attitude to job performance. For mysterious reasons, the term *attitude* in colloquial language often connotes a *negative* attitude. More accurately, an **attitude** is a predisposition to respond that exerts an influence on a person's response to a person, a thing, an idea, or a situation. Attitudes are an important part of organizational behavior because they are linked with perception, learning, and motivation. For example, your attitude toward a coworker influences your perception of how favorably you evaluate his or her work. Here we examine the components of attitudes and their relationship to organizational behavior.

Components of Attitudes

Attitudes are complex, having three components. The *cognitive* component refers to the knowledge or intellectual beliefs an individual might have about an object (an idea, a person, a thing, or a situation). A market researcher might have accumulated considerable factual information about statistics, such as sampling procedures, and software for running data. The researcher might therefore have a positive attitude toward statistics.

The feeling or *affective* component refers to the emotion connected with an object or a task. The market researcher mentioned might basically like statistical analysis due to some pleasant experiences in college associated with statistics. The *behavioral* component refers to how a person acts. The market researcher might make positive statements about statistical methods or emphasize them in his or her reports.

The cognitive, affective, and behavioral aspects of attitudes are interrelated. A change in one of the components will set in motion a change in another. If you have more facts about an object (cognitive), you form the basis for a more positive emotional response to the object (affective). In turn, your behavior toward that object would probably become more favorable.

At times, people do not experience the type of consistency just described and feel compelled to search for consistency. **Cognitive dissonance** is the situation in which the pieces of knowledge, information, attitudes, or beliefs held by an individual are contradictory. When a person experiences cognitive dissonance, the relationship between attitudes and behaviors is altered. People search for ways to reduce internal conflicts when they experience a clash between the information they receive and their actions or attitudes. The same process is used when a person has to resolve two inconsistent sets of information.

A typical example of cognitive dissonance on the job might take this form. A worker believes that the report she submits to team members is of high quality. Her teammates tell her the report is flawed and that it requires substantial rework. To reduce the dissonance, the worker might conveniently ignore the criticism. Or the worker might reason that she is the resident expert on the topic of the report, and her teammates are therefore not qualified to judge the merits of her report.

Attitudes and Job Satisfaction

Another reason attitudes are important in the study of organizational behavior is that they form the basis for how well satisfied people are with their jobs. **Job satisfaction** is the amount of pleasure or contentment associated with a job. Workers will have high job satisfaction when they have positive attitudes toward such job factors as the work itself, recognition, and opportunity for advancement. The two-factor theory of job motivation described in Chapter 5 provides more details about the contributors to job satisfaction and dissatisfaction. Exhibit 3-2 provides a sampling of issues that influence employee attitudes.

Managers are concerned about maintaining high levels of job satisfaction because of its consequences. Among the consequences of job satisfaction are the following:

- High productivity when the work involves people contact
- A stronger tendency to achieve customer loyalty
- Low absenteeism and turnover

- **"Do I know** what my boss expects of me?"
- **"Do I have** what I need to do my work properly?"
- **"Am I allowed** to do what I do best every day?"
- **"Has anyone praised** or recognized my work in the past week?"
- **"Does anyone encourage** my career growth?"
- **"Does my manager** respect my opinion?"
- **"Are my coworkers** dedicated to producing quality work?"

- **"Have I learned** something new in the past year?"

Employees who answer "Yes" to all the questions are likely to stay with their firm for the long haul.

Source: *Supervisor's Guide to Employment Practices,* Clement Communications Inc., 10 LaCrue Ave., Concordville, PA 19331.

EXHIBIT 3-2

Specific Issues That Influence Employee Satisfaction

Answers to the following questions measure employee attitudes vital to job satisfaction, increased productivity, and improved customer service.

- Less job stress and burnout
- Better safety performance
- Better life satisfaction[10]

A broader consequence of job satisfaction is that it contributes to **organizational citizenship behavior**, or the willingness to work for the good of the organization even without the promise of a specific reward. Five important components of organizational citizenship behavior are conscientiousness, altruism, civic virtue, courtesy, and sportsmanship. A good organizational citizen would engage in such behaviors as assisting a person with a computer problem outside his or her team or department, or picking up a broken bottle on the company lawn. People who are good organizational citizens are likely to achieve some of the consequences of job satisfaction including higher customer loyalty, higher productivity, and better safety performance.

Organizational citizenship behavior (OCB) has also been linked to voluntary turnover. A study conducted in 11 companies in China found that employees rated low in organizational citizenship behavior by their supervisors were more likely to quit than those who were rated as exhibiting high levels of such behavior.[11]

According to George A. Neuman and Jill R. Kickul, organizational citizenship behavior is receiving increased theoretical attention as organizations face the challenge of global competition and the need for continuous innovation. The good organizational citizen goes "above and beyond the call of duty," or engages in *extra-role* behavior.[12]

Many of the methods and techniques described in this text, such as empowerment and modified work schedules, are aimed at sustaining job satisfaction. Almost any positive management practice, however, might be linked to improving job satisfaction.

VALUES

Summarize why values are an important part of organizational behavior.

Another key factor influencing behavior in organizations is the values and beliefs of people. A **value** refers to the importance a person attaches to something that serves as a guide to action. Values are also tied in with enduring beliefs that one's mode of conduct is better than the opposite mode of conduct. One person may highly value quantitative analysis and will look down on people who present a position without providing quantitative evidence.

The topic of values has received much publicity in recent years, as baby boomers are compared to younger people, Generation X and Generation Y (also referred to as the Net Generation). With baby boomers being more conservative

Baby Boomers (1946–1964)	Generation X (1965–1977)	Generation Y (1978–1984)
Uses technology as necessary tool	Techno-savvy	Techno-savvy
Appreciates hierarchy	Teamwork very important	Teamwork very important
Tolerates teams but values independent work	Dislikes hierarchy	Culturally diverse
Strong career orientation	Strives for work/life balance but will work long hours for now	Dislikes hierarchy
		Strives for work/family balance but will work long hours for now
More loyalty to organization	Loyalty to own career and profession	Belief in informality
		Wants to strike it rich quickly
		Highly regards start-up companies
Favors diplomacy	Candid in conversation	Candid in conversation
Favors old economy	Appreciates old and new economy	Prefers the new economy
Expects a bonus based on performance	Would appreciate a signing bonus	Expects a signing bonus

Source: Several of the ideas in this table are from Robert McGarvey, "The Coming of Gen X Bosses," *Entrepreneur*, November 1999, pp. 60–64; Joanne M. Glenn, "Teaching the Net Generation," *Business Education Forum*, February 2000, pp. 6–14.

EXHIBIT 3-3

Value Stereotypes for Several Generations of Workers

and respectful of authority and hierarchy, the differences in values between the generations can cause job conflict. As with other group stereotypes, generation differences are often exaggerated. Exhibit 3-3 outlines several generational differences in values.

We discuss values from the standpoint of how they are learned, value clarification, and the mesh between individual and organizational values. Values will be mentioned again in the discussion of ethics because values are the foundation of ethics.

How Values Are Learned

People are not born with a particular set of values. Rather, values are learned in the process of growing up, and many values are learned by age 4. One important way we acquire values is through modeling. Often a person who takes considerable pride in work was reared around people who had a strong work ethic. Models can be parents, teachers, friends, siblings, and even public figures. If we identify with a particular person, the probability is high that we will develop some of his or her major values.

Communication of attitudes is another major way in which values are learned. The attitudes we hear expressed directly or indirectly help shape our values. Assume that using credit to purchase goods and services was talked about as an undesirable practice among your family and friends. You might therefore hold negative values about installment purchases.

Unstated but implied attitudes may also shape values. If key people in your life showed no enthusiasm when you talked about work accomplishment, you might not place a high value on achieving outstanding results. In contrast, if your family and friends centered their lives around their careers, you might develop similar values. (Or you might rebel against such a value because it interfered with a more relaxed lifestyle.)

51

Many key values are also learned through religion and thus become the basis for society's morals. A basic example is that all religions emphasize treating other people fairly and kindly.

SELF-ASSESSMENT

Clarifying Your Values

Directions: Rank from 1 to 21 the importance of the following values to you as a person. The most important value on the list receives a rank of 1; the least important a rank of 21. Use the space next to the two "Other" blanks to include important values of yours not on the list.

__13__ Having my own place to live

__8__ Performing high-quality work

__18__ Having one or more children

__5__ Having an interesting job and career

__14__ Owning a house or condominium

__10__ Having good relationships with coworkers

__3__ Having good health

__19__ Watching my favorite television shows

__15__ Participating in sports or other pastimes

__12__ Being neat, clean, and orderly

_____ Being active in a professional society in my field

__7__ Being a religious person

__6__ Helping people less fortunate than myself

__16__ Loving and being loved by another person

__17__ Having physical intimacy with another person

__9__ Earning an above-average income

__10__ Being in good physical condition

__4__ Being a knowledgeable, informed person

__20__ Leading a Net lifestyle

__1__ Other *Being a good parent / intill values / role model to daughter*

__2__ Other *Close relationships / being there to help / family; friends*

1. Discuss and compare your ranking of these values with the person next to you.

2. **COLLABORATE** Perhaps your class, assisted by your instructor, can arrive at a class average on each of these values. How does your ranking compare to the class ranking? What evidence will you need before you conclude that a given rank is representative of the class?

3. Are there any surprises in the class ranking? Which values did you think would be the highest and lowest?

4. How do you think average ranks for these values would be influenced by a person's culture?

Clarifying Values

The values you develop early in life are directly related to the kind of person you are now and will be and the quality of relationships that you form.[13] Recognizing this fact has led to exercises designed to help people clarify and understand some of their own values. Value-clarification exercises ask you to compare the relative importance you attach to different objects and activities. The Self-Assessment on page 52 gives you an opportunity to clarify your values.

The Mesh Between Individual and Organizational Values

Under the best of circumstances, the values of employees mesh with those required of the job and organization. When this state of congruence exists, job performance is likely to be higher. A national survey of managers investigated the fit between the values of managers and their firms. (One such mesh would be a highly ethical person working for a highly ethical firm.) A major finding was that managers who experienced a good fit were more successful and more likely to believe that they could reach their career goals. They were also more confident about remaining with their present firm and more willing to work long hours.[14]

The values stated by Eastman Kodak Company represent the type of values many business firms express in their written documents:

- Respect for individual dignity
- Uncompromising integrity
- Trust
- Credibility
- Continuous improvement and personal renewal

Not every business firm claiming to have such values carries them out in practice. As a result, problems are created for some employees. When the demands made by the organization or a manager clash with the basic values of the individual, that person suffers from **person–role conflict**. The employee wants to obey orders but does not want to perform an act that seems inconsistent with his or her values. A situation of this type might occur when an employee is asked to help produce a product or service that he or she feels is unsafe or of no value to society.

Unfortunately, both *safety* and *value to society* are not easy to specify objectively. A food manufacturer was indicted for superimposing tuna fish labels on a large batch of unsold dog food, and then selling it wholesale as tuna fish for human consumption. He contended that nobody would be harmed by such actions. One could argue that any product or service is of value to society because it creates employment for somebody.

ETHICS

Our last key factor for understanding individuals in organizations is **ethics**, the moral choices a person makes, and what he or she should do. Ethics is based on an individual's beliefs about what is right and wrong or good and bad. Ethics can also be regarded as the vehicle that converts values into action. You might value a clean environment, and the corresponding ethical behavior is not to place a television set or computer in a landfill. Ethics is a major consideration in studying the actions of managerial workers and the functioning of organizations. We will therefore refer to ethics at various places in the text.

Apply the eight-step guide to ethical decision making when faced with an ethical dilemma.

53

The ethical behavior of organizational members, whether individual contributors (nonmanagers) or managers, exerts a major force on how a firm will be perceived by outsiders and insiders. If the behavior of enough people is outrageously unethical, it may violate the law, thus leading to outside intervention. Executives at one national company engaged in such behavior:

> The Federal Communications Commission (FCC) proposed $2 million in fines against Qwest Communications International Inc., accusing the company of switching long-distance service without the subscribers' consent. The FCC charged Denver-based Qwest with illegally switching telephone service for 30 consumers without their authorization—a practice known as "slamming." The proposed fines are based on customer complaints, 22 of them in cases involving apparent forgery or falsified letters of authorization to switch service.
>
> In one case, according to the FCC, a man reported having his long-distance service switched with a "signed" authorization by his dog. For privacy reasons, the phone was listed in the local telephone directory under the dog's name. Last year, after Alda Hodgson learned from AT&T, her long-distance carrier, that she had been switched to another company, she received a letter from Qwest addressed to her husband. Hodgson called Qwest to inform the company that her husband could not have authorized the service to be switched: He had been dead for 7½ years.
>
> "If we conclude that there was any wrongdoing, the agents responsible will be terminated," a Qwest spokesperson said. The company also said it has implemented new technologies to help track and verify orders.[15]

Here we approach ethics as it relates to individuals from two perspectives. First we look at three somewhat philosophical criteria for making ethical decisions. Second, we present an eight-part guide to ethical decision making.

Ethical Decision-Making Criteria

A standard way of understanding ethical decision making is to understand the philosophical basis for making these decisions. When attempting to decide what is right and wrong, people can focus on (1) consequences; (2) duties, obligations, and principles; or (3) integrity.[16]

Focus on Consequences

When attempting to decide what is right and wrong, people sometimes focus on the consequences of their decision or action. According to this criterion, if nobody gets hurt, the decision is ethical. Focusing on consequences is often referred to as *utilitarianism*. The decision maker is concerned with the utility of the decision. What really counts is the net balance of good consequences over bad.

To focus on consequences, the decision maker would have to be aware of all the good and bad consequences of a given decision. A financial vice president might decide that if all travel expense reimbursements were delayed by ten days, the company could earn $1,000,000 per year nationwide. The earnings would stem from holding on to money longer, thus collecting interest. How would this vice president know how many family arguments and how much job stress would be created by these delayed reimbursements? How many good performers would quit in disgust?

Focus on Duties, Obligations, and Principles

Another approach to making an ethical decision is to examine one's duties in making the decision. The theories underlying this approach are referred to as *deontological* from the Greek word *deon* or duty. The deontological approach is based on universal principles such as honesty, fairness, justice, and respect for persons and property. Rights, such as the right to privacy and safety, are also important. From a deontological perspective, the principles are more important than the consequences. If a given decision violates one of these universal principles, it is automatically unethical even if nobody gets hurt.

The financial vice president pondering whether to defer payments on travel expenses would not have to spend much time with deontology. She would say to herself, "Delaying these payments may earn the company another $1,000,000 per year, but it is neither honest, fair, nor just. Furthermore, employees have a right to prompt payment."

Focus on Integrity (Virtue Ethics)

The third criterion for determining the ethics of behavior focuses on the character of the person involved in the decision or action. If the person in question has good character and genuine motivation and intentions, he or she will be judged to have behaved ethically. The criteria for good character will often include the two other ethical criteria. For example, one might judge a person to have good character if she or he follows the right principles and respects the rights of others.

The decision maker's environment, or community, helps define what integrity means. You might have more lenient ethical standards for a person selling you investment derivatives than you would for a bank vice president who accepted your cash deposit. (Derivatives are high-risk investments used to hedge other investments, with their value being derived from the existence of other securities.)

The virtue ethics of managers and professionals who belong to professional societies may be readily inferred. Business-related professions having codes of ethics include accountants, purchasing managers, and certified financial planners. To the extent that the person abides by the tenets of the code, he or she is behaving ethically. An example of such a tenet would be for a financial planner to be explicit about any commissions he or she stands to gain from a client accepting the advice.

An Eight-Step Guide to Ethical Decision-Making

Linda K. Treviño and Katherine A. Nelson have developed a guide to ethical decision making that incorporates the basic ideas in other ethical tests.[17] After studying this guide, you will be asked to ethically screen a decision. The eight steps to sound ethical decision making are described next.

1. *Gather the facts.* When making an important business decision, it is necessary to gather relevant facts. Ask yourself such questions as, "Are there any legal issues involved here?" "Is there a precedent in our firm with respect to this type of decision?" "Do I have the authority to make this decision?" "Are there company rules and regulations governing such a decision?"

2. *Define the ethical issues.* The ethical issues in a given decision are often more complicated than first glance suggests. When faced with a complex decision, it may be helpful to talk over the ethical issues with another person. The ethical issues might involve common ethical problems such as:

- Lying to customers
- Job discrimination
- Sexual harassment
- Offering or accepting bribes or kickbacks
- Overstatement of the capability of a product or service
- Use of corporate resources for personal gain

3. *Identify the affected parties.* When faced with a complex ethical decision, it is important to identify those who will feel the impact of the decision. Brainstorming may be helpful to identify all of the parties affected by a given decision. Major corporate decisions can affect thousands of people. If a company decides to shut down a plant and move manufacturing to a low-wage country, thousands of individuals and many different parties are affected. Workers lose their jobs, suppliers lose their customers, the local government loses out on tax revenues, and local merchants lose many of their customers.

   The people affected by the decision to delay expense account reimbursements include the workers owed the money and their families. In some instances, the creditors of the workers owed money may also receive late payments.

4. *Identify the consequences.* After you have identified the parties affected by the decision, the next step is to predict the consequences for each party. It may not be necessary to identify every consequence. Yet it is important to identify the consequences with the highest probability of occurring and those with the most negative outcomes.

   Both short-term and long-term consequences should be specified. The company closing a plant might create considerable short-term turmoil, but might be healthier in the long term. A healthy company would then be able to provide for more workers. The short-term consequences of delaying expense reimbursements might be a few grumbles; ill-will probably will be created for the long term.

   The symbolic consequences of an action are important. Every action and decision sends a message (the message is a symbol of something). If a company moves manufacturing out of a community to save on labor costs, it means that the short-term welfare of domestic employees is less important than the welfare of shareholders. Delaying expense account reimbursements symbolizes more concern about optimizing cash flow than treating employees fairly.

5. *Identify the obligations.* When making a complex decision, identify the obligations and the reason for each one. A manufacturer of automotive brakes has an obligation to produce and sell only brakes that meet high safety standards. The obligation is to the auto manufacturer who purchases the brakes and more importantly to the ultimate consumer whose safety depends on effective brakes. The reason for the obligation to make safe brakes is that lives are at stake.

6. *Consider your character and integrity.* A core consideration when faced with an ethical dilemma is to consider how relevant people would judge your character and integrity. What would your family, friends, significant others, teachers, and coworkers think of your actions? How would you feel if your actions were publicly disclosed in the local newspaper or over e-mail? If you would be proud for others to know what decision you made when you faced an ethical dilemma, you are probably making the right decision.

7. *Think creatively about potential actions.* When faced with an ethical dilemma, put yourself in a creative-thinking mode. Stretch your imagination to invent

several options rather than thinking you only have two choices—to do or not to do something. Creative thinking may point toward a third or even more alternatives. Visualize the ethical dilemma of a purchasing agent who is told by a sales rep that he will receive a palm computer as a token of appreciation if his company signs a contract. The agent says to himself, "I think we should award the contract to the firm, but I cannot accept the gift. Yet if I turn down the gift, I will be forfeiting a valuable possession that the company simply regards as a cost of doing business."

By thinking creatively, the agent finds another alternative. He tells the sales rep, "We will grant the contract to your firm because your product fits our requirements. I thank you for the offer of the palm computer, but instead please give it to the Jordan Street Youth Center in my name."

8. *Check your intuition.* So far we have emphasized the rational side of ethical decision making. Another effective way of conducting an ethics screen is to rely on intuition. How does the contemplated decision feel, taste, and smell? Would you be proud of yourself or would you be disgusted with yourself if you made the decision? Do you wonder how the businessperson felt who relabeled the dogfood as tuna fish? Of course, if a person lacks a conscience, checking intuition is not effective.

Another type of decision that often requires an ethical test is choosing between two rights (rather than right versus wrong). Joseph L. Badaracco, Jr., refers to these situations as *defining moments*, because such decisions over time form the basis of a person's character. The defining moment challenges people by asking them to choose between two ideals in which they deeply believe.[18] Suppose a blind worker in the group has personal problems so great that her job performance suffers. She is offered counseling but does not follow through seriously. Other members of the team complain about the blind worker's performance because it is interfering with

---

SKILL-DEVELOPMENT EXERCISE

COLLABORATE

Ethical Decision Making

Working in small groups, take one or both of the ethical dilemmas presented below through the eight steps for an ethical screening of contemplated decisions. Compare your answers for the various steps with other groups in the class.

Scenario 1: The Job Applicants with a Past. A state/ provincial government official approaches your employer, a bank, asking you to hire three people soon to be released from prison. All were found guilty of fraudulently altering a bank's computer records for personal gain. The official says that the men have paid their debt to society and that they need jobs. Your bank has three openings for computer specialists. All three men have obviously good computer skills. Your group is wondering whether to hire these people.

Scenario 2- The High-Profit Toys. You are a toy company executive starting to plan your holiday season line. You anticipate that the season's hottest item will be Robo-Woman, a battery-operated crime fighter and superheroine. Robo-Woman should have a wholesale price of $16.50 and a retail price of $36.00. Your company anticipates a gross profit of $9 per unit. You receive a sales call from a manufacturing broker who says he can produce any toy you want for one-third of your present manufacturing cost. He admits that the manufacturer he represents uses prison labor in China but that his business arrangement violates no law. You estimate that your firm can earn a gross profit of $12 per unit if you do business with the manufacturing broker. The decision you face is whether to do business with him.

the group achieving its goals. If the manager dismisses the blind worker, she may suffer severe financial consequences. (She is the only wage earner in the family.) However, if she is retained, the group will suffer consequences of its own. The manager must now choose between two rights, or the lesser of two evils.

The Skill-Development Exercise on page 57 gives you an opportunity to practice the eight-part guide to ethical decision making. The accompanying Organizational Behavior in Action describes a person who has taken the moral high ground in his career.

Organizational Behavior *in Action*

Bravo Rodrigo Baggio, Social Entrepreneur

"Rodrigo, you are crazy. Poor people can never use computers." This is what friends and business associates in Rio de Janiero told Rodrigo Baggio when he told them about his plan to bring information technology into the city's slum's, called favelas. The negative thinking bounced off Baggio. Today Baggio, age 30, operates 117 computer schools in the slums of 13 Brazilian states through his Committee for the Democratization of Information Technology (CDI). The majority of the 32,000 young people who have completed classes either have jobs or are starting their own businesses. Without Baggio's inspired dream, most of these people would have faced a life of poverty. Baggio describes his mission in these words: "To give young slum dwellers access to computers and high-tech skills as a way to improve their life."

Following the enormous success of the computer schools, Baggio intends to attempt the beginnings of a digital nation. He now intends to connect all his computer schools via the Internet. "Many times a youth in one favela never visits another one, even one in the same state," he says. "The Internet is the digital bridge."

Baggio is making a major impact on Brazil's future, one young person at a time. His computer schools would not have been possible without a jump start by Ashoka: Innovators for the Public, a nonprofit international venture-capital foundation based in Arlington, Virginia. Ashoka has given financial and professional backing for more than 1,000 social entrepreneurs in 34 countries. Just like Baggio, all of them use business techniques and expertise to help people help themselves.

A three-year stipend from Ashoka and its global alliance of executives, mentors, and consultants enabled Baggio to enlarge CDI beyond Rio. He aspires to someday enlarge beyond Brazil. Says Baggio: "We believe we can adapt it to other countries."

"The job of the entrepreneur," explains Ashoka's founder and chairman William Drayton, a Yale Law School graduate, "is to see where society is stuck and find a new way around it." As Drayton perceives the situation, there is no difference between those who apply their skills in business and those who apply them toward attaining social goals.

Tony Blair, the Prime Minister of Great Britain, emphasizes that his government embraces the idea of social entrepreneurs, describing them as "people who bring to social problems the same enterprise and imagination business entrepreneurs bring to wealth creation."

For a closer look at the social entrepeneurship practiced by CDI and Ashoka, visit their Web sites at http://www.cdi.org.br and http://www.ashoka.org, respectively.

Source: Emily Mitchell, "Getting Better at Doing Good," *Time*, (21 February 2000): B9, B10. Used by permission of the publisher.

IMPLICATIONS FOR MANAGERIAL PRACTICE

In addition to the suggestions made for applying information throughout this chapter (as is done in all chapters of this book), here we make a few additional practical suggestions.

1. Assume that you want to teach a new skill to one or more people, such as explaining a new benefits package to employees. You have no funds available for the training program, so you must do the job inexpensively, but properly. Under these circumstances, your best tactic would be to use modeling as a learning method. The trainees could observe you in action and follow up with question-and-answer sessions.

2. Be aware of the pervasive effect of selective perception in organizational behavior. Many perceptions of people, for example, are based on their needs at the time. A manager who has to fill a position by a tight deadline may overevaluate the qualifications of applicants. The judgment of a second party, who is not facing the same need, can be helpful in arriving at an objective judgment.

3. When facing a major decision, you will want to use many of the guidelines for problem solving and decision making presented in the next chapter. In addition, major decisions should be subject to the eight-step guide for ethical decision making presented here. For a quick check on the ethical soundness of your decisions, use steps 6 (consider your character and integrity) and 8 (check your intuition).

SUMMARY OF KEY POINTS

 Explain two learning processes relevant to organizational behavior.

Modeling and shaping, and cognitive learning are two ways of learning complex material. Modeling involves imitating another person performing the task correctly, then repeating the task. Shaping is learning through the reinforcement of small steps that build up to the final or desired behavior.

In cognitive learning, learners strive to learn, develop hunches, have flashes of insight, and use many aspects of personality. Cognitive learning includes informal learning, which occurs outside of a formal learning situation.

 Describe key aspects of the perceptual process, along with common perceptual problems.

Perception deals with the various ways in which people interpret things in the outside world and how they act on the basis of these perceptions. Perceptual problems are most likely encountered when the stimulus or cue to be perceived affects the emotional status of the perceiver.

The devices people use to deal with sensory information play a major role in creating perceptual problems. Among these devices are denial, stereotyping, the halo effect, projection, and selective perception.

Attribution theory is tile process by which people ascribe causes to the behavior they perceive. People attribute causes after gathering information about consensus (comparison among people), distinctiveness (comparison across tasks), and consistency (task stability over time).

 Discuss the importance of attitudes to behavior in organizations.

Attitudes influence organizational behavior in many ways. The three components of attitudes are cognitive, affective, and behavioral. A state of cognitive dissonance leads people to reduce the internal conflict when they experience a clash between the information they receive and their actions or attitudes. Attitudes are especially important because they are the basis for job satisfaction, which is linked to important consequences such as absenteeism and turnover, and job stress. Job satisfaction also contributes to organizational citizenship behavior.

 Summarize why values are an important part of organizational behavior.

A value refers to the importance a person attaches to something that serves as a guide to action. Many values are acquired early in life, often through modeling. The values a person develops early in life are directly related to the kind of person he or she is now and will be, and the quality of his or her personal relationships.

Job performance tends to be higher when there is congruence between individual and organizational values. A person suffers from person-role conflict when the demands made by the organization or a manager clash with the basic values of the individual.

 Apply the eight-step guide to ethical decision making when faced with an ethical dilemma.

A philosophical approach to understanding ethics gives three possible focuses: on consequences; on duties, obligations, and principles; or on integrity. When focusing on consequences, the decision maker is concerned with the utility, or net consequences, of a decision. The deontological approach is based on universal principles such as honesty, fairness, justice, and respect for persons and property. The integrity, or virtue, criterion focuses on the character of the ethical action.

An eight-step guide to ethical decision making follows these steps: (1) gather the facts, (2) define the ethical issues, (3) identify the affected parties, (4) identify the consequences, (5) identify the obligations, (6) consider your character and integrity, (7) think creatively about potential actions, and (8) check your intuition. Choosing between two rights, or defining moments, may require an ethical test.

KEY TERMS AND PHRASES

Learning, *42*
A relatively permanent change in behavior based on practice or experience.

Modeling, *42*
Learning a skill by observing another person performing that skill.

Shaping, *42*
Learning through the reinforcement or rewarding of small steps to build to the final or desired behavior.

Cognitive Learning Theory, *43*
A theory emphasizing that learning takes place in a complicated manner involving much more than acquiring habits and small skills.

Informal Learning, *43*
A planned learning that occurs in a setting without a formal classroom, lesson plan, instructor, or examination.

Learning Style, *44*
A person's particular way of learning, reflecting the fact that people learn best in different ways.

Perception, *45*
The various ways in which people interpret things in the outside world and how they act on the basis of these interpretations.

Attribution Theory, *47*
The process by which people ascribe causes to the behavior they perceive.

Locus of Control, *48*
The way in which people look at causation in their lives.

Attitude, *48*
A predisposition to respond that exerts an influence on a person's response to a person, a thing, an idea, or a situation.

Cognitive Dissonance, *49*
The situation in which the pieces of knowledge, information, attitudes, or beliefs held by an individual are contradictory.

Job Satisfaction, *49*
The amount of pleasure or contentment associated with a job.

Organizational Citizenship Behavior, *50*
Behaviors that express a willingness to work for the good of an organization even without the promise of a specific reward.

Value, *50*
The importance a person attaches to something that serves as a guide to action.

Person-Role Conflict, *53*
A condition that occurs when the demands made by the organization or a manager clash with the basic values of the individual.

Ethics, *53*
An individual's beliefs about what is right and wrong or good and bad.

DISCUSSION QUESTIONS AND ACTIVITIES

1. Give an example from your own life in which you have learned through modeling.

2. What relatively inexpensive steps might a company take to promote informal learning among employees?

3. How can a person capitalize upon the halo effect in managing his or her career?

4. Create a scenario in which, according to attribution theory, most people would agree that a person's success was caused by his or her inner qualities.

5. Give an example of a situation in which you would most likely experience person-role conflict within an organization.

6. If one of the tests for ethical decision making is simply to use one's intuition to evaluate the decision, why should managers study ethics?

7. Thomas M. Siebel, the Chief Executive Officer of Siebel Systems Inc., hired 27 key employees away from a competitive software company, SAP, in one year. He explained, "It's a free country, so we continue to hire their people." What is your opinion of the ethics of such behavior on the part of Siebel?

ORGANIZATIONAL BEHAVIOR ON-LINE

TO DO

Ethical Promotion-Speak

Search the Internet for an advertisement or similar promotional information about a food supplement or beauty product. Note carefully if the information is provided by the company or the individual that manufactures or sells the product or by an objective third party. Give your opinion on the ethics of the person making the claim. For example, attempt to evaluate the honesty of the claims. Use at least parts of the eight-step guide to ethical decision making to help you in your ethical evaluation.

For help getting started, go to the Paula Begoun Web site at http://www.cosmeticscop.com/.

TO BOOKMARK

Job Attitudes Survey

http://www.employeesurvey.gov/Gwjob.htm

Values in Business

http://www.WVU.edu/~finance/business/values.htm

Business Ethics

http://www.dii.org (Defense Industry Initiative on Business Ethics and Conduct)

http://www.honeywell.com/about/page1_3.html (Honeywell's Code of Ethics)

CASE PROBLEM: The Stunning Plaque

Paul Anderson, a human resources director, was asked by a magazine reporter for his opinion of Generation X managers. Anderson explained that, based on his observations, most Gen X managers emphasized a team style of management. The journalist thanked Anderson for his comments. About six months later, the journalist's article containing a one-line quote from Anderson appeared in *Entrepreneur Magazine*. Anderson was pleased to be quoted in a national magazine, and appreciated the courtesy of *Entrepreneur* sending him a copy of the magazine in which he was quoted. About 30 days after the article appeared, Anderson received the following letter on high-quality stationary at his office:

State License Documentation
22817 Ventura Blvd. Section 858
Woodland Hills, CA 91364

Dear Mr. Anderson,

Congratulations! Your write-up in *Entrepreneur Magazine* is

most impressive. You are among a select few that have had the privilege of being published in a major publication. Accomplishments like yours should be displayed proudly.

At State License Documentation we do exactly that. We professionally mount your article in a museum quality plaque preserving your feature for a lifetime. It can then be displayed in your home, office or conference room. However, your plaque is more than a decoration . . . it connotes respect and credibility.

State License Documentation has earned a reputation of producing the highest quality plaques in the industry today. Our plaques have been made for Fortune 500 companies, government dignitaries, celebrities, most medical and law universities, and numerous corporate executives.

Enclosed please find information on how you can receive a free graphic rendering of your own custom plaque. The rendering allows you to preview your plaque before you order.

Order risk free. All plaques are sold on a 100% satisfaction guarantee basis. We look forward to hearing from you and preparing your free custom layout.

Warmest Regards,

R W.

Robert B. West

Executive Vice President

The accompanying sheet to the letter includes the following information:

YES!!!

*   Send me my FREE complimentary graphic layout of what my article/write-up would look like plaqued in a museum quality wall display.

    Please provide us with the information requested so we can FAX or mail your custom layout to you. The layout includes a graphic rendering with the plaque's dimensions, color trim combinations, pricing, shipping, and ordering information.

SLD is not affiliated nor endorsed by any newspaper, journal, magazine or any other publication.

Case Questions

1. What ethical issues do you perceive in this firm calling itself "State License Documentation"?
2. What might be a more accurate name to give the firm selling the plaques?
3. What perceptions are most people likely to have when they receive an envelope in the return addressed "State License Documentation"?
3. What is the true nature of the business of SLD? (What business are they really in?)

As you may have guessed, the Better Bureau Bureau offers some useful tips on unwanted direct mail solicitatations. View the Bureau's advice at http://bbb.org/about/tipsmail/asp.

SUGGESTED READINGS

Ackroyd, Stephen, and Thompson, Paul. *Organizational Misbehavior.* London: Sage, 1999.

Becker, Thomas E. "Integrity in Organizations: Beyond Honesty and Conscientiousness." *Academy of Management Review,* January 1998, pp. 154–161.

Driscoll, Dawn-Marie, and Hoffman, W. Michael. "Handling Questions of Ethics from Job Candidates." *Workforce,* July 1998, pp. 85–86.

Lipman-Blumen, Jean, and Leavitt, Harold J. "Hot Groups 'With Attitude': A New Organizational State of Mind." *Organizational Dynamics,* Spring 1999, pp. 63–72.

Murray, Bridget. "From Brain Scan to Lesson Plan." *APA Monitor,* March 2000, pp. 22–28.

Neuman, George A., and Baydoun, Ramzi. "An Empirical Examination of Overt and Covert Integrity Tests." *Journal of Business and Psychology,* Fall 1998, pp. 65–77.

Ryan, Ann Marie et al. "Workplace Integrity: Differences in Perceptions of Behaviors and Situational Factors." *Journal of Business and Psychology,* Fall 1997, pp. 85–95.

Seibert, Kent W. "Reflection-in-Action: Tools for Cultivating On-the-Job Learning Conditions." *Organizational Dynamics,* Winter 1999, pp. 54–65.

Solomon, Charlene Marmer. "Continual Learning: Racing Just to Keep Up." *Workforce,* April 1999, pp. 66–74.

Woodward, Nancy Hatch. "The Coming of the X-Managers." *HR Magazine,* March 1999, pp. 74–76.

ENDNOTES

1. Nancy Day, "Informal Learning Gets Results," *Workforce,* June 1998, p. 31.
2. Day, "Informal Learning," pp. 31–32.
3. Sandra L. Fisher and J. Kevin Ford, "Differential Effects of Learner Effort and Goal Orientation on Two Learning Outcomes," *Personnel Psychology,* Summer 1998, pp. 397–420.
4. Wanda L. Stitt-Gohdes, "Chapter 1—Teaching and Learning Styles: Implications for Business Teacher Education," in *The 21st Century: Meeting the Challenges to Business Education* (Reston, VA: National Business Education Association, 1999), p. 10.
5. David A. Kolb, Irwin M. Rubin, and James McIntyre, *Organizational Psychology: An Experiential Approach,* 3rd ed. (Upper Saddle River, NJ: Prentice Hall, 1979), pp. 38–39.
6. Ricky W. Griffin, "Effects of Work Redesign on Employee Perceptions, Attitudes, and Behaviors: A Long-Term Investigation," *Academy of Management Journal,* June 1991, p. 426.
7. Harold H. Kelley, "The Process of Causal Attribution," *American Psychologist,* February 1973, pp. 107–128.
8. Julian P. Rotter, "Generalized Expectancies for Internal vs. External Control of Reinforcement," *Psychological Monographs* 80 (1966), pp. 1–28.
9. Terence R. Mitchell, Charles M. Smyser, and Stan E. Weed, "Locus of Control: Supervision and Work Satisfaction," *Academy of Management Journal,* September 1975, pp. 623–631.
10. Arthur P. Brief, *Attitudes In and Around Organizations* (Thousand Oaks, CA: Sage, 1998), Chapter 2; "Employee Retention...Attitudes to Make Them Stay," *Managers Edge,* November 1999, p. 8; Mildred Culp, "Employee Attitude, Perception Can Have Financial Impact on a Company," syndicated column, December 27, 1998.
11. Xiao-Ping Chen, Chun Hui, and Douglas J. Sego, "The Role of Organizational Citizenship Behavior in Turnover: Conceptualization and Preliminary Tests of Key Hypotheses," *Journal of Applied Psychology,* December 1998, pp. 922–931.
12. George A. Neuman and Jill R. Kickul, "Organizational Citizenship Behaviors: Achievement Orientation and Personality," *Journal of Business and Psychology,* Winter 1998, pp. 263–264.
13. David C. McClelland, "How Motives, Skills, and Values Determine What People Do," *American Psychologist,* July 1985, p. 815.

14. John B. Miner, *Organizational Behavior: Performance and Productivity* (New York: Random House, 1988), p. 83.

15. "Qwest on Hot Seat for 'Slamming'," Associated Press, October 20, 1999.

16. Linda K. Treviño and Katherine A. Nelson, *Managing Business Ethics: Straight Talk about How to Do It Right* (New York: Wiley, 1995), pp. 66–70.

17. Treviño and Nelson, *Managing Business Ethics*, pp. 71–75.

18. Joseph L. Badaracco, Jr., "The Discipline of Building Character," *Harvard Business Review*, March–April 1998, pp. 114–124.

Individual Decision Making and Creativity

In May 1994, 30-year old Jeff Bezos was sitting at the computer in his 39th floor office in midtown Manhattan, exploring the fledgling Internet. He found a site that claimed to measure Net usage. Bezos was astonished: the Internet was growing at a rate of 2,300 percent annually. "It was a wake-up call," he says. "I started thinking, OK, what kind of business opportunity might there be here?"

Thinking up business opportunities was Bezos's job at D. E. Shaw, a firm that prides itself on hiring some of the smartest people available and then figuring out what kind of work they might profitably do. During much of his four years at Shaw, Bezos, a computer scientist, was basically an entrepreneurial odd-jobs kind of person, recalls Shaw.

The federal government decided to get out of the Internet business and allow private companies to step in and develop it, Bezos recalls. "I'm sitting there thinking we can be a complete first mover in e-commerce." He researched mail-order companies, figuring that things that sold well by mail would do well on-line. He made a list of the top 20 mail-order products and looked for where he could create the most value for customers. "Unless you could create something with a huge value proposition for the customer, it would be easier for them to do it the old way," he reasoned. And the best way to do that was "to do something that simply cannot be done any other way."

Bezos's reasoning ultimately led to books. There weren't any huge mail-order book catalogs simply because a good catalog would contain thousands, if not millions, of listings. The catalog would need to be as big as a phone book—too expensive to mail. That, of course, made it perfect for the Internet, which is the ideal container for limitless information. Such was the reasoning process that created Amazon.com, and started the e-tailing and e-commerce revolutions.

Whereas Amazon.com and Jeff Bezos are very likely household names, D. E. Shaw very likely is not, To find out more about the company where Jeff Bezos did his non-legendary ponderings, visit the D. E. Shaw & Co. Web site at http://www.deshaw.com.

PHOTO: © LWA-DANN TARDIF/STOCK MARKET

OBJECTIVES

After reading and studying this chapter and doing the exercises, you should be able to

 Work through the classical/behavioral decision-making model when faced with a major decision.

 Identify and describe factors that influence the effectiveness of decision making.

 Understand the nature of creative decision making in organizations.

 Enhance your creative problem-solving ability.

Chapter 4

Source: Joshua Quittner, "An Eye on the Future: Jeff Bezos Merely Wants Amazon.com to be Earth's Biggest Seller of Everything," *Time* (27 December 1999): 56–58; Used with permission of the publisher. See also http://www.jeffbezosispersonoftheyear.time.com.

SO WHAT? Jeff Bezos' invention of an on-line book seller may appear intriguing and mysterious. Consider also that the reasoning process that gave birth to Amazon.com reflects a very rigorous approach to problem solving and decision making important for success in any business. (Observe particularly how Bezos systematically explored alternatives to find the best one.) To be an effective decision maker, a person must think creatively. In this chapter, we study creativity in the context of individual decision making in organizations. First, we describe a model of the decision-making process; then we examine key influences on decision making, followed by a careful look at the nature and development of creativity. We return to the study of decision making in Chapter 9 with a description of group decision making. The steps in ethical decision making have already been described in Chapter 3.

TYPES OF DECISIONS

A **decision** takes place when a person chooses among two or more alternatives in order to solve a problem. People attempt to solve problems because a **problem** is a discrepancy between the ideal and the real. Being able to make good decisions is enormously valuable for your career and job performance. If you choose the right career for yourself, you will most likely have more job satisfaction, less stress, and live longer. The reason you will most likely live longer is that stress-related disorders often shorten life. Making good business decisions is more complex and difficult than most people recognize. According to research conducted by Paul C. Nutt, one-half the decisions made in organizations fail. The typical reason is that managers employ poor decision-making tactics, such as taking shortcuts when faced with time pressures.[1]

Programmed Versus Nonprogrammed Decisions

Managerial workers sometimes face routine, uncomplicated problems involving alternatives that are specified in advance. The standard responses to these uncomplicated problems are called **programmed (or routine) decisions**. Procedures already exist for how to appropriately handle the problem. Examples of programmed decisions include the procedures for accepting a check and whether to grant an employee a day of personal leave.

Managerial workers frequently face complex, nonrecurring problems where the alternatives are not specified in advance. The unique responses to these complex problems are called **nonprogrammed (or nonroutine) decisions**. Making a nonprogrammed decision requires original or creative thinking. Higher-level managers spend more of their time making nonprogrammed decisions, while lower-level managers face a higher proportion of programmed decisions.

Degree of Risk and Uncertainty Associated with Decisions

Another useful way of classifying decisions is by the degree of risk and uncertainty associated with them. Degree of risk and uncertainty can be divided into three categories: certainty, risk, and uncertainty. A condition of *certainty* exists when the facts are well known and the outcome can be predicted accurately. A retail store manager might predict with certainty that more hours of operation will lead to more sales. (It might be uncertain, however, whether the increased sales would cover the increased expenses.) Problem solving and decision making are easiest under conditions of certainty, but few major decisions are so easy to make. In other words, few business decisions are truly "no brainers."

A condition of *risk* involves incomplete certainty regarding the outcomes of various alternative courses of action. Nevertheless, there is some awareness of the probability associated with the alternatives. Based on past experience, predictions can be made about the various outcomes. An executive might be able to estimate how employees will react to an early retirement program based on previous company experience.

A condition of *uncertainty* exists when a decision must be based on limited or no factual information. In this type of decision environment, the decision maker is unable to assign probabilities to the problem-solving alternatives. When faced with a condition of uncertainty, managers rely on intuition. Michael Dell, the founder of Dell Computer, founded his company in an uncertain business environment. He predicted intuitively that enough demand existed for purchasing personal computers by telephone. His intuition proved to be eminently correct.

Another important perspective on risk taking in decision making depends upon whether the person *frames* the decision in terms of winning or losing. Individuals tend to take fewer risks regarding choices they frame positively.[2] Conversely, they tend to take more risks about choices they frame negatively. For example, they avoid risks by choosing a proposition with a sure gain of $1,000 over one with a 25 percent chance of winning $4,000 and a 75 percent chance of winning nothing. Individuals accept more risk by choosing a proposition with a 75 percent chance of losing $4,000 and a 25 percent chance of losing nothing over one with a sure loss of $3,000.

The implication for managerial practice is that if you frame negotiations in terms of winning you are less likely to take a large risk than if you frame the situation in terms of losing. Imagine you are asking for a travel budget for your team. A positive frame would be, "If I ask for $3,000, I'm confident the vice president will approve." A negative frame might be, "There's a good chance our travel budget will be shot down anyway, so I'll ask for $6,000."

A CLASSICAL/BEHAVIORAL DECISION-MAKING MODEL

Work through the classical/behavioral decision-making model when faced with a major decision.

Two different versions of how managerial workers make decisions are widely studied. The model that emphasizes how managers *should* make decisions is based on the **classical decision model**. It views the manager's environment as certain and stable and the manager as rational. Many economists view decision making in this manner. The **behavioral decision model**, in contrast, points out that decision makers have cognitive limitations and act only in terms of what they perceive in a given situation.[3] Furthermore, decision making is influenced by many emotional and personal factors. According to the behavioral model, decision making has a messy side. For example, job performance alone may not decide who obtains big promotions in a family-controlled business.

The decision-making model described here blends the classical and behavioral decision models. Managers may make decisions in a generally rational framework. Nevertheless, at various points in the model (such as choosing creative alternatives), intuition and judgment come into play. Furthermore, the discussion in the following section about influences on decision making is based heavily on the behavioral decision model.

The seven steps in the decision-making process, reflecting both the classical and behavioral models, are outlined in Exhibit 4-1 and are described in the

EXHIBIT 4-1

The Decision-Making Process

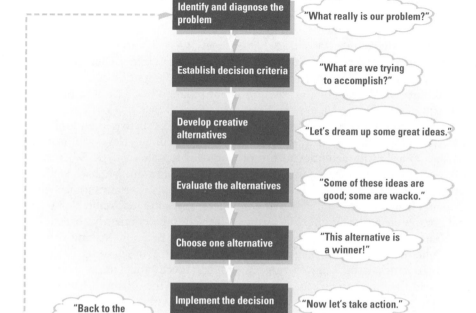

following paragraphs. The model is useful for making nonprogrammed decisions of both a personal and an organizational nature. You therefore might want to use the model in purchasing a car, choosing a career, or deciding whether to drop a product line.

Identify and Diagnose the Problem

Problem solving and decision making begin with the awareness that a problem exists. In other words, the first step in problem solving and decision making is identifying a gap between desired and actual conditions. It has been suggested that problem finding may be the key to managerial success. The more that emphasis is placed on problem finding, the less is needed for finding alternative solutions and implementation. This is especially true when lower-ranking employees are invited to participate in the problem-finding phase. Less time is required for implementation when lower-ranking workers participate from the beginning in finding and defining the problem and participating in choosing alternatives.[4]

At times, a problem is imposed on a manager, such as a demand from upper management to increase e-tailing sales by 20 percent. At other times, the manager has to search actively for a worthwhile problem or opportunity. For example, a human resources manager sought a way for her firm to celebrate cultural diversity.

A thorough diagnosis of the problem is important because the real problem may be different from the one the first look suggests. To diagnose a problem properly, you must clarify its true nature. An example is that what might appear to be a problem of quality is really one of consumer misuse of the product. To resolve the problem, one would need to better inform the consumer, not modify the product.

Establish Decision Criteria

When solving a problem, it pays to know what constitutes a good decision. **Decision criteria** are the standards of judgment used to evaluate alternatives. The more explicit the criteria, the better will be the decision. In seeking to enhance product quality, several of the decision criteria might be:

1. The customers should notice the difference in quality.
2. The price of the product should not increase.
3. Employees should be involved in making the quality improvements.
4. Job satisfaction should remain the same or increase.

A second aspect of establishing decision criteria is specifying ground rules for the decision. These include determining who will make the final decision, establishing a deadline for the decision, and determining how many resources will be invested in the decision. With respect to the last point, only so much money can be invested in a given problem.

Develop Creative Alternatives

The third step in decision making is to generate alternative solutions. This is the intellectually free-wheeling, not particularly rational, aspect of decision making. All kinds of possibilities are explored in this step even if they seem unrealistic. Often the difference between effective and mediocre decision makers is that the former do not accept the first alternative they think of. Instead, they keep digging until they find the best solution. Creativity is such a key part of decision making that it receives separate treatment later.

Evaluate the Alternatives

The next step involves comparing the relative value of the alternatives. The problem solver examines the pros and cons of each one and considers its feasibility. Part of evaluating the pros and cons of alternative solutions is to compare each one against the decision criteria established in the second step. Some alternatives would appear attractive but implementing them would be impossible or counterproductive. For example, one alternative solution a couple chose for increasing their income was to open a McDonald's restaurant. When they discovered that the franchise fee was approximately $500,000, they decided that the alternative was impossible for now.

Choose One Alternative

After investing a reasonable amount of time in evaluating the alternative solutions, it is time to choose one of them—actually make a decision. An important factor influencing the choice of alternative is the degree of uncertainty associated with it. People who prefer not to take risks choose alternatives that have the most certain outcomes. In contrast, risk takers are willing to choose alternatives with uncertain outcomes if the potential gains appear to be substantial. Despite a careful evaluation of the alternatives, ambiguity remains in most decisions. The decisions faced by managers are often complex, and the factors involved in them are often unclear.

Implement the Decision

Converting the decision into action is the next major step. Until a decision is implemented, it is not really a decision. Many decisions represent wasted effort because nobody is held responsible for implementing them. Much of a manager's job involves helping group members implement decisions. A fruitful way of evaluating a decision is to observe its implementation. A decision is seldom a good one if workers resist its implementation or if it is too cumbersome to implement.

Evaluate and Control

The final step in the decision-making framework is to evaluate how effectively the chosen alternative solved the problem and met the decision criteria. Controlling means ensuring that the results of the decision obtained are the ones set forth during the problem-identification stage.

The behavioral approach to decision making recognizes that most decision makers do not have the time or resources to wait for the best possible solution. Instead, they search for **satisficing decisions**, or those that suffice in providing a minimum standard of satisfaction. Such decisions are adequate, acceptable, or passable. Many decision makers stop their search for alternatives when they find a satisficing one.

Accepting the first reasonable alternative may only postpone the need to implement a decision that truly solves the problem and meets the decision criteria. For example, slashing the price of a pickup truck to match the competition's price can be regarded as the result of a satisficing decision. A superior decision might call for the firm to demonstrate to end users that the difference in quality is worth the higher price.

BOUNDED RATIONALITY AND INFLUENCES ON DECISION MAKING

Identify and describe factors that influence the effectiveness of decision making.

Decision making is usually not entirely rational, because so many factors influence the decision maker. Awareness of this fact stems from the research of psychologist and economist Herbert A. Simon. He proposed that bounds (or limits) to rationality are present in decision making. These bounds are the limitations of the human organism, particularly related to the processing and recall of information.[5] **Bounded rationality** means that people's limited mental abilities, combined with external influences over which they have little or no control, prevent them from making entirely rational decisions. Satisficing decisions result from bounded rationality.

Partly because of bounded rationality, decision makers often use simplified strategies, also known as **heuristics**. A heuristic becomes a rule of thumb in decision making, such as the policy to reject a job applicant who does not smile during the first three minutes of the job interview. A widely used investing heuristic is as follows: The percent of equity in your portfolio should equal 100 minus your age, with the remainder being invested in fixed-income investments. A 25-year-old would therefore have a portfolio consisting of 25 percent interest-bearing securities, such as bonds, and 75 percent in stocks. However, his or her 100-year-old grandparent should hold all debt instruments and no stocks! Heuristics help the decision maker cope with masses of information, but their oversimplification can lead to inaccurate or irrational decision making.

A host of influences on the decision-making process contribute to bounded rationality. We describe six such influences, as outlined in Exhibit 4-2.

EXHIBIT 4-2

Influences on Decision Making Contributing to Bounded Rationality

Intuition

Intuition is a key personal characteristic that influences decision making. As supported in an interview study of 60 experienced executives, making decisions by intuition is seen as a viable approach in today's business environment.[6] Effective decision makers do not rely on analytical and methodological techniques alone. Instead, they also use hunches and intuition. **Intuition** is an experience-based way of knowing or reasoning in which weighing and balancing evidence are done automatically. When relying on intuition, the decision maker arrives at a conclusion without using a step-by-step logical process. The fact that experience contributes to intuition means that decision makers can become more intuitive by solving many difficult problems. Two examples follow:

- Deborah Triant, CEO and President of Check Point Software Technologies, Inc., listens to her intuition when making decisions because intuition brings to her a kind of processing that occurs on a much deeper level than logical processing. Also, intuition helps her to synthesize and integrate information.[7]
- Ray Kroc has been described as a legend of intuition on the basis of how he started the McDonald's chain. A milkshake-mixer salesman at the time, he came to deliver eight machines to the McDonald brothers' restaurant in 1952. Kroc had a flash that fast-food hamburgers would dominate in the future. So, he made the McDonalds a buyout offer, based on what he later termed his "funny-bone instinct."[8]

The distinction between analytical and intuitive is often traced to which half of the brain is dominant. The left half of the brain controls analytical thinking, whereas the right half controls creative and intuitive thinking. (Note that many researchers have challenged the concept of left- versus right-brain dominance.) Effective problem solvers achieve a balance between analytical (left-brain) and intuitive (right-brain) thinking. Rather than operating independently of each other, the analytical and intuitive approaches should be complementary components of decision making.

Personality and Cognitive Intelligence

The personality and cognitive intelligence of the decision maker influence his or her ability to find effective solutions. One relevant personality dimension is cautiousness and conservatism. A cautious, conservative person typically opts for a low-risk solution. If a person is extremely cautious, he or she may avoid making major decisions for fear of being wrong. Cautiousness and conservatism can be in opposition to self-confidence. Confident people are willing to take reasonable risks because they have faith in the quality of their decisions.

Perfectionism has a notable impact on decision making. People who seek the perfect solution to a problem are usually indecisive because they are hesitant to accept the fact that a particular alternative is good enough. **Self-efficacy**, the feeling of being an effective and competent person, also has an influence. Researchers note, for example, that having the right amount of "gall" contributes to innovative thinking.[9]

Rigid people have difficulty identifying problems and gathering alternative solutions. People who are mentally flexible perform well in these areas. Optimism versus pessimism is another relevant personality dimension. Optimists are more likely to find solutions than pessimists are. Pessimists are likely to give up searching because they perceive situations as being hopeless.

Intelligence has a profound influence on the effectiveness of decision making. In general, intelligent and well-educated people are more likely to identify and diagnose problems and make sound decisions than are those who have less intelligence and education. A notable exception applies, however. Some intelligent, well-educated people have such a fondness for collecting facts and analyzing them that they suffer from *analysis paralysis*.

Emotional Intelligence

Emotional intelligence is important for decision making because how effective you are in managing your feelings and reading other people can affect the quality of your decisions. For example, if you cannot control your anger, you are likely to make decisions that are motivated by retaliation, hostility, and revenge. An example would be shouting and swearing at your team leader because of a work assignment you received.

Your emotional intelligence could also influence career decision making. If you understand your own feelings, you are more likely to enter an occupation, or accept a position, that matches your true attitudes. Do you remember Rodrigo Baggio, the man who became a social entrepreneur in Rio de Janiero? He recognized that he could become emotionally attached to helping poor children become computer literate. As a result, he made an excellent career choice.

Quality and Accessibility of Information

Reaching an effective decision usually requires high-quality, valid information. One of the most important purposes of management information systems is to supply managers and professionals with high-quality information. A vice president of manufacturing might be contemplating the establishment of a manufacturing plant in a distant city. She would more likely make an effective decision if the information systems group had accurate information about such factors as the quality of the workforce and environmental regulations.

Accessibility of information may be even more important than quality in determining whether or not information is used. Sometimes it takes so much time and effort to search for quality information that the manager relies on lower-quality information that is close at hand. Think of the decision-making process involved in purchasing a new automobile. Many people are more likely to rely on the opinion of friends than to search through reference sources for more systematic information.

Political Considerations

Under ideal circumstances, organizational decisions are made on the basis of the objective merits of competing alternatives. In reality, many decisions are based on political considerations, such as favoritism, alliances, or the desire of the decision maker to stay in favor with people who wield power. Political factors sometimes influence which data are given serious consideration in evaluating alternatives. The decision maker may select data that support the position of an influential person whom he or she is trying to please. For instance, one financial analyst was asked to investigate the cost effectiveness of the firm owning a corporate jet, so she give considerable weight to the "facts" supplied by a manufacturer of corporate jets. This allowed her to justify the expense of purchasing the plane.

A person with professional integrity arrives at what he or she thinks is the best decision and then make a diligent attempt to convince management of the objective merits of that solution.

Crisis and Conflict

In a crisis, many decision makers panic. They become less rational and more emotional than they would in a calm environment. Decision makers who are adversely affected by crisis perceive it to be a stressful event. As a consequence, they concentrate poorly, use poor judgment, and think impulsively. Under crisis, some managers do not bother dealing with differences of opinion because they are under so much pressure. A smaller number of managers perceive a crisis as an exciting challenge that energizes them toward their best level of problem solving and decision making. Larry Weimrach, the chairman and president of UNISYS, is such a manager. He welcomed the opportunity to bring a failing organization back to health. (UNISYS is one of the world's largest computer manufacturers and suppliers of systems.)

Conflict is related to crisis because both can be an emotional experience. When conflict is not overwhelming and is directed at real issues, not personalities, it can be an asset to decision making. By virtue of opposing sides expressing different points of view, problems can be solved more thoroughly, which leads to better decisions. One study analyzed strategic decision making by top management teams in both the food-processing and furniture-making industries. The researchers found that the quality of a decision appears to improve with the introduction of conflict. However, the conflict often had the negative side effect of creating antagonistic relationships among some members of the top management team.[10] (More will be said about the positive and negative sides of conflict in Chapter 7.)

Values of the Decision Maker

Values influence decision making at every step. Ultimately, all decisions are based on values. A manager who places a high value on the personal welfare of employees tries to avoid alternatives that create hardship for workers and implements decisions in ways that lessen turmoil. Another value that significantly influences decision making is the pursuit of excellence. A manager or professional who embraces the pursuit of excellence (and is therefore conscientious) will search for the high-quality alternative solution.

Attempting to preserve the status quo is a value held by many managers, as well as others. Clinging to the status quo is perceived as a hidden trap in decision making that can prevent making optimum decisions. People tend to cling to the status quo because by not taking action they can prevent making a bad decision.[11] If you value the status quo too highly, you may fail to make a decision that could bring about major improvements. At one company, the vice president of human resources received numerous inquiries about when the firm would begin offering benefits for domestic partners (of both the opposite or same sex). The vice president reasoned that since the vast majority of employees rated the benefit package highly, a change was not needed. A few employees took their complaints about "biased benefits" to the CEO. The vice president of human resources was then chastised by the CEO for not suggesting an initiative that would keep the company in the forefront of human resources management.

Procrastination

Many people are poor decision makers because they **procrastinate**, or delay taking action without a valid reason. Procrastination results in indecisiveness and inaction and is a major cause of self-defeating behavior. Yet research suggests that procrastination can be overcome by learning how to become more self-disciplined.[12] Part of the process involves setting goals for overcoming procrastination and conquering the problem in small steps. For example, a person might first practice making a deadline for a decision over a minor activity such as responding to a group of e-mail inquiries.

THE NATURE OF CREATIVITY

Understand the nature of creative decision making in organizations.

Creativity is an essential part of problem solving and decision making when dealing with nonprogrammed decisions. Creative thinking is an obvious asset when searching for creative alternatives yet also makes a contribution at other decision-making stages. Out-of-the-ordinary thinking, for example, makes a contribution to identifying and diagnosing problems and implementing solutions. **Creativity** can be defined simply as the process of developing good ideas that can be put into action. We approach the nature of creativity from three perspectives: steps in the creative process, characteristics of creative people, and conditions necessary for creativity.

Steps in the Creative Process

Understanding the steps involved in creativity helps a person become more creative and better manage creativity among others. An old but well-accepted model of creativity can be applied to organizations. The model divides creative thinking into five steps, as shown in Exhibit 4-3. Step 1 is *opportunity or problem recognition:* a person discovers that a new opportunity exists or a problem needs resolution. Herbert Axelrod, the CEO of THF Publications, recognized that his firm had a need to diversify beyond the publication of pet books in order to boost profits.

Step 2 is *immersion:* The individual concentrates on the problem and becomes immersed in it. He or she will recall and collect information that seems relevant, dreaming up alternatives without refining or evaluating them. Axelrod scanned pet product catalogs and spoke to pet owners about their requirements. Step 3 is *incubation:* The person keeps the assembled information in mind for a while. He or she does not appear to be working on the problem actively, yet the subconscious mind takes over. While the information is simmering, it is being arranged into meaningful patterns. CEO Axelrod did not take any action for two years on the problem he identified.

One way to capitalize on the incubation phase of creativity is to deliberately take a break from creative thinking. Instead, engage in a routine activity such as updating your electronic address book or sorting through mail. By immersing yourself in an entirely different and less taxing mental activity, a solution to the creative problem may emerge.

Step 4 is *insight:* The problem-conquering solution flashes into the person's mind at an unexpected time, such as on the verge of sleep, during a shower, or while running. Insight is also called the *Aha! Experience:* All of a sudden, something clicks. One day while walking his dog, Axelrod thought, "Why not branch into pet food with a long shelf life but that would also not last too long at home? How about a dog bone that dogs would consume quickly?"

Step 5 is *verification and application:* The individual sets out to prove that the creative solution has merit. Verification procedures include gathering supporting evidence, logical persuasion, and experimenting with new ideas. Application requires tenacity because most novel ideas are at first rejected as being impractical. Work associates first scoffed when Axelrod bounced around his idea of a pet book publisher selling short-lasting dog bones as a sideline. Yet Axelrod knew that his existing distribution channels were a natural for expansion into a delectable dog bone. Axelrod had enough capital to give his idea a pilot run. The dog bone diversification has proved to be extraordinarily profitable for THF Publications.

Note that the end product of Axelrod's creative thinking was more of a business idea than a new invention. The key technical aspect of his idea, however, was making the bones extra chewable so most dogs wouldn't stick with them for a month.

EXHIBIT 4-3

Steps in the Creative Process

Source: The original source for these stages is Graham Wallace, *The Art of Thought* (New York: Harcourt Brace, 1926).

Although creativity usually follows the same steps, it is not a mechanical process that can be turned on and off. Much of creativity is intricately woven into a person's intellect and personality. Furthermore, creativity varies among individuals, and creative people themselves have highs and lows in their creativity.[13]

Characteristics of Creative People

Creative workers are different in many ways from their less creative counterparts. The characteristics of creative people, including creative leaders, can be grouped into three key areas: knowledge, intellectual abilities, and personality. Before studying this information, compare your thinking to that of creative people by doing the accompanying Self-Assessment, found on page 77.

Knowledge

Creative problem solving requires a broad background of information, including facts and observations. This is particularly true because creativity often takes the form of combining two or more existing things in a new and different way. For example, a personal digital assistant is a combination personal computer, fax machine, and cell phone.

Intellectual Abilities

Creative problem solvers tend to be bright rather than brilliant. Intelligence and creativity tend to be moderately correlated up until an IQ of about 120 (the superior range of intelligence). Beyond that point, the relationship between intelligence and creativity become smaller.[14] Applying the triarchic theory of intelligence, the creative type of intelligence would obviously be important for creative problem solving. An important intellectual characteristic of creative people is that they are good at generating alternative solutions to problems in a short period of time. A good sense of humor and intellectual playfulness are outstanding characteristics of a creative problem solver. Humor helps release creativity, and some creativity is required to be funny.

Creative people maintain a youthful curiosity throughout their lives. The curiosity is not centered just on their own field of expertise, and they are enthusiastic about puzzling problems. Creative people are also open and responsive to the feelings and emotions of others. They score high on Openness to Experience. The accompanying Organizational Behavior in Action insert illustrates how being intellectually curious about an everyday article can virtually create a new industry.

Creative people are able to think divergently. They can expand the number of alternatives to a problem, thus moving away from a single solution. Yet the creative thinker also knows when it is time to think convergently, narrowing the number of useful solutions. For example, the divergent thinker might think of 27 different names for a Web site to sell term life insurance. Yet, at some point, he or she will have to converge toward choosing the best domain names.

Creativity can stem from both *fluid intelligence* and *crystallized intelligence*. Fluid intelligence depends on raw processing ability, or how quickly and accurately you learn information and solve problems. Like raw athletic ability, fluid intelligence begins to decline by age 30, partly because our nerve conduction slows. Crystallized intelligence is accumulated knowledge that increases with age and experience.[15] The implication for a manager who wants to assemble a creative group is to staff it with both workers of varying age. Generation X members of the group might have the wildest, most unique ideas. However, the baby boomers might have better intuition into what will work.

SELF-ASSESSMENT

The Creative Personality Test

Directions: Describe each of the following statements as "mostly true" or "mostly false."

	Mostly True	Mostly False
1. It is generally a waste of time to read articles, Web sites, and books outside my immediate field of interest.	—	✓
2. I frequently have the urge to suggest ways of improving products and services I use.	✓	—
3. Reading fiction and visiting art museums are time wasters.	—	✓
4. I am a person of very strong convictions. What is right is right; what is wrong is wrong.	✓	—
5. I enjoy it when my boss hands me vague instructions.	✓	—
6. Making order out of chaos is actually fun.	✓	—
7. Only under extraordinary circumstances would I deviate from my To Do list (or other ways in which I plan my day).	—	✓
8. Taking a different route to work is fun, even if it takes longer.	✓	—
9. Rules and regulations should not be taken too seriously. Most rules can be broken under unusual circumstances.	✓	—
10. Playing with a new idea is fun even if it doesn't benefit me in the end.	✓	—
11. Some of my best ideas have come from building on the ideas of others.	✓	—
12. Writing should try to avoid the use of unusual words and word combinations.	—	✓
13. I frequently jot down improvements in the job I would like to make in the future.	✓	—
14. I prefer to avoid using high-technology devices as much as possible.	—	✓
15. I prefer writing personal notes or poems to loved ones rather than relying on greeting cards.	—	✓
16. At one time or another in my life, I have enjoyed doing puzzles.	✓	—
17. If my thinking is clear, I will find the one best solution to a problem.	—	✓
18. It is best to interact with coworkers who think much like I do.	—	✓
19. Detective work would have some appeal to me.	✓	—
20. Tight controls over people and money are necessary to run a successful organization.	✓	—

Scoring and Interpretation: Give yourself one point for each answer in the creative direction for each question, indicated as follows:

1. Mostly False	11. Mostly True
2. Mostly True	12. Mostly False
3. Mostly False	13. Mostly True
4. Mostly False	14. Mostly False
5. Mostly True	15. Mostly True
6. Mostly True	16. Mostly True
7. Mostly False	17. Mostly False
8. Mostly True	18. Mostly False
9. Mostly True	19. Mostly True
10. Mostly True	20. Mostly False
	Total __17__

Extremely high or low scores are the most meaningful. A score of 15 or more suggests that your personality and attitudes are similar to those of creative people, including creative managers. A score of 8 or less suggests that you are more of an intellectual conformist at present. Don't be discouraged. Most people can develop in the direction of becoming more creative. The type of exercise described in Skill-Development Exercise 4-2 can help you enhance your creative problem solving.

How does your score compare to your self-evaluation of your creativity? We suggest that you also obtain feedback on your creativity from somebody familiar with your thinking and your work.

Organizational Behavior *in Action*

Breakthrough Product Still Supermarket Freezer Mainstay

on't label Gerry Thomas the father of the TV dinner, at least not when he is within earshot. "It bothers me," Thomas said, pointing to a boldface headline above a recent story on him. "I really didn't invent the dinner. I innovated the tray on how it could be served, coined the name, and developed some unique packaging."

Still, as Swanson celebrates the 45th anniversary of the archetypal home meal of convenience, the 77-year-old Thomas is receiving added recognition. A University of Nebraska graduate with a business degree, Thomas was a few years into his job as a $200-a-month salesman for Omaha-based C. A. Swanson and Sons in late 1954. The company was frantic over what to do with 520,000 pounds of excess holiday turkeys being stored in ten refrigerated rail cars.

On a sales trip to Pittsburgh, Thomas was visiting a distributor at a warehouse when he spotted a metal tray. "I was told it was something Pan American Airline was experimenting with. They thought maybe they could serve warm food on their overseas flights. Up until then, it was cold sandwiches," Thomas recalled. "It was just a single-compartment tray with foil. I asked if I could borrow it and stuck it in the pocket of my overcoat. On the flight home, I took out an envelope and did some doodling. That's when I came up with the three-compartment tray."

Back in Omaha, Thomas saw people outside an appliance store, jockeying for a look at television sets that showed only a black-and-white test pattern on a 10-inch screen. "I figured if you could borrow from that, maybe you could get some attention," Thomas said. "I think the name made all the difference in the world."

Thomas presented his idea to Clark and Gilbert Swanson, who were running the company. The first Swanson TV dinners—turkey with cornbread dressing and gravy, sweet potatoes and buttered peas—sold for about $1 a piece and could be cooked in 25 minutes.

Swanson TV dinner recently celebrated its 45th anniversary in style with a commemorative tray print on Hollywood's Walk of Fame. To read more about it, visit http://vlasic.com/swanson/celebration.html.

Personality

Creative people tend to have a positive self-image without being blindly self-confident. Because they are self-confident, creative people are able to cope with criticism of their ideas. Creative people can tolerate the isolation necessary for developing ideas. Talking to others is a good source of ideas, yet at some point the creative problem solver has to work alone and concentrate.

Creative people are frequently nonconformists and do not need strong approval from the group. Many creative problem-solvers are thrill seekers, who find developing imaginative solutions to problems to be a source of thrills. Creative people are also persistent, which is especially important for the verification and application stage of creative thinking. Creative people enjoy dealing with ambiguity and chaos. Less creative people become quickly frustrated when task descriptions are unclear and disorder exists.

SKILL-DEVELOPMENT EXERCISE

COLLABORATE

The Forced Association Technique

The task is for individuals or groups to solve a problem by making associations between the properties of two objects. Working alone or within a group, select a word at random from a textbook or dictionary. If you choose a preposition instead of a noun, verb, or adjective, try again. Next, list properties and attributes of this word.

Assume that your problem is to improve the job satisfaction of employees. Assume also that the word you chose at random was *jaguar*. Among its attributes would be "fast-moving," "energetic," "intense," "self-sufficient," "freedom-loving." The forced association is supposed to help solve the problem. Look for a link between the properties of the jaguar and the problem object. To increase job satisfaction, you might give employees more autonomy (freedom-loving) and offer them opportunities for job rotation (fast-moving).

Conditions Necessary for Creativity

Well-known creativity researcher Teresa M. Amabile has summarized 22 years of research about the conditions necessary for creativity in organizations. Creativity takes place when three components join together: expertise, creative-thinking skills, and the right type of motivation.[16] Expertise refers to the necessary knowledge to put facts together. The more facts floating around in your head, the more likely you are to combine them in some useful way. The salesman who invented a convenient way of serving TV dinners linked together knowledge about food serving and the promising technology of television.

Creative thinking refers to how flexibly and imaginatively individuals approach problems. If you know how to keep digging for alternatives and to avoid getting stuck in the status quo, your chances of being creative multiply. Persevering, or sticking with a problem to a conclusion, is essential for finding creative solutions. A few rest breaks to gain a fresh perspective may be helpful, but the creative person keeps coming back until a solution emerges. Quite often an executive will keep sketching different organization charts on paper or with a graphics program before the right one surfaces that will help the firm run smoothly.

The right type of motivation is the third essential ingredient for creative thought. A fascination with or passion for the task is more important than searching for external rewards. (Emotional intelligence also contains this type of motivation.) People will be the most creative when they are motivated primarily by the satisfaction and challenge of the work itself. Although Jeff Bezos ultimately became wealthy from building Amazon.com, he was primarily motivated by the challenge of finding a way to capitalize upon the potential of the Internet as a marketing vehicle.

Passion for the task and high intrinsic motivation contribute to a total absorption in the work and intense concentration, the **experience of flow**. It is an experience so engrossing and enjoyable that the task becomes worth doing for its own sake regardless of the external consequences.[17] Perhaps you have had this experience when completely absorbed in a hobby or being at your best in a sport or dance. (Flow also means *being in the zone*.) A highly creative businessperson, such as an entrepreneur developing a plan for worldwide distribution of a product, will often achieve the experience of flow.

In addition to the internal conditions that foster creativity, three factors outside the person play a key role. An environmental need must stimulate the setting of a goal. This is another way of saying, "Necessity is the mother of invention." For example, a manager of materials management might be told, "We've got too much inventory in the warehouse. Reduce it by 75 percent, but don't lose money for us." No standard solution is available. The manager sets the goal of reducing the inventory, including working with the marketing department to accomplish the feat.

Another condition that fosters creativity is enough conflict and tension to put people on edge. Jerry Hirschberg, founder and president of Nissan Design International, says that people should be asked to hold what appears to be conflicting ideas in the mind simultaneously while encouraging their opposition to do the same. Understanding opposing ideas helps you gain a new perspective. An example Hirschberg offers is that Nissan asked his design team to produce a "world" car. Many staff members were threatened by the idea of a world car because it implied an ordinary vehicle of mass taste. A brave design manager, however, introduced a conflicting opinion. He said, "Whether we like it or not, there are some very successful world cars out there."

Once the group said that producing such a car would not mean designing one to appease some low common denominator, the group no longer felt threatened. The group became eager to accept the assignment. By going past their fears, the group "embraced the dragon."[18] (Conquered their fears)

Another external factor in creativity is encouragement, including a permissive atmosphere that welcomes new ideas. A manager who encourages imaginative and original thinking and does not punish people for making honest mistakes is likely to receive creative ideas from employees.

ENHANCING AND IMPROVING CREATIVITY

Enhance your creative problem-solving ability.

A unifying theme runs through all forms of creativity training and suggestions for creativity improvement: Creative problem solving requires an ability to overcome traditional thinking. The concept of *traditional thinking* is relative but generally refers to a standard and frequent way of finding a solution to a problem. A nontraditional solution to a problem is thus a modal or recurring solution. For example, traditional thinking suggests that to increase revenue a retail store should conduct a sale. Creative thinking would point toward other solutions. Border's Book Stores, a chain of upscale bookstores, increased revenues substantially by also selling cassette tapes and CDs and opening cafes in their stores.

The central task in becoming creative is to break down rigid thinking that blocks new ideas.[19] A conventional-thinking manager might accept the long-standing policy that spending more than $5,000 requires three levels of approval. A creative leader might ask, "Why do we need three levels of approval for spending $5,000? If we trust people enough to make them managers, why can't they have budget authorization to spend at least $10,000?"

Overcoming traditional thinking is so important to creative thinking that the process has been characterized in several different ways. A representative concept is that *a creative person thinks outside the box*. A "box" in this sense is a category that confines and restricts thinking. Many executives have saved millions of company dollars by thinking outside the box that headquarters must be located in a major city.

Here we describe several illustrative approaches and techniques for enhancing employee creativity. Recognize also that the conditions for creativity just described can be converted into techniques for creativity enhancement. For example, given that encouragement is a condition for creativity, a manager might be able to enhance creativity by encouraging imaginative thinking.

1. *Brainstorming.* Brainstorming is the best-known technique for developing mental flexibility, which most of you have already done. As a refresher, do the Skill-Development Exercise that follows, which presents rules and guidelines for brainstorming and also gives you a challenging Net world task. Brainstorming is also accomplished through e-mail, in which participants simultaneously enter their suggestions into a computer. Each participant's input appears simultaneously on the screen of the other participants. In this way, nobody feels intimidated by a dominant member, and participants think more independently. The forced-association technique presented in the Skill-Development Exercise below is a variant of brainstorming. Electronic gift cards used by retailers and originated by Neiman Marcus were a product of brainstorming on how to improve the demand for gift certificates.

2. *Idea quotas.* A straightforward and effective technique for enhancing worker creativity is to simply demand that workers come up with good ideas. Dana Corporation sets idea quotas—two ideas per employee per month. The ideas must be generated by everyone in the company from the CEO to production workers. The company strives for 80 percent participation and 80 percent implementation. Employees are asked to focus on quality, customer service, production control, office efficiency, and security. At one Dana division, profitability increased 40 percent after idea quotas were imposed.[20] (However, an experiment was not conducted. The 40 percent increase might be attributed to factors other than idea quotas.)

3. *Heterogeneous groups.* Forming heterogeneous groups can enhance creativity because a diverse group brings various viewpoints to the problem at hand. Key diversity factors include professional discipline, job experiences, and a variety

SKILL-DEVELOPMENT EXERCISE

COLLABORATE

Brainstorming

After studying the following rules for brainstorming, organize into groups to play http://www.getreallyrich.com.

1. Use groups of five to seven people.
2. Encourage the spontaneous expression of ideas. All suggestions are welcome, even if they are outlandish or outrageous. Avoid evaluating suggestions at this point, particularly with respect to making negative statements about suggestions.
3. Quantity and variety are important. The greater the number of ideas, the greater is the likelihood of a breakthrough idea.
4. Encourage combination and improvement of ideas. This process is referred to as piggybacking or hitchhiking.

5. One person serves as the secretary and records ideas, writing them on a sheet of paper, white board, chalkboard, flip chart, or computer.
6. Do not overstructure the session by following any of the rules too rigidly. Brainstorming is a spontaneous process.

Group Activity Your group assumes the role of a team of people who want to start an Internet **COLLABORATE** company. Your task is to develop a domain name and a general explanation of your business model. In other words, explain how you intend to generate revenue (or a profit) from your site. Strive to think of a business that would actually stand a chance of making money.

of demographic factors.[21] A culturally diverse group can be effective at developing creative marketing ideas to appeal to a particular cultural group. Levi-Strauss has on occasion included an adolescent in a problem-solving group to help understand what type of jeans appeal to members of that age group.

4. *Financial incentives.* A variety of laboratory studies have concluded that working for external rewards, particularly financial rewards, dampens creativity.[22] If you focus on the reward, you may lose out on the joy (internal rewards) of being creative. In work settings, however, financial incentives are likely to spur imaginative thinking, such as in paying employees for useful suggestions, and paying scientists royalties for patents that become commercially useful.

5. *Architecture and physical layout.* A current trend is for companies to restructure space to fire up creativity, harness energy, and enhance the flow of knowledge and ideas. The general point is that any configuration of the physical environment that decreases barriers to divergence, incubation, and convergence is likely to stimulate the flow of creative thinking.[23] Among the specifics are that creative thinking is more likely to be enhanced by cubicles rather than corner offices, by elevators rather than escalators, and by atriums rather than hallways. In short, creating the opportunity for physical interaction facilitates the flow of ideas, which in turn facilitates creative thinking.

IMPLICATIONS FOR MANAGERIAL PRACTICE

1. When making nonprogrammed decisions of importance, follow carefully the decision-making steps. Although going through the steps may appear time consuming, the payout can be decisions of higher quality. Because so many decisions about organizational behavior are nonprogrammed, it is worthwhile to follow the decision-making steps.

2. Although a systematic approach to decision making is highly recommended, this does not mean that a managerial worker should avoid using intuition and insight. Intuition is particularly helpful in finding a problem to work on and in selecting from among the available alternatives. Top-level decision makers still rely heavily on intuition.

3. A key strategy for improving managerial decision making is for the manager to enhance his or her creativity. When faced with a problem, the manager should exercise discipline to search for several alternative solutions, because this is the essence of creativity.

4. To unleash creativity, it may be necessary to help group members overcome the feeling that bringing about change is almost impossible. An approach worth a try is to use the simple phrase, "Up until now" in a brainstorming session or staff meeting. Here is how it works: The group says, "Management won't let us try that." You reply, "*Up until now*, we haven't asked to try that."[24]

SUMMARY OF KEY POINTS

 Work through the classical/behavioral decision-making model when faced with a major decision.

A decision takes place when a person chooses from among two or more alternatives in order to solve a problem. Programmed decisions are made in response to uncomplicated problems, while nonprogrammed decisions are unique responses to complex problems. The degree of risk associated with a decision can be classified as certainty, risk, and uncertainty. Framing a decision in terms of a positive outcome usually leads to less risk taking than if the person frames the decision in terms of a negative outcome.

A classical/behavioral decision-making model incorporates the ideas that managers make decisions in a generally rational framework, yet intuition and judgment also enter into the model. The seven steps in the model are as follows: (1) Identify and diagnose the problem, (2) establish decision criteria, (3) develop creative alternatives, (4) evaluate the alternatives, (5) choose one alternative, (6) implement the decision, and (7) evaluate and control.

Identify and describe factors that influence the effectiveness of decision making.

Bounded rationality means that people's limited mental abilities, combined with external influences over which they have little or no control, prevent them from making entirely rational decisions. Satisficing decisions result from bounded rationality. A host of influences contribute to bounded rationality, including the following: intuition, personality and cognitive intelligence, emotional intelligence, quality and accessibility of information, political considerations, crisis and conflict, and procrastination.

 Understand the nature of creative decision making in organizations.

Understanding the steps involved in creativity helps a person become more creative and better manage creativity among others. The steps are as follows: (1) opportunity or problem recognition, (2) immersion, (3) incubation, (4) insight, and (5) verification.

Creative workers are different from others in several key areas. They typically have a broad background of knowledge, tend to be bright rather than brilliant, have a youthful curiosity, and think divergently. Both fluid intelligence and crystallized intelligence contribute to creativity. Creative workers tend to have a positive self-image and are often nonconformists who enjoy intellectual thrills, along with ambiguity and chaos.

 Enhance your creative problem-solving ability.

For creativity to occur, three components must join together: expertise, creative-thinking skills, and motivation characterized by a passion for the task. Total absorption in the work, the experience of flow, is also important. An environmental need should be present, along with some conflicting opinions, and creativity should be encouraged.

A unifying theme runs through all forms of creativity training and suggestions for creativity improvement: Creative problem solving requires an ability to overcome traditional thinking. Techniques for enhancing creativity include brainstorming, imposing idea quotas, forming heterogeneous groups, offering financial incentives for creative problem solving, and using a physical layout conducive to creative thinking.

KEY TERMS AND PHRASES

Decision, *66*
The act of choosing among two or more alternatives in order to solve a problem.

Problem, *66*
A discrepancy between the ideal and the real.

Programmed (or Routine) Decision, *66*
A standard response to an uncomplicated problem.

Nonprogrammed (or Nonroutine) Decision, *66*
A unique response to a complex problem.

Classical Decision Model, *67*
An approach to decision making that views the manager's environment as certain and stable and the manager as rational.

Behavioral Decision Model, *67*
An approach to decision making that views managers as having cognitive limitations and acting only in terms of what they perceive in a given situation.

Decision Criteria, *69*
The standards of judgment used to evaluate alternatives.

Satisficing Decision, *70*
A decision that provides a minimum standard of satisfaction.

Bounded Rationality, *70*
The idea that people's limited mental abilities, combined with external influences over which they have little or no control, prevent them from making entirely rational decisions.

Heuristics, *70*

Simplified strategies that become rules of thumb in decision making.

Intuition, *71*

An experience-based way of knowing or reasoning in which weighing and balancing evidence are done automatically.

Self-efficacy, *72*

The feeling of being an effective and competent person with respect to a task.

Procrastinate, *74*

Delaying to take action without a valid reason.

Creativity, *74*

The process of developing good ideas that can be put into action.

Experience of Flow, *79*

Being *in the zone*; total absorption in one's work.

DISCUSSION QUESTIONS AND ACTIVITIES

1. What really was the *problem* Jeff Bezos faced when he was exploring the commercial possibilities of the Internet?

2. Can you give an example of a failed decision in business? Explain why you consider the decision to be a failure.

3. Which decision criteria are relevant for you in choosing a career?

4. How would the concept of bounded rationality apply to making decisions about financial investments?

5. Give an example of a type of business-related work in which intuition is a key success factor.

6. A technique for creative problem solving is to remind oneself of the problem just before going to sleep. Upon waking up, a good solution often presents itself. How does this technique relate to the stages of creative thought?

7. Ask an experienced worker what he or she believes is the most important action a manager can take to enhance creative thinking among group members. Compare the response you get with the information in this chapter.

ORGANIZATIONAL BEHAVIOR ON-LINE

TO DO

Creativity Training

Use the Internet to learn more about what companies are doing to enhance employee creativity. Be specific when you make an entry in your search engine to avoid being deluged with a choice of Web sites far removed from your topic. A sample phrase to enter would be "creativity training program." When you have located one or two sites that give some details about a training program, compare the creativity enhancement information you have found to the information in this chapter. Note similarities and differences, and be prepared to discuss your findings in class.

About 5,000 Web search engines are now in operation.

Here are two effective engines you might have overlooked: Fast Search: All the Web, All the Time and http://www. alltheweb.com/ and http://www.google.com/.

TO BOOKMARK

Problem Solving
http://www.thinksmart.com

Intuition
http://www.intuition.org

Creativity
http://www.omega23.com/creativity.html
http://www.jamming.com

CASE PROBLEM: Penn Ball Goes to the Dogs: Arf, Arf, Arf!

Sales of tennis balls by Penn Racquet Sports have plateaued in recent years. Sales peaked at close to $100 million in 1991, then declined steadily until 1994 to about $75 million annually. From 1994 forward, sales have remained about the same. Penn, the number one manufacturer of tennis balls in the United States, has been suffering from nearly a ten-year decline in recreational tennis. In addition to a decline in sales,

the retail price of tennis balls has been about the same for 15 years, not adjusted for inflation.

Executives and other problem solvers at Penn explored various options for finding more customers. One approach the company has taken to improving sales is to invest in a Research and Development Group. The group seeks ways to improve the ball, such as looking for the best possible felt for the cover. In addition to improving the product, alternatives considered for boosting sales were going global, selling direct through a toll-free number, and selling on the Internet. Direct selling by phone (1-800-BUY-PENN) and a Web site for selling Penn products (http://www.BuyPenn.com) were implemented. However, more resources were invested in increasing sales by appealing to another species. Penn has begun marketing its familiar fuzzy, yellow balls to dog owners. The dog-ball, however, is white.

R. P. Fetchem's is a traditional tennis ball that has been dressed up as a "natural felt fetch toy" for dogs. (Customers can also purchase them for cats and toddlers.) Penn president Gregg R. Weida, who owns a schnauzer named Jake, explains that "Ten times more people own pets than play tennis." Penn hopes to boost sales of tennis balls by 5 to 10 percent through its tennis balls for dogs. For the benefit of the four-legged end user, the balls are dye-free. They carry the Ralston Purina Company logo, under a licensing agreement with the dog food manufacturer.

A major change is the price of the new line of tennis balls: $4 to $5 for a container of two Fetchem's versus around $2.50 for a container of three conventional tennis balls. PetsMart Inc. plans to test the new line of balls by ordering 400 cases for its 413 stores. "The fact that it's got the Ralston name and the natural felt are pluses," says Greg Forquer, the vice president for merchandising at PetsMart.

Penn is a small division of GenCorp Inc., a multi-division company specializing in chemicals and defense products. Making a move into dog toys is an attempt to combat the problem of declining interest in tennis in North America. Recreational play is down almost 20 percent over the last decade, and ball sales have dropped 29 percent since 1991. Yet there is still a remaining base of over 5 million players. Brad Patterson, executive director of the Tennis Industry Association says, "Twenty years ago there was no inline skating, no Blockbuster Video, no home computers. It's harder to grab mind share."

The dog-toy solution has been floating around Penn for years. Laura Kurzu, who directs the Penn account at an advertising agency, has connections at Ralston Purina. She was convinced that the two should enter into a licensing deal, but says she was at first laughed at from both sides. Yet Penn sees a growth opportunity in marketing to dog owners. Pet-pampering is a booming business. Human beings will pay $5.95 per box for doggie pasta, $59.95 for a pet canopy bed, and $500 for a heated dog house.

Of more direct relevance to Penn, pet owners buy toys. In a recent year, they spent close to $42 million on dog toys sold in pet stores. Given that many dog toys sell for as much as $25, paying $5 for a package of two tennis balls is a small expense. Jim Sweeney, a regional manager in Chicago for Pet Supplies Plus, predicts that Penn could sell 1,000 cans (really plastic containers) of Fetchum's per month.

Penn faces competitive threats with its new venture. Melia Luxury Pet Products makes six flavors of dog tennis balls including "zesty orange," and sales have reached several hundred thousand dollars per year. A representative of a pet industry trade association said about recreational products for dogs, "Everyone and their brother wants to get in."

Case Questions

1. What alternatives to increasing the sales of tennis balls for people would you recommend to Penn management?
2. What recommendations can you give Penn for increasing the market for Fetchum's?
3. Serious tennis players use a can of balls no more than twice. How can Penn encourage dog-owners to purchase Fetchum's as frequently?
4. To what extent has Penn solved the problem of declining sales of tennis balls?

Source: Dennis Berman, "Now Tennis Balls Are Chasing the Dogs," *Business Week*, July 13, 1998, p. 138; http://www.pennracquet.com.

To learn more about how Penn taught an old product a new trick, visit either of these on line magazine sites, which have reported on Penn's enterprising spirit: http://www.entrepreneurmag.com or http://fsb.com/fortunesb/.

SUGGESTED READINGS

"A Creative Dialogue." *Psychology Today*, July/August 1999, pp. 58–61.

Drazin, Robert, Gylnn, Mary Ann, and Kazanjian, Robert K. "Multilevel Theorizing about Creativity in Organizations: A Sensemaking Perspective." *The Academy of Management Review*, April 1999, pp. 286–307.

Hammonds, Keith H. "Grassroots Leadership: Ford Motor Co." *Fast Company*. April 2000, pp. 138–152.

Handy, Charles. *Beyond Creativity*. Boston, MA: Harvard Business School Publishing, 1998.

Mitroff, Ian. *Smart Thinking for Crazy Times: The Art of Solving the Right Problems*. San Francisco: Berrett-Koehler Publishers, 1998.

Rosenfeld, Jill. "Here's an Idea!" *Fast Company*, April 2000, pp. 97–130.

Runco, Mark A., and Pritzker, Steven R. (eds.) *Encyclopedia of Creativity*. San Diego, Academic Press, 1999.

Schrage, Michael. *Serious Play: How the World's Best Companies Simulate to Innovate*. Boston, MA: Harvard Business School Publishing, 1999.

Sellers, Patricia. "Big Goals Don't Work." *Fortune*, April 3, 2000, pp. 39–40, 44.

von Hippel, Eric, Thomke, Stefan, and Sonnack, Mary. "Creating Breakthroughs at 3M." *Harvard Business Review*, September–October 1999, pp. 47–57.

ENDNOTES

1. Paul C. Nutt, "Surprising but True: Half the Decisions in Organizations Fail," *Academy of Management Executive*, November 1999, p. 75.

2. Daniel Kahneman and Amos Tversky, "Rational Choices and the Forming of Decisions," *Journal of Business* 4, 1986, pp. 5251–5278.

3. James L. Bowditch and Anthony F. Buono, *A Primer on Organizational Behavior*, 3rd ed. (New York: Wiley, 1994), p. 125.

4. Min Basadur, "Managing Creativity: A Japanese Model," *Academy of Management Executive*, May 1992, p. 30.

5. Herbert A. Simon, "Rational Choice and the Structure of the Environment," *Psychological Review* 63, 1956, pp. 129–138.

6. Lisa A. Burke and Monica K. Miller, "Taking the Mystery Out of Intuitive Decision Making," *Academy of Management Executive*, November 1999, p. 91–99.

7. "Should You Trust Your Intuition?" *Manager's Edge*, December 1998, p. 4.

8. Russell Wild, "Naked Hunch," *Success*, June 1998, p. 55.

9. Michael A. West and James L. Farr (eds.), *Innovation and Creativity at Work: Psychological and Organizational Strategies* (New York: John Wiley, 1990).

10. Allen C. Amason, "Distinguishing the Effects of Functional and Dysfunctional Conflict on Strategic Decision-Making Effectiveness," *Academy of Management Journal*, February 1996, pp. 123–148.

11. John S. Hammond, Ralph L. Keeney, and Howard Rafia, "The Hidden Traps in Decision Making," *Harvard Business Review*, September–October 1998, p. 50.

12. Andrew J. DuBrin, *Getting It Done: The Transforming Power of Self-Discipline* (Princeton, NJ: Peterson's/Pacesetter Books, 1995), pp. 49–71.

13. Teresa M. Amabile, "The Social Psychology of Creativity: A Componential Conceptualization," *Journal of Personality and Social Psychology*, August 1983, pp. 357–376.

14. Dorothy Leonard and Walter Swap, *When Sparks Fly: Igniting Creativity in Small Groups* (Boston, MA: Harvard Business School Press, 1999).

15. "Why Kids Beat Adults at Video Games: The Two Types of Intelligence," *USA Weekend*, January 1–3, 1999, p. 5.

16. Teresa M. Amabile, "How to Kill Creativity," *Harvard Business Review*, September–October 1998, pp. 78–79.

17. Mihaly Csikzentmihalyi, "If We Are So Rich, Why Aren't We Happy?" *American Psychologist*, October 1999, p. 824.

18. "Creativity First," *Leadership* (American Management Association International), May 1998, pp. 5–6.

19. Alan J. Rowe and James D. Boulgarides, *Managerial Decision Making: A Guide for Successful Business Decisions* (New York: Macmillan, 1992), p. 172.

20. "Generate More Ideas with Quotas," *Managers Edge*, November 1998, p. 5.

21. Leonard and Swap, *When Sparks Fly*.

22. For a concise review of these studies, see Beth A. Hennessey and Teresa M. Amabile, "Reward, Intrinsic Motivation, and Creativity," *American Psychologist*, June 1998, pp. 674–675.

23. Dorothy Leonard and Walter Swap, "Igniting Creativity," *Workforce*, October 1999, pp. 87–89.

24. "Three 'Creative' Words," *Managers Edge*, September 1998, p. 1.

Foundation Concepts of Motivation

It was a nightmare, working-mom variety. Tori Mannes had a new job as vice president, community and media relations for Chase Bank of Texas in Dallas. To make it all work, she had hired a full-time nanny to care for her three children, who range in age from 4 to 9. Three weeks into the job, the nanny abruptly quit. "She called and left a voice mail message on Sunday night. I was really left in the lurch," Mannes said. Luckily, her employer was understanding. So were family and friends, who pitched in until she and her husband could make new arrangements. Still, "you hate to keep asking," she said.

Chase employees no longer have to scramble when they face such emergencies. In the summer of 2000, the bank opened three backup child-care centers for its Texas employees. Workers can get up to 20 days a year of free child care for times when the sitter suddenly quits or the school has an in-service day. The new centers will also serve mildly ill children and offer school holiday programs. Under another free program, parents of newborns and newly adopted children can receive up to eight consecutive weeks of free care.

"It's like insurance," Mannes said of backup child care. "You're always glad you have it, because when you need it, you really need it."

The idea for the new centers came from an employee survey, said Cynthia Peoples, vice president and employee relations manager for the bank in Dallas-Fort Worth. "It came out loud and clear that employees had a need for backup." Chase is on the cutting edge of a national trend, experts in the field say. Four percent of employers offer backup care for employees whose regular arrangements fall through. But an additional 5 percent are considering adding the care.

To learn more about key employment concerns of working women, visit Women's Wire at http://www.womenswire.com/work/.

Source: Diana Kunde, "Employers Investing in Backup Child Care for Workers," *Dallas Morning News* syndicated story, August 30, 1999.

PHOTO: © JONATHAN NOUROK/PHOTOEDIT

OBJECTIVES

After reading and studying this chapter and doing the exercises, you should be able to

1 Describe several needs theories of motivation including the needs hierarchy, the two-factor theory, and the achievement-power-affiliation triad.

2 Summarize the key propositions of goal theory and reinforcement theory.

3 Explain the expectancy theory of motivation.

4 Explain how equity and social comparison contribute to motivation.

5 Use social learning theory to motivate yourself.

6 Recognize the importance of both intrinsic and extrinsic motivators.

Chapter 5

SO WHAT? **What does Chase's program of backup child care tell us about the importance of helping workers satisfy basic needs?** Providing for the well-being of one's children while at work is not a concern of small consequence to millions of working women. Cutting-edge employers are following the tenets of need theory, the most fundamental explanation of motivation. Motivation stems from being able to satisfy needs. Need theory is one of the foundation explanations of motivation presented in this chapter. In the following chapter, we describe managerial programs to enhance motivation, all based on motivation theory. (The present chapter, however, does touch on practical approaches to motivation.) The purpose of both chapters is to enhance your knowledge and skill in a topic of perennial interest to managers and professionals: motivating people in organizations.

Motivation (in a work setting) is the process by which behavior is mobilized and sustained in the interest of achieving organizational goals. We know a person is motivated when he or she actually expends effort toward goal attainment. Motivation is complex and encompasses a broad range of behaviors, many of which are described in this and the following chapter. To assess the effectiveness of your present knowledge of motivating others, take the Self-Assessment on page 90.

NEED THEORIES OF MOTIVATION

Describe several needs theories of motivation including the needs hierarchy, the two-factor theory, and the achievement-power-affiliation triad.

The simplest explanation of motivation is one of the most powerful: People are willing to expend effort toward achieving a goal because it satisfies one of their important needs. Self-interest is thus a driving force. This principle is referred to as "What's in it for me?" or WIIFM (pronounced *wiff 'em*). Reflect on your own experience. Before working hard to accomplish a task, you probably want to know how you will benefit. If your manager asks you to work extra hours to take care of an emergency, you will most likely oblige. Yet underneath you might be thinking, "If I work these extra hours, my boss will think highly of me. As a result, I will probably receive a good performance evaluation and maybe a better-than-average salary increase."

Here we describe three classic need theories of motivation: the need hierarchy, the two-factor theory, and the achievement-power-affiliation triad.

Maslow's Hierarchy of Needs

Experiencing OB

To interact with key propositions associated with Maslow's heirarchy of needs, Herzberg's two-factor theory, and the expectancy theory of motivation, among other, visit South-Western's animated concept and activity site at *http://www.experiencingob.com*. Exclusive review tools on the topic of Motivation can help you stay ahead of the curve. Free demo available!

Based on his work as a clinical psychologist, Abraham M. Maslow developed a comprehensive view of individual motivation.[1] **Maslow's hierarchy of needs** arranges human needs into a pyramid-shaped model with basic physiological needs at the bottom and self-actualization needs at the top (see Exhibit 5-1). Lower-order needs must be satisfied to ensure a person's existence, security, and requirements for human contact. Higher-order needs are concerned with personal development and reaching one's potential. Before higher-level needs are activated, the lower-order needs must be satisfied. The five levels of needs are described next.

1. *Physiological needs.* At the first level are basic bodily needs such as the need for water, air, food, rest, and sleep. Should these needs be unfulfilled, the individual will be preoccupied with satisfying them. Once met, the second level of needs emerges.

2. *Safety needs.* At the second level are needs relating to obtaining a secure environment without threats to well-being. These include needs for security and

EXHIBIT
5-1

Maslow's Hierarchy of Needs

89

freedom from environmental threat. Many employees who work at dangerous jobs, such as loggers and miners, would be motivated by the chance to have safer working conditions. Sexual harassment is an example of frustration of the safety need for security, because the harassed person is subjected to an environmental threat. After a person feels safe and secure, a third level of needs emerges.

3. *Social and love needs.* Needs at this level include belonging to a group, affiliation with people and giving and receiving love, and sexual activity. Frustration of needs at this level can lead to serious personal problems. Managers can contribute to the satisfaction of social needs by promoting teamwork and encouraging social interaction in matters concerning work problems. When social and love needs are reasonably met, the person seeks to satisfy growth needs.

4. *Esteem needs.* Needs at this level include self-respect based on genuine achievement and respect from others, prestige, recognition, and appreciation. Occupations with high status satisfy esteem needs. Managers can satisfy the esteem needs of employees by praising their work and giving them the opportunity for recognition. After reasonable satisfaction of esteem needs, most people will strive to achieve more of their potential.

5. *Self-actualization needs.* At the top of the hierarchy are needs for self-fullfillment and personal development and the need to grow to one's fullest potential. Self-actualized people are those who have become what they are capable of becoming. Managers can help employees move toward self-actualization by giving them challenging assignments, including the chance to do creative work. The U.S. Army ad campaign, "Be all that you can be," is pitched at self-actualization needs.

A key principle of the needs hierarchy is that as needs at a given level are gratified, they lose their potency (strength). The next level of need is then activated. A satisfied need ceases to be a motivator. For instance, once employees can pay for the necessities of life, they ordinarily seek opportunities for satisfying social relationships.

Many people think that, for the vast majority of workers, the only sensible way to motivate them is to satisfy higher-level needs. Many exceptions still exist. The Chase Bank program of providing backup child care helps workers deal with social and love needs. Another consideration is that even during prosperous times, there are many corporate downsizings that pose a threat to satisfying basic needs, such as security. The many sweatshops still operating in the garment-manufacturing business pay workers wages that make paying for food and rent a major struggle.[2]

SELF-ASSESSMENT

My Approach to Motivating Others

Directions: Describe how often you act or think in the way indicated by the statements below when you are attempting to motivate another person. Use the following scale: very infrequently (VI); infrequently (I); sometimes (S); frequently (F); very frequently (VF).

	VI	I	S	F	VF
1. I ask the other person what he or she is hoping to achieve in the situation.	1	2	3	(4)	5
2. I attempt to figure out if the person has the ability to do what I need done.	1	2	(3)	4	5
3. When another person is heel-dragging, it usually means he or she is lazy.	(5)	4	3	2	1
4. I tell the person I'm trying to motivate exactly what I want.	1	2	3	4	(5)
5. I like to give the other person a reward up front so he or she will be motivated.	(5)	4	3	2	1
6. I give lots of feedback when another person is performing a task for me.	1	2	3	(4)	5
7. I like to belittle the person enough so that he or she will be intimidated into doing what I need done.	(5)	4	3	2	1
8. I make sure that the other person feels treated fairly.	1	2	3	4	(5)
9. I figure that if I smile nicely enough I can get the other person to work as hard as I need.	(5)	4	3	2	1
10. I attempt to get done what I need by instilling fear in the other person.	(5)	4	3	2	1
11. I specify exactly what needs to be accomplished.	1	2	3	(4)	5
12. I generously praise people who help me get my work accomplished.	1	2	3	4	(5)
13. A job well done is its own reward. I therefore keep praise to a minimum.	(5)	4	3	2	1
14. I make sure to let people know how well they have done in meeting my expectations on a task.	1	2	3	(4)	5
15. To be fair, I attempt to reward people about the same no matter how well they have performed.	(5)	4	3	2	1
16. When somebody doing work for me performs well, I recognize his or her accomplishments promptly.	1	2	3	4	(5)
17. Before giving somebody a reward, I attempt to find out what would appeal to that person.	1	2	3	(4)	5
18. I make it a policy not to thank somebody for doing a job he or she is paid to do.	(5)	4	3	2	1
19. If people do not know how to perform a task, their motivation will suffer.	1	(2)	3	4	5
20. If properly designed, many jobs can be self-rewarding.	1	2	3	4	(5)

Total Score 90

Scoring and interpretation: Add the numbers circled to obtain your total score.

90–100   You have advanced knowledge and skill with respect to motivating others in a work environment. Continue to build on the solid base you have established.

50–89   You have average knowledge and skill with respect to motivating others. With additional study and experience, you will probably develop advanced motivational skills.

20–49   To effectively motivate others in a work environment you will need to greatly expand your knowledge of motivation theory and techniques.

*The idea for this quiz, and a few of the items, are from David A. Whetton and Kim S. Cameron, *Developing Management Skills*, 3rd ed. (New York: HarperCollins, 1995), 358–360.

The practical implication here is that many workers today can be motivated by offering them an opportunity to satisfy basic needs through such means as job security and a living wage.

Herzberg's Two-Factor Theory

The study of the needs hierarchy led to the **two-factor theory of work motivation.** According to the research of Frederick Herzberg, there are two different sets of job factors.[3] One set, the motivators or satisfiers, can motivate and satisfy workers. The other set, dissatisfiers, or hygiene factors, can only prevent dissatisfaction. Motivators relate to higher-order needs, while hygiene factors relate to lower-order needs.

Key Points In the Theory

The two-factor theory explains how to design jobs to make them motivational. The motivational elements are the intrinsic, or job content, factors that make a job exciting. Motivator factors include achievement, recognition, advancement, responsibility, the work itself, and personal growth possibilities. The extrinsic, or job context, factors are hygienic. Although they are health maintaining and desirable, they are not motivational. Examples of hygiene factors are pay, status, job security, working conditions, and quality of leadership. Herzberg believed that motivation increases when pay combines with a motivator such as challenging work. (Money is so widely used to enhance motivation that the topic will be treated separately in Chapter 6.) Exhibit 5-2 presents examples of motivator and hygiene factors.

According to the two-factor theory, only the presence of motivator factors leads to more positive energized behavior. For example, challenging work will motivate many people to exert increased effort. If intrinsic factors such as challenging work are not present, the result is neutral rather than negative, and the worker will feel bland rather than angry or unhappy. Although the presence of hygiene (or extrinsic) factors is not motivational, their absence can cause dissatisfaction as in the following illustration.

A police captain reported that when officers were assigned old patrol cars, they complained frequently. However, when assigned brand new patrol cars, they did not express much appreciation. Nor did they increase their productivity as measured by the number of citations issued.

Evaluation

The two-factor theory has made two lasting contributions to work motivation. First, it has helped managers realize that money is not always the primary motivator. Second, it has spurred much of the interest in designing jobs to make them more intrinsically satisfying. The enrichment of individual jobs led to the enrichment of work group activities, which in turn spurred the development of self-managing work teams. All these topics are discussed in subsequent chapters.

Motivator Factors (Sources of Job Satisfaction and Motivation)	Hygiene Factors (Sources of Job Dissatisfaction; Neutral to Motivation)
Challenge of the work itself	Physical working conditions
Responsibility	Company policies
Recognition	Quality of supervision
Achievement	Coworker relationships
Job advancement and professional growth	Salary
	Status
	Job security

EXHIBIT 5-2

Examples of Motivator and Hygiene Factors

A major problem with the two-factor theory is that it de-emphasizes individual differences and glosses over the importance of hygiene factors in attracting and retaining workers. Hygiene factors such as good benefits and company management satisfy and motivate many people. Many working parents will work extra hard to keep their jobs at a company that offers on-site child care.

An example of the powerful role of employee benefits in retaining employees is Quick Solutions, Inc. The company has been giving out the perks of cleaning employee homes and a $1,200 annual voucher for vacations as a way of hiring and retaining high-tech talent. Gary Quick, president and chief executive officer, says: "I've had lots of people tell me that when they come home and see a clean house, it makes them feel the company loves them and boosts their morale and that of everyone in their family."[4] The benefits kick in after three years, and so far it appears the housekeeping service and vacation vouchers are helping with recruitment and retention.

Another problem with the two-factor theory is that some workers show no particular interest in such motivators as opportunity for growth and advancement. They work primarily so they can pay their bills and enjoy their time with family and friends.

McClelland's Achievement-Power-Affiliation Triad

Many other needs influence job behavior in addition to those mentioned specifically in the need hierarchy. (One example is the need for thrill seeking, as implied from the discussion of the trait for risk-taking and thrill-seeking described in Chapter 2.) David C. McClelland and his associates have provided a useful explanation of several of these needs.[5] They have proposed a theory of motivation based on the premise that people acquire or learn certain needs from their culture. Among the cultural influences are family, peer groups, and television shows. When a need is strong enough, it prompts a person to engage in work activities to satisfy it. Three key acquired needs are achievement, power, and affiliation.

The Need for Achievement

The **need for achievement** is the desire to accomplish something difficult for its own sake. People with a strong need for achievement frequently think of how to do a job better. They are also concerned with how to progress in their careers. Workers with a high need for achievement are interested in monetary rewards primarily as feedback about how well they are achieving. Responsibility seeking is another characteristic of people with a high need for achievement. They also set realistic yet moderately difficult goals, take calculated risks, and desire feedback on performance. (A moderately difficult goal challenges the person but is not so difficult as to most likely lead to failure and frustration.) In general, those who enjoy building business, activities, and programs from scratch have a strong need for achievement.

The Need for Power

The **need for power** is the desire to control other people, to influence their behavior, and to be responsible for them. Managers with a high need for power like to control resources (such as money and real estate) in addition to people. A person with a strong need for power spends time thinking about influencing and controlling others and about gaining a position of authority and status. Executives who have buildings named after themselves or buy professional athletic teams have strong power needs. The need for power is the primary motivator of successful managers.[6]

The Need for Affiliation

The **need for affiliation** is the desire to establish and maintain friendly and warm relationships with others. People so motivated care about restoring disrupted relationships and soothing hurt feelings. They want to engage in work that permits close companionship. Successful managers have low affiliation needs, but managers with an extremely low need for affiliation may not show adequate concern for the needs of others.

The needs described above were originally studied through a projective test, called the Thematic Apperception Test. The term *projective* means that subjects project their needs into a stimulus, such as a photograph or drawing. Visualize a photograph of a young woman carrying an attache case and entering a large office building. She is standing outside the elevator. A person with a strong need for power might make the interpretation, "The woman is hoping to become an executive some day. I can see how longingly she is looking at the offices above." A person with a strong need for achievement might say. "The woman is on her way to making a big sale. She is determined to do what it takes to close the sale today." A person with a strong need for affiliation might say, "It's lunch time. The woman is on her way to meet her friends and have a great time socializing."

In reality, the projections are much more subtle. Projective tests have elaborate scoring schemes that are interpreted only by psychologists or professionals working under their supervision.

The acquired needs theory has made an important contribution in identifying needs related to managerial performance. For example, many studies have shown that successful executives have a strong need for power. Another consistent finding is that entrepreneurs have a strong need for achievement. However, the achievement-power-affiliation triad is not a complete explanation of work motivation, because it focuses on just several key needs. Similarly, needs theories in general explain only part of motivation. The remaining sections of the chapter describe other approaches to understanding work motivation.

The direct implication of needs theories for managing and leading people is that to get the most from workers' talents, it is necessary to "push their hot buttons." Two examples are as follows:

- Employees with strong security needs are likely to seek assurance, be cautious, and carefully stay within their job description. The manager might encourage risk taking from these workers by telling them about other employees who have tried something new and been successful. It is best to avoid surprises about change and offer frequent feedback.
- Employees with strong achievement needs are likely to display initiative and set personal goals, work well independently, take pride in work well done, and seek recognition for their good work. The manager might include them when establishing work goals, give them ample resources, give them feedback on their work outcomes, and encourage professional growth opportunities.[7]

The Skill-Development Exercise that follows will help you focus on the importance of identifying psychological needs when attempting to motivate others—and perhaps motivating yourself.

SKILL-DEVELOPMENT EXERCISE

Need Identification Among Gen Xers

Following is a list of work preferences characteristic among members of Generation X. Identify what psychological need or needs might be reflected in each work preference. Jot down the needs right after the work preference on the line indicated. In addition to the information presented in this chapter, the section about personality presented in Chapter 2 will give you some concepts for analysis.

- They like variety, not doing the same thing every workday. *achievement*
- Part of their career goals is to face new challenges and opportunities. It's not all based on money, but on growth and learning. *Self-actualization need for achievement*
- They want jobs that are cool, fun, and fulfilling. *achievement*
- They believe that if they keep growing and learning then that's all the security they need. Advancing their skill-set is their top priority. *achievement self actualization*

- They have a tremendous thirst for knowledge. *Self actualization achievement*
- Unlike baby boomers, who tend to work independently, Gen Xers like to work in a team environment. *affiliation*
- They prefer learning by doing and making mistakes as they go along. *esteem achievement*
- They are apt to challenge established ways of doing things, reasoning that there is always a better way. _____
- They want regular, frequent feedback on job performance. *esteem*
- Career improvement is a blend of life and job balance. _____

Source: Reprinted with the permission from the TemPositions Group of Companies, 420 Lexington Avenue, Suite 2100, New York, NY, 10170-0002.

GOAL-SETTING THEORY

Summarize the key propositions of goal theory and reinforcement theory.

Goal setting is a basic process that is directly or indirectly part of all major theories of work motivation. Goal setting is accepted widely by managers as a means to improve and sustain performance. Based on several hundred studies, the core finding of goal-setting theory is as follows: Individuals who are provided with specific hard goals perform better than those given easy, nonspecific, "do your best," or no goals. At the same time, however, the individuals must have sufficient ability, accept the goals, and receive feedback related to the task.[8] Our overview of goal-setting theory elaborates on this basic finding.

The premise underlying goal-setting theory is that behavior is regulated by values and goals. A **goal** is what a person is trying to accomplish. Our values create within us a desire to behave consistently with them. For example, if an executive values honesty, she will establish a goal of trying to hire only honest employees. The executive would therefore make extensive use of reference checks and honesty testing. Edwin A. Locke and Gary P. Latham have incorporated hundreds of studies about goals into a theory of goal setting and task performance.[9] Exhibit 5-3 summarizes some of the more consistent findings, along with more recent developments. The list that follows describes these findings.

1. *Specific goals lead to higher performance than do generalized goals.* Telling someone to "do your best" is a generalized goal. A specific goal would be, "Decrease the cycle time on customer inquiries via the Internet to an average of three hours." (Here is an example in which common sense can be wrong. Many people believe that telling others to "do your best" is an excellent motivator.)

2. *Performance generally increases in direct proportion to goal difficulty.* The more difficult one's goal, the more one accomplishes. An important exception is that when goals are too difficult, they may lower performance. Difficulty in reaching the goal leads to frustration, which in turn leads to lowered performance.

3. *For goals to improve performance, the worker must accept them.* If one rejects a goal, one will not incorporate it into planning. This is why it is often helpful to discuss goals with employees, rather than imposing goals on them. New research, however, suggests that the importance of goal commitment may be overrated. Two meta-analyses of studies conducted in laboratories about the effect of goal commitment on performance concluded that commitment had a small impact on performance. Goals appeared to improve performance whether or not people participating in the studies felt committed to their goal.[10] Despite these recent findings, many managers think employee commitment to goals is important.

   Participating in setting goals has no major effect on the level of job performance except when it improves goal acceptance. Yet participation is valuable because it can lead to higher satisfaction with the goal-setting process.

4. *Goals are more effective when they are used to evaluate performance.* When workers know that their performance will be evaluated in terms of how well they attained their goals, the impact of goals increases.

5. *Goals should be linked to feedback and rewards.* Workers should receive feedback on their progress toward goals and be rewarded for reaching them. **Feedback** is information about how well someone is doing in achieving goals. Rewarding people for reaching goals is perhaps the most widely accepted principle of management.

6. *Group goal setting is as important as individual goal setting.* Having employees work as teams with a specific team goal, rather than as individuals with only individual goals, increases productivity. Furthermore, the combination of compatible group and individual goals is more effective than either individual or group goals alone.

7. *A learning goal orientation improves performance more than a performance goal orientation.* A person with a learning goal orientation wants to develop competence by acquiring new skills and mastering new situations. In contrast, the person with a performance goal orientation wants to demonstrate and validate his or her competence by seeking favorable judgments and avoiding negative judgments. A study with medical supply sales representatives found that a learning goal orientation had a positive relationship with sales performance. In contrast, a performance goal orientation was unrelated to sales performance.[11]

Despite the contribution of goals to performance, technically speaking, they are not motivational by themselves. Rather, the discrepancies created by what individuals do and what they aspire to creates self-dissatisfaction. The dissatisfaction in turn creates a desire to reduce the discrepancy between the real and the ideal.[12] When a person desires to attain something, the person is in a state of arousal. The tension created by not having already achieved a goal spurs the person to reach the goal. If your goal is to update your company Web site by ten days from now, your dissatisfaction with not having started would propel you into action.

An effective way to apply goal theory is for the manager to set short-term goals or to encourage others to do the same. The short-term goals should support the organization's long-term goals, but are established in "bites" that are more readily achievable. Assume, for example, that a manufacturing site wants to reduce absenteeism from 20 percent to 5 percent to remain competitive. Going from 20 percent to 5 percent in three months might not be achievable. However, moving down 2 percent per month would be feasible. As each 2-percent reduction in absenteeism is achieved, employees are fed back the results. The feedback serves as a reward for further progress.

REINFORCEMENT THEORY

A well-established explanation of motivation is **reinforcement theory,** the contention that behavior is determined by its consequences. The consequences are the rewards and punishments people receive for behaving in particular ways. In Chapter 6 we describe behavior modification programs that apply reinforcement theory to enhance motivation. Reinforcement theory, unlike needs theories of motivation, de-emphasizes understanding what needs a person is attempting to satisfy. Instead, the manager looks for rewards that will encourage certain behaviors and punishments that discourage other behaviors.

At the foundation of reinforcement theory is **operant conditioning,** or learning that takes place as a consequence of behavior. More specifically, people learn to repeat behaviors that bring them pleasurable outcomes and to avoid behaviors that lead to uncomfortable outcomes. After people learn a behavior through operant conditioning, they must be motivated by rewards to repeat that behavior.

According to the famous behaviorist B. F. Skinner, to train or condition and then later motivate people, the manager does not have to study the inner workings of the mind. (Note that a behaviorist believes in *behaviorism,* the field based on reinforcement theory. Very few behavior scientists or organizational behavior experts are true *behaviorists.*) Instead, the manager should understand the relationships between behaviors and their consequences. After these relationships are understood, the manager arranges contingencies to reward desirable behavior and discourage undesirable behaviors.[13] Four basic strategies exist for arranging contingencies, thus modifying individual (or group) behavior: positive reinforcement, avoidance motivation, extinction, and punishment.

Positive reinforcement is the application of a pleasurable or valued consequence when a person exhibits the desired response. After positive reinforcement, the probability increases that the behavior will be repeated. The term *reinforcement* means that the behavior (or response) is strengthened or entrenched. A manager who expresses appreciation when a team member works late strengthens the worker's propensity to work late.

Avoidance motivation (or **avoidance learning**) is rewarding people by taking away an uncomfortable consequence. The process is also referred to as *negative reinforcement* because a negative situation is removed. Negative reinforcement is thus a reward, not a punishment, as commonly thought. Avoidance motivation is a way of strengthening a desired response by making the removal contingent on the right response. Assume that an employee is placed on probation because of poor attendance. After 30 consecutive days of coming to work, the employer rewards the employee by removing the probation.

Extinction is weakening or decreasing the frequency of undesirable behavior by removing the reward for such behavior. It is the absence of reinforcement. Suppose an employee engages in undesirable behavior such as creating a disturbance just to get a reaction from coworkers. If the teammates ignore the disturbance, the perpetrator no longer receives the reward of getting attention and stops the disturbing behavior. The behavior is said to be extinguished.

Punishment is the presentation of an undesirable consequence for a specific behavior. An indirect form of punishment is to take away a privilege, such as working on an interesting project, because of some undesirable behavior. The most direct managerial application of reinforcement theory is to reward those behaviors that support the goals of the organization.

EXPECTANCY THEORY OF MOTIVATION

According to **expectancy theory,** motivation results from deliberate choices to engage in activities in order to achieve worthwhile outcomes. People will be well motivated if they believe that effort will lead to good performance and good performance will lead to preferred outcomes. The basic version of expectancy theory shown in Exhibit 5-4 is useful to managers and professionals. Components of the model are described next,[14] followed by the guidelines for motivation stemming from expectancy theory.

Explain the expectancy theory of motivation

Expectancy, Instrumentality, and Valence

The key components of expectancy theory are expectancy, instrumentality, and valence. Each one of these components exists in each situation involving motivation. An **expectancy** is a person's subjective estimate of the probability that a given level of performance will occur. The effort-to-performance (E → P) expectancy refers to the individual's subjective hunch about the chances that increased effort will lead to the desired performance. If a person does not believe that he or she has the skill to accomplish a task, that person might not even try to perform.

The importance of having high expectancies for motivation meshes well with a conception of work motivation that emphasizes the contribution of self-efficacy. If you have high self-efficacy about the task, your motivation will be high. Low self-efficacy leads to low motivation. Some people are poorly motivated to sky dive because they doubt they will be able to pull the rip cord while free-falling at 120 mph. A technical definition and explanation will help you appreciate the contribution of self-efficacy to motivation.

A Basic Version of Expectancy Theory

Self-efficacy refers to an individual's convictions (or confidence) about his or her abilities to mobilize the motivation, cognitive resources, and course of action needed to successfully execute a specific task within a given context.[15]

An **instrumentality** is the individual's estimate of the probability that performance will lead to certain outcomes. The $P \rightarrow O$ instrumentality refers to the person's subjective evaluation of the chances that good performance will lead to certain outcomes. Among the outcomes might be an increase in status and salary, a promotion, more job security, and appreciation from management. Performance almost always leads to multiple outcomes. In formulating the instrumentality, the employee seeks a subjective answer to the question "If I do perform well, will the organization really make good on promises to me?" Expectancies and instrumentalities range from 0.00 to 1.00 because both are probabilities.

Valence refers to the value a person places on a particular outcome. People attach positive valences to rewards and negative valences to punishments. An advertising copywriter might place a high positive valence on making a presentation to a client and assign a high negative valence to having his work insulted by the manager or client. The maximum value of a positive valence is +100, while the maximum value of a negative valence is −100. Neutral outcomes (indifference) carry a valence of zero. (Most versions of expectancy theory limit the range of valences from −1.00 to +1.00. However, such a limited range fails to capture the intensity of highly preferred or feared outcomes.) The numerical values of valences are unknown in most situations, yet it is reasonable to assume that people attach values of "good," "bad," and "neutral" to potential outcomes derived from their efforts.

The Calculation of Motivation

In expectancy theory, motivation force $M = (E \rightarrow P) \times (P \rightarrow O) \times V$. The potential of an expected outcome increasing motivation can be high only if the expectancies, instrumentalities, and valences are high. Because anything multiplied by zero is zero, a zero value for $(E \rightarrow P)$, $(P \rightarrow O)$, or V will reduce motivation to zero. Suppose an employee places a maximum value on receiving a raise ($V = 100$). The employee is confident that she can perform the task required ($E \rightarrow P = 0.85$). And the employee is even more confident that the firm will come through with the raise if she performs well ($P \rightarrow O = 0.90$). Note that the values of 0.85 and 0.90 are subjective estimates, not true calculations. The employee's motivation is consequently (100) (0.85) (0.90) = 76.5 (above average on a scale of −100 to +100).

A note of caution: The simple formula just presented does not tell the entire story because each task involves multiple expectancies, instrumentalities, and valences. Desirable and undesirable outcomes may cancel one another, resulting in a zero valence and therefore producing a zero motivational force. For example, a person might not strive for a promotion because its positive valences (such as more money and status) are neutralized by its negative valences (such as having to relocate and leave friends behind).

To create a situation of high motivation, the manager should take steps to elevate expectancies, instrumentalities, and valences. One approach would be for the manager to make sure the worker had the right training and to boost the worker's self-confidence—thus elevating expectancies. Instrumentalities could be elevated by assuring the worker that good performance would lead to a reward. Choosing meaningful rewards would elevate the valences.

Cross-Cultural Factors and Expectancy Theory

In applying expectancy theory, as well as other explanations of motivation, the manager must be alert to cross-cultural factors. Cross-cultural factors typically enter into which rewards or outcomes are likely to have the highest valence for a particular cultural group. Hispanic people, for example, generally favor outcomes that enable them to maintain cordial relations with other members of the work group. Another example would be that Asians would ordinarily prefer not to receive rewards that singled them out for attention.

As analyzed by Nancy J. Adler, expectancy theory depends on the extent to which workers believe they have control over the outcome of their efforts and how much faith they have in leaders to deliver rewards.[16] The assumption that workers believe they have control over their fate may be culturally dependent. In countries where individualism dominates, such as the United States, employees may believe more strongly that they can influence performance and outcomes. In collectivist societies, such as Taiwan, the individual feels that group effort has a stronger influence on performance and outcomes. Taiwanese are also more likely to believe that the company has a moral obligation to deliver on outcomes.

EQUITY THEORY AND SOCIAL COMPARISON

Explain how equity and social comparison contribute to motivation.

Expectancy theory emphasizes the rational and thinking side of people. Similarly, another theory focuses on how fairly people think they are being treated in comparison to certain reference groups. According to **equity theory,** employee satisfaction and motivation depend on how fairly the employees believe they are treated in comparison to peers. The theory contends that employees hold certain beliefs about the outcomes they receive from their jobs and the inputs they invest to obtain these outcomes.

The outcomes of employment include pay, benefits, status, intrinsic job factors, and anything else stemming from the job that workers perceive as useful. The inputs include all the factors that employees perceive as being their investment in the job or anything of value that they bring to the job. Among such inputs are job qualifications, skills, education level, effort, and cooperative behavior.

The core of equity theory is that employees compare their inputs and outcomes (make social comparisons) with others in the workplace.[17] When employees believe that they are receiving equitable outcomes in relation to their inputs, they are generally satisfied. When workers believe that they are being treated equitably, they are more willing to work hard. Conversely, when employees believe that they are giving too much as compared with what they are receiving from the organization, a state of tension and dissatisfaction ensues. The people used for reference are those whom the employee perceives as relevant for comparison. For example, an industrial sales representative would make comparisons with other industrial sales reps in the same industry about whom he has information.

Comparisons are of two kinds. People consider their own inputs in relation to outcomes received, and they also evaluate what others are receiving for the same inputs. Equity is said to exist when an individual concludes that his or her own outcome/input ratio is equal to that of other people. Inequity exists if the person's ratio is not the same as that of other people. All these comparisons are similar to those judgments made by people according to expectance theory—they are subjective hunches that may or may not be valid. Inequity can be in either direction and of varying magnitude. The equity ratio is often expressed as follows:

$$\frac{\text{Outcomes of Individual}}{\text{Inputs of Individual}} \text{ compared to } \frac{\text{Outcomes of Others}}{\text{Inputs of Others}}$$

According to equity theory, the highest motivation occurs when a person has ratios equal to those of the comparison person. When people perceive an inequity, they are likely to engage in one of the following actions:

1. *Alter the outcomes.* The person who feels mistreated might ask for more salary or bonus, promotional opportunities, or vacation time. Some people might even steal from the company to obtain the money they feel they deserve. Others might attempt to convince management to give less outcomes to others. One sociology professor donates $2,000 of his $60,000 annual salary to a custodial worker at his university. The professor's intent is to help create equity in the university pay system.

2. *Alter the inputs.* A person who feels treated inequitably might decrease effort or time devoted to work. The person who feels underpaid might engage in such self-defeating behavior by faking sick days to take care of personal business. Another extreme would be to encourage others to decrease their inputs so they will earn less money.

3. *Distort the perception.* To combat feelings of inequity, people can distort their perception of their own or others' inputs or outcomes. Recognizing that she is overpaid in comparison to coworkers, a financial analyst might say, "Of course, I attended a much tougher program at college, so I deserve more money." Another distortion would be to look for evidence that coworkers are contributing less effort.

4. *Change the reference source.* A convenient way of restoring equity is to change to another reference source whose outcome/input ratio is similar to one's own. A recently graduated MA accepted a job offer for $20,000 less per year than average for graduates of her program. At first she grumbled about being underpaid but then reanalyzed the situation. Her conclusion was, "The MBAs I was comparing myself with took jobs in New York City or Boston where the cost of living is much higher. If I compare myself to MBAs getting hired outside of New York or Boston, I'm being paid well."

5. *Leave the situation.* As an extreme move, the person who feels treated inequitably might quit a job. He or she would then be free to pursue greater equity in another position.

Equity theory has much face validity and has direct relevance for pay systems. No matter how well designed a program of productivity or quality improvement might be, it must still provide equitable pay.

SOCIAL LEARNING THEORY

Use social learning theory to motivate yourself.

As described in Chapter 3, people learn various behaviors by observing and imitating others. At a later point, they are motivated to repeat the learned behaviors. **Social learning** is the process of observing the behavior of others, recognizing its consequences, and altering behavior as a result. According to social learning theory, individual behavior is influenced by a combination of a person's cognitions and social environment. A person has to make some interpretations of the efficacy and suitability of the behavior being observed; otherwise the model will not be imitated.

Social learning does not take place automatically just because environmental models are available. If social learning was that easy, almost every employee would be a model worker. Effective social learning, and therefore motivated behavior, is most likely to take place when several of the following conditions are met:[18]

1. The person should have high expectancies that he or she can learn the observed behavior and high instrumentalities that the learned behavior will result in valued rewards. The high expectancies center around the person having high self-efficacy. Social learning will be facilitated when the person is confident of performing well in the task being remodeled.

2. Self-administration of rewards should take place. The person doing the modeling should find the behavior intrinsically satisfying and not have to rely exclusively on extrinsic rewards such as increased earnings and recognition. Modeling the new behavior should result in personal satisfaction and an enhanced self-image. Assume that you learned how to negotiate effectively by observing a mentor negotiate a deal. You would most likely experience increased personal satisfaction from having acquired a valuable new business skill. At a later point, external rewards would be forthcoming if your new skill led to a higher performance evaluation or saving money when purchasing a home.

3. The behavior to be learned should involve mostly tangible mechanical and verbal activities such as physical and interpersonal tasks. It is thus easier to be motivated by watching another person negotiate than engage in strategic planning. We cannot readily imitate the cognitive processes of another person.

4. Social learning can only take place when we possess the physical and mental ability needed to imitate the behavior. A frail person cannot learn to move furniture by simply watching others do it correctly. Also, one cannot imitate effective negotiating practices if he or she is not intelligent enough to figure out what the other side really wants.

Social learning may appear to be more about learning than motivation, but the motivational aspects are still important. Workers typically model the behavior of people from whom they are seeking approval, such as superiors and high-performing teammates. Part of the motivation for learning and repeating the target behavior is to receive approval from significant people in the work environment. Have you ever noticed how people from the same organization often talk alike?

The accompanying Organizational Behavior in Action describes a leader who motivates others in part by serving as a model others imitate.

INTRINSIC VERSUS EXTRINSIC MOTIVATION

Recognize the importance of both intrinsic and extrinsic motivators.

Many management experts contend that if you make jobs more interesting, there may be less need for motivating people with external rewards. The two-factor theory of motivation is based on this idea. Also, attempting to motivate people by extrinsic rewards may not be sufficient. Motivating people through interesting work is based on the principle of **intrinsic motivation.** It refers to a person's beliefs about the extent to which an activity can satisfy his or her needs for competence and self-determination. Values contribute to intrinsic motivation. People who highly value work tend to be intrinsically motivated, while people who place a low value on work have low intrinsic motivation. You will recall the contribution of intrinsic motivation to creativity in Chapter 4.

Intrinsic motivation is therefore also referred to as **self-determination theory,** the idea that people are motivated when they experience a sense of choice in initiating and regulating their actions. Instead of looking to somebody

Organizational Behavior *in Action*

The Motivational Ken Chenault of AmEx

In his college days, Ken Chenault argued that the advancement of African Americans was best met by rising to power within the Establishment instead of attacking it from the outside. Today he holds the top executive position at American Express Co., the owner of one of the world's premier consumer brands. He was recently elected to the IBM board of directors.

After graduating Bowdoin College, Chenault earned a degree from Harvard Law School. He was a member of a law firm for several years, then worked as a management consultant before joining AmEx. He rose rapidly at the consulting firm and was regarded as a person with the potential to become a corporate CEO partly because of his ability to work with and motivate others, and his strategic thinking.

Chenault makes an impressive physical appearance, is quietly charismatic and even tempered, and has exceptional drive. His admirers lavish him with praise. The chairperson of the lead advertising agency for AmEx offers this description: "Ken radiates such a depth of belief that people would do anything for him." A former AmEx executive says, "He's a true leader. I can say unequivocally that I admire Ken more than anyone else I've ever worked with. I think he will be our generation's Jack Welch."

Still rising in the corporate world, Chenault is an established star in what the president of Time Warner calls "the circle of African American professionals who have achieved." Chenault worked his way up through the giant card and travel unit (TRS), which generates most of AmEx's revenue and profits. He was instrumental in reviving and reinventing TRS, which was suffering from widespread complacency.

Former top AmEx executive Harvey Golub says he promoted Chenault to president because the challenge of developing more market share and global reach was too overwhelming to deal with alone. Golub also identified Chenault as a successor and wanted him perceived as more of a collaborator than a subordinate. "What I sought was a horizontal relationship with Ken that would enable him to do more and more of what I was doing." The two executives worked smoothly together and agreed consistently on decisions.

Work associates regard Chenault as hard-driving and pragmatic. Yet at the same time he is able to engage the emotions of his colleagues as well as their intellects. Another former AmEx executive said that "Ken has the hearts and minds of the people at the TRS company." A survey of work associates indicates that Chenault lacks the rough edges and impatience that usually accompany highly ambitious people. None of the people interviewed could recall him losing his temper or even raising his voice. He takes the time to make small talk with secretaries when he telephones their bosses. Chenault has taken the initiative to mentor dozens of high-potential AmEx managers. He has also contributed to making layoff decisions during difficult times for the company.

Chenault is a methodical decision maker who collects input from others, who leaves his door open to direct reports, and who encourages candor. A veteran AmEx employee said, "With Ken, there is no game-playing, no politics whatsoever." Yet despite his even temper, Chenault has fired managers he thought lacked the skills he needed for his organization. During a time in which AmEx was going through substantial changes to stop the slide in American Express card use, he fired most of a group of managers who resisted the changes. During the same period of turmoil, Chenault often met with major customers to resolve problems about AmEx charging them a higher

---

The Motivational Ken Chenault of AmEx (continued)

rate than did traditional credit-card companies. At one time, four restaurant owners in Boston were threatening to boycott AmEx in response to the high charges. Chenault met with them personally and was able to get the owners to back down.

An important part of Chenault's managerial approach is to interact directly with rank-and-file employees. He regularly conducts a monthly "meet the president" session over lunch. "I've gotten some of my best ideas this way," he says. An example is that Platinum card members can now purchase two international business-class airline tickets for the price of one. Chenault prefers to occupy the role of team leader, rather than its boss. He says, "It's critical to share the credit." However, Chenault is far from laid back. As he explains, "I have a psychic investment in success."

Sources: Anthony Bianco, "The Rise of a Star," *Business Week*, December 21, 1998, pp. 60–68; Carrie Shook, "Leader, Not Boss," *Forbes Magazine*, December 1, 1997; http://www. africanews.com/monitor/freeissues/03beb99/feature.html.

---

else for rewards, a person is motivated by the intrinsic or internal aspects of the task. Reinforcement theory, in contrast, emphasizes external rewards associated with the task.

The Rationale behind Intrinsic Motivation Theory

Intrinsic motivation and self-determination theory are closely related. According to self-determination theory, workers are active agents of, rather than passive reactors to, environmental forces. Two factors influence the perception of intrinsic motivation. Certain characteristics of a task, such as challenge and autonomy, promote intrinsic motivation because they allow for satisfaction of the needs for competence and self-determination. Workers' perceptions of why they perform a task can also affect intrinsic motivation. Such motivation is likely to increase when people perceive that they perform tasks for themselves rather than for an external reward. To understand intrinsic motivation, visualize a computer hacker joyously working until midnight to write software that will give her company a competitive edge in satisfying customers. She is so wrapped up in her work that she is unaware of the time. Furthermore, she gives no particular thought to whether she will receive a bonus for her outstanding work.

When an individual performs a task to achieve an external reward such as money or recognition, a shift occurs. The individual believes that the external reward caused the behavior, and money or recognition is now controlling his or her actions. The worker no longer perceives that he or she is self-determining. As a result, intrinsic motivation may decrease.[19]

Problems Associated with Extrinsic Rewards

Self-determination theory is based on the fact that external rewards have disadvantages. Extrinsic rewards can sometimes lower a person's job performance and be demotivating, particularly when a creative task is involved. The appeal of extrinsic rewards can also cause people to

- Focus narrowly on a task

IMPLICATIONS FOR MANAGERIAL PRACTICE

The explanations of motivation presented in this chapter all have implications for managerial practice. Nevertheless, we emphasize suggestions derived from expectancy theory because its components include ideas from other theories.

1. *Determine what levels and kinds of performance are needed to achieve organizational goals.* Motivating others proceeds best when workers have a clear understanding of what needs to be accomplished. At the same time, the manager should make sure that the desired levels of performance are possible.

2. *Train and encourage people.* Managers should give group members the necessary training and encouragement to be confident that they can perform the required task. Some group members who appear to be poorly motivated simply lack the right skills and self-confidence.

3. *Understand individual differences in valences.* To motivate workers effectively, managers must recognize individual differences in preferences for rewards. An attempt should be made to offer workers rewards to which they attach a high valence. Cross-cultural differences in valences may also occur.

4. *Use positive reinforcement more than punishment.* At times, punishment is necessary. Yet it can produce such negative side effects as anxiety and retaliation against the firm, including making costly mistakes intentionally.

- Rush through a job to get a reward
- Regard the task as a drudgery that must be suffered to receive the reward
- See themselves as less free and less self-determining.[20]

Despite these problems, a firm should not abandon financial bonuses and other forms of positive reinforcement. Even the people who enjoy work intensely still want recognition from management. Also, people who love their work, such as top executives, successful novelists, entertainers, and athletes, demand huge fees. The sensible solution is for managers to balance intrinsic and extrinsic rewards. For example, a purchasing agent who saved the company $300,000 by finding a low-price alternative for a component might be rewarded with the opportunity to work on a cross-sectional team. He might also be given a hefty year-end bonus.

SUMMARY OF KEY POINTS

 Describe several needs theories of motivation including the needs hierarchy, the two-factor theory, and the achievement-power-affiliation triad.

Motivation is the process by which behavior is mobilized and sustained in the interest of achieving organizational goals. As reflected in needs theories of motivation, self-interest is a driving force.

According to Maslow's needs hierarchy, human needs fall into five groups: physiological, safety, social and love, esteem, and self-actualization. As needs at one level are gratified, they lose their strength and the next level of needs is activated.

Herzberg's two-factor theory divides job factors into motivators and satisfiers versus maintenance factors or dissatisfiers. Motivational factors are the intrinsic or job content factors (such as achievement and recognition) that make a job rewarding. Maintenance factors are the extrinsic aspects of the job (such as working conditions and benefits). Dissatisfaction stems from substandard extrinsic factors.

McClelland's acquired needs theory explains that certain needs people strive to satisfy are acquired from the culture. His research centers around three needs of particular significance in understanding entrepreneurs and managers: achievement, power, and affiliation. The need for power is the primary motivator of successful managers.

 Summarize the key propositions of goal theory and reinforcement theory.

Goal setting is an important part of all major theories of motivation. Goal theory includes the following ideas: Specific and difficult goals result in high performance; goals must be accepted by workers; goals are more effective when they are linked to feedback and rewards; the combination of individual and group goals is very effective, and a learning goal orientation is more effective than a performance goal orientation.

According to reinforcement theory, behavior is determined by its consequences, or rewards and punishments, for behaving in particular ways. At the foundation of reinforcement theory is operant conditioning, or learning that takes place as a consequence of behavior. People learn to repeat behaviors that bring them pleasurable outcomes and to avoid behaviors that lead to uncomfortable outcomes. The four basic strategies for arranging contingencies to modify behavior are positive reinforcement, avoidance motivation, extinction, and punishment.

 Explain the expectancy theory of motivation.

Expectancy theory is based on the idea that work motivation results from deliberate choices to engage in certain activities in order to achieve worthwhile outcomes. The three most important components of expectancy theory are effort-to-performance expectancies, instrumentalities, and valence. Individual differences and cultural factors influence valence. Most situations have multiple outcomes and valences. Motivational force is the result of the multiplication of expectancies, instrumentalities, and valence.

 Explain how equity and social comparison contribute to motivation.

Equity theory explains that workers compare their inputs and outcomes with relevant people in the workplace. When employees believe that they are receiving equitable outputs in relation to their inputs, they are generally satisfied and motivated. When workers believe they are giving too much in relation to what they are receiving from the organization, dissatisfaction ensues. People will usually take action to bring their equity ratio into balance. Two such actions would be seeking greater outputs or decreasing input.

 Use social learning theory to motivate yourself.

According to social learning theory, individual behavior is influenced by a combination of a person's cognitions and social environment. People learn by imitating a model and are motivated to repeat the behavior. Conditions favoring social learning include high expectations, self-administration of rewards, tangible behavior to imitate, and the necessary physical and mental ability.

 Recognize the importance of both intrinsic and extrinsic motivators.

The theory of intrinsic motivation, or self-determination, emphasizes that people are active agents rather than recipients of environmental forces. Intrinsic motivation is tied in with needs for competence and self-determination. Extrinsic rewards can sometimes lower a person's job performance and be demotivating, particularly when a creative task is involved. A combination of intrinsic and extrinsic rewards is best for motivation.

KEY TERMS AND PHRASES

Motivation, *88*
In a work setting, the process by which behavior is mobilized and sustained in the interest of achieving organizational goals.

Maslow's Hierarchy of Needs, *88*
A classical theory of motivation that arranges human needs into a pyramid-shaped model with basic physiological needs at the bottom and self-actualization needs at the top.

Two-factor Theory of Work Motivation, *91*
Herzberg's theory contending that there are two different sets of job factors. One set can satisfy and motivate people (motivators); the other set can only prevent dissatisfaction (dissatisfiers).

Need for Achievement, *92*
The desire to accomplish something difficult for its own sake.

Need for Power, *92*
The desire to control other people, to influence their behavior, and to be responsible for them.

Need for Affiliation, *93*
The desire to establish and maintain friendly and warm relationships with others.

Goal, *94*
What a person is trying to accomplish.

Feedback, *95*
Information about how well someone is doing in achieving

106

goals. Also, messages sent back from the receiver to the sender of information.

Reinforcement Theory, *96*
The contention that behavior is determined by its consequences.

Operant Conditioning, *96*
Learning that takes place as a consequence of behavior.

Positive Reinforcement, *96*
The application of a pleasurable or valued consequence when a person exhibits the desired response.

Avoidance Motivation (or Avoidance Learning), *96*
Rewarding by taking away an uncomfortable consequence.

Extinction, *97*
The weakening or decreasing of the frequency of undesirable behavior by removing the reward for such behavior.

Punishment, *97*
The presentation of an undesirable consequence for a specific behavior.

Expectancy Theory, *97*
The theory that motivation results from deliberate choices to engage in activities in order to achieve worthwhile outcomes.

Expectancy, *97*
A person's subjective estimate of the probability that a given level of performance will occur.

Instrumentality, *98*
The individual's subjective estimate of the probability that performance will lead to certain outcomes.

Valence, *98*
The value a person places on a particular outcome.

Equity Theory, *99*
The motivation theory that employee satisfaction and motivation depend on how fairly the employees believe that they are treated in comparison to peers.

Social Learning, *100*
The process of observing the behavior of others, recognizing its consequences, and altering behavior as a result.

Intrinsic Motivation, *101*
A person's beliefs about the extent to which an activity can satisfy his or her needs for competence and self-determination.

Self-determination Theory, *101*
The idea that people are motivated when they experience a sense of choice in initiating and regulating their actions.

DISCUSSION QUESTIONS AND ACTIVITIES

1. How does WIIFM explain the fact that many busy managers and professionals devote considerable amounts of their time to community activities and charities?
2. In what way does Ken Chenault of AmEx use social learning theory to motivate workers—even if he never heard of the theory?
3. How would you know if a particular person had strong needs for power, achievement, or affiliation?
4. Why are goals motivational?
5. How can a manager strengthen the expectancies of group members?

6. How does a person formulate an instrumentality for estimating the extent to which hard work will lead to a promotion?
7. Scan a newspaper, search the Internet, or watch news programs on television to identify an incident of motivated behavior. Analyze whether you think the key person was motivated more by intrinsic or extrinsic rewards. Be prepared to discuss your findings in class.

ORGANIZATIONAL BEHAVIOR ON-LINE

TO DO
What Motivates Gen X?
Use the Internet to find several articles about Generation X. Analyze these articles to develop a list of five motivators likely to be effective with GenXers. If you simply search for articles about Generation X, you might be overwhelmed with choices. So, make your search more specific.

TO BOOKMARK
Thrill-Seeking Need
http://www.cineplexodeon.com/imax/thrillride/production.html

Positive Reinforcement
http://www.p-management.com/

Social Learning Theory
http://www.funderstanding.com

Intrinsic Motivation
http://www.fed.org/ (Enter *motivation* in the site's search engine and choose from among dozens of research articles on the subject.

CASE PROBLEM: Lonely Work at Home

Missed package deliveries and phone calls, and the occasional barking dog were not exactly what Tom Galloway had in mind when he launched a digital printing business from his home a few years ago. His hopes were to roll out of bed each morning, start the coffeepot and PC, and make a fortune without ever getting out of his pajamas. The reality was that within a few weeks, Galloway was buried under paperwork and E-mail messages and was lonely. After six months, he hung up his bathrobe for good. "It was such a pain," Galloway recalls.

Although he no longer works at home, Galloway still deals with that type of frustration, but now as a source of revenue. His new venture, a franchised chain of upscale small-business service centers called Your Office USA, targets people facing the same problems he did. Your Office is one among many firms serving the almost 40 million people in the United States who operate small businesses from home or are corporate telecommuters. Many of these people seek the professional services and social interaction characteristic of a traditional work environment.

Along with executive-suite operators such as HQ and Regus, Your Office positions itself as being a more elegant version of Kinko's. Superstores like Office Depot and Staples are looking to follow the lead of Kinko's by adding more in-house digital offerings.

Your Office is a subsidiary of IB Your Office, a $50 million-a-year company with more than 100 franchises in Europe and Asia. A company executive describes Your Office as a "superstore for the home-based entrepreneur." The 6,000-square foot interiors have the familiar appearance of a corporate office: a receptionist area and long hallways with art on the wall, leading to individual offices and cubicles. Yet few corporate sites house such varied activity. For instance, in one room a customer who is a security expert trains security guards, and in another room a computer specialist is at a work station.

Randolph Blatt, 41, of Raleigh, North Carolina, is one of those computer specialists. After working from home for four years, Blatt, who recruits computer professionals, became tired of the distractions. "I would get phone calls, and I had screaming babies in the background. I would duck into my laundry room to hide. It never worked. At Your Office, I regularly run into people, and I feel like I'm part of the world."

Your Office also hopes to serve millions of sales representatives who have lost their desks to downsizings and have become corporate nomads, as well as on-the-go entrepreneurs who want satellite offices in several cities. By the hour, the day, or the month, they can rent office space, hire a secretary, check their mailboxes or e-mail, or conduct a videoconference. Whenever New York City bankruptcy attorney Garret Rubin has to meet clients near the Brooklyn courts, he uses a nearby Your Office. "I wish my office was this nice," he says.

At any Kinko's outlet, day or night, graphic artists and bank presidents alike can access a uniform set of PCs, fax machines, and color copiers and printers to update résumés, and can create flyers, trade ideas, and confer with clients. "We're the intellectual meeting place in any community," claims Paul Orfalea, who started Kinko's in an old Santa Barbara, California, hamburger stand in 1970 (the name came from his kinky red hair).

Susan Cummins, a Miami public relations expert, calls Kinko's "the only office social experience I connect with. It's like the office, but without the politics." To make things cozier, Kinko's has opened a few Citibank minibranches in its stores. At Your Office, franchisees hold pizza parties and holiday bashes to bring their disparate customers together.

Case Questions

1. What needs are the small business owners and telecommuters described in this case attempting to satisfy by frequenting the small-business service centers?
2. What recommendations would you give to the operators of the service centers to make their services even more attractive to small business owners and telecommuters?
3. What recommendations can you make to the small-business owners and telecommuters for obtaining more intrinsic satisfaction in their work?

Source: Daniel Eisenberg, "Offices by the Hour," *Time* (1 February 1999): 40–41. Used with permission of the publisher.

Freed from corporate restraints, corporate refugees-turned-entrepreneurs constitute a growing phenomenon. Many, like Tom Galloway, turn to franchising to fulfill dreams of self-employment. FranNet and the International Franchise Association are two of the Web sites catering to the franchise-curious. Visit them at http://www.frannet.com/ and http://www.franchise.org/.

SUGGESTED READINGS

"Aligning Work and Rewards." *Management Review,* February 1995, pp. 19–23.

Brooker, Katrina. "Can Anyone Replace HERB? *Fortune,* April 17, 2000, pp. 186–192.

Katzenbach, Jon R. *Peak Performance: Aligning the Hearts and Minds of Your Employees.* Boston, MA: Harvard Business School Publishing, 2000.

Kerr, Steven. *Ultimate Rewards: What Really Motivates People to Achieve.* Boston, MA: Harvard Business School Press, 1997.

Komisar, Randy with Lineback, Kent. *The Monk and the Riddle: The Education of a Silicon Valley Entrepreneur.* Boston, MA: Harvard Business School Publishing, 2000.

Nelson, Bob. *1001 Ways to Energize Employees.* New York: Workman, 1997.

Potera, Carol. "Trapped in the Web." *Psychology Today,* March/April 1998, pp. 66–72.

"Rethinking Work." *Fast Company,* April 2000, pp. 254–268.

Vincola, Ann. "Good Career/Life Balance Makes for Better Workers." *HRfocus,* April 1999, p. 13.

Wood, Robert E., Atkins, Paul W. B., and Bright, E. H. "Bonuses, Goals, and Instrumentality Effects." *Journal of Applied Psychology,* October 1999, pp. 703–720.

ENDNOTES

1. Abraham H. Maslow, "A Theory of Human Motivation," *Psychological Review*, July 1943, pp. 370–396; *Motivation and Personality* (New York: Harper & Row, 1954), Chapter 5.
2. Florence M. Stone, "Motivating Employees: The Danger of Applying '60s Theories to '90s Situations," *HR/OD* (A Member Newsletter of the American Management Association International), June 1998, p. 3.
3. Frederick Herzberg, Bernard Mausner, and Barbara Snyderman, *The Motivation to Work,* 2nd ed. (New York: John Willey & Sons, 1959); Herzberg, *Work and the Nature of Man* (Cleveland: World Publishing, 1966).
4. "Boss Cleans House, Employees Applaud," *Associated Press,* October 4, 1999.
5. David C. McClelland, "Business Drive and National Achievement," *Harvard Business Review* (July–August 1962), pp. 99–112; McClelland, *The Achieving Society* (New York: Van Nostrand, 1961).
6. Edwin T. Cornelius III and Frank B. Lane, "The Power Motive and Managerial Success in a Professionally Oriented Service Industry Organization," *Journal of Applied Psychology,* February 1984, pp. 32–39.
7. Jane Churchouse and Chris Churchouse, *Managing People* (Hamshire, England: Gower Publishing Ltd. 1998); "Recognizing Workers' Needs," *Managers Edge,* March 1999, p. 1.
8. Book review in *Personnel Psychology,* Winter 1991, p. 872.
9. Edwin A. Locke and Gray P. Latham, *A Theory of Goal Setting and Task Performance* (Upper Saddle River, NJ: Prentice Hall, 1990).
10. John J. Donavan and David J. Radosevich, "The Moderating Role of Goal Commitment on the Goal Difficulty-Performance Relationship: A Meta-Analytic Review and Critical Reanalysis," *Journal of Applied Psychology,* April 1998, pp. 308–315; Howard J. Klein, Michael J. Wesson, John R. Hollenbeck, and Bradley J. Alge, "Goal Commitment and the Goal-Setting Process: Conceptual Clarification and Empirical Synthesis," *Journal of Applied Psychology,* December 1999, pp. 885–896.
11. Don VandeWalle, Steven P. Brown, William L. Cron, and John W. Slocum, Jr., "The Influence of Goal Orientation and Self-Regulation Tactics on Sales Performance: A Longitudinal Field Test," *Journal of Applied Psychology,* April 1999, pp. 249–259.
12. P. Christopher Earley and Terri R. Lituchy, "Delineating Goal and Efficacy Effects: A Test of Three Models," *Journal of Applied Psychology,* February 1991, p. 872.
13. B. F. Skinner, *Science and Human Behavior* (New York: Macmillan, 1953).
14. Victor H. Vroom, *Work and Motivation* (New York: John Wiley & Sons, 1964); Lynn E. Miller and Joseph E. Grush, "Improving Predictions in Expectancy Theory Research: Effects of Personality, Expectancies, and Norms," *Academy of Management Journal,* March 1988, pp. 107–122.
15. Alexander D. Stajkovic and Fred Luthans, "Social Cognitive Theory and Self-Efficacy: Going Beyond Traditional Motivational and Behavioral Approaches," *Organizational Dynamics,* Spring 1998, p. 66.
16. Nancy J. Adler, *International Dimensions of Organizational Behavior,* 2nd ed. (Boston: PWS-Kent, 1991), pp. 157–160.
17. J. Stacy Adams, "Toward an Understanding of Inequality," *Journal of Abnormal and Social Psychology,* Vol. 67, 1963, pp. 422–436; M. R. Carrell and J. E. Dettrich, "Equity Theory: The Recent Literature, Methodological Considerations, and New Directions, " *Academy of Management Review,* April 1978, pp. 202–210.
18. Robert Wood and Albert Bandura, "Social Cognitive Theory of Organizational Management," *Academy of Management Review,* July 1989, pp. 361–384.
19. Gregory Moorehead and Ricky W. Griffin, *Organizational Behavior: Managing People and Organizations,* 4th ed. (Boston: Houghton Mifflin, 1995), pp. 147–148; Robert P. Veccio, *Organizational Behavior,* 2nd ed. (Fort Worth, TX: Dryden Press, 1991), p. 193.
20. Richard M. Ryan and Edward L. Deci, "Self-Determination Theory and the Facilitation of Intrinsic Motivation, Social Development, and Well-Being," *American Psychologist,* January 2000, pp. 68–78; Jeffrey Pfeffer, *Human Equation: Building Profits by Putting People First* (Boston, MA: Harvard Business School Press, 1998), pp. 213–217.

Motivational Methods and Programs

Although high employee turnover rates are typical in the hospitality industry, Jeanne Bursch, director of human resources, Hotel Sofitel-Minnesota, reports her turnover has drastically declined from 84 percent to 37 percent. She credits the company culture and how it views employees for this turnaround. "If we treat our internal customers well, they'll treat our external customers well and our business will be successful." Included in this recipe for success is a $36,000 annual budget to pay for several employee rewards and recognition programs, "which is more than what most companies set aside," she admits.

The Sofitel Service Champions (one of the company recognition programs) is relatively easy to participate in, notes Bursch. Employees are selected for the Service Champion award based on weekly customer feedback, or when a manager or team member observes another employee providing outstanding service. When an employee does something noteworthy, he or she is presented with a paper resembling a French franc. Employees who receive three francs are entitled to a $35 gift certificate to one of Hotel Sofitel's restaurants. Upon receiving seven francs, employees can exchange them for dinner in one of the hotel's restaurants or a $35 gift certificate to any store or restaurant. When an employee receives 10 francs, he or she is entitled to a day off with pay or a $50 gift certificate to any store or restaurant. Sofitel maintains an impressive Web site at http://www.sofitel.com, where every facet of Sofitel service and surroundings is detailed for potential guests.

Source: Adapted from "Well-Structured Employee Reward/Recognition Programs Yield Positive Results," *HRfocus*, November 1999, pp. 1, 14–16.

PHOTO: © MARK RICHARDS/PHOTOEDIT

OBJECTIVES

After reading and studying this chapter and doing the exercises, you should be able to

1. Explain how to enhance motivation through job enrichment, the job characteristics model, and work group design.

2. Summarize the basics of a behavior modification program in the workplace.

3. Identify rules and suggestions for motivating group members through behavior modification.

4. Describe why recognition is a good motivator, and the nature of reward and recognition programs in the workplace.

5. Describe how to effectively use financial incentives to motivate others, including the use of stock options and gainsharing.

6. Choose an appropriate motivational model for a given situation.

Chapter 6

SO WHAT? **What, in particular, makes the recognition program at this Sofitel hotel an example of a successful formal program to motivate employees to work hard and stay with the firm?** Developing a shared vision for achieving excellence provides direction. But rewarding work in a manner that motivates employees to perform at the high levels expected of them will be a decisive competency for companies to develop if they are to succeed in the future. In this chapter, we describe motivational programs based on rewards and recognition, but we also examine motivation through job design and behavior modification. (Reward and recognition programs are an application of reinforcement theory and are therefore closely related to behavior modification.) We also describe choosing an appropriate motivational model, a topic that relates to both the present and previous chapter.

MOTIVATION THROUGH JOB DESIGN

Explain how to enhance motivation through job enrichment, the job characteristics model, and work group design.

A major strategy for enhancing motivation is to make the job so challenging and the worker so responsible that he or she is motivated just by performing the job. We will approach motivation through job design by explaining job enrichment, the job characteristics model, and self-managing work teams. Research and practice with motivation through job design has its roots in the two-factor theory described in Chapter 5.

Job Enrichment

Job enrichment refers to making a job more motivational and satisfying by adding variety, responsibility, and managerial decision making. At its best, job enrichment gives workers a sense of ownership, responsibility, and accountability for their work. Because job enrichment leads to a more exciting job, it often increases employee job satisfaction and motivation. People are usually willing to work harder at tasks they find enjoyable and rewarding, just as they will put effort into a favorite hobby. The general approach to enriching a job is to build into it more planning, decision making, controlling, and responsibility. Managers and professionals in organizations typically have enriched jobs.

Exciting, or enriched, jobs appeal strongly to new business graduates. A survey of 2,221 MBA students indicated that they wanted to make a quick impact on their jobs. Major employers of MBAs such as consulting firms, Intel, Disney, Microsoft, and Johnson & Johnson have responded by promising new MBAs broader exposure and the chance to work with a high-profile task force outside their functional area.[1]

Characteristics of an Enriched Job
According to Frederick Herzberg, the way to design an enriched job is to include as many of the characteristics described below as possible.[2] Exhibit 6-1 summarizes the characteristics and consequences of enriched jobs.

1. *Direct feedback.* Employees should receive immediate evaluation of their work. Feedback can be built into the job (such as the feedback that closing a sale gives a sales representative) or provided by the manager.
2. *Client relationships.* A job is automatically enriched when a worker has a client or customer to serve, whether that client is internal or external. Serving a client is more satisfying to most people than performing work solely for a

manager. An information systems specialist at a bank who interacts with loan officers is said to have a client relationship.

3. *New learning.* An enriched job allows its holder to acquire new knowledge. The learning can stem from job experiences themselves or from training programs associated with the job.

4. *Control over scheduling.* The ability to schedule one's work contributes to job enrichment. Scheduling includes the authority to decide when to tackle which assignments and having some say in setting working hours, such as flextime.

5. *Unique experience.* An enriched job has some unique qualities or features. A public relations assistant, for example, has the opportunity to interact with visiting celebrities.

6. *Control over resources.* Another contributor to enrichment is having some control over resources, such as money, material, or people.

7. *Direct communication authority.* An enriched job provides workers the opportunity to communicate directly with other people who use their output. A software engineer with an enriched job, for example, handles complaints about the software she developed. The advantages of this dimension of an enriched job are similar to those derived from maintaining client relationships.

8. *Personal accountability.* In an enriched job, workers are responsible for their results. They accept credit for a job well done and blame for a job done poorly.

A highly enriched job has all eight of the preceding characteristics and gives the job holder an opportunity to satisfy growth needs, such as self-fulfillment. A job with some of these characteristics would be moderately enriched. An impoverished job has none.

Guidelines for Implementing Job Enrichment

Before implementing a program of job enrichment, a manager must ask if the workers need or want more responsibility, variety, and growth. Some employees' jobs are already enriched enough. Many employees do not want an enriched job because they prefer to avoid the challenge and stress of responsibility. A study conducted in a government service organization indicated that employees with a strong need for growth were more likely to respond to an opportunity for performing enriched work. The independent variable studied was the manager offering a case-processing specialist the opportunity to collaborate with him on a case.[3]

Brainstorming is useful in pinpointing changes that will enrich jobs for those who want enrichment.[4] The brainstorming group would be composed of job incumbents, supervisors, and perhaps an industrial engineer. The workers' participation in planning can be useful. Workers may suggest, for example, how to increase client contact.

The Job Characteristics Model

The concept of job enrichment has been expanded to the **job characteristics model,** a method of job design that focuses on the task and interpersonal demands of a job.[5] The model is based on both needs theory and expectancy theory, with its emphasis on workers looking to satisfy needs through the job. To illustrate, a basic proposition of the model is that outcomes are valued by people to the extent that the outcomes can help satisfy their deficiency and growth needs. As Exhibit 6-2 shows, five measurable characteristics of a job improve employee motivation, satisfaction, and performance. These characteristics are:

1. *Skill variety,* the degree to which there are many skills to perform.
2. *Task identity,* the degree to which one worker is able to do a complete job, from beginning to end, with a tangible and possible outcome.
3. *Task significance,* the degree to which work has a heavy impact on others in the immediate organization or the external environment.
4. *Autonomy,* the degree to which a job offers freedom, independence, and discretion in scheduling and in determining procedures involved in its implementation.
5. *Feedback,* the degree to which a job provides direct information about performance.

As indicated in Exhibit 6-2, these core job characteristics relate to critical psychological states or key mental attitudes. Skill variety, task identity, and task significance lead to a feeling that the work is meaningful. The task dimension of autonomy leads logically to a feeling that one is responsible for work outcomes. The feedback dimension leads to knowledge of results. According to the model, a redesigned job must lead to these three psychological states for workers to achieve the outcomes of internal motivation, job satisfaction, growth satisfaction, low turnover and absenteeism, and high-quality performance.

The job characteristics model combines the five characteristics into a single index that reflects the overall potential of a job to trigger high internal work motivation. Called the Motivating Potential Score (MPS), the index is computed as follows:

The Job Characteristics Model of Job Enrichment

Source: J. R. Hackman and G. R. Oldham, *Work Redesign* (Reading, MA: Addison-Wesley, 1980), p. 77.

112

$$MPS = \frac{\text{Skill Variety} + \text{Task Identity} + \text{Task Significance}}{3} \times \text{Autonomy} \times \text{Feedback}$$

Numeric values for each of the five job characteristics are obtained by tabulating the job holder's answers to the Job Diagnostic Survey, a written questionnaire. After computing the MPS, a researcher can evaluate whether redesigning a job actually changed employees' perceptions of its motivational value.

Researchers have been able to demonstrate the potential of the job characteristics model. A large southwestern bank-holding company decided to enrich the job of bank teller. The enrichment involved making tellers feel more professional and fulfilled by enhancing responsibility, authority, and accountability. For example, tellers no longer had to refer commercial checking customers to special tellers. A total of 526 tellers participated in the study at intervals of 6, 24, and 48 months.

Enriching the job of bank teller improved the tellers' perceptions. They thought the newly defined job was more motivational, as measured by increases in the MPS. Job satisfaction and commitment increased quickly but then returned to its initial level. Performance did not increase within 6 months, yet increased significantly when measured at 24 and 48 months.[6]

A potential problem in implementing the job characteristics model, as well as job enrichment in general, is that supervisors and group members may not agree on what constitutes an enriched job. A study conducted in a university office setting with a variety of jobs found that supervisors and subordinates perceived their job characteristics differently. (The dimensions studied were the same as those contained in the job characteristics model.)

The most notable difference was found for task significance, with the supervisors rating this dimension higher than did group members. A possible interpretation was that the supervisors had a clearer view of the "big picture," thereby having a better understanding of the potential impact of a task. Another finding was that the group members' perception of the enriched quality had a bigger impact on job outcomes than did the supervisor's perception. Your perception of task significance has a bigger impact on your satisfaction and motivation than your supervisor's perception of the same factor. An implication of these findings is that employees should play a major role in job redesign since their perceptions of enrichment differ from their supervisor's perceptions.[7]

Self-Managed Work Teams

A dominant trend in job design is to organize workers into teams with considerable authority to direct themselves. A majority of U. S. corporations use some form of team structure in their organizations, and often these team structures[8] are the type of self-managed teams in question here. Team structures are also prevalent in European and Asian industry. A **self-managed work team** is a formally recognized group of employees who are responsible for an entire work process or segment that delivers a product or service to an internal or external customer.[9] Other terms for self-managed work teams include *self-directed work teams, autonomous group, semi-autonomous team, production work team,* and *work team.* The difference in title sometimes refers to varying amounts of authority held by the group. Self-managed work groups originated as an outgrowth of job enrichment. Working in teams broadens the responsibility of team members.

Small as well as large companies are making use of this form of job design. Self-directed teams are found in businesses as diverse as food processing, furniture manufacturing, telecommunications, insurance, government agencies, and health care.[10] The accompanying Organizational Behavior in Action illustrates the application of self-managed teams in a manufacturing setting of a well-known consumer products firm.

Organizational Behavior *in Action*

S e l f - M a n a g i n g   T e a m s   a t   E a s t m a n   K o d a k   C o .

The single-use camera factory at an Eastman Kodak Co. plant made a simple change that saved millions of dollars: It stopped shutting down lines for lunch. Staggered breaks added 90 minutes to two hours of productive time per day to a plant thought to be running at full capacity. The move boosted potential output of a fast-selling product by hundreds of thousands and perhaps by more than 1 million cameras a year, based on rough industry estimates.

The decision was not an edict from the corporate office or from plant management. It came from the workers themselves. To take the inefficiency and complacency out of its worldwide manufacturing operations, Kodak has vested teams with unprecedented power to shape their jobs. "There's a cultural change going on in this company," said Tom Wright, 40, a single-use factory mechanic. "We, as a company, are recognizing we have to change to compete differently. We're to work with managers to make it happen. That's been communicated very well."

So far, the teams are rewarding Kodak for its confidence. In one six-month period, the company said it found $355 million in cost cuts of $1 billion pledged as part of the previous year's restructuring. The savings came largely on the strength of advances in manufacturing efficiency. Some of the savings, however, stemmed from layoffs. At the same time, Kodak's cost of goods sold has declined in seven straight quarter-over-quarter periods and is poised to hit a four-year low.

The daily focus for manufacturing workers is on simple common-sense strategies for working better and smarter. The single-use camera employees, according to both managers and hard-core performance measurements, have provided an array of grass-roots ideas designed in some instances to cut mere seconds from production times. One example is a project tackled by 22-year-old Daniel Butler and 30-year-old Dan Van Guilder. The two men were charged with redesigning the plant's supply chain to keep fewer bins of raw material on the floor at any particular time.

The unit had operated with a six-hour supply of spools, counters, camera backs and other parts. Having so much material in bins that stretched across the shop floor led to confusion during breakdowns and mistakes during line changes. That translated into a waste of time and resources. Van Guilder and Butler needed to figure out where key materials had to go, make clear new signs for each area, and interview members of each shift for their ideas, all the while carrying on regular duties.

"It's a lot better for us. We definitely have reduced the defects," Van Guilder said. According to plant officials, the cost of making cameras has been reduced as waste is cut and production runs more smoothly. The company also says that its output of single-use cameras that survive quality tests has increased 34 percent since the raw material was reconfigured.

For more information about how Kodak uses employee networks to apply collective talents to achieve share objectives, visit the Jobs at Kodak page at http://www.kodak.com.

Source: Ben Rand, "Look Who's Running Kodak: Workers on the Shop Floor Flex New Muscle—and Produce Results," *Democrat and Chronicle, (*Rochester, New York), 6 September 1998, by permission of the *Democrat and Chronicle.*

The key purposes for establishing self-managed teams are to increase productivity, enhance quality, reduce cycle time (the amount of time required to complete a transaction), and to respond more rapidly to a changing workplace. Next we describe the method of operation of these teams and take a brief look at the results.

Method of Operation

Members of the self-managed work team typically work together on an ongoing, day-by-day basis, thus differentiating it from a task force or committee. The work team is often given total responsibility or "ownership" of a product or service. A work team might be assigned the responsibility for preparing a merchandise catalog. At other times, the team is given responsibility for a major chunk of a job, such as building a truck engine (but not the entire truck). The self-managed work team is taught to think in terms of customer requirements, thus fitting well into the quality movement. The team members might ask, "How easy would it be for a left-handed person to use this can opener?"

To promote the sense of ownership, workers are taught to become generalists rather than specialists. Each team member learns a broad range of skills and switches job assignments periodically. Members of the self-directed work team also receive training in team skills. Cross-training in different organizational functions is also important to help members develop an overall perspective of how the firm operates. As compiled by a team of experts,[11] the distinguishing characteristics of a self-directing work team are presented in Exhibit 6-3. Studying these characteristics will provide insight into work teams.

As a result of having so much responsibility for a product or service, team members usually develop pride in their work and team. At best, the team members feel as if they are operating a small business, with the profits (or losses) directly attributable to their efforts. An entry-level worker, such as a data-entry specialist in a market research firm, is less likely to have such feelings.

Self-Managed Work Team Effectiveness

Self-managed work teams have a good record of improving productivity, quality, and customer service. Corporate executives and small-business owners are finding that self-managed work teams are a highly effective form of work group design. Consultant Jon Katzenbach believes there is virtually no environment in which teams—if implemented properly—cannot have a measurable impact on an organization's performance.[12]

EXHIBIT 6-3

Characteristics of a Self-Managed Work Team

1. Team members are empowered to share many management and leadership functions, such as making job assignments and giving pep talks.
2. Members plan, control, and improve their own work processes.
3. Members set their own goals and inspect their own work.
4. Members create their own schedules and review their group performance.
5. Members often prepare their own budgets and coordinate their work with other departments.
6. Members typically order materials, keep inventories, and deal with suppliers.
7. Members are sometimes responsible for obtaining any new training they might need. (The organization, however, usually mandates the start-up training as described above.)
8. Members are authorized to hire their own replacements or assume responsibility for disciplining their own members.
9. Members assume responsibility for the quality of their products and services, whether provided to internal or external customers.

SELF-ASSESSMENT

Mental Readiness for Being Assigned to a Work Team

Directions: Respond to each statement on the following scale: SD, strongly disagree; D, disagree; N, neutral; A, agree; SA, strongly agree.

Amount of Agreement

1. Employees should make the majority of decisions related to their work.   SD D N (A) SA
2. It is possible for corporate employees to take as much pride in their work as if it were their own business.   SD D N A (SA)
3. Workers who lack advanced training and education are capable of making useful work improvements.   SD D N A (SA)
4. Groups can work effectively without a clear-cut center of authority.   SD D N A (SA)
5. It is worth sacrificing some specialization of labor to give workers a chance to develop multiple skills.   SD D N A (SA)
6. Competent workers do not require too much supervision.   SD D N A (SA)
7. Having authority over people is not as important to me as being part of a smooth-working team.   SD D N A (SA)
8. Given the opportunity, many workers could manage themselves without much supervision.   SD D N A (SA)
9. Cordial relationships are important even in a factory setting.   SD D N A (SA)
10. The more power workers are given, the more likely they are to behave responsibly.   SD D N A (SA)

Scoring and Interpretation: Score the answers as 1 through 5, with SD being 1 and SA being 5. Add the numerical value you assigned to each statement and total your scores. The closer your score is to 50, the higher your degree of mental readiness to lead or participate on a work team. If your score is 30 or less, attempt to develop a more optimistic view of the capabilities and attitudes of workers. Start by looking for evidence of good accomplishments by skilled and semiskilled workers.

A specific example of positive results with a self-managed work team took place at a General Electric plant in Salisbury, North Carolina. The company introduced work teams in addition to flexible automation and computerized systems. Productivity increased 250 percent in comparison to other GE plants producing the same product. The results were so encouraging that 20 percent of 120,000 GE employees now work in teams.[13] The evidence from GE could mean that the combination of work teams and the right type of automation improves productivity.

A major contributor to work team effectiveness is the suitability of its members to a team operation. The Self-Assessment above gives you a chance to think about your mental readiness to work on a team.

Work teams also have some potential disadvantages. Absenteeism tends to be higher than in traditional work group designs. The reason might be that team members believe that other team members can cover for them because they are multiskilled. A high-quality workforce is needed because team members have to be flexible and intelligent and think broadly. In a manufacturing setting, establishing work modules for the team can require substantial space. Costs can skyrocket when each group has its own equipment.

ORGANIZATIONAL BEHAVIOR MODIFICATION

One of the more elaborate systems for motivating employees is based upon reinforcement theory. **Organizational behavior modification (OB Mod)** is the application of reinforcement theory for motivating people in work settings. OB Mod programs typically use positive reinforcement rather than punishment to modify behavior. Linking behavior with positive consequences is more effective than using negative motivators, and positive consequences arouse less controversy. Here we present a framework for a formal OB Mod program, followed by suggestions for everyday managerial application of behavior modification.

Summarize the basics of a behavior modification program in the workplace.

Steps in a Formal OB Mod Program

As outlined in Exhibit 6-4, the OB Mod program begins with identifying behaviors that require change.[14] For example, the regional manager of a chain of convenience stores might believe strongly that cashiers should always ask before a customer pays, "What else can I get for you?" Market research has shown that this statement enhances sales. The behavior for change is that the cashiers are not asking this question frequently enough.

The next step is for the manager to measure baseline performance, for example, how frequently cashiers are asking the sales-inducing question. The behavior is stated in terms of a percentage frequency for various intervals. Store observers assigned by the regional manager might find, for example, that cashiers are asking "What else can I get you?" only about 20 percent of the time.

Step three is to analyze the behavioral antecedents and contingent consequences in the performance-related context (analyze functional consequences). This analysis attempts to answer two questions: (1) What are the antecedents of the performance-related behavior measured in the first two steps? and (2) What are the contingent consequences when workers make the desired response? Antecedents can include many factors such as equipment, technological processes, job design, and/or performance training. However, here we are concerned with antecedents that set the occasion for the behavior to occur, a customer bringing goods to the counter.

The contingent consequences are the outcomes that stem from the behavior. The behavior is what the cashier does (asking the question). Consequences are the outcomes that stem from the behavior, such as the customer saying, "Yes, please get me six Beef Jerkies." A more general consequence would be that sales increase an average of $2.50 per customer when the cashier asks, "What else can I get for you?"

Next the manager decides upon an intervention strategy appropriate to the situation. Environmental variables affecting the linkage between reward and behavior include industry, structure, size, processes, and technology. For example, the information technology built into the cash registers will influence how easy it is to record sales above baseline. The manager is now ready to apply an appropriate contingency strategy. Positive reinforcement is applied to increase functional behaviors and decrease dysfunctional behaviors. Punishment of dysfunctional behaviors might also be used as a last resort. Punishment, however, is followed by positive reinforcement as the worker improves.

After intervening, the manager measures performance again to assess whether the desired effect—asking the sales-inducing question frequently—has been achieved. If the appropriate behavior does not occur frequently, the manager must choose a new intervention strategy or repeat the entire process.

OB Mod Application Model

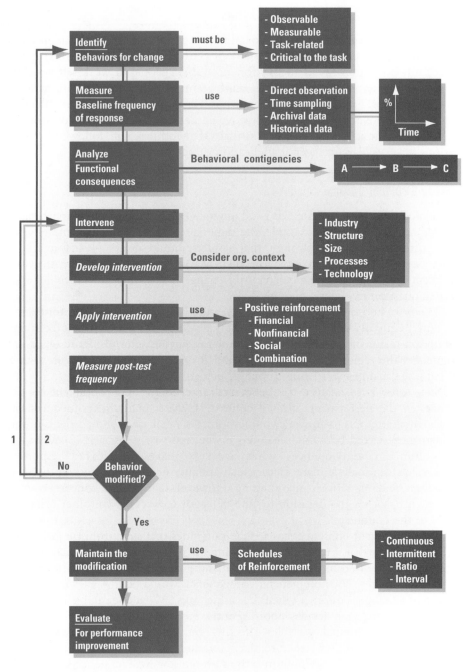

Note: A = antecedent, B = behavior, C = consequences.

Source: Fred Luthans and Alexander D. Stajkovic, "Reinforce for Performance: The Need to Go Beyond Pay and Even Rewards," *Academy of Management Executive*, May 1999, p. 53.

If performance increases as planned, the manager must maintain the desirable behavior through a schedule of reinforcement. Under a continuous schedule, the cashier receives a reward each time a customer responds positively to the question. An intermittent schedule offers rewards from time to time. (A ratio schedule is giving the reward on a ratio such as one reward per six right responses; an interval schedule gives the reward based on the amount of time between the right responses.) The cashier might receive continuous reinforcement in terms of earning a small commission on every sale. The fact that customers will not always respond "Yes" to the key question creates an intermittent schedule.

The last step answers the question of whether the OB Mod program led to performance improvement in observable and measurable terms. The manager looks for improvements in the employee's behavior. A store observer might monitor how often the key question is asked; receipts might provide an index of change in sales volume.

RULES FOR THE APPLICATION OF OB MOD

Principles of behavior modification can also be applied outside of a structured company program. Our focus here is with managers' day-by-day application of OB Mod, with an emphasis on positive reinforcement. An individual contributor attempting to motivate somebody else can also apply these rules. Following these eight rules increases the probability that an OB Mod program will achieve its intended result of increasing the motivation and productivity of individuals and groups. Although the rules have generally been developed with individuals, they also apply to rewarding group performance.

Identify rules and suggestions for motivating group members through behavior modification.

Rule 1: Choose an appropriate reward or punishment. An appropriate reward or punishment is effective in motivating a worker or group and is feasible from the company standpoint. Rewards should have a high positive attraction and punishments a negative one. If one reward does not work, another should be tried. Feasible rewards include money, company stock, recognition, challenging new assignments, and status symbols such as a private work area. It is generally best to use the mildest form of punishment that will motivate the person, such as expressing disappointment. Although widely used, fear is a generally ineffective form of punishment because it may cause resentment, revenge, and a degree of immobilization.

Rule 2: Reinforce the behaviors you really want to encourage. An axiom of behavior modification is that you get what you reinforce. If you give rewards to help-desk workers based on the number of requests for help they process, you will increase the number of calls. Customer service may not improve, however, because the help-desk workers will feel compelled to quickly process the calls for help. Rewards for resolving customer problems have a greater probability of enhancing customer service. (It takes time and patience to resolve some problems called in to a help desk.)

Rule 3: Supply ample feedback. OB Mod tactics cannot work without frequent feedback to individuals. Feedback can take the form of simply telling people they have done something right or wrong. Brief e-mail messages or handwritten notes are another common form of feedback. Be aware, however, that many employees resent seeing a message with negative feedback on their computer screen.

Rule 4: Rewards should be commensurate with the good deed. Average performance is encouraged when all forms of accomplishment receive the same reward. Suppose one employee made substantial progress in reducing customer complaints. She should receive more recognition (or other reward) than a group member who makes only a minor contribution to solving the problem.

Rule 5: Schedule rewards intermittently. Intermittent rewards sustain desired behavior longer and slow the process of behavior fading away when it is not rewarded. A reward that is given continuously may lose its impact. A practical value of intermittent reinforcement is that it saves time. Few managers have enough time to dispense rewards for every appropriate response forthcoming from group members.

Rule 6: Rewards and punishments should follow the observed behavior closely in time. For maximum effectiveness, workers should be rewarded shortly after doing something right and punished shortly after doing something wrong. A built-in feedback system, such as software working or not working, capitalizes on this principle. If you are administering rewards and punishments, strive to administer them the same day they are earned.

Rule 7: Make rewards visible to the recipient and to others. The person who receives the reward should be aware that it has been received. A person might receive a small bonus for good performance with the payment being virtually hidden in the paycheck. Because the reward is not noticed, it has a negligible impact on behavior.[15] Ideally, rewards should also be made visible to other employees besides the recipient. Rewards that are made public increase the status of the recipient and also let other employees know what kind of behavior gets rewarded.

Rule 8: Change the reward periodically. Rewards do not retain their effectiveness indefinitely. A major criticism of positive reinforcement as a motivational technique is that rewards go stale. Employees and customers lose interest in striving for a reward they have received many times previously. This is particularly true with a repetitive statement such as "Nice job" or "Fantastic." It is helpful for the manager to formulate a list of feasible rewards and try different ones from time to time.

Now do the Skill-Development Exercise that follows to practice several of these rules for using behavior modification.

Behavior modification has a long history of improving productivity on the job. Fred Luthans and Alexander D. Sajkovic performed a meta-analysis of all the empirical findings of research conducted with the OB Mod method over a 20-year period. The study indicated a substantial 17 percent average improvement in performance. The overall improvement in manufacturing settings was 33 percent

SKILL-DEVELOPMENT EXERCISE

COLLABORATE

Organizational Behavior Modification

In both of the following scenarios, one student plays the role of the manager attempting to modify the behavior of (or motivate) the other individual. Another student plays the role of the recipient of these attempts at motivation.

Scenario 1: Rewarding a Customer Service Representative. The customer service manager reviews customer service reports to discover that one service rep has resolved the most complaints for four consecutive weeks. Since this rep has only been on the job for six months, the manager wants to ensure that the rep feels amply rewarded and appreciated. The manager also wants to sustain this high level of performance. The manager calls the rep into the office to discuss this outstanding performance and administer an appropriate reward.

Scenario 2: Punishing a Customer Service Representative. The customer service manager reviews customer service reports and discovers that one service rep has resolved the fewest complaints for four consecutive weeks. Furthermore, three customers have written the company complaining of rude treatment by this representative. Since this rep has only been on the job six months, the manager wants to make sure that the rep makes substantial improvements. The manager calls the rep into the office to discuss this poor performance and administer an appropriate punishment.

Others in the class observe the two scenarios so they can provide feedback on how well OB Mod principles were applied.

and 17 percent in service settings. Another notable finding was that social rein-forcers such as recognition and positive feedback were as effective as monetary rewards.[16]

MOTIVATION THROUGH RECOGNITION

Motivating workers by giving them praise and recognition can be considered a direct application of positive reinforcement. Nevertheless, recognition is such a potentially powerful motivator that it merits separate attention. Also, reward and recognition programs are a standard practice in business and nonprofit firms. An example would be rewarding high performing employees with electronic gift cards or designating them "employee of the month." A reward and recognition program essentially focuses on rewards as a form of recognition. The gift card just mentioned might have a commercial value of $100, but its main value is to rec-ognize a job well done.

Recognition is a strong motivator because it is a normal human need to crave recognition. At the same time, recognition is effective because most workers feel they do not receive enough recognition. Several studies conducted over a 50-year time span indicated that employees welcome praise for a job well done as much as a regular paycheck. This finding should not be interpreted to mean that praise is an adequate substitute for compensation. Employees tend to regard compensa-tion as an entitlement, whereas recognition is perceived as a gift.[17] Workers, includ-ing your coworkers, want to know that their output is useful to somebody.

To appeal to the recognition need of others, identify a meritorious behavior and then recognize that behavior with an oral, written, or material reward. The rules for the use of behavior modification are directly applicable. An example of employee recognition is as follows: As the team leader of a production unit, you observe that Janice, one of the manufacturing technicians, has the best safety record in the plant—zero accidents in five years. You send an e-mail message noti-fying every company employee of Janice's accomplishment.

An outstanding advantage of recognition, including praise, as a motivator is that it is low cost or no cost, yet powerful. Recognition thus has an enormous return on investment in comparison to a cash bonus. Following are several more points to better understand and implement reward and recognition programs:

1. *Feedback is an essential part of recognition.* Specific feedback about what the worker did right makes recognition more meaningful. For example, "The clever cartoon you inserted on our Web site increased sales by 22 percent for replacement keyboards."
2. *Praise is one of the most powerful forms of recognition.* Praise works well because it enhances self-esteem if the praise is genuine. As indicated above, praise is a supplement to other rewards such as compensation. A challenge in using praise as a form of recognition is that not everybody responds well to the same form of praise. A germane example is that highly technical people tend not to like general praise like "Great job." Instead, they prefer a laid-back, factual state-ment about how their output made a contribution.
3. *Reward and recognition programs should be linked to organizational goals.* Many organizations today understand that the biggest return on reward and recog-nition programs takes place when the rewards and recognition are linked to business strategy.[18] If the company strategy is to develop a more culturally diverse workforce at all levels, an employee should be recognized for recruit-ing a Latino computer scientist.

Describe why recognition is a good motivator, and the nature of reward and recog-nition programs in the workplace.

121

4. *Employee input into what type of rewards and recognition are valued is useful.* A company might spend a lot of money giving away grandfather clocks only to find that employees would prefer gift certificates to movies as a form of reward and recognition. Exhibit 6-5 illustrates how a not-for-profit firm solicited employee input to enhance the possibility of having a reward and recognition program meaningful to employees.

5. *It is important to evaluate the effectiveness of the reward and recognition program.* As with all organizational behavior and human resources interventions, it is useful to assess how well the reward and recognition program is working. For example, the company would establish baseline measures of performance, administer the reward and recognition program, and then measure performance again. (Review the section about research methods in Chapter 1.)

MOTIVATION THROUGH FINANCIAL INCENTIVES

Describe how to effectively use financial incentives to motivate others, including the use of stock options and gainsharing.

A natural reinforcer for workers at any level is to offer them financial incentives for good performance. Using financial incentives as a motivator is another application of behavior modification. Financial incentives, however, predate behavior modification in the workplace and are also an application of common sense. The following sections describe four current issues about money as a reinforcer: linking pay to performance, stock options, gainsharing, and problems associated with financial incentives.

EXHIBIT 6-5

Survey to Measure Employee Attitudes Toward Rewards and Recognition

Linking Pay to Performance

Financial incentives are more effective when they are linked to (or contingent upon) good performance. Linking pay to performance generally motivates people

---

1. Do you receive positive feedback from your supervisor on a regular basis? Does your supervisor thank you for the work you do?
    ___✓ Mostly yes   ·___ No or rarely

2. Have you ever wanted to be able to recognize good work done by coworkers?
    ___✓ Frequently   ____ Seldom

3. Would you prefer to receive recognition initiated by supervisors and managers or by your peers? Or both? (check all that apply)
    ___✓ Managers   ___✓ Supervisors   ___✓ Peers

    Keeping in mind that this program is intended to involve "non-cash" tangible rewards that are limited by University and IRS regulations, please respond to the following:

4. What kind of "rewards" would you like to see given?
    ___✓ Mugs, other items with a special department of University logo
    ____ Flowers   ____ Certificates of appreciation   ___✓ Catalog of gift certificates
    ____ T-shirts   ____ CDs   ___✓ Parking passes
    ____ Transit passes   ___✓ Dinner certificates   ___✓ Tickets to events
    ____ Other: List suggestions below

5. How could we be sure such a program would work effectively and positively?

6. What drawbacks do you see to such a program?

7. Would you be willing to participate in a work group to implement a program?

For more information on Berkeley's reward/recognition program, check out the University's Web site for human resources at http://www.berkeley.edu.

Source: University of California, Berkeley, as reprinted in "Employee Input Can Maximize Recognition/Reward Program Success," *HRfocus,* (November 1999): 15. By permission of the University of California, Berkeley.

to work harder because the link acts as a reinforcer. The recommended approach is to tie employee pay to specific performance criteria and link it directly to value-adding business results.[19]

Managers and human resource specialists continue to fine-tune methods of linking pay to individual performance. A method used by many companies calculates base pay according to a variety of factors. Among them are ability to communicate, customer focus, dealing with change, interpersonal skills, and job knowledge. Teamwork is often included as a performance factor with good team players receiving more money. In some firms, members of self-managed teams receive part of their compensation based on team performance. Managers are rated on employee development, team productivity, and leadership. Merit pay for both individuals and the team is based on actual results. Merit pay runs from 5 percent to over 15 percent of total compensation.[20]

Although many employers believe they link pay to performance, research suggests that merit pay may not be so closely linked to performance. A team of researchers meta-analyzed the results of 39 studies about the relationship between pay and performance. A striking conclusion was that pay had little relationship to quality of work, but did show a moderately positive relationship with quantity of work. However, managers are not completely to blame. It is often easier to measure how much work employees are performing than how well they are performing. The meta-analysis in question also confirms the obvious: People will produce more work when money is at stake.[21] In defense of employers, it is easier to elevate quantity than quality.

Stock Options

An increasingly popular way of motivating workers with financial incentives is to make them part owners of the business through stock purchases. Stock ownership can be motivational because employees participate in the financial success of the firm as measured by its stock price. If employees work hard, the company may become more successful and the value of the stock increases. **Stock options** give employees the right to purchase a certain number of company shares in the future at a specified price, generally the market price on the day the option is granted. If the stock rises in value, you can purchase it at a discount. If the stock sinks below your designated purchase price, your option is worthless (or "under water"). As with many employee benefits, stock options are used to attract and retain employees, as well as reward them. Thousands of workers in the information technology field, particularly in Silicon Valley, have become millionaires and multimillionaires with their stock options. Exhibit 6-6 shows the mathematics behind a stock option.

One of the best publicized uses of stock options is at a low-technology firm, Starbucks Corp. More than 10,000 of the 26,000 Starbucks employees participate in the plan. After exercising their options, these employees have made down payments on houses, purchased cars, and paid for their college education. Stock options have also helped reduce turnover to approximately one-third the industry norm.[22]

The true impact of stock options as a motivational device is difficult to evaluate. A major confounding factor is that firms that offer stock options (an extrinsic motivator) also offer exciting work (an intrinsic motivator). As explained by Mike Butler, a compensation specialist, many of the workers who are attracted to high-tech, entrepreneurial companies find the work stimulating. "Pay isn't the only issue or even the primary issue for some workers. It's the ability to have an impact and do something exciting."[23]

How a Stock Option Works

Employee decides to exercise option for 400 shares at $10.57 each when stock reaches $35 per share.

Brokerage sells 400 shares of company stock at $35 each (400 shares × $35)	=	$14,000
Brokerage deducts exercise price (400 shares × $10.57)		– 4,228
		9,772
Taxes withheld (28% for federal income tax + 7.56% for social security tax)		– 3,475
		6,297
Brokerage deducts fees/commissions/interest		–100
		6,197
Brokerage pays profit to employee		$ 6,197

Source: Carrington Nelson, "Exercising Your Stock Options," Gannett News Service, 26 July 1998. Copyright 1998, Gannett Co., Inc. Reprinted with permission.

A major potential problem with stock options as a motivational tool is that they are worthless if a stock plunges because the employee has the option to purchase stock at above the market value! The employee suffers from disappointed expectations, and the company looks foolish. Another problem is particularly acute with high-tech start-ups that offer relatively low salary combined with generous stock options. If the stock price never rises or if it plunges, the employee has worked for less than equitable total compensation.

Gainsharing

Many organizations attempt to increase motivation and productivity through a company-wide plan of linking incentive pay to increases in performance. **Gainsharing** is a formal program of allowing employees to participate financially in the productivity gains they have achieved. Gainsharing Inc. is the institute that helps promote this motivational method (see http://www.gainsharing.com). Gainsharing is based on principles of positive reinforcement and it also emphasizes the motivational impact of money.

The formula used in gainsharing varies widely, but there are common elements. Managers begin by comparing what the employees are paid to what they sell or produce. Assume that labor costs make up 50 percent of production costs. Any reduction below 50 percent is placed in a bonus pool. The company's share of productivity savings in the pool can be distributed to stockholders as increased profits. The savings may allow managers to lower prices, a move that could make the company more competitive.

The second element of gainsharing is employee involvement. Managers establish a mechanism that actively solicits, reviews, and implements employee suggestions about productivity improvement. A committee of managers and employees reviews the ideas and then implements the most promising suggestions.[24]

Gainsharing plans have a 60-year history of turning unproductive companies around and making successful companies even more productive. Gainsharing Inc. contends that most companies will achieve an increase in their productive output of between 10 percent and 30 percent within 30 to 90 days after implementing gainsharing. The reason is that it becomes the employees' self-interest to maximize company output.[25]

Lincoln Electric is often cited as an ideal example of gainsharing because its productivity is almost double the industry average. In addition, motivation is high, absenteeism and turnover are exceedingly low, and no layoffs have occurred. Over the life of the system, bonuses have averaged 95.5 percent of base pay. Bonuses are paid at the end of the year in one check, thus magnifying the perception of the importance of the bonus.[26] Although the year-end bonus does not fit the suggestion of giving rewards close in time to the good behavior, it does make the bonus a reward of higher valence.

A research team recently did an experimental evaluation of gainsharing in two hubs of a *Fortune 500* company. One hub served as the experimental group where the gainsharing plan was implemented, and the other served as the control group (no gainsharing). Survey data were collected from several thousand employees participating in the study. The data were analyzed before the beginning of the program and at 7 and 24 months into the program. Another data analysis took place at 20 months, 3 months after the gainsharing bonus had been eliminated.

The researchers found that even a short-lived gainsharing program can foster and sustain long-term job performance. It was also found that gainsharing contributes to positive employee attitudes, even after the program is terminated. A conclusion reached in the study was that the gainsharing program enhanced peer communication. In turn, the improved communication became a source of learning that eventually led to behavioral changes in the workers.[27]

Gainsharing's popularity is growing and is expected to be used with increasing frequency by service firms. The allure of gainsharing is that the organization achieves significant productivity gains and employees elevate their real wages.[28]

Problems Associated with Financial Incentives

Although financial incentives are widely used as motivators, they can create problems. For example, workers may not agree with managers about the value of their contributions. Financial incentives can also pit individuals and groups against each other. The result may be unhealthy competition rather than cooperation and teamwork.

The most researched argument against financial rewards is that it focuses the attention of workers too much on the reward such as money or stocks. (This follows the logic of the opposition to extrinsic motivation in general.) In the process, the workers lose out on intrinsic rewards such as joy in accomplishment. Instead of being passionate about the work they are doing, people become overly concerned with the size of their reward. One argument is that external rewards do not create a lasting commitment. Instead, they create temporary compliance, such as working hard in the short run to earn a bonus. A frequent problem with merit pay systems is that a person who does not receive a merit increase one pay period often feels that he or she has been punished. Another argument against financial incentives is that rewards manipulate people, as do bribes.

Organizational theory specialist Jeffrey Pfeffer explains that people do work for money, but they work even more for meaning in their lives. Work brings people a meaningful type of fun. Pfeffer believes that people who ignore this truth are essentially bribing their employees and will pay the price in lack of loyalty and commitment. He illustrates his position with the SAS Institute, a successful software company that emphasizes excellent benefits and exciting work rather than financial incentives.[29]

In reality, workers at all levels want a combination of internal rewards and financial rewards along with other external rewards such as praise. The ideal combination is to offer exciting (internally rewarding) work to people and simultaneously pay them enough money so they are not preoccupied with matters such as salary and bonuses. Money is the strongest motivator when people have financial problems. Another reality is that even if a firm offers exciting work, great benefits,

125

and wonderful coworkers, they usually need to offer financial incentives to attract quality workers.

CHOOSING AN APPROPRIATE MOTIVATIONAL MODEL

Choose an appropriate motivational model for a given situation.

In this and the previous chapter, 13 approaches to understanding an enhancing motivation have been presented. Although these approaches have different labels, most of them have elements in common. In quick review, the 13 approaches are (1) the needs hierarchy, (2) the two-factor theory, (3) the achievement-power-affiliation triad, (4) goal theory, (5) reinforcement theory, (6) expectancy theory, (7) equity theory, (8) social learning theory, (9) intrinsic versus extrinsic motivation, (10) job design, (11) organizational behavior modification, (12) recognition, and (13) financial incentives.

A fruitful approach to choosing an effective motivation theory or program for a given situation is for the manager (or other would-be motivator) to carefully diagnose the situation. Choose a motivational approach that best fits the deficiency or neglected opportunity in a given situation. Observe the people to be motivated, and also interview them about their interests and concerns. Then apply a motivational approach that appears to match the interests, concerns, deficits, or missed opportunity. Two examples will help clarify the diagnostic approach:

1. The manager observes that group members are performing their jobs well enough to meet standards, but they are not excited about their work. Introducing job enrichment and intrinsic motivation could be just what the organizational behaviorist ordered.

2. The manager observes that group members appear interested in their work and that they like the company and their coworkers. Yet they spend too much time grumbling about personal financial problems. The most direct approach to enhancing motivation in this situation would be to introduce a program of financial incentives. To be effective, the financial payouts should be large enough to make a difference in the financial welfare of the workers.

IMPLICATIONS FOR MANAGERIAL PRACTICE

1. Although motivation through job design is complex, time consuming, and expensive, it must be given careful consideration in any strategic attempt to enhance motivation and productivity. This is especially true because motivation through job design is the conceptual core for a revolution taking place in the organization of work—the shift to self-managed work teams.

2. Employees chosen for work teams should be those who show pride in their work and enjoy working cooperatively with others. Self-nomination, or asking for volunteers for the self-directed work team, will decrease selection errors. After employees are selected, they must be trained thoroughly to become productive members of work teams. Essential training areas include problem-solving techniques, technical skills, and interpersonal and leadership skills.

3. No motivational program is a substitute for adequate compensation, including pay and benefits. One of the many reasons that money remains an all-important reinforcer is that most people have financial worries. One problem is that family income has not kept up with the high cost of housing, creating financial pressures for many wage earners.

3. The manager is attempting to use recognition to motivate workers at different occupational levels. He or she should choose recognition methods that are likely to have the highest valence for the particular level of worker. Symbolic forms of recognition such as company hats, ties, and desk clocks are likely to have the highest valence for people at lower occupational levels, such as clerical and production workers. Professional-level workers are likely to be more motivated by written forms of recognition including a letter to the file documenting their contribution.

4. The manager is attempting to motivate members of the contingent workforce such as temporary workers and part-time workers. Recognizing these workers' needs for security, company benefits might prove to have high valence, since many contingent workers lack a good benefits package.

SUMMARY OF KEY POINTS

 Explain how to enhance motivation through job enrichment, the job characteristics model, and work group design.

A major strategy for enhancing motivation is to increase the challenge and responsibility in a job. An enriched, and therefore motivational, job includes some of the following characteristics: direct feedback, client relationships, new learning, control over scheduling, unique experience, control over resources, direct communication authority, and personal accountability. Job enrichment works best when workers want or need more responsibility, variety, and growth.

Job enrichment has been expanded to create the job characteristics model, which focuses on the task and interpersonal dimensions of a job. Five characteristics of a job improve employee motivation, satisfaction, and performance: skill variety, task identity, task significance, autonomy, and feedback. These characteristics relate to critical psychological states which, in turn, lead to outcomes such as internal motivation, satisfaction, low-absenteeism, and high quality.

A dominant trend in job design is to organize workers into self-managed work teams in order to increase productivity and quality and reduce cycle time. The team is given total responsibility for a product or service in dealing with an external or internal customer. Each team member learns a broad range of skills and switches job assignments periodically. Team members plan, control, and improve their own work processes. They usually order materials, keep inventories, and deal with suppliers.

Self-managed work team members have to be mentally flexible and alert and possess at least average interpersonal skills. They must take pride in their work and enjoy working cooperatively.

 Summarize the basics of a behavior modification program in the workplace.

Organizational behavior modification (OB Mod), an application of reinforcement theory, is an elaborate motivational system. A formal program includes steps such as: identifying behavior performance problems, developing a contingency intervention strategy, maintaining desirable behavior, and measuring improvement. OB Mod programs are well documented as a method of enhancing productivity in manufacturing and service settings. Social reinforcers work as well as financial ones.

 Identify rules and suggestions for motivating group members through behavior modification.

Behavior modification can also be applied outside of a formal program by the manager following these rules: Choose an appropriate reward or punishment; reinforce the behaviors you want to encourage; supply ample feedback; make rewards commensurate with the good deed; schedule rewards intermittently; give rewards and punishments promptly; make the rewards visible to the recipient and others; and change the reward periodically.

Describe why recognition is a good motivator, and the nature of reward and recognition programs in the workplace.

Recognition is a strong motivator because it is a normal human need to crave recognition, and most workers feel they do not receive enough recognition. To appeal to the recognition need of others, identify a meritorious behavior and then recognize that behavior with an oral, written, or material reward. Praise is a powerful form of recognition. Reward and recognition programs should be linked to organizational goals. Employee input into what type of rewards and recognition are valued is useful.

Describe how to effectively use financial incentives to motivate others, including the use of stock options and gainsharing.

Financial incentives are a widely used motivator at all worker levels. Such incentives are more effective when they are linked to performance. In some firms, members of self-managed work teams receive part of their compensation based on team performance.

An increasingly popular way of motivating workers with financial incentives is to make them part owners of the business through stock purchases. Stock options give employees the right to purchase a certain number of company shares in the future at a specified price. If the stock price drops, the option is worthless.

Gainsharing, which is growing in popularity, is a formal program that allows employees to participate financially in the productivity gains they have achieved, thus enhancing motivation. Bonuses are distributed to employees based on how much they decrease the labor cost involved in producing or selling goods. Employee involvement in increasing productivity is an important part of gainsharing.

Financial incentives can create problems such as poor cooperation and focusing too much attention on the reward such as money or stocks. Instead of being passionate about the work they are doing, people become overly concerned with the size of the reward. In reality, workers at all levels want a combination of internal rewards and financial rewards along with other external rewards such as praise.

Choose an appropriate motivational model for a given situation.

A fruitful approach to choose an effective motivation theory or program for a given situation is for the manager to carefully diagnose the situation. A motivational approach is then chosen that best fits the deficiency or neglected opportunity in the situation. An example would be to understand that part-time workers might be strongly motivated by good benefits.

KEY TERMS AND PHRASES

Job Enrichment, *110*

The process of making a job more motivational and satisfying by adding variety, responsibility, and managerial decision making.

Job Characteristics Model, *112*

A method of job design that focuses on the task and interpersonal demands of a job.

Self-managed Work Team, *113*

A formally recognized group of employees responsible for an entire work process or segment that delivers a product or service to an internal or external customer.

Organizational Behavior Modification (OB Mod), *117*

The application of reinforcement theory for motivating people in work settings.

Stock Option, *123*

A financial incentive that gives the option owner the future right to purchase a certain number of company shares at a specified price, generally the market price of the stock on the day the option is granted.

Gainsharing, *124*

A formal program of allowing employees to participate financially in the productivity gains they have achieved.

DISCUSSION QUESTIONS AND ACTIVITIES

1. How might the job of a store associate (sales clerk) be enriched?

2. In your own words, what does the following statement mean: "You get what you reinforce"?

3. Critics of behavior modification contend that it is a method of manipulating workers. What is your assessment of this criticism?

4. What forms of recognition would be the most effective in motivating you?

5. In what way do stock options interfere with intrinsic motivation?

6. Why does gainsharing enhance cooperation rather than competition?

7. **COLLABORATE** Ask a friend which he or she would prefer to take: a new position that offered (a) below-average pay but with some stock options, or (b) above-average pay but without stock options. What might the answer tell you about your friend's personality?

ORGANIZATIONAL BEHAVIOR ON-LINE

TO DO

Problems with Stock Options

Use the Internet to learn more about the dark side of stock option plans as motivational devices. See if you can find an example of dissatisfaction with stock options or somebody quitting because of worthless stock options. Potentially productive search phrases include, "problems associated with stock options," and "negative side of stock options." Additional searches on recent collapses of high-profile dot.coms such as Boo.com, Toysmart, and Nickelodeon's Red Rocket should also provide unique insights into the relative merit of options.

TO BOOKMARK

Recognition Programs

http://www.cornellphysicians.com/applause

Salary Comparisons

http://www.wageweb.com

Gainsharing

http://www.gainshare.com/profile.html

CASE PROBLEM: Seasonal Workers

Skiing and golf, two of the best amenities in the Bend, Oregon, region, are not designed just for visitors. However, most working-class locals struggle to find the time and the money to fit such costly recreational activities into their daily lives. Mount Bachelor Inc., which during the ski season hires about 450 employees, and Sunriver resort, which has 350 jobs to fill each summer, have teamed together to create a year-round recreational industry. Employees receive medical and dental benefits, free skiing and golf, and an opportunity to shift jobs each season.

Although a group within the local workforce already transfers between these two employers each season, the companies are enticing workers to return to their positions each year with added medical benefits. Pat Gerhart, human resources director at Mount Bachelor, said creating the benefits package was a natural evolution from job fair efforts and active recruitment. Benefits bridge the gap between seasons if the first job is cut short before the next one begins.

"Workforce availability shortages have prompted the human resources departments to put their heads together and find a way to bring people back year after year because once a seasonal employee leaves the area, it's hard to get them (him or her) back," Gerhart said.

Experience Wanted

Both companies would like to benefit from the return of experienced and well-trained employees. Sunriver human resources director Joyce Luckman said the resort hopes to retain its core staffs, who will increase their customer-service skills in the reciprocal-employment program. "There's a need in central Oregon for year-round employment, and there's a perfect niche in this partnership," Luckman said.

The program benefits both sides. Although paying for the insurance for the employees adds a cost for the businesses, Luckman and Gerhart said it's worth it. Plus, Luckman

added, the employees won't file for unemployment insurance benefits when their seasons end.

The program is available to all employees, but this year was limited to 25 employees on a first-come, first-served basis because the human resources directors wanted to keep the program small in its first year. "We wanted to keep it manageable to see what pitfalls we might run into," Gerhart said, adding that they are still working out details.

Program Will Grow

Eventually, Gerhart said, she hopes that there are no number limits and that anyone who wants to participate can. Gerhart said the program will grow to include Eagle Crest employees, the Inn of the Seventh Mountain, and maybe the Riverhouse or rafting companies, too. But employers would have to meet some minimum coverage requirement close to the packages offered by Sunriver and Mount Bachelor. Benefits don't kick in until the employees enter their second season, so last summer's Sunriver employees working at the winter resort would now be covered.

Most Jobs Pay Low

Gerhart acknowledges that the majority of resort jobs don't pay family wages. She therefore hopes to see more people take advantage of the program who fit on the higher end of the pay scale, like groomers and golf course technicians. These workers could make a year-round family wage while bringing their families in on the recreational benefits. Besides a season pass for the whole family, Mount Bachelor employees in the program receive a company-paid medical and dental program worth $185 a month. It's a major medical program with a $250 deductible and dental insurance with a $25 deductible. Employees also have 80 percent of most medical expenses paid and up to $300 worth of preventative care.

Sunriver offers employees in the program a full recreation package, including free golf at Meadows and

Woodlands, as well as bike and canoe rentals and other discounts at the resort.

The employees in the reciprocal program receive health insurance for the entire family. The company picks up two-thirds of the premium, which can be worth as much as $450 per family.

Management at Mount Bachelor and Sunriver hope that their initiatives in providing year-round pay and more employee benefits will help develop a more experienced and stable workforce.

Case Questions

1. What does this case have to do with motivation?
2. Referring to the two-factor theory, which set of job factors is management emphasizing: motivators or hygiene? Explain your answer.

3. What other steps should managers at the golf resorts and ski resorts take to motivate experienced workers to return?
4. What is your prediction of the success of the new pay and benefits in building a stable workforce?

Source: Anne Aurand, "Resorts Offer Benefits to Seasonal Employees," Bulletin of *Bend*, (Oregon) 11 March 2000, by permission of Western Communications, Inc. (Wescom).

Want to live and work where others only visit? Cool Works.com (http://www.coolworks.com/) carries loads of information about jobs in great places.

SUGGESTED READINGS

Bernstein, Aaron. "Down and Out in Silicon Valley." *Business Week,* March 27, 2000, pp. 76–92.

Borden, Mark, and Koudsi, Suzanne. "America's 40 Richest Under 40." *Fortune,* September 27, 1999, pp. 89–118.

Fishman, Charles. "Total Teamwork, Imagination Ltd." *Fast Company,* April 2000, pp. 156–168.

Jesperson, Fred. "Executive Pay: It Continues to Explode—and Options Alone Are Creating Paper Billionaires." *Business Week,* April 7, 2000, pp. 100–112.

Kerr, Steven. *Ultimate Rewards: What Really Motivates People to Achieve.* Boston: Harvard Business School Publishing, 1997.

Laabs, Jennifer J. "Targeted Rewards Jump-Start Motivation." *Workforce,* February 1998, pp. 88–96.

Mandel, Michael J., "The Prosperity Gap: The Economy Is Booming, Profits Are Soaring—So Why Isn't Everyone Riding High?" *Business Week,* September 27, 1999, pp. 90–102.

Sempler, Ricardo. *Maverick: The Success Story Behind the World's Most Unusual Workplace.* New York: Warner Books, 1993.

Solomon, Charlene Marmer. "Using Cash Drives Strategic Change: Owens-Corning's Renewed Compensation Program Supports Business Goals." *Workforce,* February 1998, pp. 78–81.

Wood, Robert E., Atkins, Paul W. B., and Bright, James E. "Bonuses, Goals, and Instrumentality Effects." *Journal of Applied Psychology,* October 1999 pp. 703–720.

ENDNOTES

1. Shelly Branch, "MBAs: What They Really Want," *Fortune,* March 16, 1998, p. 167.
2. Frederick Herzberg, "The Wise Old Turk," *Harvard Business Review,* September–October 1974, pp. 70–80.
3. George B. Graen, Terri A. Scandura, and Michael R. Graen, "A Field Experimental Test of the Moderating Effects of Growth Need Strength on Productivity," *Journal of Applied Psychology,* August 1986, pp. 484–491.
4. J. Barton Cunningham and Ted Eberle, "A Guide to Job Enrichment and Redesign," *Personnel,* February 1990, p. 59.
5. John Richard Hackman and Greg R. Oldham, *Work Redesign* (Reading, MA: Addison-Wesley, 1980).
6. Ricky W. Griffin, "Effects of Work Redesign on Employee Perceptions, Attitudes, and Behaviors: A Long-Term Investigation," *Academy of Management Journal,* June 1991, pp. 425–435.
7. Marc C. Marchese and Robert P. Delprino, "Do Supervisors and Subordinates See Eye-to-Eye on Job Enrichment?" *Journal of Business and Psychology,* Winter 1998, pp. 179–191.
8. Anthony M. Towsend, Samuel M. DeMarie, and Anthony R. Hendrickson, "Virtual Teams: Technology and the Workplace of the Future," *Academy of Management Executive,* August 1998, p. 18.
9. Richard S. Wellings, William C. Byham, and Jeanne M. Wilson,

Empowered Teams: Creating Self-Directed Work Groups that Improve Quality, Productivity, and Participation (San Francisco: Jossey Bass, 1991), p. 3.
10. For case studies of self-managed work teams, see Deale E. Yeatts and Cloyd Hyten, *High-Performing Self-Managed Work Teams* (Thousands Oaks, CA: Sage, 1998).
11. This list is paraphrased from Welling, Byham, and Wilson, *Empowered Teams,* p. 4.
12. Quoted in Shari Caudron, "Are Self-Directed Work Teams Right for Your Company?" *Personnel Journal,* December 1993, p. 78.
13. Jana Schilder, "Work Teams Boost Productivity," *Personnel Journal,* February 1992, p. 67.
14. Fred Luthans and Alexander D. Stajkovic, "Reinforce for Performance: The Need to Go Beyond Pay and Even Rewards," *Academy of Management Executive,* May 1999, pp. 52–54.
15. Stephen Kerr, "Practical, Cost-Neutral Alternatives that You May Know, but Don't Practice," *Organizational Dynamics,* Summer 1999, p. 65.
16. Luthans and Stajkovic, "Reinforce for Performance," pp. 54–55.
17. Jennifer Laabs, "Satisfy Them More Than Money," *Workforce,* November 1998, p. 43.
18. Gillian Flynn, "Is Your Recognition Program Understood?" *Workforce,* July 1998, p. 30.
19. Barbara Davison, "Strategies for Managing Retention," *Human*

Resources Forum (A supplement to *Management Review*), November 1997, p. 1.

20. Linda Thornburg, "Pay for Performance: What You Should Know, *HRMagazine*, June 1992, p. 59; Shari Caudron, "Tie Individual Pay to Team Success," *Personnel Journal*, October 1994, p. 43.

21. G. Douglas Jenkins, Jr., "Are Financial Incentives Related to Performance? A Meta-Analytic Review of Empirical Research," *Journal of Applied Psychology*, October 1998, pp. 777–787.

22. Samuel Greengard, "Stock Options Have Their Ups & Downs," *Workforce*, December 1999, p. 44.

23. Quoted in Greengard, "Stock Options," p. 46.

24. Larry L. Hatcher and Timothy L. Ross, "Organization Development through Productivity Sharing," *Personnel*, October 1985, p. 44.

25. Cited in "Why Gainsharing Works Even Better Today Than in the Past," *HRfocus*, April 2000, p. 3.

26. Richard S. Sabo, "Linking Merit Pay with Performance at Lincoln Electric," in *The Quest for Competitiveness: Lessons from America's Productivity and Quality Leaders*, Y. K. Shetty and Veron M. Buehler (eds.) (Westport, CT: Quorum Books, 1993).

27. Susan C. Hanlon, David C. Meyer, and Robert R. Taylor, "Consequences of Gainsharing: A Field Experiment Revisited," *Group and Organizational Management*, Vol. 19, 1994, pp. 87–111.

28. "Why Gainsharing Works Even Better," p. 5.

29. Jeffrey Pfeffer, "Six Dangerous Myths about Pay," *Harvard Business Review*, May–June 1998, p. 110.

Conflict, Stress, and Well-Being

After two years of managing the corporate headquarters in Chicago of Spencer Stuart, a worldwide executive search firm, Gail H. Vergara, a senior director specializing in the health-care industry, decided to relinquish her managerial responsibilities and instead devote all her time to her clients—and family, friends, and herself.

"Even though it means less money, I wanted more flexibility," said Vergara, 51, who is married to Dr. Herman Vergara, a psychiatrist. The executive, who says she's happy with the new balance of work and family responsibilities she now has, observes that "you always hear how difficult it is to create a work/life balance, but more and more women executives are doing it."

A survey by Spencer Stuart of 57 female executives reinforces her optimistic outlook: Forty-seven percent say they are "usually satisfied" with the balance between personal and professional responsibilities. And an additional 31 percent state they are "sometimes satisfied."

Though achieving balance doesn't always involve reducing work responsibilities, as Vergara did (66 percent of the executives work from 46 to 60 hours a week), the survey shows that 28 percent of the women surveyed now spend 26 to 30 hours a week with friends and family, up from 13 percent in 1994.

Spencer Stuart publishes a number of its studies at http://www.spencerstuart.com/ (such as the migration of executive talent from traditional corporate sectors to the Internet arena) online.

Source: "Female Bosses Finding Needed Balance in Job and Personal Lives," Knight Ridder, January 9, 2000.

OBJECTIVES

After reading and studying this chapter and doing the exercises, you should be able to

1 Understand the nature of conflict in organizations and its leading causes.

2 Have the necessary information to resolve many workplace conflicts.

3 Understand the nature of work stress, its causes and consequences.

4 Explain what organizations can do to manage and reduce stress.

5 Do a more effective job of managing your own stress.

Chapter 7

SO WHAT? What does the situation of Gail Vergara tell us about how individuals and organizations are resolving one of the most prevalent conflicts in the modern workplace: work/family conflict? Many sources of conflict and stress brought into clearer perspective can be better managed through knowledge of organizational behavior. The purpose of this chapter is to present information that will help the reader better understand two closely related processes: conflict and stress.

CONFLICT IN ORGANIZATIONS

Understand the nature of conflict in organizations and its leading causes.

Conflict refers to the opposition of persons or forces that gives rise to some tension. Conflict occurs when two or more parties perceive mutually exclusive goals, values, or events. Each side believes that what it wants is incompatible with what the other wants. Conflict can also take place at the individual level when a person has to decide between two incompatible choices. For example, a person might have to choose between accepting a job transfer and remaining in town with family and friends. Refusing to transfer could mean job loss, whereas accepting the transfer would mean less contact with family and friends. Conflict has enough emotional content to lead to stress for the individuals involved. This is why conflict is presented here as the final chapter in the section of the text dealing with individual behavior.

Our study of conflict concentrates on how people frame conflict, sources of conflict, and various methods, including negotiation, for resolving conflict. We also discuss briefly how and why managers sometimes deliberately stimulate conflict.

Conflict Frames

The type of conflict people enter into depends somewhat on how they define, perceive, or frame a situation in which disagreement exists.[1] A **conflict frame** is the lens through which disputants view a conflict situation. The frames that disputants choose lead them to focus on some characteristics of a conflict situation while ignoring others. A manager who frames conflict in terms of negative personality traits might miss out on the technological and financial aspects of the conflict. Three dimensions of conflict frames have been identified: relationship versus task, emotional versus intellectual, and cooperate versus win.

1. *Relationship versus task* refers to differences in the extent to which the people in conflict focus on the relationship aspects of a conflict. Disputants with a relationship orientation would focus on the interpersonal aspects of a conflict. In contrast, disputants with a task orientation would focus on the material aspects of a dispute such as money or property settlements.
2. *Emotional versus intellectual* refers to the degree of attention the opposing parties pay to the affective components of a dispute. Some people in conflict focus on the feelings involved such as anger, revenge, hatred, and frustration. Other disputants focus instead on the actions and overt behaviors in the conflict situation.
3. *Cooperate versus win* refers to the degree to which the disputants share the blame for the conflict. People with a cooperate frame see both parties as responsible for the conflict and focus on maximizing the benefits to both parties. In contrast, disputants with a win orientation blame the other party. As a result, they concentrate on winning or at least minimizing personal gains, even at the other party's expense.

Sources and Antecedents of Conflict

Conflict is pervasive in organizations. Managers allegedly spend about 20 percent of their work activities directly or indirectly resolving conflict. The sources, antecedents, or outright causes of conflict are numerous, and the list is dynamic. At various times, a new and potent source of conflict surfaces such as management's current emphasis on hiring temporary workers rather than offering full-time employment. Here we describe five illustrative sources of workplace conflict.

Perceived Adverse Changes

A high-impact source of conflict is a change in work methods, conditions of work, or employment opportunities that the people involved perceive negatively. **Downsizing,** the laying off of workers to reduce costs and increase efficiency, is one such change. The people eliminated from the payroll do not remain in conflict with the organization. Survivors, however, suffer from guilt, anger, and bereavement as they feel sorry for the departed coworkers.[2] Continuous downsizing even when business conditions improve can precipitate labor versus management conflict. In the words of a labor union (AFL-CIO) coordinator:

> Why did 75,000 Teamsters walk off the job in April? What they fought for and won, after three weeks of picketing, is the American worker's vanishing right to earn a decent living, refusing to allow their livelihoods to be mutated into low-paid part-time jobs without health and pension benefits.[3]

Despite these comments, downsizing is not perceived as an adverse change by all parties. Company executives may believe that downsizing is *rightsizing,* leading to an efficient, competitive firm that will attract investors.

Line Versus Staff Differentiation

A major form of conflict takes place between line and staff units. Line units deal with the primary purposes of the firm, such as the sales group in a business firm. Staff units deal with the secondary purposes of the firm, such as the environmental protection unit in a business firm. They also deal with the activities necessary to make the line activities more efficient and effective. Staff units might do the hiring and the labor contract interpretations and verify that the line group complies with environmental laws. Yet they would not manufacture or sell the product or service.

Staff managers and professionals advise managers but cannot make certain decisions about themselves. A human resources professional, for example, might advise top management about the adverse consequences of downsizing following a merger. Nevertheless, the professional does not have the authority to halt the downsizing.

Line and staff workers may conflict when the line manager perceives that the staff professional is attempting to heavily influence his or her decisions. Another source of conflict is that staff professionals are often more loyal to their discipline than to the organization. An organizational behavior specialist working for a large firm might feel that attending professional meetings is her right. In contrast, her manager feels she should only attend such meetings while on vacation.

Sexual Harassment

Many employees experience conflict because they are sexually harassed by a manager, coworker, customer, or a vendor. **Sexual harassment** is generally defined as unwanted sexually oriented behavior in the workplace that results in discomfort and/or interference with the job. Sexual harassment is divided into two types. In *quid pro quo* harassment, the employee's submission to or rejection of unwelcome sexual advances of conduct is used as the basis for a tangible employment action about the employee. (A tangible employment action is defined by the Supreme Court as "hiring, firing, failing to promote, reassignment with significantly different responsibilities, or a decision causing a significant change in benefits.") The demands of a harasser can be explicit or implied.

Hostile working environment harassment is the other form of sexual harassment. It occurs when someone in the workplace creates an intimidating, hostile, or offensive working environment. A tangible employment advantage or adverse economic consequence does not have to exist. The hostile environment type of harassment is subject to considerable variation in perception and interpretation. A company executive might decide to hang a French impressionist painting of a partially nude woman in the lobby. Some people would find this offensive and intimidating, and complain that they were harassed. Others might compliment the executive for being a patron of the arts.

The meanings and interpretations of what constitutes sexual harassment continue to evolve with judicial rulings. Three U. S. Supreme Court decisions in 1998 are now given considerable weight by lower courts and employers:

- In *Oncale vs. Sundowner Offshore Services Inc.,* the Court unanimously declared that sexual harassment is actionable, even when the people involved are of the same sex. What matters is the conduct at issue, *not* the sex of the people involved and *not* the presence or absence of sexual desire. The case involved a roustabout (a waterfront laborer) who was forcibly subjected on numerous occasions to humiliating sex-related actions. His harassers were three crew members, including two supervisors.
- In *Burlington Industries, Inc. vs. Ellerth,* the Court ruled that an employer can be liable for sexual harassment and can be sued regardless of whether a supervisor's threats against an employee are carried out. However, employers can assert an *affirmative defense.* This means that the employer may be relieved of liability if it genuinely tried to prohibit and remedy sexual harassment, and the employee did not take advantage of corrective opportunities offered by the employer. The case involved a marketing assistant who claimed that her boss made repeated passes at her and advised her to wear short skirts.
- In *Faragher vs. City of Boca Raton, Florida,* the Court ruled that an employer is liable for a pervasive, hostile atmosphere of harassment and is potentially liable for its supervisors' misconduct whether the company was aware of the harassment or not. The case involved an ocean lifeguard who claimed she endured repeated sexual harassment from two male supervisors during five years of employment.[4]

At least 50 percent of women perceive that they have been harassed at some point in their career. Several different theoretical explanations have been offered as to why sexual harassment is so widespread: the gender, role, and power approaches. According to the *gender approach,* sexual harassment is a likely outcome of interactions between men and women in the workplace. Furthermore, greater work-related interaction between men and women results in a more sexualized work environment and a higher frequency of sexual harassment. Adherents of the *role approach* state that sexual harassment results from the inappropriate carryover of sex-based behavior expectations into the workplace. Advocates of the *power approach* perceive sexual harassment as a mechanism for maintaining the economic and political superiority of men over women.[5]

Sexual harassment is widely considered an ethical and legal problem, and harassment also has negative effects on the well-being of its victims. The harassed person may experience job stress, lowered morale, severe conflict, and lowered productivity. A study with both business and university workers documented some of the problems associated with sexual harassment. It was found that even at low levels of frequency, harassment exerts a significant impact on women's psychological well-being, job attitudes, and work behaviors. For both business and university workers, women who had experienced high levels of harassment reported the worst job-related and psychological effects. The study also found that women who had experienced only a moderate level of harassment also suffered from negative outcomes.[6]

Although sexual harassment receives most of the publicity, writing, and research, racial and ethnic harassment is also a problem in the workplace. Restrictions against other forms of harassment are generally covered by the same laws forbidding sexual harassment. A study was conducted with 575 men and women workers (mostly Hispanics) in various educational settings. The researchers found that most incidences of ethnic harassment related to ethnic slurs, derogatory ethnic comments, or ethnic jokes. Similar to the data for sexual harassment, about half the sample experienced ethnic harassment. The harassed workers reported lower levels of well-being, as did the workers who experienced discrimination by being excluded from favorable work-related interactions, such as being invited to meetings.[7]

Exhibit 7-1 presents information employers can use to minimize the frequency of harassment in the workplace, as well as defend themselves against charges of harassment.

Competing Work and Family Demands

Balancing the demands of career and family has become a major challenge facing today's workforce. The challenge is particularly intense for employees who are part of a two wage-earner family. **Work-family conflict** occurs when the individual has to perform multiple roles: worker, spouse, and, often, parent.[8] This type of conflict is frequent because the multiple roles are often incompatible. Imagine having planned to attend your child's championship soccer game and then being ordered at the last minute to attend a late-afternoon meeting. A survey revealed the following evidence of work-family conflict and the potential of such conflict:

EXHIBIT 7-1

Guidelines for Minimizing Sexual Harassment and Protecting the Company Against Harassment Charges

- Develop a zero-tolerance policy on harassment and communicate it to employees. Inform employees that harassment between members of the same sex is also forbidden. Ensure that victims can report abuses without fear of retaliation.
- Deflect the sexual harassment charge with an affirmative defense. First, take reasonable care to prevent and correct promptly any sexually harassing behavior. Second, show that an employee failed to use internal procedures for reporting abusive behavior.
- Publicize the antiharassment policies as aggressively and regularly as possible—in handbooks, on posters, in training sessions, in reminders in paychecks, and on the intranet.

- Ensure that employees will not face reprisals if they report offending behavior. Appoint several managers to take complaints, and train these managers in sexual harassment issues. Have at least two methods of reporting charges available such as an 800 number, an open-door policy, or internal review procedures.
- Conduct training for employees and all levels of managers on antidiscrimination and antisexual harassment policies and practices.
- Punishments against employees found guilty of harassment should be swift and sure.

Sources: Susan B. Garland, "Finally, A Corporate Tip Sheet on Sexual Harassment," *Business Week,* July 13, 1998; Jennifer Laabs, "Steps to Protect Your Company Against Sexual Harassment," *Workforce,* October 1998, p. 41.

137

- About 45 percent of college students say their top consideration in selecting a first employer is the opportunity to achieve a balance between work and life outside of work.
- Approximately 80 percent of workers consider their effort to balance work and personal life as their first priority.
- More than one-third of employed Americans are working ten or more hours a day, and 39 percent work on weekends.
- One-third of employees say they are forced to choose between advancing in their jobs or devoting attention to their family or personal lives.[9]

Work-family conflict is significant for the individual. A meta-analysis of 50 studies with 50 groups found a negative relationship among all forms of work-family conflict and both job and life satisfaction. A tendency was found for women to be more adversely affected by work-family conflict. Family-to-work conflict (family life interfering with work) was less strongly related to dissatisfaction than was work-to-family conflict, or conflict that ran in two directions.[10]

Organizational programs to help reduce work-family conflict include flexible working hours, work-at-home programs, dependent care centers, and parental leave programs. Francine M. Deutsch, a specialist in gender equality, advises that parents must also take responsibility for reducing work-life conflicts. She says, "Both parents can have successful work lives and also well-balanced personal lives by fully sharing all responsibilities."[11]

Personal Dispositions and Personality Clashes

Many instances of workplace conflict stem from personal dispositions of individuals as well as personality clashes. (A *disposition* is a characteristic attitude.) People who are rude, aggressive, inconsiderate, hostile, or intensely pessimistic readily enter into conflict. Incivility (or rudeness) is gaining attention as a cause of workplace conflict. (Think of making a presentation at a meeting while one of the participants chats on a cellular phone about personal matters.) The underlying problem is that workplace incivility can spiral because the offended party reciprocates with a counterincivility. More rudeness results, and the interpersonal conflict becomes intense. On a larger scale, an organizational climate characterized by rudeness can result in aggressive behavior, higher turnover, and lost customers.[12] Visualize a person dousing coffee on the person making the telephone call. People with low self-esteem and those with authoritarian (rigid-thinking) attitudes are also conflict prone. They are predisposed to defend themselves against objectively trivial threats.[13]

Many other workplace conflicts arise because people simply dislike each other. A **personality clash** is thus an antagonistic relationship between two people based on differences in personal attributes, preferences, interests, values, and styles. People involved in personality clashes often have difficulty in specifying why they dislike each other. Generational differences can result in personality clashes based on differences in values. As described in Chapter 2, members of different generations often have different values, and these differences can lead to workplace conflict. Members of older generations often place more value on seniority and hierarchy, whereas members of younger generations may place more value on merit and team structures. Opinions vary, however, on which generation harbors which values. According to one analysis, baby boomers have embraced a team-based approach to leadership because they are eager to shed the command-and-control style of their predecessor generation. The children of the baby boomers may well thrive in a workplace that resembles what they once rejected—one characterized by centralized authority.[14] Whatever the differences in values between generations, these differences can lead to conflict.

FUNCTIONAL AND DYSFUNCTIONAL CONSEQUENCES OF CONFLICT

Although conflict sparks images of negative behavior, it has both positive and negative consequences. Exhibit 7-2 illustrates that conflict in the right amount improves performance, while too little or too much conflict can decrease performance. **Functional conflict** occurs when the interests of the organization are served as a result of a dispute or disagreement. **Dysfunctional conflict** occurs when a dispute or disagreement harms the organization. When destructive conflict erupts, the manager may wish to intervene.

Have the necessary information to resolve many workplace conflicts.

139

Functional conflict fosters higher levels of performance through such means as arousing motivation, problem-solving ability, creativity, and constructive change. For example, conflicts between various functions such as engineering and manufacturing have led to the establishment of cross-functional teams. Because these teams contain representatives from the different functions, it has been easier to resolve areas of conflict.

Dysfunctional conflict is disruptive in many ways including wasting time and placing personal welfare above the interests of the firm. For example, a labor union may call a strike or a company may eliminate some jobs primarily to demonstrate power. Conflict can divert time and energy away from reaching important goals. It is not uncommon for two managers in conflict to spend time exchanging e-mail messages proving each other wrong in a particular dispute. Another dysfunctional consequence of conflict is that it may result in one party retaliating for the perceived wrongdoing of another party.

Many of the negative consequences of conflict take place because conflict leads to anger. According to one report, angry employees are sabotaging employers' equipment and operations in sophisticated and novel ways. The anger-induced sabotage can be as simple as acts of vandalism or pranks, or as complex as disabling software. Angry employees have put rodents into food products, put needles into baby food, set companies on fire, and wiped out entire company databases.[15] Anger against employers is so common that a forum for disgruntled present and former employees has emerged: http://www.disgruntled.com.

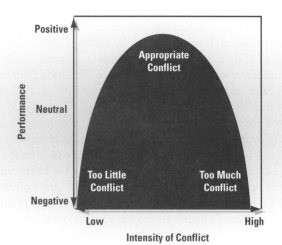

EXHIBIT 7-2

The Relationship between Conflict Intensity and Performance

Workplace violence is a dysfunctional consequence of growing concern, and workplace homicide is a leading cause of workplace death. Most of these deaths result from a robbery or commercial crime. Many of these killings, however, are perpetrated by disgruntled workers or former employees harboring an unresolved conflict. John Byrnes, a workplace violence consultant, advises employers to be aware of behavior that could lead to violence. Extreme acts of violence are preceded by a series of incidents—screaming, verbal threats, or throwing something such as a stapler or floppy disk.[16]

Workplace violence is usually attributed to a conflicted and deranged individual seeking revenge. It is also important to examine organizational forces that trigger unstable employees into dysfunctional behavior. Michael D. Kelleher believes that being downsized or fired can trigger an angry outburst in an unstable worker. Many instances of violence can be prevented if managers ensure that employees perceive their value and if managers communicate openly with employees.[17]

An implication of Exhibit 7-2 is that a manager may need to stimulate the right amount of conflict to enhance performance. One method of introducing a moderate degree of conflict would be to assign two groups the same problem and have them compete for the best solution. Another method is for the manager to play the role of the devil's advocate. The manager looks for something to criticize in any proposal made by an individual or the group. Potential flaws in the proposal are therefore uncovered, leading to a superior result.

Stimulating the Right Type of Conflict within Teams

The right amount of conflict can enhance performance. Recent case history analysis in organizations suggests that stimulating the right *type* of conflict is perhaps more important. Building on earlier knowledge about conflict, a team of researchers classifies the conflict found in teams into two types.[18] (Note the similarity to the conflict frames described earlier in this chapter.) **C-type conflict** focuses on substantive, issue-related differences. The *C* stands for *cognitive,* indicating that the conflict relates to tangible, concrete issues that can be dealt with more intellectually than emotionally. **A-type conflict** focuses on personalized, individually oriented issues. The *A* stands for *affective,* indicating that the conflict relates to subjective issues that are dealt with more emotionally than intellectually.

C-type conflict is functional because it requires teams to engage in activities that foster team effectiveness. Team members engaged in C-type conflict would critically examine alternative solutions and incorporate different points of view into their mission statement. Because frank communication and different points of view are encouraged, C-type conflict encourages innovative thinking. In contrast, A-type conflict undermines group effectiveness by blocking constructive activities and processes. By such means as directing anger toward individuals and blaming one another for mistakes, A-type conflict leads to cynicism and distrust.

Four attributes characterize teams that are able to engage mostly in C-type conflict and minimize A-type conflict: focused activity, creativity, open communication, and integration. *Focused activity* refers to getting to the core issues of a problem and sticking closely to the task at hand. Instead of drifting into tangents, the team stays with the agenda. *Creativity* refers to encouraging thinking beyond traditional options. CSX Railroad, for example, encourages creative thinking by using stretch goals that force teams to search for innovative solutions. *Open communication* refers to an atmosphere that allows team members to speak freely and challenge the premises of one another's viewpoints. At the same time, there is no implied threat of anger, actual threat, or retribution. *Integration* refers to making nearly full use of all team members, instead of one or two members making most of the contributions.

Conflict Management Styles

Before describing specific methods of resolving conflict, it is useful to understand five styles of handling conflict. As shown in Exhibit 7-3, the five styles are based on a combination of satisfying ones own concerns (assertiveness) and satisfying the concerns of others (cooperativeness).[19]

1. *Competitive.* The competitive style is a desire to win one's own concerns at the expense of the other party, or to dominate. A person with a competitive orientation is likely to engage in win-lose power struggles.
2. *Accommodative.* The accommodative style favors appeasement, or satisfying the other's concerns without taking care of one's own. People with this orientation may be generous or self-sacrificing just to maintain a relationship. A dissatisfied employee might be accommodated with a larger-than-average pay raise just to calm down the person and obtain his or her loyalty.
3. *Sharing.* The sharing style is halfway between domination and appeasement. Sharers prefer moderate but incomplete satisfaction for both parties, which results in a compromise. The term "splitting the difference" reflects this orientation and is commonly used in such activities as negotiating a budget or purchasing equipment.
4. *Collaborative.* In contrast to the other styles, the collaborative style reflects a desire to fully satisfy the desires of both parties. It is based on an underlying philosophy of **win–win,** the belief that after conflict has been resolved, both

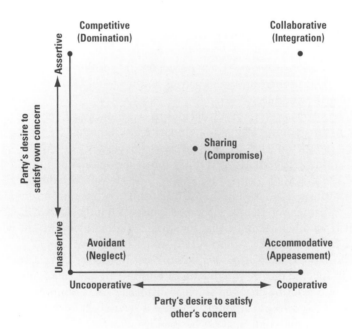

EXHIBIT 7-3

Conflict-Handling Styles According to Degree of Cooperation and Assertiveness

Source: Kenneth W. Thomas, "Organizational Conflict," in Steven Kerr (ed.), *Organizational Behavior* (Columbus, Ohio: Grid Publishing, 1979). p. 156.

sides should gain something of value. A win-win approach is genuinely concerned with arriving at a settlement that meets the needs of both parties, or at least does not badly damage the welfare of the other side. When a collaborative approach is used, the relationship between the parties improves.

A win-win approach to labor-management conflict might take this form: The union would agree for workers to relax tight job definitions, thus lowering wage costs, if management would agree to hire fewer temporary workers. Labor wins by retaining more full-time jobs, and management wins by stabilizing the cost of wages.

5. *Avoidant.* The avoider is a combination of uncooperative and unassertive. He or she is indifferent to the concerns of either party. The person may actually be withdrawing from the conflict or be relying on fate. The avoidant style is sometimes used by a manager who stays out of a conflict between two team members, who are left to resolve their own differences.

Conflict Resolution Methods

Styles of dealing with conflict are closely related to methods of resolving conflict. For example, a collaborative style is a way of managing *and* resolving conflict. Here we present a sampling of conflict resolution methods by describing confrontation and problem solving, and several structural methods.

Confrontation and Problem Solving

A widely applicable approach to resolving conflict is **confrontation and problem solving,** a method of identifying the true source of conflict and resolving it systematically. The confrontation approach is gentle and tactful rather than combative and abusive. Reasonableness is important because the person who takes the initiative in resolving the conflict wants to maintain a harmonious working relationship with the other party. D. H. Stamatis has developed six steps for confronting and problem solving:

Step 1: Awareness. Party A recognizes that a conflict exists between himself or herself and Party B.

Step 2: The decision to confront. Party A decides the conflict is important enough to warrant a confrontation with Party B and that such a conflict is preferable to avoiding the conflict.

Step 3: The confrontation. Party A decides to work cooperatively and confronts Party B. At this point, Party B may indicate a willingness to accept the confrontation or may decide to gloss over its seriousness. Often the conflict is resolved at this step, particularly if it is not of a serious and complicated nature.

Step 4: Determining the cause of the conflict. The two parties discuss their own opinions, attitudes, and feelings in relation to the conflict and attempt to identify the real issue. For example, the real cause of conflict between a manager and a team member might be that they have a different concept of what constitutes a fair day's work.

Step 5: Determining the outcome and further steps. In this step, the parties attempt to develop specific means of reducing or eliminating the cause of the conflict. If the cause cannot be changed (such as changing one's opinion of a fair day's work), a way of working around the cause is devised. If both parties agree on a solution, then the confrontation has been successful.

Step 6: Follow-through. After the solution has been implemented, both parties should check periodically to ensure that their agreements are being kept.[20]

The collaborative style of conflict resolution meshes with confrontation and problem solving. A major factor is that trust builds between two parties as they search for the real reason for conflict.

Confront, Contain, and Connect for Anger

A variation of confrontation and problem solving has developed specifically to resolve conflict with angry people: confront, contain, and connect. *Confront* in this context means that you jump right in and get agitated workers talking to prevent future blowups. The confrontation, however, is not aimed at arguing with the angry person. If the other person yells, you talk more softly. *Contain* refers to moving an angry worker out of sight and out of earshot. At the same time, you remain impartial. The supervisor is advised not to choose sides or appear to be a friend.

You *connect* by asking open-ended questions such as "What would you like us to do about your concern?" to get at the real reasons behind an outburst. Using this approach, one worker revealed he was upset because a female coworker got to leave early to pick up her daughter at day care. The man also needed to leave early one day a week for personal reasons but felt awkward making the request. So instead of being assertive (explicit and direct) about his demands, he flared up.

An important feature of the confront, contain, and connect technique is that it provides angry workers a place where they can vent their frustrations and report the outbursts of others. Mediator Nina Meierding says that "Workers need a safe outlet to talk through anger and not feel they will be minimized or put their job in jeopardy."[21]

Structural Methods

A structural method of resolving conflict emphasizes juggling work assignments and reporting relationships so that disputes are minimized. One structural method for resolving conflict is for a manager to have direct control over all the resources he or she needs to get the job done. In this way, the manager is less likely to experience conflict when attempting to get the cooperation of people who do not report to him or her.

Conflict can often be reduced or prevented by one or more members from one organizational unit exchanging places with those of another unit. Working in another unit, such as shifting from purchasing to manufacturing, fosters empathy. Reassigning people in this way can achieve the benefit of different viewpoints in the affected groups. As the group members get to know one another better, they tend to reduce some of their distorted perceptions of one another. (As described previously, cross-functional teams accomplish the same purpose.) Exchanging members works best when the personnel exchanged have the technical competence to perform well in the new environment.

A long-standing structural approach to conflict resolution is an appeals procedure. When the person cannot resolve a problem with his or her manager, the person appeals to a higher authority. The higher authority is ordinarily the next level of management or a member of the human resources department. However, top management in some firms maintains an **open-door policy,** in which any employee can bring a gripe to its attention without checking with his or her immediate manager. The open-door policy is a popular grievance procedure because it allows the problem to be settled quickly.

Understand the nature of work stress, its causes and consequences.

WORK STRESS

Stress is closely related to conflict because conflict is a major contributor to stress. As used here, **stress** is the mental and physical condition that results from a perceived threat that cannot be dealt with readily. Stress is therefore an internal response to a state of activation. The stressed person is physically and mentally aroused. Stress will ordinarily occur in a threatening or negative situation such as worrying about losing one's job or being reprimanded. However, stress can also be caused by a positive situation such as receiving a large cash bonus.

The topic of work stress is of enormous interest to managers and other professionals because of its productivity, legal consequences, and human consequences. A group of industrial health specialists noted that American workers are working harder and longer than they have in the past two decades simply to maintain their standard of living. The result is a workforce more at risk than ever for psychological, physical, and behavioral health problems.[22] The International Labor Organization estimates the cost of job stress in the United States and Canada to be about $230 billion annually. The cost stems from worker compensation claims, reduced productivity, absenteeism, and added health insurance costs.[23]

Our study of work stress centers around its consequences and sources, along with individual and organizational methods for managing stress. Because stress deals heavily with personal perceptions, you will be invited to take three different questionnaires, starting with the stress questionnaire that follows in the Self-Assessment on page 145.

A Cybernetic Theory of Stress, Coping, and Well-Being in Organizations

A theory of work stress developed by Jeffrey R. Edwards serves as a useful framework for understanding the symptoms, consequences, and management of stress. The **cybernetic theory of stress, coping, and well-being in organizations** views stress as a discrepancy between an employee's perceived state and desired state.[24] The worker must consider the discrepancy important to experience stress. Consistent with other theories, stress damages psychological and physical well-being. As a result, the person engages in coping—attempts to reduce the negative impacts of stress on well-being.

Coping influences stress by altering the perceptions, desires, and importance surrounding the stressful discrepancy. If coping is successful, it can also improve well-being directly, such as taking constructive action about a troublesome experience. The total stress a person experiences is determined by all of his or her discrepancies.

An important implication of the cybernetic theory of stress is that to manage stress properly, a person must seek to narrow the discrepancies between actual conditions and a desired state.

Symptoms and Consequences of Work Stress

A person experiencing stress displays certain symptoms indicating that he or she is trying to cope with a **stressor,** any force creating the stress reaction. These symptoms can include a host of physiological, emotional, and behavioral reactions. A problem with stress symptoms is that they lead to **strain,** or an adverse impact on employee health and well-being.

Experiencing OB

Test your understanding of the sources of stress and conflict, the relationship between stress level and performance, stress management, conflict management, and related issues by visiting South-Western's animated concept and activity site at *http://www. experiencingob.com.* Exclusive review tools on the topics of Stress and Conflict & Negotiation when you need them. Free demo available!

SELF-ASSESSMENT

The Stress Questionnaire

Directions: Apply each of the following questions to the last six months of your life. Check the appropriate column.

	Mostly Yes	Mostly No
1. Have you been feeling uncomfortably tense lately?	—	✓
2. Are you engaged in frequent arguments with people close to you?	—	✓
3. Is your social life very unsatisfactory?	—	✓
4. Do you have trouble sleeping?	—	✓
5. Do you feel lethargic about life?	—	✓
6. Do many people annoy or irritate you?	—	✓
7. Do you have constant cravings for candy and other sweets?	—	✓
8. Is your cigarette or alcohol consumption way up?	—	✓
9. Are you becoming addicted to soft drinks or coffee?	—	✓
10. Do you find it difficult to concentrate on your work?	—	✓
11. Do you frequently grind your teeth?	—	✓
12. Are you increasingly forgetful about little things such as mailing a letter?	—	✓
13. Are you increasingly forgetful about big things such as appointments and major errands?	—	✓
14. Are you making too many trips to the restroom?	—	✓
15. Have people commented lately that you do not look well (or "good")?	—	✓
16. Do you get into verbal fights with people too frequently?	—	✓
17. Have you been involved in more than one physical fight lately?	—	✓
18. Do you have a troublesome number of tension headaches?	—	✓
19. Do you feel nauseated much too often?	—	✓
20. Do you feel light-headed or dizzy almost every day?	—	✓
21. Do you have churning sensations in your stomach too often?	—	✓
22. Are you in a big hurry all the time?	✓	✓
23. Are far too many things bothering you?	—	✓
24. Do you frequently feel tired and exhausted for no particular reason?	—	✓
25. Do you have difficulty shaking colds or other infections?	—	✓

Scoring: The following guidelines are only of value if you answered the questions sincerely:

0–7   Mostly Yes answers: You seem to be experiencing an normal amount of stress.

8–17   Mostly Yes answers: Your stress level seems high. Become involved in some kind of stress management activity, such as those described later in this chapter.

18–25   Mostly Yes answers: Your stress level appears much too high. Discuss your stress levels with a mental health professional or visit your family doctor (or both).

Physiological symptoms of stress include increased heart rate, blood pressure, breathing rate, pupil size, and perspiration. Men in particular who respond most intensely to mental stress have a higher risk of blocked blood vessels, which increases their risk of heart attack and stroke.[25] If stress symptoms are severe or persist over a prolonged period, the result can also be other stress–related disorders such as hypertension, migraine headache, ulcer, colitis, or allergy. Stress also leads to a chemical imbalance that adversely affects the body's immune system. Thus, the overly stressed person becomes more susceptible to disease and suffers more intensely from existing health problems.

Emotional symptoms of stress include anxiety, tension, depression, discouragement, boredom, prolonged fatigue, feelings of hopelessness, and various kinds of defensive thinking. Behavioral symptoms include nervous habits such as facial twitching, and sudden decreases in job performance due to forgetfulness and errors in concentration or judgment. If the stress is particularly uncomfortable or distasteful (large and enduring discrepancies), it will lower job performance. The effect is greater for more complex jobs. An example of a stressor that will lower job performance for all people is a bullying, abrasive boss who wants to see the employee fail. Also, an 8-hour meeting on a Monday is a stressor for most managers and professionals who have other urgent work to perform.

Similar to conflict, not all stress is bad. People require the right amount of stress to keep them mentally and physically alert. A person's perception of something or somebody usually determines whether it will be a positive or negative stressor. For example, one manager might perceive a quality audit by a corporate executive to be so frightening that he is irritable toward team members. Another manager might welcome the visit as a chance to proudly display her department's high-quality performance.

After prolonged exposure to job stress, a person runs the risk of feeling burned out—a drained, used up feeling. **Burnout** is a pattern of emotional, physical, and mental exhaustion in response to chronic job stressors. The same syndrome (collection of symptoms) is sometimes regarded as work exhaustion.[26] Cynicism, apathy, and indifference are the major behavior symptoms of the burned-out worker. Personal accomplishment finally diminishes as a result of burnout.[27]

Because burnout results from prolonged stress, some of its causes parallel those of stress to be described in the next sections. In addition, Christina Maslach and Michael P. Leiter attribute most of burnout to a mismatch between the nature of the job and the nature of the person performing the job in one or more of the following six areas:

- Work overload (longer hours and less free time)
- Lack of control over one's work
- Lack of reward for one's contributions (low pay and the absence of recognition)
- Lack or breakdown of a work community (lack of connections among people)
- Lack of fair treatment (lack of affirmation of self-worth or uneven application of rules particularly with respect to performance evaluation and promotion)
- Value conflicts between job demands and one's personal code of ethics[28]

Factors Contributing to Work Stress

A host of factors within a person as well as adverse organizational conditions can cause or contribute to job stress. As with sources of conflict, the list is dynamic. New sources of stress surface as the work environment changes. For example, today thousands of industrial and retail salespeople feel less job security because so much of the sales function is being moved to the Internet.

Factors within the Individual

A general stressor that encompasses both individual and organizational factors is having to cope with significant change. The more significant the change you have to cope with in a short period of time, the greater is the probability that you will experience a stress disorder.[29] Exhibit 7-4 presents the impact of various life changes, measured in *life-change units*. Hostile, aggressive, and impatient people find ways of turning almost any job into a stressful experience. Such individuals are labeled Type A personality, in contrast to their more easygoing Type B personality counterparts. In addition to being angry, the outstanding trait of Type A personality people is their strong sense of time urgency, known as "hurry sickness." This sense of urgency compels them to achieve more and more in less and less time. Type A personality people are prone to cardiovascular disorders.[30] Recognize, however, that not every hard-driving, impatient person is correctly classified as Type A personality. Managers and professionals who love their work and enjoy other people are not particularly prone to heart disease.

Having an external locus of control predisposes people to job stress because they do not believe they can control key stressors in their environment. Managers and professionals with a limited tolerance for ambiguity are prone to frustration and stress because high-level job responsibilities are often ambiguous. Another behavior pattern predisposing one to job stress is **negative lifestyle factors.** Among them are poor exercise and eating habits and heavy consumption of caffeine, alcohol, tobacco, and other drugs.

Another factor predisposing a person to stress is being pessimistic. Being optimistic, in contrast, helps you ward off stress. Take the Self-Assessment that follows to measure your own tendencies toward pessimism versus optimism.

Adverse Organizational Conditions

Under ideal conditions, workers experience just enough stress to prompt them to respond creatively and energetically to their jobs. Unfortunately, high stress levels created by adverse organizational conditions lead to many negative symptoms. According to the **job demands–job control model,** workers experience the most stress when the demands of the job are high yet they have little control over the activity[31] (see Exhibit 7-5). A customer service representative dealing with a major blooper by the firm would fit into this category. In contrast, when job demands are high and the worker has high control, the worker will be energized, motivated, and creative. A high-level planning job might fit here.

A major contributor to work stress is role overload. Demands on managers and professionals are at an all-time high as companies attempt to increase work output

EXHIBIT 7-4

The Top 25 Stressors as Measured by Life-Change Units

CHANGE		

The numbers to the right of each life event represent the scale value in life-change units.

1. Death of a spouse (100)	**16.** Mortgage or loan for major purpose (31)
2. Divorce (73)	**17.** Foreclosure of mortgage or loan (30)
3. Marital separation (65)	**18.** Change in responsibilities at work (29)
4. Jail term/imprisonment (63)	**19.** Son or daughter leaving home (29)
5. Death of a family member (63)	**20.** Trouble with in-laws (29)
6. Major personal injury or illness (53)	**21.** Outstanding personal achievement (28)
7. Marriage (50)	**22.** Spouse begins or stops work (26)
8. Fired from the job (47)	**23.** Begin or end school (26)
9. Marital reconciliation (45)	**24.** Change in living conditions (20)
10. Retirement (45)	**25.** Revision of personal habits (15)
11. Major change in health of family member (44)	*Daughter ∆'d school*
12. Pregnancy (40)	**Sources:** These stressors have changed over time. This version is from
13. Sexual difficulties (39)	Thomas H. Holmes and Richard H. Rahe, "The Social Adjustment Rating
14. Change in financial state (38)	Scale," *Journal of Psychosomatic Research*, 15, 1971, pp. 210–223; with an
15. Change in number of arguments with spouse (35)	interview updating it from Sue MacDonald, "Battling Stress," *The Cincinnati Enquirer*, October 23, 1995, p. C4.

148

Are You an Optimist?

A widely used method for assessing optimistic or pessimistic disposition is the Life Orientation Test developed by psychologists Micheal Scheier and Charles Carver. To gauge your optimism level with this test, indicate your response to each item below:

A—strongly agree; B—agree; C—feel neutral; D—disagree; E—strongly disagree. Don't let your answer to one question influence another.

1. In uncertain times, I usually expect the best.
2. It's easy for me to relax.
3. If something can go wrong for me, it will.
4. I'm always optimistic about my future.
5. I enjoy my friends a lot.
6. It's important for me to keep busy.
7. I hardly ever expect things to go my way.
8. I don't get upset too easily.
9. I rarely count on good things happening to me.
10. Overall, I expect more good things to happen to me than bad.

Total your score

Ignore answers to items 2, 5, 6 and 8. Those are fillers.

Subtotal your scores for items 1, 4 and 10 as follows: A scores 4 points; B scores 3; C scores 2; D scores 1; E scores 0.

Subtotal your scores for items 3, 7, and 9 as follows: A scores 0 points; B scores 1; C scores 2; D scores 3; E scores 4.

Add these totals for an overall optimism score. The range is from 0 to 24, from extreme pessimism to extreme optimism, with virtual neutrality being the midpoint, 12.

Expecting good things

Most people who have taken this test are slightly optimistic, Carver said. For instance, among 2,000 college students, the average score was 14, with two-thirds scoring between 10 and 18. A group of 159 patients awaiting coronary artery bypass surgery had an average score of 15, possibly suggesting that a serious challenge may boost one's optimism a bit.

"People tend to run a little toward the optimistic end of the dimension, but not by a whole lot," Carver said. "Also, people tend to be moderate in their self-descriptions. Not many are saying they are enormously optimistic or pessimistic."

Source: Terence Monmaney, "Cheer Up: It Just May Help You Live Longer," *Los Angeles Times*, 23 January 2000. Copyright 2000. *Los Angeles Times*. Reprinted with permission.

---

and decrease staffing at the same time. Worrying about being next on the "hit list" during downsizing is another major job stressor. In contrast to being overloaded, many other workers suffer from role underload (too little to do) or the job monotony associated with repetitive work. In one situation, a manager left town for three weeks, without giving his newly hired executive assistant an assignment. The assistant suffered anxiety attacks after the fifth day of make-work activities.

A long-recognized contributor to work stress is **role conflict,** having to choose between competing demands or expectations. We have already touched upon role conflict in the study of value conflicts in Chapter 3 and work-family conflicts in the present chapter. If a person complies with one aspect of a role, compliance with the other is difficult. Role conflict has been divided into four types:[32]

	Low Job Demands	High Job Demands
Low Control	Passive Job	High-strain Job
High Control	Low-strain Job	Active Job

EXHIBIT 7-5

The Job Demands-Job Control Model

149

1. *Intrasender* conflict occurs when a person is asked to accomplish two objectives that are in apparent conflict. A request by a manager for a group member to increase speed and decrease errors could result in this type of conflict.

2. *Intersender* conflict occurs when two or more senders give a person incompatible directions. A worker's manager might request that he begin a project immediately, but upper management insists that new projects should be postponed for now.

3. *Interrole* conflict results when two different roles a person occupies are in conflict. Work-family conflict fits the interrole category, as does the situation of a mentor who must give a harsh performance evaluation to the person she is mentoring.

4. *Person-role* conflict occurs when the role(s) an employer expects a worker to perform conflict with the person's basic values. A clerk in the bursar's office at a vocational technical school in Montréal experienced role conflict because the administration asked her to pressure students to pay their outstanding bills. The woman, herself in poor financial condition, sympathized with the students.

The wider the gap between the two or more roles in role conflict, the more intense the stress. Assume that a sales representative's spouse threatened divorce if the rep's travel exceeded two nights per month. The sales rep would experience intense stress if job demands suddenly required 15 nights away from home per month.

Another role-related stressor is **role ambiguity,** a condition in which the job holder receives confusing or poorly defined expectations. Role ambiguity involves several aspects. First, there is insufficient information about the worker's expected performance. Second, there is unclear or confusing information about expected job behaviors. Third, there is uncertainty about the outcomes (such as promotion or dismissal) of certain on-the-job behaviors.[33] The person facing extreme role ambiguity proclaims, "I don't know what I'm supposed to be doing or what will happen to me if I do it."

Another contributor to stress and burnout is **emotional labor,** the burden of having to modify or fake emotions, or at least facial expression, when dealing with customers. Alicia Grandey contends that sales workers and customer service representatives carry the biggest emotional labor of any occupational group.[34] Similar to other stressors, faking emotion can overwork the cardiovascular and nervous systems and weaken the immune system. An example of the problem took place at Safeway Stores Inc. in California. Five employees filed a lawsuit over the company's Superior Service rules that require employees to smile, make prolonged eye contact, and speak to every customer. The plaintiffs said the policy encouraged sexual harassment by some male customers. At some companies, however, such behavior rules are successful.

Repetitive strain injuries (RSI), including carpal tunnel syndrome, account for two-thirds of all work-related injuries. Computer workers, as well as interpreters for the deaf who use sign language, are at high risk for repetitive strain injuries. Repetitive strain injury victims often suffer severe mental stress as well as physical pain. Among the many stressors are worrying about not being able to work again in one's chosen field because of the physical disability. Although physical pain is at the root of the problem, emotional stress can lead to more muscle tension and intensify the physical pain.[35]

A final organizational stressor mentioned here is being part of a culturally diverse workforce. Although cultural diversity brings many advantages to organizations (as will be described in Chapter 15), it may lead to interpersonal stress. As analyzed by Richard S. DeFrank and John M. Ivancevich, these stressors include competition among groups for attention and resources, and decreased interaction because of the perceived need for political correctness in dealing with demographic groups other than one's own. Not knowing how to respond well in a diverse setting is also a stressor, such as a 55-year old white man feeling awkward because his manager is a 25-year-old African-American woman. Furthermore, it is stressful for a person to feel that he or she is not a good cultural fit with most members of the organization.[36]

ORGANIZATIONAL APPROACHES TO STRESS MANAGEMENT

4

Explain what organizations can do to manage and reduce stress.

Negative stress is disruptive to both productivity and employee well-being. As a consequence, organizations are actively involved in stress management. Several illustrative approaches to stress management include providing emotional support to employees, a wellness and fitness program, giving on-site massages, and providing the opportunity to nap on the job. The accompanying Organizational Behavior in Action provides details about a corporate program designed to combat work overload stress and burnout.

Creating a high-job-demand, high-control job, as described previously, is one approach to stress prevention. Two other illustrative approaches are providing emotional support to employees and establishing a wellness and physical fitness program.

Emotional support from their immediate superior can help group members cope better with job stress. One study compared the illness rate between two groups of employees who faced comparable heavy stressors. Those employees who felt they had their manager's support suffered only half as much illness in 12 months as those who felt they lacked such support. The most helpful managers ask themselves the question, "How can I make my subordinates feel as effective as I do?" Supportive behaviors that help employees feel more effective include the following:

1. Keep communication channels open.
2. Provide the right kind of help (such as verbal encouragement or time off from work to recover from a heavy stressor).
3. Act as a catalyst (such as helping an employee look at a troublesome problem in a new perspective).
4. Hold back on disseminating stressful information (such as passing along rumors about downsizing).[37]

Organizational Behavior *in Action*

Hewlett-Packard Reduces and Redesigns Workloads

"Today, it's a different environment entirely in that team members trust each other, support each other and even encourage each other to take vacations without checking voice mail and e-mail; it really wasn't like that a few years ago," says Kristi Bolas, a marketing specialist in Hewlett's Great Lakes area division. Bolas is one of today's chosen few—a participant in HP's experimental program to reduce and redesign workloads. The program asks employees to set goals not just for productivity, but for personal goals as well.

If you think mastering golf as a career goal sounds gimmicky, you're mistaken. The program was a godsend for sales manager Linda Davis, who jumped at the chance to volunteer for the pilot program after realizing that she had a crisis on her hands. Davis says her sales team was showing impressive revenue figures, but the effect of staffers putting in long hours was taking its toll.

For HP, the pressure on the job had taken a visible and alarming turn. The attrition rate rose to 20% in a tight labor market and the company's annual employee survey revealed a staggering statistic: over 50% of those polled said they "experienced excessive pressure" on the job, a dramatic increase over the previous survey.

"The survey showed that stress had gone up dramatically. We read comments that people were on antidepressants and marriages were ending. These kinds of riveting comments told us that these were not just comments by people working too hard," says Davis. She notes that fortunately top management allowed her and her staff of 75 people to take unusual steps to retool and rework the workload process.

Hewlett-Packard takes its leisure goals seriously, requiring employees to meet personal goals as defined. If they fall short, supervisors are held accountable. Here is how it works: At monthly meetings, team members are asked to list three business goals and three personal goals. When a staff member achieves a milestone, such as leaving at 2:00 P.M. to take a daughter roller-blading, coworkers are encouraged to applaud with the same enthusiasm they would applaud someone landing a sales order.

The emphasis on leisure goals and the added focus on personal life add a whole new dimension to work-life balance. Says Davis, "It creates a comfort zone because it creates a family-like environment in a large company. If I were to ask people if they felt less stressed out, they would probably say no; but fewer people are leaving the organization because they now have a better way of dealing with stress."

Davis believes that Hewlett-Packard has hit upon something: "While expectations have been lowered to how much an individual can accomplish in a day, productivity has not been compromised and the Great Lakes area has stayed on top both numbers-wise and people-wise," she says.

Davis explains how "shooting under par" affects sales: "First there is the subjective or immeasurable part that tells us people are more open and communicative about their life and that improves morale—people feel they can trust each other, and that builds rapport and a support structure. The other factor is that people stay; we have a higher retention level. During the first two years of the program, I haven't lost any person externally who hasn't come back."

For additional information about options HP employees can exercise to manage work-life demands, go to http://www.hp.com then click on Jobs at hp, choose a region, then click on the Diversity & Work/Life Balance link on the Jobs at hp page.

Source: Joanne Cole, "De-Stressing the Workplace: Hewlett-Packard Pushes the Envelope," *HRfocus* (October 1999) 1, 10-11, by permission of the Institute of Management and Administration.

To help combat negative stress, as well as to promote wellness, many employers offer programs that encourage employees to stay in physical and mental shape. A **wellness program** is thus a formal organization-sponsored activity to help employees stay well and avoid illness. Workshops, seminars, activities, and medical procedures offered in a wellness program include the following: medical examinations, stress management techniques, smoking cessation programs, and preventive health care.[38]

Closely related to wellness programs is providing on-site massages to employees to help relieve muscle tension. Massage therapy has become a common antidote for work-related stress. The massage sessions are typically given in the company wellness center, but some firms offer quick back and neck massages at a person's office or cubicle. On-site massages are also considered an employee benefit to help attract and retain workers.

An emerging approach to help employees combat stress is to give them the opportunity to nap on company premises. Napping is one of the most effective methods of treating and preventing stress. Everyday job stress can often be alleviated by taking a 15- to 20-minute nap to restore alertness and memory and to decrease the effects of fatigue. Naps beyond 30 minutes place people in their normal sleep cycle, with people often waking up feeling groggy and disoriented. 42IS, a California information systems firm, is an example of a company that commits resources to facilitate employee napping. 42IS created a sleeping loft complete with queen-size bed, pillows and blankets.[39] For career-minded people, the slogan "You snooze, you win" replaces, "You snooze, you lose."

Individual Approaches to Stress Management

Techniques individuals can use to manage stress can be divided into three categories: control, symptom management, and escape.[40]

Control
Control and reduction of stress include getting the right emotional support. Receiving social support—encouragement, understanding, and friendship—from other people is a key strategy for coping with work and personal stress.

An equally important control technique is to practice good work habits and time management. By establishing priorities and minimizing procrastination, people can gain better control of their lives. Gaining control is especially important because being out of control is a major stressor. The lowly To Do list could thus save you an ulcer! Demanding less than perfection from oneself can also help prevent stress. Not measuring up to one's own unrealistically high standards is a substantial stressor.

Symptom Management
Dozens of symptom management techniques have been developed, and no stress management program is complete without using at least one. Getting appropriate physical exercise is an excellent starting point in symptom management. Physical exercise helps dissipate some of the tension created by work stress and also helps the body ward off future stress-related disorders. One way in which exercise helps combat stress is by releasing endorphins. These are morphine-like chemicals produced in the brain that act as painkillers and antidepressants.

IMPLICATIONS FOR MANAGERIAL PRACTICE

1. A manager's goal should be to maintain optimal levels of conflict in his or her unit. Sometimes this will involve the reduction of conflict, while, at other times, conflict stimulation may be necessary.

2. Approximately 20 percent of a manager's time involves resolving conflict. It is therefore important for a manager to develop effective conflict resolution skills. A good starting point is to use confrontation and problem solving.

3. A manager should encourage C-type conflict within the organizational unit and at the same time discourage A-type conflict. A mechanism for doing this would be for the manager to take the steps necessary within the group to encourage focused activity, creative problem solving, open communication, and integration.

4. Given that an optimal amount of stress facilitates performance, a manager should strive to design the appropriate amount and kinds of stressors for both individuals and groups. Manipulating stressors is much like manipulating job challenge. Stress can be increased or decreased by manipulating the amount of job responsibility, goal difficulty, tightness of deadlines, amount of supervision, and critical feedback.

5. Managers should encourage team members to embark upon a systematic program of stress management, considering today's turbulent work environment. Workers who are already managing stress well should be encouraged in their efforts.

Another widely, applicable symptom management technique is the **relaxation response,** a general-purpose method of learning to relax by yourself. The key ingredient of this technique is to make yourself quiet and comfortable. At the same time, think of the word "one" (or any simple chant or prayer) with every breath for about ten minutes. The technique slows you down both physiologically and emotionally and at the same time reduces the adverse effects of stress. Much of the benefit of the relaxation response can also be achieved by napping or

EXHIBIT 7-6

Stress Busters

- Take a nap when facing heavy pressures. "Power napping" is regarded as one of the most effective techniques for reducing and preventing stress.
- Give in to your emotions. If you are angry, disgusted, or confused, admit your feelings. Suppressing your emotions adds to stress.
- Take a brief break from the stressful situation and do something small and constructive such as washing your car, emptying a waste basket, or cleaning out a drawer.
- Get a massage because it can loosen tight muscles, improve your blood circulation, and calm you down.
- Get help with your stressful task from a coworker, manager, or friend.
- Concentrate intensely on reading, a sport, or hobby or surfing the Internet. Contrary to common sense, concentration is at the heart of stress reduction.
- Have a quiet place at home and enjoy a brief idle period there every day.
- Take a leisurely day off from your routine.
- Finish something you have started, however small. Accomplishing almost anything reduces some stress.
- Stop to smell the flowers, make friends with a young child or elderly person, or play with a kitten or puppy.
- Strive to do a good job, but not a perfect job.
- Work with your hands, doing a pleasant task.
- Find somebody or something that makes you laugh, and have a good laugh.
- Minimize drinking caffeinated or alcoholic beverages, and drink fruit juice or water instead. Eat fruits or vegetables for snacks rather than junk food.

153

visualizing a pleasant fantasy for about ten minutes. The stress busters listed in Exhibit 7-6 are mostly aimed at symptom management.

Escape

Escape methods of stress management are actions and reappraisals of situations that provide the stressed individual some escape from the stressor. Eliminating the stressor is the most effective escape technique. For example, if a manager is experiencing stress because of serious understaffing in his department, he should negotiate to receive authorization to hire additional staff. Mentally blocking out a stressful thought is another escape technique, but it may not work in the long run. Without constructive action about the problem, a stressor will usually return.

SUMMARY OF KEY POINTS

 Understand the nature of conflict in organizations and its leading causes.

The type of conflict people enter into depends somewhat on how they frame (perceive) a situation in which disagreement exists. The three dimensions of conflict frames are relationship versus task, emotional versus intellectual, and cooperate versus win.

Workplace conflict has many sources, including the following: perceived adverse changes, line versus staff differentiation, sexual harassment, competing work and family demands, and personal dispositions and personality clashes.

Functional conflict occurs when the interests of the organization are served as a result of a dispute or disagreement. Dysfunctional conflict occurs when a dispute or disagreement harms the organization, calling for managerial intervention. At times, the manager may want to stimulate conflict to enhance performance. Team performance is enhanced by stimulating C-type conflict, which deals with substantive, work-related issues. A-type conflict, which deals with personal issues and emotions, generally lowers team performance.

 Have the necessary information to resolve many workplace conflicts.

Five styles of handling conflict based on a combination of assertiveness (looking out for oneself) and cooperativeness have been identified: competitive, accomodative, sharing, collaborative (win-win), and avoidant. A widely applicable approach to resolving conflict is confrontation and problem solving, in which the true source of the conflict is identified and then resolved systematically. The recommended confrontation approach is a gentle and tactful one. To resolve conflict with angry people, you might confront, contain the angry situation, and connect with the person. A structural method of resolving conflict emphasizes juggling work assignments and

reporting relationships so that disputes are minimized. An appeals procedure is a structural approach.

 Understand the nature of work stress, its causes and consequences.

Stress is an internal response to a state of activation and ordinarily occurs in a threatening or negative situation. The cybernetic theory of stress views stress as an important discrepancy between an employee's perceived state and a desired state. To manage stress properly, the person attempts to narrow the discrepancy.

Stress symptoms include a host of physiological, emotional, and behavioral reactions. Many of these symptoms can adversely affect job performance. After prolonged job stress, a person may experience burnout. A general stressor that encompasses both individual and organizational factors is having to cope with significant change. Factors within the person contributing to work stress include a Type A personality, an external locus of control, negative lifestyle factors, and being pessimistic.

Adverse organization conditions are another set of stressors. According to the job demands-job control model, workers experience the most stress when the demands of the job are high yet they have little control over the activity. Other stressors include role overload and worry about potential job loss. Role conflict in its various forms and role ambiguity are other stressors of significance. Emotional labor, or the burden of having to fake emotions to please customers, is a recently recognized stressor.

 Explain what organizations can do to manage and reduce stress.

Organizational approaches to stress management include providing emotional support to employees, the establishment of a wellness program, providing on-site massages, and allowing for napping on the job.

Do a more effective job of managing your own stress.

Individual methods of preventing and controlling stress can be divided into three categories: attempts to control stressful situations, symptom management, and escape from the stressful situation. Specific tactics include eliminating stressors, getting sufficient physical exercise, using relaxation techniques, getting emotional support from others, and improving work habits. Also see the stress buster list in Exhibit 7-6.

KEY TERMS AND PHRASES

Conflict, *134*

The opposition of persons or forces that gives rise to some tension.

Conflict Frame, *134*

The lens through which disputants view a conflict situation.

Downsizing, *135*

The laying off of workers to reduce costs and increase efficiency.

Sexual Harassment, *135*

Unwanted sexually oriented behavior in the workplace that results in discomfort and/or interference with the job.

Work-Family Conflict, *137*

Conflict that ensues when the individual has to perform multiple roles: worker, spouse, and, often, parent.

Personality Clash, *138*

An antagonistic relationship between two people based on differences in personal attributes, preferences, interests, values, and styles.

Functional Conflict, *139*

A situation that occurs when the interests of the organization are served as a result of a dispute or disagreement.

Dysfunctional Conflict, *139*

A situation that occurs when a dispute or disagreement harms the organization.

C-Type Conflict, *140*

Conflict that focuses on substantive, issue-related differences.

A-Type Conflict, *140*

Conflict that focuses on personalized, individually oriented issues.

Win-Win, *141*

The belief that, after conflict has been resolved, both sides should gain something of value.

Confrontation and Problem Solving, *142*

A method of identifying the true source of conflict and resolving it systematically.

Open-Door Policy, *143*

An understanding in which any employee can bring a gripe to the attention of upper-level management without checking with his or her immediate manager.

Stress, *144*

The mental and physical condition that results from a perceived threat that cannot be dealt with readily.

Cybernetic Theory of Stress, Coping, and Well-Being in Organizations, *144*

The view that stress is a discrepancy between an employee's perceived state and desired state.

Stressor, *144*

Any force creating the stress reaction.

Strain, *144*

An adverse impact on employee health and well-being.

Burnout, *146*

A pattern of emotional, physical, and mental exhaustion in response to chronic job stressors.

Negative Lifestyle Factors, *147*

A behavior pattern predisposing a person to job stress, including poor exercise and eating habits and heavy consumption of caffeine, alcohol, tobacco, and other drugs.

Job Demands-Job Control Model, *147*

An explanation of job stress contending that workers experience the most stress when the demands of the job are high yet they have little control over the activity.

Role Conflict, *148*

Having to choose between competing demands or expectations.

Role Ambiguity, *149*

A condition in which the job holder receives confused or poorly defined role expectations.

Emotional Labor, *148*

A contributor to stress and burnout, emotional labor is having to modify and fake emotions and facial expressions when dealing with customers.

Wellness Program, *152*

A formal organization-sponsored activity to help employees stay well and avoid illness.

Relaxation Response, *153*

A general-purpose method of learning to relax by oneself, which includes making oneself quiet and comfortable.

DISCUSSION QUESTIONS AND ACTIVITIES

1. Is the pursuit of the same customers by traditional retailers and e-tailers a conflict? Why or why not?

2. Ask two managers what percent of work time they spend in resolving conflict. Compare this to the 20 percent figure given in the text.

3. Several analyses have concluded that sexual harassment is costly to the organization. What do you think are the costs associated with sexual harassment?

4. Why are entrepreneurs and other business owners more likely to experience work-family conflict than corporate employees?

5. What should employers do about the problem of employees being rude to one another and to customers?

6. Give an example from your own life of how the cybernetic model of stress might be valid.

7. Identify a Net age job that you think creates negative stress for most incumbents, and pinpoint the stressors.

ORGANIZATIONAL BEHAVIOR ON-LINE

TO DO

Stress Management on the Web

Many Web sites help you manage stress and stay well. Here are several to consider. Which site gets your vote for best functionality and design?

- Aerobics and Fitness Association of America (http://www.afaa.com): features recent research, personalized answers to fitness questions, and fitness counseling

- Find a free stress control plan at http://www.managingstress.com.

- Learning Meditation (http://www.learningmeditation.com) provides brief meditation sessions

- Adversity Quotient (http://www.doogee.com) gives a test measuring your tendencies toward being able to rebound from adversity thereby warding off long-lasting stress

TO BOOKMARK

Learning to Disagree without Being Disagreeable
http://www.fastcompany.com/online/01/disagree.html

American Institute of Stress
http://www.stress.org

Institute for Stress Management
http://www.hyperstress.com

Evaluation of Resistance to Stress
http://www.pressanykey.com/stresstest.html

Employee Assistance Program
http://www.eapintl.com

CASE PROBLEM: Net Warfare between Home Depot and Toro

Lynde Sorenson, Toro's executive in charge of e-commerce, faces a quandary common among manufacturers these days: how to use the Internet to develop a tighter bond with consumers without alienating dealers and retailers. Weighing on her mind is a letter the Bloomington, Minnesota-based outdoor maintenance equipment maker received from Home Depot earlier this summer. The letter, sent to 1,000 vendors, implies that selling products directly to consumers via the Internet is grounds for having your products yanked out of the Atlanta-based home-improvement giant's stores.

As a result, Toro is proceeding with caution as it develops its site. "It's such an important question, and we want to take a conservative approach," Sorensen said.

While Target has yet to issue any edicts à la Home Depot, it is also watchful of its vendors. "We do not view it as a friendly action to compete with us," said Gerald Storch, president of credit and new businesses for Target's parent company, Minneapolis-based Dayton Hudson.

Storch argues that multichannel retailers, not the suppliers, are best suited to sell products over the Internet. Retailers know the consumer best, they have the widest and deepest array of products, and they are the most convenient place to shop for, buy, service, or return merchandise. He cites studies from the Boston Group consulting firm that retailers already account for more than half the sales over the Internet.

It makes poor sense for vendors to cut the retailer out of the equation, Storch said. After all, most consumers check out products in stores before they order online, whether it be the smell of perfume, the feel of the cloth, or the fit of a blouse. Retailers spend a lot of money to advertise, stock, and showcase products. If they don't make the sale, they won't make the effort.

"Everyone wants to paint Home Depot as blocking the path to progress," Storch said. "It's a wonderful company. They hire licensed trade people for their floors, and that's an expensive service. What's wrong with getting the sale if you provide the advice?"

Like Home Depot, Dayton Hudson is encouraging its vendors to be partners and grow their sales together on the Internet through target.com, or any of the upcoming sites for Dayton Hudson's other divisions.

Toro is treading carefully about developing an Internet strategy, searching for ways to sell their wares online without angering other retailers. "The overall goal is convenience. We want to be able to sell our products, where, when, and how our customers want to buy them," Sorensen said. Toro recognizes a lot of its customers like to buy its lawn mowers and snowblowers at Home Depot and other retailers, and it's striving to develop an Internet strategy that won't cut off that channel.

Jim Datovech, an Internet consultant, said that someone like Scott's (lawn and garden products) has much more leverage than small, captive, vendors. "Who's the dog, and who's the tail? If you're going to buy weed killer, you're going to buy Scott's or Ortho, and if Home Depot doesn't have it, you'll go somewhere else."

Case Questions

1. How would you frame the conflict between Toro and Home Depot, as well as between other vendors and retailers?

2. What should Toro and Home Depot do to resolve their conflict about selling Toro equipment?

3. How could the conflict between Toro and Home Depot have been prevented?

Source: Jim McCartney, "It's a Tangled Web When Manufacturers, Retailers Clash," Knight Ridder, October 25, 1999.

To evaluate Home Depot's and Toro's Internet strategies for yourself, go online and visit http://www.homedepot.com/ and http://www.toro.com/.

SUGGESTED READINGS

Anthony, William, and Anthony, Camille. *The Art of Napping at Work: The No-Cost, Natural Way to Increase Productivity and Satisfaction.* (Burdett, New York: Larson Publishing, 1998).

Leonetti Dannhauser, Carol. "Attacking Anxiety: When Stress Goes Down, Productivity Goes Up." *Working Woman,* May 2000, pp. 40–42.

"Don't Burn Out!" *Fast Company,* May 2000, pp. 101–132.

Epstein, Robert. "Stress Busters: 11 Quick, Fun Games to Tame the Beast." *Psychology Today,* March/April 2000, pp. 30–36.

Hammonds, Keith H., and Palmer, Ann Therese. "The Daddy Trap." *Business Week,* September 21, 1998, pp. 56–64.

"It's About Time." *Fast Company,* November 1999, pp. 141–176.

Kruger, Pamela. "Jobs for Life." *Fast Company,* May 2000, pp. 236–252.

Munson, Liberty J., Hulin, Charles, and Drascow, Fritz. "Longitudinal Analysis of Dispositional Influences and Sexual Harassment: Effects on Job and Psychological Outcomes." *Personnel Psychology,* Spring 2000, pp. 21–46.

Spaeder, Karen E. "Is Your Business Killing You? How to Break Your Bad Habits and Pick Up Better Ones." *Entrepreneur,* October 1999, pp. 98–106.

Spector, Paul E., Chen, Peter Y., and O'Connell, Brian J. "A Longitudinal Study of Relations Between Job Stressors and Job Strains While Controlling for Prior Negative Affectivity and Strains." *Journal of Applied Psychology,* April 2000, pp. 211–218.

Taylor, Alex III. "Behind Bill's Boardroom Struggle: The Fight at Ford." *Fortune,* April 3, 2000, pp. 140–146.

ENDNOTES

1. Robin L. Pinkley and Gregory P. Northcraft, "Conflict Frames of Reference: Implications for Dispute Processes and Outcomes," *Academy of Management Journal,* February 1994, p. 193.

2. David M. Noer, *Healing the Wounds: Overcoming the Trauma of Layoffs and Revitalizing Downsized Organizations* (San Francisco: Jossey Bass, 1993).

3. Christopher Garlock, "Down Side of Downsizing," *Rochester Democrat and Chronicle,* May 2, 1994, p. 7A.

4. These rulings are summarized in Jennifer Laabs, "What You're Liable for Now," *Workforce,* October 1998, pp. 34–42.

5. Based on a review of the literature in Anne M. O'Leary-Kelly, Ramona L. Paetzold, and Ricky W. Griffin, "Sexual Harassment as Aggressive Behavior: An Actor-Based Perspective," *Academy of Management Review,* April 2000, p. 372.

6. Kimberly T. Schneider, Suzanne Swan, and Louise F. Fitzgerald, "Job-Related and Psychological Effects of Sexual Harassment in the Workplace: Empirical Evidence from Two Organizations," *Journal of Applied Psychology,* June 1997, p. 406.

7. Kimberly T. Schneider, Robert T. Hitlan, and Phanikiran Radhakrishan, "An Examination of the Nature and Correlates of Ethnic Harassment Experiences in Multiple Contexts," *Journal of Applied Psychology,* February 2000, pp. 3–12.

8. Linda Elizabeth Duxbury and Christopher Alan Higgins, "Gender Differences in Work-Family Conflict," *Journal of Applied Psychology,* February 1991, p. 64.

9. "When Work and Private Lives Collide," *Workforce,* February 1999, p. 27.

10. Ellen Ernst Kossek and Cynthia Ozeki, "Work-Family Conflict, Policies, and the Job-Life Satisfaction Relationship: A Review and Directions for Organizational Behavior—Human Resources Research," *Journal of Applied Psychology,* April 1998, pp. 139–149.

11. Quoted in Carol Kleiman, "Finding Balance with Work, Family," *Chicago Tribune* syndicated story, November 23, 1998. See also Francine M. Deutsch, *Having It All: How Equally Shared Parenting Works* (Boston, MA: Harvard University Press, 1998).

12. Lynne M. Andersson and Christine M. Pearson, "Tit for Tat? The Spiraling Effect of Incivility in the Workplace," *Academy of Management Review,* July 1999, pp. 452–471.

13. J. M. Rabbie and F. K. Bekkers, "Threatened Leadership and Intergroup Competition, " *European Journal of Social Psychology,* Vol. 8, 1978, pp. 19–20. (As cited in Robert P. Vecchio, *Organizational Behavior,* 2nd ed. (Chicago: Dryden Press, 1991), p. 415.

158

14. Katharine Mieszkowski, "Generation *# #@**# #@!!" *Fast Company,* October 1999, pp. 106–108.

15. Jennifer Laabs, "Employee Sabotage: Don't Be a Victim," *Workforce,* July 1999, p. 33.

16. Cited in Susan Strother, "He's Defusing the Workplace," Rochester *Democrat and Chronicle,* December 27, 1999, p. 3F.

17. Michael D. Kelleher, *Profiling the Lethal Employee: Case Studies of Violence in the Workplace* (Westport, CT: Praeger, 1997), p. 12. Understanding how the environment contributes to violence is also an underlying theme in Ricky W. Griffin, Ann O'Leary-Kelly, and Judith M. Collins (eds.), *Dysfunctional Behavior in Organizations, Part A: Violent and Deviant Behavior, Part B: Non-Violent Dysfunctional Behavior in Organizations, Volume 23* (Stamford, CT: JAI Press, 1998).

18. Allen C. Amson, Wayne A. Hockwarter, Kenneth R. Thompson, and Allison W. Harrison, "Conflict: An Important Dimension in Successful Management Teams," *Organizational Dynamics* (Autumn 1995), pp. 20–33.

19. Kenneth Thomas, "Conflict and Conflict Management," in Marvin D. Dunnette (ed.), *Handbook of Industrial and Organizational Psychology* (Chicago: Rand McNally College Publishing, 1976), pp. 900–902.

20. D. H. Stamatis, "Conflict: You've Got to Accentuate the Positive," *Personnel,* December 1987, pp. 48–49.

21. The quote and technique are both from Kathleen Doheny, "It's a Mad, Mad Corporate World," *Working Woman,* April 2000, pp. 71–72.

22. Patrick A. McGuire, "Worker Stress, Health, Reaching Critical Point," *APA Monitor,* May 1999, p. 1.

23. Charlene Marmer Solomon, "Stressed to the Limit," *Workforce,* September 1999, p. 50.

24. Jeffery R. Edwards, "A Cybernetic Theory of Stress, Coping, and Well-Being in Organizations," *Academy of Management Review,* April 1992, pp. 256–257.

25. Research reviewed in "Mental Stress Is Linked to Blocked Blood Vessels," *APA Monitor,* February 1998, p. 7.

26. Jo Ellen Moore, "Why Is This Happening? A Causal Attribution Approach to Work Exhaustion Consequences," *Academy of Management Review,* April 2000, pp. 335–349.

27. Cynthia L. Cordes and Thomas W. Dougherty, "A Review and Integration of Research on Job Burnout," *Academy of Management Review,* October 1993, p. 622.

28. Christina Maslach and Michael P. Leiter, *The Truth About Burnout: How Organizations Cause Personal Stress and What to Do About It.* (San Francisco: Jossey-Bass, 1997).

29. Rabi S. Bhagat, "Effects of Stressful Life Events on Individual Performance and Work Adjustment Processes within Organizational Settings: A Research Model," *Academy of Management Review,* October 1983, pp. 660–671.

30. Cynthia Lee, Susan J. Ashford, and Philip Bobko, "Interactive Effects of 'Type A' Behavior and Perceived Control of Worker Performance, Job Satisfaction, and Somatic Complaints," *Academy of Management Journal,* December 1990, p. 870.

31. Marilyn L. Fox, Deborah J. Dwyer, and Daniel C. Ganster, "Effects of Stressful Job Demands and Control on Physiological and Attitudinal Outcomes in a Hospital Setting," *Academy of Management Journal,* April 1993, pp. 290–292.

32. Daniel Katz and Robert L. Kahn, *The Social Psychology of Organizations* (New York: Wiley, 1966); updated in "Working Smart," *Personal Report for the Executive* (May 15, 1988), p. 3.

33. J. B. Teboul, "Facing and Coping with Uncertainty during Organizational Encounter," *Communication Quarterly,* Vol. 8, 1994, pp. 190–224.

34. "Emotional Labor Causes Stress, Burnout, Researcher Finds," Knight Ridder, March 13, 2000. The article is based on research published in the *Journal of Occupational Health Psychology.*

35. Haeyoun Park, "Emotional Impact on RSI Sufferers Is Often Overlooked," Knight Ridder, August 2, 1999.

36. Richard S. DeFrank and John M. Ivancevich, "Stress on the Job: An Executive Update," *Academy of Management Executive,* August 1998, p. 56.

37. Sandra L. Kirmeyer and Thomas W. Dougherty, "Work Load, Tension, and Coping: Moderating Effects of Supervisor Support," *Personnel Psychology,* Spring 1988, pp. 125–139.

38. Kelly Dunn, "Roche Chooses Health by Promoting Prevention," *Workforce,* April 2000, pp. 82–84; Fred W. Shott and Sandra Wendel, "Wellness with a Track Record," *Personnel Journal,* April 1992, pp. 98–104.

39. M. Waters, "Naps Could Replace Coffee as Workers' Favorite Break," *APA Monitor,* July 1998, p. 6.

40. The framework for this section is from Janina C. Latack, "Coping with Job Stress: Measures and Future Directions for Scale Development," *Journal of Applied Psychology,* August 1986, pp. 522–526.

Interpersonal Communication

Ryobi Die Casting USA (http://www.ryobi.com), with headquarters in Shelbyville, Indiana, has 1,000 employees and $1 billion in annual revenues. President and CEO James C. Smith, says, "When I became CEO of Ryobi Die Casting, my primary goal was to change the company from an aluminum die cast manufacturer into an information and knowledge enterprise that competes in the aluminum die casting market. In my view, this is the only way for our company to build long-term, sustainable growth in both market share and number of customers.

"But to achieve this kind of change, it is important to believe that every employee has the ability to do more than management has allowed him or her to do in the past. By developing a clear road map and delivering it to all employees as part of an ongoing communication plan, every employee knows what is expected of him or her, the path to getting there, and the role or she will play in the process.

"At our company, this road map is not simply printed and distributed to every employee, but rather is presented through a series of small information meetings, which I personally host, across all of our departments and shifts. With this process, each employee has the opportunity to meet with the company's leadership team in small groups. We can communicate the four cornerstones that will guide us toward our organization's goals: leadership systems, innovative processes, people partnerships and customer focus.

"How has the use of the road map affected results? In the past 14 months, we have doubled our revenues and our number of customers. We also received a World Excellence Achievement Award from Ford Motor Co., presented each year to only a top few suppliers from the thousands that do business with Ford."

Ford maintains its own road map of what it takes to do business with Ford. Visit http://fsn.ford.com/dbwf/table_of_contents.html for details.

Source: James C. Smith, "Do Your Employees KNOW the Plan?" *Management Review*, October 1999, p. 11.

OBJECTIVES

After reading and studying this chapter and doing the exercises, you should be able to

1. Describe the communication process.

2. Describe the impact of information technology on interpersonal communication in organizations.

3. Explain how nonverbal communication can be used to enhance communication.

4. Present details about the various channels of communication in organizations.

5. Summarize barriers to effective communication and how to overcome them.

6. Explain how to overcome cross-gender and cross-cultural communication problems.

7. Recognize the basics for becoming a more power-oriented communicator.

159

Chapter 8

SO WHAT? A fundamental truth about many successful organizations is that their leaders make a conscious and deliberate effort to communicate their intentions and plans to all workers. Furthermore, such communication is enhanced by interacting with employees at all levels about issues large and small. Face it. Communication is the basic process by which managers and professionals accomplish their tasks, and people in positions of authority consistently rank communication skills as vital for success. The Nierenberg Group's survey on the top job skills for the 21st century identified interpersonal communication skills as the number one workplace skill. Communication was also rated as a top 5 skill by 95 percent of Nierenberg survey respondents.[1]

The key purpose of this chapter it to explain key aspects of interpersonal communication in organizations and make suggestions for improved communication. To achieve this purpose, we include information about the communication process, the impact of information technology on communication, overcoming various barriers to communication, and how to develop a more power-oriented communication style.

THE COMMUNICATION PROCESS

Describe the communication process.

Interpersonal communication takes place through a series of steps, as illustrated in Exhibit 8-1. For effective communication to take place, six components must be present: a communication source or sender, a message, a channel, a receiver, feedback, and the environment. As you study this model, you will observe that perception and communication are closely linked. To help explain the communication process, assume that a production manager wants to inform a team leader that quality in his department slipped last month.

1. *Source (the sender).* The source of a communication event is usually a person attempting to send a spoken, written, sign language, or nonverbal message to another person or persons. The perceived authority and experience of the sender are important factors in influencing how much attention the message will receive.

2. *Message.* The heart of a communication event is the **message,** a purpose or an idea to be conveyed. Many factors influence how a message is received. Among them are clarity, the alertness of the receiver, the complexity and

EXHIBIT 8-1

The Communication Process

Various sources of interference can prevent a message getting from sender to receiver as intended.

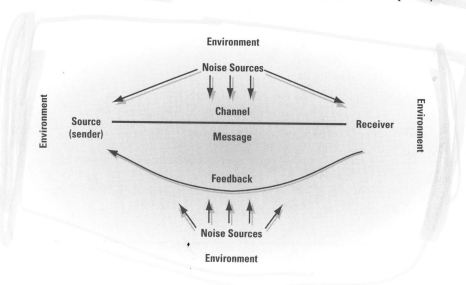

length of the message, and how the information is organized. The production manager's message will most likely get across if she says directly, "I need to talk to you about last month's below-average quality figures."

3. *Channel (medium).* Several communication channels, or media, are usually available for sending messages in organizations. Typically messages are written, spoken, or a combination of the two. Some kind of nonverbal cue such as a smile or hand gesture accompanies most spoken messages. Heavy reliance is now placed on electronic transmission of messages. As the punch line to a cartoon in a business newspaper reads, "Hello. You've reached a live receptionist. The first available recording will be with you shortly."[2] In the production manager's case, she has chosen to drop by the team leader's office and deliver her message in a serious tone.

4. *Receiver.* A communication event can only be complete when another party receives the message and understands it properly. In the example being examined, the team leader is the receiver. Perceptual distortions of various types (as described in Chapter 3) act as filters that can prevent a message from being received as intended by the sender. If the team leader is worried that his job is at stake, he might get defensive when he hears the production manager's message.

5. *Feedback.* Without feedback, it is difficult to know whether a message has been received and understood. The feedback step also includes the reactions of the receiver. If the receiver takes action as intended by the sender, the message has been received satisfactorily. The production manager will know her message got across if the team leader says, "OK, when would you like to review last month's production figures?" Effective interpersonal communication therefore involves an exchange of messages between two people. The two communicators take turns being receivers and senders.

6. *Environment.* A full understanding of communication requires knowledge of the environment in which messages are transmitted and received. The organizational culture is a key environmental factor that influences communication. It is easier to transmit controversial messages when trust and respect are high than when they are low.

7. *Noise.* Distractions such as noise have a pervasive influence on the components of the communication process. In this context, **noise** is anything that disrupts communication, including the attitudes and emotions of the receiver. Noise includes work stress, fear, ambivalence, and strong advocacy for an opposing position. The whir of machinery, piped-in music, and the chatting of coworkers with each other and on cell phones are among the many examples of noise in the workplace.

COMMUNICATION AND INFORMATION TECHNOLOGY

Advances in information technology have influenced the quantity and quality of interpersonal communications in the workplace. Quite often the influence has been positive, but at other times communication effectiveness has decreased. Four developments that illustrate the impact of information technology on interpersonal communication are e-mail, the alternative workplace, slide presentations by computer, and voice-recognition systems.

161

Experiencing OB

Learn more about barriers to effective communication and how to overcome them by visiting South-Western's animated concept and activity site at *http://www.experiencingob.com*. Exclusive review tools on the topic of Communication shed light on this intricate subject, with unique insights into issues associated with high-tech communication channels. Free demo available!

Describe the impact of information technology on interpersonal communication in organizations.

E-mail

E-mail has had two major impacts on interpersonal communication. First, written messages replace many telephone and in-person interchanges, with an estimated 23 million workers in the United States and Canada being connected by e-mail networks. Group members often keep in regular contact with one another without having lengthy meetings or telephone conversations. Second, people receive many more messages than they did by paper and telephone. Many managers and professionals process over 100 e-mail messages per day.

E-mail facilitates communication in many ways, including people in various parts of the world exchanging information without worrying about trying to connect through different time zones. A more subtle consequence of e-mail is that it enhances industrial democracy. Ray Maghroori, dean of the business school at San Francisco State University, notes that "Ten or 20 years ago, there was no way for average workers to communicate with leaders."[3] Today messages are no longer filtered through layers of management.

A widespread problem with e-mail is that it encourages the indiscriminate sending of messages including trivial information, mass distribution of information of interest to a limited number of people, the exchange of jokes and personal philosophies, and requests for seemingly unimportant information. The blitz of messages requires many people to work extra hours just to sort through their mail on matters that do not add value to the organization. The problems associated with e-mail are widely recognized, leading various specialists to suggest ways for more productive use of this mode of communication. The accompanying Organizational Behavior in Action presents representative ideas for the proper use of e-mail.

The Alternative Workplace

A major deviation from the traditional work schedule is the **alternative workplace,** a combination of nontraditional work practices, settings, and locations that supplements the traditional office. An estimated 30 million to 40 million people in the United States work at home as corporate employees or for self-employment.[4] In addition to working at home, the alternative workplace can include working from a small satellite office, sharing an office or a cubicle, or being assigned a laptop computer and a cell phone as a substitute for a private work space. Here we concentrate on working at home because it represents the most substantial communication challenges.

Telecommuting is an arrangement in which employees use computers to perform their regular work responsibilities at home or in a satellite office. Employees who telecommute usually use computers tied to the company's main office. People who work at home are referred to as telecommuters or *teleworkers.* The vast majority of people who work at home are either assigned a computer by the company or possess their own computer and related equipment. Yet a person might do piecework at home, such as making garments or furniture without using a computer. In addition to using computers to communicate to their employer's office, telecommuters attend meetings on company premises and stay in contact by telephone and teleconferences.

A major communication challenge to telecommuters is that they rely so heavily on e-mail, thereby losing out on the social interaction of work, so important to many people. You will recall the case at the end of Chapter 5 about telecommuters and small business people spending some time congregating in

Organizational Behavior *in Action*

E - M a i l   E t i q u e t t e

Elsa Steo, vice president of HR Works, a human resources management firm, and the staff of Office Team, a temporary worker firm, offer tips on e-mail etiquette. Observing these tips will also enhance your electronic communication effectiveness.

Keep it simple. Each message should have only one piece of information or request for action so that it's easier for the executive to respond.

Include an action step. Clearly outline what type of reply you're looking for, as well as any applicable deadlines.

Use the subject line to your advantage. Generic terms such as "details" or "reminder" do not describe the contents of your message or whether it's time sensitive. So the executive may delay opening it.

Take care in writing e-mails. Clearly organize your thoughts to avoid sending e-mails with confusing, incomplete or missing information. Never use profane or harsh language (referred to as *flaming*).

Proofread. Use business writing style, and check carefully for grammatical and typographical errors. (Also, avoid the trend to spell "I" in lower case.)

Be considerate. Use "please" and "thank you" even in brief messages.

Don't include confidential information. E-mail is occasionally forwarded to unintended recipients. If your message is in any way sensitive or confidential, set up a meeting or leave a voice mail in which you request confidentiality.

Want more? Everyone from Martha Stewart to self-proclaimed Web wizard Barbara J. Feldman of *i*Village.com has advice about e-mail netiquette. Visit http://www.ivillage.com/click/experts/webwizard/ for an additional take on the subject.

Source: Todd Grady, "Even via E-Mail, Courtesy Matters," *Democrat and Chronicle* (Rochester, New York) 1 May 2000, by permission of the *Democrat and Chronicle*.

---

office centers that cater to people who work independently. Teleworkers are also encouraged to spend some time in the traditional office in face-to-face communication with other workers. Avoiding such contact can lead to feelings of isolation and not being part of the office communication network.

Presentation Technology

Virtually every reader of this text has witnessed or given a talk using presentation technology. Computer-generated slides, such as PowerPoint, are currently in vogue, yet overhead projectors are also part of presentation technology. Speakers in all types of organizations supplement their talk with computer slides and often organize their presentation around them. Some speakers sit slumped in a chair, narrating the slides. Many people want presentations reduced to bulleted items and eye-catching graphics. (Have you noticed this tendency among students?) The ability to prepare a slide presentation has become in indispensable corporate survival skill.[5] Audiences have become accustomed to watching an array of impressive graphics during oral presentations.

The communication challenge here is that during an oral presentation the predominant means of connection between sender and receiver is eye contact.

When an audience is constantly distracted from the presenter by movement on the screen, sounds from the computer, or lavish colors, eye contact suffers and so does the message. Another problem is that the speaker who relies on multimedia to the exclusion of person-to-person contact may be communicating the subtle message, "I am not really necessary."[6]

The implication for presenters is to find a way to integrate speaking skills with the new technology. One of the biggest challenges is to learn how to handle equipment and maintain frequent eye and voice contact at all times. Jean Mausehund and R. Neil Dortch offer these sensible suggestions:

- *Reveal points only as needed.* Project the overhead transparencies or computer slides only when needed and use a cursor, laser pointer, or metal pointer for emphasis.
- *Talk to the audience and not the screen.* A major problem with computer slides is that the presenter as well as the audience is likely to focus continually on the slide. If the presenter minimizes looking at the slide, and spends considerable time looking at the audience, it will be easier to maintain contact with the audience.
- *Keep the slide in view until the audience gets the point.* A presenter will often flash a slide or transparency without giving the audience enough time to comprehend the meaning of the slide. It is also important for presenters to synchronize the slides with their comments.[7]

Voice Recognition Systems

A growing technology centers around methods for communicating with electronic devices by voice rather than through computer commands or touching buttons. A **voice-recognition system** is an electronic device that can be commanded by human voices. Many customer service systems, such as calling in a meter read or ordering from a catalog, already use voice recognition. A voice-recognition system for the office can function as a virtual secretary. Built with a human voice, the machine can place telephone calls, direct incoming calls to a specified number, put through other calls, and take incoming phone messages. The most widespread use for voice-recognition systems will be to supplement or replace keyboarding, with commands such as instructing your spreadsheet program, "Show me what would happen to profits if we eliminated our 100 smallest customers."

A communications challenge with voice-recognition systems is that the sender must articulate clearly and slowly. Microsoft employees refer humorously to the "wreck a nice beach" syndrome. You instructed the computer to print, "recognize speech," but it interpreted your input as "wreck a nice beach." The systems work best when used with a limited vocabulary and carefully structured commands. Jim Baumann explains that the difficulty in using voice as computer input lies in the fundamental difference between human speech and the more traditional forms of computer input. Computer programs rely upon precise input, whereas spoken words are usually imprecise. Each human voice is unique, and identical words can have different meanings if spoken with different inflections or in different contexts.[8] For example, "The leader led the group to get rid of the lead in the old building."

Some voice-recognition systems are customized to adapt to the regional intonation and accents of the sole, or typical, user of the system. In this way, the computer could differentiate between such subtleties as the pronunciation of "ing" at the end of a gerund. ("My computer needs *fixin*" versus "My computer needs *fixeen*" or "*fixingah*" [hard g].) Even with custom features, voice-recognition systems require emphasis on clear and precise speech.

Despite these key advances in applying information technology to communication, the process model of communication remains valid. Workers at all organizational levels must be cognizant of such factors as effectively sending and receiving messages and being aware of potential noise.

NONVERBAL COMMUNICATION

The most obvious modes of communication are speaking, writing, and sign language. (Many large business meetings today include an interpreter who signs for deaf members of the audience.) A substantial amount of interpersonal communication also occurs through **nonverbal communication,** the transmission of messages by means other than with words. Body language refers to those aspects of nonverbal communication directly related to movements of the body, such as gestures and posture. Nonverbal communication usually supplements rather than substitutes for writing, speaking, and sign language.

Explain how nonverbal communication can be used to enhance communication.

The general purpose of nonverbal communication is to express the feeling behind a message. Suppose that a sales representative stands tall when saying, "Our payroll processing service is devoid of bugs and glitches." The representative's posture reveals confidence in making this pitch. The same message delivered in a slouched position with one hand over the mouth would communicate a feeling of limited confidence.

Nonverbal communication incorporates a wide range of behavior. Nevertheless, it can be divided into the following eight categories.[9]

1. *Environment.* The physical setting in which the message takes place communicates meaning. Included here would be the office décor, the type of automobile, and the restaurant or hotel chosen for a business meeting. Bigger deals are typically negotiated and consummated in more luxurious restaurants, whereas discussions about work assignments might be held in a family-style restaurant.
2. *Body placement.* The placement of one's body in relation to someone else is widely used to transmit messages. Facing a person in a casual, relaxed style indicates acceptance. Moving close to another person is also a general indicator of acceptance. However, moving too close may be perceived as a violation of personal space, and the message sender will be rejected.
3. *Posture.* Another widely used clue to a person's attitude is his or her posture. Leaning toward another person suggests a favorable attitude toward the message one is trying to communicate. Leaning backward communicates the opposite. Standing up straight is generally interpreted as an indicator of self-confidence, while slouching is usually a sign of low self-confidence.
4. *Hand gestures.* Included here are gestures of the hand, such as frequent movements to express approval and palms spread outward to indicate perplexity.
5. *Facial expressions and movement.* The particular look on a person's face and movements of the person's head provide reliable cues as to approval, disapproval, or disbelief.
6. *Voice tone.* Aspects of the voice such as pitch, volume, quality, and speech rate may communicate confidence, nervousness, or enthusiasm. Intelligence is often judged by how people sound. Research suggests that the most annoying voice quality is a whining, complaining, or nagging tone.[10]

7. *Clothing, dress, and appearance.* The image a person conveys communicates such messages as "I feel powerful" and "I think this meeting is important." For example, wearing one's best business attire to a performance appraisal interview would communicate the idea that "I think this meeting is very important."

8. *Mirroring.* To mirror is to build rapport with another person by imitating his or her voice tone, breathing rate, body movement, and language. Mirroring relies 10 percent on verbal means, 60 percent on voice tone, and 30 percent on body physiology. A specific application of mirroring is to conform to the other person's posture, eye movements, and hand movements. The person feels more relaxed with you as a result of your imitation.

One of many practical applications of nonverbal communication is to project enthusiasm and confidence with body language. Ron Huff recommends the following:

- *Loosen your facial expression.* A tight, grim look gives the appearance of being unapproachable. Relax your muscles, and look for opportunities to smile and offer encouraging nods.

- *Move closer to message senders.* Work associates feel you are listening intently when you lean slightly toward them when they speak. It is a subtle way of showing that you want to hear every word.

- *Gesture to reinforce a point.* If you are excited or pleased with an idea, do not rely exclusively on words to communicate these feelings. Pump a fist, clap your hands, or point approvingly at the speaker. Use the gesture that feels the most natural to you.[11]

Despite the recommendations and implications of the information about nonverbal communication, keep in mind that many nonverbal signals are ambiguous. For example, a smile usually indicates agreement and warmth, but can also indicate nervousness.

ORGANIZATIONAL CHANNELS OF COMMUNICATION

Present details about the various channels of communication in organizations.

Messages in organizations travel over many different channels, or paths. Communication channels can be formal or informal and can be categorized by the direction they follow.

Formal Communication Channels

Formal communication channels are the official pathways for sending information inside and outside an organization. The primary source of information about formal channels is the organization chart. It indicates the channels the messages are supposed to follow. By carefully following the organization chart, an entry-level worker would know how to transmit a message to the CEO.

The formal communication channels are precisely specified in a bureaucratic organization with its many layers. Communication channels are more difficult to follow in the modern **network organization,** a spherical structure that can rotate self-managing teams and other resources around a common knowledge base. The key purpose of the network organization is to enter into temporary alliances with other firms in order to capitalize on the combined talents. A *strategic alliance* is the term often used to describe these temporary, multifirm ventures.

An outstanding example of the network organization is Technical and Computer Graphics in Sydney, Australia, an interactive network of 24 companies.

It is one of its country's most significant innovators in portable data terminals, computer graphics, and other applications of information and computer technology.[12] Similarly, IBM and Apple Computer have entered into strategic alliances for certain products and services. Later on, they terminated some of their strategic alliances, pointing to the fluid nature of network organizations.

Exhibit 8-2 shows the contrast between a bureaucracy (pyramid-shape) and a network organization (spherical shape). The connecting lines can be considered formal communication channels. Formal communication channels are often bypassed through information technology. Using e-mail, anybody can send a message to anybody else in the organization. During a crisis, formal channels may also be ignored as a lower-ranking person sends a message about an urgent problem directly to top management.

Informal Communication Channels

An **informal communication channel** is the unofficial network of channels that supplement the formal channels. Most of these informal channels arise out of necessity. For example, people will sometimes depart from the official communication channels to consult with a person with specialized knowledge. Suppose an administrative assistant in the inventory control department spoke and wrote fluent German. Employees from other department would regularly consult her when they were dealing with a customer who sends a message in German.

The **grapevine** is the major informal communication channel in organizations. The grapevine refers to the tangled pathways that can distort information. The term referred originally to the snarled telegraph lines on the battlefield during the U.S. Civil War. The grapevine is often thought to be used primarily for passing along negative rumors and gossip. The grapevine, however, is sometimes used purposely to disseminate information along informal lines. For example, top management might want to hint to employees that certain work will be outsourced unless the employees become more productive. Although the plans are still tentative, feeding them into the grapevine may result in improved motivation and productivity.

Rumors are an important communication force within organizations, and they tend to thrive in organizations with poor corporate communication, such as a penitentiary. Furthermore, an active grapevine is correlated with higher levels of stress, threat, and insecurity. Respondents to a worldwide survey agreed that

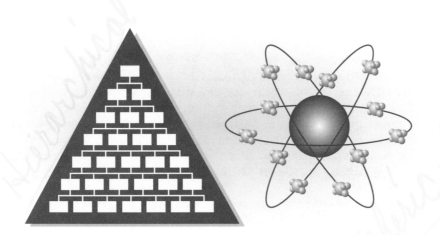

Communication Pathways in a Hierarchical Organization and a Spherical Organization

Communication pathways are more complex in a spherical organization than in a hierarchical organization.

rumors are an important early source of information. Executives from the United Kingdom and the United States agreed most strongly, whereas those from Switzerland and Japan agreed the least. To ensure that rumors are more helpful than harmful, management might do the following:

- Be wary of vague communication, which fosters misinterpretation and anxiety.
- Promote healthy, accurate communication.
- Avoid concealing bad news.
- Correct erroneous communications that relate to organizational policies, practices, and strategic plans.[13]

A problem with inaccurate rumors is that they can distract workers, create anxiety, and decrease productivity. A frequent by-product of false rumors about company relocation or a pending merger is that some of the more talented workers leave in the hopes of more stable employment.

Another informal channel of significance is chance encounters. Unscheduled informal contact between managers and employees can be an efficient and effective communication channel. John P. Kotter found that effective managers do not confine their communication to formal meetings.[14] Instead, they collect valuable information during chance encounters. Spontaneous communication events may occur in the cafeteria, near the water fountain, in the halls, and on the elevator. In just two minutes, the manager might obtain the information that would typically be solicited in a 30-minute meeting or through a series of e-mail exchanges.

One important communication channel can be classified as formal or informal. **Management by walking around** involves managers intermingling freely with workers on the shop floor, in the office, and with customers. By spending time in personal contact with employees, the manager enhances open communication. Because management by walking around is systematic, it could be considered formal. However, a manager who circulates throughout the company is not following the formal paths prescribed by the organization chart. Management by walking around differs from chance encounters in that the latter are unplanned events; the former occurs intentionally.

Communication Directions

Messages in organizations travel in five directions: downward, upward, horizontally, diagonally, and spherically. *Downward communication* is the flow of messages from one level to a lower level. It is typified by a middle manager giving orders to a lower-level supervisor or by top management sending announcements to employees. Information is sometimes transmitted from a higher level to a lower one without the sender inviting a response. When this occurs, the feedback built into two-way communication is lost.

Upward communication is the transmission of messages from lower to higher levels in an organization. It is the most important channel for keeping management informed about problems within the organization. Management by walking around, chance encounters, and simply talking regularly to employees are factors that improve upward communication. An **open-door policy** is a more formal upward communication channel. This policy allows employees to bring a gripe to top management's attention without first checking with their manager. Upward communication is more widely used in less bureaucratic firms than in highly bureaucratic firms.

Horizontal communication is sending messages among people at the same organization level. It often takes the form of coworkers from the same department talking to one another. When coworkers are not sharing information with and responding to one another, they are likely to fall behind schedule. Also, efforts are duplicated and quality suffers.[15] Another type of horizontal communication takes place when managers communicate with other managers at the same level. Horizontal communication is the basis for cooperation.

Diagonal communication is the transmission of messages to higher or lower organizational levels in different departments. A typical diagonal communication event occurs when a manager from one department contacts a lower-ranking person from a department outside of his or her chain of command.

Spherical communication is communication among members from different teams in the network organization. The communication events take place with team members from the same of different organizations. Visualize a team member from Nike Corporation communicating directly with a team member from Panasonic Corporation. He wants to talk about a strategic alliance to develop a basketball shoe with a built-in radio!

BARRIERS TO INTERPERSONAL COMMUNICATION

Summarize barriers to effective communication and how to overcome them.

The information presented so far is helpful in understanding how communication takes place in organizations. Let us now explore further why messages sent from one person to another are often not received exactly as intended. As was shown in Exhibit 8-1, barriers (or noise) exist at every step in the communication process. Interference is the most likely to occur when a message is complex, arouses emotion, or clashes with a receiver's mental set. An emotionally arousing message may deal with such topics as money or personal inconvenience. A message that clashes with a mental set challenges the receiver to make a radical shift in thinking. For example, a human resources manager had difficulty getting across the message that managers could no longer request specifically for a woman to fill an administrative assistant position.

Seven communication barriers are described here. The first four relate primarily to the sending of messages; the last three relate more to receiving them. Exhibit 8-3 lists the barriers to communication as well as the means for overcoming them to be described in the next section of the chapter.

1. *Semantics.* Many communication problems are created by **semantics,** the varying meanings people attach to words. The symbols (both words and nonverbal behavior) used in communication can take on different means for different people. Consequently, it is possible for a person to misinterpret the intended meaning of the sender. One phrase fraught with varying interpretations is "essential personnel." When a CEO announces before a downsizing that only essential personnel will be retained, many people are left wondering about their status. Few people can accept the message that they are "nonessential."

2. *Filtering of negative information.* A formidable upward communication barrier is **filtering,** the coloring and altering of information to make it more acceptable to the receiver. Many managers and individual workers filter information to avoid displeasing their superiors, such as when describing an inventory buildup. Filtering is most likely to take place when top-level management has a history of punishing the bearer of bad news.

3. *Credibility of the sender.* The more trustworthy the source or sender of a message, the greater the probability that the message will get through clearly. In contrast, when the sender of the message has low credibility, many times it will

be ignored. Credibility in sending messages is so important that it is a major contributor to effective leadership.

4. *Mixed signals.* Communications can break down for a subtle variation of low credibility. The disconnect occurs from **mixed signals**—sending different messages about the same topic to different audiences.[16] For example, a company might brag about the high quality of its products in its public statements. Yet on the shop floor and in the office, the company tells its employees to cut corners whenever possible to lower costs. Another type of mixed signal occurs when you send one message to a person about desired behavior, yet behave in another way yourself. A mixed signal of this type would occur when an executive preaches the importance of social responsibility, yet practices blatant job discrimination.

5. *Different frames of reference.* People perceive words and concepts differently depending on their **frame of reference,** a perspective and vantage point based on past experience. A typical example of the frame of reference problem took place in a financial service company that was instituting work streamlining teams to improve productivity. The vice president of operations announced the program with great enthusiasm, only to find that the message was received in a distorted, negative fashion. The problem was that the vice president perceived productivity improvement as a vehicle for ensuring increased profits and survival. Lower-ranking employees, however, perceived productivity improvement as a way of maintaining output while laying off workers.

6. *Value judgments.* Making value judgments prior to receiving an entire message interferes with the communication if its intended meaning. A **value judgment** is an overall opinion of something based on a quick perception of its merit. When value judgments are made too hastily, the receiver hears only the part of the message that he or she wishes to hear. A manager might begin to read an announcement about a dependent-care center to be sponsored by the company. The manager might make a quick value judgment that this program is "just another human resources initiative to keep people happy." By so doing, the manager will block out the information that dependent-care facilities often increase productivity by reducing absenteeism and turnover. It is also possible that a hasty value judgment will prompt a person to discount a message despite listening to it fully.

7. *Communication overload.* Electronic communication has contributed to the problem of too much information being disseminated throughout most private and public firms. **Communication** (or **information**) **overload** occurs when people are so overloaded with information that they cannot respond

Barriers	Overcoming Barriers
Semantics	Clarify ideas before sending.
Filtering of negative information	Motivate the receiver.
Credibility of the sender	Discuss differences in paradigms.
Mixed signals	Foster informal communication.
Different frames of reference	Communicate feelings behind the facts.
Value judgements	Be aware of nonverbal behavior.
Communication overload	Obtain feedback.
	Adapt to the other person's communication style.

effectively to messages. As a result, they experience work stress. Managers and staff professionals alike are exposed to so much printed, electronic, and spoken information that their capacity to absorb it is taxed. The human mind is capable of processing only a limited quantity of information at a time.

Communication overload is a communication barrier contributed to by both the receiver and the sender. The receiver's "circuits are jammed," yet many senders contribute to the problem by disseminating too much information to the same person.

OVERCOMING COMMUNICATION BARRIERS

An effective strategy for improving communication in organizations is to overcome communication barriers. Improving communication is important because successful firms are characterized by an abundance of straightforward communication.[17] The following sections provide an overview of tactics and techniques for improving the sending and receiving of messages. In addition, they describe methods of overcoming problems in communicating with people of the opposite sex and from different cultures.

Improving the Sending of Messages

Improving the way messages are sent will help overcome communication barriers. Implementing the following suggestions will improve the chances that messages are received as intended.

1. *Clarify ideas before communicating.* Many communications fail because of inadequate planning and lack of understanding of the true nature of the message to be communicated. To plan effectively, managers and professionals must consider the goals and attitudes of those who will receive the message and those who will be affected by it. Part of clarifying ideas is to present them in a clear, exciting manner, at a level appropriate for the audience.

2. *Motivate the receiver.* The recipient of the message has to be motivated to attend to the message. This is best accomplished by appealing to the receiver's interests or needs. In sending a message to higher-level management, it is important to frame it in terms of how it contributes to earning money, saving money, or productivity.

3. *Discuss differences in paradigms.* A method for understanding and dealing with differences in frames of references is to recognize that people have different **paradigms** that influence how they interpret events. A paradigm is a model, framework, viewpoint, or perspective. When two people look at a situation with different paradigms, a communication problem may occur. For instance, a business owner might say, "We should be able to get this order ready for shipment by Monday morning if we work all day Saturday and Sunday." The employee may respond "How horrible. Nobody works on Saturday and Sunday; those are family days." From the paradigm of the business owner, you work as much as necessary to meet a business goal. From the standpoint of this worker in particular, a person works a limited number of hours, and reserves other times for personal activities.

   The solution to this communication clash is to discuss the paradigms. Both people live by different rules or guidelines (a major contributor to a paradigm). If the two people can recognize that they are operating with different paradigms, the chances for agreement are improved. Keep in mind that people can change their paradigms when the reasons are convincing.[18] For example, the worker in the preceding situation may never have thought about investing time on weekends to help the employer succeed.

4. *Foster informal communication.* An abundance of informal, open communication enhances trust within an organization. Negative rumors are less likely to appear on the grapevine when talking about sensitive topics is a natural event. Ample casual meeting areas such as lounges and conference rooms also contribute to informal communication. Management by walking around and chance encounters are other contributors to the flow of informal communication.

5. *Communicate feelings behind the facts.* The facts in a message should be accompanied by the appropriate feelings. Feelings add power and conviction to the message. The sender of the message should explain his or her personal feelings and encourage the receiver to do the same. For example, a manager who is disappointed with the quality of a finished product might say, "The product has a cheap look. I'm disappointed with the attention you paid to product design. How do you feel about my criticism?" A less-effective approach would be to simply criticize the poor design without mentioning feelings.

6. *Be aware of nonverbal behavior.* A speaker's tone of voice, expression, and apparent receptiveness to the responses of others have an impact on the receiver. These subtle nonverbal aspects of communication often affect the listener's reaction to a message even more than the content of the communication. When sending messages to others, it is important to keep in mind all the aspects of nonverbal behavior previously described.

7. *Obtain feedback.* The best efforts at communication may be wasted if feedback on how well the message came across is not received. Asking questions, encouraging the receiver to express reactions, following up on contacts, and subsequently reviewing performance are ways of obtaining feedback. A powerful method of obtaining feedback is to request, "Could you please summarize what you heard me say?"

8. *Adapt to the other person's communication style.* People communicate more freely with those who match their communication style. If you want to assume the burden for decreasing communication barriers with another person, then make some adaptations to his or her style. If your communication target prefers e-mail messages to telephone calls, emphasize e-mail when communicating with him or her. If your manager prefers brief, bulleted summaries rather than well-developed narrative reports, prepare such brief reports for him or her. If your target responds best to anecdotes, develop anecdotes to support your major points. In contrast, if the receiver prefers statistics to anecdotes, prepare statistics to support major points. It is usually possible to learn the other person's style by careful observation, and my posing a question such as, "How do you like your information presented?"

Improving the Receiving of Messages

Listening is a basic part of communication, and many communication problems stem from the intended receiver not listening carefully. Reducing communication barriers requires a special type of listening. **Active listening** means listening for full meaning without making premature judgments or interpretations. The active listener listens intently, with the goal of empathizing with the speaker. As a result of listening actively, the listener can feed back to the speaker what he or she thinks the speaker meant. Observing nonverbal cues is another facet of active listening. For example, if an employee laughs slightly whenever he mentions a deadline, dig for more information. The laughter may signal that he thinks the deadline is unrealistic.[19]

An active listener also avoids traps such as reacting too quickly to a word that stirs emotion. Instead he or she carefully interprets the word and analyzes what the word might mean to the sender. The active listener might hear a speaker say, "People with a weak work ethic have no place in this company." Before getting angry or accepting the entire message, the active listener would wait to find out what the sender really means by a "weak work ethic."

Listening can be an important factor in business success. Many companies invest considerable time and energy to better understand the thinking, values, and behavior patterns of their customers. Quite often the same processes the companies use to gain insights into their external customers can be used to learn more about their own employees. One executive who emphasized the importance of listening to employees was Sam Walton, founder of Wal-Mart. Walton was fanatical about visiting his stores, listening and learning and watching.[20] More recent Wal-Mart executives have followed in his tradition.

The suggestions for effective listening presented in Exhibit 8-4 support active listening. In addition, do the Skill-Development Exercise to build your ability to listen actively.

DEALING WITH GENDER DIFFERENCES IN COMMUNICATION STYLE

Explain how to overcome potential cross-gender and cross-cultural communication problems.

Despite the trend toward equality in organizations, substantial interest has arisen in identifying differences in communication style between men and women. People who are aware of these differences will face fewer communication barriers between themselves and members of the opposite sex. As we describe these differences, recognize them as group stereotypes. Individual differences in communication style are usually more important than group (men versus women) differences. Key differences in sex-related communication styles are as follows:[21]

- Women prefer to use communication for rapport building.
- Men prefer to use talk primarily as a means of preserving independence and status, by displaying knowledge and skill.
- Men prefer to work out their problems by themselves, whereas women prefer to talk out solutions with another person.
- Women want empathy, not solutions. When women share feelings of being stressed out, they seek empathy and understanding.
- Women are more likely to compliment the work of a coworker, while men are more likely to be critical.
- Men tend to be more directive in their conversation, while women emphasize politeness.
- Women tend to be more conciliatory when facing differences, while men become more intimidating.
- Men are more interested than women in calling attention to their accomplishments or hogging recognition.
- Men tend to dominate discussions during meetings.
- Women tend to downplay their certainty, while men are more likely to minimize their doubts. As a result, women tend to appear less confident than men even when their confidence levels are equal.

Understanding these differences can help you interpret the behavior of people, thus avoiding a communication block. For example, if a male team member is not as effusive with praise as you would like, remember that he is simply engaging in gender-typical behavior. (Again, this is a gender stereotype that is not universally applicable.) Factor in this gender difference before taking the shortfall personally.

Overcoming Cross-Cultural Communication Barriers

The modern workforce has become more culturally diverse in two major ways. Many subgroups within our own culture have been assimilated into the workforce, and there is increasing interaction with people from other countries. Cultural differences within a diverse country, such as the United States or Canada, can be as pronounced as differences between two countries. Managers therefore face the challenge of preventing and overcoming communication barriers created by differences in language and customs. Sensitivity to cultural differences goes a long way toward overcoming these potential communication barriers. In addition, communicators should keep in mind several suggestions.

1. *Be sensitive to the fact that cross-cultural communication barriers exist. If you are aware of these potential barriers, you will be ready to deal with them.* When you are dealing with a work associate with a different cultural background than yours, solicit feedback in order to minimize cross-cultural barriers to communication.

EXHIBIT 8-4

Eleven Keys to Effective Listening

These keys are a positive guideline to better listening. In fact, they're at the heart of developing better listening habits that could last a lifetime.

Eleven Keys to Effective Listening	The Bad Listener	The Good Listener
1. Find areas of interest	Tunes out dry subjects	Seeks opportunities; asks "What's in it for me?"
2. Judge content, not delivery	Tunes out if delivery is poor	Judges content, skips over delivery errors
3. Hold your fire	Tends to enter into argument	Doesn't judge until comprehension is complete
4. Listen for ideas	Listens for facts	Listens for central themes
5. Be flexible	Takes intensive notes using only one system	Takes fewer notes; uses four or five different systems, depending on speaker
6. Work at listening	Shown no energy output; fakes attention	Works hard; exhibits active body state
7. Resist distractions	Is distracted easily	Fights or avoids distractions, tolerates bad habits, knows how to concentrate
8. Exercise your mind	Resists difficult expository material; seeks light, recreational material	Uses heavier material as exercise for the mind
9. Keep your mind open	Reacts to emotional words	Interprets color words; does not get hung up on them
10. Capitalize on the fact that *thought* is faster than speech	Tends to daydream with slow speakers	Challenges, anticipates, mentally summarizes, weighs the evidence, listens between the lines to tone of voice
11. Restate what you hear	Reacts to what he or she hears	Clarifies what he or she hears until other person says, "Yes, this is what I'm saying."

Sources: John W. Richter, "Listening: An Art Essential to Success," (September 1980): p. 26; Lyman K. Steil, "How Well Do You Listen?" *Executive Female*, Special Issue No. 2 (1986): p. 37.

SKILL-DEVELOPMENT EXERCISE

COLLABORATE

Actively Listening to a Coworker

Before conducting the following role plays, review the keys to effective listening presented in Exhibit 8-4. Suggestion 11 about summarization is particularly important when listening to a person who is talking about an emotional topic.

One student plays the role of a coworker who has just been offered the position of manager of another department. He or she will be receiving 10 percent higher pay and be able to travel overseas twice a year for the company. He or she is eager to describe full details of this good fortune to a coworker. At the same time, the person has some concerns about the

promotion. The person is concerned that his or her spouse might not appreciate the idea of overseas travel.

Another student plays the role of the coworker to whom the first worker wants to describe his or her good fortune. The second worker wants to listen intently to the first worker. At the same time, the listener is facing some urgent work problems and therefore may have to fight being distracted.

Other class members will rate the second person on his or her listening ability.

2. *Show respect for all workers.* The same behavior that promotes good cross-cultural relations in general helps overcome communication barriers. A widely used comment that implies disrespect is to say to a person from another culture, "You have an accent." If you were in that person's culture, you, too, might have an accent.

3. *Use straightforward language and speak slowly and clearly.* When working with people who do not speak your language fluently, speak in an easy-to-understand manner. Minimize the use of idioms and analogies specific to your language. Particularly difficult for foreigners to interpret are sports analogies such as "This should be a slam dunk." Also perplexing are general idioms such as "My manager passed the buck," or "Our competitor is over the hill."

4. *Be alert to cultural differences in customs and behavior.* To minimize cross-cultural communication barriers, recognize that many subtle job-related differences in customs and behavior may exist. For example, Asians typically feel uncomfortable when asked to brag about themselves in the presence of others. From their perspective, calling attention to oneself at the expense of another person is rude and unprofessional. Exhibit 8-5 presents a sampling of cross-cultural differences in customs and behavior that relate to communications.

5. *Be sensitive to differences in nonverbal communication.* All cultures use nonverbal communication, but the specific cues differ across cultures. To receive messages accurately when working with people from diverse cultures, one must be sensitive to these differences. When visiting another country, Americans must be careful not to use the OK signal of a circle formed by the thumb and forefinger. Such a signal is considered an extreme vulgarity in several other cultures, including Germany. (It could be argued that the OK signal is really verbal communication because it is a symbol.)

6. *Do not be diverted by style, accent, grammar, or personal appearance.* Although these superficial factors all relate to business success, they are difficult to interpret when judging a person from another culture. It is therefore better to judge the merits of the behavior.[22] (This is also good advice in dealing with people from your own culture.) A brilliant individual from another culture may be still learning your language and thus make basic mistakes when speaking in your

tongue. He or she might also not have yet developed a sensitivity to dress style in your culture.

THE POWER-ORIENTED LINGUISTIC STYLE

Recognize the basics for becoming a more power-oriented communicator.

A major part of being persuasive involves choosing the right **linguistic style,** a person's characteristic speaking pattern. According to Deborah Tannen, linguistic style involves such behaviors as amount of directness, pacing and pausing, word choice, and the use of such communication devices as jokes, figures of speech, anecdotes, questions, and apologies.[23] A linguistic style is complex because it includes the culturally learned signals by which people communicate what they mean, along with how they interpret what others say and how they evaluate others. The complexity of linguistic style makes it difficult to offer specific prescriptions for using one that is power-oriented. Nevertheless, here are many components of a linguistic style that would give power and authority to the message sender.[24]

- Choose words that show conviction, such as "I'm convinced" or "I'm confident that." Similarly, avoid expressions that convey doubt or hesitancy, such as "I think" or "I hope." Be bold in expressing ideas, yet do not attack people.
- Use the pronoun *I* to receive more credit for your ideas. (Of course, this could backfire in a team-based organization.)
- Emphasize direct rather than indirect talk, such as saying, "I need your report by three tomorrow afternoon," rather than, "I'm wondering if your report will be available by noon tomorrow."
- Frame your comments in a way that increases your listener's receptivity. The *frame* is built around the best context for responding to the needs of others. An example would be to use the frame "let's dig a little deeper" when the other people present know something is wrong, but pinpointing the problem

EXHIBIT 8-5

Cross-Cultural Differences in Communication

- Members of Asian and some Middle-Eastern cultures consider direct eye contact rude.
- Japanese people rarely use the word "no." When they say "yes" ("hai"), it only acknowledges they have heard what was said.
- When Japanese people say "We'll consider it," they probably mean "No."
- Korean people are hesitant to say "no," even when they have rejected a proposal. Koreans feel it is important to have visitors leave with good feelings.
- British people understate their feelings. If a British person says "Your report does raise a few questions," the real meaning is probably "Your report is atrocious."
- People from Latin America are very conscious of rank, and they expect the manager to be the voice of authority. Consequently, Latin Americans may be hesitant to make suggestions to a superior.
- Americans are eager to get down to business quickly and will therefore spend less time than people from other cultures in building a relationship.

- Americans value time much more than do people from other cultures. They are therefore more likely than people from other cultures to appear perturbed when a person shows up late for a meeting.
- French-speaking people tend to use polite forms of greeting, particularly in business settings, while Americans are less formal. When greeting a business contact in a French-speaking country, it is therefore important to include the prefix *sir, monsieur, madame, ms., mademoiselle,* or *miss.*

Skill Development: The above information will lead to cross-cultural skill development if practiced in the right setting. During the next 30 days, look for an opportunity to relate to a person from a given culture in the way described above. Observe the reaction of the other person to provide feedback on your cross-cultural effectiveness.

is elusive. Your purpose is to enlist the help of others in finding the underlying nature of the problem.

- Speak at length, set the agenda for a conversation, make jokes, and laugh. Be ready to offer solutions to problems, as well as suggesting a program or plan. All of these points are more likely to create a sense of confidence in listeners.
- Minimize the number of questions you ask that imply you lack information on a topic, such as, "What do mean that most dot.com companies are burning cash?"
- Apologize infrequently and particularly minimize saying, "I'm sorry."
- Take deep breaths to project a firm voice. People associate a firm voice with power and conviction.
- Occupy as much space as possible when speaking before a group. Stand with your feet approximately 18 inches apart, and place your hands on the top of your hips occasionally. The triangles you create with arms occupy space, and the hand-on-hip gesture symbolizes power to most people.

Despite these suggestions for developing a power-oriented linguistic style, Tannen cautions that here is no one best way to communicate. How to project your power and authority is often dependent upon the people involved, the organizational culture, the relative rank of the speakers, and other situational factors. The power-oriented linguistic style should be interpreted as a general guideline.

IMPLICATIONS FOR MANAGERIAL PRACTICE

1. Interpersonal communication is the basic process by which managers and professionals carry out their functions. It is therefore critical to work toward unclogging communication channels in all directions. Part of unclogging these channels is to overcome communication barriers following some of the guidelines presented in this chapter. It is particularly important to be aware of communication barriers and to recognize the receiver's frame of reference.

2. Two-way communication is usually superior to one-way communication. Interact with the receiver to foster understanding. While delivering your message, ask for verbal feedback and be sensitive to nonverbal signals about how your message is getting across. By so doing, many communication barriers (such as value judgments) will be overcome.

3. Managers and professionals are well advised to pay attention to the nonverbal messages they send and receive. A starting point is to become more conscious of one's facial expression and those of other people. Managerial workers can also listen more carefully to vocal inflections, look closer to see what other people's eyes show about their true feelings, and pay attention to what they wear to transmit the desired messages about themselves. By paying close attention to nonverbal communication, managerial workers can improve communication and consequently improve productivity.

SUMMARY OF KEY POINTS

 Describe the communication process.
Interpersonal communication takes place through the following steps: source (the sender), message, channel (medium), receiver, and feedback. The environment in which the message is sent and noise are also part of the communication process.

 Describe the impact of information technology on interpersonal communication in organizations.
Advances in information technology have influenced the quantity and quality of interpersonal communications in the workplace. Four such advances are e-mail, the alternative workplace, presentation technology, and voice-recognition systems.

E-mail facilitates communication but contributes to information overload. People working from alternative workplaces can lose out on face-to-face human interaction. People who make extensive use of presentation technology sometimes neglect to connect with the audience. Voice-recognition systems require emphasis on clear and precise speech.

 Explain how nonverbal communication can be used to enhance communication.
Nonverbal communication helps express the feeling behind a message and includes the following forms: environment (physical setting), body placement, hand gestures, facial expressions and movements, voice tone, dress and appearance, and mirroring (to establish rapport). One of the many practical applications of nonverbal communication is to project enthusiasm and confidence with body language, such as loosening your facial expression.

 Present details about the various channels of communication in organizations.
Formal communication channels are specified precisely in bureaucratic organizations. These channels are more difficult to follow in a network organization because of its spherical structure of self-directed teams. Informal communication channels supplement the formal channels, with the grapevine being the major informal communication channel. Rumors are an important communication

force within organizations and provide information early. Management by walking around can be classified as both a formal and an informal channel.

Messages in organization travel in five directions: downward, upward, horizontally, diagonally, and spherically (in the network organization). An open-door policy is an example of a formal upward communication channel.

 Summarize the barriers to effective communication and how to overcome them.
Key barriers to communication are as follows: semantics, filtering of negative information, credibility of the sender, mixed signals, different frames of reference, value judgments, and communication overload. Overcoming these barriers can involve such activities as clarifying ideas before sending, motivating the receiver, discussing differences in paradigms, fostering informal communication, communicating feelings behind the facts, being aware of nonverbal behavior, obtaining feedback, and adapting to the other person's communication style. Active listening facilitates receiving messages more accurately.

 Explain how to overcome potential cross-gender and cross-cultural communication problems.
Sensitivity to gender differences in style is important for overcoming communication barriers. For example, men tend to be more directive in their conversation, whereas women emphasize politeness. Cross-cultural communication barriers can be overcome in general by sensitivity to cultural differences. Two specific tactics are to show respect for all workers and to use straightforward language and speak slowly and clearly.

 Recognize the basics for becoming a more power-oriented communicator.
To become a more power-oriented communicator, it is important to choose the right linguistic style. Among the features of a power-oriented linguistic style are choosing words that show conviction, emphasizing direct talk, and apologizing infrequently.

KEY TERMS AND PHRASES

Message, *160*
A purpose or an idea to be conveyed in a communication event.

Noise, *161*
Anything that disrupts communication, including the attitude and emotions of the receiver.

Alternative Workplace, *162*

A combination of nontraditional work practices, settings, and locations, including working from a small satellite office, sharing offices or cubicles, or working from home.

Telecommuting, *162*

Working at home and sending output electronically to the office.

Voice-Recognition System, *164*

An electronic device that can be commanded by human voice.

Nonverbal Communication, *165*

The transmission of messages by means other than words.

Formal Communication Channels, *166*

The official pathways for sending information inside and outside an organization.

Network Organization, *166*

A spherical structure that can rotate self-managing teams and other resources around a common knowledge base.

Informal Communication Channels, *167*

The unofficial network of channels that supplements the formal channels.

Grapevine, *167*

The major informal communication channel in organizations.

Management by Walking Around, *168*

The process of managers intermingling freely with workers on the shop floor, in the office, and with customers.

Open-Door Policy, *168*

An understanding in which any employee can bring a gripe to the attention of upper-level management without checking with his or her immediate manager.

Semantics, *169*

The varying meanings people attach to words.

Filtering, *169*

The coloring and altering of information to make it more acceptable to the receiver.

Mixed Signals, *170*

Communication breakdown resulting from the sending of different messages about the same topic to different audiences.

Frame of Reference, *170*

A perspective and vantage point based on past experience.

Value Judgment, *170*

An overall opinion of something based on a quick perception of its merit.

Communication (or Information) Overload, *170*

A situation that occurs when people are so overloaded with information that they cannot respond effectively to messages, resulting in stress.

Paradigm, *171*

A model, framework, viewpoint, or perspective.

Active Listening, *172*

Listening for full meaning without making premature judgments or interpretations.

Linguistic Style, *176*

A person's characteristic speaking pattern, involving amount of directness, pacing and pausing, word choice, and the use of jokes, figures of speech, questions, and apologies.

DISCUSSION QUESTIONS AND ACTIVITIES

1. Why is communication referred to as "the basic process by which managers get their job done"?
2. A manager recently said, "By the time I answer all my e-mail and voice mail, it's time to go home." What advice can you offer this manager?
3. Watch a business executive on television and evaluate how effectively the person uses nonverbal communication. Be ready to report your findings back to class.
4. What barriers to communication are being created by cellular phones?
5. How can an organization benefit from good upward communication?
6. What ethical problems, if any, do you see in being a power-oriented communicator?
7. Ask a successful person his or her impression of the importance of being a power-oriented communicator. Be prepared to share your observations with classmates.

ORGANIZATIONAL BEHAVIOR ON-LINE

TO DO

Workforce Capabilities

To reinforce your understanding of the importance of good communication skills for professional success, visit The Workforce Skills Website at http://www.scans.jhu.edu. As you work your way through the site, identify the communication skills the federal government commission in question thinks are essential for success in today's workplace. Make a notation to yourself about which of these skills are already strong for you and where you need development.

TO BOOKMARK

Presentation Tips
http://www.fastcompany.com/online/07/124present.html

Telecommuting
http://www.sangabriel.com/telecommuting.htm

Cross-cultural Communication Barriers
http://www.bena.com/ewinters/xculture.html

Nonverbal Communication
http://www.selfgrowth.com/bodyl.html

C A S E   P R O B L E M :   The Scrutinized Team Member Candidate

HRmanagerPLUS.com is a human resources management firm that provides human resource services such as payroll, benefits administration, affirmative action programs, and technical training to other firms. By signing up with HRmanagerPLUS.com, other firms can outsource part or all of their human resources functions. During its seven years of operation, HRmanagerPLUS.com has grown from 3 to 50 employees, and last year had total revenues of $21 million.

Most of the work of the firm is performed by teams, led by a rotating team leader. Each team member takes an 18-month turn at being a team leader. The four-person new ventures team is regarded by CEO and founder, Jerry Clune, as vital for the future of the company. In addition to developing ideas for new services, the team members are responsible for obtaining clients for any new service they propose that is approved by Clune. The new ventures team thus develops and sells new services. After the service is launched and working well, the sales group is responsible for developing more clients.

As with other teams at HRmanagerPLUS.com, the team members have a voice as to who is hired to join their team. In conjunction with Clune, the new ventures team decided it should expand to five members. The team posted the job opening for a new member on an Internet recruiting service, ran classified ads in the local newspaper, and also asked present employees for referrals. One of the finalists for the position was Gina Cleveland, a 27-year-old business school graduate. In addition to interviewing with Clune and the two company vice presidents, Cleveland spent one-half day with the new ventures team, breakfast and lunch included. About two-and-one-half hours of the time was spent in a team interview in which Gina sat in a conference room with the four team members.

The team members agreed that Cleveland appeared to be a strong candidate on paper. Her education and experience were satisfactory, her résumé was impressive, and she presented herself well during a telephone screening interview. After Cleveland completed her time with the new ventures team, the team leader, Lauren Nielsen, suggested that the group hold a debriefing session. The purpose of the session would be to share ideas about Cleveland's suitability for joining the team. Nielsen commented, "It seems like we think that Gina is a strong candidate based on her credentials and what she said. But I'm a big believer in nonverbal communication. Studying Gina's body language can give us a lot of valuable information. Let's each share our observations about what Gina's body language tells us she is *really* like. I'll go first.

Lauren: I liked the way Gina looks so cool and polished when she joined us for breakfast. She's got all the superficial movements right to project self-confidence. But did anybody else notice how she looked concerned when she had to make a choice from the menu? She finally did choose a ham-and-cheese omelet, but she raised her voice at the end of the sentence when she ordered it. I got the hint that Gina is not very confident.

I also noticed Gina biting her lips a little when we asked her how creative she thought she was. I know that Gina said she was creative and gave us an example of a creative project she completed. Yet nibbling at her lips like that suggests she's not filled with fire power.

Michael: I didn't make any direct observations about Gina's being self-confident or not, but I did notice something that could be related. I think Gina is on a power trip, and this could indicate high or low self-confidence. Did anybody notice how Gina put her hands on her hips when she was standing up? That's a pure and clear signal of somebody who wants to be in control. Her haircut is almost the same length and style like most women who've made it to the top in Fortune 500 companies. I think she cloned her hairstyle from Carly Fiorina, the HP honcho.

Another hint I get of Gina's power trip is the way she eyed the check in the restaurant at lunch. I could see it in her eyes that she really wanted to pay for the entire team. That could mean a desire to control and show us that she is very important. Do we want someone on the team with such a strong desire to control?

Brenda: I observed a different picture of Gina based on her nonverbal communication. She dressed just right for the occasion—not too conservatively, not too far business casual. This tells me she can fit into our environment. Did you notice how well-groomed her shoes were? This tells you she is well organized and good at details. Her attaché case was a soft, inviting leather. If she was really into power and control, she would carry a hard vinyl or aluminum attaché case. I see Gina as a confident and assertive person who could blend right into our team.

Larry: I hope that because I'm last, I'm not too influenced by the observations that you three have shared so far. My take is that Gina looks great on paper, but she may have a problem in being a good team player. She's too laid back and distant. Did you notice her handshake? She gave me the impression of wanting to have the least possible physical contact with me. Her handshake was so insincere. I could feel her hand and arm withdrawing from me as she shook my hand.

I also couldn't help noticing that Gina did not lean much toward us during the round table discussion. Do you remember how she would pull her chair back ever so slightly when we got into a heavy discussion? I interpreted that as a sign that Gina does not want to be part of a close-knit group.

Lauren: As you have probably noticed, I've been typing as fast as I can with my laptop, taking notes on what you have said. We have some mixed observations here, and I want to summarize and integrate them before we make a decision. I'll send you an e-mail with an attached file of my summary observations by tomorrow morning. Make any changes you see fit and get back to me. After we have finished evaluating Gina carefully, we will be able to make our recommendations to Jerry (Clune).

Case Questions

1. To what extent are new ventures team members making an appropriate use of nonverbal communication to size up Gina Cleveland?

2. Which team member do you think made the most realistic interpretation of nonverbal behavior? Why?

3. Should Lauren, the team leader, have told Gina in advance that the team would be scrutinizing her nonverbal behavior? Justify your answer.

SUGGESTED READINGS

Balu, Rekha. "Listen Up!" *Fast Company,* May 2000, pp. 304–316.

Conger, Jay A. "The Necessary Art of Persuasion." *Harvard Business Review,* May–June 1998, pp. 84–95.

DeLaat, Jacqueline. *Gender in the Workplace: A Case Study Approach.* Thousand Oaks, CA: Sage Publications, 1999.

DiFonzo, Nicholas, and Bordia, Prashant. "How Top PR Professionals Handle Corporate Hearsay: Corporate Rumors, Their Effects, and Strategies to Manage Them." *Public Relations Review,* Summer 2000, pp. 173–198.

Knight, Sue. *NLP Solutions: How to Model What Works In Business— And Make It Work For You.* London: Nicholas Brealey Publishing, 1995.

Lieber, Ron. "Information is Everything..." *Fast Company,* November 1999, pp. 246–254.

Maggio, Rosalie. *How to Say It: Choice Words, Phrases, Sentences & Paragraphs for Every Situation.* Paramus, NJ: Prentice Hall, 1998.

Rogers, Carl, and Roethlisberger, F. J. "Barriers and Gateways to Communication." *Harvard Business Review,* 1952. (*HBR* classic reprinted November–December 1991) pp. 105–111.

ENDNOTES

1. Cited in "The Top Job Skills for the 21st Century," *People@work,* May 1999, Professional Training Associates *Inc.*

2. Quoted from "Bottom Liners" by Eric and Bill, Inc., in Rochester *Democrat and Chronicle,* April 24, 1995, p. 2.

3. Quoted in "Like It or Not, You've Got Mail," *Business Week,* October 4, 1999, p. 178.

4. Mahlon Apgar, IV, "The Alternative Workplace: Changing Where and How People Work," *Harvard Business Review,* May–June 1998, p. 121.

5. Geoffrey Nunberg, "The Trouble with PowerPoint," *Fortune,* December 20, 1999, pp. 330, 334.

6. Jean Mausehund and R. Neil Dortch, "Presentation Skills in the Digital Age," *Business Education Forum,* April 1999, pp. 30–32.

7. Mausehund and Dortch, "Presentation Skills," pp. 31–32.

8. Jim Baumann, "Voice Recognition," http://www.hitl.washington.edu/scivw/EVE/I.D.2.d.VoiceRecognition.html.

9. Michael Argyle, *Bodily Communication,* 2nd ed. (Madison, CT: International Universities Press, 1990).

10. Jeffrey Jacobi, *The Vocal Advantage* (Upper Saddle River, NJ: Prentice Hall, 1996).

11. Research cited in "Use Body Language to Gain Their Trust," *Managers Edge,* April 2000, p. 5

12. Raymond E. Miles and Charles C. Snow, "The New Network Firm: A Specialized Structure Built on a Human Investment Philosophy," *Organizational Dynamics,* Spring 1995, pp. 6–7.

13. Cited in Mildred L. Culp, "Rumor Important, Say Managers Worldwide," *WorkWise®* syndicated column, March 28, 1999.

14. John P. Kotter, *The General Managers* (New York: Free Press, 1991).

15. Valorie A. McClelland and Richard E. Wilmot, "Improve Lateral Communication," *Personnel Journal,* August 1990, pp. 32–38.

16. Valorie A. McClelland, "Mixed Signals Breed Mistrust," *Personnel Journal,* March 1987, pp. 24–29.

17. Robert A. Dilenschneider, *A Briefing for Leaders: Communication as the Ultimate Exercise of Power* (New York: Harper/Business 1991).

18. Suzette Haden Elgin, *Genderspeak* (New York: Wiley, 1993).

19. The comment about nonverbal cues is from "See How Much You're Missing? How to Listen When You'd Rather Talk," *Working Smart,* April 2000, p. 7.

20. "Listen and Respond: The Communication Two-Step," *Leadership* (American Association International), June 1998, p. 4.

21. Deborah Tannen, *Talking from 9 to 5* (New York: William Morrow, 1994); Tannen, *You Just Don't Understand* (New York: Ballantine, 1990); John Gray, *Men Are from Mars, Women Are from Venus* (New York: HarperCollins, 1992).

22. Roger E. Axtell, *Gestures: The Do's and Taboos of Body Language Around the World* (New York: Wiley, 1990).

23. Deborah Tannen, "The Power of Talk: Who Gets Heard and Why?" *Harvard Business Review,* September–October 1995, pp. 138–148.

24. Tannen, "The Power of Talk," pp. 138–158; "How You Speak Shows Where You Rank," *Fortune,* February 2, 1998, p. 156; "Proven Strategies for Gaining Cooperation," *Managers Edge,* April 2000, p. 4.

Group Dynamics and Teamwork

At Volvo Commercial Finance Inc., in Minneapolis, Minnesota, vice president Doug Olson needed to develop a greater sense of teamwork between his sales force and that of Prévost Car, Inc., a Volvo bus manufacturer in Saint Clair, Quebec. Olson's Group offers financing to Prévost's customers, but bus purchasers can get financing anywhere they choose. So the group is dependent on the Prévost sales force to steer buyers its way.

To help build cooperation and teamwork between the two groups, Olson sent representatives from each group to corporate race-driving school. Olson says that race-car driving was not only appropriate for their two companies, given their respective line of business, but also provided a strong bonding experience. Participants drove around an oval track at Sebring racetrack in Florida at speeds up to 120 mph on straightaways—and they weren't alone on the track. Although the school's instructors took all the real danger out of the experience by staggering the drivers, participants still felt strong rushes of fear-driven adrenaline. The neophyte race-car drivers saw that their safety was as dependent on the driving of their coworkers as on their own newly acquired skills.

"They realized how reliant they were on the person in front and behind them," says Olson. The experience reinforced the message that sales often is both an individual and a team effort, he adds. And despite its pedagogic aspects, it was an exhilarating experience that Olson's employees still relish. "They're still talking about it to this day," he says.

Driving school for the corporate crowd is not a trivial pursuit. The cars, the adrenaline, and the excitement can be had at any of a growing number of driving schools catering to team-building exercises. Two favorite sites are the Porsche Driving Experience at http://www.porschedriving.com and Justin Bell's Viper Driving School at http://www.viperschool.com/.

Source: Reprinted from Michael Hickins, "A Day at the Races," *Management Review* (May 1999): 59. Copyright © 1999 American Management Association International, New York, NY. All rights reserved. http://www.amanet.org.

OBJECTIVES

After reading and studying this chapter and doing the exercises, you should be able to

 Describe the various types of groups in organizations.

 Summarize the stages of group development and key roles members occupy within a work group.

 Identify characteristics of an effective work group.

 Be able to implement two different methods of group problem solving and decision making.

 Pinpoint several potential problems with group effort and know how to prevent them.

 Explain how to foster teamwork.

Chapter 9

183

SO WHAT? **What does sending workers to race-car driving school really mean?** Top management, if it truly believes strongly in the importance of developing teamwork among interdependent individuals and groups, doesn't balk at pursuing high-performance thrills to achieve it. (For workers with less intense needs for thrill-seeking, tamer approaches to achieving the same goal also exist, such as classroom exercises.) The heavy emphasis on teams and group decision making in organizations increases the importance of understanding teams and groups. In modern organizations, standard practice is to organize all sorts of work around groups and teams.[1] Groups are vital to the understanding of organizational behavior because they are the building blocks of the larger organization.

TYPES OF GROUPS AND TEAMS

Describe the various types of groups in organizations.

A **group** is a collection of people who interact with one another, are working toward some common purpose, and perceive themselves to be a group. The head of a customer service team and her staff would be a group. In contrast, 12 people in an office elevator would not be a group because they are not engaged in collective effort. According to Jon R. Katzenbach and Douglas K. Smith, groups and teams function differently.[2] A **team** is a special type of group. Team members have complementary skills and are committed to a common purpose, a set of performance goals, and an approach to the task. An important part of team functioning is **teamwork,** an understanding and commitment to group goals on the part of all team members.

Groups and teams can also be differentiated in other ways. A working group has a strong, clearly focused leader, while a team leader shares leadership roles. A group is characterized by individual accountability, while a team has individual and mutual accountability. Another distinction is that the team delivers actual joint work products. Also, a group strives to run efficient meetings, while a team encourages open-ended discussion and full participation in problem solving.

Groups and teams have been classified in many different ways. Here we describe the distinction between formal versus informal groups and among four different types of work teams.

Formal Versus Informal Groups

Some groups are formally sanctioned by management and the organization itself, while others are not. A **formal group** is one deliberately formed by the organization to accomplish specific tasks and achieve goals. Examples of formal or work groups include departments, projects, task forces, committees, and quality circles. In contrast, **informal groups** emerge over time through the interaction of workers. Although the goals of these groups are not explicitly stated, informal groups typically satisfy a social or recreational purpose. Members of a department who dine together occasionally would constitute an informal group. Yet the same group might also meet an important work purpose of discussing technical problems of mutual interest.

Types of Work Teams

All workplace teams have the common elements of people working together cooperatively and members possessing a mix of skills. We have already described self-directed work teams in Chapter 6. Four other representative work teams include cross-functional teams, top-management teams, affinity groups, and virtual teams. Projects, task forces, and committees are quite similar in design to cross-functional teams, so they do not receive separate mention here. No matter what label the team carries, its broad purpose is to contribute to a *collaborative workplace* in which people help one another achieve constructive goals. The idea is for workers to collaborate (a high level of cooperation) rather than compete with or prevent others from getting their work done.

As teams have become more common in the workplace, much effort has been directed toward specifying the skills and knowledge needed to function effectively on a team, particularly a self-directed work team. The Self-Assessment that follows presents a representative listing of team skills perceived as necessary by employers. How many team skills do you possess?

Cross-Functional Teams

It is common practice for teams to be composed of workers from different specialties. A **cross-functional team** is a work group composed of workers from different specialties, but about the same organizational level, who come together to accomplish a task. The purpose of the cross-functional team is to get workers from different specialties to blend their talents toward a task that requires such a mix.

Product development is the most frequent purpose of a cross-functional team. In addition, cross-functional teams are used for such purposes as improving quality, reducing costs, and running a company (in the form of a top-management team). Northwestern Mutual Life has been using cross-functional teams for various purposes almost as long as the company has been in business. In recent years, a cross-functional team created the company's Web site (http://www.northwesternmutual.com). Most Northwestern cross-functional teams now include an individual who has no responsibility for the problem—one who is not a stakeholder. The outside perspective is thought to be effective in stimulating the thinking of other team members.

The largest British design firm, Imagination Ltd., successfully uses cross-functional teams to accomplish their client assignments. The company does a variety of design work including graphic design, Web sites, production introductions, and visitor centers. A recent assignment called for the company to make a waiting line at Britain's Millennium Dome more manageable. The firm started with a team of in-house employees—an architect, a lighting designer, a graphic designer, and a film director. Eventually the core Imagination team brought a choreographer in to join the group. Workers at Imagination practiced true teamwork and recognized that the talent of the team is greater than the talent of its individual members.[3]

To perform well on a cross-functional team, a person would have to think in terms of the good of the larger organization, rather than in terms of his or her own specialty. For example, a manufacturing technician might say, "If I propose using expensive components for the Net-access pager, would the product cost too much for its intended market?"

Top Management Team

The group of managers at the top of most organizations is referred to as a team, the management team, or the top-management team. Yet as team expert Jon R. Katzenbach observes, few groups of top managers function as a team in the sense of the definition presented earlier in this chapter.[4] The CEO gets most of the publicity, along with credit and blame for what goes wrong. Nevertheless, groups of top managers are teams in the sense that most major decisions are made

SELF-ASSESSMENT

Team Skills

A variety of skills are required to be an effective member of various types of teams. Several different business firms use this skill inventory to help guide team members toward the competencies they need to become high-performing team members. Review each team skill listed and rate your skill level for each one, using the following classification:

S = strong (capable and comfortable with effectively implementing the skill)
M = moderate (demonstrated skill in the past)
B = basic (minimum ability in this area)
N = not applicable (not relevant to the type of work I do)

Skill Level (S, M, B, or N)

Communication Skills

Speak effectively _____
Foster open communications _____
Listen to others _____
Deliver presentations _____
Prepare written communication _____

Self-management Skills

Act with integrity _____
Demonstrate adaptability _____
Engage in personal development _____
Strive for results _____
Commitment to work _____

Thought Process Skills

Innovate solutions to problems _____
Use sound judgment _____
Analyze issues _____
Think "outside the box" _____

Organizational Skills

Know the business _____
Use technical/functional expertise _____
Use financial/quantitative data _____

Strategic Skills

Recognize big picture impact _____
Promote corporate citizenship _____
Focus on customer needs _____
Commit to quality _____
Manage profitability _____

collaboratively with all members of the top-management group included. Michael Dell (Dell Computers) and Steve Jobs (Apple Computers) are examples of highly visible and brilliant CEOs who regularly consult with their trusted advisors before making major decisions.

The term *top-management team* has another less frequent meaning. A handful of companies are actually run by a committee of two or more top executives who claim to share power equally. In this way, they are like a husband-and-wife team running a household. An example of power sharing at the top to form a two-person team is the merger of Exxon and Mobil. Some observers are skeptical that a company can really be run well without one key executive having the final decision. Can you imagine your favorite athletic team having two head coaches, or your favorite band having two leaders?

Affinity Groups

Different types of work teams continue to emerge to meet organizational needs. A recent example of a new variation of a team is the **affinity group,** an employee-involvement group composed of professional-level (or knowledge) workers. The members are colleagues who meet regularly to share information, capture opportunities, and solve problems affecting the work group and the larger organization. The group is self-directing and has a formal charter.[5] An application of an affinity group took place at a large branch of Merrill Lynch. A group of investment counselors met regularly to discuss how they could better meet the needs of their many clients who were accepting early retirement. The group developed a package of investments that met the special needs of people who retired young and had a long life expectancy. The new program met with high acceptance from the clients it intended to serve.

Virtual Team

Some teams conduct most of their work by sending electronic messages to one another rather than conducting face-to-face meetings. A **virtual team** is a small group of people who conduct almost all of their collaborative work by electronic communication rather than face-to-face meetings. In the language of information technology, they engage in "cybercollaboration" by conducting "cybermeetings." E-mail is the usual medium for sharing information and conducting meetings. *Groupware* is another widely used approach to conducting a cybermeeting. Using groupware, several people can edit a document at the same time or in sequence. Desktop videoconferencing is another technological advance that facilitates the virtual team.[6] Electronic brainstorming, as described in Chapter 4, is well suited for a virtual team.

Most high-tech companies make some use of virtual teams and cybermeetings. Strategic alliances in which geographically dispersed companies work with one another are a natural for virtual teams. It's less expensive for the field technician in Iceland to hold a cybermeeting with her counterparts in South Africa, Mexico, and California than to bring them all together in one physical location. IBM makes some use of virtual teams in selling information technology systems, partially because so many IBM field personnel work from their homes and vehicles. Virtual teams are also an effective way of responding to new workforce demographics where the most talented employees may be located anywhere in the world, and may demand personal flexibility in terms of when and where to perform work.[7]

Despite the efficiency of virtual teams, there are times when face-to-face interaction is necessary to deal with complex and emotional issues. Negotiating a new contract between management and a labor union, for example, is not well suited to a cybermeeting.

The accompanying Organizational Behavior in Action is mostly about self-directed teams. However, the employees also belong to affinity groups.

Organizational Behavior *in Action*

S E I   I n v e s t m e n t s   I n v e s t   i n   T e a m s

from the moment you step into headquarters of SEI Investments, you know you're not in old-fashioned corporate America anymore. Spread out on a rural hillside near Valley Forge, Pennsylvania, the large asset-management company inhabits five industrial-style buildings. SEI manages or acts as an administrator for $121 billion in assets, mostly in mutual funds. The company manages back-office operations for the trust departments at 85 of the largest 200 U.S. banks and also runs an investment advisory service for wealthy individuals.

Inside, exposed structural steel, pipes, and ducts—painted fuchsia and blue in one building and yellow, gold, and red in another—carry through the factory motif. Most striking, however are the thick coils of wire hanging from the ceiling—staffers call them "pythons"—containing phone, computer, and electrical wiring. The coils carry electricity, a dial tone, and Internet access. Looking closer, you see that all the office equipment, desks, chairs, computers, and filing cabinets are on wheels.

The design was inspired by SEI's need to change—frequently, quickly, and cheaply. The business began in 1973 making software for bank trust companies. With accelerating speed, it has added services and products such as mutual funds and 401(k) administration, and cash-management programs for investment advisors. Out of necessity, employees are constantly shifting and recombining to develop new services and products to meet customers' shifting groups of needs. CEO Al West says he got tired of paying $2,000 per move per person to relocate furniture and redo wiring under the floors. These days, when teams switch assignments—which may happen at least once a year—they just unplug their pythons, wheel their chairs and desks to the next location, plug into a new python, and go to work. SEI can get a new team resettled and working in an hour or two.

The rolling furniture isn't the only thing that's flexible at SEI. The defining unit of operation at SEI is the team, with work being distributed among approximately 140 self-managed teams. Teams have as few as 2 members or as many as 30. Different teams have different structures. Most employees belong to one base team and to three or four ad hoc teams. The ad hoc teams give SCI a feel of perpetual motion. A batch of teams organizes and delivers the company's products and services. Tasks not central to business—personnel benefits and food services, for example—are outsourced. Teams do their own recruiting for new employees and perform all the secretarial work themselves, and they definitely get their own coffee. SEI awards annual productivity bonuses to teams, and their leaders decide how to split the money. "Working on different teams allows you to be totally outside the box with no physical or emotional barriers," says Alice Lidenauer, a team business manager.

When CEO West reorganized SEI over ten years ago, he tore down the corporate pyramid. "We disenfranchised the upper-level people and enfranchised the lower-level people."

For an inside look at SEI's office architecture—pythons included—view the photographs at Meyer, Scherer & Rockcastle, Ltd., the firm's architects, at http://www.msrltd.com/sei.html.

Sources: Jeremy Main, "The Shape of the New Corporation," *Working Woman*, October 1998, pp. 61–62; Scott Kirsner, "Everyday It's A New Place," *Fast Company*, May 1998, pp. 132–134.

STAGES OF GROUP DEVELOPMENT

Key to understanding the nature of work groups is what the group is doing (the content) and how it proceeds (the process). A key group process is how a group develops over time. To make this information more meaningful, relate it to any group to which you have belonged for at least one month. Understanding the stages of group development can lead to more effective group leadership or membership. The five group stages are shown in Exhibit 9-1 and described next.[8]

Stage 1: Forming. At the outset, members are eager to learn what tasks they will be performing, how they can benefit from group membership, and what constitutes acceptable behavior. Members often inquire about rules they must follow. Confusion, caution, and communality are typical during the initial phase of group development.

Stage 2: Storming. During this "shakedown" period, individual styles often come into conflict. Hostility, infighting, tension, and confrontation are typical. Members may argue to clarify expectations of their contributions. Coalitions and cliques may form within the group, and one or two members may be targeted for exclusion. Subgroups may form to push for an agenda of interest to them. (Despite the frequency of storming, many workplace groups work willingly with one another from the outset, thus skipping stage 2.)

Stage 3: Norming. After the storm comes the quiet of overcoming resistance and establishing group standards of conduct (norms). Cohesiveness and commitment begin to develop. The group starts to come together as a coordinated unit, and harmony prevails. Norms stem from three sources. The group itself quickly establishes limits for members, often by effective use of glares and nods. For example, the team member who swears at the leader might receive angry glances from other members. Norms may also be imposed that are derived from the larger organization and from professional codes of conduct. A third source of norms might be an influential team member who inspires the group to elevate its performance or behavior. A member of a sales team at Western New York Computing (systems and software) said to the other team members, "Why stop at being the best in this city? Let's develop a regional reputation."

Stage 4: Performing. When the group reaches the performing stage, it is ready to focus on accomplishing its key tasks. Issues concerning interpersonal relations and task assignment are put aside as the group becomes a well-functioning unit. Intrinsic motivation and creativity are likely to emerge as the group performs. At their best, members feel they are working "for the cause," much like a political campaign team or one team bringing a breakthrough product to market.

Summarize the stages of group development and key roles members occupy within a work group.

189

South-Western's animated concept and activity site at *http://www. experiencingob.com* provides a neat extension of key issues regarding the nature of work groups, including stages in group development, team cohesiveness, and social loafing. Exclusive review tools on the topic of Teams add dimension to your study of group dynamics. Free demo available!

EXHIBIT
9-1

The Stages of Group Development

Most groups follow a predictable sequence of stages.

Stage 5: Adjourning. Temporary work groups are abandoned after their task has been accomplished, much like a project team to erect an office tower. The same group members, however, have developed important relationships and understandings they can bring with them should they be part of the same team in the future. The link between adjourning and forming shown in Exhibit 9-1 is that many groups do reassemble after one project is completed. The link between Stages 1 and 5 would not apply for a group that disbanded and never worked together again.

A key managerial challenge is to help the group move past the first three stages into performing. At times, group members may have to be challenged that they are spending too much time on process issues and not enough on the task.

Roles within Groups

Another perspective on group process is to identify team members' roles.[9] Positive roles are described here to help you identify areas of possible contribution in group effort.

1. *Knowledge contributor.* Being technically proficient, the knowledge contributor provides the group with useful and valid information. He or she is intent upon helping with task accomplishment and also values sharing technical expertise with team members.

2. *Process observer.* A person occupying this role forces the group to look at how it is functioning with statements such as: "We've been at it for two and a half hours, and we have only taken care of one agenda item. Shouldn't we be doing better?" The process observer might also point to excellent team progress.

3. *People supporter.* A person occupying this role assumes some of the leader's responsibility for providing emotional support to teammates and resolving conflict. He or she serves as a model of active listening, while others are presenting. The people supporter helps others relax by smiling, making humorous comments, and appearing relaxed. He or she supports and encourages team members even when disagreeing with them.

4. *Challenger.* To prevent complacency and noncritical thinking, a team needs one or more members who confront and challenge bad ideas. A challenger will criticize any decision or preliminary thinking that is deficient in any way, including being ethically unsound. Effective interpersonal skills are required to be a challenger. Antagonistic, attack-style people who attempt the challenger role lose their credibility quickly because they appear more interested in attack than solving problems.

5. *Listener.* Listening contributes so substantially to team success that it comprises a separate role, even though other roles involve listening. If other people are not heard, the full contribution of team effort cannot be realized. As a result of being a listener, a team member or team leader is able to summarize discussion and progress for the team.

6. *Mediator.* Disputes within the group may become so intense and prolonged that two people no longer listen or respond to each other. The two antagonists develop such polarized viewpoints that they are unwilling to move toward each other's point of view. Furthermore, they have moved beyond the point that conciliation is possible. At this point, the team leader or a team member must mediate the dispute.

7. *Gatekeeper.* A recurring problem in group effort is that some members may fail to contribute because other team members dominate the discussion. Even when the viewpoints of the timid team members have been expressed, they may not be remembered because one or two other members contribute so frequently to discussion. When the opportunity gate is closed to several members, the gatekeeper pries it open. He or she requests that a specific team member be allowed to contribute or that the member's past contribution be recognized.

8. *Take-charge leader.* Some teams cry out for direction because either a formal leader has not been appointed or the appointed leader is unusually laid-back. In such situations, a team member can assume the role of the take-charge leader. The problem could be that team members are hesitant to make even simple decisions or take a stand on controversial matters. A starting point for the take-charge leader is to encourage the team to define its mission and list its three main objectives.

The Skill-Development Exercise on page 192 gives you an opportunity to identify and observe the roles just described. Recognize, however, that these roles may overlap; they are not entirely independent of each other.

Job Design

Effective work groups follow the principles of job design embodied in job enrichment and the job characteristics model described in Chapter 6. For example, task significance and task identity are both strong. A major theme is self-management, as practiced by self-managing work teams. A closely related attribute is participation in key decisions by work group members, such as how to improve quality.

Interdependence

Effective work groups are characterized by several types of interdependence. Such groups show *task interdependence* in the sense that members interact and depend on one another to accomplish the work. Task interdependence is valuable because it increases motivation and enhances the sense of responsibility for the work of other group members.

CHARACTERISTICS OF EFFECTIVE WORK GROUPS

Groups, like individuals, have characteristics that contribute to their uniqueness and effectiveness. As shown in Exhibit 9-2, these characteristics can be grouped into eight categories. Our description of work group effectiveness follows this framework.[10]

Identify characteristics of an effective work group.

Job Design

Effective work groups follow the principles of job design embodied in job enrichment and the job characteristics model described in Chapter 6. For example, task significance and task identity are both strong. Group members therefore perceive their work as having high intrinsic motivation.

A Feeling of Empowerment

An effective group or team believes that it has the authority to solve a variety of problems without first obtaining approval from management. Empowered teams share four experiences: potency, meaningfulness, autonomy, and impact. *Potency* refers to teams members believing in themselves and exhibiting a confident can-do attitude. Teams with a sense of *meaningfulness* have a strong collective commitment

SKILL-DEVELOPMENT EXERCISE

COLLABORATE

Team Member Roles

Small teams are formed to conduct a 45-minute meeting on a significant topic. Possibilities include (1) a management team deciding on whether to lay off one-third of the workforce in order to increase profits, or (2) a group of fans who have volunteered to find a new team mascot name to replace "Redskins."

While the team members are conducting their heated discussion, other class members make notes of which team members carry out which roles. Watching for the seven different roles can perhaps be divided among class members, such as people in the first row looking for examples of Knowledge Contributor. Use the role worksheet below to help you make your observations. Summarize the comments indicative of the role.

Knowledge Contributor: _____
_____
_____

Process Observer: _____
_____
_____

People Supporter: _____
_____
_____

Challenger: _____
_____
_____

Listener: _____
_____
_____

Mediator: _____
_____
_____

Gatekeeper: _____
_____
_____

Take Charge Leader: _____
_____
_____

to their mission and see their goals as valuable and worthwhile. *Autonomy* refers to the freedom, discretion, and control the teams experience (the same as in job enrichment). A team experiences *impact* when members see the impact of their work on other interested parties such as customers and coworkers.[11]

Interdependence

Effective work groups are characterized by several types of interdependence. Such groups show *task interdependence* in the sense that members interact and depend on one another to accomplish work. Task interdependence is valuable because it increases motivation and enhances the sense of responsibility for the work of other group members.

Goal interdependence refers to the linking of individual goals to the group's goals. A member of a sales team might establish a compensation goal for herself, but she can realize this goal only if the other team members achieve similar success. Aside from the fact of interdependence, clearly defined goals are a major requirement for group effectiveness. *Interdependent feedback and rewards* also contribute to group effectiveness. Individual feedback and rewards should be linked to group performance to encourage good team play.

Right Mix and Size

A variety of factors relating to the mix of group members are associated with effective work groups. A diverse group of members with respect to factors such as experience, knowledge, and education generally improves problem solving. Cultural diversity tends to enhance creativity because various viewpoints are brought into play. Current research cautions, however, that only when each member of the group enjoys high-quality interactions can the full benefits of diversity be realized. The interactions relate to both the task itself (such as talking about improving a motorcycle starter) and social interactions (such as chatting about children during a break).[12]

Groups should be large enough to accomplish the work, but when groups become too large, confusion and poor coordination may result. Also, larger groups tend to be less cohesive. Cross-functional teams, work teams, committees, and task forces tend to be most productive with seven to ten members. Another important composition factor is the quality of the group or team members. Bright people with constructive personality characteristics contribute the most to team effectiveness. A study involving 652 employees composing 51 work teams found that

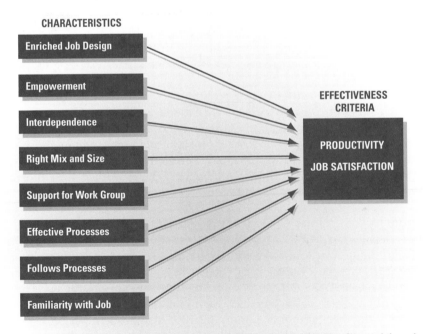

EXHIBIT 9-2

Work Group Characteristics Related to Effectiveness

Sources: Michael A. Campion, Ellen M. Papper, and Gina Medsker, "Relations between Work Team Characteristics and Effectiveness: A Replication and Extension," *Personnel Psychology,* Summer 1996, p. 431; David E. Hyatt and Thomas M. Ruddy, "An Examination of the Relationship between Work Group Characteristics and Performance: Once More into the Breech," *Personnel Psychology,* Autumn 1997, p. 579; Brian D. Janz, Jason A. Colquitt, and Raymond A. Noe, "Knowledge Worker Team Effectiveness: The Role of Autonomy, Interdependence, Team Development, and Contextual Support Variables," *Personnel Psychology,* Winter 1997, pp. 877–904; Bradley L. Kirkman and Benson Rosen, "Powering Up Teams," *Organizational Dynamics,* Winter 2000, pp. 48–52.

teams with members higher in mental ability, conscientiousness, extraversion, and emotional stability received higher supervisor ratings for team performance.[13] (Put winners on your team, and you are more likely to have a winning team.)

Support for the Work Group

The resources available to support the group and the context (environment) influence effectiveness. Key support factors include giving the group the information it needs, coaching group members, providing the right technology, and receiving recognition and other rewards. *Training* quite often facilitates work group effectiveness. The training content typically includes group decision making, interpersonal skills, technical knowledge, and the team philosophy. *Managerial support* in the form of investing resources and believing in group effort fosters effectiveness. *Communication and cooperation between groups* improves group effectiveness, and management must help create the right environment for it to occur.

A contributing factor to the success of the highly productive Kansas City Harley plant is that workers say the higher-ups pay more than lip service to the concept of "partnership": They pay attention in such ways as granting worker requests about funding for new equipment and machinery.

Effective Processes within the Group

Many processes (activities) that influence effectiveness take place within the group. One is the belief that the group can do the job, reflecting high team spirit. Effectiveness is also enhanced when workers provide *social support* to one another through such means as helping one another have positive interactions. *Workload sharing* is another process characteristic related to effectiveness. *Communication and cooperation* within the work group also contribute to effectiveness. Collectively, the right amount of these process characteristics contributes to *cohesiveness,* or a group that pulls together. Without cohesiveness, a group will fail to achieve synergy.

Follows Processes and Procedures

Teams that can be trusted to follow work processes and procedures tend to perform better. Adhering to such processes and procedures is also associated with high-quality output. Although following processes and procedures might appear to be a routine expectation, many problems are created by workers who fail to do so. For example, a group might show a productivity dip if workers on a project fail to back up computer files and a computer virus attacks.

Familiarity with Jobs, Coworkers, and the Environment

Another important set of factors related to work-group effectiveness is familiarity. It refers to the specific knowledge group members have of their jobs, coworkers, and the environment. Familiarity essentially refers to experience, and for many types of job experience—at least to the point of proficiency—is an asset. The contribution of familiarity is evident also when new members join an athletic team. Quite often the team loses momentum during the adjustment period.

To help you pull together loads of information about the characteristics of effective work groups and teams, study the following summary of research conducted with professional-level workers in a financial services firm. The researchers concluded:

> The high-performing teams performed a variety of tasks that members perceived to be significant. They were allowed a high degree of self-management,

were interdependent in terms of tasks, goals and feedback, and functioned as a single team. They tended to have members with complementary skills who were flexible in the tasks they performed. They were not too large for the tasks assigned them. They were well supported by the organization in terms of training, managerial support, and cooperation and communication from other teams. They had confidence in their teams' abilities, and members supported one another, communicated, cooperated, and fairly shared the workload.[14]

The characteristics of an effective work group or team should be supplemented by effective leadership. Team leaders must emphasize coaching more than controlling. Instead of being a supervisor, the leader becomes a team developer.

GROUP PROBLEM SOLVING AND DECISION MAKING

Be able to implement two different methods of group problem solving and decision making.

The use of teams in industrial, military, and medical contexts is on the rise and is likely to continue. The majority of U.S. business firms now use some types of teams.[15] A major activity of many of these teams is to make decisions. Furthermore, most major decisions in organizations are made by teams and other groups. In general, decision making by groups has proven superior to individual decision making. An exception is that individuals can generate more creative solutions to problems by themselves than in group brainstorming.[16]

One method of group problem solving, brainstorming, was described in Chapter 4. Here we describe group decision-making styles, along with two other methods of group decision making and problem solving—the nominal group and delphi techniques.

Group Decision-Making Styles

The term *group decision making* refers to the fact that the group plays a role in making the decision. Group decision making takes place in different degrees. One extreme is *consultative* in which the group leader consults with members before making a decision. The other extreme is *democratic* in which the problem at hand is turned over to the group, and they are empowered to make the decision themselves.

Midway between the two is *consensus* decision making in which the manager shares the problem with group members. Together they generate and evaluate alternatives and attempt to reach agreement on a solution. Consensus is achieved when every member can say, "I have had an opportunity to express my views fully, and they have been thoughtfully considered by the group. Even though this solution is not the one I believe is optimal, it is acceptable and I will support it. I endorse the validity of the process we have undertaken."[17]

The Nominal Group Technique

The opposite of an interacting group is a nominal group whose distinguishing characteristic is silent effort during part of group problem solving. Brainstorming by computer allows for the same noninteractive input by group members. The steps in the **nominal group technique (NGT)** proceed as follows:

1. Members of the target group are chosen and brought together.
2. If the group is too large, it is divided into subgroups of eight or fewer.
3. The group leader presents a specific question.
4. Individual members silently and independently record their ideas in writing.

5. Each group member (one at a time, in turn. around the table) presents one idea to the group without discussion. The ideas are summarized and recorded on a chalkboard, flipchart, or sheet of paper on the wall. If computers are used, the output can be displayed on a large monitor.

6. After all members have presented their ideas, a discussion takes place to clarify and evaluate the ideas.

7. The meeting terminates with a silent, and independent, voting by individuals through a rank ordering (such as using a 1-to-10 scale). The nominal group decision is the pooled outcome of the individual rankings.[18]

The NGT has met with acceptance because it results in a disciplined decision. An advantage of this technique is that it combines the merits of individual reflection with the scrutiny of collective thought. Also, the NGT helps introverted people become actively involved in group activity.

The Delphi Technique

In some decision-making situations, group input is needed, yet it is difficult to bring people together because of the cost or time away from the office. Managers might also believe that teleconferencing is not appropriate for decision making. The **Delphi technique** is well suited for these purposes. It is a group decision-making technique designed to provide group members with one another's ideas and feedback, while avoiding some of the problems associated with interacting groups.[19]

As outlined in Exhibit 9-3, the Delphi technique incorporates a carefully structured sequence of questionnaires distributed to each group member. Each person answers the questionnaire about the problem at hand and transmits his or her responses and thoughts to the coordinator. As the questionnaires go through successive iterations, feedback is provided to the people working on the problem. Problem solving ordinarily improves with each successive input. In the last round of the questionnaire, group members are asked to vote for their choice of solutions. Responses are sometimes averaged. At other times, some people's choices are given more weight than others'.

A modern way to implement the Delphi technique is to use e-mail. Each person receiving the report makes his or her modification on the attached file and then passes it to the next recipient. The coordinator edits the final version containing successive input from all the participants. The Delphi technique becomes a type of chain letter.

An important part of group decision making is not apparent from the discussions of the NGT and Delphi techniques. Asking tough questions often enhances group decision making, as illustrated in the accompanying Organizational Behavior in Action.

POTENTIAL PROBLEMS WITHIN GROUPS

Pinpoint several potential problems with group effort and know how to prevent them.

Group activity, including group decision making, does not always lead to superior results. Failure to attain outstanding results typically stems from lacking the characteristics of effective work groups, as summarized in Exhibit 9-2. For example, a work team might fail if it was not empowered, the members all had the same functional background, and the group was poorly trained. Furthermore, the team lacked the support of management, members did not support one another, and members were quite unfamiliar with the task and one another. For these and perhaps other reasons, informal studies, formal studies, and anecdotal evidence from consultants estimate a failure rate of at least 50 percent for self-directed teams.[20]

EXHIBIT 9-3

Steps in the Delphi Process

The Delphi technique allows for refining a questionnaire or report by participants building on inputs from one another.

Source: R. J. Tersine and W. E. Riggs, "The Delphi Technique: A Long-Range Planning Tool," *Business Horizon* (April 1976): p. 53. Copyright © 1976 by the Foundation for the School of Business at Indiana University.

Work group failures also stem from dysfunctional processes. Here we look at three major processes within groups that can hamper their effectiveness: group polarization, social loafing, and groupthink.

Group Polarization

During group problem solving, or group discussion in general, members often shift their attitudes. Sometimes, the group moves toward taking greater risks, called the risky shift. At other times, the group moves toward a more conservative position.

Organizational Behavior *in Action*

A s k i n g   T o u g h   Q u e s t i o n s   a t   G o r e

W L. Gore & Associates, makers of GoreTex™ (the waterproof fabric), is known for organizing small teams around business opportunities. President Bob Gore participates in group problem-solving sessions. He is known for his skill in asking the right question. "Sometimes it's a bit embarrassing," said one associate. "Here you've been working on a project for six months to a year and you're overlooking what proves to be an obvious question. Bob comes in, and in ten minutes he's asking what everybody else hasn't noticed. So you don't feel great that you've missed it, but at least the project is back running again."

Bob Gore once had a discussion with an associate who wanted to lead a Gore-Tex fabrics effort into a new market segment. Gore made almost no statements during the whole 90-minute meeting, but instead asked hundreds of questions—from market forecasts to the associate's "dream" for a business. Afterward, the associate marveled at the thoroughness of Gore's questioning. The list of questions was subsequently typed up and circulated among associates responsible for developing new market segments.

Fortune recently named W.L. Gore to its list of the "100 Best Companies to Work for in America." Not surprising, considering how much the CEO challenges his associates. To learn more, visit http://www.gore.com.

Source: Michael Pacanowsky, "Team Tools for Wicked Problems," *Organizational Dynamics* (Winter 1995): p. 40.

The general term for moving in either direction is **group polarization,** a situation in which postdiscussion attitudes tend to be more extreme than prediscussion attitudes.[21] For example, as a result of group discussion, members of an executive team become more cautious about entering a new market.

Group discussion facilitates polarization for several reasons. Discovering that others share our opinions may reinforce and strengthen our position. Listening to persuasive arguments may also strengthen our convictions. The "it's not my fault" attitude is another contributor to polarization. If responsibility is diffused, a person will feel less responsible—and guilty—about taking an extreme position.

Group polarization has a practical implication for managers who rely on group decision making. Workers who enter into group decision making with a stand on an issue may develop more extreme postdecision positions. For example, a group of employees who were seeking more generous benefits may decide as a group that the company should become an industry leader in employee benefits.

Social Loafing

An unfortunate by-product of group effort is that an undermotivated person can often squeeze by without contributing a fair share. **Social loafing** is freeloading, or shirking individual responsibility, when a person is placed in a group setting and removed from individual accountability. If you have worked on group projects for courses you may have encountered this widely observed dysfunction of collective effort.

Two motivational explanations of social loafing have been offered. First, some people believe that because they are part of a team, they can "hide in the crowd."

Second, group members typically believe that others are likely to withhold effort when working in a group. As a consequence, they withhold effort themselves to avoid being played for a sucker.

An experiment by Tina L. Robbins demonstrated that social loafing can occur even when a task is thought provoking, personally involving, and allows for unique contribution. She concludes that "the performance of self-directed work teams or groups which are formed for the purpose of brainstorming, product idea generation, or for making proposal implementation decisions may suffer the consequences of social loafing.[22] Even some workers involved in exciting tasks look for a free ride.

Groupthink

A potential disadvantage of group decision making is **groupthink,** a deterioration of mental efficiency, reality testing, and moral judgment in the interest of group cohesiveness. Simply put, groupthink is an extreme form of consensus. The group atmosphere values getting along more than getting things done.[23] The group thinks as a unit, believes it is impervious to outside criticism, and begins to have illusions about its own invincibility. As a consequence, the group loses its powers of critical analysis.

Groupthink is most likely to take place under certain conditions. A highly cohesive group favors groupthink because members identify strongly with the group. Other contributing factors include directive leadership, high stress, insulation of the group, and no built-in mechanisms for evaluating decisions. Having to choose between two unfavorable alternatives can lead to groupthink. An example would be an executive group deciding whether to recall a potentially unsafe product (and taking a huge loss) or leaving the product in distribution (and risking human suffering and negative publicity). Having limited time to make a major decision is another contributor to groupthink because the contributors may rush through the process.[24]

Groupthink appears to take place at the many long-distance service providers who engage in *slamming,* or illegally switching people to its long-distance service without permission. The management group in the companies involved in this practice assume that the customers who were involuntarily switched to their service either won't notice or won't complain about the problem. However, many customers do complain, such as the 1,400 complaints against the group of long-distance companies known as The Fletcher Companies. The owner of the companies was ultimately fined $5 million for violating federal rules against slamming.[25]

A negative implication of groupthink is that it interferes with effective decision making. The emotional factors of wanting to achieve consensus and not wanting to be perceived as an irritant by other group members interferes with a person making an optimum decision. You might think that the alternative chosen by the group is terrible, yet you suppress your dissent to avoid being perceived as a dissident.

Groupthink can often be prevented if the team leader or member encourages all group members to express doubts and criticism of proposed solutions to the problem. It is also helpful to periodically invite qualified outsiders to meet with the group and provide suggestions.

BUILDING TEAMWORK

Explain how to foster teamwork.

The team player roles described previously point to actions the individual can take to become a team player. The Self-Assessment below gives you the opportunity to gauge your current mental readiness to be a contributing team member. Here we highlight managerial actions and organizational practices that facilitate teamwork.[26] Good teamwork enhances, but does not guarantee, a successful team.

The manager can begin by helping team members believe that they have an *urgent constructive purpose.* A demanding performance challenge helps create and sustain the team. Early in the history of the group, the manager should establish trust by *empowering the group to determine how to meet the objectives.* Teamwork is fostered when the team leader establishes the direction, then steps aside to allow the group to work out the details of getting the job done. A major strategy for teamwork is to promote the attitude that *working together effectively is the established norm.* Developing such a culture of teamwork will be difficult when a strong culture of individualism exists within the firm. The team leader can communicate the norm of teamwork by *making frequent use of words and phrases that support teamwork.* Emphasizing the words *team members* or *teammates,* and de-emphasizing the words *subordinates* and *employees* helps communicate the teamwork norm.

Using the *consensus decision-making style* is another way to reinforce teamwork. A sophisticated approach to enhancing teamwork is to *feed team members valid facts*

SELF-ASSESSMENT

Team Player Attitudes

Directions: Describe how well you agree with each of the following statements, using the scale: disagree strongly (DS); disagree (D); neutral (N); agree (A); agree strongly (AS).

	DS	D	N	A	AS
1. I am at my best working alone.	5	4	③	2	1
2. I have belonged to clubs and teams ever since I was a child.	1	②	3	4	5
3. It takes far too long to get work accomplished with a group.	5	④	3	2	1
4. I like the friendship of working in a group.	1	2	3	④	5
5. I would prefer to run a one-person business than to be a member of a large firm.	5	4	③	2	1
6. It's difficult to trust others in the group on key assignments.	5	④	3	2	1
7. Encouraging others comes naturally to me.	1	2	3	4	⑤
8. I like the give and take of ideas that is possible in a group.	1	2	3	4	⑤
9. It is fun for me to share responsibility with other group members.	1	2	3	④	5
10. Much more can be accomplished by a team than by the same number of people working alone.	1	2	3	④	5

Total Score __38__

Scoring and interpretation: Add the numbers you have circled to obtain your total score.

41–50   You have strong positive attitudes toward being a team member and working cooperatively with other members.

30–40   You have moderately favorable attitudes toward being a team member and working cooperatively with other members.

10–29   You much prefer working by yourself than being a team member. To work effectively in a company that emphasizes teamwork, you may need to develop more positive attitudes toward working jointly with others.

and information that motivate them to work together. New information prompts the team to redefine and enrich its understanding of the challenge it is facing, thereby focusing on a common purpose. A subtle yet potent method of building teamwork is for the team to *use language that fosters cohesion and commitment.* In-group jargon bonds a team and sets the group apart from others. An example is a team of information technology specialists saying "Give me a core dump" to mean "Tell me your thoughts."

To foster teamwork, the manager should *avoid* **micromanagement,** or supervising group members too closely and second-guessing their decisions. Micromanagement can hamper a spirit of teamwork because team members do not feel in control of their own work.

Creating physical structures suited for teams is an effective organizational intervention to support teamwork. Group cohesiveness, and therefore teamwork, is enhanced when teammates are located close together and can interact frequently and easily. Frequent interaction often leads to camaraderie and a feeling of belonging. A useful method for getting people to exchange ideas is to establish a shared physical facility, such as a conference room, research library, or break lounge. A key strategy for encouraging teamwork is to *reward the team as well as individuals.* The most convincing team incentive is to calculate compensation partially on the basis of team results.

Another option available to organizations for enhancing teamwork is to *send members to outdoor (or off-site) training,* a form of experiential learning. Participants acquire leadership and teamwork skills by confronting physical challenges and exceeding their self-imposed limitations. Rope activities are typical of outdoor training. Participants attached to a secure pulley with ropes will climb up a ladder and jump off to another spot. All of these challenges are faced in teams rather than individually, hence the development of teamwork. Outdoor training is likely to

IMPLICATIONS FOR MANAGERIAL PRACTICE

1. Be aware of group norms and the extent to which they facilitate or inhibit reaching organizational objectives. Reward systems must be developed that encourage high group performance. For example, if a group performs well on a given task and management then elevates performance standards, a norm toward lowered productivity may result.

2. When forming a new work group or team, recognize that time is needed before the group will be able to achieve maximum performance. Be alert to somewhat predictable stages of group formation and development: forming, storming, norming, and performing.

3. Be aware that group effectiveness is not a random occurrence. Strive to incorporate into the group many of the characteristics associated with work group effectiveness, such as proper job design, the right composition, and workload sharing.

4. When accepting advice from a group, recognize that the group's decision may involve a more extreme position than the members would take individually.

5. Managers can remove themselves as impediments to self-management of teams, while retaining the role of adviser and resource person, by asking these questions of team members: (a) What is the cause of the problem? (b) What are you doing to fix it? (c) How will you know when it is accomplished? (d) How can I help?[28]

have the most favorable outcomes when the trainer helps the team members comprehend the link between such training and on-the-job behavior.

Many companies invest in off-site training. A case in point is Daniel Hubbard, director of corporate communications at Charles Schwab, the large brokerage firm. He created an adventure kayak racing club for employees at the company's San Francisco headquarters. Hubbard believes that adventure racing develops personal and team skills. He also thinks that kayak racing together will help Schwab employees get to know one another better or meet for the first time and will promote loyalty to the company. Hubbard chose an activity that he thought would fit employee demographics and personal characteristics. The average Schwab employee is around 30, educated, affluent, competitive, and team oriented.[27]

SUMMARY OF KEY POINTS

 Describe the various types of groups in organizations.

Groups and teams can be classified in various ways. Formal groups are deliberately formed by the organization, whereas informal groups emerge over time through worker interaction. Four types of work teams described here are cross-functional teams, top-management teams, affinity groups, and virtual teams (ones that meet electronically).

 Summarize the stages of group development and key roles members occupy within a work group.

Groups are thought to go through five predictable stages of development: forming, storming, norming, performing, and adjourning. Group member roles include knowledge contributor, process observer, people supporter, challenger, listener, mediator, gatekeeper (letting others into the discussion), and take-charge leader.

 Identify the characteristics of an effective work group.

Effective work group characteristics are well documented. The jobs should be enriched, and the members should have a feeling of empowerment. Group members should be interdependent in terms of tasks, goals, and feedback and rewards. The group should be composed of heterogeneous members who are flexible and have a preference for group work. The group should have support including giving the group the information it needs, coaching group members, providing the right technology, and receiving recognition and other rewards. The group process should include team spirit, social support, and workload sharing. Teams that follow work processes and procedures tend to perform better.

Members should be familiar with the jobs, coworkers, and the work environment.

 Be able to implement two different methods of group problem solving and decision making.

Group decision-making styles follow a continuum from consultative, through consensus, to democratic. When consensus is reached, all group members are at least willing to support the decision. The nominal group and Delphi techniques capitalize on the value of collective thought yet minimize some of the problems that occur in interacting groups. Using the NGT, each person writes down ideas separately and later shares ideas with the group before all the ideas are ranked by group members. With the Delphi technique, each member responds to a questionnaire about the problem, passing along his or her input to others. Finally, group members vote on the best solution.

 Pinpoint several potential problems with group effort and know how to prevent them.

Group effectiveness can be hampered in several ways. Polarization, or taking extreme positions, can result. Members may engage in social loafing, or freeloading, Groupthink, an extreme form of consensus and lack of critical reasoning, may occur as members strive for solidarity.

Explain how to foster teamwork.

Managers and leaders can enhance teamwork through many behaviors, attitudes, and organizational actions including the following: give the team an urgent, constructive purpose; develop a norm of teamwork, refrain from micromanagement, create physical structures suited for teams, and support outdoor (or off-site) training.

KEY TERMS AND PHRASES

Group, *184*

A collection of people who interact with one another, are working toward some common purpose, and perceive themselves to be a group.

Team, *184*

A special type of group in which the members have complementary skills and are committed to a common purpose.

Teamwork, *184*

A situation in which there is understanding and commitment to group goals on the part of all team members.

Formal Group, *184*

A group deliberately formed by the organization to accomplish specific tasks and achieve goals.

Informal Group, *184*

A group that emerges over time through the interaction of workers, typically to satisfy a social or recreational purpose.

Cross-functional Team, *185*

A work group, composed of workers with different specialties but from about the same organizational level, who come together to accomplish a task.

Affinity Group, *187*

An employee-involvement group composed of professional-level (or knowledge) workers.

Virtual Team, *187*

A group that conducts almost all its collaborative work via electronic communication rather than in face-to-face meetings.

Nominal Group Technique (NGT), *195*

An approach to developing creative alternatives that requires group members to generate alternative solutions independently.

Delphi Technique, *196*

A group decision-making technique designed to provide group members with one another's ideas and feedback, while avoiding some of the problems associated with interacting groups.

Group Polarization, *198*

A situation in which postdiscussion attitudes tend to be more extreme than prediscussion attitudes.

Social Loafing, *198*

Freeloading, or shirking individual responsibility when placed in a group setting and removed from individual accountability.

Groupthink, *199*

A deterioration of mental efficiency, reality testing, and moral judgment in the interest of group cohesiveness.

Micromanagement, *201*

Supervising group members too closely and second-guessing their decision.

DISCUSSION QUESTIONS AND ACTIVITIES

1. Explain the meaning of this sentence: "All teams are groups, but not all groups are teams."

2. Why are novels never written by more than one person, whereas texts, scholarly books, and research reports are frequently written by groups of two or more people?

3. Why is membership on a cross-functional team such good experience for becoming an executive?

4. To what extent have you observed the stages of group development in any group to which you have belonged?

5. How might you use the Delphi technique to help you prepare a more effective job résumé?

6. Identify an example of groupthink in a work or social setting that you have observed or read about.

7. Outdoor (or off-site) training has achieved enormous popularity as a method for developing teamwork (even without research substantiation). What factors do you think account for its popularity?

ORGANIZATIONAL BEHAVIOR ONLINE

TO DO

The Effective Team

Use the Internet to locate a description of an effective work team in action. While reading the description, identify at least three characteristics that conform to the characteristics of effective work groups presented in the chapter. Make a notation such as, "This group showed *high familiarity* because the team members had worked with one another for over one year. Also, they were highly trained specialists."

Here are several search words and phrases you might enter into your search engine: "Successful cross-functional team," "Example of effective work group," "High-performing team," or "Successful business team." If within 20 minutes you do not achieve the results you need, shift your focus to analyzing a sports team. A good starting point is to use the team's name as a search word, such as "New York Liberty," or "Florida Marlins."

TO BOOKMARK

Center for the Study of Work Teams
http://www.workteams.unt.edu

The Nominal Group Technique
http://www.epsincor.com/nomgrtec.htm

Groupthink Links
http://www.groupthink.ca

Studies of Social Loafing
http://www.theabc.org/work.htm

CASE PROBLEM: The Unbalanced Team

Bluestone Security Systems is one of the largest security systems distributors in its city with annual sales of $15 million. Two years ago, Bill Scovia, the vice president of marketing and sales, reorganized the sales force. Previously the sales force consisted of inside sales representatives (who took care of phone-in orders) and outside sales representatives (who called on accounts). The reorganization divided the outside sales force into two groups: direct sales and major accounts. The direct sales representatives were made responsible for small commercial customers and individual homeowners. As before, they would service existing customers and prospect for new accounts. Servicing existing customers usually involves adding fire protection to burglary protection and upgrading burglary systems.

Three of the people who were direct sales representatives were promoted to major account executives. The account executives would service Bluestone's largest accounts, including prospecting for new business within those accounts. An example would be expanding the security system to other stores of a retailer. To promote teamwork and cooperation, Scovia assigned group sales quotas to the account representatives. Collectively, their goal was to bring in 21 new large accounts per month.

Given that the sales quota was a group quota, the account representatives were supposed to work together on strategy for acquiring new accounts. If a particular account executive did not have the expertise to handle his or her customer's problems, another account executive was supposed to offer help. Brian Marcos, for example, was the resident expert on the unique security problems of warehouses. If invited, Brian would join one of the two other account executives to call on a customer who owned a warehouse.

After the new sales organization had been in place 19 months, Elizabeth Kato, an account executive, was having lunch with Larry Starks, the manufacturing director at

Bluestone. "I've about had it," said Elizabeth. "I'm tired of single-handedly carrying the team."

"What do you mean, you're single-handedly carrying the team?" asked Larry.

"You're a trusted friend, Larry. So let me lay out the facts. Each month the group is supposed to bring in 21 new sales. If we don't average those 21 sales per month, we don't get our semiannual bonus. That represents about 25 percent of my income. So a big chunk of my money comes from group effort.

"My average number of new accounts brought in for the last 12 months has been 11. And we are averaging about 18 new sales per month. This translates into the other account execs averaging about 7 sales among them. I'm carrying the group, but overall sales are still below quota. This means I didn't get my bonus last month.

"The other account execs are friendly and helpful in writing up proposals. But they just don't bring in their share of accounts."

Larry asked, "What does your boss say about this?"

"I've had several conversations with him about the problem. He tells me to be patient and to remember that the development of a fully balanced team requires time. He also tells me that I should develop a stronger team spirit. My problem is that I can't pay my bills with team spirit."

CASE QUESTIONS

1. What does this case illustrate about teamwork?
2. What role or roles is Elizabeth occupying in the group?
3. To what extent are Elizabeth's complaints justifiable?

On-line resources for sales professionals are plentiful. One of the best sites is the Marketing Library available at http://www.sell.org/. Use it to uncover useful insights into sales force reorganizations.

SUGGESTED READINGS

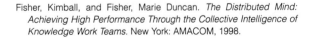

Fisher, Kimball, and Fisher, Marie Duncan. *The Distributed Mind: Achieving High Performance Through the Collective Intelligence of Knowledge Work Teams.* New York: AMACOM, 1998.

Guzzo, Richard R., Salas, Eduardo, and Associates. *Team Effectiveness and Decision Making in Organizations.* San Francisco: Jossey-Bass, 1995.

Imperato, Gina. "Their Specialty? Teamwork." *Fast Company,* January/February 2000, pp. 54–56.

Kets De Vries, Manfred F. R. "High Performance Teams: Lessons from the Pygmies." *Organizational Dynamics,* Winter 1999, pp. 66–76.

Maani, Kambiz E., and Benton, Campbell. "Rapid Team Learning: Lessons from Team New Zealand's America Cup Campaign." *Organizational Dynamics,* Spring 1999, pp. 48–62.

Nagler, Ben. "Recasting Employees into Teams." *Workforce,* January 1998, pp. 101–106.

Pappas, Charles. "Missionary Position: Recruiting Your Team is Your Toughest Sales Job." *Success,* May 1999, pp. 40–41.

Parcells, Bill. *"The Tough Work of Turning Around a Team."* Harvard Business Review, November-December 2000, pp. 179–184.

Uhl-Bien, Mary, and Graen, George B. "Individual Self-Management: Analysis of Professionals' Self-Managing Activities in Functional and Cross-Functional Work Teams." *The Academy of Management Journal,* June 1998, pp. 340–350.

ENDNOTES

1. John E. Sawyer, William R. Latham, Robert D. Pritchard, and Winston R. Bennett Jr., "Analysis of Work Group Productivity in an Applied Setting: Application of a Time Series Panel Design," *Personnel Psychology,* Winter 1999, p. 927.

2. Jon R. Katzenbach and Douglas K. Smith, "The Discipline of Teams," *Harvard Business Review,* March–April 1993, p. 113.

3. Charles Fishman, "Total Teamwork: Imagination Ltd, " *Fast Company,* April 2000, p. 158.

4. Jon R. Katzenbach, "The Myth of the Top Management Team," *Harvard Business Review,* November–December 1997, pp. 82–99.

5. Eileen M. Van Aaken, Dominic J. Monetta, and D. Scott Sink, "Affinity Groups: The Missing Link in Employee Involvement," *Organizational Dynamics,* Spring 1994, p. 38.

6. James L. Creighton and James W. R. Adams, "The Cybermeeting's About to Begin," *Management Review,* January 1998, pp. 29–31.

7. Anthony M. Townsend, Samuel M. DeMarie, and Anthony R. Hendrickson, "Virtual Teams: Technology and the Workplace of the Future," *Academy of Management Executive,* August 1998, p. 17.

8. J. Steven Heinen and Eugene Jacobsen, "A Model of Task Group Development in Complex Organizations and A Strategy of Implementation," *Academy of Management Review,* October 1976, pp. 98–111; Bruce W. Tuckman and Mary Ann C. Jensen, "Stages of Small Group Development Revisited," *Group & Organization Studies* Vol. 2, 1977, pp. 419–427.

9. Glen M. Parker, *Team Players and Teamwork: The New Competitive Business Strategy* (San Francisco: Jossey-Bass, 1990); Thomas L. Quick, *Successful Team Building* (New York: AMACOM, 1992), pp. 40–52; "Lead or Lay Back? How to Play the Right Role on a Team," *Executive Strategies,* November 1999, p. 2.

10. Based on literature reviews and original material in Michael A. Campion, Ellen M. Papper, and Gina Medsker, "Relations between Work Team Characteristics and Effectiveness: A Replication and Extension," *Personnel Psychology,* Summer 1996, p. 431; David E. Hyatt and Thomas M. Ruddy, "An Examination of the Relationship between Work Group Characteristics and Performance: Once More into the Breech, *Personnel Psychology,* Autumn 1997, p. 579; Brian D. Janz, Jason A. Colquitt, and Raymond A. Noe, "Knowledge Worker Team Effectiveness: The Role of Autonomy, Interdependence, Team Development, and Contextual Support Variables, *Personnel Psychology,* Winter 1997, pp. 877–904; Bradley L. Kirkman and Benson Rosen, "Powering Up Teams," *Organizational Dynamics,* Winter 2000, pp. 48–52.

11. Kirkman and Rosen, "Powering Up Teams," pp. 48–52.

12. Priscilla M. Elsass and Laura M. Graves, "Demographic Diversity in Decision-Making Groups: The Experiences of Women and People of Color," *Academy of Management Review,* October 1997, p. 968.

13. Murray R. Barrick, Greg L. Stewart, Mitchell J. Neubert, and Michael K. Mount, "Relating Member Ability and Personality to Work-Team Processes and Team Effectiveness," *Journal of Applied Psychology,* June 1998, pp. 377–391.

14. Campion, Papper, and Medsker, "Relations between Work Team Characteristics and Effectiveness," p. 450.

15. Anthony M. Townsend, Samuel M. DeMarie, and Anthony R. Hendrickson, "Virtual Teams: Technology and the Workplace of the Future," *Academy of Management Executive,* August 1998, p. 18.

16. Larry K. Michaelsen, Warren E. Watson, and Robert H. Black, "A Realistic Test of Individual versus Group Decision Making," *Journal of Applied Psychology,* October 1989, pp. 834–839.

17. William B. Eddy, *The Manager and the Working Group* (New York: Praeger, 1985), pp. 150–151.

18. Andrew J. Van de Ven and André L. Delberq, "The Effectiveness of Nominal, Delphi, and Interacting Group Decision-Making Processes," *Academy of Management Journal,* December 1974, p. 606.

19. Normal Dalkey, *The Delphi Method: An Experimental Study of Group Opinions* (Santa Monica, CA: Rand Corporation, 1969).

20. Carla Joinson, "Teams at Work," *HRMagazine,* May 1999, p. 32; Jac Fitz-Enz, "Measuring Team Effectiveness," *HRfocus,* August 1997, p. 3.

21. Our discussion is based on Gregory Moorhead and Ricky W. Griffin, *Organizational Behavior: Managing People and Organizations,* 4th ed. (Boston: Houghton Mifflin, 1995), pp. 278–279.

22. Tina L. Robbins, "Social Loafing on Cognitive Tasks: An Examination of the 'Sucker Effect'," *Journal of Business and Psychology* (Spring 1995), pp. 278–279.

23. Irving L. Janis, *Victims of Groupthink: A Study of Foreign Policy Decisions and Fiascoes* (Boston: Houghton Mifflin, 1972), pp. 39–40; Glenn Whyte, "Groupthink Reconsidered," *Academy of Management Review,* January 1989, pp. 40–56.

24. A review of the research on groupthink antecedents is provided by Debra L. Nelson and James Campbell Quick, *Organizational Behavior: Foundations, Realities, & Challenges,* 3rd ed. (Cincinnati, OH: South-Western College Publishing, 2000), pp. 332–333.

25. "FCC Pulls the Plug on Phone Slammer," The Associated Press syndicated story, April 22, 1998.

26. Many of the ideas in this section come from Ruth Wagemen, "Critical Success Factors for Creating Superb Self-Managing Teams," *Organizational Dynamics,* Summer 1997, p. 57; Robert Fisher and Bo Thomas, *Real Dream Teams: Seven Practices that Enable Ordinary People to Achieve Extraordinary Results as Team Leaders* (Delray Beach, FL: St. Lucie Press, 1995); Katzenbach and Smith, "The Discipline of Teams," pp. 118–119; Rebecca Winters, "Extreme Offsites," *Time,* August 9, 1999, pp. 75A–76A.

27. Valerie Marchant, "Am I Up to This?" *Time,* August 9, 1999, p. 79A.

28. Milan Moravec, Odd Jan Johannessen, and Thor A. Hjelmas, "The Well-Managed SMT," *Management Review,* June 1998, p. 58.

Leadership in Organizations

In May 2000, Anne M. Mulcahy was elevated to president and chief operating officer of Xerox Corp., setting the stage for the first woman to lead the company. In her previous position with the company, Mulcahy was the top executive at the General Markets Organization of Xerox, a division that sold mid-size machines on the Internet and through retail outlets. Mucahy replaced CEO G. Richard Thoman, who was asked to resign mostly because his business strategies were not working fast enough and because of his apparent inability to inspire workers. Thoman held the CEO position for 13 months.

Rebecca Runkle, an investment analyst and a Xerox observer, has said that Mulcahy is quite well liked by the employees, and that her ability to inspire and motivate employees will be critical. Before being named to the head of the 6,000-employee General Markets group, Mulcahy was senior vice president and chief staff officer responsible for human resources, advertising, Internet marketing, and government relations. She joined the company 24 years previously as a sales representative. Mulcahy's human resources experience is thought to be critical as Xerox entered contract negotiations with its largest union seven months after she was appointed to her new position.

Although it may take some time before Wall Street investors fully endorse Mulcahy's leadership at Xerox, the company itself hasn't been shy about promoting Mulcahy's new role. Visit Xerox's News Room at http://www.xerox.com and click on "News & Events."

Source: Richard Mullins, "Mulcahy Known to Inspire, Motivate Workers," *Democrat and Chronicle*, (Rochester, New York) 12 May 2000, by permission of the *Democrat and Chronicle*.

PHOTO: © MARK RICHARDS/PHOTOEDIT

OBJECTIVES

After reading and studying this chapter and doing the exercises, you should be able to

 1 Differentiate between leadership and management.

 2 Describe key leadership traits, styles, and behaviors.

 3 Explain the basics of four different contingency theories of leadership.

 4 Present an overview of transformational and charismatic leadership.

 5 Explain how 360-degree feedback is used to improve leadership effectiveness.

 6 Identify gender differences in leadership style.

 7 Identify forces that can sometimes decrease the importance of leadership.

Chapter 10

SO WHAT? Does this glimpse of Anne Mulcahy hint at any key justifications for studying organizational leadership? In a word, yes. A person who combines the ability to inspire and motivate others with thorough knowledge of the business holds promise of strengthening even already strong organizations, but leadership ability is especially crucial to beleaguered companies such as Xerox, which has been losing market value. Leadership has always been a topic of major importance to scholars and practitioners, and current interest is intense as organizations struggle to survive in our hyper-competitive world. Turning to a *Fortune* magazine analysis of the 10 most-admired companies in the world to sum up our argument: "The truth is that no one factor makes a company admirable, but if you were forced to pick the one that makes the most difference, you'd pick leadership."[1]

Leadership is not just the domain of a few members of top management. Today, take-charge ability is important at all levels of management. Employees who are in direct contact with customers and clients often require stronger leadership than do higher-level workers. This is true because entry-level workers often lack experience, direction, and a strong work ethic. Furthermore, the current emphasis on teams means that effective team leaders are needed throughout the organization.

The discussion of leadership in this chapter centers around several topics of interest to managers and professionals: leadership traits, styles, and behaviors: contingency theories of leadership; transformational and charismatic leadership; 360-degree feedback for improving leadership effectiveness, and substitutes for leadership. Let us first, however, look at the nature of leadership.

THE NATURE OF LEADERSHIP

Differentiate between leadership and management.

Leadership involves influencing others to achieve objectives important to them and the organization. Recently **leadership** has been defined as the ability to inspire confidence and support among the people on whose competence and commitment performance depends.[2] Although leadership is a major function of management, it is not the same thing as management. In the view of John Kotter, management copes with complexity, which requires preserving order and consistency. Leadership, in comparison, copes with change in a competitive, rapidly changing world. Effective leaders deal with change by formulating a vision of the future and setting a direction for that vision.[3] Leaders are also heavily involved in persuading, inspiring, and motivating others and spearheading useful changes.

Exhibit 10-1 presents a stereotype of the difference between leadership and management. The same information provides more insight into the nature of leadership. Effective leadership and management are both required in the modern workplace. Managers must be leaders, but leaders must also be good managers. Workers need to be inspired and persuaded, but they also need assistance in developing and maintaining a smoothly functioning workplace. Sometimes a company will use a pair of executives at the top: one to emphasize leadership and one to emphasize management. The duo who run Oracle Corp. fit this concept. Larry Ellison, the flamboyant founder and visionary, is the company's public face and promotes his grand new business strategies such as interactive TV. Ray Lane spends his time directing sales and day-to-day operations, while he painstakingly builds the organization. Ellison attempts to change the world, and Lane attempts to change Oracle into an ever-more-efficient company.[4] (Lane has since left Oracle.)

Another important perspective on leadership is that it contributes to organizational effectiveness. The leaders featured in this chapter are people whose personal attributes help them achieve good results for the organization. A new conception

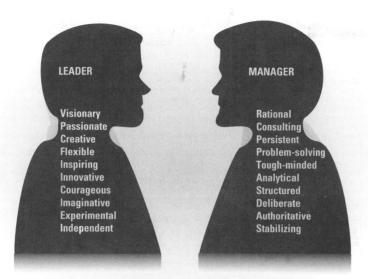

Leaders versus Managers

of leadership states: effective leadership = attributes × results. The equation indicates that truly effective leaders are capable of demonstrating desired attributes (such as trustworthiness) *and* achieving desired results (such as gross profit margins). A low standing on either attributes or results lowers a leader's effectiveness.[5]

A growing body of evidence supports the common-sense belief that leadership matters. (You will recall how the board of directors at Xerox Corp. reasoned that bringing in a new leader would lead to improved business results and morale.) For example, a comprehensive study of many organizations concluded that incompetent managers are responsible for billions of dollars of lost productivity each year.[6] The opposing view is presented later in this chapter.

LEADERSHIP TRAITS AND CHARACTERISTICS

Describe key leadership traits, styles, and behaviors.

A logical approach to understanding leadership is to study the traits and characteristics of effective leaders (the great person theory). For many years, scholars downplayed the study of leadership characteristics, but an interest in the inner qualities of leaders has reawakened. The traits of leaders are related closely to the degree to which others perceive these people to be leaders. For example, a person who exudes self-confidence would generally be perceived by others as having leadership qualities. Research evidence confirms that effective leaders are different from other people—that they have the "right stuff." Their differences relate to the traits and characteristics described in this section.[7] The current interest in leadership traits is also reflected in a demand for leaders with vision and charisma.

Hundreds of traits and personal characteristics of leaders have been researched over the years, dating back to the early 1900s. Here we discuss key leadership qualities that are supported by research or careful observation. They are grouped under the categories of cognitive skills and personality traits and motives.

An effective leader must have appropriate **cognitive skills,** or mental ability and knowledge. Organizational leaders possess effective problem-solving ability. They anticipate problems before they occur and persevere until the problems are solved. In the process, they demonstrate imagination, creativity, and a willingness to experiment with unproven methods. Leadership positions place a continuously increasing demand on problem-solving ability. An example is that managers are pressured to perform tasks in a shorter time with a smaller staff.

Technical and professional competence, or knowledge of the business, is another cognitive requirement for effective leadership. When outsiders are brought into a company to fill senior management positions, they usually need a specialty to complement their leadership and administrative skills. One reason Carly Fiorina was recruited from Lucent Technologies to become the CEO of Hewlett Packard was because of her extensive knowledge of how to provide Internet equipment and services to other businesses. In lesser leadership positions, technical competence is important because it is difficult to establish rapport with group members when the leader does not understand the technical details of their work.

Personality traits and characteristics have an important influence on leadership effectiveness. Which traits and characteristics are the most relevant varies with the situation. For example, enthusiasm may be more important for a sales manager for term life insurance than for an inventory control manager. The sale manager's enthusiasm may be needed to help sales representatives cope with rejection by customers.

A realistic degree of *self-confidence* is frequently associated with leadership effectiveness. A leader who is self-confident without being overbearing instills confidence among group members. The concept of self-confidence is useful in studying leadership because it illustrates the relationship between traits and behavior. A manager who is inwardly self-confident will behave confidently and will be perceived as acting cool under pressure. Jack Welch, the highly-acclaimed GE executive, said that one of his most important responsibilities was to help his managers become more self-confident so they could become more effective leaders.

Trustworthiness contributes to leadership effectiveness in most situations. Being perceived as trustworthy involves many different behaviors. At the top of the list, however, are behavioral consistency and integrity. Consistency refers to being reliable and predictable, such as conducting performance evaluations and reimbursing for expenses as agreed. Integrity centers around telling the truth, and keeping promises.[8] Judy George, the founder of the home furnishings retail chain, Domain, makes this comment about trustworthiness: "Running a successful business has a lot to do with integrity, work ethic, treating people fairly and kindly, and being honest in all your dealings."[9]

Emotional intelligence is considered a major contributor to leadership effectiveness. As described in Chapter 2, the concept refers to managing ourselves and our relationships effectively. A recent conception of emotional intelligence is so broad it encompasses many traits and behaviors related to leadership effectiveness, including self-confidence, empathy, and visionary leadership.[10] Passion for the work and the people is a particularly important aspect of emotional intelligence for leadership effectiveness. It is difficult to inspire others if you are not passionate about your major work activities.

Many leaders have failed because of glaring deficits in emotional intelligence. When Frank Lorenzo took over Eastern Air Lines (which he later led into bankruptcy), the animosity that developed between him and union bosses grew so great that it hastened the airline's demise. Leona Helmsley played evil stepmom to all the employees of her real estate mogul husband. She fired employees at whim (one for taking an apple while she worked through lunch). Eventually Helmsley was convicted of tax evasion and sent to prison.[11]

The power and achievement motives were described in Chapter 5 in relation to motivation. Both motives are closely associated with leadership effectiveness. A strong power motive propels the leader to be interested in influencing others. When a power motive is too intense, it can manifest itself in ruthless leadership behavior. The two leaders just cited for having low emotional intelligence fit here, as does Chainsaw Al Dunlap described in the case problem for Chapter 1.

A need for achievement often facilitates leadership effectiveness. As a leader, a person with a strong need for achievement will typically have a strong sense of time urgency. In turn, this strong sense of time urgency can be a positive force for innovation,[12] such as wanting to be the first mover on a product.

A sense of humor is another example of how traits are related to leadership effectiveness. The right amount of humor helps relieve tension and boredom among group members and often defuses hostility. If people can be made to see the humor in a situation, some of their anger will dissipate. Furthermore, shared laughter enhances teamwork. An elaborate study of humor was conducted in a large Canadian financial institution. A key finding was that the use of humor was significantly and positively related to individual and work unit performance. A complexity noted was that for managers who were described as inspirational by their subordinates, humor was linked to strong work unit performance. For managers who used a more methodical approach to motivation (emphasizing rewards and punishments) humor was associated with lower individual and work unit performance.[13]

Leadership Styles and Behavior

After the trait approach came a focus on the activities carried out by leaders to enhance productivity and morale. Referred to as the **behavioral approach to leadership,** it attempts to specify how the behavior of effective leaders differs from their less-effective counterparts. The behavioral approach assumes that leaders are relatively consistent in how they attempt to influence group members in different situations. A key concept here is **leadership style,** the relatively consistent pattern of behavior that characterizes a leader. Much of this consistency occurs because a leadership style is based somewhat on an individual's personality. Despite this consistency, some managers can modify their style as the situation requires.

Our presentation of leadership styles and behaviors consists of three parts: the pioneering Ohio State University and University of Michigan studies, the Leadership Grid, and the leader-member exchange model. Before reading ahead, assess your leadership style in the Self-Assessment that follows.

Pioneering Studies on Leadership Dimensions

Much of theory underlying leadership styles traces back to studies conducted at Ohio State University and the University of Michigan beginning in the late 1940s. A major output of the Ohio State studies was the emphasis placed on two leadership dimensions, initiating structure and consideration.

Initiating structure describes the degree to which the leader establishes structure for group members. Structure is initiated by activities such as assigning specific tasks, specifying procedures to be followed, scheduling work, and clarifying expectations. **Consideration** describes the degree to which the leader creates an environment of emotional support, warmth, friendliness, and trust. He or she does so by engaging in such behaviors as being friendly and approachable, looking out for the personal welfare of the group, keeping the group informed of new

SELF-ASSESSMENT

How Participative Is Your Leadership Style?

Directions: The purposes of this quiz are to (1) specify what kind of behaviors are represented by an ideal participative leader and (2) give you an opportunity to compare your behavior (or potential behavior) to that ideal. Be more concerned about giving yourself the gift of candid self-appraisal than attempting to give the "right" answer. Grade your leadership style by rating the frequency with which you use (or *would use* if placed in the situation) the behaviors listed: 3 = Almost always; 2 = Sometimes; 1 = Never.

	AA	S	N
1. I believe that employee involvement is critical to my work group's success.	(3)	2	1
2. I hardly ever review our corporate mission statement with our group.	3	(2)	1
3. My work group develops its own measurable goals.	(3)	2	1
4. I communicate how my work group contributes to the success of the entire organization.	3	(2)	1
5. I allow my group to establish its own performance measures.	3	(2)	1
6. I provide informal performance feedback to my group.	(3)	2	1
7. My group members play an active role in determining their own recognition and rewards.	3	(2)	1
8. I appropriately delegate my responsibilities to my work group.	3	(2)	1
9. I support my work group by providing the resources they need.	(3)	2	1
10. I emphasize the importance of work.	(3)	2	1

Scoring and Interpretation: Subtract your answers to questions 2, 3, 5, and 7 from the sum of your remaining questions.

11–14 You are already a participative leader (or already think and act like one).

7–10 You are well on your way to becoming a participative leader.

4–6 You have begun the shift to participative leadership (or you are beginning to think in that direction).

0–3 You are still leading in a traditional manner (or are thinking like one who does).

Source: Adapted from a quiz from Suzanne W. Goglio, *The Participative Leader* (Doylestown, Pa.: Tower Hill Press, 1994).

developments, and doing small favors for group members.[14] Exhibit 10-2 shows how leadership style can be based on a combination of these two key dimensions.

Many of the Ohio State studies were conducted with first-level supervisors and therefore may not apply well to executive leadership. It was discovered that employee turnover was lowest and job satisfaction highest under leaders who were rated highest in consideration. Research also indicated that leaders high on initiating structure were generally rated highly by superiors and had higher-producing work groups.

Researchers at the University of Michigan also investigated the differences in results obtained by production-centered and employee-centered managers. Production-centered managers set tight work standards, organized tasks carefully, prescribed the work methods to be followed, and supervised closely. Employee-centered managers encouraged group members to participate in goal setting and other work decisions and helped to ensure high performance by engendering trust and mutual respect.

A dominant finding of the Michigan studies was that the most productive work groups tended to have leaders who were employee centered rather than production centered. In addition, it was found that the most effective leaders were those who had supportive relationships with group members. They also tended to

EXHIBIT
10-2

*Leadership Styles Based on a
Combination of Initiating
Structure and Consideration*

use group rather than individual decision making and encouraged subordinates to set and achieve high performance goals. Despite this dominant finding, exceptions were found. A study conducted with 20,000 employees at a heavy-equipment manufacturer indicated that supervisors with the best production records were both production and employee centered.[15]

In practice, effective leaders exhibit a wide range of behaviors in addition to the key behaviors mentioned here. A behavior recently identified is the leader's ability to manage polarities, or extremes of positions and interests. Philosopher Peter Koestenbaum believes that the central leadership attribute is the ability to *manage polarity.* In every aspect of life, these polarities are inevitable. On-the-job polarities include: How can I invest myself heavily in both family and career? Am I a boss or a friend? How do I reconcile my own needs for glory with those of the team? How do I cut costs drastically yet not lay off good employees? Koestenbaum believes that how a leader manages polarity separates greatness from mediocrity.[16]

To personalize the concept of having the right traits and behaviors for leadership, take the Self-Assessment quiz that follows.

The Leadership Grid

The **Leadership Grid**® is a framework for classifying leadership styles that simultaneously examine a leader's concerns for task accomplishment and people. With roots in the Ohio State leadership dimensions, the Grid has been updated several times and is the nucleus of a system of leadership training and organization development. As shown in Exhibit 10-3, the Leadership Grid describes leadership style in terms of concerns for production and people. The concerns reflect attitudes rather than actual behavior.

Concern for production includes results, the bottom line, performance, profits, and mission. Concern for people includes group members and coworkers. Each of these concerns (or dimensions) exists in varying degrees along a continuum from 1 to 9. A manager's standing on one concern is not supposed to influence his or her standing on the other. Leaders can also combine their concerns for people

SELF-ASSESSMENT

Check Your Leadership Potential

Do you have what it takes to be a leader? Place a check mark next to the abilities you feel you have.

Ask a coworker (or a fellow student) to rate you. Then compare the results.

Do you:

_____   Communicate effectively?

_____   Set priorities and action plans?

✓   Learn and improve procedures?

✓   See how your responsibility relates to the big picture?

✓   Analyze problems and make sound decisions?

✓   Adapt to changing conditions, influences, and environments?

✓   Accept risk and take on difficult assignments?

✓   Inspire excellence and commitment in others?

✓   Stand up when under fire?

✓   Exhibit strong social and interpersonal skills?

✓   Focus on the end product?

✓   Demonstrate a high tolerance for stress and pressure?

Scoring: If you checked 8 or more abilities, your leadership potential is high. Take corrective action on the items you or your coworker left unchecked.

Source: The Center for Creative Leadership, Greensboro, NC, 910-288-7210.

and production to be either opportunistic or paternalistic/maternalistic. The opportunistic leader shifts to any Grid style needed to achieve personal gain and self-promotion. The paternalistic/maternalistic leader takes the high 9 level of concern from 9,1 and 1,9 to create a combined style of controlling with parent-like behavior.

According to the Grid, a 9,9 style (team management) is the best because it leads to such positive consequences as high productivity, satisfaction, and creativity. The 9,9 style has built-in flexibility, rather than a "one size fits all" philosophy. With it, the manager evaluates the situation and then uses principles of human behavior to handle problems.[18]

The Leader-Member Exchange Model

The behavioral models presented so far assume that the leader relates in approximately the same manner toward all group members. George Graen and his associates have developed a leadership model that challenges the reality of such consistency in behavior. The **leader-member exchange model** recognizes that leaders develop unique working relationships with each group member.[18] A leader might be considerate and compassionate toward one team member yet structured and unfeeling toward another.

Each relationship between the leader/manager differs in quality. One subset of employees, the in-group, is given additional rewards, responsibility, and trust in exchange for their loyalty and performance. In contrast, another subset of employees (the out-group) is treated in accordance with a more formal understanding of

EXHIBIT
10-3

The Leadership Grid Figure★

In Opportunistic Management, people adapt and shift to any Grid style needed to gain the maximum advantage. Performance occurs according to a system of selfish gain. Effort is given only for an advantage for personal gain.

9+9 Paternalism/Maternalism
Rewards and approval are bestowed to people in return for loyalty and obedience; failure to comply leads to punishment.

*Formerly the Managerial Grid by Robert R. Blake and Jane S. Mouton.

Source: Robert R. Blake and Anne Adams McCarse, *Leadership Dukennas—Grid Solutions.* Houston: Gulf Publishing Company, Grid figure: p. 29, Paternalism/Materialism figure: p. 30, Opportunism figure: p. 31. Copyright © 1991 by Scientific Methods, Inc. Reproduced by permission of the owners.

the supervisor–subordinate relations. The leader's first impression of a group member's competency heavily influences where he or she becomes a member of the in-group or out-group.

In-group members have attitudes and values similar to the leader and interact frequently with the leader. Out-group members have less in common with the leader and operate somewhat detached from the leader. The one-to-one relationships have a major influence on the subordinate's behavior in the group. Members of the in-group become part of a smoothly functioning team headed by the formal leader. Out-group members are less likely to experience good teamwork.

Interest in the leader-member exchange model has intensified in recent years, with many field studies being conducted. Here we highlight research findings with the most direct implications for organizational behavior.

1. Being a member of the in-group facilitates achieving high productivity and satisfaction. Out-group members receive less challenging assignments and are more likely to quit because of their job dissatisfaction.[19]
2. High-quality leader-member exchanges lead to more effective delegation, in addition to higher productivity and satisfaction. The study in question showed that the quality of exchanges from the standpoints of both supervisors and group members were associated with improved delegation, which in turn enhanced performance and satisfaction.[20]
3. Despite the many consequences of positive leader-member exchanges, most supervisors are not overly influenced by them in making performance appraisals. Supervisors may have their "pets," but research has shown that supervisors can overcome these biases to make objective performance appraisals.[21]

An important implication of the leader-member exchange is that the quality of the relationship between the leader/manager and each group member has important job consequences. Favorable exchanges can lead to such important effects as higher productivity and satisfaction, improved motivation, and smoother delegation.

CONTINGENCY THEORIES OF LEADERSHIP

Explain the basics of four different contingency theories of leadership.

The behavioral theories of leadership provided general guidelines for leadership effectiveness, such as emphasizing both production and people. After the behavioral theories came an attempt to specify the conditions under which various leadership styles would lead to the best results. The intent was to make explanations of leadership precise and scientific. According to **contingency theory of leadership**, the best style of leadership depends on factors relating to group members and the work setting. Here we present four contingency theories, or explanations, of leadership: Fiedler's contingency theory, the path-goal theory, the situational leadership model, and the normative decision model.

Fiedler's Contingency Theory of Leadership

Fred E. Fiedler developed an elaborate contingency model, which holds that the best style of leadership is determined by the situation in which the leader is working. Fiedler's model specifies the conditions under which leaders should use task-motivated and relationship-motivated styles.[22] To implement Fiedler's theory, measurements are taken of both leadership style and the situation.

Fiedler measures the leader's style by means of the *least-preferred coworker scale (LPC)*. Whether the leader is primarily task or relationship motivated is measured by how favorably the leader describes his or her least-preferred coworker. The LPC is defined as the past coworker with whom he or she would least like to work. Ratings of coworkers are made on a scale with polar-opposite adjectives such as pleasant versus unpleasant. The logic is that people who describe their least-preferred coworker in relatively positive terms are relationship oriented. In contrast, people who describe their least-preferred coworker in very negative terms are task oriented.

Situational control is the degree to which the leader can control and influence the outcomes of group effort. Measurements of situational control (or favorableness to the leader) are based on three factors. Listed in order of importance, they are:

1. *Leader-member relations:* The extent to which group members accept and support their leader.
2. *Task structure:* The extent to which the leader knows exactly what to do and how well and in what detail the tasks to be completed are defined.
3. *Position power:* The extent to which the organization provides the leader with the means of rewarding and punishing group members and with appropriate formal authority to get the job done.

Numerous studies have investigated the relationship among leadership style situational control by the leader, and leadership effectiveness. Exhibit 10-4 summarizes the major findings of these studies with over 800 groups in various settings. The task-motivated style generally produces the best results when the leader has very high or very low control of the situation. The relationship-motivated style is best when the situation is under moderate or intermediate control. Fiedler has also added an intermediate style of leadership called *socio-independent leadership,* which falls midway between relationship-motivated and task-motivated. Socio-independent leaders tend to perform best when their control is high.

The Path-Goal Theory of Leadership

The **path-goal theory of leadership** specifies what the leader must do to achieve high morale and productivity in a given situation.[23] *Path-goal* refers to a focus on helping employees find the correct path to goal attainment. A model of the theory is presented in Exhibit 10-5. It indicates that the leader chooses the right leadership style to match the contingency factors in order to achieve results.

An important contribution of the path-goal theory is that it both specifies what leaders need to do in different situations and explains the reasoning behind such behavior. The key propositions relate to motivation, satisfaction, and performance. (Path-goal theory is based on the expectancy theory of motivation.)

EXHIBIT 10-4

Summary of Findings from Fiedler's Contingency Theory

EXHIBIT 10-5

The Path-Goal Theory of Leadership

The leader chooses the right leadership style to match the contingency factors in order to achieve outcomes.

(Contingency factors)

Personal Characteristics of Group Members

Leadership Styles

- Directive
- Supportive
- Participative
- Achievement-oriented

OUTCOMES

- Productivity
- Morale

Demands of the Task

(Contingency factors)

1. Leaders perform a motivational function by increasing personal payoffs (rewards) to group members for achieving work objectives and by making the path to payoffs smoother. Clarifying the path, reducing roadblocks and pitfalls, and increasing opportunities for satisfaction on the way to the goal are behaviors that make the path smoother.
2. When group members perceive that clear paths to work goals exist, they will be motivated because they will be more certain of how to reach the goals.
3. Attempts by the leader to clarify path-goal relationships will be seen as redundant by group members if the work system already carefully defines the path to the goal. Under these conditions, control may increase performance, but it will also result in decreased satisfaction.

According to path-goal theory, the leader needs to consider choosing among four different leadership styles to handle the contingency demands of a given situation. *Directive leadership* is about the same as initiating structure and involves setting guidelines on standards and conveying expectations. *Supportive leadership* emphasizes showing concern for the well-being of group members and developing mutually satisfying relationships. *Participative leadership* involves consulting with group members to solicit their suggestions and then using this input for decision making. In *achievement-oriented leadership,* the leader sets challenging goals, promotes work improvement, sets high expectations, and expects group members to assume responsibility.

Each of the above leadership styles works well in some situations but not in others. As shown in Exhibit 10-5, one set of contingency factors involves personal characteristics of group members, such as personality traits and abilities. Another set of contingency factors is the demands of the task, such as degree of ambiguity, repetitiveness, and amount of structure. A statement of the circumstances, or contingency factors, appropriate to each of the four leadership styles is presented in Exhibit 10-6.

The Situational Leadership Model

The **situational leadership model** of Paul Hersey and Kenneth H. Blanchard explains how to match leadership style to the readiness of group members.[24] The

EXHIBIT 10-6

Contingency Relationships in Path-Goal Leadership

219

Leadership Style	Situation in which Appropriate
Directive	Positively affects satisfaction and expectancies of subordinates working on ambiguous tasks.
	Negatively affects satisfaction and expectancies of subordinates working on clearly defined tasks.
Supportive	Positively affects satisfaction of subordinates working on dissatisfying, stressful, or frustrating tasks.
Participative	Positively affects satisfaction of subordinates who are ego-involved with nonrepetitive tasks.
Achievement-oriented	Positively affects confidence that effort will lead to effective performance of subordinates working on ambiguous and nonrepetitive tasks.

situational leadership training program is widely used in business and government because it offers practical suggestions for dealing with everyday leadership problems.

Leadership in the situational model is classified according to the relative amount of task and relationship behavior the leader engages in (quite similar to initiating structure and consideration). Task behavior is the extent to which the leader spells out the duties and responsibilities of the individual or group. Relationship behavior is the extent to which the leader engages in two-way or multi-way communication. It includes such activities as listening, providing encouragement, and coaching. As Exhibit 10-7 shows, the situational model places combinations of task and relationship behaviors into four quadrants. Each quadrant calls for a different leadership style.

The situational leadership model states that there is no one best way to influence group members. The most effective leadership style depends on the readiness level of group members. **Readiness** in situational leadership is defined as the extent to which a group member has the ability and willingness or confidence to accomplish a specific task. The concept of readiness is therefore not a characteristic, trait, or motive; it relates to a specific task.

Readiness has two components—ability and willingness. Ability is the knowledge, experience, and skill an individual or a group brings to a particular task or activity. Willingness is the extent to which an individual or group has the confidence, commitment, and motivation to accomplish a specific task.

The key point of the situational leadership model is that as a group member's readiness increases, a leader should rely more on relationship behavior and less on task behavior. As a person becomes more skilled, he or she needs less direction about the job, but motivation and encouragement might still be important. When a group member becomes very ready (or self-sufficient), a minimum of task or relationship behavior is required by the leader. Notice that at the readiness condition R4 (as shown in Exhibit 10-7), the group member is able and willing or confident. The manager therefore uses a delegating leadership style (quadrant 4). He or she turns over responsibility for decisions and implementation.

The situational model represents a consensus of thinking about leadership behavior in relation to group members: Competent people require less specific direction than do less competent people. The situational model also supports common sense and is therefore appealing. You can benefit from the model by attempting to diagnose the readiness of group members before choosing the right leadership style.

EXHIBIT 10-7

The Situational Model of Leadership

The situational model offers precise guidelines for supervising group members, depending on their readiness.

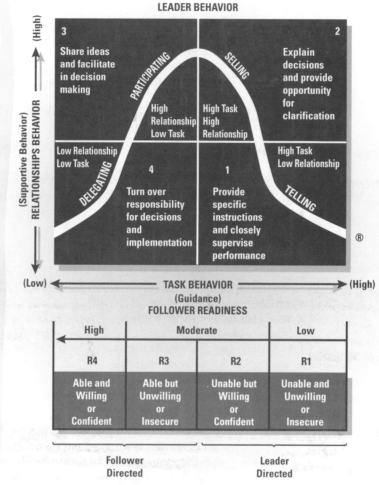

LEADER BEHAVIOR

3 Share ideas and facilitate in decision making — PARTICIPATING — High Relationship Low Task

2 Explain decisions and provide opportunity for clarification — SELLING — High Task High Relationship

4 Turn over responsibility for decisions and implementation — DELEGATING — Low Relationship Low Task

1 Provide specific instructions and closely supervise performance — TELLING — High Task Low Relationship

(High) ← (Supportive Behavior) RELATIONSHIPS BEHAVIOR → (Low)

(Low) ← TASK BEHAVIOR (Guidance) → (High)

FOLLOWER READINESS

High	Moderate		Low
R4	R3	R2	R1
Able and Willing or Confident	Able but Unwilling or Insecure	Unable but Willing or Confident	Unable and Unwilling or Insecure

Follower Directed   Leader Directed

Nevertheless, the model presents categories and guidelines so precisely that it gives the impression of infallibility. In reality, leadership situations are less clear-cut than the four quadrants suggest. Also, the prescriptions for leadership will work only some of the time. For example, many supervisors use a telling style with unable and unwilling or insecure team members (R1) and still achieve poor results.

The Normative Decision Model

Another contingency viewpoint is that leaders must choose a style that elicits the correct degree of group participation when making decisions. Given that much of a leader's interactions with group members involves decision making, this perspective is sensible. The **normative decision model** views leadership as a decision-making process in which the leader examines certain factors within the situation to determine which decision-making style will be the most effective. Here we present the latest version of the model that Victor Vroom and his associates have been evolving for 30 years, based on research with over 100,000 managers.[25]

The normative model (formerly known as the leader-participation model) identifies five decision-making styles, each reflecting a different degree of participation by group members.

Decide. The leader makes the decision alone and either announces or sells it to the group. The leader might use expertise in collecting information from the group or others who appear to have information relevant to the problem.

Consult (Individually). The leader presents the problem to group members individually, gathers their suggestions, and then makes the decision.

Consult (Group). The leader presents the problem to group members in a meeting, gathers their suggestions, and then makes the decision.

Facilitate. The leader presents the problem, then acts as a facilitator, defining the problem to be solved and the boundaries in which the decision must be made. The leader wants concurrence and avoids having his or her ideas receive more weight based on position power.

Delegate. The leader permits the group to make the decision within prescribed limits. Although the leader does not directly intervene in the group's deliberations unless explicitly asked, he or she works behind the scenes, providing resources and encouragement.

The leader diagnoses the situation in terms of seven variables. Based on answers to those variables, the leader/manager follows the path through decision matrices to choose one of the five decision-making styles. The model includes two versions: one when time is critical and one when a more important consideration is the development of group member decision-making capabilities receiving high priority.

Exhibit 10-8 depicts the matrix for time-driven group problems, a situation in which a decision must be reached rapidly. The situational factors, or problem attributes, are listed at the top of the matrix. Specifying the situational factors makes the model a contingency approach. The decision-making style chosen depends on these factors and are defined as follows:

Decision Significance: The significance of the decision to the success of the project or the organization.

Importance of Commitment: The importance of team members' commitment to the decision.

Leader's Expertise: Your knowledge or expertise in relation to this problem.

Likelihood of Commitment: The likelihood that the team would commit itself to a decision that you might make on your own.

Group Support for Objectives: The degree to which the team supports the organization's objectives at stake in the problem.

Group Expertise: Team members' knowledge or expertise in relation to the problem.

Team Competence: The ability of the team members to work together in solving problems.

Accurate answers to these seven situational factors are not always easy to obtain. The leader may have to rely heavily on intuition, and also minimize distorted thinking such as believing he or she has expertise when it might be lacking.

To use the model, the decision maker begins at the left side of the matrix, at "Problem Statement." At the top of the matrix are seven situational factors, each of which may be present (H for high) or absent (L for low) in that problem. You begin by ascertaining if the decision is significant. If so, you select H and answer the second question, concerning the importance of gaining group commitment. If you continue the process without crossing any horizontal line on the matrix, you will arrive at one of the five recommended decision styles. Sometimes a conclusive determination can be made based on two factors, such as L, L. Others require three, [such as L, H, H, four (H, H, H, H,) or as many as seven factors (such as H, H, L, L, H, H, H)].

Different people giving different answers to the situational factors will arrive at different conclusions about the recommended decision style in the situation.

To help you apply the model, the following Skill-Development Exercise presents a scenario developed by Vroom, along with the suggested answer or path.

EXHIBIT 10-8

The Time-Driven Model

Instructions: The matrix operates like a funnel. You start at the left with a specific decision problem in mind. The column headings denote situational factors that may or may not be present in the problem. You progress by selecting High or Low (H or L) for each relevant situational factor. Proceed down from the funnel, judging only those situational factors for which a judgment is called for, until you reach the recommended process.

	Decision Significance	Importance of Commitment	Leader Expertise	Likelihood of Commitment	Group Support	Group Expertise	Team Competence	
PROBLEM STATEMENT	H	H		H	–	–	–	Decide
			H	L	H	H	H	Delegate
						H	L	
						L	–	Consult (Group)
					L	–	–	
			L	H	H	H	H	Facilitate
						H	L	
						L	–	Consult (Individually)
					L	–	–	
				L	H	H	H	Facilitate
						H	L	
						L	–	Consult (Group)
					L	–	–	
		L	H	–	–	–	–	Decide
			L	–	H	H	H	Facilitate
						H	L	
						L	–	Consult (Individually)
					L	–	–	
	L	H	–	H	–	–	–	Decide
				L	–	–	H	Delegate
							L	Facilitate
		L	–	–	–	–	–	Decide

Source: Victor H. Vroom's Time-Driven Model reproduced from *A Model of Leadership Style,* Copyright 1998.

SKILL-DEVELOPMENT EXERCISE

Applying the Time-Driven Model

Setting: Auto Parts Manufacturer
Your Position: County Manager

Your firm has just acquired a small manufacturer of spare auto parts in Southeast Asia. A recent collapse of the economies in the region made values very attractive. Your senior management decided to acquire a foothold in this region. It was less interested in the particular acquired firm, which produces parts for the local market, than it was in using it as a base from which to produce parts at reduced cost for the worldwide market.

When you arrived at your new assignment two weeks ago, you were somewhat surprised by the less than enthusiastic reception that you received from the current management. You attribute the obvious strain in working relations not only to linguistic and cultural differences but also to a deep-seated resentment to their new foreign owners. Your top management team members seem to get along very well with one another, but the atmosphere changes when you step into the room.

Nonetheless, you will need their help in navigating your way through this unfamiliar environment. Your immediate need is to develop a plan for land acquisition on which to construct new manufacturing and warehouse facilities. You and your administrative assistant, who accompanied you from your previous assignment, should be able to carry out the plan, but its development would be hazardous without local knowledge.

How much should you involve the team in developing the plan about constructing new manufacturing and warehouse facilities?

Source: Victor H. Vroom, "Leadership and the Decision-Making Process," *Organizational Dynamics*, Spring 2000, p. 90. (Question added.)

ANALYSIS FOR TIME-DRIVEN DECISION:
H L L L – CONSULT INDIVIDUALLY

The normative model provides a valuable service to practicing managers and leaders. It prompts them to ask questions about important contingency variables in decision-making situations. It has been found that for previous versions of the model, managers who follow its procedures are likely to increase their decision-making effectiveness. Furthermore, managers who make decisions consistent with the model (again, based on previous versions) are more likely to be perceived as effective managers.[26] These same good results are probable for Vroom's new model.

When the leader concludes that group decision making is appropriate, morale will often be elevated. Lois Juliber, a Colgate-Palmolive executive, implemented a program of encouraging people throughout the organization to make decisions. She noted,

> All of a sudden, people got the sense that they could really make a decision, and no one was going to second-guess them. And for morale, that was just fantastic. Second-guessing is the absolute paralyzer of an organization, and not what you do in a turnaround, when you need speed.[27]

TRANSFORMATIONAL AND CHARISMATIC LEADERSHIP

Considerable attention is now being paid to a type of leader who goes beyond merely conducting transactions with people, such as rewarding and disciplining them. The **transformational leader** is one who helps organizations and people make positive changes in the way they conduct their activities. Transformational leadership is closely linked to strategic leadership, which provides the direction and inspiration to an organization. However, the emphasis in transformational

Present an overview of transformational and charismatic leadership.

leadership is on sweeping, positive changes. A major contributing factor to transformational leadership is **charisma,** the ability to lead others based on personal charm, magnetism, inspiration, and emotion. The study of transformational leadership and charismatic leadership is based on trait theory because the focus of analysis is the leader's personal characteristics.

Transformational Leadership

The transformational leader exerts a higher level of influence than does a transactional (routine) leader, thereby motivating people to do more than expected. Transformational leadership is seen as a key to revitalizing large organizations of many types. In recent years, a new leader was brought into the Internal Revenue Service to help revitalize that organization in terms of its technology and responsiveness to the needs of taxpayers. A transformational leader can develop new visions for a firm and mobilize employees to accept and work toward attaining these visions. Transformations take place in one or more of the following ways:[28]

1. By raising people's level of consciousness about the importance of and value of designated rewards and ways to achieve them.
2. By getting people to transcend their self-interests for the sake of the work group and the firm.
3. By raising people's focus on minor satisfactions to a quest for self-fulfillment. At the same time, group members are encouraged to seek satisfaction of higher-level needs.
4. By helping workers to adopt a long-range, broad perspective and focus less on day-by-day concerns.
5. By helping people understand the need for change. The transformational leader must help group members understand the need for change both emotionally and intellectually. A transformational leader recognizes this emotional component to resisting change and deals with it openly.
6. By investing managers with a sense of urgency. If managers throughout the organization do not perceive a vital need for change, the leader's vision will not be realized.
7. By committing to greatness. Greatness encompasses striving for business effectiveness such as profits and high stock value, as well as impeccable ethics.

Several different concepts of the characteristics and qualities of transformational leaders have been developed. A recent analysis of the components of transformational leaders was based on 1,440 subordinates who assess the leader behavior of 695 branch managers in a large Australian financial institution.[29] As summarized in Exhibit 10-9, the results are useful because they reinforce other understandings of transformational leadership. The statements accompanying each leadership dimension are essentially behavioral descriptions as expressed in survey statements about transformational leadership. For example, empowerment is defined as "My manager fosters trust, involvement, and cooperation among team members."

A concern about transformational leadership is that sometimes it is not necessary. The transformational leader might attempt to make sweeping changes in a system that only needs modification. Furthermore, Michael E. McGill and John W. Slocum contend that in many situations, small acts of leadership, such as listening to workers, is all that is needed. They observe, "A little leadership is what followers want and what leaders can do. Moreover, it can be learned. No less important, it is exactly the amount and kind of leadership that most organizations need."[30]

1. **Vision**
   Communicates a clear and positive vision of the future
2. **Staff Development**
   Treats staff as individuals, supports and encourages their development
3. **Supportive leadership**
   Gives encouragement and recognition to staff
4. **Empowerment**
   Fosters trust, involvement, and cooperation among team members
5. **Innovative Thinking**
   Encourages thinking about problems in new ways and questions assumptions

6. **Lead by Example**
   Is clear about his or her values, and practices what he or she preaches
7. **Charisma**
   Instills pride and respect in others and inspires me by being highly competent

Source: Sally A. Carless, Alexander J. Wearing, and Leon Mann, "A Short Measure of Transformational Leadership," *Journal of Business and Psychology,* Spring 2000, p. 396.

EXHIBIT
10-9

Dimensions and Corresponding Behaviors of Transformational Leadership

The Organizational Behavior in Action on the next page describes a transformational leader who has achieved remarkable results.

Charismatic Leadership

Charisma in a leader generally inspires group members and facilitates bringing about transformations. However, charisma to a large extent lies in the eye of the beholder and involves a relationship between the leader and the follower. A good example is Steve Jobs, considered by many to be the number-one visionary of Silicon Valley. One of his latest visions is to make his Pixar Animation Studios the next Disney studios. His earlier visions for Apple Computer may have changed personal computing. Despite Job's wide popularity, for many people he is too arrogant, sarcastic, and impatient to be charismatic and therefore inspirational. When the charismatic leader has good ethics, the transformations will be beneficial to society. A less-than-moral charismatic leader, in contrast, can lead people toward evil ends. Who in your mind is an *evil charismatic?*

A key characteristic of charismatic leaders is their *vision.* They offer a vision (or lofty goal) of where the organization is headed and how it can get there (a plan). According to Jay A. Conger and Rabindra N. Kanungo, a vision is multifaceted, extending beyond organizational goals. It also involves a way of identifying with the organization, aligning the organization's actions and strategies, and even building a collective identity for the firm.[31] A sense of vision inspires employees to perform well.

Charismatic leaders are masterful *communicators.* They formulate believable dreams and portray their vision of the future as the only path to follow. Charismatics also use metaphors to inspire people. An example is a favorite of Richard Marcus, the president of Neiman-Marcus stores: "If you follow in someone else's footsteps, you never get ahead."

Charismatic leaders at their best *inspire trust.* Quite often their followers are willing to gamble with their careers to follow their chief's vision, such as accepting a low starting salary with stock options based on the start-up's vision of great success. Charismatic leaders are *energetic* and use an action-oriented leadership style. They exude energy (like John Chambers), serving as a model for getting things done well and on time.

Charismatic leaders are adept at managing their impression well, which helps them be perceived as charismatic.[32] Impression management can take place at the

Organizational Behavior *in Action*

The Transformational John Chambers of Cisco Systems

A few years ago at a technology conference, John T. Chambers, the CEO of networking giant Cisco Systems Inc., was talking with Carl Russo, the CEO of the telecom-equipment start-up Cerent Corp. After a few pleasantries, Chambers got right to the point. With his typical broad smile, he asked "How much would it cost me to buy you?" Virtually no price would dissuade Chambers. Cisco agreed to pay a staggering $6.9 billion in stock for Cerent, even though the two-year start-up had sold only $10 million worth of equipment. Convinced that Cerent's technology was critical for linking the Internet and telephone-system worlds, Chambers would not back down. The offer also included a measure of job security for the 285 Cerent employees.

Much of Cisco's growth has come through acquisitions, having bought over 60 companies through 2000. At the same time, the company has invested heavily in internal R & D (research and development). The strategy has led to tremendous growth in sales and stock price, with the stock having climbed 100,000 (yes, one hundred thousand) percent in the first ten years since it went public.

A *Fortune* reporter said that Cisco, with John Chambers at the helm, must be considered one of America's outstanding companies. When Chambers became CEO in 1995, Cisco had a market cap of $9 billion. Five years later, the cap was $486 billion (a figure that fluctuates regularly).

Chambers is considered the leading salesperson in the Internet world. He persistently hawks the Internet. One day he is preaching Net religion to Chinese President Jiang Zemin, and the next he's meeting with six geeks in a garage who are sketching a new networking technology. Chambers approaches managing his company with the same zeal. He has helped Cisco become the ultimate model of an efficient Net company. The company sells about 80 percent of its products over the Internet, speeding up the process of and eliminating costly and needless steps between order-taking and delivery. Chambers evangelizes about how he can do the same for every other industrial company. A chairperson of an Internet Service Provider said, "What Bill Gates is to PCs, John Chamber has become for the Net."

Chambers spins a far-reaching vision of an Internet future. He declares that there will be a day when a New World Network will seamlessly blend the technology of the Internet with the high-speed optical fibers, cable, and wireless systems to carry voice and data everywhere. Chamber thinks that his company can become the top supplier for the New World Network. "If we do it right, we have the chance to become one of the most influential companies in history," he says. Chambers frequently makes statements such as, "We want to change the world." When Chambers speaks on a one-to-one level, he looks you in the eye. He always wears a suit and tie to work, owing somewhat to his early days at IBM.

Jack Welch, of GE, had Chambers address a quarterly management meeting. "He was very impressive. John has always impressed me. He's the leader of a very deep team that is really winning," stated Welch. Others agree that Chambers has built one of the deepest management teams in Silicon Valley. Managers are empowered more than at other well-known high-tech firms. One Cisco executive says, "One thing John does well is stretch people's responsibilities and change the boxes they are in. It makes our jobs new all the time."

Despite the warmth Chambers projects when he assumes a sales role, some competitors perceive him as a bully. "Cisco's competitors hate the company—I mean really hate it," says Shannon Pleasant, a networking analyst.

The Transformational John Chambers of Cisco Systems *(continued)*

Chambers has adopted the role of industry statesman. He has frequent meetings at the White House and spends face time with Washington insiders during their pilgrimages to Silicon Valley. In a one-year period, he met with more than 30 heads of state and George W. Bush before the latter became U. S. President.

Chambers heavily emphasizes customer relations in his approach to leading Cisco. When Chambers joined the company, it was engineering oriented. Today the emphasis is strongly marketing oriented despite being so high tech. All company executives have their bonuses tied to customer-satisfaction ratings. Cisco managers and professionals emphasize listening to their customers and often buy whatever technology they think their customers want. Chambers invests considerable time building customer relationships, making good use of his folksy charm.

Chambers works relentlessly, although he takes off Sunday to spend time with his family. He spends 30 hours per week meeting with customers. Chambers's work ethic helps set the tone for Cisco employees. A former Cisco-ite says, "It's a very demanding place. The peer pressure is intense. For Type A personalities only. To be successful, you have to commit to it. It's *not* an eight-hour day."

Chambers has a tremendous thirst for knowledge related to his business, but dyslexia has made reading a struggle for him. Nevertheless, he attended Duke University and West Virginia University as an undergraduate, earned a law degree at W.V.U., and an MBA from Indiana University. Chambers uses a sharp memory to compensate for his mediocre reading skills.

Want to read about the latest acquisitions of networking giant Cisco? Cnet.com (http://www.cnet.com) tracks the latest Cisco happenings.

Sources: Andy Reinhardt, "Meet Mr. Internet: Cisco Systems CEO John Chambers Has a Vision of a New World Order—with Cisco as its No. 1 Supplier," *Business Week*, September 13, 1999, pp. 128–140; Andy Serwer, "There's Something About Cisco," *Fortune*, May 15, 2000, pp. 114–138.

---

physical level, such as an appealing appearance, yet can also take place at an intellectual level. An intellectual example would be making it known that the person has powerful contacts, such as saying, "Steve Jobs and I were discussing the future of the PC just last week."

Charisma is not necessarily a mystical, inborn set of characteristics and behaviors. As the Skill-Development Exercise that follows shows, charisma is an attainable skill if you have the discipline to practice the techniques it outlines. Observe that several of the suggestions are geared toward impression management.

360-DEGREE FEEDBACK FOR IMPROVING LEADERSHIP EFFECTIVENESS

A widely used method for improving leadership effectiveness is for the manager/leader to receive feedback on his or her traits, attitudes, and behaviors from multiple raters. A **360-degree survey** is a formal evaluation of superiors based on input from people who work for and with them, sometimes including customers and suppliers. The 360-degrees refers to the fact that people all around you are making the ratings and evaluations. Such evaluations can also be used as part of the performance appraisal. Particularly when used for learning about leadership effectiveness, the individual completes the same form that all others used to describe his or her behavior. The feedback is communicated to the leader and interpreted with the assistance of a psychologist or organizational behavior specialist.

Explain how 360-degree feedback is used to improve leadership effectiveness.

SKILL-DEVELOPMENT EXERCISE

Developing Charisma

Establishing the goal of becoming more charismatic is the starting point for developing charisma. In addition, you then discipline yourself to develop some of the traits and characteristics described in the text. Here are eight specific suggestions for skill development.[33]

1. *Use visioning.* If you are the leader of an organizational unit, develop a dream about its future. Discuss your vision with others in the unit and with your immediate superior.
2. *Make frequent use of metaphors.* Develop metaphors to inspire people around you. A commonly used one after a group has suffered a substantial setback is, "Like the phoenix, we will rise from the ashes of defeat."
3. *Inspire trust and confidence.* Make your deeds consistent with your promises. Get people to believe in your competence by making your accomplishments known in a polite, tactful way.
4. *Make others feel capable.* Give out assignments on which others can succeed, and lavishly praise their success.

5. *Be highly energetic and goal oriented.* Impress others with your energy and resourcefulness. To increase your energy supply, exercise frequently, eat well, and get ample rest.
6. *Express your emotions frequently.* Freely express warmth, joy, happiness, and enthusiasm.
7. *Smile frequently, even if you are not in a happy mood.* A warm smile seems to indicate a confident, caring person, which contributes to a perception of charisma.
8. *Make everybody you meet feel that he or she is quite important.* For example, at a company meeting, shake the hand of every person you meet.
9. *Focus on the positive.* Charismatic people are optimists who minimize complaints and emphasize what positive steps can be taken to overcome a problem.
10. *Maintain positive body language.* To radiate authenticity and confidence, stand and sit up straight. When standing, keep your feet about 12 inches apart. When sitting, do not tap your feet nervously.

The data from the survey can be used to help leaders fine-tune their attitudes and behaviors. For example, if all the raters gave the leader low ratings on "sensitive to the needs of others," the leader might be prompted to improve his or her sensitivity to the needs of others. Action plans for improving sensitivity would include reading about understanding others, attending a seminar, taking a suitable on-line course, and making a deliberate attempt to understand the feelings and needs of others.

A standard approach to a 360-degree survey is for a sampling of work associates to complete a lengthy questionnaire about dozens of specific behaviors.[34] Self-ratings are then compared to ratings by others. Assume that a leader rates himself in the 90th percentile on "Displays warmth and a good sense of humor." If others rated him at the 15th percentile on this dimension, the leader might be counseled about how to put others at ease. The example just cited hints at the importance of professionally trained counselors being involved in 360-degree surveys. Some people feel emotionally crushed when they find a wide discrepancy between their self-perception on an interpersonal skill and the perception of others.

GENDER DIFFERENCES IN LEADERSHIP

Identify gender differences in leadership style.

Controversy continues as to whether men and women have different leadership styles and characteristics. Several researchers and observers argue that women have certain acquired traits and behaviors that suit them for relationship-oriented leadership. Consequently, women leaders more frequently exhibit a cooperative, empowering style that includes nurturing of team members. Women are more likely than men to praise group members and will more frequently temper criticism with small amounts of praise.

According to this same perspective, men are inclined toward a command-and-control, militaristic leadership style. Women find participative management more natural than do men because women feel more comfortable interacting with people and building relationships. The same stereotype contends that women's natural sensitivity to people gives them an edge over men in encouraging group members to participate in decision making.

Adding to the controversy about gender differences in leadership style is a five-year study comparing how well men and women managers are perceived by work associates. Lawrence A. Plaff, a human resources consultant, found that female managers scored higher than their male counterparts in 20 skill areas. Included in the study were 2,482 managers at all levels from more than 400 organizations across 19 states. To evaluate the managers, 360-degree feedback was used. Plaff said that the sex differences extend beyond the softer skills such as communication, feedback, and empowering other employees to such hard areas as decisiveness, planning, and setting standards.

Plaff believes that women have acquired nontraditional strengths in recent years, but that men have not broadened their strengths in the same way. His study also suggests that male managers still rely on a more autocratic style, emphasizing individual accomplishment and competition. Women place more emphasis on facilitating group processes, using positive motivation, and developing group members' abilities.[35]

To what extent these stereotypes of men and women leaders are true is difficult to judge. For example, many women contend that women managers are meaner than men managers. A more important issue is how to capitalize on both male and female leadership tendencies. Connie Glaser believes that the best approach to leadership takes advantage of the positive traits from both men and women. She sees a new management style that blends the male and female sides:

> While the female may impart that sense of nurturing, the sensitivity to individual and family needs, that's offset by certain traits the male brings to the table. The ability to make decisions quickly, the sense of humor, the risk-taking—these are qualities that traditionally have been associated with the male style of management.[36]

LEADERSHIP SUBSTITUTES AND FOLLOWERSHIP

An implicit theme of this chapter has been that leadership is important because it affects such outcomes as productivity and satisfaction. At times, however, competent leadership is not necessary, and incompetent leadership can be counterbalanced by certain factors in the work situation. Under these circumstances, leadership is of little consequence to the performance and satisfaction of team members. According to this viewpoint, many organizations have **substitutes for leadership.** Such substitutes are factors in the work environment that provide guidance and incentives to perform, making the leader's role almost superfluous.[37] Leadership substitutes, in effect, neutralize the effects of leadership.

Group member characteristics that can substitute for leadership include ability, experience, training, and professional orientation. For example, a highly capable

Identify forces that can sometimes decrease the importance of leadership.

employee with strong professional values will accomplish the job with any plausible person acting as the formal leader. Task characteristics that can substitute for leadership include standardized methods, jobs with built-in feedback, and intrinsically satisfying work. Information technology can also substitute for leadership (or at least supervision) when instructions for tasks are entered into the computer. Organizational factors that can substitute for leadership include explicit plans and goals and cohesive work groups. The cohesive work group, for example, will exert its own influence over group members.

Another way of framing the leadership substitute issue is that good followers require less leadership. Although a negative term for many, *follower* in this context means a person who is not presently assigned to a leadership position. A good follower would have many of the traits and skills described throughout this text including high cognitive intelligence, emotional intelligence, motivation, and communication skills. As observed by Robert E. Kelly, effective followers share four essential qualities: *Self-management* is the ability to work well without close supervision. *Commitment* refers to being committed to something beyond yourself, be it a cause, a product, a department, an organization, an idea, or a value. *Competence and focus* refer to mastering skills useful to the organization and concentrating effort on important tasks. *Courage* refers to being an independent, critical thinker who will fight for what he or she believes is right.[38]

Choosing an Appropriate Leadership Model

Thirteen different leadership theories, models, or other explanations of leadership have been presented. Although these approaches have different labels, there are many common elements. Furthermore, all the different theories, models, and explanations are useful for guiding and influencing group members. In quick review, the thirteen approaches are (1) developing the right traits, (2) the initiating structure and consideration dimensions of leadership, (3) the Leadership Grid, (4) the leader–member exchange model, (5) Fiedler's contingency theory of leadership, (6) the path-goal theory of leadership, (7) the situational leadership model, (8) the normative decision model, (9) transformational leadership, (10) charismatic leadership, (11) 360-degree feedback, (12) gender differences in leadership, and (13) substitutes for leadership and followership.

A fruitful approach to choosing an effective leadership theory, model, or explanation is for the manager to carefully diagnose the situation. Choose a leadership approach that best fits the deficiency or neglected opportunity in a given situation. Observe the people to be led, and also interview them about their interests, goals, and concerns. Then apply a leadership approach that appears to match the interests, concerns, deficits, or missed opportunities. The following two examples will help clarify this diagnostic approach:

1. The manager observes that many important decisions are being made and that group members are eager to get involved. Nevertheless, the group members are overworked and pressed for time. The leader would be advised to use the normative decision model to help decide how important it is to involve the group in a particular decision. (The leader wants to involve group members, but needless involvement will intensify the overwork problem.)
2. The manager observes that the group is accomplishing its job, and morale is satisfactory. Yet something is missing; a sense of urgency and excitement does not pervade the atmosphere. In this situation, the leader is advised to take the steps in his or her power to behave like a transformational and charismatic leader.

IMPLICATIONS FOR MANAGERIAL PRACTICE

1. Technically competent and well-motivated employees require less guidance and control than do their less-competent and poorly motivated counterparts.
2. When time is critical and the situation is favorable to the leader (for example, when the leader has good relationships with the group), a task-oriented style may contribute to goal attainment.
3. When group members are facing ambiguity, heavy work demands, and heavy job stress, a relationship-oriented leadership style may lead to increased morale and productivity.
4. Exhibiting charisma can benefit the vast majority of leaders. Although charisma is somewhat dependent on longstanding personality characteristics, it can be enhanced through such means as suggested in the Skill-Development Exercise on page 228.
5. Although the modern organization emphasizes team-oriented, collaborative leadership, decisive, creative, and independent-thinking leaders are still needed.

SUMMARY OF KEY POINTS

 Differentiate between leadership and management. Leadership involves influencing others to achieve important objectives. Leaders are heavily involved in persuading, inspiring, and motivating others and spearheading change. Managers are more involved with stability and control.

 Describe key leadership traits, styles, and behaviors. Certain traits and characteristics contribute to leadership effectiveness in many situations. These personal attributes fall into the general categories of cognitive skills and personality characteristics, including emotional intelligence.

A foundation concept of the behavioral approach to leadership is the two dimensions of initiating structure and consideration and, similarly, production centered and employee centered. The Leadership Grid® describes a manager's leadership style along the dimensions of concern for production and concern for people. Each of these concerns exists in varying degrees. The leader-member exchange model emphasizes that leaders have unique relationships with group members. In-group members have good relationships with the leader, whereas out-group members have poor relationships. Being part of the in-group enhances productivity and satisfaction.

 Explain the basics of four different contingency theories of leadership.
Fiedler's contingency theory specifies the conditions under which leaders need to use task-motivated and relationship-motivated styles. In situations of high control and low control, the task-motivated style is better. Socio-independent leaders tend to perform best when their control is high.

According to the path-goal theory, leaders can enhance motivation by increasing personal payoffs to group members for achieving work objectives and by making the paths to payoffs smoother. The effective leader will choose among leadership styles according to two sets of contingency factors: characteristics of subordinates and task demands.

The situational leadership model explains how to match leadership style to the readiness of group members. Leadership is classified according to the amount of task and relationship behavior. Readiness is the extent to which a group member has the ability and willingness or confidence to accomplish a specific task. As a group member's readiness increases, a leader should rely more on relationship behavior and less on task behavior. When a group member becomes very ready, a minimum of task or relationship behavior is required by the leader.

The normative decision model explains that leadership is a decision-making process. A leader examines certain contingency factors in the situation to determine which decision-making style will be the most effective in either a time-driven or a developmental situation. The model identifies five decision-making styles: two individual and three group. By answering a series of seven diagnostic questions in a matrix, the manager follows the path to a recommended decision style.

Present an overview of transformational and charismatic leadership.

The transformational leader is a charismatic person who helps bring about profound changes in people and the organization, often transforming the culture. Charismatic leaders are known to have vision, be masterful communicators, and inspire trust. They are also adept at managing their impression well. Charisma can be developed to some extent.

Explain how 360-degree feedback is used to improve leadership effectiveness.

Using 360-degree feedback, a person receives feedback on his or her traits, attitudes, and behaviors from multiple raters. Self-evaluation is often included. The data from the 360-degree survey can be used to help the leaders fine-tune their attitudes and behaviors.

Identify forces that can sometimes decrease the importance of leadership.

Although leadership is important, in certain situations, other factors may function as substitutes for leadership. These factors can be found within group members, the task, or the organization. Effective followers also decrease the need for leadership.

Identify gender differences in leadership style.

Gender differences in leadership are thought to exist, with women using a more cooperative, empowering style that also involves frequent praise. Men are thought to be more inclined toward a command-and-control, militaristic style of leadership with less inclination toward participative decision making. The case can be made for blending the positive aspects of the male and female approaches to leadership—to the extent that these stereotypes are valid.

KEY TERMS AND PHRASES

Leadership, *208*
The ability to inspire confidence and support among the people on whose competence and commitment performance depends.

Cognitive Skills, *209*
Mental ability and knowledge.

Behavioral Approach to Leadership, *211*
An attempt to specify how the behavior of effective leaders differs from their less-effective counterparts.

Leadership Style, *211*
The relatively consistent pattern of behavior that characterizes a leader.

Initiating Structure, *211*
The degree to which a leader establishes structure for group members.

Consideration, *211*
The degree to which the leader creates an environment of emotional support, warmth, friendliness, and trust.

Leadership Grid®, *213*
A framework for classifying leadership styles that simultaneously examines a leader's concerns for task accomplishment and people.

Leader-member Exchange Model, *214*
The model that recognizes that leaders develop unique working relationships with each group member.

Contingency Theory of Leadership, *216*
The position that the best style of leadership depends on factors relating to group members and the work setting.

Situational Control, *217*
The degree to which the leader can control and influence the outcomes of group effort.

Path-goal Theory of Leadership, *217*
An explanation of leadership that specifies what the leader must do to achieve high morale and productivity in a given situation.

Situational Leadership Model, *218*
The model that matches leadership style to the readiness of group members.

Readiness, *219*
The extend to which a group member has the ability and willingness or confidence to accomplish a special task.

Normative Decision Model, *220*
A contingency viewpoint of leadership that views leadership as a decision-making process in which the leader examines certain situational factors to determine which decision-making style will be most effective.

Transformational Leader, *223*
One who helps organizations and people make positive changes in the way they conduct their activities.

Charisma, *224*

The ability to lead others based on personal charm, magnetism, inspiration, and emotion.

360-degree Survey, *227*

A formal evaluation of superiors based on input from people who work for and with them, sometimes including customers and suppliers.

Substitutes for Leadership, *229*

Factors in the work environment that provide guidance and incentives to perform, making the leader's role almost superfluous.

DISCUSSION QUESTIONS AND ACTIVITIES

1. Describe how a person might be a good leader but a poor manager.
2. Describe how a person might be a good manager but a poor leader.
3. Give an example of a leadership task that you think would require considerable cognitive skill.
4. Give an example of a business leader you think has an enormous power motive, and explain your reasoning.

5. How would the situational theory help you do a better job of managing or leading poorly motivated workers?
6. If gender differences in leadership style really exist, what implications would that have for assigning people to team leader positions in organizations?
7. What do you perceive to be a major difference between a contingency leader and a charismatic leader?

ORGANIZATIONAL BEHAVIOR ON-LINE

TO DO

Charisma Tips from the Net

The Skill-Development Exercise on page 228 offered suggestions for becoming more charismatic. Search the Internet for additional suggestions and compare them to the suggestions in the text. Be alert to contradictions, and offer a possible explanation for the contradiction. Use a search phrase such as "How to become more charismatic." An all-encompassing phrase such as "developing leadership effectiveness" is unlikely to direct you to the information you need. You might consult a search engine and look for information about developing charisma.

TO BOOKMARK

Center for Creative Leadership
http://www.ccl.org

Journeyman Leadership
http://www.coxegroup.com/articles/leader.html

GE Leaders—Our Values
http://www.ge.com/ibinta18.htm

Servant-Leadership
http://greenleaf.org

CASE PROBLEM: Yahoo! What Type of Leader is Tim Koogle?

Yahoo! has been one of the wonderful success stories in the commercial history of the Internet. Founded in 1994 by Jerry Yang and David Filo, two Stanford University graduate students in engineering who created a Web directory mostly for fun, Yahoo is a dominant player in its niche. Its management team, led by Chairman and CEO Tim Koogle, has built Yahoo into a powerful portal and one of the best-known brands in cyberspace. The company is a portal with 145 million registered users, making it the largest in the world. Koogle is now boosting the economy of this huge virtual bazaar with on-line wallets, shopping services, and other features. Koogle says, "We've set out to make Yahoo the only place anyone needs to go to get connected to anything. There's nothing in the real world to compare to that."

The company's strategic moves, such as the acquisition of GeoCities and Broadcast.com, have been praised by financial analysts. The company's ability to attract viewers (or "aggregate eyeballs") is unquestioned. Although Yahoo has the most registered users, it still trails No. 1 AOL in terms of on-line visitors per month. Yahoo is one of the rare profitable Net companies. Much of its income stems from the fees it charges retailers for transactions generated on its Web site. Its gross margins are 83 percent, more than four times that of Amazon.com, because Yahoo does not have to pay for warehouses and labor.

Although Yahoo stock has had an incredible growth, the management team is much more concerned about building the business than in running up the company's market valuation. Venture capitalist Michael Moritz made the following comment about the Yahoo management team: "These guys

234

have never allowed themselves to be distracted by the hoopla over the stock. They've always understood that they are building a business and not promoting a stock. In all the conversations I've had with the team, I don't think we've spent five minutes talking about the stock. Not five minutes."

Koogle had wanted to delay doing an IPO, partly because Yahoo already had received $100 million as an investment from the Japanese Company, Softbank. Koogle said, "I really wanted a few more quarters. I wanted to be sure we could deliver our numbers consistently ahead of Wall Street's expectations." In the end, Koogle was forced to offer stock to the public. Two competitors, Lycos and Excite, had announced plans for IPOs, and Koogle felt Yahoo could not be left behind.

Koogle and other Yahoo executives believed that it was necessary for the company to show profits early if it didn't want to have a reputation as another profitless Net company whose stock floated on air. Koogle and the rest of the Yahoo management team also made a point of not acting like a bunch of wild and crazy start-up guys. They went low-key and professional, never talking up the stock, and always talking about the business. They dealt in real numbers, not blue-sky projections. Today, Yahoo is considered one of the safer Internet investments and is regarded by some analysts as a blue-chip stock.

At Yahoo, the new millennium began with a major challenge. Koogle heard that archrival America Online was about to acquire Time Warner. The deal raised questions about the effectiveness of Yahoo's strategy of forming partnerships with lots of companies instead of buying a big one. Koogle and two other top Yahoo executives hustled off to a conference room with a white board. Remaining cool under pressure, Koogle led a reevaluation of the strategy. The three resolved to stand firm. "He really held the group together," said President Jeff Mallett.

Koogle shuns geeky Net-speak. He prefers instead folksy phrases that draw on his southern roots. "Mamby-pamby," for example, is his term for ideas that lack substance. There's also the "rowboat syndrome" to describe people who spend too much time looking backward instead of forward.

A *Business Week* reporter observed that Koogle's business savvy, drawn from 3 engineering degrees and 15 years in high-tech management, has been critical to the success of the company where the average age is under 30. Koogle is the voice of reason in an environment heavy with breathless

Net enthusiasts. "He's very decisive and focused," says a board member.

The founders of Yahoo were reluctant to turn their enterprise into an advertising-driven enterprise. But the pragmatic Koogle persuaded them that they could make money and still deliver their on-line treats gratis. He turned them around by building consensus through lively, and sometimes painstaking, debate. While working out problems with the executive team, Koogle plays the role of the seasoned veteran.

Transforming Yahoo into a profitable business seems as natural to Koogle as rebuilding a car. "It's a full circle for me," he says. "The whole process of taking raw parts and building something that runs appeals to me." He also says he is into businesses that make money, unlike many of the dot.com businesses of recent years.

Koogle enjoys fixing things. He learned auto mechanics from his late father, a Navy machinist. He put himself through graduate school by rebuilding the engines of students' cars and founding an industrial design company. He graduated first in his class at the University of Virginia. He later earned an MS and a PhD in engineering at Stanford University, and then worked at Motorola Inc. in the operations and venture-capital groups. Koogle has an artistic and fun side, too, with his network of friends including a group of glass blowers and painters near Venice. He plays the electric guitar and has tuned his Mercedes to exceed legal speed limits. He also enjoys car racing on a track.

Case Questions

1. Using any system of classifying leadership styles you choose, identify the dominant leadership style of Tim Koogle.

2. Identify key traits and behaviors of Koogle, as revealed in this case.

3. What suggestions can you offer Tim Koogle to make him an even more-effective leader?

Source: Steve Rosenbush, "How Can Tim Koogle Stay So Cool In the Face of AOL's Assault?" *Business Week* **E.Biz,** May 15, 2000, p. **EB 27**; Joseph Nocera, "Do You Believe? How Yahoo! Became a Blue Chip," *Fortune,* June 7, 1999, pp. 76–92; Linda Himmelstein, "Yahoo! The Company, the Strategy, the Stock," *Business Week,* September 7, 1998, pp. 66–76.

Yahoo maintains an archive of Yahoo!® Events at http://www.broadcast.com. Koogle and other Yahoo notables often show up on Yahoo!® Events pages, giving radio or televised addresses and interviews.

SUGGESTED READINGS

Bennis, Warren, and O'Toole, James. "Don't Hire the Wrong CEO." *Harvard Business Review,* May–June 2000, pp. 170–176.

Buckingham, Marcus, and Coffman, Curt. *First, Break All the Rules: What the World's Greatest Managers Do Differently.* New York: Simon and Schuster, 1999.

Cashman, Kevin. *Leadership from the Inside Out.* Provo, Utah: Excellence Publishing, 1998.

Caudron, Shari. "The Looming Leadership Crisis." *Workforce,* September 1999, pp. 72–79.

Grossman, Robert J. "Heirs Unapparent: Leaders Wanted for the New Century." *HR Magazine,* February 1999, pp. 36–44.

Hill, Linda, and Wetlaufer, Suzy. "Leadership When There Is No One to Ask: An Interview with ENI's Franco Bernabè." *Harvard Business Review,* July-August 1998, pp. 80–94.

Maccoby, Michael. "Narcissistic Leaders: The Incredible Pros, the Inevitable Cons." *Harvard Business Review,* January–February 2000, pp. 68–77.

Reingold, Jennifer. "Big Headhunter Is Watching You." *Business Week,* March 1, 1999, pp. 54–56.

Smith, Scott S. "You Got Personality." *Entrepreneur,* September 1999, pp. 135–138.

Stewart, Thomas A. "Have You Got What It Takes?" *Fortune,* October 11, 1999, pp. 318–322.

Waldroop, James, and Butler, Timothy. "Eight Failings That Bedevil the Best." *Fortune,* November 23, 1998, p. 293.

ENDNOTES

1. Thomas A. Stewart, "America's Most Admired Companies," *Fortune,* March 2, 1998, p. 72.
2. W. Chan Kim and Renee A. Mauborgne, "Parables of Leadership," *Harvard Business Review,* July–August 1992, p. 123.
3. John P. Kotter, "What Leaders Really Do," *Harvard Business Review,* May–June 1990, pp. 103–111.
4. Steve Hamm, "Behind the Larry & Ray Show," *Business Week,* August 3, 1998, p. 88.
5. Dave Ulrich, Jack Zenger, and Norman Smallwood, *Results-Based Leadership: How Leaders Build the Business and Improve the Bottom Line* (Boston: Harvard Business School Press, 1999).
6. Robert Hogan, Gordon J. Curphy, and Joyce Hogan, "What We Know about Leadership Effectiveness and Personality," *American Psychologist,* June 1994, p. 494.
7. Shelly A. Kirkpatrick and Edwin A. Locke, "Leadership: Do Traits Matter?" *Academy of Management Executive,* May 1991, pp. 48-60; Edwin A. Locke and Associates, *The Essence of Leadership: The Four Keys to Leading Successfully* (New York: Lexington/Macmillan, 1991), pp. 13–34.
8. Ellen M. Whitener, Susan E. Brodt, M. Audrey Korsgaard, and Jon M. Werner, "Managers as Initiators of Trust: An Exchange Relationship Framework for Understanding Managerial Trustworthy Behavior," *Academy of Management Review,* July 1998, p. 516.
9. Quoted in "The Top 500 Women-Owned Businesses," *Working Woman,* June 1999, p. 44.
10. Daniel Goleman, "Leadership that Gets Results," *Harvard Business Review,* March–April 2000, p. 80
11. Joel Stein, "Bosses from Hell," *Time,* December 7, 1998, p. 181.
12. Martin L. Maher and Douglas A. Klieber, "The Greying of Achievement Motivation," *American Psychologist,* July 1981, pp. 787–793.
13. Bruce J. Avolio, Jane M. Howell, and John J. Sosik, "A Funny Thing Happened on the Way to the Bottom Line: Humor as a Moderator of Leadership Style Effects," *Academy of Management Journal,* April 1999, pp. 219–227.
14. Ralph M. Stogdill and Alvin E. Coons (eds.), *Leader Behavior: Its Description and Measurement* (Columbus, OH: Ohio State University Bureau of Business Research, 1957); Carroll L. Shartle, *Executive Performance and Leadership* (Upper Saddle River, NJ: Prentice Hall, 1956).
15. Arnold S. Tannenbaum, *Social Psychology of the Work Organization* (Monterey, CA: Wadsworth, 166), p. 74; Robert Dubin, "Supervision and Productivity: Empirical Findings and Theoretical Considerations," in Walter Nord (ed.), *Concepts and Controversies in Organizational Behavior* (Glenview, IL: Scott, Foresman and Company, 1972), pp. 524–525.
16. Polly Labarre, "Do You Have the Will to Lead?" *Fortune,* March 2000, pp. 227–228.
17. Robert R. Blake and Anne Adams McCanse, *Leadership Dilemmas—Grid Solutions* (Houston: Gulf Publishing Company, 1991).
18. George Graen and J. F. Cashman, "A Role-Making Model of Leadership in Formal Organizations: A Developmental Approach," in J. G. Hunt and L. I. Larson (eds.), *Leadership Frontiers* (Kent, OH: Kent State University Press, 1975), pp. 143-165; Robert P. Vecchio, "Leader-Member Exchange, Objective Performance, Employment Duration, and Supervisor Ratings: Testing for Moderation and Mediation," *Journal of Business and Psychology,* Spring 1998, pp. 327–341.
19. Robert P. Vecchio, "Are You In or OUT with Your Boss?" *Business Horizons,* vol. 29, 1987, pp. 76–78.
20. Chester A. Schriesheim, Linda L. Neider, and Terri A. Scandura, "Delegation and Leader-Member Exchange: Main Effects, Moderators, and Measurement Issues," *Academy of Management Journal,* June 1998, pp. 298–318.
21. Vecchio, "Leader-Member Exchange," p. 340.
22. Fred E. Fiedler, Martin M. Chemers, and Linda Mahar, *Improving Leadership Effectiveness: The Leader-Match Concept,* 2nd ed. (New York: John Wiley & Sons, 1984; Martin M. Chemers, *An Integrative Theory of Leadership* (Mahwah, NJ: Lawrence Erlbaum Associates, 1997), pp. 28–38.
23. Robert J. House and Terence R. Mitchell, "Path-Goal Theory of Leadership," *Journal of Contemporary Business* (Fall 1974), p. 83.
24. Paul Hersey, Kenneth H. Blanchard, and Dewey E. Johnson, *Management of Organizational Behavior: Utilizing Human Resources,* 7th ed. (Upper Saddle River, NJ: Prentice Hall, 1996), pp. 188–227.
25. Victor H. Vroom, "Leadership and the Decision-Making Process," *Organizational Dynamics,* Spring 2000, pp. 82–93.
26. Richard H. G. Field and Robert J. House, "A Test of the Vroom-Yetton Model Using Manager and Subordinate Reports," *Journal of Applied Psychology,* June 1990, pp. 362–366.
27. Susan Caminiti, "Turnaround Titan," *Working Woman,* December/January 1999, p. 57.
28. John J. Hater and Bernard M. Bass, "Supervisors' Evaluations and Subordinates' Perceptions of Transformational and Transactional Leadership," *Journal of Applied Psychology,* November 1988, p. 695; Noel M. Tichy and May Anne Devanna, *The Transformational Leader* (New York: Wiley, 1990).
29. Sally A. Carless, Alexander J. Wearing, and Leon Mann, "A Short Measure of Transformational Leadership," *Journal of Business and Psychology,* Spring 2000, pp. 389–405.
30. Michael E. McGill and John W. Slocum Jr., "A Little Leadership, Please?" *Organizational Dynamics,* Winter 1998, p. 48.
31. Jay A. Conger and Rabindra N. Kanungo, *Charismatic Leadership in Organizations* (Thousand Oaks, CA: Sage, 1998).
32. William L. Gardner and Bruce J. Avolio, "The Charismatic Relationship: A Dramaturgical Perspective," *Academy of Management Review,* January 1998, p. 33.
33. Several of the suggestions are from Roger Dawson, *Secrets of Power Persuasion: Everything You'll Need to Get Anything You'll Ever Want* (Upper Saddle River, NJ: Prentice Hall, 1992), pp. 179-194: "Secrets of Charismatic Leadership," *WorkingSMART,* February 1998, p. 1.

34. Craig T. Chappelow, "360-Degree Feedback," in Cynthia D. McCauley, Russ S. Moxley, and Ellen Van Velsor, *The Center for Creative Leadership Handbook of Leadership Development* (San Francisco: Jossey-Bass, 1998), pp. 29–65; Angelo S. DeNisi and Avraham, N. Kluger, "Feedback Effectiveness: Can 360-Degree Appraisals Be Improved?" *Academy of Management Executive,* February 2000, pp. 129–139.

35. Research reported in S. Kass, "Employees Perceive Women as Better Managers than Men, Finds Five-Year Study," *APA Monitor,* September 1999, p. 6.

36. Cited in Debra Phillips, "The Gender Gap," *Entrepreneur,* May 1995, p. 112.

37. Jon P. Howell, David E. Bowen, Peter W. Dorfman, Steven Kerr, and Philip Podsakoff, "Substitutes for Leadership: Effective Alternatives to Ineffective Leadership," *Organizational Dynamics,* Summer 1990, p. 23.

38. Robert E. Kelley, "In Praise of Followers," *Harvard Business Review,* November–December 1988, pp. 142–148.

Power, Politics, and Influence

Sylvain Marchand, a division manager of a Montreal food-processing company, received a below-average performance appraisal and a below-average salary increase from his regional manager, Guy LeBlanc. Marchand disagreed strongly with the assessment and attempted to persuade LeBlanc to change his opinion. LeBlanc would not comply, explaining that he had carefully documented why Marchand's performance did not meet expectations.

Marchand plotted his revenge. He reasoned that because he and the CEO were former golfing partners, he could capitalize on this friendship to get LeBlanc in trouble. Marchand sent the CEO a scathing letter about LeBlanc's performance, including the assertion that LeBlanc only gave favorable performance appraisals to Yes-people. Marchand was pleasantly surprised when the CEO responded to the letter by inviting him to a meeting at his office the following Friday. Yet when Marchand arrived at the meeting, he was unnerved to find LeBlanc also present. After three minutes of warm-up conversation, the CEO said calmly, "Guy and I agree that since your performance is below average and you are unhappy here, you are terminated as of 5:00 this afternoon. You will receive two weeks' severance pay. Goodbye."

Power relationships are a pervasive fact of organizational life and a pervasive theme of the 1972 film classic *The Godfather*. Much has been written about the chilling effects of political behavior in Coppola's trilogy of the Corleone family. Go to the Movie Review Query Engine at http://www.mrqe.com to find out more.

Source: Case history researched by Lorraine Dubeau, the Salvation Army of Canada, April 1995.

OBJECTIVES

After reading and studying this chapter and doing the exercises, you should be able to

1. Identify sources of power for individuals and sub-units within organizations.

2. Describe the essence of empowerment.

3. Pinpoint factors contributing to organizational politics.

4. Identify and describe a variety of political and influence tactics.

5. Explain how managers can control dysfunctional politics.

6. Differentiate between the ethical and unethical use of power, politics, and influence.

Chapter 11

SO WHAT? **What does the demise of Sylvain Marchand tell us about how managers use political tactics to hold on to power?** Among other things, the incident shows that managers sometimes choose unethical tactics (in this case, backstabbing) that can sometimes backfire. Power, politics, and influence are such a major part of the workplace that they have become a standard topic of organizational behavior. How they are invoked—whether with aggression or to achieve closer cooperation—presents interesting dilemmas suitable for our analysis.

In this chapter, we approach power, politics, and influence from multiple perspectives. We describe the meaning of these concepts, how power is obtained, and how it is shared (empowerment). We then examine why organizational politics is so prevalent, along with a description of tactics of politics and influence. In addition, we describe the control of dysfunctional politics, and ethical considerations about the use of power, politics and influence. As you read the chapter, you will learn that some tactics of power, politics, and influence violate ethical codes and therefore should be avoided.

THE MEANING OF POWER, POLITICS, AND INFLUENCE

A challenge in understanding power, politics, and influence in organizations is that the terms appear close in meaning. Here we present meanings of these terms aimed at providing useful distinctions. **Power** is the potential or ability to influence decisions and control resources. Many definitions of power center around the ability of a person to overcome resistance in achieving a result. Yet some researchers suggest that power lies in the potential, while others focus on use.[1] As a hedge, our definition includes both potential and use. If you have a powerful battery in your car, isn't it still powerful whether or not it is in use?

Politics is a way of achieving power. As defined by Jeffrey Pfeffer, "Organizational politics involves those activities taken in organizations to acquire, develop, and use power and other resources to obtain one's preferred outcomes in a situation in which there is uncertainty or dissensus about choices."[2] Or as used here, **organizational politics** refers to informal approaches to gaining power through means other than merit or luck.

Influence is close in meaning to power. Influence is also the ability to change behavior, but it tends to be more subtle and more indirect than power. Power indicates the ability to affect outcomes with greater facility and ease than does influence.[3]

Managers and professionals often need to use political tactics to achieve the power and influence they need to accomplish their work. An example would be a customer service manager cultivating the support of a top executive so she can proceed with a program of total customer satisfaction. Without the ethical and effective use of politics, the company would not be able to work toward total customer satisfaction.

SOURCES OF INDIVIDUAL AND SUBUNIT POWER

Identify sources of power for individuals and subunits within organizations.

The sources or bases of power in organizations can be classified in different ways. A useful starting point is to recognize that power can be used to forward the interests of the organization or personal interests. **Socialized power** is the use of power to achieve constructive ends. An example would be the manager who was attempting to gain power to spearhead a program of total customer satisfaction. **Personalized power** is the use of power primarily for the sake of personal aggrandizement and gain.[4] An example would be a new CEO using his power to insist that company headquarters be moved to a location near his home.

Here we classify the sources (also bases or origins) of power into those stemming from the position, from the person, and from providing resources.[5]

Power Granted by the Organization (Position Power)

Managers and professionals often have power because of the authority, or right, granted by their positions. The power of a manager's position stems from three sources: legitimate power, coercive power, and reward power. **Legitimate power** is based on the manager's formal position within the hierarchy. A government agency head, for example, has much more position power than a unit supervisor in the same agency. Managers can enhance their position power by formulating policies and procedures. For example, a manager might establish a requirement that she must approve all new hires, thus exercising authority over hiring.

Coercive power is controlling others through fear of punishment or threat of punishment. Typical organizational punishments include bypassing an employee for promotion and terminating employment. The threat of a lawsuit by an employee who is treated unjustly serves as a constraint on legitimate power, and is referred to as *subordinate power*. **Reward power** is controlling others through rewards or the promise of rewards. Examples of this are promotions, challenging assignments, and recognition given to employees.

The effectiveness of coercive power and reward power depends on the perceptions and needs of group members. For coercive power to be effective, the employee must fear punishment and care about being a member of the firm.

Power Stemming from the Individual (Personal Power)

Managers and professionals also derive power from two separate personal characteristics: knowledge and personality. **Expert power** is the ability to influence others because of one's specialized knowledge, skills, or abilities. For expertise to be an effective source of power, group members must respect that expertise. Exercising expert power is the logical starting point for building one's power base.

Powerful people in business, government, and education almost invariably launched their career by developing expertise in a specialty of value to their employers. A telling example is Mary G. Meeker, a managing director at the investment firm of Morgan Stanley Dean Witter. While an industry analyst, she developed expertise as a trend spotter, and is considered to have laser-sharp analytical skills. She was one of the first people to see the possibilities of the Internet for conducting business. John Chambers of Cisco Systems says this about Meeker: "She gets it, got it earlier than most, and was able to articulate it to the business community in a way they could understand."[6]

Referent power is the ability to influence others that stems from one's desirable traits and characteristics. It is based on the desire of others to be led by or identify with an inspiring person. Having referent power contributes to being perceived as charismatic, but expert power also makes a contribution.[7]

Power from Providing Resources

Another way of understanding the sources of power is through the **resource dependence perspective.** According to this perspective, the organization requires a continuing flow of human resources, money, customers, technological inputs, and material to continue to function. Subunits or individuals within the organization who can provide these resources derive power from this ability.[8]

An important consequence of the resource dependence perspective is that when managers start losing their ability to control resources, their power declines. A case in point is that of Donald Trump. When his vast holdings were generating a positive cash flow and his image was one of extraordinary power, he found many willing investors. The name *Trump* on a property escalated its value. As his cash flow worsened, Trump found it difficult to find investment groups willing to buy his properties at or near the asking price. At one point, the Trump organization was $9.2 billion in debt. Finally, when Trump's financial position improved again, he found a stream of willing investors. By 1999, Trump felt so powerful that he explored the possibilities of running for president of the United States, and launched a Web site for that purpose.[9]

A variation on power from providing resources is to derive power from being a good source of gossip, which is an important resource in many organizations. Most people know that being an influential member of the grapevine accrues a small degree of power, and a recent scientific analysis supports this idea. The authors of the analysis define gossip as "informal and evaluative talk in an organization, usually among no more than a few individuals, about another member of that organization who is not present."[10] According to the model developed, a supplier of gossip will develop the sources of power already described such as reward, expert, and coercive power. However, if the person provides mostly negative gossip, his or her referent power will decrease.

EMPOWERMENT OF GROUP MEMBERS

Describe the essence of empowerment.

Distributing power throughout the organization has become a major strategy for improving productivity, quality, and satisfaction. Employees experience a greater sense of self-efficacy (self-confidence for a particular task) and ownership in their jobs when they share power. **Empowerment** is the process of sharing power with group members, thereby enhancing their feelings of self-efficacy.[11] You can begin to personalize the meaning of empowerment by doing the Skill-Development Exercise that follows.

A model of the empowerment process is shown in Exhibit 11-1. According to this model, managers must act in specific ways to empower employees, such as those mentioned in Stage 2. Participative management is the general strategy for empowering workers. The techniques of participative management listed in Stage 2, such as goal setting, modeling, and job enrichment, have been described in previous chapters. The information about empowering teams presented in Chapter 8 is also relevant here.

To bring about empowerment, managers must remove conditions that keep employees powerless, such as authoritarian supervision or a job over which they have little control. An example of a person in a low-control job would be a manager who cannot shut off interruptions even to prepare budgets or to plan. Employees must also receive information that increases their feelings of self-efficacy. As shown in Exhibit 11-1, when employees are empowered, they will take the initiative to solve problems and strive hard to reach objectives.

Empowerment may not proceed smoothly unless certain conditions are met. A major consideration is that the potential empowerees must be competent and interested in assuming more responsibility. Otherwise the work will not get

SKILL-DEVELOPMENT EXERCISE

Becoming an Empowering Leader

To empower employees, leaders and managers must convey appropriate attitudes and develop the right interpersonal skills. The following list of attitudes and skills will help you become an empowering manager and leader. To the best of your self-evaluation, indicate which skills and attitudes you have and which ones require development.

Empowering Attitude or Behavior	Can Do Now	Would Need to Develop
1. Believe in the ability of team members to be successful.	✓	____
2. Be patient with people and give them time to learn.	✓	____
3. Provide group members with direction and structure.	✓	____
4. Teach group members new skills in small, incremental steps so they can easily learn those skills.	✓	____
5. Ask group members questions that challenge them to think in new ways.	✓	____
6. Share information with team members, sometimes just to build rapport.	✓	____
7. Give group members timely feedback and encourage them throughout the learning process.	✓	____
8. Offer group members alternative ways of doing things.	✓	____
9. Exhibit a sense of humor and demonstrate caring for workers as people.	✓	____
10. Focus on group members' results and acknowledge their personal improvement.	✓	____

Source: Reprinted from Richard Hamlin, "A Practical Guide to Empowering Your Employees," *Supervisory Management* (April 1991): 8. Copyright © 1991 American Management Association International. Reprinted by permission of American Management Association International, New York, NY. All rights reserved. http://www.amanet.org.

accomplished. W. Alan Randolph observed ten companies that made the transition to empowerment.[12] The first key to effective empowerment is *information sharing.* Lacking information, it is difficult for workers to act with responsibility.

Another critical factor for successful empowerment is for management to *provide more structure* as teams move into self-management. To initiate empowerment, managers must teach people new skills and make the parameters clear. Workers need to know, for example, "What are the limits to my empowerment?" A case in point is InfoServ. Employee empowerment did not include employees making more strategic decisions for the business. Yet empowerment did mean that employees would gradually make more operational decisions.

The third critical factor Randolph observed was that *teams must gradually replace the traditional organizational hierarchy.* Empowered teams do not only recommend, they make and implement decisions and are held accountable. A major contributor to successful empowerment at Food Corp. was that teams acted as managers. They hired and fired people, appraised performance, scheduled work, and managed a budget.

Empowerment is also more effective when the empowered individuals and teams are told what needs to be done but are *free to determine how to achieve the objectives.* Consultant Norman Bodek says, "Allowing people to determine the most efficient work techniques is the essence of empowerment."[13]

Source: Jay A. Conger and Rabindra N. Kanungo, "The Empowerment Process: Integrating Theory and Practice," *Academy of Management Review* (July 1988): p. 475.

Five Stages in the Process of Empowerment

A final consideration for successful empowerment is implied in the other conditions. *Unless managers trust employees,* empowerment will not be effective or even take place. For example, when employees are trusted, they are more likely to be given the information they need and be granted the freedom to choose an appropriate method. Without trusting employees, according to Oren Harari, companies cannot capitalize on intellectual assets to the optimal extent in achieving competitive advantage.[14]

Exhibit 11-2 provides additional insight into empowerment by listing indicators of whether group members show signs of being empowered or disempowered.

Now that we have described the sources of' power and empowerment, we shift focus to more details about political behavior and influence tactics.

FACTORS CONTRIBUTING TO AND EXAMPLES OF POLITICAL BEHAVIOR

Pinpoint factors contributing to organizational politics.

The most fundamental reason for organizational politics is the political nature of organizations. Coalitions of interests and demands arise both within and outside organizations. Similarly, organizations can be viewed as loose structures of interests and demands in competition with one another for attention and resources. The interaction among different coalitions results in an undercurrent of political tactics, such as one group trying to promote itself and discredit another.

Another contributor to political activity is the pyramidal shape of organizations. The people at the top of the organization hold most of the power, while people at each successive level down the hierarchy hold less power. The amount of power that can be distributed in a hierarchy is limited. Power-oriented managers sometimes cope with the limited amount of power available by expanding their sphere of influence sideways. For example, the director of the food stamp program in a government agency might attempt to gain control over the housing assistance program, which is at the same level.

One valuable way to track progress in empowerment is to look for the behaviors exhibited by employees who are moving toward effective empowerment. Compare those behaviors with the behaviors you might see from disempowered employees:

Empowered Employees	Disempowered Employees
Take initiative in ambiguous situations and define problems in a way that enables further analysis of decisions	Wait for a designated authority to define the problem and assign responsibilities
Identify opportunities in ambiguous situations, such as when customers complain or competitive threats arise	Address a problem effectively but fail to notice the possible opportunity
Apply critical thinking skills, such as surfacing and testing assumptions or evaluating arguments	Accept information, reasoning, or conclusions without testing (especially when presented by an authority)
Offer judgments about how and why specific decisions or actions support the shared purpose	Discuss but may not be able to apply the available information about shared purpose
Build consensus for decisions and actions both within and across functional groups	Expect to attempt consensus building, but appeal to hierarchical authority if the attempt fails
Identify and act on opportunities to systematize activities, document and communicate system information, identify and resolve systemic problems, and adapt or dismantle systems that no longer add value	Focus on improving individual or team effectiveness, yet fail to notice problems that extend beyond the group, create good one-time solutions yet fail to systematize them, rely on existing systems even if they are less valuable
Optimize resources by reducing expenses and finding opportunities to invest new resources (process improvements, technology upgrades, etc.)	Focus on the resources question only when and as directed by a designated authority

Source: Reprinted from Kyle Dover, "Avoiding Empowerment Traps," *Management Review* (January 1999): 53. Copyright © 1999 American Management Association International. Reprinted by permission of Association International, New York, NY. All rights reserved. http://www.amanet.org.

EXHIBIT
11-2

Signs of Empowerment and Disempowerment

Downsizing and team structures create even less opportunity for climbing the hierarchy, thus intensifying political behavior for the few remaining powerful positions. Worrying about being laid off themselves, many workers attempt to discredit others so that the latter would be the first to go.

Decentralization contributes to political behavior in another, less-significant way. Under decentralization, power is widely dispersed and decision making often takes place without the benefit of formal policy. As a consequence, coalitions emerge with each group fighting for self-interest.[15] For example, one group might be formed to push for the type of quality standard its members are the most familiar with.

Organizational politics is also fostered by the need for power. Executives have much stronger needs than others, thus being propelled toward frequent political behavior. Because executives are responsible for controlling resources, their inner desire to do so helps them in their jobs. A personalized power need is more likely to trigger political behavior than is a socialized power need.

Finally, a devious reason for the existence of politicking is **Machiavellianism,** a tendency to manipulate others for personal gain. One study found that people who scored very high on an organizational politics questionnaire also scored high on a test of Machiavellianism.[16] A current analysis suggests that many ambitious and successful corporate executives have strong Machiavellian tendencies, such as acquiring other companies just to give the appearance of true corporate growth.[17]

To make effective use of organizational politics, managerial workers must be aware of specific political strategies and tactics. The accompanying Organizational Behavior in Action illustrates how political skill (in this case, essentially well-developed interpersonal skills) can contribute to high-level success. To identify and explain the majority of political behaviors would require years of study and

Organizational Behavior *in Action*

M e r r i l l ' s   T e f l o n   T i g e r

Stanley O'Neal caught the public's attention in February 2000 when he was named to lead Merrill Lynch & Co.'s brokerage operation, the world's largest. However, 48-year-old O'Neal, one of the highest-ranking African Americans on Wall Street, had been selected by Merrill's top management as a high-potential manager years earlier. The executive, who joined Merrill from General Motors Corp. 14 years ago, is considered a skilled manager and an excellent communicator. O'Neal can get things done without antagonizing people in his wake. He even emerged unscathed in 1998 when he was a chief financial officer during a bloodbath that led to Merrill's first quarterly loss in nine years. "At that point, you knew he was golden within the firm," says a Wall Street analyst.

The latest promotion makes O'Neal the leading candidate to succeed chairman and chief executive David H. Komansky, age 60, who is expected to retire in five years. Whether O'Neal attains the top position at Merrill will be contingent on one challenge: his ability to lead Merrill's 14,200 U.S. brokers through the most turbulent time ever in the retail brokerage industry.

O'Neal's formidable task is to continue to remake a brokerage firm that grew up—and grew prosperous—on schmoozing with clients, recommending investments, and earning rich commissions on every trade. The boom in on-line trading makes much of that irrelevant. "O'Neal's appointment is indicative of a sea of change at Merrill and the brokerage industry in general. Because of the Internet, it's becoming much less of an old-boy's network. They've really got to focus on meeting stated financial goals," says a securities industry analyst.

O'Neal said he plans little change in the strategy of his predecessor, John L. (Launny) Steffens: "Launny put in place a magnificent business. He's had a clear vision that proved to be right."

Where O'Neal may be able to improve his predecessor's record is in patching up brokers' morale. O'Neal's outsider status (he has never worked as a broker) and people skills may help smooth the way as he pushes through needed change. "The biggest obstacle he faces is that brokers aren't happy with the status quo," says another industry analyst. "The way Merrrill introduced a lot of their on-line strategy was a blow to brokers," adds a brokerage recruiter. O'Neal says he plans to add bodies to the brokerage ranks: "We need more people—the best we can find."

O'Neal's success reenergizing brokers may stem from how well he does the other half of his job: ensuring that Merrill's explosive growth on-line isn't primarily coming out of their hides. "O'Neal's got to make on-line work without cannibalizing traditional revenue," says one of the security industry analysts quoted above.

If O'Neal can steer Merrill's brokerage business through these tumultuous times, he may prove himself golden once again. O'Neal intends to stay focused on keeping brokers happy.

Merrill Lynch Direct, available at http://www.mldirect.ml.com/, is the brokerage's offering to the on-line traders who want to manage their own portfolios.

Source: Marcia Vickers, "Merrill's Teflon Tiger: Can Stanley O'Neal Reenergize the Brokers?" *Business Week*, February 28, 2000, pp. 41–42.

observation. Managers so frequently need support for their programs that they search for innovative political maneuvers. Furthermore, new tactics continue to emerge as the workplace becomes increasingly competitive. Here we present twelve political tactics, with the first eight being mostly ethical and the last four most unethical.

1. *Develop power contacts.* A fundamental principle of success is to identify powerful people and then establish alliances with them. Cultivating friendly, cooperative relationships with powerful organizational members and outsiders can make the managerial worker's cause much easier to advance. These contacts can support a person's ideas and recommend him or her for promotions and visible temporary assignments. A challenge in the era of electronic communications is that face time is helpful for building contacts. (Face time refers to having in-person contact.) This means that it is important to converse with powerful people in person in addition to sending them electronic messages. Although still electronic, an occasional telephone call is a useful supplement to e-mail for purposes of building a network.

2. *Manage your impression.* You will recall that charismatic leaders rely heavily on impression management, and the same technique is important for other success-oriented people. An example of an ethical impression-management tactic would be to contribute outstanding performance and then make sure key people know of your accomplishments. When tactics of impression management appear insincere, they are likely to create a negative impression and thus be self-defeating. A key person to impress is your immediate superior. The accompanying Self-Assessment will help you think through how sensitive you are to effectively managing your impression.

3. *Control vital information.* Power accrues to those who control vital information, such as knowing how to maneuver contracts through private and governmental bureaucracies. Here *control* generally refers to keeping the information covert until it serves one's purpose. If the information is made public, the person loses control.

4. *Keep informed.* In addition to controlling vital information, it is politically important to keep informed. Successful managers and professionals develop a pipeline to help them keep abreast, or ahead, of developments within the firm. For this reason, a politically astute individual befriends a major executive's assistant.

5. *Be courteous, pleasant, and positive.* According to employment specialist Robert Half, courteous, pleasant, and positive people are the first to be hired and the last to be fired (assuming they are also technically qualified).[18]

6. *Ask satisfied customers to contact your manager.* A favorable comment by a customer receives considerable weight because customer satisfaction is a top corporate priority. If a customer says something nice, the comment will carry more weight than one from a coworker or subordinate. The reason is that insiders might praise you for political reasons, whereas a customer's motivation is thought to be pure.

7. *Avoid political blunders.* A strategy for retaining power is to refrain from making power-eroding blunders. Committing these politically insensitive acts can also prevent you from attaining power. Leading blunders include strong criticism of a superior in a public forum and going around your manager with a complaint. (Remember the case introduction to this chapter?) Another blunder is burning your bridges by creating ill will with former employees.

8. *Sincere flattery.* A powerful tactic for ingratiating yourself to others is to flatter them honestly and sincerely. Although one meaning of the term *flattery* is insincere praise, another meaning refers to a legitimate compliment. Charismatic people use flattery regularly. The Skill-Development Exercise that follows on page 247 will help you develop flattery skills. Such development should come easy to you because Organizational Behavior students typically

Integrate your knowledge of the political nature of working and managing by visiting South-Western's animated concept and activity site at *http://www. experiencingob.com*. Exclusive review tools on the topics of Power & Politics help you comprehend workplace realities. Free demo available!

Ethical

SELF-ASSESSMENT

The Manager Impression Survey

Respond to each of the following statements on a 1 to 5 scale: very infrequently (VI), infrequently (I), sometimes (S), frequently (F), or very frequently (VF). If you do not have a manager currently, think of a previous relationship with a manager or how you would behave if you were placed in the situation being described.

To what extent do you

	Frequency				
	(1)	(2)	(3)	(4)	(5)
1. Do personal favors for your manager (such as getting him or her coffee or a soft drink)	(VI)	I	S	F	VF
2. Offer to do something for your manager that you are not required to do, as a personal favor	VI	(I)	S	F	VF
3. Compliment your immediate manager on his or her dress or appearance	(VI)	I	S	F	VF
4. Praise your immediate manager on his or her accomplishments	VI	I	(S)	F	VF
5. Take an interest in your manager's personal life	VI	I	(S)	(F)	VF
6. Try to be polite when interacting with your manager	VI	I	S	F	(VF)
7. Try to be a friendly person when interacting with your manager	VI	I	(S)	F	VF
8. Try to act as a "model" employee such as never taking longer than the established time for lunch	VI	I	S	(F)	VF
9. Work hard when you know the results will be seen by your manager	VI	I	(S)	F	VF
10. Let your manager know that you try to do a good job in your work	VI	I	(S)	F	VF

Total Score ___34___

Scoring and Interpretation: Score each circled response 1, 2, 3, 4, or 5, according to the scale indicated above. Use the following interpretive guide:

45–50   You are working diligently at creating a good impression with your manager. You show good political savvy. Be aware, however, that insincere attempts at impressing management will backfire because they will appear as unethical.

30–44   You show moderate concern for creating a good impression with your manager. Become more sensitive to the impression you are making on your manager.

10–29   You are not making enough effort to create a good impression with your manager. If you want to be recognized, do a more effective job of managing your impression.

Source: Sandy J. Wayne and Robert C. Liden, "Effects of Impression Management on Performance Ratings: A Longitudinal Study." *Academy of Management Journal* (February 1995): p. 246.

have great potential interpersonal skills, along with high cognitive and emotional intelligence.

9. *Backstabbing.* The ubiquitous backstab requires that you pretend to be nice but all the while plan someone's demise. A frequent form of backstabbing is to inform your rival's immediate superior that he or she is faltering under the pressure of job responsibilities. The recommended approach to dealing with a backstabber is to confront the person directly, ask for an explanation of his or her behavior, and demand that he or she stop. Threaten to complain to the person's superior.[19]

10. *Embrace-or-demolish.* The ancient strategy of embrace-or-demolish suggests that you remove from the premises rivals who suffered past hurts through your efforts. (The same tactic is called "take no prisoners.") Otherwise the wounded rivals might retaliate at a vulnerable moment. An illustration of embrace-or-

unethical

SKILL-DEVELOPMENT EXERCISE

A Short Course in Effective Flattery

Flattering others is an effective way of building personal relationships (or engaging in organizational politics) if done properly. Suggestions for effective flattery are presented below. Flattery in the sense used here refers to pleasing by complimentary remarks or attention. We are not referring to flattery in the sense of giving insincere or excessive compliments. To build your skills in flattering others, practice these suggestions as the opportunity presents itself. Rehearse your flattery approaches until they feel natural. If your first attempt at flattery does not work well, analyze what went wrong the best you can.

- *Use sensible flattery.* Effective flattery has at least a spoonful of credibility, implying that you say something positive about the target person that is quite plausible. Credibility is also increased when you point to a person's tangible accomplishment. Technical people in particular expect flattery to be specific and aimed at genuine accomplishment.
- *Individualize your compliments.* Avoid using the same old compliment on everybody to avoid appearing insincere. Everyday compliments such as "nice tie" or "nice dress" are sometimes referred to as *throwaway* compliments. An assist toward individualizing compliments is to carefully research what others have done to merit flattery.
- *Compliment what is of major importance to the flattery target.* You might find out what is important to the person by observing what he or she talks about with the most enthusiasm.
- *Flatter others by listening intently.* Listening intently to another person is a powerful form of

flattery. Use active listening (see Chapter 8) for best results.
- *Flatter by referring to or quoting the other person.* By referring to or quoting (including paraphrasing) another person, you are paying that person a substantial compliment.
- *Use confirmation behaviors.* Use behaviors that have a positive or therapeutic effect on other people, such as praise and courtesy. Because confirmation behaviors have such a positive effect on others, they are likely to be perceived as a form of flattery.
- *Give positive feedback.* A mild form of flattering others is to give them positive feedback about their statements, actions, and results. The type of feedback referred to here is a straightforward and specific declaration of what the person did right.
- *Remember names.* Remembering the names of people with whom you have infrequent contact makes them feel important. To help remember the person's name, study the name carefully when you first hear it and repeat it immediately.
- *Avoid flattery that has a built-in insult or barb.* The positive effect of flattery is eradicated when it is accompanied by a hurtful comment, such as "You have good people skills for an engineer" or "You look good. I bet you were really beautiful when you were younger."

Source: Andrew J. DuBrin, *Personal Magnetism: Discover Your Own Charisma and Learn to Charm, Inspire, and Influence Others* (New York: AMACOM, 1997), pp. 75–92; Karen Judson, "The Fine Art of Flattery," *Kiwanis*, March 1998, pp. 34–36, 43.

---

demolish is when, after a hostile takeover, many executives lose their jobs because they opposed the takeover.

11. *Setting up a person for failure.* The object of the setup is to place a person in a position where he or she will either fail outright or look ineffective. For example, a supervisor who the agency head dislikes might be given responsibility for a troubled department. The newly appointed supervisor cannot improve productivity, is then reprimanded for poor performance, and the negative evaluation becomes part of the person's permanent record.

12. *Territorial games.* Also referred to as turf wars, **territorial games** involve protecting and hoarding resources that give a person power, such as information, relationships, and decision-making authority. The purpose of territorial games is to compete for three kinds of territory in the modern corporate survival

game: information, relationships, or authority. A relationship is "hoarded" in such ways as not encouraging others to visit a key customer, or blocking a higher performer from getting a promotion or transfer by such means as informing other managers that he or she is mediocre.[20] Other examples of territorial games include monopolizing time with clients, scheduling meetings so someone cannot attend, and shutting out coworkers from joining you on an important assignment.

ORGANIZATIONAL INFLUENCE TACTICS

④

Identify and describe a variety of political and influence tactics.

In addition to using power and political tactics to get people to their way of thinking, managerial workers also use a variety of influence tactics. Extensive research has been conducted on social influence tactics aimed at upward, horizontal, and downward relations.[21] The person doing the influencing chooses which tactic seems most appropriate for a given situation. Seven of the most frequently used influence tactics are leading by example, assertiveness, rationality, ingratiation, exchange, inspirational appeal and emotional display, and joking and kidding.

1. *Leading by example* means that the manager influences group member by serving as a positive model of desirable behavior. A manager who leads by example shows consistency between actions and words. For example, suppose a firm has a strict policy on punctuality. The manager explains the policy and is always punctual. The manager's words and actions provide a consistent model.

2. *Assertiveness* refers to being forthright in your demands. It involves a person expressing what he or she wants done and how he or she feels about it. A manager might say, for example, "Your report is late, and that makes me angry. I want you to get it done by noon tomorrow." Assertiveness, as this example shows, also refers to making orders clear.

3. *Rationality* means appealing to reason and logic. Strong managers and leaders frequently use this influence tactic. Pointing out the facts of a situation to group members to get them to do something exemplifies rationality. Intelligent people respond the best to rational appeals.

4. *Ingratiation* refers to getting someone else to like you, often through the use of political skill. A typical ingratiating tactic would be to act in a friendly manner just before making a demand. Effective managerial workers treat people well consistently to get cooperation when it is needed.

5. *Exchange* is a method of influencing others by offering to reciprocate if they meet your demands. Managers with limited expert, referent, and legitimate power are the most likely to use exchange and make bargains with group members. When asking favors in a busy workplace, it is best to specify the amount of time the task will take, such as saying "I will need ten minutes of your time sometime between now and next Wednesday." Be aware of what skills or capabilities you have that you can barter with others. Perhaps you are good at retrieving crashed computer files or explaining the tax code. You can then offer to perform these tasks in exchange for favors granted to you. [22]

6. *Inspirational appeal and emotional display* is an influence method centering on the affective (as opposed to the cognitive) domain. Given that leaders are supposed to inspire others, such an influence tactic is important. As Jeffrey Pfeffer observes, "Executives and others seeking to exercise influence in organizations often develop skill in displaying, or not displaying, their feelings in a strategic fashion.[23] An inspirational appeal usually involves an emotional display by the

person seeking to influence. It also involves appealing to group members' emotions.

7. *Joking and kidding,* according to one survey, are widely used to influence others on the job.[24] Good-natured ribbing is especially effective when a straightforward statement might be interpreted as harsh criticism. A manager concerned about the number of errors in a group member's report might say, "Now I know what you are up to. You planted all those errors just to see if I really read your reports."

Which influence tactic to choose? Managers are unlikely to use all the influence tactics in a given situation. Instead, they tend to choose an influence tactic that fits the demands of the circumstance. Researchers found support for this conclusion in a study with 120 managers, along with about 1,200 subordinates, peers, and superiors. (The tactics studied were similar to many of those mentioned in this chapter.) An effective tactic was one that led to task commitment and that was used by managers who were perceived to be effective by the various raters.

The results suggested that the most effective tactics were rational persuasion, inspirational appeal, and consultation. In contrast, the least effective influence tactics were pressure, coalition formation, and appealing to legitimate authority. The researchers cautioned that the outcome of a specific influence attempt is also determined by such factors as the target's motivation and organizational culture.[25] Also, any influence tactic can trigger target resistance if it is inappropriate for the situation or it is applied unskillfully. Tact, diplomacy, and insight are required for effective application of influence (and political) tactics.

THE CONTROL OF DYSFUNCTIONAL POLITICS AND ETHICAL CONSIDERATIONS

Explain how managers can control dysfunctional politics.

Carried to excess, organizational politics and influence tactics can hurt an organization and its members. One consequence is that when political factors far outweigh merit, competent employees may become unhappy and quit. Another problem is that politicking takes time away from tasks that could contribute directly to achieving the firm's goals. Many managers spend more time developing political allies (including "kissing up") than coaching group members or doing analytical work.

The most comprehensive antidote to improper, excessive, and unethical organizational politics is to rely on objective measures of performance. This is true because people have less need to behave politically when their contributions can be measured directly. With a formal system of goal setting and review, the results a person attains should be much more important than the impression the person creates. However, even a goal-setting program is not immune from politics. Sometimes the goals are designed to impress key people in the organization. As such, they many not be the most important goals for getting work accomplished. Another political problem with goal setting is that some people will set relatively easy goals so they can look good by attaining all their goals.

Meshing individual and organizational objectives would be the ideal method of controlling excessive, negative political behavior. If their objectives, needs, and interests can be met through their jobs, employees will tend to engage in behavior that fosters the growth, longevity, and productivity of the firm. L. A. Witt investigated how goal congruence between the individual and the organization affected political behavior. When employees perceived considerable politics in the workplace, their commitment to the organization and job performance both suffered. However, when employees and their superiors shared the same goals, commitment and performance were less negatively affected by politics. Witt concluded that one way to reduce the negative impact of organizational politics is for the manager to ensure that his or her subordinates hold the appropriate goal priorities. In this way, group members will have a greater sense of controversy over and understanding of the workplace and thus be less affected by the presence of organizational politics.[26]

Finally open communications can also constrain the impact of political behavior. For instance, open communication can let everyone know the basis for allocating resources, thus reducing the amount of politicking. Organizational politics can also be curtailed by threatening to discuss questionable information in a public forum. If one employee engages in backstabbing of another, the manager might ask her or him to repeat the anecdote in a staff meeting. It has been said that sunlight is the best disinfectant to deviousness.

Our discussion of sources of power, political tactics, and influence tactics should not imply an endorsement of all of these methods of gaining advantage. Each strategy and tactic must be evaluated on its merit by an ethical test, such as those described in Chapter 3. One guiding principle is to turn the strategy or tactic inward. Assume that you believe that a particular tactic (for example, ingratiation) would be ethical in working against you. It would then be fair and ethical for you to use this tactic in attempting to influence others.

Another guiding principle is that it is ethical to use power and influence to help attain organizational goals. In contrast, it is generally unethical to use the same tactics to achieve personal agenda and goals not sanctioned by the organization. Yet even this guideline involves enough "grayness" to be open for interpretation. The following Skill-Development Exercise provides an opportunity to evaluate the ethics of behavior.

Another perspective on organizational politics is to recognize that both the means and the ends of political behavior must be considered. A study of the subject cautioned, "Instead of determining whether human rights or standards of justice are violated, we are often content to judge political behavior according to its outcomes."[27] The authors of the study suggest that when it comes to the ethics of organizational politics, respect for justice and human rights should prevail for their own sake.

SKILL-DEVELOPMENT EXERCISE

The Ethics of Influence Tactics

You decide if the following manager made ethical use of influence tactics.

Jack Green, a manager at an internationally prominent telecommunications company, wanted to start a new venture for the firm. He believed the organization's best interests would be served by producing a system for wireless communication among computers (much like a cellular phone). Green realized that the organization culture so strongly favored teams that recommendations from individuals received scant attention. Green formed a new-ventures team. (The

team meetings consisted mostly of the team members listening to Green's proposals and presenting supporting data.) Three months later, the team proposed that the company move into a system of wireless communication among computers. At that point, Green brought forth his team's proposal to upper management.

1. Was Jack Green behaving ethically?
2. What influence tactic did he use in attempting to achieve his goals?

IMPLICATIONS FOR MANAGERIAL PRACTICE

1. Recognize that a significant portion of the efforts of organizational members will be directed toward gaining power for themselves or their group. At times, some of this behavior will be directed more toward self-interest than toward organizational interest. It is therefore often necessary to ask, "Is this action being taken to help this person or is it being done to help the organization?" Your answer to this question should influence your willingness to submit to that person's demands.

2. If you want to establish a power base for yourself, a good starting point is to develop expert power. Most powerful people began their climb to power by demonstrating their expertise in a particular area. (This tactic is referred to as becoming a subject matter expert.)

3. In determining if a particular behavior is motivated by political or merit considerations, evaluate the intent of the actor. The same action might be based on self-interest or concern for others. For instance, a team member might praise you because he believed that you accomplished something of merit. Or that same individual might praise you to attain a favorable work assignment or salary increase.

SUMMARY OF KEY POINTS

Identify sources of power for individuals and sub-units within organizations.

Power, politics, and influence are needed by managers to accomplish their work. In the model presented here, managers and professionals use organizational politics to achieve power and influence, thus attaining desired outcomes.

Socialized power is used to forward organizational interests, whereas personalized power is used to forward personal interests. Power granted by the organization consists of legitimate power, coercive power, and reward power. Power stemming from the individual consists of expert power and referent power (the basis for charisma). According to the resource dependence perspective, subunits or individuals who can provide key resources to the organization accrue power. At times, gossip can be a power-giving source.

Describe the essence of empowerment.

Managers must act in specific ways to empower employees, including removing conditions that keep employees powerless and giving information that enhances employee feelings of self-efficacy. Five critical conditions for empowerment are for an organization to share information with employees, provide them structure, use teams to replace the traditional hierarchy, grant employees the freedom to determine how to achieve objectives, and trust employees.

Pinpoint factors contributing to organizational politics.

Contributors to organizational politics include: the political nature of organizations, the pyramidal shape of organizations, decision making in the absence of formal policy, the need for power, and Machiavellianism.

Identify and describe a variety of political and influence tactics.

Among the ethical tactics of organizational politics are the following: develop power contacts; manage your impression; control vital information; keep informed; be courteous, pleasant, and positive; ask satisfied customers to contact your manager; avoid political blunders; and use sincere flattery. Among the unethical tactics are backstabbing, embrace-or-demolish, setting up a person for failure, and playing territorial games.

Influence tactics frequently used by managerial workers include leading by example, assertiveness, rationality, ingratiation, exchange, inspirational appeal and emotional display, and joking and kidding.

Explain how managers can control dysfunctional politics.

Approaches to controlling dysfunctional politics include: relying on objective performance measures, meshing individual and organizational objectives, minimizing political behavior by top management, and open communications, including threatening to discuss poli-ticking publicly.

 Differentiate between the ethical and unethical use of power, politics, and influence.

Political behaviors chosen by an individual or organizational unit must rest on ethical considerations. A guiding principle is to use only those tactics you would consider fair and ethical if used against you. Also recognize that both the means and the ends of political behavior must be considered.

KEY TERMS AND PHRASES

Power, *238*

The potential or ability to influence decisions and control resources.

Organizational Politics, *238*

Informal approaches to gaining power through means other than merit or luck.

Socialized Power, *238*

The use of power to achieve constructive ends.

Personalized Power, *238*

The use of power primarily for the sake of personal aggran-dizement and gain.

Legitimate Power, *239*

Power based on one's formal position within the hierarchy of the organization.

Coercive Power, *239*

Controlling others through fear of punishment or the threat of punishment.

Reward Power, *239*

Controlling others through rewards or the promise of rewards.

Expert Power, *239*

The ability to influence others because of one's specialized knowledge, skills, or abilities.

Referent Power, *239*

The ability to influence others that stems from one's desirable traits and characteristics; it is the basis for charisma.

Resource Dependence Perspective, *239*

The need of the organization for a continuing flow of human resources, money, customers, technological inputs, and material to continue to function.

Empowerment, *240*

The process of sharing power with group members, thereby enhancing their feelings of self-efficacy.

Machiavellianism, *243*

A tendency to manipulate others for personal gain.

Territorial Games, *247*

Also known as *turf wars,* territorial games refer to behaviors involving the hoarding of information and other resources.

DISCUSSION QUESTIONS AND ACTIVITIES

1. What might be the negative consequences to a manager if he or she ignored power, politics, and influence tactics?
2. In your own words, make a distinction among power, pol-itics, and influence tactics.
3. Describe how the exercise of personal power can lead to position power for the individual.
4. Using concepts from the theory presented about power, explain why people who are skilled at enterprise soft-ware, such as SAP, Siebel, and PeopleSoft, have so much power today.

5. Why does the replacement of hierarchy by teams assist the empowerment process?
6. Which two of the political tactics and strategies described in this chapter do you think would help you most in your career? Explain your reasoning.
7. **COLLABORATE** What can you do today to start increasing your power? Compare your observations with classmates.

ORGANIZATIONAL BEHAVIOR ON-LINE

TO DO

Power Analysis

The object of this exercise is to identify a powerful person and analyze the source of his or her power. A direct way to approach the task is to think of a powerful businessperson, such as Bill Gates, Oprah Winfrey, Bill Joy, or Martha Stewart. Search for an in-depth article about your chosen powerful person. Identify the sources of the person's power or the types of power he or she possesses. Another approach to the exercise is to use a search term such as "powerful person in business," and then analyze the person identified. If your powerful person's e-mail address is given, send the person an e-mail message asking how he or she became so powerful.

TO BOOKMARK

Employee Empowerment at the U.S. Equal Employment Opportunity Commission
http://www.eeoc.gov

Employee Empowerment
http://www.geocities.com/TimesSquare/1848/org.html

Office Politics
http://www.fastcompany.com/online/14/politics.html

CASE PROBLEM: To Kiss Up or Not to Kiss Up, That Is the Question

Stanley Bing, a *Fortune* staff writer known for his tongue-in-cheek attitude, offers you three scenarios and questions to test your political savvy.

Scenario 1

A man likes to play platform tennis. He plays every morning before he arrives at work to put in his 12-hour day at the office. One morning he receives a telephone call from the CEO of his company. "Todd?" says the CEO. "This is Marty. It's come to my attention that you play platform tennis every morning. I do, too. Would you like to play with me?"

"When do you play?" asks Todd, very laid-back. "At 5:00 A.M., 5:30 maybe," says Marty, who is wondering why at this point a torrent of sucking up in response to his offer is not forthcoming. "Gee, Marty," says Todd, "I don't think so. I don't get started until about seven. Thanks anyway." He hangs up.

Complete the following sentence: "I think Todd is …"

(a) a really cool guy who does what he wants to do within the confines of his job. His platform tennis is personal. He doesn't have to mortgage that precious time for a little favor in high places. This is one dude who has his hair on straight.

(b) stupid.

Scenario 2

Todd is invited to a corporate retreat in Sedona, Arizona. Day two after lunch, everybody takes off for the desert, some to shoot at cans with six-guns, others to play golf among the dunes. One guy heads for the lonely buttes in a rented Maserati. Guess who? "Where the heck is Todd?" several people remark.

Complete the following sentence: "I think Todd is …"

(a) an amazing person who seized the opportunity for personal revelation, a moment of beauty and abandon that may never be recaptured in a narrow, frenetic business life bounded by duty, discipline, and location.

(b) a complete lunkhead.

Scenario 3

It is several years later. Numbers are bad. Todd has a meeting with his chief executive, who reads him the riot act. There is some yelling, all of it going one way. After a while, the yelling is over and it is time for Todd to leave the chief executive's office. On his way out the door, Todd…

(a) says something provocative that re-enrages the chief executive to the point where the meeting continues for another ten minutes with more yelling, accompanied by that throbbing vein in the chief executive's forehead that usually precedes the moment when his head flies off.

(b) smiles politely and remains silent.

Case Questions

1. What are your answers to the three scenarios?
2. What political mistakes would Todd be making by choosing alternative "a" in each of the scenarios?
3. What positive political tactics would Todd be using by choosing alternative "b" in each of the scenarios?
4. What type of power might accrue to Todd by choosing to play platform tennis with the CEO at 5 A.M.?

Source: Stanley Bing, "Rebel Without Applause," *Fortune* (27 September 1999): 65–66. Used with permission of the publisher.

New media journalists love recounting the exploits of corporate rebels. Visit Wired's archives for a case in point at http://www.wirednews.com/wired/archives/5.05/rebels.html.

SUGGESTED READINGS

Dulebohn, James H., and Ferris, Gerald R. "The Role of Influence Tactics in Perceptions of Performance Evaluations' Fairness." *Academy of Management Journal*, June 1999, pp. 288–303.

Kirkman, Bradley L., and Rosen, Benson. "Beyond Self-Management: Antecedents and Consequences of Team Empowerment." *Academy of Management Journal*, February 1999, pp. 58–74.

Lyness, Karen S., and Thompson, Donna E. "Climbing the Corporate Ladder: Do Female and Male Executive Follow the Same Route?"

Journal of Applied Psychology, February 2000, pp. 86–101.

"The Most Influential People in Electronic Business." *Business Week E. Biz*, pp. EB 24–51.

Roberts, Paul. "The Art of Getting Things Done." *Fast Company*, June 2000, pp. 162–164.

Warner, Melanie. "The Young and the Loaded." *Fortune*, September 27, 1999, pp. 79–88.

Wetlaufer, Suzy. "Organizing for Empowerment: An Interview with AES's Roger Sant and Dennis Bakke." *Harvard Business Review,* January–February 1999, pp. 110–123.

Wolfe, Rebecca Luhn. *Office Politics: Positive Results from Fair Practices.* Menlo Park, CA: Crisp Publications, 1997.

ENDNOTES

1. Daniel J. Brass and Marlene E. Burkhardt, "Potential Power and Power Use: An Integration of Structure and Behavior," *Academy of Management Journal,* June 1993, pp. 441–442.

2. Jeffrey Pfeffer, *Power in Organizations* (Marshfield, MA: Putman, 1981), p. 7.

3. Robert P. Vecchio, *Organizational Behavior,* 2nd ed. (Chicago: Dryden Press, 1991), p. 270.

4. Leonard H. Chusmir, "Personalized vs. Socialized Power Needs among Working Men and Women," *Human Relations,* February 1986, p. 149.

5. John R. P. French and Bertram Raven, "The Basis of Social Power," in Dorwin Cartwright and Alvin Zander, eds. *Group Dynamics: Research and Theory* (Evanston, IL: Row, Peterson and Company, 1962), pp. 607–623.

6. Heather Green, "The Most Influential People in Electronic Business," *Business Week* **E.BIZ,** September 27, 1999, p. **EB 43.**

7. Jeffrey D. Kudisch, Mark L. Poteet, Gregory H. Dobbins, Michael C. Rush, and Joyce E. A. Russell, "Expert Power, Referent Power, and Charisma: Toward the Resolution of a Theoretical Debate," *Journal of Business and Psychology,* Winter 1995, p. 189.

8. Jeffrey Pfeffer, *Managing with Power* (Boston: Harvard Business Review Publications, 1990), pp. 100–101.

9. Maureen Dowd, "Vain Trump Is 'Me' Politics at Its Silliest," *The New York Times* syndicated column, September 21, 1999.

10. Nancy B. Kurland and Lisa Hope Pelled, "Passing the Word: Toward a Model of Gossip and Power in the Workplace," *Academy of Management Review,* April 2000, p. 429.

11. Jay A. Conger and Rabindra N. Kanungo, "The Empowerment Process: Integrating Theory and Practice," *Academy of Management Review,* July 1988, pp. 473–474.

12. W. Alan Randolph, "Navigating the Journey to Empowerment," *Organizational Dynamics,* Spring 1995, pp. 19–31.

13. Phillip M. Perry, "Seven Errors to Avoid When Empowering Your Staff," *Success Workshop,* A supplement to *Managers Edge,* 1999, p. 4.

14. Oren Harari, "The Trust Factor," *Management Review,* January 1999, p. 28.

15. Robert E. Coffey, Curtis W. Cook, and Phillip L. Hunsaker, *Management and Organizational Behavior* (Burr Ridge, IL: Austen Press, Irwin, 1994), p. 274.

16. Gerald Biberman, "Personality and Characteristic Work Attitudes of Persons with High, Moderate, and Low Political Tendencies," *Psychological Reports,* 1985, pp. 1303–1310.

17. Stanley Bing, *What Would Machiavelli Do?* (New York: HarperCollins, 2000).

18. "'Career Insurance' Protects DP Professionals from Setbacks, Encourages Growth," *Data Management,* June 1986, p. 33. The same principle is equally valid today.

19. "Face Cowardly Backstabbers in the Workplace," Knight Ridder story, February 13, 2000.

20. Annette Simmons, *Territorial Games: Understanding & Ending Turf Wars at Work* (New York: AMACOM, 1998).

21. Several of the tactics are from Gary Yukl and Cecilia M. Falbe, "Influence Tactics and Objectives in Upward, Downward, and Lateral Influence Attempts," *Journal of Applied Psychology,* April 1990, pp. 132–140.

22. "Aloofness Doesn't Pay," *Executive Strategies,* April 2000, p. 1.

23. Pfeffer, *Managing with Power,* p. 224.

24. Andrew J. DuBrin, "Sex Differences in the Use and Effectiveness of Tactics of Impression Management," *Psychological Reports,* Vol. 74, 1994, pp. 531–544.

25. Gary Yukl and J. Bruce Tracey, "Consequences of Influence Tactics Used with Subordinates, Peers, and the Boss," *Journal of Applied Psychology,* August 1992, pp. 525–535.

26. L. A. Witt, "Enhancing Organizational Goal Congruence: A Solution to Organizational Politics," *Journal of Applied Psychology,* August 1998, pp. 666–674.

27. Gerald F. Cavanagh, Dennis J. Moberg, and Manuel Velasquez, "The Ethics of Organizational Politics," *Academy of Management Review,* July 1981, p. 372.

Organization Structure and Design

Jennifer Johnson knew she had a problem when she discovered that some of her 15 employees were taking their complaints to someone other than her. "People were going to a senior consultant at the company for the real scoop, as opposed to coming to me," Johnson says. "I found it kind of troubling."

The 37-year-old founder of Johnson & Co., a two-year old Santa Cruz, California, marketing consulting and media relations firm, knew it was important to understand who is talking to whom, who is listening, and how most of the information and influence really flows in her company.

Disturbed by the fact that she wasn't the hub of information at her media relations firm, Johnson created a new position—account planner—to keep everyone connected. In this way, all workers in the small company would get the information they needed. The account planner would keep Johnson informed of information flow and problems. Furthermore, nobody (including the owner) would be left out of the information loop.

Source: Mark Henricks, "The Shadow Knows," *Entrepreneur* (January 2000): 110. Used with permission of the publisher.

OBJECTIVES

After reading and studying this chapter and doing the exercises, you should be able to

1 Identify and define the foundation concepts of organization structure, including the informal organization.

2 Specify the basic features of the bureaucratic form of organization structure, including how it is divided into departments.

3 Describe three key modifications of a bureaucratic structure: matrix, flat, and outsourcing.

4 Describe the two contemporary organizational designs referred to as horizontal structures and network organizations.

5 Understand why a new type of organization chart called an *organigraph* can contribute to understanding organization structure.

Chapter 12

SO WHAT? No matter how small a business is, the help of an informed communications support team is critical to its success. The problem facing the small-business owner just described and the solution she chose hints at the importance of understanding organization structure. At the media relations firm, the informal approach to exchanging information was bypassing the formal structure, so the owner adjusted the structure to facilitate better working relationships. In this chapter, we describe organization structure because understanding structure, including informal networks, is part of organizational behavior. Structure and behavior influence each other. For example, a loose organization structure, such as a collection of teams, requires employees to work productivity without the benefit of close supervision. In contrast, some employees need careful guidelines for conducting their work, and therefore need a tighter structure, such as a bureaucracy.

The purpose of this chapter is to understand the various types of organization structures and factors that influence the structure for a given purpose. Let us first clarify three key terms. An **organization** is a collection of people working together to achieve a common purpose (or simply a big group). **Organization structure** is the arrangement of people and tasks to accomplish organizational goals. The structure is usually indicated on the organization chart, along with specifying who reports to whom. **Organizational design** is the process of creating a structure that best fits a purpose, strategy, and environment. For example, a giant motor company like Ford Motors emphasizes organizing by product such as having a separate division for Jaguar Motors.

FOUNDATION CONCEPTS OF ORGANIZATIONAL STRUCTURE

Identify and define the foundation concepts of organization structure, including the informal organization.

Organizations are so complex that many different variables are required to describe them, similar to describing people or machines. To get started understanding how organizations are structured, we look at six key concepts: mechanistic versus organic, formal versus informal, degree of formalization, degree of centralization, complexity, and coupling. You will observe that several concepts about organization structure overlap, thus simplifying the understanding of organizations.

Mechanistic versus Organic

A major variable for understanding organization structure is whether it is mechanistic or organic. A **mechanistic organization** is primarily hierarchical with an emphasis on specialization and control, vertical communication, and heavy reliance on rules, policies, and procedures. An old-fashioned manufacturing organization such as General Motors of yesteryear is an example of a mechanistic organization. The term has become synonymous with the earlier term *bureaucracy.*

An **organic structure** is laid out like a network and emphasizes horizontal specialization, extensive use of personal coordination, extensive communication among members, and loose rules, policies, and procedures. Knowledge resides wherever it is most useful to the organization. Organic structures are known for their responsiveness to a changing environment. A small high-tech start-up would be an example of an organic structure. Also, a shop that makes custom racing cars would have an organic form.

Formal versus Informal Structure

The **formal organization structure** is an official statement of reporting relationships, rules, and regulations. The rules and regulations are designed to cover all the events and transactions that are likely to take place in conducting the business of the organization. For example, the formal organization structure tells managers how to respond to employee requests for an education leave of absence or what to do with damaged parts from vendors.

The **informal organization structure** is a set of unofficial working relationships that emerges to take care of the events and transactions not covered by the formal structure. The informal structure supplements the formal structure by adding a degree of flexibility and speed. At a training and development firm, a television monitor needed for a training session had poor reception. The formal structure dictated telephoning the contracted repair shop, but at best this fix would have required several hours. Pressed for time, one of the trainers borrowed a television monitor from the employee lounge. In repayment for his impromptu borrowing, he bought for the lounge a bag of donuts and bagels from the bakery across the street. This humble act demonstrated how the real mission and work of the organization can sometimes best be done by avoiding formal channels.

Another perspective on the informal organization structure is that all companies have hidden shadow organizations where much of the real work gets accomplished. The shadow organization is revealed by *social network analysis,* which traces who is talking to whom, who is listening, and how most of the information and influence really flows (as in the chapter introduction). Consultants Ernst & Ernst LLP reported finding opportunities to save a large auto industry supplier more than $14 million by using social network analysis to uncover inefficient communication that was deterring innovation.[1]

Social network analysis reveals the informal social relationships and the unofficial communication channels, so it also helps to understand informal groups and informal communication channels. Tracking the informal relationships within an organization can help explain how and why new hires either succeed or fail to assimilate into the corporate culture. Workers who connect to the right information flow will perform better because of the connections they make.

Network mappers begin by surveying company employees to find answers to several key questions. The basic one is "To whom do you go for information about what's going on?" Other questions are asked about the frequency of interaction or differentiate between requests for information and requests for influence. Based on the answers, the mappers draw diagrams that graphically show who is connected to whom.[2] (In the past, such diagrams were referred to as sociograms.)

Social network analysis can benefit managers by revealing if people are getting the information they need to perform their job well. The same analysis can point to which employees are in the best position to disseminate useful information to other workers.

Formalization

The dimension of **formalization** is the degree to which expectations regarding the methods of work are specified, committed to writing, and enforced. The more policies, rules, and procedures specifying how people should behave, the more formalized the organization. An organization with a high degree of formalization is likely to have a high degree of specialization of labor and high delegation of authority. The more formalized an organization, the more mechanistic and bureaucratic it is. A motor vehicle bureau usually has a high degree of formalization, especially in dealing with the public. (People cannot order vanity license plates without paying a fee no matter how sweetly they ask!)

Centralization

Centralization refers to the extent to which executives delegate authority to lower organizational units. The smaller the amount of delegation, the more centralized the organization. In a decentralized firm, however, some decisions are more centralized than others. Strategic decision—those involving the overall functioning of the firm—are more likely to be centralized than operational decisions. An organization that relies heavily on functional (specialized) units will be more centralized because top management needs to coordinate the functions of the various units.

Domino's Pizza is a highly centralized firm. Company headquarters makes all the major decisions about matters such as menu, quality, décor, and policy regarding speed of delivery. An example of a highly decentralized firm is Laura Ashley, a worldwide chain of British stores with quaint storefronts that feature women's wear and fabrics. Laura Ashley, the founder, grants her store operators considerable leeway in merchandising.

Complexity

Complexity refers to the number of different job titles and organizational units. Large organizations often have hundreds of departments and thousands of job titles. In a complex organization, many of the job titles are esoteric, such as risk analyst, contract administrator, and fleet manager. The more complex the organization, the more difficult it is to manage. Complexity typically increases in direct proportion to size. Small organizations have fewer job titles and departments.

The concept of *differentiation* is closely linked to complexity. A horizontally differentiated organization has many different job titles, whereas a vertically differentiated organization has many levels. A giant bureaucracy such as Mellon Bank has considerable horizontal and vertical differentiation.

Tight versus Loose Coupling

A contemporary perspective for understanding organizations is to examine the interdependency of the various parts of the organization. **Coupling** reflects the extent to which the parts are interdependent. If a minor change in one variable in the organization creates a major response in another variable, the two elements are tightly coupled. In contrast, if a change in one variable in the organization has a negligible impact on another variable, the two elements are loosely coupled.[3]

Organizations are more tightly coupled today than previously because of the interdependence of the parts or subsystems. For example, if the marketing group detects a sudden change in customer preferences, other parts of the organization have to pull together to help meet changing customer needs.

Coupling is also an important concept because it influences contemporary organizational designs. In the present example, an organization structure may need to be designed in a hurry to meet substantial shifts in consumer preferences. A major customer such as Honda of America might demand that its suppliers now conduct all their business with them over the Internet. As a result, the suppliers would have to upgrade their e-commerce capabilities to continue as Honda suppliers.

THE BUREAUCRATIC FORM OF ORGANIZATION

Specify the basic features of the bureaucratic form of organization structure, including how it is divided into departments.

259

As already implied, a **bureaucracy** is a rational, systematic, and precise form of organization in which rules, regulations, and techniques of control are precisely defined. *Bureau* is the French word for office, indicating that a bureaucracy is a form of organization with many different offices. Exhibit 12-1 depicts the basic concept of the bureaucratic form of organization. A bureaucracy was conceived of by Max Weber to be the ideal organization, having the following characteristics.[4]

- Rules and procedures controlling organizational activities
- A high degree of differentiation among organizational functions
- A high degree of job specialization
- An organization of offices determined by hierarchy, with each unit reporting to a higher unit and no unit free-floating
- A heavy emphasis on rules and norms to regulate behavior
- Interpersonal relations characterized by impersonality in place of favoritism
- Selection and promotion based on merit
- All administrative actions recorded in writing

The ideal organization just described is called a **machine bureaucracy** because it standardizes work processes and is efficient. It is best suited to large organizations whose work is largely performed by production, technical, and support workers. In contrast, a **professional bureaucracy** standardizes skills for coordination and is composed of a core of highly trained professionals.

Professional bureaucracies include organizations such as accounting firms, consulting firms, hospitals, and universities. Because it is difficult to regulate the work of professionals performing complex work, the professional bureaucracy decentralizes decision making and is less formal than a machine bureaucracy. The professional bureaucracy is relatively flat, with considerable differentiation across units.[5]

In visualizing a typical bureaucracy, it appears that one person is in charge of every function, including running the enterprise. In reality, authority is shared to some extent in top-level positions. You will recall the existence of top-management teams as described in Chapter 9, in which major executives share

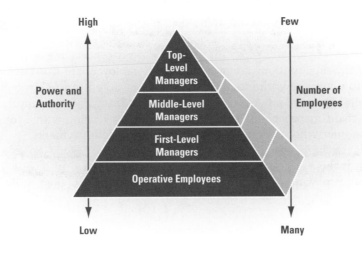

EXHIBIT 12-1

The Bureaucratic Form of Organization

In a bureaucracy, power is concentrated at the top.

Note that team leaders are typically found at the first level or middle level of management.

responsibility for directing an enterprise. A dual-executive team is becoming more frequent in major corporations. As mentioned previously, two people share most of the power at Oracle Corp. A company founder will often divest day-to-day responsibilities to another executive, so the former can concentrate more on strategy and building relationships with the outside world. Starbucks, Infospace Inc., and Amazon.com have recently had major changes in leadership to create two-person executive teams who share a company vision. Bill Gates of Microsoft transferred his role as chief executive to company president Steve Ballmer. Gates assumed the job of chief software architect.[6]

Despite this power sharing in the above examples, one person still stands out as the symbolic leader of each firm. The arrangement is a softening of having one person in charge, but not an abandonment of the principle.

Before reading about the good and bad side of bureaucracy, do the accompanying Self-Assessment, which follows on page 261. It will help you assess how well you might fit into a bureaucracy.

The Contribution of Bureaucracy

Bureaucratic forms of organization have persisted because, used properly, they make possible large-scale accomplishments that cannot be achieved by small groups of people working independently. The Social Security Administration is an example of a large bureaucracy that accomplishes an astonishing amount of work each month in paying benefits to perhaps 20 million Americans. Also, the major food processing companies, such as General Mills, are prime examples of bureaucracy on a large scale. The contribution of bureaucracy has been aptly expressed by Elliot Jacques:[7]

> Thirty-five years of research has convinced me that managerial hierarchy (or bureaucracy) is the most efficient, hardiest, and in fact the most natural structure ever devised for large corporations. Properly structured, hierarchy can release energy and creativity, rational productivity, and actually improve morale.

A current analysis by Paul S. Adler also points to the important contributions of bureaucracy. One of his major arguments is that slashing bureaucracy can backfire. Many firms have discovered that the layers of managers eliminated to reduce bureaucracy are often the repository of precious skills and expertise.[8] After many middle manager positions have been eliminated, their loss is recognized and regretted.

A similar argument is that dumping the policies and procedures characteristic of bureaucracy can weaken an organization. In many cases, these procedures embody a vast organizational memory of best practices. Having tossed out the manuals, many organizations discover that their employees are frustrated because they have to improvise with little guidance. A lot of time is wasted in reinventing and redeveloping useful procedures that have been discarded. For example, a newly appointed credit manager might not have a policy for dealing with a long-term, reliable customer who suddenly becomes delinquent with payments.

The hierarchical form of organization called bureaucracy emerged from necessity. It is the only form of organization that enables a firm to employ large numbers of people and still hold them clearly accountable for their results.

SELF-ASSESSMENT

- creativity is discouraged
-
-

The Bureaucratic Orientation Scale

+ reward seniority
+ know what's expected of you
+ little uncertainty / routine

Directions: Answer each question "mostly agree" (MA) or "mostly disagree" (MD). Assume the mental set of attempting to learn something about yourself rather than attempting to impress a prospective employer.

	MA	MD
1. I value stability in my job.	✓	—
2. I like a predictable organization.	✓	—
3. I enjoy working without the benefit of a carefully specified job description.	✓	—
4. I would enjoy working for an organization in which promotions are generally determined by seniority.	—	✓
5. Rules, policies, and procedures tend to frustrate me.	—	✓
6. I would enjoy working for a company that employed 95,000 people worldwide.	✓	—
7. Being self-employed would involve more risk than I'm willing to take.	—	✓
8. Before accepting a job, I would like to see an exact job description.	—	✓
9. I would prefer a job as a freelance landscape artist to one as a supervisor for the Department of Motor Vehicles.	✓	—
10. Seniority should be as important as performance in determining pay increases and promotion.	—	✓
11. It would give me a feeling of pride to work for the largest and most successful company in its field.	✓	—
12. Given a choice, I would prefer to make $100,000 per year as a vice president in a small company than $110,000 per year as middle manager in a large company.	—	✓
13. I would feel uncomfortable if I was to wear an employee badge with a number on it.	—	✓
14. Parking spaces in a company lot should be assigned according to job level.	✓	—
15. I would generally prefer working as a specialist to performing many different tasks.	✓	—
16. Before accepting a job, I would want to make sure that the company has a good program of employee benefits.	✓	—
17. A company will not be successful unless it establishes a clear set of rules and regulations.	—	✓
18. Regular working hours and vacation are more important to me than finding thrills on the job.	✓	—
19. You should respect people according to their rank.	—	✓
20. Rules are meant to be broken.	—	✓

Scoring and Interpretation: Give yourself one point for each question that you answered in the bureaucratic direction:

1. Mostly agree	11. Mostly agree
2. Mostly agree	12. Mostly disagree
3. Mostly disagree	13. Mostly disagree
4. Mostly agree	14. Mostly agree
5. Mostly disagree	15. Mostly disagree
6. Mostly agree	16. Mostly agree
7. Mostly agree	17. Mostly agree
8. Mostly agree	18. Mostly agree
9. Mostly disagree	19. Mostly agree
10. Mostly agree	20. Mostly disagree

15–20 You would enjoy working in a bureaucracy.

8–14 You would experience a mixture of satisfaction and dissatisfaction if working in a bureaucracy.

0–7 You would most likely be frustrated by working in a bureaucracy, especially a large one.

Source: *Human Relations: A Job Oriented Approach*, 5th ed., by DuBrin, Andrew J., © 1988. Reprinted by permission of Prentice-Hall, Inc. Upper Saddle River, NJ.

Potential Dysfunctions of a Bureaucracy

Not all bureaucracies work like Max Weber intended. The major problem is that members of the bureaucracy often carry out its characteristics to the extreme. Organizations that rely heavily on formal controls to direct people sometimes suppress initiative and decision making at lower levels of management. Too many controls and too much review of decisions can also lower productivity. A bureaucracy is subject to rigidity in handling people and problems. Its well-intended rules and regulations sometimes create inconvenience and inefficiency. Some experts blame the demise of the Pontiac Fiero, five years after it was introduced, on a bureaucracy that was rigid and inefficient. For example, the car died after the company decided not to spend enough money to make changes as basic as power steering.

Another frequent problem in a bureaucracy is high frustration accompanied by low satisfaction. The sources of these negative feelings include red tape, slow decision making, and an individual's limited influence on how well the organization performs.

Departmentalization

In bureaucratic and other forms of organization, the work is subdivided into departments or other units. The departmentalization capitalizes upon the classic bureaucratic principle of specialization and also helps avoid confusion. Can you imagine the chaos if all the workers in an organization of more than 50 people worked in one large department? The process of subdividing work into departments is called **departmentalization.**

Here we will use charts to illustrate five frequently used forms of departmentalization: functional, territorial, product-service, and customer. Most organization charts show a combination of the various types. The majority of business firms use a combination of the first four structures, and are therefore the fifth type—a hybrid.

Functional Departmentalization

Functional departmentalization is grouping people according to their expertise. Bureaucracies are almost always organized into functional departments. Within a given department, the work may be further subdivided. For instance, finance may include subunits for accounts receivable, accounts payable, and payroll. The names of functional departments vary widely with the nature of the business or enterprise. Exhibit 12-2 illustrates a generic type of functional structure. The advantages and disadvantages of functional departmentalization follow those of a bureaucracy.

Territorial Departmentalization

Grouping subunits according to the geographic area served is **territorial departmentalization.** In this structure, those responsible for all the activities of a firm in a given geographic area report to one manager. The internationalization of business has increased the relevance of organizing by territory. Service organizations make extensive use of territorial departmentalization. For example, large insurance and financial services firms organize territorially. Territorial departmentalization is used frequently to supplement functional groupings. For example, a corporate headquarters might departmentalize by function while the field forces are organized by territory.

EXHIBIT 12-2

Functional Departmentalization

263

Product/Service Departmentalization

Product–service departmentalization is the arrangement of departments according to the products or services they provide. When specific products or services are so important they almost become independent companies, product departmentalization makes sense. Exhibit 12-3 presents a version of product-service departmentalization. Notice that the organization depicted offers products and services with unique demands of their own. For example, the manufacture and sale of airplane engines is an entirely different business from the development of real estate.

Customer Departmentalization

Customer departmentalization creates a structure based on customer needs. When the demands of one group of customers are quite different from the demands of another, customer departmentalization often results. Many manufacturing companies organize their efforts according to business and retail departments, such as the marketing of Hewlett Packard personal computers.

Many manufacturers and retailers now have an e-commerce or e-tailing division. Such divisions are customer departmentalization because the divisions cater

EXHIBIT 12-3

Product-Service Departmentalization

to the customer group that chooses to trade over the Internet. Sometimes the e-groups have their own physical facilities such as a distribution center and dedicated servers.

The overriding advantage of organizing by territory, product-service, or customer is that it gives major attention to enhancing that product's growth or providing good service to customers. Such units also foster employee pride. The same types of departmentalization present identical problems as any other form of decentralization. It can be expensive because of duplication of effort and the difficulty of controlling the organization units.

Hybrid Organization Structure

Almost all complex organizations contain several forms of departmentalization either in the overall organization chart or in various divisions. Referring back to Exhibit 12-3, imagine that the Airplane Engines Division departmentalized into engines for government airplanes, commercial airplanes, and private airplanes. You would then have an organization that featured product-service departmentalization yet also contained a division with customer departmentalization. A **hybrid (or mixed) organization structure** combines the advantages of two or more types of organization forms into one structure. Some functions may be highly specialized and located at corporate headquarters, whereas other units (such as product or territorial units) may be self-contained and located elsewhere. Exhibit 12-4 illustrates a hybrid organization structure. It is doubtful any large, complex organization could function effectively or efficiently without using a hybrid design.

Line versus Staff Units

In Chapter 7, line and staff groups were mentioned in relation to conflict. Line and staff groups are present in most forms of departmentalization, yet the organization chart rarely makes such designations. In Exhibit 12-2 the human resources unit would undoubtedly be considered a staff group; the finance group would sometimes be considered a staff group; the other groups are line.

EXHIBIT 12-4

Hybrid Organization Structure

Most organizations use different organization structures at each organizational level or at various places throughout the organization.

Keep in mind that the distinction between line and staff is often blurred. (Line groups are responsible for the primary purposes of the firm, whereas staff groups are responsible for the secondary purposes.) Members of some departments are not sure if they are perceived as line or staff by top management, leading to role ambiguity. A marketing executive said, "The key purpose of our firm is to provide goods to customers. Yet when cutbacks take place, marketing people get chopped first. It makes no sense to me."

KEY MODIFICATIONS OF THE BUREAUCRATIC STRUCTURE

To overcome several of the disadvantages of the bureaucratic and functional forms of organization, several other structures have developed. Typically these less bureaucratic structures are used to supplement or modify the bureaucratic structure. Teams, as described in Chapter 5 in the context of job design, have emerged as the most widely used supplement to the bureaucratic structure. Task forces and projects follow a similar departure from bureaucracy as do teams. Here we describe matrix, flat structures, and outsourcing.

Describe three key modifications of a bureaucratic structure: matrix, flat, and outsourcing.

Matrix Organization Structure

Traditional organizations can be slow to respond to change. A frequently used antidote to this problem is the **matrix organization,** which consists of a project structure superimposed on a functional structure. A **project** is a temporary group of specialists working together under one manager to o accomplish a fixed objective such as launching a major new product. The word *matrix* refers to the feature of something contained in something else, similar to a grid with numbers in the cells (see Exhibit 12-5). The distinguishing feature of the matrix organization is

EXHIBIT 12-5

Matrix Organization in an Electronics Company

In a matrix organization, a project structure is superimposed on a functional structure.

the responsibility of the project or program manager to achieve results through employees who also report directly to another manager or have dual reporting responsibilities. For example, a person assigned to a project in a matrix organization might report to both the project manager and the manager in his or her regular department.

A major purpose of the matrix organization is to allow the firm to take advantage of new opportunities and solve special problems. Instead of developing a new organization containing functional departments, the firm leaves the original organization intact. The project or program managers within the matrix structure have access to the resources of the functional departments.

A key advantage of the matrix organization is its ability to implement important projects that demand intense, sustained attention for a limited time. It has been used, for example, to build a prototype for an e-commerce system. On the negative side, the matrix structure often creates problems because people assigned to projects within the matrix have a dual reporting relationship. One study concluded that matrix organizations have proved unworkable, particularly in international settings. Separated by the barriers of distance, language, culture, and different time zones, international managers could not overcome the confusion created by matrix structures.[9]

Despite this potential disadvantage, a project manager in a matrix organization is not doomed to failure. The challenge for the manager is to use a high level of interpersonal skill (such as the ability to resolve conflict) as well as technical skill to achieve goals.

Flat Organization Structures and Downsizing

A **flat organization structure** is one that has relatively few layers. A flat structure is less bureaucratic for two reasons. First, few managers in this form of organization are available to review the decisions of other people. As a by-product, customer service is often improved because many customer problems can be resolved without waiting for layers of approval. Second, because the chain of command is shorter, there is less concern about authority differences among people. Most large organizations have moved toward flatter structures, continuing a trend that began over 20 years ago. General Motors, for example, has moved from a peak of 29 layers to about 15 today (the number fluctuates somewhat). Small- and medium-size businesses have held on to their traditionally flat structures, which are usually imposed by not having enough money to build management depth.

Flatter organization structures created by downsizing sometimes do lead to greater organizational efficiency. GE, one of the world's most successful companies, has downsized over 100,000 workers in the last two decades. AT&T, another profitable and well-known company, laid off 19,000 workers in 1998 alone. Sunglass Hut, a major retailer of sunglasses and wristwatches, returned to profitability after closing 280 unprofitable stores in 1998. A controversial aspect of flat structures created by downsizing is that they result in substantial human suffering. Even when jobs are plentiful, losing a job can result in considerable emotional turmoil for the individual. Survivors of the downsizing also experience problems, such as guilt. The accompanying Organizational Behavior in Action illustrates how one successful company has avoided downsizing and therefore its negative human consequences. More will be said about the problems associated with downsizing as a change strategy in Chapter 13.

An important implication for managers when creating flat structures is to deal with the human element. As one study about downsizing concluded, ". . . maintaining an open dialogue with employees and providing them with opportunities to affirm themselves in a positive manner will help to eliminate some of the negative outcomes which accompany layoffs."[10]

Organizational Behavior *in Action*

Lincoln Electric Finds Humane Alternatives to Downsizing

Looking for alternatives to downsizing has been the policy at Lincoln Electric Holdings, a manufacturer of arc-welding products including welding machines and motors. Based in Cleveland, Ohio, Lincoln's productivity rate is double to triple that of many other manufacturing operations that use steel as its raw materials and that has 1,000 or more employees. The company offers no paid holidays or sick days, but has a no-layoff policy. The no-layoff policy began during the Depression, which started in the early 1930s. As a result, there have been no layoffs at Lincoln, even though the company has faced several economic downturns. In 1992, for instance, it suffered severe losses following an expansion into Europe, Asia, Russia, and Latin America. The departments involved with the international operation were in trouble.

Roy Morrow, director of corporate relations, explains what Lincoln did: "We redeployed people, turning 54 factory workers into salespeople who brought in $10 million in sales their first year. We called that our Leopard Program. We also used the slow time to upgrade facilities." Upgrading the facilities included modernizing machines, conducting maintenance on machinery, rearranging machines for greater efficiency, cleaning, and painting. All of these activities contribute only indirectly to productivity, but taken together the impact can be substantial.

Lincoln pulled out of its 1992 tailspin, returning a bonus to all employees and top management that has averaged between 52 percent and 56 percent of salary for 65 consecutive years. Lincoln has been a pioneer in the application of gainsharing and other profit-sharing plans to enhance worker motivation. Many production workers earn over $100,000 per year, salary and profit-sharing bonus included. "Our people are too valuable. The loss of one person costs us $100,000 to replace. We don't want to do business that way," concluded Morrow.

In more than 60 years without downsizing, Lincoln has learned how to balance business peaks and valleys with its commitment to employees. Top management has developed a set of principles they believe might also be effective for other companies:

- Avoid thinking of downsizing as a viable management strategy.
- If you don't overhire, you won't have to downsize. (*Rightsizing* prevents downsizing.)
- Set aside funds for growth and productivity.
- Introduce new products and services during a business downturn so that your company remains innovative.
- When customers demand a discount during downtimes, form a partnership with them to deliver services or products faster or cheaper. The goal is to deliver 10 percent to 20 percent in added value instead of giving a discount.

Lincoln Electric's pays-for-performance systems are among the oldest in the country. To learn more about its proud history of employee motivation through profit sharing, visit http://www.lincolnelectric.com/.

Source: Marlene Piturro, "Alternatives to Downsizing," *Management Review*, October 1999, p. 38; Carolyn Wiley, "Incentive Plan Pushes Production," *Personnel Journal*, August 1993, pp. 86-91.

Outsourcing as an Organizational Arrangement

An increasingly common practice among organizations of all types and sizes is to **outsource,** or have work performed for them by other organizations. Outsourcing is linked to organization structure because it is a method of dividing work: certain activities are assigned to groups outside the organization. Another way of framing outsourcing is that it is a vast network of interconnected enterprises that depend on one another for services.[11] By outsourcing, a company can reduce its need for employees and physical assets and reduce payroll costs. Many firms outsource the development and start-up phases of their e-commerce units to outside information technology consultants. Much to the chagrin of labor unions and local workers, many companies outsource work to geographic areas where workers are paid lower wages.

Among the many examples of outsourcing would be for a small company to hire another company to manage its payroll and employee benefits and for a large manufacturing firm to have certain components made by another firm. Even IBM is a contractor for other employers, such as making the hard drives for other computer manufacturers or managing their computer systems. The outsourcing movement has been a boon for small- and medium-size firms who perform stable work for larger organizations.

A key implication of outsourcing as an organization design strategy is that work is being performed for your firm by people over whom you have no control. Other managers are responsible for leading and managing employees who perform important functions for the organization. A frequent concern in the clothing, toy, and consumer electronics industries is that subcontractors sometimes engage in unsavory practices such as violating wage and salary laws and child-labor laws. Outsourcing has led to sweatshops as smaller firms compete to offer the lowest possible price for manufacturing goods. Outsourcing can therefore create ethical dilemmas.

LEADING-EDGE ORGANIZATION STRUCTURES

Describe the two contemporary organizational designs referred to as horizontal structures and network organizations.

Spin-offs from traditional organization structures continue to emerge as organizations strive to improve their efficiency and effectiveness. A major reason for these changes is that a traditional mechanistic organization can be too cumbersome to respond to changes in the environment. Two leading-edge forms are the horizontal structure and the network organization.

The Horizontal Structure

A major current development in organizational design is to work horizontally rather than vertically. A **horizontal structure** is the arrangement of work by teams that are responsible for accomplishing a process. The virtual organization is thereby similar to the establishment of work teams. A major difference, however, is that team members are responsible for a process rather than a product or service. The difference is subtle in that the team aims at delivering a product or service to a customer rather than focusing on the product or service itself. Instead of focusing on a specialized task, all team members focus on achieving the purpose of all the activity, such as getting a product in the hands of a customer. In a horizontal structure or process organization, employees take collective responsibility for customers.[12]

One approach to switching from a task emphasis to the process emphasis in a horizontal structure is through **reengineering,** the radical redesign of work to achieve substantial improvements in performance. Reengineering searches for the most efficient way to perform a large task. The emphasis is on uncovering wasted steps, such as people handing off documents to one another to obtain their approval. Eliminating workers who are performing nonessential tasks is another goal of reengineering. E-commerce can be considered a way of reengineering the work of sales representatives. If goods are exchanged over the Internet, the need for industrial sales representatives shrinks considerably. Fewer purchasing agents are needed also because buying over the Internet is more efficient than speaking directly to sales representatives.

As a result of reengineering, work is organized horizontally rather than vertically. The people in charge of the process act as team leaders who guide the team toward the completion of an important core process such as new product development or filling a complicated order. Key performance objectives for the team would include "reduce cycle time," "reduce costs," and "reduce throughput time." Exhibit 12-6 illustrates the horizontal structure, as do the projects embedded in the matrix organization shown in Exhibit 12-5.

A caution to managers and prospective managers is to recognize that the push toward the horizontal structures and reengineering should not be embraced without qualification. Having a "task mentality" is still important because expertise is still crucial in many endeavors. A surgical team, for example, still relies on highly proficient specialists such as a brain surgeon and an anesthetist. Also, wouldn't you prefer that the operating system on your cellular telephone be designed by a specialist when you need to call somebody to rescue you from a life-threatening situation?

The Network Structure

Another fast-growing development in organization structure is for organizations to affiliate with one another based on their need to share resources. Few companies have all the assets and resources in their firm to accomplish new endeavors. The key in many modern firms is not to own the resources, but to have access to them.[13] The best resources and talents are borrowed as needed. A **network structure (or virtual organization)** is a temporary association of otherwise independent firms that are linked by technology to share expenses, employee talents, and access to one another's markets.[14] Outsourcing is somewhat like forming a network structure, except that the relationship is more limited and contractual.

A pure network structure would have neither corporate headquarters nor an organization chart. Hierarchy would be sacrificed to speed of decision making, and vertical integration would be supplanted by horizontal integration across company boundaries. Each contributor to the network would stick to its core

EXHIBIT 12-6

A Horizontal Structure

In a horizontal structure, even though specialists are assigned to the team, they are expected to understand one another's tasks and perform some of those tasks as needed.

competency—what it does best such as manufacturing a particular component, marketing the finished product, or new product development.

For most organizations, the network structure supplements the regular structure, much like a large project. Many large organizations have small units that use the network structure for forming strategic alliances with other companies. Digital cameras, for example, are typically the product of a strategic alliance among several companies. Strategic alliances are also formed to market products. An example is that Xerox Corp. formed a strategic alliance with several office products stores to provide new channels for customers to obtain many Xerox products. Also, many companies form partnerships with Internet portals to one another's advantage. The portal, such as Yahoo, benefits because of a link on the Web site of the partner. Companies even form alliances with rivals, such as Apple Computer and Microsoft Corp. working jointly on a few products.

Proponents of the network structure see it as a fluid and flexible entity taking the form of a group of collaborators who link together to capitalize on a specific opportunity. After the opportunity has been met, the venture will typically disband. However, some alliances and partnerships are relatively permanent. An essential requirement is that members of the alliance must trust one another. One incompetent or dishonest member of the network can ruin or severely damage the multiple venture. It is not uncommon for an overseas member of a strategic alliance to steal the other's technology and become a direct competitor.

The horizontal and virtual structures place additional demands on the interpersonal skills of the workers involved. Relationships tend to be more stable in a functional structure, whereas horizontal and virtual structures involve more temporary relationships. A person has to get up to speed quickly in establishing working relationships. Furthermore, the authority structure is less clear, so the individual may have to rely more on informal influence tactics. Personal power becomes more important than positional power.

ORGANIGRAPHS: DRAWING HOW COMPANIES REALLY WORK

Understand why a new type of organization chart called an *organigraph* can contribute to understanding organization structure.

The typical approach to providing an overview of reporting relationships in an organization is to draw an organization chart. Simplified versions of these charts have been presented throughout this chapter. Henry Mintzberg and Ludo Van der Heyden have developed what they believe is a more revealing way to depict the people and operations within an organization. The **organigraph** is a map that provides an overview of the company's functions and the way people organize themselves at work. An organigraph is potentially useful because it depicts the many relationships among people in the organization.[15] Network analysis, as described earlier, provides a similar type of analysis within a small work unit. An organigraph helps you understand several important aspects of organizational functioning:

- What parts connect to one another?
- How should processes and people be linked to one another?
- Whose ideas have to flow to which other people?

According to Mintzberg and Van der Heyden, an organigraph can help a company see untapped competitive opportunities. To illustrate, one such map drawn for Electrocomponents, a British distributor of electrical and mechanical products, led managers to see clearly the company's true expertise—business-to-business relationships. Based on this insight, the company decided to expand in Asia and to increase its Internet business.

Exhibit 12-7 presents three organigraphs for a Canadian Bank, illustrating how understanding work relationships can enhance customer service. A traditional organizational chart would not include information about customer interactions.

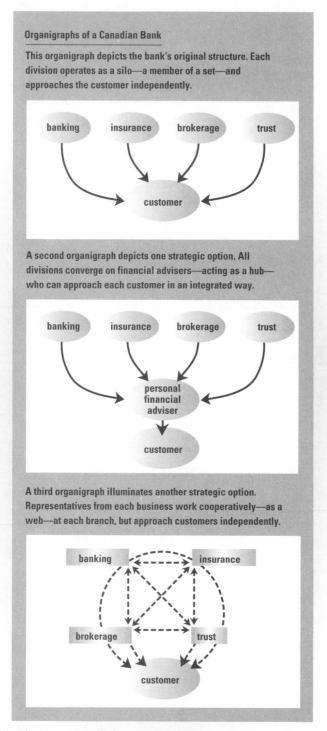

EXHIBIT 12-7

271

Organigraphs of a Canadian Bank

Organigraphs of a Canadian Bank

This organigraph depicts the bank's original structure. Each division operates as a silo—a member of a set—and approaches the customer independently.

A second organigraph depicts one strategic option. All divisions converge on financial advisers—acting as a hub—who can approach each customer in an integrated way.

A third organigraph illuminates another strategic option. Representatives from each business work cooperatively—as a web—at each branch, but approach customers independently.

IMPLICATIONS FOR MANAGERIAL PRACTICE

1. An overriding decision in organizational design is the choice between a mechanistic or an organic structure. Mechanistic structures are better suited for repetitive tasks in a stable environment and in which centralized control is desirable. Organic structures are better suited for creative tasks in a rapidly changing environment and in which decentralized control is desirable.

2. A design decision for a large organization is usually not an issue of mechanistic versus organic but instead choosing between which units should be mechanistic and which ones should be organic.

3. Organization structure influences behavior in many ways. A key factor is that specialization can lead to job dissatisfaction and boredom for many workers. An exception is that some highly trained workers prefer to be superspecialists, such as a package designer. Yet even here, the person would probably prefer to design a variety of packages.

4. Workers with a strong bureaucratic orientation thrive best in a controlled environment with tight job descriptions and predictability in their jobs. Workers with a low bureaucratic orientation prefer a looser and less predictable work environment.

5. The leading-edge organizational designs such as the network organization are the wave of the future. Managers and nonmanagers alike need high-level interpersonal skills to function effectively in such structures because they must often rely more on informal than formal authority.

SUMMARY OF KEY POINTS

 Identify and describe foundation concepts of organization structure.

Organization structure is the arrangement of people and tasks to accomplish organizational goals, whereas organizational design is the process of creating an appropriate structure. Mechanistic organizations are hierarchical, with an emphasis on specialization and control, and rules and regulations. In contrast, an organic structure is laid out like a network and is much looser.

An informal organization emerges to take care of the events and transactions not covered by the formal structure. Social network analysis is useful in depicting the informal structure. The more formalized an organization, the more it is mechanistic and bureaucratic. The more centralized an organization, the more extensively top managers delegate responsibility. Organizations vary in their complexity, or differentiation among subunits.

 Specify the basic features of the bureaucratic form of organization, including how it is divided into departments.

A bureaucracy is a rational, systematic, and precise form of organization. In it, rules, regulations, and techniques of control are defined precisely. Properly used, bureaucracy allows for large-scale accomplishments. Problems associated with bureaucracy include suppression of initiative through overcontrol, and high job frustration, and low job satisfaction.

Departmentalization is the grouping of work into manageable units. The basic forms of departmentalization are functional, territorial, product-service, and customer. Most firms use a hybrid structure composed of several types of departmentalization. The functional organization has both the advantages and disadvantages of a bureaucracy. The other forms give major attention to a customer or market, but can be expensive because of duplication of effort and are also difficult to control. Line and staff units are frequently built into a departmentalized structure.

 Describe three key modifications of a bureaucratic structure: matrix, flat, and outsourcing.

Bureaucratic structures are commonly supplemented by organic, or highly adaptable, organizational units. A matrix structure consists of a project structure imposed on a functional structure. The matrix manager must achieve results through employees who are also responsible to another manager. A flat structure has relatively few layers, which speeds up decision making. Outsourcing is an arrangement whereby one organization has work performed by another. Outsourcing is linked to structure because it is a method of dividing work.

 Describe the two contemporary organizational designs referred to as horizontal structures and network organizations.

Two leading-edge organization structures are the horizontal structure and the network organization. A horizontal organization arranges work by teams that are responsible for accomplishing a process. A network

structure, or virtual corporation, is a temporary association of otherwise independent firms that join forces to exploit an opportunity. Each network member contributes its core competency.

 Understand a new type of organization chart called an *organigraph* that can contribute to understanding organization structure.

The organigraph is a map that provides an overview of the company's functions and the way people organize themselves at work. Aside from depicting interpersonal relationships in the organization, an organigraph can help a company see untapped competitive opportunities.

273

KEY TERMS AND PHRASES

Organization, *256*
A collection of people working together to achieve a common purpose (or simply a big group).

Organization Structure, *256*
The arrangement of people and tasks to accomplish organizational goals.

Organizational Design, *256*
The process of creating a structure that best fits a purpose, strategy, and environment.

Mechanistic Organization, *256*
A primarily hierarchical organization with an emphasis on specialization and control, vertical communication, and heavy reliance on rules, policies, and procedures.

Organic Structure, *256*
An organization laid out like a network, emphasizing horizontal specialization, extensive use of personal coordination, extensive communication among members, and loose rules, policies, and procedures.

Formal Organization Structure, *257*
An official statement of reporting relationships, rules, and regulations.

Informal Organization Structure, *257*
A set of unofficial working relationships that emerges to take care of the events and transactions not covered by the formal structure.

Formalization, *257*
The degree to which expectations regarding the methods of work are specified, committed to writing, and enforced.

Centralization, *258*
The extent to which executives delegate authority to lower organizational units.

Complexity, *258*
The number of different job titles and units within an organization.

Coupling, *258*
The extent to which the parts of an organization are interdependent.

Bureaucracy, *259*
A rational, systematic, and precise form of organization in which rules, regulations, and techniques of control are precisely defined.

Machine Bureaucracy, *259*
An ideal organization that standardizes work processes and is efficient.

Professional Bureaucracy, *259*
An organization that standardizes skills for coordination and is composed of a core of highly trained professionals.

Departmentalization, *262*
The process of subdividing work into departments.

Functional Departmentalization, *262*
The grouping of people according to their expertise.

Territorial Departmentalization, *262*
An organizational structure in which those responsible for all the activities of a firm in a given geographic area report to one manager.

Product-Service Departmentalization, *263*
The arrangement of departments according to the products or services they provide.

Customer Departmentalization, *263*
An organizational structure based on customer needs.

Hybrid (or Mixed) Organization Structure, *264*
An organization structure that combines two or more types of organization forms into one structure.

Matrix Organization, *265*

An organization consisting of a project structure imposed on a functional structure.

Project, *265*

A temporary group of specialists working together under one manager to accomplish a fixed objective.

Flat Organization Structure, *266*

An organization structure with relatively few layers.

Outsource, *268*

The practice of having work performed by groups outside the organization.

Horizontal Structure, *268*

The arrangement of work by teams that are responsible for accomplishing a process.

Reengineering, *268*

The radical redesign of work to achieve substantial improvements in performance.

Network Structure (or Virtual Organization), *269*

A temporary association of otherwise independent firms linked by technology to share expenses, employee talents, and access to one another's markets.

Organigraph, *270*

A map that provides an overview of a company's functions and the way people organize themselves.

DISCUSSION QUESTIONS AND ACTIVITIES

1. Many readers of this text are not already in a position to lay out an organization structure. How might they make use of information about organization structure and design?
2. Explain whether Starbucks (or choose Pizza Hut or McDonalds) is a mechanistic or an organic organization.
3. What hints would you look for to analyze the degree of formalization in the company for which you were being interviewed?
4. Speculate about the personality traits of a person who

scores 20 on the Bureaucratic Orientation Scale in the Self-Assessment on page 261.
5. Obtain an annual report or visit the Web site of any organization of your choosing. What type of departmentalization does this firm use?
6. Why is the network organization so well suited to a highly competitive, rapidly changing work environment?
7. Why might an organigraph provide more useful information for organizational behavior than would the standard organization chart?

ORGANIZATIONAL BEHAVIOR ON-LINE

TO DO

Analyzing an Organization Structure

The purpose of this exercise is to find an example of organization structure on the Internet and then classify it by structural type (or types). We recommend two approaches. One approach is to search directly for examples of an organization structure by using a search phrase such as "example of organization structure." Another approach is to visit the Web site of a company of your choosing. (It might be necessary to visit the sites of several companies to find an organization chart.) You might not find the organization structure laid out on the Web site. In this case, send the company an e-mail message, asking for a copy of a company organization chart. Ask the company representative to classify a typical organization structure the company uses.

TO DO

Designing a Flat Organization

COLLABORATE You and your teammates are assigned the task of

creating a flatter structure for the organization depicted on the following page. Draw a new chart with each box carefully labeled. You might first sketch your chart on notebook paper and then draw a final version on (a) an overhead transparency, (b) a white board, (c) a chalkboard, or (d) a computer slide. Explain why you made the cuts you did, what happens to any managers who might be downsized, and why your new structure is an improvement.

Organization Charts
http://www.rff.com

An Example of a Machine Bureaucracy
http://www.gm.com

An Example of Divisional Structures
http://www.valero.com

Virtual Organizations
http://www.virtual-organization.net

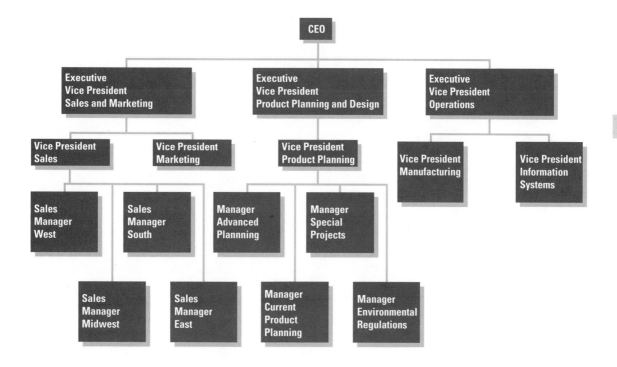

SUGGESTED READINGS

Banner, David K., and Gagné, T. Elaine. *Designing Effective Organizations: Traditional and Transformational Views.* Thousand Oaks, CA: Sage Publications, 1995.

Das, Somnath, Sen, Pradyot K., and Sengupta, Sanjit. "Impact of Strategic Alliances on Firm Valuation." *Academy of Management Journal,* February 1998, pp. 27–41.

Fisher, Susan Reynolds, White, Margaret A. "Downsizing in a Learning Organization: Are There Hidden Costs?" *Academy of Management Review,* January 2000, pp. 244–251.

Forrester, Russ, and Drexler, Allan B. "A Model for Team-Based Organization Performance." *Academy of Management Executive,* August 1999, pp. 36–49.

Mishra, Aneil K. and Spreitzer, Gretchen M. "Explaining How Survivors Respond to Downsizing: The Roles of Trust, Empowerment, Justice, and Work Redesign." *Academy of Management Review,* July 1998, pp. 567–588.

Sparks, Debra. "Conseco's Morning After." *Business Week,* June 5, 2000, pp. 108–110.

Sylvia, Egan M. "Reorganization as Rebirth." *HR Magazine,* January 1995, pp. 84–88.

Tullar, William L. "Compensation Consequences of Reengineering." *Journal of Applied Psychology,* December 1998, pp. 975–980.

ENDNOTES

1. Henricks, "The Shadow Knows," p. 110.
2. Henricks, "The Shadow Knows," p. 112.
3. Steven Cavellere and Obloj Kryzstof, *Management Systems: A Global Perspective* (Belmont, CA: Wadsworth, 1993), pp. 29–30.
4. Max Weber, *The Theory of Social and Economic Organization* (New York: Free Press, 1947).
5. Henry Mintzberg, *Structure in Fives: Designing Effective Organizations* (Upper Saddle River, NJ: Prentice-Hall, 1983), pp. 189–214.
6. "More Dual Executives Teams Running Companies," Associated Press, June 2, 2000.
7. Elliot Jacques, "In Praise of Hierarchy," *Harvard Business Review,* January–February 1990, p. 127.
8. Paul S. Adler, "Building Better Bureaucracies," *Academy of Management Executive,* November 1999, p. 36.
9. Christopher A. Bartlett and Sumantra Ghosal, "Matrix Management: Not a Structure, a Frame of Mind," *Harvard Business Review,* July–August 1990, p. 145.

10. Barbara J. Petzall, Gerald E. Parker, and Philipp A. Stoeberl, "Another Side to Downsizing: Survivors' Behavior and Self-Affirmation," *Journal of Business and Psychology,* Summer 2000, p. 601.
11. "Outsourcing Proves Value for Doing Business Cheaper," Knight Ridder, May 21, 2000.
12. Ann Majchrzak and Qianwei Wang, "Breaking the Functional Mind-Set in Process Organizations," *Harvard Business Review,* September–October 1996, p. 93.
13. Oren Harari, "Transform Your Organization into a Web of Resources," *Management Review,* January 1998, p. 21.
14. William H. Davidow and Michael S. Malone, *The Virtual Corporation: Structuring and Revitalizing the Corporation for the 21st Century* (Edward Burlingame Books/Harper Business, 1992).
15. Henry Mintzberg and Ludo Van der Heyden, "Organigraphs: Drawing How Companies Really Work," *Harvard Business Review,* September–October 1999, pp. 87–94.

Organizational Culture and Change

Costs were rising too rapidly in Margaret Jordan's department. Top management told her she would have to reduce her staff of 300 by approximately 25 percent. But Jordan knew she needed the entire department's effort to make the transition to a reduced size workforce. Jordan felt like she was "asking employees to help build a house that most of them wouldn't live in." Jordan was careful not to disguise that fact. Instead, as soon as she knew the details, Jordan told everyone exactly what was going to happen and what she needed from them. Here are the steps Jordan took:

During an "all-hands" meeting, Jordan discussed the reasons for the transition and the phases it would take. Then she asked for questions about the scenario she painted. No one raised a hand. Many leaders would breathe a sigh of relief and end the meeting at that point. Jordan, however, knew she couldn't make the transition work without everyone's support. She had to dig deeper. So she asked the employees to take a moment and think about their concerns, then write down any questions that came to mind. When they were done, she called a break in the meeting so she could read their questions and organize her responses.

After the break, Jordan read the questions aloud and answered them one by one. Some were based on rumors circulating in the company. Some were straightforward requests for more information. She addressed them all. By the time Jordan returned to her office, e-mail was already pouring in. Employees appreciated Jordan's up-front attitude. They also thanked her for setting a standard for collaboration.

Jordan's approach paid off. The transition went smoothly and most of the employees stayed to help.

The U.S. Office of Personnel Management has published an on-line survival guide for federal employees at http://safetynet.doleta.gov/ because of ongoing efforts to reduce the size and budgets of federal agencies. Although Margaret Jordan chose a different route to engage employees in a discussion about the transition to a smaller workforce, her up-front approach to communication is well reflected at this U.S. O.P.M. Web site.

Source: Adapted from facts reported in Lisa Friedman and Herman Gyr, *The Dynamic Enterprise: Tools for Turning Chaos into Strategy and Strategy into Action* (San Francisco: Jossey-Bass Inc., 1999). Copyright © 1999, Jossey-Bass, Inc. Reprinted by permission of Jossey-Bass, Inc., a subsidiary of John Wiley & Sons, Inc.

OBJECTIVES

After reading and studying this chapter and doing the exercises, you should be able to

 Present an analysis of the importance of organizational culture.

 Present two models of the change process in organizations.

 Describe why people resist change and how to manage such resistance.

 Describe several strategies for bringing about organizational change.

 Explain the nature of organization development.

 Develop useful insights into managing change in your job and career.

277

Chapter 13

SO WHAT? **What does Margaret Jordan's approach to delivering seriously bad news tell us about organizational culture?** Bringing about organizational change and overcoming potential resistance to change—even when the change centers on the very sensitive issue of staff reductions—can be managed both wisely and humanely. By first examining organizational culture, which is much like the personality of an organization, we can dig deeper into three key aspects of organizational change: strategies for bringing about change, the role of organization development in making organizations more adaptive, and dealing with change on a personal level.

ORGANIZATIONAL CULTURE

Present an analysis of the importance of organizational culture.

As implied in previous mentions of the term, **organizational culture** is a system of shared values and beliefs that influence worker behavior. Our study of organizational culture focuses on its determinants, its dimensions, how it is learned, and its consequences.

The Determinants of Organizational Culture

Many forces shape a firm's culture. Often its origin lies in the values, administrative practices, and personality of the founder or founders. Also, the leader's vision can have a heavy impact on culture, such as John Chambers's dream of Cisco Systems being one of the world's greatest companies. A much-publicized example of the impact of a leader on culture is Herb Kelleher, the founder of Southwest Airline, who is considered pivotal in shaping one of the most distinctive organizational cultures. Up until Kelleher's recent retirement, Southwest was considered very dependent on his personality and character. After his retirement for health reasons, his personality could still be felt. At the core of Southwest are the values of humor and altruism. For example, Southwest employees have established a catastrophe fund to help workers who need more assistance than usual employee benefits cover.[1]

Organizational culture responds to and mirrors the conscious and unconscious choices, behavior patterns, and prejudices of top-level managers. As the founders leave or become less active, other top-level managers help define the culture. One of the ways in which Lou Gerstner, the CEO and chair of IBM, changed the IBM culture was to relax its dress standards. His intent was to create a more relaxed (and less rigid) atmosphere at IBM.

The culture in which a society operates also helps determine the culture of the firm. Sooner or later, society's norms, beliefs, and values find their way into the firm. Societal values are communicated through such means as the media, conversations, and education. The emphasis on sexual and racial equality in U. S. society has become incorporated into the value culture of many employers. The culture at the Finnish electronics company, Nokia, emphasizes collegiality, as does the Finnish character. CEO Jorma Ollila says, "We don't snap our suspenders."[2] The same emphasis on collegiality translates into harmony and cooperation in the workplace at many Scandinavian companies. Another perspective on national culture is that the introduction of values from another society into a retail business can be a competitive advantage. For example, the Western values of speed, good service, and clean work areas helped fuel the success of McDonald's in Moscow.

The industry to which a firm belongs helps shape its culture, such as the culture of a high-tech information technology firm being quite different from the culture of the meat-packing industry. A study of 15 firms representing four industries in the service sector demonstrated the impact of the industry on organizational culture. It was found, for example, that household goods carriers have a culture different from consulting firms.[4] A public utility will have a culture different from a food manufacturer of comparable size. Heavy competition and low profit margins may force the food manufacturer to operate at a faster pace than the utility, which has more limited competition.

A firm's code of conduct is another key determinant of culture. The code of conduct establishes the workplace culture and communicates the employer's true attitudes.[5] For instance, a discipline system with little regard for due process leads to a harsh, threatening work environment. In contrast, a discipline system with checks and balances leads to a warmer, less-threatening culture.

Dimensions of Organizational Culture

The dimensions, or elements, of culture help explain the nature of the subtle forces that influence employee actions. For example, a culture that values risk taking encourages employees to try new ways of doing things. The employees will do so without concern that they will be punished for failed ideas. The following list describes eight influential dimensions of culture.

1. *Values.* The foundation of any organizational culture is values. A firms's philosophy is expressed through values, and values guide behavior on a daily basis. A study demonstrated, for example, that when top management has a lax attitude toward honesty, employee theft increases above the norm of 30 percent. (Two studies have shown that about 30 percent of respondents admitted to having stolen from their employers.)[5]

2. *Organizational stories that have underlying meanings.* Stories are circulated in many organizations to reinforce principles that top management thinks are important. A story circulates at Steelcase about how two night-shift workers shipped prototype models to waiting customers, thus illustrating how much the firm values good customer service. (Prototype models are ordinarily not sold, but are for internal purposes only.)

3. *Myths.* Myths are dramatic narratives or imagined events about the firm's history. They contribute to corporate legends, help unify groups, and can build competitive advantage. At United Parcel Service (UPS), for example, stories are repeated about drivers overcoming severe obstacles or reaching inaccessible locations to deliver packages.

4. *Degree of stability.* A fast-paced, dynamic firm has a different culture from that of a slow-paced, stable one. Top-level managers send out signals by their own energetic or lethargic stance regarding how much they welcome innovation. The degree of stability also influences whether or not a culture can take root and how strong that culture can be.

5. *Resource allocations and rewards.* The ways in which money and other resources are allocated have a critical influence on culture. The investment of resources sends a message about what the firm values.

6. *Rites and rituals.* Part of a firm's culture is made up of its traditions, or rites and rituals. Few companies think they have rites and rituals, yet an astute observer can identify them. Examples include regular staff meetings, retirement banquets (even for fired executives), and receptions for visiting dignitaries.

7. *A sense of ownership.* The movement toward stock ownership for an increasing

number of employees has created an ownership culture in many firms whereby workers are inspired to think and act like owners. An ownership culture includes increased loyalty, improved work effort, and the alignment of worker interests with those of the company. An ownership culture can be reflected in such everyday actions as conserving electricity, making gradual improvements, and not tolerating sloppy work by coworkers. An ownership culture can backfire, however, if employee wealth stays flat or decreases as a result of stock ownership.[6]

8. *Corporate spiritualism and organizational spirituality.* Organizations differ substantially in two closely related concepts that influence culture. *Corporate spiritualism* takes place when management is just as concerned about nurturing employee well-being as they are about profits. Many practices, such as work/life programs, contribute to this style of spiritualism.[7] *Organizational spirituality* refers to workers at all levels believing in something bigger than themselves in addition to traditional religion. This type of spirituality is also seen as an invisible means of support and an ever-reliable resource that keeps you and your career on track when the going gets rough.[8] Workers in a pharmaceutical firm, for example, might believe that the grand purpose of the company is to alleviate and prevent human suffering. Workers at a yo-yo factory might believe that their spirituality centers around bringing people moments of happiness. In firms with either corporate spiritualism or organizational spirituality (or both), people go about their work with a true sense of purpose. Both of these cultural dimensions contribute to a firm having a soul. (You will recall that the purpose of work/life programs is to help workers balance the demands of career and personal life.)

In addition to the dominant culture of a firm, the subculture also influences behavior. A **subculture** is a pocket in which the organizational culture differs from that of other pockets and the dominant culture. In a bank, the consumer loan division may have a culture different from that of the mortgage group, because the consumer group has to work with much shorter time frames in processing loans.

How Workers Learn the Culture

Employees learn the organizational culture primarily through **socialization,** the process of coming to understand the values, norms, and customs essential for adapting to the organization. Socialization is therefore a method of indoctrinating employees into the organization in such a way that they perpetuate the culture. The socialization process takes place mostly by learning through imitation and observation.

Another important way in which workers learn the culture is through the teachings of leaders, as implied in the cultural dimension of resource allocations and rewards. Organizational members learn the culture to some extent by observing what leaders pay attention to, measure, and control.[9] Suppose a coworker of yours is praised publicly for doing community service. You are likely to conclude that an important part of the culture is to help people outside the company.

The Consequences and Implications of Organizational Culture

Depending on its strength, a firm's organizational culture can have a pervasive impact on organizational effectiveness. Employees of a firm with a strong culture

EXHIBIT
13-1

*Consequences and
Implications of
Organizational Culture*

*Although organizatonal
culture is a soft concept, it
has many hard consequences.*

281

will follow its values with little questioning. A weaker culture provides only broad guidelines to members. Six major consequences and implications of organizational culture are outlined in Exhibit 13-1 and summarized next.

1. *Competitive advantage and financial success.* The right organizational culture contributes to gaining competitive advantage and therefore achieving financial success. A study of 34 firms investigated the relationship between a high-involvement/participative culture and financial performance. Firms perceived by employees to link individual efforts to company goals showed higher returns on investments and sales than firms without such linkages.[10] The consistently strong performance of Southwest Airlines is partially attributed to its humane and fun-loving culture.

2. *Productivity, Quality, and Morale.* A culture that emphasizes productivity, including high quality, encourages workers to be productive. Productivity and competitive advantage are closely linked because being productive contributes heavily to gaining on the competition. A representative example is the unique culture CEO Christos Cotsakos has created at E★Trade, the on-line stockbroker. The culture is characterized by a "lust for being different" that propels the professional staff to work unusually hard. The culture emphasizes high enthusiasm and bizarre behavior with such stunts as having workers wear propeller beanies.[11] Cotsakos believes that a remarkable culture is crucial for achieving corporate success. A culture that values the dignity of human beings fosters high morale and job satisfaction.

3. *Innovation.* A major contributor to innovation is a corporate culture that encourages creative behavior, as described in Chapter 4 about decision making and creativity. Gary Hamel has identified specific features of a culture that inspire innovation. Included are setting very high expectations, creating a cause that workers can be passionate about, encouraging radical ideas, and allowing talented people in the company to easily transfer to different business areas within the firm. Also, innovators must be paid exceptionally well. As Hamel states, "Entrepreneurs won't work for peanuts, but they'll work for a share of the equity, a piece of the action."[12]

4. *Compatibility of mergers and acquisitions.* A reliable predictor of success in merging two or more firms is compatibility of their respective cultures. When the cultures clash, such as a mechanistic firm merging with an organic one, the result can be negative synergy. A positive example is that top management at Cisco Systems makes all acquisitions (over 60 companies through year 2001) feel that they are part of the company, thus softening any possible culture barriers. A negative example is that when Chrysler and Daimler/Benz merged in 1999, their cultures clashed considerably, creating many transition problems. A

small example of the culture clash was that the American executives objected to the German executives spending so lavishly on hotel suites and meals. Another problem was that American managers were paid up to four times more than the German counterparts.[13]

5. *Person-organization fit.* An important success factor for the individual is finding an organization that fits his or her personality. Similarly, an organization will be more successful when the personality of most members fits its culture. In one study, organizations were measured on such dimensions as stability, experimenting, risk taking, and being rule-oriented. The preferences of professional employees regarding culture were measured and compared to the culture of their firms. Good person-organization fits result in more commitment and higher job satisfaction.[14]

6. *Direction of leadership activity.* Much of a top-level manager's time is spent working with the forces that shape the attitudes and values of employees at all levels. A key leadership role is to establish what type of culture is needed for the firm and then shaping the existing culture to match that ideal. This is particularly true when an outsider is brought in to head a company. When Michael Armstrong joined AT&T as its top executive, he acted quickly to shake up a culture that was too smug about competition. Armstrong also eliminated company chauffeur privileges for many managers because he thought they had developed an imperial attitude. Charles D. Moran, the top executive at Acxicom Corp., sums up the link between culture and company leadership in these words: "Your culture should be everything you do as a business. It should be how you solve problems, build products and work in teams. For the CEO and other leaders, it's about how you lead."[15]

The accompanying Organizational Behavior in Action provides more information about the implication and importance of organizational culture.

GENERAL CONSIDERATIONS ABOUT MANAGING CHANGE

Present two models of the change process in organizations.

For starters, experiment with Lewin's model of the change process. Next, engage with some of the forces underlying resistance to change. Visit South-Western's animated concept and activity site at *http://www.experiencingob. com* for exclusive review tools on the topics of Innovation & Change. Free demo available!

"The only constant is change" is a frequently repeated cliché in the workplace. To meet their objectives, managers and professionals must manage change effectively almost daily. Even companies that appear from the outside to work in a stable environment are faced with change. A surprising example is Hershey Foods Corporation, which has been making chocolate products since 1905—including the remarkably stable brands, Hershey's milk chocolate and Reese's Peanut Butter Cups. However, the technology for distributing chocolate products, including Internet sales, has created enormous challenges for the chocolate maker. Delays with a new automated distribution system hampered delivery of Halloween and Christmas candy one year. A company executive recently said, "Keeping up with the technology is probably the greatest challenge. Imagine how different it is to make chocolate now than when Milton Hershey was making his first caramel. From the time chocolate is made to the time it reaches the consumer, it's dealing with new technology the whole way."[16]

The many types of change in organizations include changes in technology, organizational structure, and the people with whom one works, such as customers and company insiders. Here we examine the change process itself, downsizing, information technology and change, disruptive technology and change, and the transition from jobs to performing work. We will also describe organization development—a formal approach to creating change.

282

Organizational Behavior *in Action*

C o r p o r a t e   C u l t u r e   T a k e s   A   K - T u r n

 Kansas City Star reporter prepared the following report on cultural changes taking place at the local transportation authority:

How do you turn a bus around on a city street? Deliberately and skillfully. It's a fitting analogy for corporate culture changes being attempted at the Kansas City Area Transportation Authority. Fourteen years of budget cuts had traumatized the largely unionized workforce. And years of unfriendly negotiations had created a rift between supervisors and drivers. But in 1996 a breakthrough contract agreement allowed the authority to work more efficiently by using part-time drivers and smaller buses where routes called for them. Federal funding has also stabilized in the last couple of years, and the ridership leveled off.

"We finally got to the point where we had a mutual appreciation of our serious problems," said Dick Davis, the authority's general manager. After the financial emergencies were handled, though, some workplace relationships remained troubled.

"The ATA unfortunately had become too oriented to dealing with the problem operator," Davis said. "We'd become a disciplinarian. We needed to move more toward a culture that spent a lot more time supporting and recognizing the good ones."

The authority found what most organizations have learned in the 1990s: Workers want to be asked for their suggestions. They want to share experiences. They don't want to just take orders. Recognizing that evolution, the authority's board hired organizational behavior consultant Jerry Haney to work with a "culture change team" of supervisors and union members, people handpicked to lead the transformation.

"We looked for respected employees who were thinkers or natural leaders, not just yes persons or complainers," said Fern Koehler, the authority's deputy general manager. They are working on such issues as conflict management, rudeness, and personal safety. A major goal is to have a workforce that works well without supervision, that makes the "right" decision because it's the right thing to do based on the circumstance—not because a company rule or schedule says so. My limited experiences riding buses indicates that the goal isn't universally met yet. It will take time.

"We're trying for open, two-way communication, not order giving," Davis said. "When we opened one of our first change meetings to questions and comments, we got remarkable feedback. We heard customer and employee issues that had never been raised in union talks."

"It's an amazing thing when organizations finally get to a place of mutual respect and common purpose. Everybody at the authority isn't there yet, but the organization is en route. Let's see if riders appreciate the change."

The Kansas City ATA can be found at http://www.keata.org/.

Source: Diane Stafford, "Changes in Corporate Culture," *Kansas City Star* syndicated story, November 1, 1999.

Models of the Change Process

Organizational change has been studied from different perspectives. Collectively, the two models described next help explain change from the organizational and individual perspectives.

The Growth Curve Model of Change in Organizations

The **growth curve model** traces the inevitability of change through a firm's life cycle, as shown in Exhibit 13-2. According to this model, businesses pass through three phases in sequence.[17] First is the *formative phase,* characterized by a lack of structure, trial and error, and entrepreneurial risk taking. Mistakes are seen as learning opportunities, and innovation is extremely important. The firm focuses on its market, with the goal of becoming predictable, stable, and successful.

Second is the *normative phase,* in which stability occurs. An emphasis is placed on maintaining the existing structure and developing predictability. Mistakes are frowned upon and perhaps punished, which leads to less risk taking. The firm becomes bureaucratized, and innovation is mostly given lip service or relegated to the research and development unit. The goal is survival, and the focus is less on the market and more on maintaining the status quo. However, changes continue to occur in the environment, which forces this phase to end.

Third is the *integrative phase,* in which the firm redefines itself and finds a new direction. During this phase, top-level managers attempt many changes such as introducing a new vision and policies. At the same time, the most resistance to change occurs as many members of the firm attempt to resist the discomfort it brings. The integrative phase is associated with ambiguity and uncertainty. In addition, the firm experiences an "organ rejection" of the new systems. During this phase, leadership, inspiration, and interpersonal skills become more important than routine management and technical skills.

During the integrative phase, there is a pulling and tugging between forces for and against change. According to the **force-field theory,** an organization simultaneously faces forces for change (the driving forces) and forces for maintaining the status quo (the restraining forces). Forces for change include new technology, competition from other groups, and managerial pressures. Forces for the status quo include group performance norms, fear of change, employee complacency, and well-learned skills. Considerable managerial skill is required in order for driving forces to outweigh restraining forces. As managers push for change, there is an equal push in the opposite direction from those who want to maintain the status quo.[18]

Another observation about change is that the ability to change is somewhat related to size: large organizations are more resistant to change than are small- or medium-size organizations. For example, some analysts have criticized IBM for not growing as fast as other information technology firms. Chairman Louis V. Gerstner Jr., points out that double-digit revenue growth is not possible for a company of IBM's size. Other company defenders note that a company with about $85 billion in annual sales cannot change as rapidly as a smaller company can.[19]

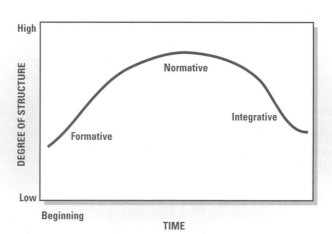

EXHIBIT 13-2

The Growth Curve Model of Organizational Change

Organizations go through predictable life stages.

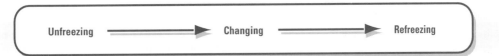

| Unfreezing | ⟶ | Changing | ⟶ | Refreezing |

The Unfreezing-Changing-Refreezing Model

Psychologist Kurt Lewin presented a three-step analysis of the change process.[20] His unfreezing-changing-refreezing model is widely used by managers to help bring about constructive change. Many other approaches to initiating change stem from this simple model, illustrated in Exhibit 13-3.

Unfreezing involves reducing or eliminating resistance to change. As long as employees oppose a change, it will not be implemented effectively. To accept change, employees must first deal with and resolve their feelings about letting go of the old. Only after people have dealt effectively with endings are they ready to make transitions.[21]

Changing, or moving on to a new level, usually involves considerable two-way communication, including group discussion. According to Lewin, "Rather than a one-way flow of commands or recommendations, the person implementing the change should make suggestions. The changees should be encouraged to contribute and participate." *Refreezing* includes pointing out the success of the change and looking for ways to reward people involved in implementing the change. For the change process to be complete, refreezing must take place.

WHY PEOPLE RESIST CHANGE

Before a company's managers can gain support for change, they need to understand why people resist change. People resist change for reasons they think are important, the most common being the fear of an unfavorable outcome. This outcome could be less money, personal inconvenience, more work, and so forth. People also resist change for such varied reasons as not wanting to disrupt social relationships and not wanting to break well-established habits.

Even when people do not view a change as potentially damaging, they may sometimes resist it because they fear the unknown. People will sometimes cling to a system they dislike rather than change. According to folk wisdom, "People would rather deal with the devil they know." Workers may also resist change because they are aware of weaknesses in the proposed changes that may have been overlooked or disregarded by management.[22]

> A sales manager resisted her company's proposal to shift a key product to dealer distribution. She explained that dealers would give so little attention to the product that sales would plunge. Despite her protests, the firm shifted to dealer distribution. Sales of the product did plunge, and the company returned to direct selling.

Gaining Support for Change

Gaining support for change, and therefore overcoming resistance, is an important managerial responsibility. Let us look at nine of these techniques for gaining support for change. Exhibit 13-4 provides an overview of most of these methods, as described in a classic article.

EXHIBIT 13-3   285

The Change Process

Change is a three-step process.

Describe why people resist change and how to manage such resistance.

Approach	Commonly Used	Advantages	Drawbacks
Education and communication	Where there is a lack of information or inaccurate information and analysis.	Once persuaded, people will often help with the implementation of the change.	Can be very time-consuming if lots of people are involved.
Participation and involvement	Where the initiators do not have all the information they need to design the change, and where others have considerable power to resist.	People who participate will be committed to implementing change, and any relevant information they have will be integrated into the change plan.	Can be very time-consuming if participants design an inappropriate change.
Facilitation and support	Where people are resisting because of adjustment problems.	No other approach works as well with adjustment problems.	Can be time-consuming, expensive, and still fail.
Negotiation and agreement	Where someone or some group will clearly lose out in a change, and where that group has considerable power to resist.	Sometimes it is a relatively easy way to avoid major resistance.	Can be too expensive in many cases if it alerts others to negotiate for compliance.
Manipulation and co-optation	Where other tactics will not work or are too expensive.	It can be a relatively quick and inexpensive solution to resistance problems.	Can lead to future problems if people feel manipulated.
Explicit and implicit coercion	Where speed is essential, and the change initiators possess considerable power.	It is speedy and can overcome any kind of resistance.	Can be risky if it leaves people mad at the initiators.

Source: Adapted and reprinted by permission of *Harvard Business Review.* From "Choosing Strategies for Change" by John P. Kotter and Leonard A. Schlesinger, March–April 1979, p. 111. Copyright © 1979 by the President and Fellows of Harvard College. All rights reserved.

EXHIBIT 13-4

Methods for Dealing with Resistance to Change

1. *Allow for discussion and negotiation.* Support for change can be increased by discussing and negotiating the more sensitive aspects of the change. The two-way communication incorporated into the discussion helps reduce some employee concerns. Discussion often leads to negotiation, which further involves employees in the change process.

2. *Allow for participation.* The best-documented way of overcoming resistance to change is to allow people to participate in the changes that will affect them. An application of this concept is allowing employees to set their own rules to increase compliance. A powerful participation technique is to encourage people who already favor the change to help in planning and implementation. These active supporters of the change will be even more strongly motivated to enlist the support of others.

3. *Point out the financial benefits.* Because so many employees are concerned about the financial effects of work changes, it is helpful to discuss these effects openly. If employees will earn more money as a result of the change, this fact can be used as a selling point. For example, the CEO of a small company told his employees, "I know you are inconvenienced and ticked off because we have cut way back on secretarial assistance. But some of the savings will be invested in bigger bonuses for you." Much of the grumbling subsided.

4. *Avoid change overload.* Too much change in too short a time leads to negative stress. So it is helpful to avoid overloading employees with too many sweeping changes in a brief time period. Too much simultaneous change also causes confusion, leading to foot-dragging about the workplace innovation. The more far-reaching the innovation is, such as restructuring a firm, the greater is the reason for not attempting other innovations simultaneously.

5. *Gain political support for change.* Few changes get through organizations without the change agent's forming alliances with people who will support his or her proposals. Often this means selling the proposed changes to members of top-level management before proceeding down the hierarchy. It is much more difficult to create change from the bottom up.

6. *Provide education.* A standard method of reducing resistance to change is through education and communication of relevant information. The method is likely to be the most effective when people resist change because they lack sufficient information. For example, workers may resist making the necessary preparations for outsourcing part of their work until they are informed about the scale of the outsourcing program and how it will affect their jobs.

7. *Use manipulation and co-optation.* Managers will sometimes resort to manipulating employees into supporting change. In this context, manipulation involves the selective use of information and the conscious structuring of events. Co-optation is a common form of manipulation used in overcoming resistance to change. Co-opting a group member usually involves giving him or her a role in the design or implementation of the change.

8. *Avoid citing poor performance as the reason for change.* Instead of criticizing, the change agent should accurately describe market challenges or budget restraints and show employees why change is necessary for survival. For example, do not say to employees, "If things hadn't become so sloppy around here, we wouldn't need to change." Instead, tell them, "Our competitors can deliver finished product in half the time because of this new technology. If we don't make the change, too, we'll lose all our key accounts."[23]

9. *Use explicit and implicit coercion.* Managers will sometimes force people to accept change by using direct or indirect threats. The threat can involve loss of job, a negative reference after leaving the company, demotion, or geographical transfer. As with manipulation, coercion is an unethical and risky tactic. Workers who feel they have been manipulated, coerced, or lied to may rebel at change. They may show more resistance to change than if other tactics for gaining support for change had been implemented.

To practice the concepts of managing change, do the Skill-Development Exercise that follows.

DOWNSIZING AND RESTRUCTURING AS A CHANGE STRATEGY

Describe several strategies for bringing about organizational change.

Downsizing has already been mentioned as a significant stressor and as a method of achieving a flat structure. Downsizing is also the most often used deliberate organization change in recent years. More than 85 percent of the Fortune 100 firms initiated major restructuring in the early 1990s. The pace of downsizing diminished only slightly at the end of the decade and in the 2000–2001 period, with major contributors being company mergers and acquisitions, and a slower economy. Cost reductions are often necessary because the survival of the firm is at stake. Downsizing can sometimes make a firm more competitive by lowering costs,

COLLABORATE

SKILL-DEVELOPMENT EXERCISE

Overcoming Resistance to Change

One student plays the role of a team leader who is to meet today with team members to sell them on the idea that the company plans to shift from a standard work week to a 4/40 workweek (work 10 hours per day, four days per week). About six other students play the role of the team members, several of whom have mixed reactions to the proposed change. The team leader should use the techniques for overcoming resistance to change described in this section. Team members who do not like the contemplated change should express what they consider valid reasons for resisting the change. Other class members should observe and then provide feedback.

but at the same time cause enormous confusion and resentment. Downsizing can also leave a firm so understaffed that it cannot capitalize on new opportunities. Another concern is that downsizing depletes human assets and interferes with organizational learning (see Chapter 14) because so much information stored in people's memories leaves the firm.[24]

An important perspective on downsizing as a change strategy is to specify the conditions under which it has the best chance of contributing to organizational effectiveness.[25] To begin, top management should ponder whether downsizing be avoided. Instead of laying off employees, a way should be sought to better utilize their expertise. Some cost cutting can be achieved by involving employees in improving work methods and processes. Under ideal circumstances, key people can look to penetrate new markets.

The first key to a successful restructuring is to integrate downsizing with the company's long-term strategies. The firm must determine where the business is headed and which employees are needed to ensure that future. The company must identify and protect high-potential individuals who are needed to carry the firm forward. After delayering, firms must decentralize and empower key individuals to conduct their jobs. The downsizing survivors must be revitalized by redefining their positions. (A problem is that survivors often have to assume the workload of several people.) It is therefore essential to eliminate low-value and non-value activities such as multiple reviews of other people's work and meetings without meaningful agendas.

After restructuring, teamwork must be emphasized more than previously because much cooperation is required to accomplish the same amount of work with fewer personnel. The downsized organization may require a new structure. It should be redesigned to reflect the changed jobs, processes, and responsibilities. Horizontal as well as vertical relationships must be specified.

Considerable attention must be paid to the human element before and after downsizing. GE emphasizes carefully evaluating the performance of all employees, grading each worker, A, B, or C. The lowest-performing workers are the first to go should a downsizing be necessary. However, GE gives employees a chance to move out of the bottom bracket through coaching and counseling. Grade A "players" are carefully cultivated and promoted so that when downsizing takes place they do not leave the company voluntarily. A carefully implemented system of performance appraisal increases the chances that good work performance and the possession of vital skills should receive more weight than favoritism in retaining employees.

A progressive approach some large companies take is to offer training to employees designated for downsizing so they might qualify for any vacant positions in the company. Downsizing survivors in all companies need an outlet to talk about their grief and guilt in relation to laid-off coworkers. As is often done, laid-off workers should be given assistance in finding new employment and redirecting their careers.

Information Technology and Organizational Change

Advances in information technology have facilitated a variety of profound changes in organizations. Your knowledge of information systems and information technology will help you visualize many organizational changes created by the digitalization of information. A major change is that electronic access to information has made much of the delayering of organizations possible. Many middle management and coordinator positions have been eliminated because there is less need for people to act as conduits of information. Instead, information seekers obtain information via computers.

Information technology has played a key role in making organizations more democratic. Democracy is enhanced because more people have access to information. John Gage of Sun Microsystems said, "Sun's organization structure is who sends e-mail to whom."[26] As implied by this quote, e-mail makes it easier for lower-ranking members to communicate directly with higher-ranking members. Before the surge in information technology, such direct interaction was rare in large firms.

The Internet is changing the nature of many businesses, such as companies interacting more directly with customers and suppliers. Many retail sales positions and industrial sales positions have been eliminated by e-commerce. Industries have been transformed by the Internet. A good example is the newspaper industry whose changes mirror what is happening in other industries. To survive, the industry has had to rely on its traditional strength of offering detail and depth. Services must now also be offered in both hard copy and on-line. Newspapers were among the first commercial entities on the Internet. Information on the Net is now offered free, pay-per-view, and by subscription. *The Wall Street Journal* actually makes money with its on-line subscription service.[27]

Enterprise software that links together the various functions of the enterprise to one another and to customers is starting to affect job behavior. As Tom Peters contends, "They are your nightmare, these white-collar robots. The complex products from German software giant SAP will do to your company's innards what forklifts and robots and containerization did to the blue-collar world circa 1960."[28] One likely scenario is already happening. A smaller number of managers will be needed because fewer employees will be needed. The remaining key workers will be skilled in information technology, problem solving, and interpersonal skills.

Information technology has created substantial changes in how long and where people work. Accessing and responding to e-mail has added hours to the workweek of many employees. Another change is that managers and professionals feel obliged to stay in frequent contact with the office, even during nights, weekends, and vacations. A report on technology in the 21st century put it this way:

> The problem today is that we haven't yet learned to manage technology. All too often our cellular telephones and notebook computers control us. Increasingly, we work all the time, everywhere. We use every available second to handle and prioritize voice mail, e-mail, and paperwork. In the Information Age, it's

becoming impossible to know when work is completed. And unless something changes, all this ultimately affects everything from customer service to burnout.[29]

Disruptive Technology and Organizational Change

Imagine that you are an executive at a profitable regional airline. You learn that a start-up company called JetYou is selling jet packs that enable people to fly within a 500-mile radius without having to purchase an airline ticket or visit an airport. You laugh at the idea that a jet pack is a serious competitor. But gradually one-half your customers shift to JetYou instead of flying commercially. You have been blindsided by **disruptive technology.** The phenomenon generally refers to large successful companies losing sight of small emerging markets served by a company with new technologies. In essence, a large industry leader is subject to attacks from a shoestring start-up.[30] So now you think to yourself, "Should we get into the jet pack business?"

Disrputive technologies create an entirely new market by introducing a new kind of product or service. The product or service is inferior in terms of what the best customers demand. (Flying 200 miles in the rain by jet pack rather than seated in an airplane might be considered inferior service.) Charles Schwab's initial entry as a bare-bones stock brokerage firm was a disruptive technology for big brokerage firms like Merrill Lynch. Early PCs were a disruptive innovation in comparison to mainframes and minicomputers. Full-service brokerage firms said, "Who would want to buy investments without full professional advice?" Mainframe manufacturers at first said, "Why bother with those junkie toys with slim profit margins?" However, discount brokers and PCs have become dominant forces in the fields of financial services and computers.

The point of disruptive technology as it relates to organizational behavior is that a new technology or start-up can create havoc for an organization. Several larger, well-established firms have been able to cope with the innovation. Dayton-Hudson, for example, is the only department store company that has been successful in the discount business. Dayton-Hudson staved off the competition by founding the Target Stores division. Clayton M. Christensen and Michael Overdorf offer three solutions for organizations to meet the challenge of disruptive change:

- Create new organizational structures within the existing corporation in which new processes can be developed. An example might be a traditional book publisher developing a project team in a remote location to develop electronic books.
- Spin out an independent organization from the existing organization and develop within it the new processes and values required to solve the problem. Hewlett-Packard finally met with success in the ink-jet printer business when it transferred the ink-jet unit to a separate division in Vancouver, British Columbia.
- Acquire another company whose processes and values closely match the requirements of furnishing the new product or service. Cisco Systems routinely purchase start-ups that have a technology that could threaten their business, such as improved software for linking computers together.[31]

The accompanying Organizational Behavior in Action provides an illuminating description about how a firm you have probably used regularly is adapting to disruptive technology.

Organizational Behavior *in Action*

The U.S. Postal Service Adapts to Disruptive Technology

Wary of losing its lucrative bill and payment delivery business to the Internet, the Postal Service has decided to offer one-stop bill paying via computer. Many Americans have grown comfortable paying bills electronically, and now they will be able to do all their business at a single site, Postmaster General Henderson announced recently.

It doesn't matter if the bill is from the electric company or the phone company, the local hardware store or the dentist's office. Henderson predicted that "the generation that has grown up with PCs will move to transacting business on the Internet."

He said that the service is being made available immediately (in April 2000), with new customers getting the first six months of service free. People interested in the service, USPSeBillPay, can get details and sign up at http://www.usps.gov. The Postal Service said it worked with CheckFree Corp. and YourAccounts.Com, a division of Output Technology Solutions, to develop the system. Companies can send bills electronically, and individuals will be able to pay all of them electronically. If someone wants to make a payment to a company that does not have an electronic connection to the service, the Postal Service will simply issue a check.

After the initial six months of free service, there are two plans. "Pay Everyone," at $6 a month, includes 20 payments and costs 40 cents for each additional payment. "Pay As You Go" costs $2 a month, plus 40 cents per payment.

You can visit the U.S. Postal Service and its partners in bill payment via the Internet at http://www.usps.gov, http://www.checkfree.com, and http://www.youraccounts.com.

Source: "Postal Service Offers Bill Paying Over the Internet," The Associated Press, April 6, 2000.

The Transition from Carrying out a Job to Performing Work

A subtle change in the workplace of concern to organizations and individuals is that traditional job descriptions are becoming too rigid to fit the flexible work roles carried out by many workers. An emerging trend is for companies to hire people to "work" rather than to fill a specific job slot. At both Amazon.com and Koch Industries, job descriptions are rarely used. At Amazon, a person might still hold the same essential job but three months later be performing entirely different work. The "Amazonian" might be working out a software glitch one day and helping lay out a new wing of a distribution center the next.

This sea of change in work design can be overwhelming for people whose paradigm is to think of work as occupying a particular job. A starting point in the shift is to think about how to accomplish work rather than fill a job. Both Koch and Amazon have developed a model to make this shift from filling a job to carrying out a work role. These companies look more for a good person-organization fit than for candidates to fill a particular job. At Amazon, this means hiring people with entrepreneurial drive who are customer focused. The director of strategic growth (human resources) says, "We try not to be too rigid about qualifications, but on the kind of people we hire and how they can apply what they know."[32]

To make this approach to work roles function well, the organization structure has to be flexible and employees have to have access to different opportunities.

Also, managers have to be willing to let employees experiment and work in different positions. A cornerstone idea is that workers' skills have to be matched to the project, such as a creative person from anywhere in the firm being assigned to a cross-functional product development team.

The implication for managers is that shifting away from relatively fixed job descriptions to emphasizing work roles is part of dealing with change in organizations. For many managers, this shift is difficult because job descriptions are the essence of bureaucracy.

ORGANIZATION DEVELOPMENT AS A CHANGE STRATEGY

Explain the nature of organization development.

When it is necessary to bring about long-term, significant changes in a firm, a formal method of organizational change is sometimes used. **Organization development (OD)** is any strategy, method, or technique for making organizations more effective by bringing about constructive, planned change. In its ideal form, organization development attempts to change the culture toward being more democratic and humanistic. At other times, organization development aims to help change the technology or structure of the firm.[33]

An appreciation of the number of OD techniques available can be gained from studying Exhibit 13-5. Various techniques are grouped according to whether they deal primarily with individuals, small groups, or the total organization. Several of the techniques, such as work teams, conflict resolution, and stress management, have been described in previous chapters. Labeling all of these interventions *organization development* is somewhat arbitrary because they are practiced in organizations not even aware of such a label. Here we describe a process model of organization development, followed by more information about two other OD approaches.

A Process Model of Organization Development

To be effective, OD methods must be made to fit a particular firm. Nevertheless, a process model has been developed that incorporates the important features of many different OD change efforts.[34] The model builds on earlier strategies for

EXHIBIT 13-5

A Sampling of Organization Development Interventions

Individual Level

Executive coaching
Employee assistance programs (EAPs)
Career development programs
Organizational behavior modification (OB Mod)
Job enrichment
Wellness programs, including stress reduction
Sexual harassment avoidance training

Small-Group Level

Team development
Cultural diversity training (including valuing
    differences)
Modified work schedules
Brainstorming
Intergroup conflict resolution
Quality improvement teams
Self-managing teams

Organization Level

Total quality management (TQM)
Grid organization development
Gainsharing
Survey feedback (attitude surveys)
Action research (employees participate in
    implementing changes identified as needed
    by a consultant)
Helping an organization learn
Knowledge management

organization development. A key feature is that the OD specialist and staff members are both involved in bringing about constructive change. The model, which is summarized here, is outlined in Exhibit 13-6.

Step 1: Preliminary Problem Identification
The manager recognizes that a problem exists that is interfering with work effectiveness. The problem could include the manager's behavior.

Step 2: Managerial Commitment to Change
The manager must commit to taking the necessary steps to implement the change program. The manager is warned that the change program could involve negative feedback about his or her behavior.

Step 3: Data Collection and Analysis
Before organization development can proceed, the climate must be assessed through interviews, observations, and a written survey. Information is obtained about such topics as the manager's alertness and open-mindedness. cooperation with other departments, problem-solving ability, and trust. This information is used to develop objectives for constructive changes.

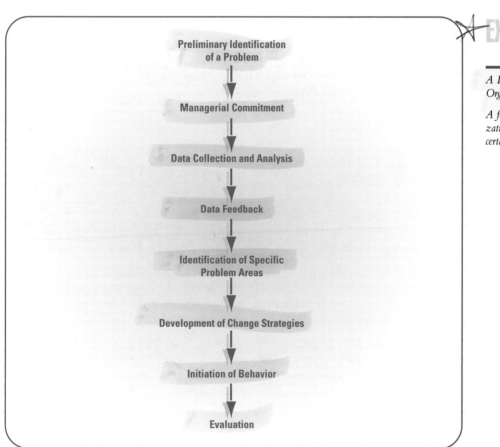

EXHIBIT 13-6

A Process Model of Organization Development

A formal program of organization development follows certain steps.

Source: Joseph A. Young and Barbara Smith, "Organizational Change and the HR Professional," *Personnel,* October 1988: p. 48.

Step 4: Data Feedback

Data collected in Step 3 are shared with the manager and staff members. In this way, staff members can compare their perceptions with those of others, and the manager shows ownership of the problem.

Step 5: Identification of Specific Problem Areas

The OD specialist helps staff members give the manager feedback regarding strengths and weaknesses. Although the manager may not agree with the feedback, he or she must accept the perceptions. Problem areas among the staff members can also be identified in this step.

Step 6: Development of Change Strategies

The emphasis is on identifying root problems and developing action steps. A spirit of teamwork often develops as problems are identified that can be attributed to both the manager and staff members.

Step 7: Initiation of Behavior

An action step(s) is selected and implemented that seems to be the best solution to the problem. The behavioral change strategy considers who, what, when, and where. For example, the manager (who) will make sure that the planning and priority setting (what) are accomplished during staff meetings (when) in the conference room (where).

Step 8: Evaluation

An attempt is made to evaluate whether the behavior changes made in Step 7 by both the manager and staff members have improved behavior and work results. Evaluation data may be collected through more interviews and observations, including speaking to the manager's superior.

Process Consultation

A widely used OD intervention at the small-group level is called **process consultation.** Using this technique, the OD specialist (process consultant) examines the pattern of a work unit's communications. A team leader typically asks for process consultation because team meetings have not been highly productive. The process consultant directly observes team meetings. At opportune times, the consultant will raise questions or make observations about what has been happening. The role of the process consultant is to challenge the status quo by asking such questions as:

- "Why doesn't anybody ever respond to Larry's questions?"
- "How come nobody challenges Jennifer's remarks when she is way off base?"
- "Why does everybody shake their heads in agreement when the CEO speaks? Are you all yes-people around here?"

Why process consultation makes a contribution has been explained in these terms: "It points out the true quality of the emperor's new clothes even when everyone is pretending they are quite elegant." Also, the process consultant can be helpful in changing a closed communication style.[35]

Large-Scale Organizational Change

At best, organization development is a method of change aimed at breathing new life into a firm. **Large-scale organizational change** is the method used to accomplish a major change in the firm's strategy and culture. The process is some-times referred to as *bending the frame*, to indicate that the firm is changed in a sig-nificant way.[36] To accomplish such a far-reaching change, a large proportion of the workforce must be involved. Richard H. Alexrod explains that efficient and effec-tive implementation of change requires a critical mass of people throughout the organization who are committed to the outcomes—not just consultants and lead-ers—but everyone.[37] (A knowledge of individual differences suggests that such total commitment to improving the organization is highly unlikely, even though an ideal worth striving for.) If the program described in the process model of organization development is used throughout the firm, large-scale organizational change will be feasible.

Certain warning signs suggest that a company needs large-scale organizational change, or a turnaround, as gathered by consultant John H. Collard. A key sign is when top executives are *micromanaging instead of delegating*. As a consequence, employees are being underused and talent is going to waste. A *high turnover rate* suggests that the company is not a good place to work for a variety of possible rea-sons. When a company develops a reputation for high turnover, it will be difficult to attract talented, motivated replacements. *Ineffective communication,* as indicated by low-quality communication, suggests the need for major overhaul. A *compensation system that rewards people actions unrelated to business success* could spell major trou-ble. For example, many workers might find ways to receive overtime pay by sim-ply not getting their work accomplished during normal working hours. *Loss of established business and the failure to obtain new business* is virtual proof that the com-pany is in trouble. (The previous five conditions are symptoms that lead to poor results.) If relationships with established customers are weakening and their indus-tries are not slowing down, then the problem most likely comes from the vendor, not the customers.[38]

Shifting from an authoritarian (or command and control) style organization to a team-style organization would be a typical example of a large-scale change. Closely related is the shift from a slow-moving bureaucracy to a more nimble, entrepreneurial-style firm. Ford Motor Company and IBM are examples of famous companies that have transformed themselves into more nimble entities in the last decade. One of the most stunning turnarounds of all, however, was Continental Airlines, which went from an airline headed for its third bankruptcy, with low morale and poor customer service to becoming an industry leader. A key part of the large-scale organizational change was to establish a results-oriented cul-ture. Two components of the culture change were to (a) let people do their job without interference, and (b) treat one another with dignity and respect.[39]

As with most forms of organization development, an external or internal con-sultant is usually required to bring about large-scale change. Line managers may be responsible for implementing the change, but advisors help in the process.

Total Quality Management and Six Sigma as Organization Development

The shift to a more quality-conscious firm can be classified as a total systems approach to organization development. Defined with some focus, **total quality management (TQM)** is a management system for improving performance throughout a firm by maximizing customer satisfaction, making continuous improvements, and relying heavily on employee involvement. Defined more broadly, total quality management "is a fundamental change in the organization's culture to one that includes a focus on the customer, an environment of trust and openness, formation of work teams, breaking down of internal barriers, team leadership and coaching, share power, and communication improvement."[40] A definition of this scope implies that TQM encompasses much of organizational behavior and organization development.

Although the term TQM has fallen into almost disuse, and many people consider the quality movement to have passed, the quest for high quality remains an important thrust. Having high-quality goods and services is considered a necessary minimum to compete effectively. To qualify as vendors to well-established customers, it is necessary to maintain high-quality standards. One such standard is *six sigma,* or 3.4 errors in one million opportunities. (The figure is derived from the area under the normal curve from −6 to +6 standard deviations from the mean.) This quality standard has taken the form of company-wide programs for attaining high quality. With capital first letters, Six Sigma also refers to a philosophy of driving out waste, improving quality, and the cost and time performance of a company. Three examples of companies with Six Sigma programs are GE, AlliedSignal/Honeywell, and Motorola Corp.

Six Sigma is regarded as a data-driven method for achieving near-perfect quality with an emphasis on preventing problems. The approach emphasizes statistical analysis and measurement in design, manufacturing, and the entire area of customer-oriented activities. Six Sigma also has a strong behavioral aspect with an emphasis on motivating people to work together to achieve higher levels of productivity. As with all programs of organizational improvement, top-management commitment is critical. Six Sigma is seen as a fusion of technical and social systems because of the emphasis on both technical programs and creating a culture of quality. Six Sigma teams are formed to carry out most of the quality improvement.[41]

Six Sigma, as with other quality programs, can help an organization achieve reliable products and services. However, good quality alone does not attract large numbers of customers and job candidates. Products that offer passion, fun, and excitement (such as the Ford Motor Company Jaguar) are bigger draws than flawless construction.

MANAGING CHANGE YOURSELF

Develop useful insights into managing change in your job and career.

A major factor in managing change is coping well with change yourself. All the approaches to organizational and small-group change described in this chapter work more effectively with individuals who are predisposed to managing change well. Our approach to providing insight into managing change yourself is divided into relevant research and personal suggestions. To help you think through your flexibility about dealing with change, do the Self-Assessment that follows.

Empirical Research about Coping with Organizational Change

The well-accepted belief by practicing managers that some employees adapt better to organizational change than others was supported in a study involving over 500 employees in six organizations and five countries. Ability to cope with change was measured both by self-reports and managerial assessments of how the workers coped with change. Seven personality factors presumed to be related to change were measured: locus of control, generalized self-efficacy, self-esteem, positive affectivity (similar to being optimistic), openness to experience, tolerance for ambiguity, and risk aversion. The seven traits were reduced to two factors: positive self-concept and risk tolerance.

SELF-ASSESSMENT

How Flexible Are You?

To succeed as a managerial worker, a person needs a flexible attitude, an ability to be open to others and a willingness to listen. Where do you stand on being flexible? Test yourself by answering Often, Sometimes, or Rarely to the following questions.

		Frequency	
	Often	**Sometimes**	**Rarely**
1. Do you tend to seek out only those people who agree with your analysis on issues?	___	✓	___
2. Do you ignore most of the advice from coworkers or other students about doing your work more efficiently?	___	___	___
3. Do your team members go along with what you say just to avoid an argument?	___	___	___
4. Have people referred to you as "rigid" or "close-minded" on several occasions?	___	___	___
5. When presented with a new method, do you immediately look for a flaw?	___	___	___
6. Do you make up your mind early with respect to an issue and then hold firmly to your opinion?	___	___	___
7. When people disagree with you, do you tend to belittle them or become argumentative?	___	___	___
8. Do you often feel you are the only person in the group who really understands the problem?	___	___	___
9. Do you prefer to hang on to old software even though more than one new update has been published?	___	___	___
10. Do you resist trying new foods?	___	___	___

Check Your Score: If you answered "rarely" to eight questions, you are unusually adaptable and therefore probably cope well with change. If you answered "sometimes" to at least six questions, you are on the right track, but more flexibility would benefit your ability to deal with change. If you answered "often" to five or more questions, you have a long way to go to improve your flexibility and adaptability to change. You are also brutally honest about your faults, which could be an asset.

A key result was that having a positive self-concept and a tolerance for risk were positively related to both measures of coping with change. The strongest and most consistent dispositional, or personality, variables among the seven traits in terms of their relationship to coping with change were tolerance for ambiguity and positive affectivity.[42] The implication supports what you probably suspected: People who can tolerate a lack of clarity and structure and who are optimistic cope well with change.

Other findings in the study are also useful for managing one's career. The dispositional factors studied were related to both intrinsic and extrinsic dimensions of career success. The intrinsic success factors studied were job satisfaction and organizational commitment, whereas the external factors were salary, being on a career plateau, and job performance. These findings reinforce the idea that personality factors are related to career success.

Suggestions for Coping with Change

The research just reported has a few implications for your being able to manage change well: Practice dealing with ambiguous tasks (such as unclear assignments) and work on having a positive general disposition. Consider also the following practical suggestions:[43] *Look for the personal value that could be embedded in a forced change.* If you are downsized, take the opportunity to assume responsibility for your own career rather than being dependent on the organization. Many downsizing victims find a new career for themselves that better fits their interests. One woman laid off twice by a small companies took a job with the federal government so she could enjoy job security.

When faced with a significant change, *ask "What if?" questions* such as "What if my company is sold tomorrow?" "What if I went back to school for more education?" "What if I did accept that one-year assignment in China?" When confronting major change, *force yourself to enjoy at least some small aspect of the change.* Suppose the edict comes through the organization that purchases can now only be made over the Internet. This means you will no longer be able to interact with a few of the sales reps you considered to be buddies. With the time you save, however, you will have spare hours each week for leisure activities.

You are less likely to resist change if you *recognize that change is inevitable.* Dealing with change is an integral part of life, so why fight it? Keep in mind also to *change before you have to and you'll get a better deal.* If your manager announces a new plan, get on board as a volunteer before you are forced to accept a lesser role. If your company has made the decision to start a Six Sigma program, study the subject early and ask for a role as a facilitator or team leader. Finally, *stop trying to be in control all the time.* Many changes will occur that you cannot control, so relax and enjoy the ride.

IMPLICATIONS FOR MANAGERIAL PRACTICE

1. To manage organizational culture, one must first understand the culture of the firm and then use that knowledge to guide one's own behavior and that of group members. For example, an executive at Donna Inc., the manufacturer of the DKNY line of clothing, was approached by a small firm that wanted to market a low-priced running shoe with the DKNY label. The executive declined the offer, stating that selling licensing rights to the use of the DKNY name was inconsistent with the quality values of the firm.

2. The biggest challenge in implementing workplace innovations is bringing about cultural change. Workers' attitudes and values have to change if the spirit of innovation is to keep smoldering. An effective vehicle for bringing about such change is for top-level managers and others to exchange ideas. Formal arrangements such as regularly scheduled staff meetings facilitate exchanging ideas, reflecting on values. and learning what behavior is in vogue. Encouraging informal meetings can often achieve the same purpose with a higher degree of effectiveness.

3. Learning how to cope well with change yourself is a key part of managing change.

SUMMARY OF KEY POINTS

 Present an analysis of the importance of organizational culture.

The origins of organizational culture often lie in the values, administrative practices, and personality of its founders. Other key influences are the societal culture, the industry, and the organization's code of conduct. Organizational culture has various dimensions, such as the values, stories, and myths maintained by the organization, the sense of ownership within the firm, and corporate spiritualism.

The culture is taught primarily through socialization and the teaching of leaders. The consequences of organizational culture include: competitive advantage, productivity and morale, innovation, compatibility of mergers and acquisitions, person-organization fit, and direction of leadership activity.

 Present two models of the change process in organizations.

The growth curve model of change in organizations traces the inevitability of change through a firm's life cycle. During the integrative phase, there is a pulling and tugging between forces for change and against change. Another model of change views it as a three-step process: the unfreezing, changing, and refreezing of behavior.

 Describe why people resist change and how to manage such resistance.

People resist change for a variety of reasons they think are important, the most common being the fear of an unfavorable outcome. Techniques for overcoming resistance include: (1) allow for discussion and negotiation, (2) allow for participation, (3) point out the financial benefits, (4) avoid change overload, (5) gain political support for change, (6) provide education, (7) use manipulation and co-optation, (8) avoid citing poor performance as the reason for change, and (9) use explicit and implicit coercion.

 Describe several strategies for bringing about organizational change.

Downsizing as a change strategy is most likely to be effective when it is integrated into the company's long-term strategies. Low-value work must be eliminated, teamwork must be emphasized, and considerable attention must be paid to the human element. Information technology has facilitated change in organizations, including making them more democratic because of the increased accessibility of information. The Internet is changing the nature of many businesses, such as companies interacting more directly with customers and suppliers. Information technology has created substantial changes in how long and where people work.

Disruptive technology occurs when large successful companies lose sight of small emerging markets served by a company with new technologies. The new technology creates havoc for the more established firm. Another force for change in organizations is the transition from a job holder meeting the demands of a job description to carrying out a variety of work roles, or different kinds of work.

 Explain the nature of organization development.

Organization development brings about constructive, planned change including modifying the culture. Using the process model of organization development, both the OD consultant and staff members are involved in bringing about constructive change. Process consultation is used to examine the pattern of a work unit's communications. Large-scale organization development is used to accomplish a major change in the firm's strategy and culture. Signs that large-scale OD is necessary include micromanagement by top management, loss of established business, and the failure to obtain new business.

Total quality management, including Six Sigma programs, is an important organization development strategy.

 Develop useful insights into managing change in your job and career.

Recent research has shown that people who score high on the personality factors of positive self-concept and risk tolerance adapt better to change. Two specific traits related to dealing well with change are tolerance for ambiguity and positive affectivity. Among the suggestions for managing change well are searching for the personal value that could be embedded in forced change, asking "What if," forcing yourself to enjoy at least some small aspect of the change, and recognizing that change is inevitable.

KEY TERMS AND PHRASES

Organizational Culture, *278*

A system of shared values and beliefs that influence worker behavior.

Subculture, *280*

A pocket in which the organizational culture differs from that of other pockets and the dominant culture.

Socialization, *280*

The process of coming to understand the values, norms, and customs essential for adapting to an organization.

Growth Curve Model, *283*

A model that traces the inevitability of change through a firm's life cycle.

Force-field Theory, *284*

The theory contending that an organization simultaneously faces forces for change (the driving forces) and forces for maintaining the status quo (the restraining forces).

Disruptive Technology, *290*

A new technology or start-up that blindsides a large successful company.

Organization Development (OD), *292*

Any strategy, method, or technique for making organizations more effective by bringing about constructive, planned change.

Process Consultation, *294*

An intervention in which the organization development specialist examines the pattern of a work unit's communications.

Large-Scale Organizational Change, *294*

The method used to accomplish a major change in the firm's strategy and culture.

Total Quality Management (TQM), *295*

A management system for improving performance throughout an organization by maximizing customer satisfaction, making continual improvements, and relying heavily on employee involvement.

DISCUSSION QUESTIONS AND ACTIVITIES

1. How would you describe the organizational culture of Wal-Mart (or any other retailer) based on whatever evidence you have? If necessary, visit your local Wal-Mart (or other retailer) for firsthand observations.
2. Why do so many CEOs believe that their primary responsibility is managing organizational culture? What happened to making a profit?
3. How can a manager tell if an employee is resisting change?
4. Identify a *disruptive technology* that could be threatening the PC industry.
5. Why might the transition from "jobs to work" lead to resistance to change for many people?
6. Describe any organization you think should go through large-scale organizational change.
7. Identify a major change you will have to cope with in the next several years and describe your plan of action for coping with it.

ORGANIZATIONAL BEHAVIOR ON-LINE

TO DO

Learning about OD Consultants

Locate the Web sites of at least two organization development consultants. You might find them with search terms such as "organization development consultants," or "organization change consultants." Find out what type of changes and results the consultants contend they will be able to bring about. What similarities and differences do you find between what they offer and the change programs mentioned in this chapter?

TO BOOKMARK

Culture at Two Corporate Giants

Hewlett Packard: http://www.hp.com

IBM: http://ibm.com

Culture at Two Start-ups

Napster: http://www.napster.com

Covisint: http://www.covisint.com

Managing Change, as Proposed by the Center for Quality of Management

http://www.cqm.org

The American Productivity & Quality Center

http://www.apqc.org

Behavior On-line

http://www.behavior.net

Process Consultation

http://www.cape.org/2000/schein.html

CASE PROBLEM: Change Now & Survive: Do Nothing and Die

Chuck Volo, the plant director of restructuring at the Rochester, New York, plant of Valeo SA sent an illustrated report printed on glossy paper to the homes of all local employees. "As it stands today," said the report, "Rochester is not a financially viable business. We are in trouble."

The former ITT Automotive plant, which has 3,000 employees in Rochester, was purchased by France-based Valeo several years ago. Valeo SA, based in Paris, is Europe's second-largest automobile parts manufacturer. The company's American headquarters are in Detroit, Michigan. The Rochester operation produces windshield wiper systems and electrical motors for automobiles. It has been struggling with global competition since becoming an independent supplier in the late 1990s because it was no longer guaranteed that the major automakers would buy its parts.

Valeo spokesperson Chadra Lewis said, "It is not our intent to close the plant. But certainly competitive issues must be managed successfully." The company has fired or demoted about 30 assembly-line supervisors and department heads this week alone. Sam Galusha, 54, was among the group. With 24 years at the automotive plant, he is six years shy of retirement. Galusha said he was asked to decide between a severance package, early retirement, or a lesser-paying hourly position. Other supervisors were not given choices and were escorted out of the building.

Several employees confirmed the fact that about 100 manufacturing supervisors were given skills-assessment tests. Those who did not meet Valeo's standards were let go, in many cases ending the near-retirement careers of people with more than 20 years of service.

Rumors had been swirling for over a year that Valeo would move out of Rochester. The company responded publicly with a statement that it still might invest $100 million to refurbish the local plant or expand—if the plant met its productivity and cost-reduction goals.

It was against this backdrop that Valeo issued its report. Titled *Change Now & Survive: Do Nothing and Die,* it is a point-by-point comparison of Rochester and a similar Valeo parts operation in San Luis Potosi, Mexico. The report says the Rochester operation is Valeo's "poster plant" on how *not* to operate. The following comparisons were cited in the report, by first stating what was seen in San Luis Potosi, followed by what was not seen. The "not seen" items are characteristics of the Rochester operation in the perception of Chuck Volo.

- 99.6% of the workforce on the job. 25% absenteeism in Rochester.
- A pristine, inviting work environment in every single part of the facility at SLP. Not seen were coffee concessions, vending machines, personal belongings at the workstations, books, newspapers, food wrappers, clutter.
- A workforce as pristine as their environment that reflects as much pride in personal appearance as in workplace appearance. Not seen were operators out of uniform.
- Action plans with up-to-date information. Aged or incomplete data were not seen.
- Daily meetings, workshops, weekly quality meetings, training—a high degree of involvement of personnel. Employees refusing to participate or disrupting the process were not seen.
- A glass wall as the only separation between administrative and engineering functions and production. Columns, concrete interior walls were not seen.
- Team leaders or facilitators in every work unit. Confusion, turmoil, or disorder of teams operating without focus or direction were not seen.
- A motivated workforce enthusiastic about the advantages of working for a quality company offering a wealth of tools and resources. Did not see a "that's not my job" attitude or any sense of entitlement—that Valeo owes them something.
- A sense of urgency and importance in completing all tasks at hand. Not seen were extended breaks, early quits, slacking off once quotas are met, anyone not giving a full day's work for a full day's pay.
- Community involvement in the form of workplace mentoring for children from a local orphanage. Not seen were uncaring attitudes toward those less fortunate in the community.

In addition to these perceptions, Volo cited a list of facts for comparison. The pay scale at SLP is 10% of wages in Rochester; SLP had 267 accident-free days in 1999, and Rochester had no accident-free days; SLP had 139 end-of-line rejects in 1999; Rochester Wipers had 8,098 and Rochester Motors had 9,767. Volo wrote that, "It's a humbling experience to visit Valeo sites in Mexico and see them outperforming us on nearly every front."

The union president in Rochester accused Volo of trying to destroy employee morale. He said that "Every real American knows big business throughout the world exploits the Mexican work for more profits to line their pockets. Rochester cannot be threatened or bullied. We know management is creating a negative environment. They are doing it on purpose in order to beat this membership down."

The managing directors for Rochester retorted, "Like it or not, we are in a fight for our survival. Now is not the time to be divided or unclear as to what is the reality."

Case Questions

1. How motivational do you think the *Change Now* would be for the Rochester workers?

2. What approach to organizational improvement would you recommend for the Rochester Valeo plant, assuming the report is accurate?

3. As a Valeo executive in company headquarters in Detroit or Paris, what would be your recommendations about keeping the Rochester plant open?

Source: Chuck Volo, "Change Now & Survive: Do Nothing and Die," Company report of Valeo Wipers and Motors made public, March, 2000; J. Leslie Sopko, "Valeo Plant Gripped by Uncertainty and Friction," Rochester, New York, April 14, 2000, pp. 1A, 11A.

For more information about Valeo and its Rochester production facility, visit http://www.valeo.com, where an eight-year contract with its Rochester union was announced on August 14, 2000.

SUGGESTED READINGS

Amabile, Teresa M., and Conti, Regina. "Changes in the Work Environment for Creativity During Downsizing." *The Academy of Management Journal,* December 1999, pp. 630–640.

Galpin, Timothy. "Connecting Culture to Organizational Change." *HRMagazine,* March 1996, pp. 84–90.

Godin, Seth. "In My Humble Opinion." *Fast Company,* May 2000, pp. 324–328.

Grensing-Pophal, Lin. "Hiring to Fit Your Corporate Culture." *HRMagazine,* August 1999, pp. 50–54.

James, Jennifer. *Thinking in the Future Tense: Leadership Skills for a New Age.* New York: Simon & Schuster, 1997.

Karbo, Karen. "Change Is a Circus." *Fast Company,* December 1999, pp. 426–437.

Maruca, Regina Fazio. "Retailing: Confronting the Challenges that Face Brick-and-Mortar Stores." *Harvard Business Review,* July–August 1999, pp. 159–168.

Sunoo, Brenda Paik. "Relying on Faith to Rebuild a Business." *Workforce,* March 1999, pp. 54–59.

Strebel, Paul. "Why Do Employees Resist Change?" *Harvard Business Review* (May-June 1996), pp. 86–92.

Thompson, Kenneth R. "Confronting the Paradoxes in a Total Quality Environment." *Organizational Dynamics,* Winter 1998, pp. 62–72.

ENDNOTES

1. Katrina Brooker, "Can Anyone Replace Herb?" *Fortune,* April 17, 2000, pp. 186–192; James Campbell Quick, "Crafting an Organization Culture: Herb's Hand at Southwest Airline," *Organizational Dynamics,* Autumn 1992, pp. 50–53.

2. "Can CEO Ollila Keep the Cellular Superstar Flying High?" *Business Week,* August 10, 1998, p. 54.

3. Jennifer A. Chatman and Karen A. Jehn, "Assessing the Relationship between Industry Characteristics and Organizational Culture: How Different Can You Be?" *Academy of Management Journal,* June 1994, pp. 522–533.

4. James R. Redecker, "Code of Conduct as Corporate Culture," *HRMagazine,* July 1990, p. 83.

5. John Kamp and Paul Brooks, "Perceived Organizational Climate and Employee Counterproductivity," *Journal of Business and Psychology,* Summer 1991, p. 455.

6. Scott Hays, "'Ownership Cultures' Create Unity," *Workforce,* February 1999, pp. 60–64.

7. Joanne Cole, "Building Heart and Soul," *HRfocus,* October 1998, pp. 9–10.

8. Milldred L. Culp, "Spirituality Brings Connectedness, Profit in Today's Fragmented Workplace," *WorkWise®* syndicated column, September 5, 1999.

9. Literature reviewed in Gerard George, Randall G. Sleeth, and Mark A. Siders, "Organizing Culture: Leader Roles, Behaviors, and Reinforcement Mechanisms," *Journal of Business and Psychology,* Summer 1999, p. 548.

10. Daniel R. Denison, *Corporate Culture and Organizational Effectiveness* (New York: Wiley, 1990).

11. Louise Lee, "Tricks of E*Trade," *Business Week **E.BIZ,*** February 7, 2000, pp. 18–20.

12. Gary Hamel, "Reinvent Your Company," *Fortune,* June 12, 2000, pp. 97–118. The quote is from page 118.

13. Bill Vlasic & Bradley A. Stertz, "How the DaimlerChrysler 'Marriage of Equals' Crumbled," *Business Week,* June 5, 2000, p. 90.

14. Charles A. O'Reilly III, Jennifer A. Chatman, and David F. Caldwell, "People and Organizational Culture: A Profile Comparison Approach to Assessing Person-Organization Fit," *Academy of Management Journal,* September 1991, pp. 487–516.

15. Charles D. Morgan, "Culture Change/Culture Shock," *Management Review,* November 1998, p. 13.

16. "Hershey Thinks Its Delivery Problems Are Now Over," Associated Press, April 20, 2000.

17. Harry Woodward and Steve Bucholtz, *Aftershock: Helping People Through Corporate Change* (New York: Wiley, 1987).

18. Kurt Lewin, *Field Theory in Social Science: Selected Theoretical Papers* (New York: Harper & Brothers, 1951).

19. David Rocks, "Is Big Blue Thinking Big Enough?" *Business Week,* May 22, 2000, p. 132.

20. Kurt Lewin, *Field Theory and Social Science* (New York: Harper & Row, 1951), Chapters 9 and 10.

21. Woodward and Bucholtz, *Aftershock.*

22. James A. F. Stoner and R. Edward Freeman, *Management,* 4th ed. (Upper Saddle River, NJ: Prentice Hall, 1989), p. 369.

23. "When Employees Resist Change," *Success Workshop,* A supplement to *Managers Edge,* January 2000, p. 1.

24. Susan Reynolds Fisher and Margaret A. White, "Downsizing in a Learning Organization: Are There Hidden Costs?" *Academy of Management Review,* January 2000, pp. 244–251.

25. Sherry Kuczynski, "Help! I Shrunk the Company," *HRMagazine,* June 1999, pp. 40–45; Dean Elmuti and Yunus Kathawaia, "Rightsizing for Individual Competitiveness: Important Thoughts to Consider," *Business Forum,* Fall 1993, pp. 8–11.

26. Quoted in "At Crossroads of Change: An Interview with Tom Peters," *Leadership* (A Member Newsletter of the American Management Association International), May 1998, p. 3.

27. Eric Shoeniger, "Turning a Page on the Internet Economy," *Unisys Exec,* May–June 2000, pp. 8–10.

28. Tom Peters, "What Will We Do for Work?" *Time,* May 22, 2000, p. 68.

29. Samuel Greengard, "How Technology Will Change the Workplace," *Workforce,* January 1998, p. 78.

30. Clayton M. Christensen and Michael Overdorf, "Meeting the Challenge of Disruptive Change," *Harvard Business Review,* March–April 2000, pp. 66–76; Del Jones, "Are MBAs Going Out of Style?" *USA Today,* May 23, 2000; Christensen, "Should You Fear Disruptive Technology?" *Fortune,* April 3, 2000, pp. 249–250.

31. Christensen and Overdorf, "Meeting the Challenge," p. 73.

32. Shari Caudron, "Jobs Disappear: When Work Becomes More Important," *Workforce,* January 2000, pp. 30–32.

33. Robert T. Golembiewski, *Organization Development: Ideas and Issues* (New Brunswick, NJ: Transaction Books, Rutgers University, 1989).

34. Joseph A. Young and Barbara Smith, "Organizational Change and the HR Professional," *Personnel,* October 1988, p. 46; Wendell L. French, "Organization Development, Objectives, Assumptions, and Strategy," *California Management Review,* Vol. 2, 1969, p. 26.

35. Leonard D. Goodstein and W. Warner Burke, "Creating Successful Organizational Change," *Organizational Dynamics,* Spring 1991, p. 14.

36. Goodstein and Burke, "Creating Successful Organizational Change," p. 4.

37. Richard H. Axelrod, *Terms of Engagement: Changing the Way We Change Organizations* (Williston, VT: BK Publishers, 2000).

38. George Milite, "Turnaround Management: Charting a New Beginning," *HRfocus,* November 1999, pp. 9–10.

39. Greg Brenneman, "Right Away and All at Once: How We Saved Continental," *Harvard Business Review,* September–October 1998, pp. 162–179.

40. Carol A. Reeves and David A. Bednar, "Defining Quality: Alternatives and Implications," *Academy of Management Review,* July 1994, p. 419.

41. Joseph A. Defeo, "Six Sigma: Road Map for Survival," *HRfocus,* July 1999, pp. 11–12.

42. Timothy A. Judge, Carl J. Thoresen, Victor Pucik, and Theresa M. Welbourne, "Managerial Coping with Organizational Change: A Dispositional Perspective," *Journal of Applied Psychology,* February 1999, pp. 107–122.

43. The first two items on the list are from Fred Pryor, "What Have You Learned from Change?" *Managers Edge,* September 1998, p. 2.

The Learning Organization and Knowledge Management

Buckman Laboratories, based in Memphis, Tennessee, pioneered workers sharing organizational knowledge. About 10 years ago, the specialty chemical manufacturer established a series of private forums on CompuServe so employees could share wisdom within the 1,200-person company. Using on-line forums, connected knowledge bases, electronic bulletin boards, libraries, and virtual conference rooms, employees began exchanging proposals, presentations, spreadsheets, technical specs, and more. Suddenly, they could pose questions and swap ideas, whether in Boston or Beijing.

It didn't take long to reap the rewards. Within months, employees had become hooked on using the forums to improve the quality of work and close deals. Once a sales representative approached the management of an Indonesian paper mill with a potential business deal. The plant's senior executives asked to see a detailed proposal within two weeks—a deadline that seemed impossible to meet.

Undaunted, the sales rep ventured into the on-line forum, mentioned that he had a potential $6 million deal, but needed sample proposals and information. Within 48 hours, he had responses from other Buckman employees scattered across the globe. The rep went back to the customer, handed over a customer proposal, and nailed the deal. It wasn't one individual putting together a proposal, it was one sales rep leveraging the knowledge and expertise of the entire organization.

A unique aspect of Buckman's corporate Web site is the opportunity to drill down to a Knowledge Nurture Web site, where the company has established a resource for people beyond its own employees to learn about knowledge management. Go to http://www.knowledge_nurture.com/ for more information.

Source: Samuel Greengard, "Storing, Shaping, and Sharing Collective Wisdom," *Workforce* (October 1998): 82–83. Used with permission of the publisher.

OBJECTIVES

After reading and studying this chapter and doing the exercises, you should be able to

 Describe the 4I framework of a learning organization.

 Identify the building blocks, or key characteristics, of a learning organization.

 Recognize organizational conditions favoring knowledge management (KM).

 Pinpoint strategies and techniques for knowledge management.

 Specify methods for sharing information within an organization.

Chapter 14

SO WHAT? Why is finding a way to manage knowledge so relevant to our study of organizational behavior? Useful information that can be shared among workers at all levels is a rich repository of lessons learned and engagements won. The concept of managing knowledge and sharing information stems from the idea of learning organizations, so in this chapter we look at both. We first examine the nature of learning organizations, then follow that discussion with a description of knowledge management, including knowledge sharing. Being a learning organization sets the stage for managing knowledge well and making optimum use of human capital.

THE LEARNING ORGANIZATION

Describe the 4I framework of a learning organization.

Closely related to organization development is the idea that an effective organization engages in continuous learning by proactively adapting to the external environment. Scholars and managers agree that organizational learning is desirable, yet not all agree on the nature of a learning organization. A **learning organization** is one that is skilled at creating, acquiring, and transferring knowledge, and at modifying behavior to reflect new knowledge and insights.[1] Or as Peter Senge puts it, a learning organization can be looked upon simply as a group of people working together to enhance their capacities to create results they value.[2]

Our approach to understanding the learning organization will be to first describe a recent model framework of a learning organization, followed by a list of its building blocks or components. Before proceeding, however, the Self-Assessment that follows will give you a sense of the day-by-day characteristics of a learning organization.

The 4I Framework of a Learning Organization

As interest in learning organizations has increased, attempts have been made to develop an overall understanding, or framework, for them. The 4I framework is instructive because it describes the processes that are involved in a firm making systematic use of information. A portion of the model that appears most useful to practitioners is presented here and shown in Exhibit 14-1. A premise behind this framework is that organizational learning that results in organizational renewal encompasses the entire enterprise, not simply the individual or group. Another premise is that the organization operates in an open system, rather than having solely an individual focus. As is well known, an organization must satisfy the demands of the external world or it will perish.

EXHIBIT 14-1

The 4I Framework of Organizational Learning

Organizational learning takes place at three levels and involves four processes.

Source: Mary M. Crossan, Henry W. Lane, and Roderick E. White, "An Organizational Learning Framework: From Intuition to Institution," *Academy of Management Review,* July 1999, p. 525.

SELF-ASSESSMENT

Do You Work for a Learning Organization?

Directions: Indicate for each of the following statements whether it is mostly true or mostly false in relation to your current or most recent place of work.

Indicate a question mark when the statement is either not applicable or you are not in a position to judge.

	Mostly true	?	Mostly false
1. Company employees often visit other locations or departments to share new information or skills they have learned.		✓	
2. Our company frequently repeats mistakes.		✓	
3. We get most of our market share by competing on price.			✓
4. Loads of people in our organization are aware of and believe in our vision.	✓	·	✓
5. Top management assumes that the vast majority of employees are experts at what they do.		✓	
6. Almost all of our learning takes place individually rather than in groups or teams.			✓
7. In our company, after you have mastered your job you do not have to bother with additional learning such as training programs or self-study.			✓
8. Our firm shies away from inviting outsiders into our company to discuss our business because few outsiders could understand our uniqueness.			✓
9. If it weren't for a few key individuals in our company, we would be in big trouble.			✓
10. Our new product launches go smoothly and quickly.		✓	
11. Our company creates a lot of opportunities for employees to get together and share information, such as conferences and meetings.		·	✓
12. We are effective at pricing the service we provide to customers.			✓
13. Very few of our employees have any idea about company sales and profits.		✓	
14. I often hear employees asking questions about why the company has taken certain major actions.	✓		
15. The company maintains a current database about the knowledge and skills of almost all our employees.			✓
16. Having specialized knowledge brings you some status in our company.	·	✓	
17. It would be stretching the truth to say that many of our employees are passionate about what our organization is attempting to accomplish.		✓	
18. Our performance appraisal system makes a big contribution to helping employees learn and improve.			✓
19. Following established rules and procedures is important in our company, so creativity and imagination are not encouraged.			✓
20. Most of our employees believe that if you do your own job well, you don't have to worry about what goes on in the rest of the organization.			✓
21. We get loads of useful new ideas from our customers.		✓	
22. I have frequently heard our managers talk about how what goes on in the outside world has an impact on our company.		✓	
23. We treat customer suggestions with a good deal of skepticism.		✓	
24. During breaks, you sometimes hear employees discussing the meaning and implication of the work they are doing.	✓		
25. Employees at every level tend to rely on facts when making important decisions.		✓	
26. If a process or procedure works well in our company, we are hesitant to experiment with other approaches to a problem.	✓		

(continued)

SELF-ASSESSMENT

Do You Work for a Learning Organization? (continued)

	Mostly true	?	Mostly false
27. Our company treats mistakes as valuable learning experiences about what not to do in the future.	___	___	✓
28. Our company rarely copies ideas from the successful practices of other companies.	___	✓	___
29. Each time we face a significant problem, our company seems to start all over to find a solution.	___	✓	___
30. It's a waste of time to be reading about a learning organization, when my real interest is in learning how to prevent problems.	___	___	✓

Total score: _____

Scoring and Interpretation: A. Record the number of Mostly true answers you gave to the following questions: 1, 4, 5, 10, 11, 12, 14, 15, 16, 18, 21, 22, 24, 25, 27. ③

B. Record the number of Mostly false answers you gave to the following questions: 2, 3, 6, 7, 8, 9, 13, 17, 19, 20, 23, 26, 28, 29, 30.   ⑧

C. Add the numbers for A and B.   il

D. Add half of your ? responses to A, and half to B.

25 or higher   You are most likely a member of a learning organization. This tendency is so pronounced that it should contribute heavily to your company's success.

13–24   Your company has an average tendency toward being a learning organization, suggesting an average degree of success in profiting from mistakes and changing in response to a changing environment.

0–12   Your firm is definitely not a learning organization.

Source: Andrew J. DuBrin, *Looking Around Corners: The Art of Problem Prevention* (Madison, WI; CWL Publishing Enterprises, 1999), 181–183. Used with permission of the publisher.

As explained by Mary M. Crossan, Henry W. Lane, and Roderick E. White, organizational learning is composed of four processes: intuiting, interpreting, integrating, and institutionalization.[3] The four processes work together to link the individual, group, and organizational levels. The four processes are the glue that binds the structure together. The three learning levels define the structure through which organizational learning takes place (as does all of organizational behavior).

Individual Level: Intuiting and interpreting take place at the individual level. *Intuiting* is the preconscious (not quite explicit or conscious) recognition of the pattern and/or possibilities inherent in a personal stream of experience. Intuiting is essentially intuition and relies on hunches about events taking place in the organization. *Interpreting* is the explaining through words and/or actions of an insight or idea to one's self and to others. A manager might develop the intuition that the company is not getting its fair share of repeat business. He might then say to coworkers, "Could we be facing some problem with our products that prompts many customers to forget about us after one try?"

Group Level: Taking place at the group level is *integrating,* the process of developing shared understanding among individuals and of taking coordinated action. Dialogue about the problem and joint action are critical to the development of shared understanding. The group might bat around the problem, "What is it about us that prompts so many customers to try us once and not come back?"

Organization Level: Taking place at the organization level is *institutionalizing,* or the process of ensuring that routinized actions occur. At first, the integrating taking place at the group level will be ad hoc and informal. However, if the coordinated action is recurring and substantial, it will become institutionalized. Tasks become defined, actions specified, and organizational mechanisms put in place to ensure that certain actions occur. Institutionalizing can also be regarded as the process of embedded learning achieved by individuals and groups into the organization. In the example at hand, an institutionalized process might be to follow up with first-time customers as to the reasons they intend to return or not return.

An implication of the 4I framework for managers is that for organizational learning to take place, individuals should be encouraged to share their intuition and insights with other individuals and the group. In this way, the best insights will eventually become institutionalized.

BUILDING BLOCKS OF A LEARNING ORGANIZATION

To become and remain a learning organization, certain characteristics and behaviors are required of organizational members, as described next.[4] Although organizational theorists speak of a learning *organization,* the workers do the learning. The collective wisdom of the workers might then translate into a learning organization.

Identify the building blocks, or key characteristics, of a learning organization.

Double-Loop Learning

An in-depth, nondefensive type of learning takes place in a learning organization. **Double-loop learning** occurs when people use feedback to confront the validity of the goal or the values implicit in the situation. A conventional-thinking manager (one who engages in *single-loop* learning) at a tire distributor might ask, "How can we more effectively market retread tires for automobiles?" As a double-loop learner, the same manager might ask, "Why are we even selling retreads for the automotive market? The demand is declining and they are not very safe." Note that the sales manager is being open and nondefensive about his or her product line.

Action Learning

Learning while working on real problems, or **action learning,** is a fundamental part of a learning organization. Participants in action learning are asked to work in teams to attack a significant organizational problem, such as decreasing the cycle time on a project. In the process of resolving an actual work problem, the participants acquire and use new skills, tools, or concepts. As the project progresses, new skills are applied later in the process of working with the problem. For example, if the team learned how to eliminate duplication of effort in one aspect of the work process, they would look to eliminate duplication at other points in the cycle. Motorola is one company that uses action learning systematically. Teams of 20 to 25 senior managers from various parts of the company work on significant problems as defined by executives to whom the managers report. Quite often a starting point in problem solving is to enhance product quality.

Systems Thinking

In the learning organization, members regard the organization as a system in which everybody's work affects the activities of everybody else. Systems thinking also means keeping the big picture foremost in everybody's mind and being keenly aware of the external environment. This is true because the organization is part of a system that includes the outside world. A systems thinker at Brooks Brothers said a few years ago, "The trend even among affluent businesspeople is away from our ultraconservative image. Our customer base is declining. If we don't want Brooks Brothers to be perceived as a museum of fashions past, we had better modify our product line." Brooks Brothers was able to modify its product image just enough to satisfy the modern conservative dresser without alienating its remaining die-hard conservatives. Each store has elegant products to satisfy the conservative and ultraconservative dresser.

Shared Vision

Organization members must develop a common purpose and commitment for the organization to keep learning. If the vision inspires enough people, they will keep learning to make the vision come true. A designer at Waterman, for example, might ask, "What can I learn this month that will help us realize our dream of remaining the premier supplier of a full range of high-quality, high-fashion writing instruments?" Developing a shared vision is contingent upon effective leadership. If workers at all levels believe that the company is headed toward greatness, they will be motivated to learn to help deliver greatness.

The Challenging of Mental Models

Organization members must unearth the powerful assumptions that prevent people from working together. For example, higher-level managers might have the assumption that entry-level workers are not capable or interested in strategic thinking. The managers therefore never engage entry-level workers in dialogue about the purpose of the firm and its long-range vitality. As a result, managers miss out on valuable input. To help you challenge mental models, practice asking "Why?" and "Why not?" Challenging mental models and questioning assumptions can open up a world of opportunities.

Team Learning

A learning organization emphasizes collective problem solving. Members freely share information and opinions with one another to facilitate problem solving. Xerox Corporation holds learning conferences in which hundreds of people gather to exchange ideas and teach one another. One participant said he was amazed that the loose agenda and informal setting at these gatherings led to so much constructive learning. He said, "I came away with some wonderful ideas that I probably would not have thought of myself. Just one small suggestion I picked up about using a new chain of residence hotels for extended field trips is now saving us several hundred thousand dollars per year."

Personal Mastery of the Job

Continuous learning usually is required to master a job in the modern organization. For continuous learning to take place, each member must develop expertise. Quite often this detail is overlooked because of the emphasis on learning in groups. Collective learning is much more productive when every member of the group brings something valuable to the table. As mentioned above, in a learning organization it is still people who are doing the learning. To say an organization adapts to it environment really means that a handful of perceptive workers spot environmental trends and figure out how the organization can capitalize on them.

Translation of New Knowledge into New Ways of Behaving

Given that learning involves a change in behavior, a true learning organization translates knowledge into action. Learning at a superficial level would occur if managers attended a seminar on expectancy theory and simply retained key principles. Members of a learning organization would apply expectancy theory. Similarly, if you are a learning person, you will incorporate organizational behavior knowledge into your repertoire of skills.

The challenge of translating new knowledge into new ways of behavior became evident during the beginnings of the e-commerce revolution. Companies who learned about e-commerce, then simply used the Internet as an electronic sales catalogue did not profit much from e-commerce. The true winners were firms that made more far-sweeping changes related to e-commerce such as also transforming the ways they dealt with suppliers, dealers, and distributors.

Systematic Investigation and Problem Solving

A key building block of a learning organization is the widespread use of systematic investigation and problem solving based on the scientific method. A systematic approach can prevent overlooking important facts and not gathering enough information to make an informed decision. As important as problem-solving tools may be, even more important is the disciplined mind-set necessary for creating a learning organization. Employees must think with greater discipline and pay more attention to details.

As David A. Garvin notes, workers must continuously ask, "How do we know that's true?" They must "push beyond obvious symptoms to assess underlying causes, often collecting evidence when conventional wisdom says it is unnecessary."[5] A corporate travel coordinator might say to her boss, "Why is it true that at the vice-president level and above, managers must fly first-class and stay at premier hotels? Have we recently collected data on their travel preferences? Suppose we showed how the company could save $150,000 per year by less luxurious flight and hotel accommodations? Isn't it worth investigating?"

Experimentation

One approach to seeking out new opportunities and learning is through experimentation. Most successful companies continuously experiment with new ways of improving their manufacturing or services. The efforts of the United States Postal Service to retain market share, as described in Chapter 13, is a good example of organizational learning. Experimentation can be done on a large scale by conducting demonstration projects or pilot programs. For example, McDonald's Corporation will often try out a new restaurant theme such as 1950s-style diners in a test market. If the project is profitable, the concept will be expanded. Experimentation requires a risk-taking attitude, characteristic of the entrepreneurial mind-set.

312

Learning from Other Organizations

Some of the best insights an organization can acquire stem from studying competitors and other firms. Borrowing ideas from the competition, also known as benchmarking, took place long before the concept of a learning organization arose. A learning organization systematizes the process, while at the same time attempting to be ethical. "Learning from others" is most ethical when the learning does not directly capitalize on an idea a competitor spent considerable time and money developing.

Substantial learning can take place in copying the practices of firms not directly in your line of business. Suppose you would like to establish a worldwide method of distributing hard-to-get automobile parts, like a carburetor for a 1956 Edsel. You carefully study the marketing techniques of Amazon.com and Barnes andNoble.com, distributors of books, music, and other products. You set up an elaborate system, copy the order and shipping process of these firms, and call yourself Oldautoparts.com. Since you don't distribute books, music, and videos and your benchmarking targets don't distribute hard-to-find auto parts, nobody gets hurt. You are a learning organization without directly copying another company's ideas.

Healthy Disrespect for the Status Quo

A general characteristic of a learning organization is to challenge whatever exists and see if anything can be improved in any way. The status quo to be challenged can refer to work processes, products, services, policies, organization structure, organizational culture, or physical location of offices and plants. Managers and other employees should challenge whatever can be changed to prevent the problem of being a less effective organization. When an organization is successful, the desire to change can be weak because success is self-rewarding. (This problem was discussed in relation to disruptive technology in Chapter 13.) Yet highly effective leaders should see the need to change to prevent problems in the long run. A telling example is Gateway Computer in the late 1990s.

> Although a very successful company, the executive group of Gateway decided to relocate its headquarters and technical division from North Sioux City, South Dakota, to San Diego, California. Part of the reasoning was that the company could not attract the type of talent it needed to grow unless it was located in a geographic area more appealing to many technical and marketing personnel. The Gateway cow logo was also softened (cow markings but no cow face) to create a less rural image that might have stronger appeal to future customers and employees.

Another interesting way in which Gateway disrespected the status quo was to depart slightly from their strategy of selling products and services by telephone and the Internet. Instead, the company added showrooms for displaying products and ordering them over the Internet, and providing computer training.

High-Impact Learning

Another perspective on a learning organization is that the significance of the learning must be taken into account. The more significant the learning, the more likely it will move the firm forward and prevent substantial problems. According to one team of researchers, learning capability is demonstrated only if the ideas have impact or add value for the firm's stakeholders for a long time. Three steps facilitate high-impact learning.[6]

The first step to facilitate high-impact learning is to build a commitment to learning capability. The challenge in this step is getting managers intellectually and emotionally committed to learning. One way of getting managers and other workers excited about learning is to incorporate ideas about learning into business strategy and mission statements.

The second step is to generate ideas with impact. Companies that are successful at high-impact learning have deliberate approaches for acquiring knowledge. Many companies choose continuous improvement as a method for generating new ideas. Two other useful methods for generating ideas are suggestions systems and process-improvement task forces.

The third step is to work to disseminate ideas with impact. One way to share ideas is the widespread use of cross-functional teams. Individuals from different functions share some of the best ideas while carrying out group tasks. More ideas about information sharing are presented later in this chapter.

KNOWLEDGE MANAGEMENT

A major consequence of a learning organization is that knowledge is managed more effectively. **Knowledge management (KM)** is the systematic sharing of information to achieve such goals as innovation, nonduplication of effort, and competitive advantage. When knowledge is managed effectively, information is shared as needed whether it is printed, stored electronically, or resting in the brains of workers. The justification for knowledge management is that intellectual capital is a resource that allows for survival and competitive advantage. Although a learning organization leads to knowledge management, it is also true that managing knowledge well helps an organization learn. Our study of knowledge management encompasses the conditions favoring knowledge management, strategies and techniques of knowledge management, and methods for sharing knowledge.

Recognize organizational conditions favoring knowledge management (KM).

Organizational Conditions Favoring Knowledge Management

Certain organizational conditions favor the effective management of knowledge. As already mentioned, *being a learning organization* facilitates knowledge management because the learning organization creates the conditions for making good use of information. Such an organization is prepared to make good use of knowledge. A closely related condition is an *organizational culture* that emphasizes sharing information. A knowledge management system is unlikely to work without an organization undergoing a significant cultural change. Incentives must exist for knowledge sharing. Those who contribute to the knowledge base and generate the most useful or frequently used information might receive a cash bonus, stock, a plaque, or a company-paid luxury vacation. More important than the incentives themselves is for workers to develop a social obligation to share.[7]

Another organizational condition for making knowledge management a reality is to *provide leadership for the effort*. Senior management should understand the value of knowledge management and support the development of programs and policies to make it a reality. Mark T. Stone, a director of internal knowledge management at Arthur Anderson, says: "Organizations that succeed with knowledge management always have high-level support."[8] The right kind of leadership usually means more than financial support for a KM initiative. Senior executives must understand the potential contribution of knowledge management and play an active role in making decisions about knowledge management activities. For example, a senior executive might make a decision about new initiatives to retain creative people within the firm.

Another key organizational condition is to *demonstrate the value of knowledge management to encourage commitment.* Workers must understand why the organization has formalized knowledge management and how it will benefit the organization. Thomas Koulopoulos, president of a consulting firm specializing in knowledge management, notes that "Most of us were raised in a culture that doesn't believe in sharing. We've built our careers around proprietary ideas, information, and knowledge."[9] Explaining the benefits of KM can only go so far in creating favorable attitudes. Workers should be shown how the sharing knowledge makes their job easier or better. A high-impact approach is to explain how knowledge management leads to new products, increased sales, cost savings, and more money available for salaries.

KNOWLEDGE MANAGEMENT STRATEGIES AND TECHNIQUES

Pinpoint strategies and techniques for knowledge management.

Given that knowledge management has become one of the fastest growing trends in management of the decade, various strategies and techniques have been developed to foster the process. We make no rigid distinction between strategies and techniques for KM versus conditions favoring knowledge management. The building blocks of a learning organization are also closely tied in with the knowledge management strategies and techniques to be described next.

Hire the Right Persons

If you want to achieve an important organizational goal, hire the right people. Hiring people who are good at learning and teaching makes a substantial difference in the effectiveness of knowledge management. Human resources consultant Tom O. Davenport explains: "Not enough companies have built into their competency models how well people learn and pass on their knowledge informally on the job. If you've got people who are hungry to learn and people who are good at transferring knowledge, the organization will be much more alive."[10]

People with the right stuff for KM are most likely to be those who have demonstrated intelligence, accumulation of knowledge, and intellectual curiosity in the past. Interview probing and reference checks would be helpful. Two relevant interview questions would be, "Describe to me how you have shared knowledge with others so far in your career or at school" and "What new development in your field have you learned in the past month or so?" Psychological testing about cognitive ability and openness to experience would also be appropriate.

Create Knowledge

Creating knowledge is an important first step for managing knowledge. The strategy is easily stated but not so easy to implement. First you need intelligence to create the knowledge, and you also need the conditions favoring creativity and innovation described in Chapter 4. Knowledge is the raw material that allows people to innovate new products, services, processes, and management methods. The 4I model of organizational learning provides a partial explanation of how knowledge is created. To understand the need for creating new knowledge, it is useful to perceive every product, service, and work process as a bundle of knowledge. For example, the Chrysler PT Cruiser is the intelligence bundled in the ability to transform a 63-year old design to fit modern tastes for the retro look, do the appropriate engineering and manufacturing, and market and distribute the product to customers. The idea of creating knowledge is not new; it has been the foundation of successful organizations for a long time. KM, however, underscores the value of large numbers of people creating knowledge.[11]

Competitive Knowledge Management

An aggressive approach to knowledge management is to develop mechanisms for enabling workers to track knowledge and expertise outside the company. This approach has traditionally been referred to as *competitive intelligence*. With the Internet and company-developed databases now available to the public, company employees might be able to find out useful information about the competition that is public knowledge. If this approach is carried too far, it could move into the area of stealing trade secrets.

Michael Dell of Dell Computer makes an Internet search of industry trends part of his work routine. He believes that considerable useful information about industry trends is available on various Web sites. A person needs high-level Internet search skills—knowing where to look—to derive useful information.

Codification versus Personalizing Knowledge

To better understand different approaches to knowledge management, a team of researchers studied KM practices at management consulting firms, health-care providers, and computer manufacturers.[12] The researchers classified the various knowledge management activities into two different strategies. A major finding was that companies dealing with standardized products and services have a different approach to knowledge management than companies that provide highly customized solutions to problems.

In companies that manufacture and sell relatively standardized products that fit the needs of many customers, knowledge is carefully codified and stored in databases. In this way, the information can be readily accessed and used repeatedly by anyone in the firm. The authors of the study call this the *codification strategy*. In companies that provide highly customized solutions to unique customer or client problems, knowledge is shared primarily through interpersonal contacts. (The same strategy could be described as informal learning.) The chief purpose of computers, including e-mail, is to help people communicate. The approach just described is labeled the *personalization strategy*. The researchers noted that a company's choice of knowledge management strategy is not arbitrary; it should be driven by the company's competitive strategy of standardization versus customization. Emphasizing the wrong approach or attempting to do both simultaneously can interfere with productivity and profitability. To help identify whether codification or personalization is the best approach to KM, top management should find accurate answers to the following questions:

- Do you offer standardized or customized products? (If your products are standardized, it is best to codify knowledge. For customized products, use the personalization model because codified knowledge will generally be of little value.)
- Do you have a mature or an innovative product? (Use codified knowledge for mature products and personalized knowledge for innovative products.)

- Do your people rely on explicit or tacit knowledge to solve problems? (Explicit knowledge fits better for a codified strategy of knowledge management. For tacit knowledge, a person-to-person approach works best.)

These guidelines are probably less precise than the authors of the study think. One problem is that products are sometimes a combination of standardization and customization, such as shoes made to fit unusual sizes. Also, knowledge is not always readily classifiable as explicit (well structured) versus tacit (intuitive).

Appointing a Chief Knowledge Officer

To help foster knowledge management, about 100 large firms have created a position labeled chief knowledge officer, chief learning officer, or chief information officer. Contrary to popular expectation, this person is not in charge of training and development. A chief knowledge officer is in charge of systematically collecting information and connecting people who need information with others who might have the information they need. Specific parts of the job description or role include:

- Arranging conferences where workers share information
- Assimilating databases of company knowledge
- Teaching people how to learn at a deeper level
- Getting people to reflect on their experiences and profit from their mistakes
- Selling people on the idea that brainpower is the company's true source of competitive advantage

Because knowledge is the primary output of professional service firms, they were the first to create the position of chief knowledge officer. John Peetz, CKO of Ernst & Young, describes his role: "For us, knowledge management is critical. It's one of our four core processes—sell work, do work, manage people, and manage knowledge."[13]

Closing the Gap between Knowing and Doing

Jeffrey Pfeffer and Robert I. Sutton have investigated why companies don't accomplish more if they have so much knowledge and expertise. (This is a Stanford University Business School twist on the age-old question, "If you're so smart, why aren't you rich?") Pfeffer and Sutton believe that companies have fallen into the know-doing gap because doing something requires the hard work of making something happen. Managing knowledge is not enough; it must be converted into action. It is easier and safer to have intellectual discussions, to gather large databases, and to invest in technical infrastructure, than to actually execute. The challenge for companies and the people in them is to build a culture of action.[14] Often this means taking decisive action that results in repeat business, such as an airline having a high percent of on-time flights, offering commissions to retail store sales representatives.

METHODS FOR SHARING INFORMATION

Specify methods for sharing information within an organization.

A major goal of the learning organization and knowledge management is for organizational members to share relevant information. Many of the strategies and techniques already described in this chapter contribute directly or indirectly to information sharing. Also, the accompanying Organizational Behavior in Action describes how a small company developed an effective method of information sharing. Here we describe briefly five focused methods for sharing information.

316

Organizational Behavior *in Action*

S k i   C e n t e r   E m p l o y e e s   S h a r e   K n o w l e d g e

The Swan Mountain Ski Center had problems with its season pass system. The equipment used for the season pass system was old and worn down, causing customers to wait a long time in line to obtain their passes. Another problem was that the same type of photograph and laminate was used every year. As a result, an increasing number of people made counterfeit passes. Swan Mountain management knew that changes had to be made. The Center needed a new season pass system that was faster and would give the passes a new look.

Management decided to install a computerized season pass system. The database system Access was used for inputting, storing, and outputting all season pass information. A digital camera was acquired to take the photographs to be inserted on the season passes. Management thought that by applying state-of-the art technology it had resolved the problems with its system.

Management's optimism did not last long; a new set of problems arose. Most of the office staff who had worked at the ski center for years either did not know how to operate a computer at all or had very limited computer skills. A few of the employees were so frightened by working with a new computer system that they contemplated resigning. The ski area needed to find an inexpensive and relatively quick way of training the employees to use the new system for issuing season passes.

Elizabeth Simon, the office manager, decided to solve the training problem in stages. First, she put the ten office employees at ease by telling them not to worry about using the new computerized system and digital camera. She assured the employees that they would all be trained at their own pace on how to use the computer and digital camera. Second, Simon queried the employees about the extent of their computer knowledge. She found that three people had substantial computer knowledge and experience. She trained these individuals first on how to use Access and the digital camera. Simon started with these employees because she knew that they would be a good resource for the other employees who needed assistance in learning the new system. Simon then continued to train the other two groups of employees in a similar manner. However, she proceeded in baby steps when needed.

After all of the employees received this initial technical training, they were brought back in for simulated on-the-job training. Each of the employees took a turn operating the computer and camera, and then being a customer. The three employees with the most computer knowledge assisted the less experienced. The simulations gave the Swan Mountain office staff an opportunity to use the acquired knowledge without feeling much pressure.

This method of training employees and giving them the opportunity to share knowledge proved to be effective. None of the employees resigned, and they are now all comfortable working on the new computerized system of issuing season passes.

Source: Case researched by Theresa Whitman, Rochester Institute of Technology, 1998.

1. *In-house Yellow Pages.* The basic idea of company Yellow Pages is to compile a directory of the skills, talents, and special knowledge of employees throughout the firm. To be useful, the Yellow Pages have to go far beyond basic information and job experience. The directory should indicate the specialized knowledge of the people listed and their level of expertise. When faced with

a problem requiring specialized talent, employees can consult the Yellow Pages for a person to help.

2. *Intranet communication systems.* A growing number of firms use intranets and on-line forums to spread and share knowledge. Buckman Laboratories (see the introductory case in this chapter) has a knowledge sharing system known as K'Netix, used by 1,200 employees in 80 countries including CEO Bob Buckman. Employees working from home or a customer's office can receive information instantaneously on everything from HR practices to perfecting a new chemical process.[15]

3. *Personal explanations of success factors.* An advanced method of information sharing is for key organizational members to teach others what they know through explanations of success factors. Noel Tichy refers to these stories as the *teachable point of view* because they help leaders become teachers. The teachable point of view is a written explanation of what a person knows and believes about what it takes to succeed in his or her own business, as well as in business in general. About two pages in length, the document focuses on critical success factors such as "What would it take to knock out the competition?" Tichy claims that this hard-hitting method of information sharing is used in hundreds of companies.[16]

4. *Foster dialogue among organization members.* To promote the importance of information sharing, company leaders should converse about the importance of intellectual capital and the development of core competencies.[17] At the same time, workers throughout the firm should be encouraged to share useful suggestions, tidbits of knowledge, and success stories about problem solving. This type of information sharing can take place face-to-face, yet e-mail exchanges also play a vital role.

5. *Shared physical facilities and informal learning.* An important method of fostering dialogue is to develop shared physical facilities as described in Chapter 9 about developing teamwork. Considerable information sharing is likely to take place in a snack lounge or company information resource center. At the same time, informal learning takes place, which is almost synonymous with information sharing.

IMPLICATIONS FOR MANAGERIAL PRACTICE

1. The most important and the most practical aspect of the learning organization and knowledge management is for workers to share useful information with one another. In your role as a manager, you should therefore make a systematic effort to ensure that information is shared in the total organization or your organizational unit. Establish both formal steps (for example, an intranet) and informal methods (such as simply encouraging people to exchange good ideas) to accomplish information sharing.

2. Several theorists have mentioned that a company's true competitive advantage derives from intellectual capital. If this observation is valid, then one of the highest organizational priorities is to recruit and retain knowledgeable and intelligent workers. Even during a downsizing, maximum effort should be invested in retaining the best thinkers and most knowledgeable people in the company.

SUMMARY OF KEY POINTS

Describe the 4I framework of a learning organization.
According to the 4I framework, organizational learning that results in organizational renewal encompasses the entire enterprise. Organizational learning is composed of four processes: intuiting, interpreting, integrating, and institutionalization. The four processes work together to link the individual, group, and organizational levels. Intuiting and interpreting take place at the individual level; integrating takes place at the group level; and institutionalizing takes place at the organizational level.

Identify the building blocks, or key characteristics, of a learning organization.
Components of the learning organization include: (a) double-loop learning, (b) action learning (learning while doing), (c) systems thinking, (d) shared vision, (e) the challenging of mental models, (f) team learning, (g) personal mastery of the job, (h) translation of new knowledge into new ways of behaving, (i) systematic investigation and problem solving, (j) experimentation, (k) learning from other organizations, (l) healthy disrespect for the status quo, and (m) high-impact learning.

Recognize organizational conditions favoring knowledge management (KM).
Among the conditions favoring KM are being a learning organization; having an organizational culture that emphasizes information sharing, leadership for knowledge management, and demonstrating the value of knowledge management.

Pinpoint strategies and techniques for knowledge management.
Strategies and techniques for knowledge management include: (a) hire the right persons, (b) create knowledge, (c) competitive knowledge management, (d) codification versus personalizing knowledge, (e) appointing a chief knowledge officer, and (f) closing the gap between knowing and doing.

Specify methods for sharing information within an organization.
Information sharing is at the heart of a learning organization and knowledge management. Five specific methods are (a) in-house Yellow Pages, (b) intranet communication systems, (c) personal explanations of success factors, (d) foster dialogue among organizational members, and (e) shared physical facilities and organizational learning.

KEY TERMS AND PHRASES

Learning Organization, *306*
An organization that is skilled at creating, acquiring, and transferring knowledge and at modifying behavior to reflect new knowledge and insights.

Double-loop Learning, *309*
A change in behavior that occurs when people use feedback to confront the validity of the goal or the values implicit in the situation.

Action Learning, *309*
Learning that occurs while working on real problems, involving the acquisition of new skills, tools, and concepts.

Knowledge Management (KM), *313*
The systematic sharing of information to achieve advances in innovation, efficiency, and competitive advantage.

DISCUSSION QUESTIONS AND ACTIVITIES

1. Give an example from your own life when it would have been advantageous for you to have used double-loop learning.
2. What is the difference between a learning organization and simply an organization that offers its employees considerable training and development?
3. Why do mental models sometimes interfere with the goals of diversity?
4. Give an example of how your instructor for this course would be able to be a systems thinker in his or her role as a teacher.
5. How would you explain the observation that managers and professional workers in pharmaceutical firms tend to be strongly interested in the topic of information sharing?
6. How might being a generous information sharer interfere with a person's career success?
7. Ask an experienced manager what type of information should be included in the in-house Yellow Pages. Be prepared to share your findings with classmates.

ORGANIZATIONAL BEHAVIOR ON-LINE

TO DO

Sorting Out Information on Information Sharing

Knowledge management makes extensive use of digitized information, so the Internet should be a useful source for researching knowledge sharing. The problem is that most search engines list thousands of entries under "knowledge management." Your task is to find at least five methods of information sharing, using your favorite search engines. You might use the search term "knowledge sharing" to narrow down your search. See if your search uncovers any specific technique of knowledge sharing not already mentioned in this chapter.

TO BOOKMARK

The Learning Organization—an international journal
http://www.mcb.co.uk/tlo.htm

Resources for Learning Organizations
http://www.Smartbiz.com

Knowledge Management
http://www.amsinc.com/KnowledgeMgmt
http://www.advisor.com/ZKM

CASE PROBLEM: The Reluctant Information Sharers

The Flagstaff Marketing Group specializes in offering marketing assistance to business firms. Most of their accounts are small- and medium-size firms without large marketing staffs of their own. The Flagstaff Group often helps a client market a product by assisting in such matters as finding prospective customers and developing marketing slogans. One client, a manufacturer of foot-powered scooters, sought advice on opening a new market. Flagstaff helped them market their product to city dwellers as a vehicle for going to work. The marketing theme was "Scoot Your Way to Success." Sales quadrupled for the scooter manufacturer.

Flagstaff also has several large firms as clients. For these firms, Flagstaff offers specialized expertise that the client firm may lack. For example, Flagstaff develops company logos and names that help give a firm a distinctive identity, such as finding a new name for a company after a merger or spin-off. Although not developed by Flagstaff, an example is the name "Lucent Technologies" for the former equipment-manufacturing division of AT&T.

Peter Flagstaff, the founder of the firm, has been concerned lately that his firm develops ideas inefficiently. He said to Lindsay Gibson, the executive vice president at Flagstaff, "I keep hearing the same discussions over and over about solving a particular client problem. The account executives keep sifting through the alternatives that others have done before. People don't capitalize on all the good problem solving that has taken place in the past. We go through the same agonizing process of dealing with similar problems."

Gibson replied, "Are you suggesting, Peter, that we should offer canned solutions to clients so we could save lots of time?"

"Not at all," responded Peter. "We could at least save some time and offer similar types of assistance to clients that we offered to other clients in the past. I'll give you a good example. Reggie Whitson recently had a pet-clothing manufacturer for a client. The client wanted to expand the market for items like dog raincoats, dog shoes for cold weather, and a luxury line of dog sweaters for special occasions. So Reggie spent a week researching dog clothing before coming up with some recommendations for his client.

"If Reggie could have picked up some ideas in-house, he could have found some good ideas a lot more quickly. Also, if he had spent less time, the client would not have been so taken back by the large fee."

Looking perplexed, Lindsay said, "But how would Reggie have known about who had tackled a similar client problem in the past?"

Peter jumped in, "Lindsay, you have pinpointed the problem. We have done a poor job of systematically pooling all that great information in our heads. Not only do we reinvent the wheel, we reinvent the idea that a wheel would be useful.

"I'm proposing that we find a way of sharing knowledge that will pay big dividends for the firm. The major consulting firms have developed pretty effective systems of knowledge management and knowledge sharing in recent years.

"I'm not implying that we hire somebody to be our chief knowledge officer or that we invest $500,000 in sophisticated software. I just want us to do a better job of sharing ideas with one another."

"I've got an idea," said Lindsay, "let's schedule a combination dinner and focus group for the professional staff. The subject will be why we aren't doing a better job of information sharing."

Among the comments that emerged from the dinner/focus group were the following:

GARY: I would like to share more of my experiences with the other account executives. I'm concerned, though, about the good of the firm. Suppose I give some of my best ideas to another account exec, and then he or she leaves the firm. My good ideas are fed right to the competition.

BRENDA: Unlike Gary, I have no hesitancy in sharing ideas. The problem is the time involved. We were encouraged at one time to do a write-up of how we solved unusual client problems. The task proved to be busywork. We had to follow a complicated format. Maybe we should use a briefer method of recording good ideas.

SHARON: I'm not opposed to sharing ideas, but it makes me a little self-conscious. To ask someone else for ideas suggests that I'm not so creative myself. Take that dog-clothing account. If I asked others for ideas, it would have been like I can't think of any good ideas for promoting dog clothing myself. (Laughter from the group.)

JASON: So long as we are all being brutally honest here, let me get to the heart of the problem. We're creative types. Our careers are dependent on having good ideas. After you share an idea with another exec, the idea becomes public knowledge. It loses its originality. So if you use that idea again, you are no longer creative because other account execs are using it.

ANNE: Jason has a point. Teamwork is nice, but you still have to look out for numero uno. Sure I have warm, fuzzy feelings toward top management and the other account executives. Yet I'm still evaluated by Flagstaff in terms of my originality.

Peter Flagstaff said to the group, "Lindsay and I both thank you for being so candid. I see a few glimmers of hope in terms of knowledge sharing in our firm. But this is just the start of a continuing dialogue. We have a long way to go to manage knowledge well at Flagstaff marketing."

Lindsay nodded in agreement.

Case Questions

1. What suggestions can you offer Peter Flagstaff and Lindsay Gibson to improve knowledge sharing at the Flagstaff Marketing Group?
2. How valid are the points made by the account executives for not doing a better job of sharing information?
3. What cultural changes might be needed at Flagstaff to improve knowledge sharing?

BrandEra.com calls itself the "marketer's marketplace," aggregating news, advice, career information, and more at its Web site at http://www.brandera.com/. On the surface, BrandEra.com evinces few of the qualms about sharing ideas discussed by Flagstaff's staff. View the site for an additional perspective.

SUGGESTED READINGS

Davenport, Thomas H., and Prusak, Laurence. *Working Knowledge: How Organizations Manage What They Know.* Boston, MA: Harvard Business School Publishing, 1997.

DiBella, Anthony J., and Nevis, Edwin C. *How Organizations Learn: An Integrated Strategy for Building Learning Capability.* San Francisco: Jossey-Bass, 1998.

Pfeffer, Jeffrey and Sutton, Robert I. *The Knowing-Doing Gap: How Smart Companies Turn Knowledge Into Action.* Boston, MA: Harvard Business School Publishing, 1999.

Roth, George, and Kleiner, Art. "Developing Organizational Memory through Learning Histories." *Organizational Dynamics,* Autumn 1998, pp. 43–60.

Senge, Peter M. *The Fifth Discipline.* New York: Doubleday, 1990.

ENDNOTES

1. David A. Garvin, "Building a Learning Organization," *Harvard Business Review,* July–August 1993, p. 80.
2. Quoted in Robert M. Fulmer and J. Bernard Keys, "A Conversation with Peter Senge: New Developments in Organizational Learning," *Organizational Dynamics,* Autumn 1998, p. 35.
3. Mary M. Crossan, Henry W. Lane, and Roderick E. White, "An Organizational Learning Framework: From Intuition to Institution," *Academy of Management Review,* July 1999, pp. 522–537.
4. Robert M. Fulmer and Philip Gibbs, "The Second Generation Learning Organizations: New Tools for Sustaining Competitive Advantage," *Organizational Dynamics,* Autumn 1998, pp. 7–20; Senge, *The Fifth Discipline;* Daniel R. Tobin, *The Knowledge-Enabled Organization* (New York: AMACOM, 1998). William E. Brenneman, Robert M. Fulmer, and J. Bernard Keys, "Learning Across a Living Company: The Shell Companies' Experiences," *Organizational Dynamics,* Autumn 1998, pp. 61–70.
5. David A. Garvin, "Building a Learning Organization," *Harvard Business Review,* July-August 1993, pp. 81–82.
6. Dave Ulrich, Todd Jick, and Mary Ann Von Glinow, "High-Impact Learning: Building and Diffusing Capability," *Organizational Dynamics,* Autumn 1993, p. 60.
7. Samuel Greengard, "How to Make KM a Reality," *Workforce,* October 1998, p. 91.
8. Greengard, "How to Make KM a Reality," p. 90.
9. Greengard, "How to Make KM a Reality," p. 91.
10. Quoted in Louisa Wah, "Making Knowledge Stick," *Management Review,* May 1999, p. 27.
11. William Miller, "Building the Ultimate Resource," *Management Review,* January 1999, p. 43.
12. Morten T. Hansen, Nitin Nohria, and Thomas Tierney, "What's Your Strategy for Managing Knowledge?" *Harvard Business Review,* March–April 1999, pp. 106–116.
13. Thomas A. Stewart, "Is This Job Really Necessary?" *Fortune,* January 12, 1998, p. 154.
14. Cited in Alan Webber, "Why Can't We Get Anything Done?" *Fast Company,* June 2000, pp. 168–180.
15. Greengard, "Storing, Shaping, and Sharing Collective Wisdom," *Workforce,* October 1998, p. 84.
16. Noel Tichy, "The Teachable Point of View," *Harvard Business Review,* March–April 1999, p. 82.
17. Miller, "The Ultimate Resource," p. 45.

Cultural Diversity and International Organizational Behavior

Three years ago, Jerry DiMonti decided to recruit employees among various ethnic groups to better reflect changes in the Elmont, New York, home of his Century 21 People Services Realty franchise. Once primarily an Irish and Italian neighborhood, the suburban community on the border of New York City now hosts about 90 different nationalities. "I feel that you should have some kind of diversity in the workplace," he says.

Today DiMonti's 33 agents include people with Italian, Irish, French, African-American, Guatemalan, Puerto Rican, Jamaican, Nigerian, Jewish, Indian, and South African backgrounds. That scope of diversity has better helped the real estate agency reach the surrounding market. If clients prefer to deal in Spanish or Hindi, DiMonti will accommodate them. In the first year after his diversity drive, sales at his agency spiked by 33 percent. In the third year, they increased by an additional 12 percent.

Cultural diversity, long the province only of the Equal Employment Opportunity Commission and affirmative action stalwarts like the National Urban League, increasingly occupies the attention of America's corporate officers. AT&T, Levi Strauss, and Philip Morris are three widely admired U.S. companies with regard to community relations and diversity. At http://www.levistrauss.com/, you can read about Levi Strauss's take on corporate social responsibility.

PHOTO: © ANDY SACHS/STONE

OBJECTIVES

After reading and studying this chapter and doing the exercises, you should be able to

1 Understand the scope, competitive advantages, and success factors associated with cultural diversity.

2 Identify and explain key dimensions of cultural differences.

3 Describe what is required for managers and organizations to become multicultural.

4 Be more aware of barriers to good cross-cultural relations.

5 Explain how motivation, ethics, conflict resolution, and skills needed for negotiation can vary across cultures.

6 Appreciate the nature of diversity training and cultural training.

323

Chapter 15

Source: Adapted from Chris Sandlund, "There's a New Face to America," *Success*, April 1999, p. 38.

SO WHAT? **Are there business advantages to having a culturally diverse workforce?** If so, exactly how can organizational behavior inform our abilities to harness and capitalize on the talents of diversity? Even though our case hero, Jerry DiMonti, operates in one locale close to New York City, he deals with people from many different cultures and, more importantly, actively recruits them. Including people of all backgrounds in its decision-making processes helps Century 21 better appreciate its customers' needs and points the way to continual improvement of its services.

We have already mentioned demographic and cultural diversity at several places in this text. Chapter 2 included a description of demographic factors as a source of individual differences; Chapter 8 described cross-cultural communication barriers; Chapter 13 described how cross-cultural differences can hamper a merger; and cross-cultural issues were raised in relation to many other concepts throughout the text. One purpose of this chapter is to provide additional insights that managers and professionals can use to capitalize upon diversity within and across countries.

The fact that business has become increasingly international has elevated the importance of understanding international organizational behavior. Small- and medium-size firms, as well as corporate giants, are increasingly dependent on trade with other countries. An estimated 10 to 15 percent of jobs in the United States depend on imports or exports. Furthermore, most manufactured goods contain components from more than one country. For example, the Jeep Cherokee manufactured by the Chrysler division of DaimlerChrysler is made in Toledo, Ohio, but the motor is made in Japan.

Our description of cultural diversity and cross-cultural organizational behavior will include a presentation of key concepts, and ideas for developing diversity and cross-cultural skills. Before reading on, do the Self-Assessment on skills and attitudes that follows. It will help you think through how multicultural you are now.

CULTURAL DIVERSITY: SCOPE, COMPETITIVE ADVANTAGES, AND SUCCESS FACTORS

Understand the scope, competitive advantages, and success factors associated with cultural diversity.

Cultural diversity can be approached from many different perspectives relating both to its interpersonal and business aspects. In this section, we describe the scope of cultural diversity, how it affects business results, and factors associated with successful cultural diversity initiatives. Diversity training is given separate attention later.

The Scope of Cultural Diversity

Improving cross-cultural relations includes understanding the true meaning of appreciating demographic and cultural diversity. To appreciate diversity, a person must go beyond tolerating and treating people from different racial and ethnic groups fairly. The true meaning of valuing diversity is to respect and enjoy a wide range of cultural and individual differences. To be diverse is to be different in some measurable way. Although the diversity factor is *measurable* in a scientific sense, it may not be *visible* on the surface. Upon meeting a team member, it may not be apparent that the person is diverse from the standpoint of being dyslexic, color-blind, gay, lesbian, or vegetarian. However, all of these factors are measurable.

As just implied, some people are more visibly diverse than others because of physical features or disabilities. Yet the diversity umbrella is supposed to include

SELF-ASSESSMENT

Cross-Cultural Skills and Attitudes

Listed below are various skills and attitudes that employers and cross-cultural experts think are important for relating effectively to coworkers in a culturally diverse environment. Check the appropriate column.

	Applies to Me Now		Not There Yet
1. I have spent some time in another country.	✓		✓
2. At least one of my friends is deaf, blind, or uses a wheelchair.			✓
3. Currency from other countries is as real as the currency from my own country.	✓		
4. I can read in a language other than my own.		✓	
5. I can speak in a language other than my own.		✓	
6. I can write in a language other than my own.			✓
7. I can understand people speaking in a language other than my own.			✓
8. I use my second language regularly.			
9. My friends include people of races different from my own.	✓		
10. My friends include people of different ages.	✓		
11. I feel (or would feel) comfortable having a friend with a sexual orientation different from mine.		✓	
12. My attitude is that although another culture may be very different from mine, that culture is equally good.	✓		
13. I would be willing to (or already do) hang art from different countries in my home.	✓		
14. I would accept (or have already accepted) a work assignment of more than several months in another country.		✓	
15. I have a passport.			✓

Scoring and Interpretation: If you answered "Applies to Me Now" to 10 or more of the above questions, you most likely function well in a multicultural work environment. If you answered "Not There Yet" to 10 or more of the above questions, you need to develop more cross-cultural awareness and skills to work effectively in a multicultural work environment.

You will notice that being bilingual gives you at least five points on this quiz.

Source: Ruthann Dirks and Janet Buzzard, "What CEOs Expect of Employees Hired for International Work," *Business Education Forum,* April 1997, pp. 3–7; Gunnar Beeth, "Multicultural Managers Wanted," *Management Review,* May 1997, pp. 17–21.

everybody in an organization. The goal of a diverse organization is for persons of all cultural backgrounds to achieve their full potential, not restrained by group identities such as sex, nationality, or race.[1] Exhibit 15-1 presents a broad sampling of the ways in which work associates can differ from one another. Studying this list can help you anticipate the types of differences in cultural as well as individual factors. Individual factors are also important because people can be discriminated against for personal characteristics as well as group factors. Many people, for example, believe they are held back from promotion because of their weight-to-height ratio.

The Competitive Advantage Of Diversity

Encouraging cultural and demographic diversity within an organization helps an organization achieve social responsibility goals. Also, diversity brings a competitive advantage to a firm. Before diversity can offer a competitive advantage to a firm,

326

- Race
- Sex or gender
- Religion
- Age (young, middle-aged, and old)
- Generation differences including attitudes (for example, baby boomers versus Net Generation)
- Ethnicity (country of origin)
- Education
- Abilities
- Mental disabilities (including attention deficit disorder)
- Physical disabilities (including hearing status, visual status, able-bodied, wheelchair user)
- Values and motivation
- Sexual orientation (heterosexual, homosexual, bisexual, transsexual)
- Marital status (married, single, divorced, cohabitating, widow, widower)

- Family status (children, no children, two-parent family, single parent, grandparent, opposite-sex parents, same-sex parents)
- Personality traits
- Functional background (area of specialization, such as marketing, HR)
- Technology interest (high tech, low tech, technophobe)
- Weight status (average, obese, underweight, anorexic)
- Hair status (full head of hair, bald, wild hair, tame hair, long hair, short hair)
- Style of clothing and appearance (dress up; dress down; professional appearance; casual appearance; tattoos; body piercing including multiple ear rings, nose rings, lip rings)
- Tobacco status (smoker versus nonsmoker, chewer versus nonchewer)
- Your addition to the list _____

○ *Veteran status*

The Diversity Umbrella

Diversity has evolved into a wide range of group and individual characteristics.

it must be managed in the sense of being woven into the fabric of the organization. This stands in contrast to simply having a "diversity program" offered periodically by the human resources department. Instead, the human resource efforts toward accomplishing diversity should be part of organizational strategy. The potential competitive (or bottom-line) benefits of cultural diversity, as revealed by research and observations, are described next:[2]

1. *Managing diversity well offers a marketing advantage, including increased sales and profits.* A representational workforce facilitates reaching a multicultural market as indicated in the opening case in this chapter. Allstate Insurance Company invests considerable effort into being a culturally diverse business firm. More than coincidentally, Allstate is now recognized as the nation's leading insurer of African-Americans and Hispanics. A study of racial diversity and business strategy in banking indicated that cultural diversity adds value, and within the proper context, contributes to a competitive advantage for the firm. The proper context, however, was that the banks have a growth strategy. Racial diversity did not increase profits for firms with a downsizing strategy.[3] The Skill-Development Exercise that follows gives you an opportunity to engage in problem solving about diversity and profits.

2. *Effective management of diversity can reduce costs.* More effective management of diversity may increase job satisfaction of diverse groups, thus decreasing turnover and absenteeism and their associated costs. A diverse organization that welcomes and fosters the growth of a wide variety of employees will retain more of its minority and multicultural employees. Also, effective management of diversity helps avoid costly lawsuits over being charged with discrimination based on age, race, or sex.

3. *Companies with a favorable record in managing diversity are at a distinct advantage in recruiting talented people.* Those companies with a favorable reputation for welcoming diversity attract the strongest job candidates among women and racioethnic minorities. A shortage of workers has given extra impetus to cultural diversity. During a tight labor market, companies cannot afford to be seen as racist, sexist, ageist, or even antiunion.

SKILL-DEVELOPMENT EXERCISE

COLLABORATE

Diversity Equals Profits

The Reverend Jesse Jackson said recently that General Motors Corp. would improve its business if it had more African-American customers and executives. (The Rainbow/PUSH coalition headed by Jackson owns GM shares.) Jackson also said that GM could add more sales if it did a better job of selling in urban areas, noting that Washington, D. C., had about 600,000 residents but no GM dealerships.[4]

Assemble into a GM task force to develop a plan for selling more vehicles to African Americans and other minorities. Part of your plan must include leveraging diversity, as suggested by Jackson. Work for about 15 minutes on the task. The team leader you appoint might present your plan to the rest of the class.

4. *Workforce diversity can provide a company with useful ideas for favorable publicity and advertising.* A culturally diverse workforce or its advertising agency can help a firm place itself in a favorable light to targeted cultural groups. During Kwanzaa, the late December holiday celebrated by many African Americans, McDonald's Corp. has run ads aimed at showing its understanding of and respect for African Americans' sense of family and community. For such ads to be effective, however, the company must also have a customer-contact workforce that is culturally diverse. Otherwise, the ads would lack credibility.

5. *Workforce heterogeneity may also offer a company a creativity advantage.* As mentioned in relation to effective groups (Chapter 9), creative solutions to problems are more likely when a diverse group attacks a problem. A study of organizational innovation found that innovative companies had above-average records on reducing racism, sexism, and classism.[5]

Factors Associated with Diversity Success

Business firms, as well as public organizations, achieve varied success with cultural diversity initiatives. Jacqueline A. Gilbert and John M. Ivancevich studied two comparable-size companies that achieved different levels of success with cultural diversity. Both firms were established units of *Fortune* 500 conglomerates. Employee surveys, managerial interviews, and company records were used to provide a detailed account of the diversity efforts over time.[6] One firm, designated the Multicultural Organization, has made substantial progress toward becoming more diverse. Evidence for the success included regional and local diversity awards and mention in prominent business publications. The firm designated the Plural Organization was less successful with inclusion of diverse employees and wanted to improve its efforts. Five factors highlight the differences between the Multicultural Organization's fundamental cultural change and the Plural Organization's superficial diversity commitment:

1. *CEO Initiation and Support.* The CEO of the Multicultural Organization played a more active and assertive role in bringing about cultural diversity. For example, he established a clear vision of how a more diverse workforce contributes to the bottom line. Also, he helped established values that defined its culture as one embracing diversity.

2. *Human Resource Initiatives.* The Multicultural Organization had more human resource programs aimed at achieving diversity. Among these many initiatives

include a vice president of diversity position, an annual diversity conference that features best practices from plants corporatewide, and an active women and minority recruitment program. The Plural Organization had fewer human resource initiatives for promoting diversity.

3. *Organizational Communication.* At the Multicultural Organization, a wide range of employees were involved in shaping human resource policies. A representative example is the Equality Council, a cross section of employees who meet once a month on issues related to a diverse workforce. Among its many suggestions were an anonymous suggestion box named "Dr. Equality." Employees also designed material to promote diversity such as posters, calendars, and coffee mugs. Efforts to involve employees at the Plural Organization were much less systematic.

4. *Corporate Philosophy.* A corporatewide philosophy governed diversity policies in the Multicultural Organization, whereas in the Plural Organization each plant had the freedom to develop its own philosophy. Lack of accountability made it easier for plants of the Plural Organization to discontinue diversity initiatives found to be too costly and time-consuming.

5. *Measures of Company Success.* At the Multicultural Organization, human capital objectives—including diversity—are presented as essential components of achieving profit and customer satisfaction. Also, the efforts of the human resources department were considered as adding value to the corporation. At the Plural Organization, cultural diversity was seen as a public relations tool and not as a vehicle for creating competitive advantage.

All five success factors can be interpreted as suggestions to management for gaining true advantage from cultural diversity. For example, include achieving cultural diversity as a measure of company success along with financial measures. The accompanying Organizational Behavior in Action provides pinpointed insights into how cultural diversity translates into competitive advantage for Allstate. Note that the initiatives taken are consistent with the five success factor just mentioned. Despite its success with cultural diversity, Allstate has faced bitter conflict with its agents over the company also selling insurance over the Internet. This extensive conflict, resulting in legal problems, suggests that cultural diversity initiatives do not resolve and prevent all organizational problems.

CROSS-CULTURAL VALUES

Identify and explain key dimensions of cultural differences.

Useful background information for understanding how to work well with people from different cultures is to examine their values. We approach this task by first looking at how cultures differ with respect to certain values, and second how cultural values shape management style.

Key Dimensions of Differences in Cultural Values

One way to understand how national cultures differ is to examine their values. Here we examine eight values and how selected nationalities relate to them, based on the work of several researchers.[7] Geert Hofstede identified the first five value dimensions in research spanning 18 years, involving over 160,000 people from over 60 countries. The other three on the list have been observed by several researchers. A summary of these values is presented next.

Organizational Behavior *in Action*

Diversity as a Competitive Weapon at Allstate

Since 1993, Allstate Insurance Co., based in Northbrook, Illinois, has been managing diversity as a central business. The focus is to drive greater levels of employee and customer satisfaction by taking an integrated approach to diversity in the workplace and the market.

Joan Crockett, senior vice president for human resources at Allstate, emphasizes that the company's diversity initiative isn't a nice-to-do, social conscience program. "It's a compelling business strategy," she says. Clinton Yearwood, director of diversity management, adds, "Diversity has become an initiative that has clear business outcomes. If you start having customers say they want to interact with knowledge workers who are like themselves, that gives the customers absolute best services and products. Through the diversity initiative, we demonstrate our commitment to a diverse marketplace."

Allstate is one of few companies that attempt to measure the impact of diversity on performance. The giant insurer boasts a rigorous measurement system as part of its initiative, and that process has proven a strong link between the diversity strategy and business growth. Crockett says, "We measure our environment through a survey process. We are able to set goals and hold the leaders responsible and tie their rewards to diversity. That really gives us an edge."

In the heated competitive environment of the insurance business, Allstate not only faces renewed competition from traditional insurance companies, but also new challenges from financial services firms and direct marketers who skip over agents and sell via 800 numbers and the Internet. Phil Lawson, vice president of sales, says the competition became especially intense in the late 1990s.

An ability to make positive use of the diversity in its workforce and customer base thus helps Allstate strengthen its competitive edge. Lawson says, "Being in a relationship business, how can you not look like and sound like your clients? It's an obvious competitive advantage when you can mirror the clients that you serve."

For Allstate, the concept of diversity is not limited to ethnicity and gender. It is based on a wider perspective that includes diversity in age, religion, sexual orientation, and disability, among others. Managing diversity at Allstate has six components:

- **Recruitment.** Recruiting employees with diverse backgrounds is the first step to ensure fair representation. Leaders in the organization are responsible for proactive hiring and promotion. Prospects can generally choose their employers, so creating an environment where people feel comfortable working is a priority. One of Allstate's recruiting techniques is making job offers to people who approach the company as potential customers.
- **Proactive Retention.** From the moment employees join Allstate, they hear a clear message from management that they will enjoy a bias-free work environment. Career development is also part of retention. A diverse slate of candidates is given the training and opportunities needed to advance their careers.
- **Diversity Education.** Continuing education is the lifeblood of Allstate's diversity initiative. Every new employee receives diversity training within the first six months of employment. Beyond this one-shot training, the diversity education team provides support to managers on how to sustain a diverse and trustful environment. For example, short exercises are provided on how diversity affects the bottom line.
- **Measuring Diversity.** One of the methods used to gauge leadership effectiveness in managing diversity is an employee feedback

> *Diversity as a Competitive Weapon at Allstate* (continued)
>
> system (see Exhibit 15-2). All 53,000 employees are surveyed twice a year through a leadership measurement system. This on-line feedback system measures employees' perception of how well the company is achieving aspirations for its customer, shareholders, and employees. A key result has been that when employees are satisfied with diversity efforts, their job satisfaction increases and so does customer satisfaction and retention.
>
> - **Leadership Accountability.** The compensation system at Allstate is closely linked to the goal of upholding diversity in the workplace. For managers at all levels, 25 percent of merit pay is tied to the diversity measures mentioned above.
> - **Sensitivity to Customers and Community Outreach.** Allstate's leading position in market share among minorities reflects its commitments to local communities consisting of many ethnic backgrounds. Allstate's director of relationship marketing, Andre Howell, says that learning from customers is the best way to develop products and services that serve their specific needs. Howell works with a team of six to create community outreach programs whose ultimate aim is to capture a larger market share. These programs include financial and expert contributions to ethnic, local and other organizations.
>
> Read more about Allstate's competitive advantage at its corporate Web site at http://www.allstate.com/.
>
> **Source:** Louisa Wah, "Diversity at Allstate: A Competitive Weapon," *Management Review,* July-August 1999, pp. 24–30; Joan Crockett, "Winning Competitive Advantage through a Diverse Workforce," *HRfocus,* May 1999, pp. 9–10.

1. *Individualism versus collectivism.* At one end of the continuum is **individualism,** a mental set in which people see themselves first as individuals and believe that their own interests take priority. **Collectivism,** at the other end of the continuum, is a feeling that the group and society receive top priority. Members of a society that values individualism are more concerned with their careers than with the good of the firm. Members of a society that values collectivism, in contrast, are typically more concerned with the organization than with themselves.

   Highly individualistic cultures include the United States, Canada, Great Britain, Australia, and the Netherlands. Japan, Taiwan, Mexico, Greece, and Hong Kong are among the countries that strongly value collectivism.

2. *Power distance.* The extent to which employees accept the idea that members of an organization have different levels of power is referred to as **power distance.** In a high-power-distance culture, the boss makes many decisions simply because she or he is the boss. Group members readily comply because they have a positive orientation toward authority. In a low-power-distance culture, employees do not readily recognize a power hierarchy. They accept directions only when they think the boss is right or when they feel threat-

EXHIBIT 15-2

The Diversity Index at Allstate

The diversity index at Allstate asks the following questions on employee surveys:

1. To what extent does our company deliver quality services to customers?
2. To what extent are you treated with respect and dignity at work?
3. To what extent does your immediate manager/team leader seek out and utilize diverse backgrounds and perspectives?
4. How often do you observe insensitive behaviors at work, for example, inappropriate comments or jokes?
5. To what extent do you work in an environment of trust?

Source: Courtesy of Allstate Insurance Co.

ened. High-power-distance cultures include France, Spain, Japan, Mexico, and Brazil. Low-power-distance cultures include the United States, Israel, Germany, and Ireland.

3. *Uncertainty avoidance.* People who accept the unknown and tolerate risk and unconventional behavior are said to have low **uncertainty avoidance**. In other words, these people are not afraid to face the unknown. A society ranked high in uncertainty avoidance contains a majority of people who want predictable and certain futures. Low-uncertainty-avoidance cultures include the United States, Canada, Australia, and Singapore. Workers in Israel, Japan, Italy, and Argentina are more motivated to avoid uncertainty in their careers.

4. *Materialism versus concern for others.* In this context, **materialism** refers to an emphasis on assertiveness and the acquisition of money or material objects. It also means a deemphasis on caring for others. At the other end of the continuum is **concern for others,** an emphasis on personal relations and a concern for the welfare of others. Materialistic countries include Japan, Austria, and Italy. The United States is considered to be moderately materialistic (according to Hofstede's research). Scandinavian nations all emphasize caring as a national value.

5. *Long-term orientation versus short-term orientation.* Workers from a culture with a **long-term orientation** maintain a long-range perspective, thus being thrifty and not demanding quick returns on their investments. A **short-term orientation** is characterized by a demand for immediate results and a propensity not to save. Pacific Rim countries are noted for their long-term orientation. In contrast, the cultures of the United Stated and Canada are characterized by a more short-term orientation.

6. *Formality versus informality.* A county that values **formality** attaches considerable importance to tradition, ceremony, social rules, and rank. At the other extreme, **informality** refers to a casual attitude toward tradition, ceremony, social rules, and rank. Workers in Latin American countries highly value formality, such as lavish public receptions and processions. Americans, Canadians, and Scandinavians are much more informal.

7. *Urgent time orientation versus casual time orientation.* Individuals and nations attach different importance to time. People with an **urgent time orientation** perceive time as a scarce resource and tend to be impatient. People with a **casual time orientation** view time as an unlimited and unending resource and tend to be patient. Americans are noted for their urgent time orientation. They frequently impose deadlines and are eager to get started doing business. Asians and Middle Easterners, in contrast, are patient negotiators.

   A paradox about the time orientation dimension is that Chinese get major projects completed quickly despite a casual time orientation. A key part of the ability of Chinese to move projects along so quickly is the value they place on personal relationships. To Chinese managers, a handshake is more important than extensive documentation that has been reviewed and signed off by lawyers.

8. *High-context versus low-context cultures.* Cultures differ in how much importance they attach to the surrounding circumstances, or context, of an event. **High-context cultures** make more extensive use of body language. Some cultures, such as the Asian, Hispanic, and African-American cultures, are high context. In contrast, northern European cultures are **low-context** and make less use of body language. The American culture is considered to be medium-low context. People in low-context cultures seldom take time in business dealings to build relationships and establish trust.

Although the dimensions of cultural values described above are broad national stereotypes, they still relate to meaningful aspects of organizational behavior. A study related the extent of role conflict, role ambiguity, and role overload reported by middle managers from 21 nations to national scores on power distance, individualism, uncertainty avoidance, and materialism. Middle managers from cultures with high power distance and collective attitudes experience less role ambiguity. However, high power distance and collectivism were positively related to role overload. The researchers also found that role stress varies substantially more by country than by demographic or organizational factors.[8]

How might a person use information about cultural differences to enhance interpersonal effectiveness? A starting point would be to recognize that a person's national values might influence his or her behavior. Assume that the managerial worker wanted to establish a good working relationship with a person from a high context culture. To begin, he or she might emphasize body language when communicating with the individual.

Culturally-Based Differences in Management Style

The impact of culture on management and leadership style is another important influence of culture on organizational behavior. Although personality factors are a major contributor to management style, culture is also important because it serves as a guide to acceptable behavior. Culture provides the values that guide behavior. For example, a person raised in a collectivist culture would find it natural to be a consensus style manager/leader. Because management deals so heavily with people, it is part of the society in which it takes place. To be effective, a manager transplanted to a different culture may have to make some concessions to the national stereotype of an effective leader. National stereotypes of management styles, according to the research of Geert Hofstede and his collaborators, are as follows:[9]

1. *Germany:* German managers are expected to be primarily technical experts, or *meisters,* who assign tasks and help solve difficult problems. Like their counterparts in many cultures, top-level German executives can be authoritarian and power-grabbing such as Jürgen Schrempp, the chairman of DaimlerChrysler.
2. *Japan:* Japanese managers rely on group consensus before making a decision, and the group controls individual behavior to a large extent. Japanese managers are perceived as more formal and businesslike, and less talkative and emotional, than their American counterparts. Japanese managers in large, successful firms are more likely to fit the consensus stereotype. Many Japanese managers in family-owned businesses have imperial attitudes and behaviors, and have strong sexist attitudes toward women.
3. *France:* French managers, particularly in major corporations, are part of an elite class (having attended select business schools called Les Grandes Écoles). As a consequence, they behave in a superior, authoritarian manner. The rigid class distinctions of French society also help shape the managers' attitudes and behaviors. Higher-level managers perceive themselves to be superior to managers at lower levels.
4. *The Netherlands:* Dutch managers emphasize quality and consensus, and do not expect to impress group members with their status. Dutch managers give group members ample opportunity to participate in problem solving. Following the tradition of consensus, most problems are resolved through lengthy discussion.

5. *China:* Many managers from China work in Pacific Rim countries such as Taiwan, Hong Kong, Singapore, Malaysia, and the Philippines. In companies managed by Chinese, major decisions are made by one dominant person, quite often people over 65. The Chinese manager maintains a low profile.

MULTICULTURAL MANAGERS AND ORGANIZATIONS

A major message from the study of international and cross-cultural organizational behavior is that managers and their organizations need to respond positively to cultural diversity. Here we look separately at the multicultural manager and the multicultural organization.

Describe what is required for managers and organizations to become multicultural.

The Multicultural Manager

The **multicultural manager** has the skills and attitudes to relate effectively to and motivate people across race, gender, age, social attitudes, and lifestyles. A multicultural manager has the ability to conduct business in a diverse, international environment. Achieving such competence is a combination of many factors, including some of the traits associated with effective leadership described in Chapter 10. A few skills and attitudes are especially relevant for achieving the status of a multicultural manager. A good starting point is to make strides toward becoming bilingual. International business people respect the fact that a managerial worker is bilingual even if the second language is not their primary language. For example, if an American speaks French, the American can relate well to Italians and Spanish people. The tortuous reasoning is that many Italians and Spanish speak French as a *third language,* and respect the American who speaks a little French.

A major requirement for becoming a multicultural manager is to develop **cultural sensitivity,** an awareness of and a willingness to investigate the reasons why people of another culture act as they do.[10] A person with cultural sensitivity will recognize certain nuances in customs that will help build better relationships with people from different cultural backgrounds than his or her own. Exhibit 15-3 provides specific examples of nuances to consider. In addition, the information in Chapter 8 about overcoming cross-cultural communication barriers is directly relevant.

Being able to deal effectively with cultural differences can be a make-or-break factor (or mediating variable) in the success of overseas ventures. An example of this problem took place with the merger of Deutsche Bank (Germany) and Bankers Trust (U.S.A.). Terry Garrison, a professor who specializes in cultural conflict issues, noted:

> German banks have a culture of long-term commitment, especially when they work in a retail banking environment like those at Deutsche Bank. They are having some trouble understanding American investment bankers who think of themselves as "hotshots," who really don't look beyond the deal of the moment.[11]

An effective strategy for becoming a multicultural manager is to simply respect others in the workplace. To respect another culture is to recognize that although the other culture is different, it is equally good. A person from one culture might therefore say, "Eating rattlesnakes for dinner is certainly different from my culture, yet I can see that eating rattlesnakes is as good as eating cows." (Which living organisms constitute palatable food is a major day-by-day cultural difference.) Respect comes from valuing differences. Respecting other people's customs can

EXHIBIT 15-3

Protocol Dos and Don'ts in Several Countries

334

Dorothy Manning, of International Business Protocol, suggests adhering to the following dos and don'ts in the countries indicated. Remember, however, that these suggestions are not absolute rules.

Great Britain

DO say please and thank you often.
DO arrive promptly for dinner.
DON'T ask personal questions because the British protect their privacy.
DON'T gossip about British royalty.

France

DO shake hands when greeting. Only close friends give light, brushing kisses on cheeks.
DO dress more formally than in the United States. Elegant dress is highly valued.
DON'T expect to complete any work during the French two-hour lunch.
DON'T chew gum in a work setting.

Italy

DO write business correspondence in Italian for priority attention.
DO make appointments between 10:00 A.M. and 11:00 A.M. or after 3:00 P.M.
DON'T eat too much pasta, as it is not the main course.
DON'T hand out business cards freely. Italians use them infrequently.

Greece

DO distribute business cards freely so people will know how to spell your name.
DO be prompt even if your hosts are not.
DON'T expect to meet deadlines. A project takes as long as the Greeks think is necessary.
DON'T address people by formal or professional titles. The Greeks want more informality.

Japan

DO present your business cards with both hands and a slight bow as a gesture of respect.
DO present gifts, American made and wrapped.
DON'T knock competitors.
DON'T present the same gift to everyone, unless all members are the same organizational rank.

Sources: *TWA Ambassador* (October 1990): p. 69: *Inc Magazine's Going Global: Japan Inc.* (January 1994).

translate into specific attitudes such as respecting one group member for wearing a yarmulke on Friday or another for wearing an African costume to celebrate Kwanzaa.

A final point for becoming a multicultural manager is to avoid a set of twin dangers. One is **parochialism,** the assumption that the ways of one's culture are the *only* ways of doing things. (An American might say, "Of course, we give merit pay to workers. There is no other way of motivating them.") The other danger is **ethnocentrism,** the assumption that the ways of one's culture are the *best* ways of doing things. ("Merit pay is the most effective method of motivating workers.")[12]

The Multicultural Organization

As more workers in a firm develop multicultural skills, the organization itself can achieve the same skill level. A **multicultural organization** values cultural diversity and is willing to encourage and even capitalize on such diversity. Developing a multicultural organization helps achieve the potential benefits of valuing diversity.

In addition, the multicultural organization helps avoid problems of not managing for diversity such as increased turnover, interpersonal conflict, and communication breakdowns.

An organization passes through developmental stages as it moves from a monocultural organization to a multicultural one, as shown in Exhibit 15-4. At the *monocultural level,* there is implicit or explicit exclusion of racial minorities, women, and other groups underrepresented in powerful positions in society.

The *nondiscriminatory level* is characterized by a sincere desire to eliminate the majority group's unfair advantage. Yet the organization does not significantly change its culture. The organization may strive to ensure that the racial and ethnic mix matches the racial and ethnic mix of society in general or its customer base. The organization may also attempt to influence its climate so it is not a hostile environment for the new members of the workforce. Full compliance with a government-mandated affirmative action program helps an organization reach the nondiscriminatory level.

At the *multicultural level,* the organization is becoming or has become profoundly diverse. The organization reflects the contributions and interests of the diverse cultural and social groups in the organization's mission, operations, products, and services. A pluralism exists when both minority and majority group members are influential in creating behavioral norms, values, and policies. Another characteristic is full structural integration. The term means that that no one is assigned a specific job just because of his or her ethnicity or gender.[13]

The multicultural organization strives to be bias-free, because bias and prejudice create discrimination. Northern Telcom, for example, offers a 16-hour program designed to help employees identify and modify cultural biases and prejudices.

BARRIERS TO GOOD CROSS-CULTURAL RELATIONS

Be more aware of barriers to good cross-cultural relations.

An important part of achieving a multicultural organization and good cross-cultural relations in general is to understand barriers to such harmony. Major barriers of this type are described as follows:[14]

1. *Perceptual expectations.* Achieving good cross-cultural relations is hampered by people's predisposition to discriminate. They do so as a perceptual shortcut, much like stereotyping. Psychologist Diane Halpern explains how the process works: "Even if you have absolutely no prejudice, you are influenced by your expectations. A small woman of color doesn't look like a corporate executive. If you took at heads of corporations, they are tall, slender, white males. They are not fat. They are not in a wheelchair. They are not too old. Anything that doesn't conform to the expectations is a misfit."[15]

   Halpern's perception about all corporate executives being slim and not too old may be a misperception (check out a few annual reports), yet the message is important. Because people are not naturally nondiscriminatory, a firm has to put considerable effort into becoming multicultural.

MONOCULTURAL	NONDISCRIMINATORY	MULTICULTURAL
Exclusion of minorities and women from power	Unfair advantage of majority group removed, but no culture change	Shares power and influence with all; major culture change

EXHIBIT 15-4

Developmental Stages for the Multicultural Organization

2. *Ethnocentrism.* As stated previously, the multicultural manager avoids ethnocentrism. The same attitude impairs intercultural relations in general. Most cultures consider themselves to be the center of the world. One consequence of this attitude is that people from one culture prefer people from other cultures more similar to themselves. English people would therefore have more positive attitudes toward the Scottish than they would toward Brazilians. Despite this generalization, some countries that appear to have similar cultures are intense rivals. Many Japanese and Korean people dislike one another, as do French and Belgians.

3. *Intergroup rather than interpersonal relations.* In *intergroup* relations, we pay attention only to the group membership of the person. In *interpersonal* relations, we pay attention to a person's characteristics. An interpersonal relationship requires more effort because we have to attend to details about the other person. Automobile manufacturers have in recent years developed extensive training programs to help sales representatives develop interpersonal rather than intergroup relations with women buyers. In the past, many sales reps would lose valuable sales prospects because they assumed that women were not the decision makers about an automobile purchase.

4. *Stereotypes in intergroup relations.* As a result of stereotypes, people overestimate the probability that a given member of a group will have an attribute of his or her category. People tend to select information that fits the stereotype and reject inconsistent information. As a consequence, we readily draw conclusions about people from another cultural group without carefully listening and observing. As a Chinese-American woman reports, "I'm tired of people assuming that I like math and science and that I'm good with details. I'm a people person with a creative bent. I actually hate math." (A problem here is that the woman may be excluded from job assignments that fit her true capabilities.)

CROSS-CULTURAL PROCESSES

Explain how motivation, ethics, conflict resolution, and skills needed for negotiation can vary across cultures.

Another approach to understanding international and cross-cultural organizational behavior is to examine similarities and differences in important processes. Four such areas in which cross-cultural differences may surface are motivation, ethics, negotiations, and conflict resolution methods.

Cross-Cultural Motivation

For managers to effectively lead and influence workers from another culture, they must use a motivational approach that fits the culture in question. Motivational concepts apply across cultures providing that the manager has relevant information about two key factors. The manager must know which needs the people are attempting to satisfy and which rewards will satisfy those needs. A case in point is reinforcement theory. All human beings are motivated by rewards, yet which rewards have high valence varies across cultures. An American worker might respond well to individual recognition, while a South Korean worker might respond better to sharing a reward with the group.

Be aware that some scholars are skeptical about the universality of American-based theories of motivation and other aspects of organizational behavior. These researchers conclude that what is true for American workers in the United States usually does not apply to people in other countries.[16]

A study conducted in the Russian Republic of the former Soviet Union illustrates how motivation theory can apply across cultures. Dianne H. B Welsh, Fred Luthans, and Steven M. Sommer selected three motivational theories and accompanying techniques to test in a Russian factory. Extrinsic rewards, behavioral management, and participation were studied because all three approaches have historical roots in Russian human resource management. The study took place in a cotton mill, using 99 male weavers from three different shifts. All the weavers also assisted other weavers but did not occupy formal supervisory roles.

The extrinsic rewards were American goods that the weavers received contingent upon increasing the amount of top grade fabric they produced. The behavioral management intervention consisted of the weavers' supervisors administering recognition and praise for functional behaviors. The participative intervention asked for the workers' input and involved elements of job enrichment.

The extrinsic rewards and behavioral management interventions had a positive impact on the job performance of Russian workers. The participation intervention not only failed to improve performance, it actually contributed to a performance decline. The researchers concluded that American-based motivation theories do apply in Russia, but that participative management is a poor cultural fit.[17]

Cross-Cultural Ethics

Coping with cross-cultural ethical codes challenges many international managers. When faced with an ethical dilemma, should managers abide by ethical codes of their own country or those of the country they are visiting? A recurring ethical dilemma is that in many countries, including Pakistan and Mexico, government officials demand payments to expedite certain transactions. In the United States, direct payments to government officials to win contracts is illegal and unethical. The Foreign Corrupt Practices Act does not outlaw payment to foreign government officials providing such payoffs are part of the country's business practices.

Another cross-cultural difference in ethics is that in the United States, ethical values and behavior are the responsibility of the individual. In Europe and Japan, managers typically make ethical decisions based on the shared values and responsibilities of the organization. Another point of differentiation is that American companies are more likely to have a written code of ethics.[18]

One questionable way in which managers cope with cross-cultural differences in ethics is to outsource to another country work that would be unethical, or illegal, in their own culture. A lethal example is the recycling of automobile and truck batteries. During recycling, acid leaks from these batteries and the fumes are extraordinarily toxic. Several countries, including Australia, contract with small firms in India to recycle these batteries. The small Indian firms take virtually no safety precautions for the workers.

Cross-Cultural Negotiations

As world trade increases, so does the need for negotiating with people from different cultures. Negotiation is one of the single most important skills for the international manager or specialist. A major challenge in skill development is that negotiation styles vary from one culture to another. Managers should negotiate when the value of the exchange and the relationship is important.

Managerial negotiation requires significant adaptation when conducted in a foreign culture. A do-or-die attitude is often self-defeating. A list of suggestions for negotiation abroad follows. Each point includes the American attitude that could be self-defeating and explains how it can be improved.[19]

1. *Use a team approach.* Most American managers are convinced they can handle any negotiation by themselves, while other countries rely on negotiation teams. Bringing several Americans to the negotiating table may convey a seriousness of purpose and commitment.

2. *Do not push for informality.* More than any other national group, Americans value informality and equality in interpersonal relationships. To negotiate successfully, Americans should not persist in using first names. Calling company officials by their first name, however, is becoming more acceptable worldwide. To be safe, ask people how they prefer to be addressed. Americans also need to pay attention to other status indicators such as the organizational rank of foreign negotiators.

3. *Be patient.* A striking difference between American negotiations and those in many foreign cultures concerns time. Japanese, Chinese, and Arab negotiators, for example, are willing to spend many days negotiating a deal. Much of their negotiating activity seems to be ceremonial (including elaborate dining) and unrelated to the task. This often frustrates the "strictly business" American.

4. *Learn to tolerate less than full disclosure of information.* Many Americans believe that "laying one's cards on the table" is a valuable negotiating tactic. As a consequence, they expect honest information and are frustrated when it is not forthcoming. Because many foreign negotiators routinely practice small deceptions at the negotiating table, less than full disclosure must be tolerated.

5. *Accept silence as part of negotiating.* Unlike Asian negotiators, Americans often become uncomfortable when more than 10 seconds elapses without somebody making a task-related comment. It is sometimes fruitful to remain silent and wait for the other side to make an offer or reveal the nature of its thinking.

6. *Take no for an answer sometimes.* American are highly competitive in a negotiating session and take each loss personally. Foreign customers and suppliers, in contrast, are often willing to lose one negotiating session to build a solid long-term relationship among people and firms.

7. *Be adaptable.* Negotiating tactics that are developed for use in Western countries may have to be modified to work effectively in different cultures.

A useful perspective on these suggestions is that a person is rarely on a level playing field when negotiating in another country. Adapting to the other side's negotiating tactics may help to place negotiations on an equal footing. However, Americans should not necessarily be the only group adapting their negotiating tactics to fit different cultures. Business people from around the world may have to develop a cross-cultural negotiating style.

Conflict Resolution Models across Cultures

Current research provides some quantitative evidence that national culture influences which method of conflict resolution a manager chooses. Catherine Tinsley sorted conflict-resolution models into three types: resolving conflict by (a) deferring to status power, (b) applying regulations, and (c) integrating interests. According to her observations, preference for a model, or method, is influenced by culture that filters information and guides members toward a particular model.

The 396 participants in the study were managers from Japanese, German, and American cultures. All participants had been educated by business programs in their culture and were currently working for a company in their culture. Participants completed surveys about resolving conflict over different approaches to solving a business problem.

A major finding was that Japanese, German, and American managers tended to use different models when resolving workplace conflict. Half the variance (reasons for something taking place) in choosing a conflict model could be accounted for by a manager's cultural group membership. Japanese preferred a status power model (using their authority). Germans preferred a regulations model (appealing to rules and regulations), and Americans preferred an interests (win-win) model. Tinsley cautions that these cross-cultural differences may complicate the work life for the expatriate managers who find themselves trying to manage conflict in a foreign cultural system. A particular concern is that American managers may be surprised to learn that colleagues from Japanese and German cultures do not favor the interests model.[20]

DIVERSITY TRAINING AND CULTURAL TRAINING

Appreciate the nature of diversity training and cultural training.

Many training programs have been developed to help employees value diversity and improve cross-cultural relations, especially overseas relations. The type of information presented so far in this chapter is likely to be included in such programs. In this section, we describe a cultural diversity program and one for improving cross-cultural relations.

Diversity Training

Cultural training aims to help workers understand people from another culture. Understanding can lead to dealing more effectively with them as work associates or customers. **Diversity training** has a slightly different purpose. It attempts to bring about workplace harmony by teaching people how to get along better with diverse work associates. Quite often the program is aimed at minimizing open expressions of racism and sexism. All forms of diversity training center around increasing people's awareness of and empathy for people who are different from themselves.

Diversity training sessions focus on the ways that men and women or people of different races reflect different values, attitudes, and cultural backgrounds. These sessions can vary from several hours to several days. Sometimes the program is confrontational, sometimes not. As described by diversity consultant H. Roosevelt Thomas, Jr., the objectives of diversity training include one or more of the following:[21]

- Fostering awareness and acceptance of individual differences
- Helping participants understand their own feelings and attitudes about people who are "different"
- Exploring how differences might be tapped as assets in the workplace
- Enhancing work relations between people who are different from each other

An essential part of relating more effectively to diverse groups is to empathize with their point of view. To help training participants develop empathy, representatives of various groups explain their feelings related to workplace issues. The Skill-Development Exercise on page 340 provides an opportunity to simulate a cultural diversity training program.

340

SKILL-DEVELOPMENT EXERCISE

COLLABORATE

Developing Empathy for Differences

Class members come up to the front of the room one by one and give a brief presentation (perhaps two or three minutes) of any way in which they have been perceived as different and how they felt about this perception. The difference can be of any kind, relating to characteristics such as ethnicity, race, choice of major, physical appearance, height, weight, hair color, or body piercing. After each member of the class has presented (perhaps, also the instructor), class members discuss what they learned from the exercise. It is also important to discuss how this exercise can improve workplace relationships.

Cultural diversity programs have several potential problems. The diversity trainers and participants are sometimes too confrontational and express too much hostility. Companies have found that when employees are too blunt during these sessions, it may be difficult to patch up interpersonal relations in the work group later on. Another concern about diversity training is that it exaggerates stereotypes in order to promote understanding, such as Latinos not starting meetings on time.[22]

In recent years, mentoring of minority group members has been effective in fostering some of the goals of diversity training. Many companies rely on both informal mentoring and formal mentoring (assigning a mentor to a person) as a way to help minorities and women advance in their careers. A survey of successful minority executives indicated that 48 percent of the respondents said they had a role model who guided them toward early career goals. The role model/ mentors were primarily of the same ethnic, racial, or cultural origin. A specific finding was that successful minorities with supportive managers and coworkers have faster compensation growth and progress more rapidly in their firms. A sponsor of the survey said, "Minority executives believe that mentors are very helpful in advocating for upward mobility and teaching them how to navigate through the corporation."[23]

Training in Cross-Cultural Relations

For many years, companies and government agencies have prepared their workers for overseas assignments. The method most frequently chosen is **cultural training,** a set of learning experiences designed to help employees understand the customs, traditions, and beliefs of another culture. In today's diverse business environment, training employees in cross-cultural relations has increased in importance.

A major goal of cultural training, especially for workers on overseas assignments, is to help them avoid **culture shock.** The condition refers to a group of physical and psychological symptoms that can develop when a person is abruptly placed in a foreign culture. Among the symptoms are excessive hand washing and concern for sanitation, fear of physical contact with others, fear of being mugged, and strong feelings of homesickness.[24] A partial explanation for culture shock is that when placed in an unfamiliar environment, and when people behave in ways we do not understand, we feel out of control. Culture shock is a major contributor to the high failure rate of overseas assignments.

Learning a foreign language is often part of cultural training, yet it can also be a separate activity. Knowledge of a second language is important because it builds better connections with people from other cultures than does relying on a translator.

Many workers, aside from international business specialists, also choose to develop skills in a target language. Speaking another language can help build rapport with customers and employees who speak that language.

Cultural training can be used to improve effectiveness in one's own country as well as overseas. For example, the home-building and real estate industries use cultural training. Selected workers in these industries are learning the Asian culture. Such training does not necessarily involve taking a crash course in Chinese or Japanese. Instead, it means the workers have been learning about subtle cultural differences between Eastern and Western people.

Builders and real estate agents hire cultural diversity specialists to help them learn how to communicate and accommodate their customers from China, Japan, Taiwan, Korea, Vietnam, and the Philippines. Home builders and real estate agents receive cultural training in such issues as:[25]

- Negotiating styles
- Money matters in terms of who is the decision maker in the Asian family
- Use of body language, such as eye contact
- Business etiquette
- Design preferences in a home, such as *feng shui*. (The term refers to the ancient Chinese philosophy of creating a harmonious home and work environment leading to good fortune and prosperity for the inhabitants. Other Asian cultures and many Westerners now embrace *feng shui* principles.)

IMPLICATIONS FOR MANAGERIAL PRACTICE

1. As a manager or cultural diversity specialist, it is important to keep selling the idea that diversity initiatives do not regard white males as the enemy. In contrast, diversity is meant to be inclusive. Many white males are concerned that diversity initiatives are a form of reverse discrimination and that they are accused of being "advantaged" because of their skin color.[26]

2. Diversity training contributes to multiculturalism, especially when conducted by insightful and experienced consultants. Guard against, however, diversity training that is needlessly confrontational and mean-spirited. The Federal Aviation Administration is one organization that found cultural diversity training to be dysfunctional. During role reversal exercises, women were encouraged to sexually harass males in physical ways. In other exercises, whites and African Americans were encouraged to engage in heated exchanges. Such activities led to hard feelings and lawsuits.

3. A managerial success factor is to become multicultural in terms of conducting business effectively with people from different cultures. The demand for multicultural managers continues to increase despite some disenchantment with the success of overseas business in recent years.

4. To perform well in many positions in the modern world, it may be necessary for you to develop a *global mind-set,* a feeling of comfort and confidence in dealing with workers from diverse countries. Developing a global mind-set requires perspective, a sincere interest in another country, and a sense of humor to recover from obvious slips.[27] Similarly, second-language proficiency is becoming a key success factor in the global workplace.

SUMMARY OF KEY POINTS

 Understand the scope, competitive advantages, and success factors associated with cultural diversity.

The true meaning of valuing diversity is to respect a wide range of cultural and individual differences. To be diverse is to be different in some measurable, though not necessarily visible, way. Encouraging cultural diversity within an organization is socially responsible and also offers these potential advantages: increased sales and profits; cost reduction associated with turnover and lawsuits; better employee recruitment; better ideas for publicity and advertising; and creativity.

Five factors associated with successful diversity initiatives are: CEO initiation and support; a variety of human resource initiatives; widespread communication about diversity programs; a corporate philosophy favoring diversity; and including diversity in measures of company success.

 Identify and explain key dimensions of cultural differences.

Eight values particularly helpful in understanding how national cultures differ are as follows: individualism versus collectivism; power distance (respect for hierarchy); uncertainty avoidance; materialism versus concern for others; long-term versus short-term orientation; formality versus informality; urgent time orientation versus casual time orientation; and high-context versus low-context realities.

The impact of culture on management and leadership style is another important influence of culture on organizational behavior. Culture serves as a guide to acceptable behavior. For example, a person raised in a collectivist culture would find it natural to be a consensus-style manager/leader. Also, French managers tend to be highly authoritarian.

 Describe what is required for managers and organizations to become multicultural.

Multicultural managers have the skills and attitudes to relate effectively to and motivate people across race, gender, social attitudes, and lifestyles. Multiculturalism is enhanced by bilingualism, cultural sensitivity, and an absence of parochialism and ethnocentrism.

A multicultural organization values cultural diversity and is willing to encourage and even capitalize upon such diversity. The developmental stages of such an organization are monocultural, nondiscriminatory, and multicultural.

 Be more aware of barriers to good cross-cultural relations.

Barriers to the good cross-cultural relations required of a multicultural organization include perceptual expectations that lead to discriminatory stereotypes and ethnocentrism, and intergroup (based on group differences) versus interpersonal (based on individual differences) relations.

 Explain how motivation, ethics, conflict resolution, and skills needed for negotiation can vary across cultures.

Certain motivational approaches can apply cross-culturally. For example, extrinsic rewards and behavior management techniques were found to be effective with Russian factory workers. Coping with cross-cultural ethical codes challenges many international managers. A major issue is whether to abide by the home ethical codes or those of the foreign company and country.

Managers need good negotiating skills to achieve their objectives in international business. Americans must adapt their traditional negotiating tactics to fit other cultures. For example, people from other cultures may want to work more slowly than Americans on reaching agreement. When working in other countries, managers must be sensitive to differences in the preferred model of resolving conflict. One study showed that Japanese managers prefer a status power model of conflict resolution, Germans preferred to appeal to rules and regulations, and Americans preferred an interests model.

 Appreciate the nature of diversity training and cultural training.

Diversity training attempts to bring about workplace harmony by teaching people how to get along better with diverse work associates. Cultural training is helpful in overcoming culture shock and contributing to better relations with various groups at home. Learning a foreign language is often part of cultural training, yet it can also be a separate activity.

342

KEY TERMS AND PHRASES

Individualism, *330*

A mental set in which people see themselves first as individuals and believe that their own interests take priority.

Collectivism, *330*

A value emphasizing that the group and society receive top priority.

Power Distance, *330*

The extent to which employees accept the idea that members of an organization have different levels of power.

Uncertainty Avoidance, *331*

The extent to which people accept the unknown and tolerate risk and unconventional behavior.

Materialism, *331*

An emphasis on assertiveness and the acquisition of money and material objects. Usually measured along a continuum, with concern for others at the opposite end.

Concern for Others, *331*

An emphasis on personal relations and a concern for the welfare of others. Usually measured along a continuum, with materialism at the opposite end.

Long-term Orientation, *331*

In describing national culture, taking a long-range perspective.

Short-term Orientation, *331*

In describing a national culture, a demand for immediate results.

Formality, *331*

Attaching considerable importance to tradition, ceremony, social rules, and rank.

Informality, *331*

A casual attitude toward tradition, ceremony, social rules, and rank.

Urgent Time Orientation, *331*

The perception of time as a scarce resource, therefore leading to impatience.

Casual Time Orientation, *331*

The perception of time as an unlimited and unending resource, leading to patience.

High-context Culture, *331*

A culture that makes more extensive use of body language.

Low-context Culture, *331*

A culture that makes less use of body language.

Multicultural Manager, *333*

A manager with the skills and attitudes to relate effectively to and motivate people across race, gender, age, social attitudes, and lifestyles, and to conduct business in a diverse, international environment.

Cultural Sensitivity, *333*

An awareness of and a willingness to investigate the reasons why people of another culture act as they do.

Parochialism, *334*

The assumption that the ways of one's culture are the only way of doing things.

Ethnocentrism, *334*

The assumption that the ways of one's culture are the *best* ways of doing things.

Multicultural Organization, *334*

An organization that values cultural diversity and is willing to encourage and even capitalize on such diversity.

Diversity Training, *339*

Training that attempts to bring about workplace harmony by teaching people how to get along better with diverse work associates.

Cultural Training, *340*

Training that attempts to help workers understand people from another culture.

Culture Shock, *340*

A group of physical and psychological symptoms that can develop when a person is abruptly placed in a foreign culture.

DISCUSSION QUESTIONS AND ACTIVITIES

1. What steps can you take to better prepare yourself to become a multicultural manager?

2. What hints can you find in an organization's annual report about whether the organization is culturally diverse?

3. Diversity specialists argue that a firm's employee mix (or base) should match its customer mix. Assume you are the general manager of a nursing home or a retirement village. Explain whether your employee base (or mix) should match your client base.

4. If you knew that group members all had "low uncertainty avoidance," how would this information help you do a better job as a manager?

5. **COLLABORATE** In recent years, several employees who have changed sexes (transsexuals) have complained about severe discrimination by their employer after they

return to work with their sex change completed. Working alone or in a group, develop a policy for a large company to deal with the rights of employee transsexuals.

6. What is your evaluation of the ethics of countries sending their "dirty work" to countries that have more liberal laws on issues of worker safety?

7. A criticism made of cultural training and diversity training is that they usually emphasize Americans adjusting to other cultures rather than the reverse. Where do you stand on this issue?

ORGANIZATIONAL BEHAVIOR ON-LINE

TO DO
Developing Your Multicultural Skills through the Internet
A useful way of developing skills in a second language and learning more about another culture is to create a bookmark, or favorite, written in your target language. In this way, each time you go the Internet on your own computer, your cover page will contain fresh information in the language you want to develop.

To get started, use a search engine like Yahoo! or Excite that offers choices in several languages. Enter a key word like "newspaper" or "current events" in the search probe. Once you find a suitable choice, enter the edit function for "Favorites" or "Bookmarks" and insert that newspaper as your cover page. For example, imagine that French was your choice. The Yahoo! France search engine might have brought you to www.france2.fr. This Web site keeps you abreast of French and international news, sports, and cultural events—

written in French. Now every time you access the Internet, you can spend five minutes becoming multicultural. You can save a lot of travel costs and time using the Internet to help you become multicultural.

TO BOOKMARK
Cultural Diversity
http://www.DiversityInc.com

Cultural Diversity—What Managers Need to Know
http://www.Katzassoc.com

Mentoring
http://www.mentoringgroup.com

International Organizational Behavior
http://www.ciber.bus.msu.edu

CASE PROBLEM: The Domestic Partner Benefit Controversy

Giantcom, a telecommunications company, announced that it will offer employees $1,500 per year to purchase health-care insurance for domestic partners, including those of the same sex. By extending limited benefits to domestic partners, Giantcom joined ranks with about 100 other private employers in the United States. According to the International Foundation of Employee Benefit Plans, these 100 companies offer some form of benefits to same-sex couples or unmarried heterosexual partners.

The same study found that dozens of colleges, governments, and unions offer some benefits to domestic partners. In addition, some U.S. firms offer full health-care benefits to domestic partners. Among them are Apple Computer, Ben & Jerry's, Levi Strauss, and Lotus Development Corp. Also, in 2001, Coca-Cola, Co. extended health insurance benefits to the same-sex domestic partners of its U.S. employees, and the benefits may become worldwide. President Jack Stahl said, "Coca-Cola is committed to attracting and retaining the most diverse workforce in the world."[28]

A spokesperson for a caucus group for homosexuals at Giantcom, and in the community, said, "We think it's a major step in the journey to eventual inclusion in equality. Giantcom

is saying that they want to help us satisfy the need for medical coverage. This is a recognition of our families and our needs."

Six business days after the announcement, an electronic message was sent to the company chairman/CEO and to the vice president of human resources. A copy was sent to a companywide distribution list. The message read as follows:

We as a group are tolerant of our fellow employees who are gay and lesbian. We are also tolerant of people of the opposite sex who live together without the benefit of marriage. They have a right to their lifestyle, as we do to ours. What we cannot accept, however, is using company money to subsidize immoral lifestyles that are leading to the breakdown of families worldwide. If this benefit money were not given to "domestic partners" it could be used for benefits to promote healthy lifestyles such as extended dental benefits for the families of married employees.

Signed,

The Giantcom Employee Group for Morality and Common Sense

After receiving this message, the chairman/CEO said he wanted to meet immediately with the vice president of human resources to decide on a course of action.

Case Questions

1. How should top management respond to this message?
2. What can top management do to change the attitudes of the dissenting employee group?

3. How does the new benefit plan support a strategy of multiculturalism?

To find out more about health insurance benefits for domestic partners, visit http://www.insure.com/health/domestic/html.

SUGGESTED READINGS

Dass, Parshotam, and Parker, Barbara. "Strategies for Managing Human Resource Diversity: From Resistance to Learning." *Academy of Management Executive,* May 1999, pp. 68–80.

Gentile, Mary C., ed. *Differences that Work: Organizational Excellence through Diversity.* Prospect Heights, IL: Waveland Press, 1999.

Halcrow, Allan. "Expats: The Squandered Resource." *Workforce,* April 1999, pp. 42–48.

Leonard, Bill. "Linking Diversity Initiatives: A High-tech Network in Seattle is Causing a Positive Chain Reaction." *HRMagazine,* June 1999, pp. 60–64.

Minehan, Maureen. "Worldwide Progress on Removing Gender Barriers." *HRMagazine,* May 1998, p. 168.

Petrick, Joseph A., Scherer, Robert F., Brodzinski, James D., Quinn, John F., and Ainina, M. Fall. "Global Leadership Skills and Reputa-tional Capital: Intangible Resources for Sustainable Competitive Advantage." *Academy of Management Executive,* February 1999, pp. 58–69.

Robinson, Edward, and Hickman, Jonathan. "The Diversity Elite." *Fortune,* July 19, 1999, pp. 62–70.

Rosner, Bob. "How Do You Diversify a Workforce?" *Workforce,* March 1999, p. 18–19.

Simons, Tony, Pelled, Lisa Hope, and Smith, Ken A. "Making Use of Difference: Diversity, Debate, and Decision Comprehensiveness in Top Management Teams." *Academy of Management Journal,* December 1999, pp. 662–673.

Sunoo, Brenda Palk. "Around the World in HR Ways." *Workforce,* March, 2000, pp. 54–58.

ENDNOTES

1. Joan Crockett, "Winning Competitive Advantage through a Diverse Workforce," *HRfocus,* May 1999, p. 9.

2. Orlando C. Richard, "Racial Diversity, Business Strategy, and Firm Performance: A Resource-Based View," *Academy of Management Journal,* April 2000, pp. 164–177; Crockett, "Winning Competitive Advantage," *HRfocus,* pp. 9–10; Taylor H. Cox and Stacy Blake, "Managing Cultural Diversity: Implications for Organizational Competitiveness," *Academy of Management Executive,* August 1991, pp. 45–56.

3. Richard, "Racial Diversity," pp. 164–177.

4. "Jackson Tells GM Diversity Equals Profits," The Associated Press, June 7, 2000.

5. Rosabeth Moss Kanter, *The Change Masters* (New York: Simon and Schuster, 1983).

6. Jacqueline A. Gilbert and John M. Ivancevich, "Valuing Diversity: A Tale of Two Organizations," *Academy of Management Executive,* February 2000, pp. 93–105.

7. Geert Hostede, *Culture's Consequences: International Differences in Work-Related Values* (Beverly Hills, CA: Sage, 1980); updated and expanded in "A Conversation with Geert Hofstede," *Organizational Dynamics* (Spring 1993), pp. 53–61; Jim Kennedy and Anna Everest, "Put Diversity in Context," *Personnel Journal,* September 1991, pp. 50–54.

8. Mark F. Peterson et al, "Role Conflict, Ambiguity, and Overload: A 21-Nation Study," *Academy of Management Journal,* April 1995, pp. 429–452.

9. Geert Hofstede, "Cultural Constraints in Management Theories," *Academy of Management Executive,* February 1993, pp. 81–94; Hofstede, "The Universal and the Specific in 21st-Century Global Management," *Organizational Dynamics,* Summer 1999, pp. 35–41.

10. Arvand V. Phatak, *International Dimensions of Management* (Boston: Kent, 1983), p. 167.

11. Andrew Rosenbaum, "Testing Cultural Waters," *Management Review,* July–August 1999, p. 41.

12. Harry C. Triandis, *Culture and Social Behavior* (New York: McGraw-Hill, 1994), pp. 249-259.

13. The model in Exhibit 15-4 is an integration of Badi G. Foster, Gerald Jackson, William E. Cross, Bailey Jackson, and Rita Hardiman, "Workforce Diversity and Business," *Training and Development Journal,* April 1988, pp. 39–40, and Taylor Cox, "The Multicultural Organization," *Academy of Management Executive,* May 1991, pp. 34–47.

14. Triandis, *Culture and Social Behavior,* pp. 249–259.

15. Quoted in "Discrimination is Brain's Way," *Los Angeles Times* story, May 7, 1995.

16. Nancy J. Adler, *International Dimensions of Organizational Behavior,* 2nd ed. (Boston: PWS-Kent, 1991), p. 160.

17. Dianne H. B. Welsch, Fred Luthans, and Steven S. Sommer, "Managing Russian Factory Workers: The Impact of U.S.-based Behavioral and Participative Techniques," *Academy of Management Journal,* February 1993, pp. 58–79.

18. David Vogel, "Is U.S. Business Obsessed with Ethics?" *Across the Board,* November–December 1993, pp. 58–79.

19. John L. Graham and Roy A. Herberger, Jr., "Negotiators Abroad— Don't Shoot from the Hip," *Harvard Business Review,* July–August 1983, p. 167.

20. Catherine Tinsley, "Models of Conflict Resolution in Japanese, German, and American Cultures," *Journal of Applied Psychology,* April 1998, pp. 316–323.

21. R. Roosevelt Thomas, Jr., *Beyond Race and Gender: Unleashing the Power of Your Total Work Force by Managing Diversity* (New York: AMACOM, 1991), p. 25.

22. Gillian Flynn, "The Harsh Reality of Diversity Programs," *Workforce,* December 1998, p. 27.

23. Jerry Langdon, "Minority Executives Benefit from Mentors," Gannett News Service, December 7, 1998. See also Letty C. Hardy, "Mentoring: A Long-term Approach to Diversity," *HRfocus,* July 1998, p. S11.

24. Triandis, *Culture and Social Behavior,* p. 263.

25. Marcia Forsberg, "Cultural Training Improves Relations with Asian Clients," *Personnel Journal,* May 1993, pp. 79–89.

26. Gillian Flynn, "White Males See Diversity's Other Side," *Workforce,* February 1999, pp. 52–55.

27. Mildred L. Culp, "New Mentality Compels Business Effectiveness. . .Global Mind-Set: Don't Leave Home without It," *WorkWise*®, December 6, 1998.

28. "Coca-Cola Extends Benefits to Gays," Rochester, New York *Democrat and Chronicle,* June 23, 2000, p. 11D.

360-degree Survey A formal evaluation of superiors based on input from people who work for and with them, sometimes including customers and suppliers.

Action Learning Learning that occurs while working on real problems, involving the acquisition of new skills, tools, and concepts.

Active Listening Listening for full meaning without making premature judgments or interpretations.

Affinity Group An employee-involvement group composed of professional-level (or knowledge) workers.

Alternative Workplace A combination of nontraditional work practices, settings, and locations, including working from a small satellite office, sharing offices or cubicles, or working from home.

Attitude A predisposition to respond that exerts an influence on a person's response to a person, a thing, an idea, or a situation.

Attribution Theory The process by which people ascribe causes to the behavior they perceive.

A-Type Conflict Conflict that focuses on personalized, individually oriented issues.

Avoidance Motivation (or Avoidance Learning) Rewarding by taking away an uncomfortable consequence.

Behavioral Approach to Leadership An attempt to specify how the behavior of effective leaders differs from their less-effective counterparts.

Behavioral Approach to Management The belief that specific attention to the workers' needs creates greater satisfaction and productivity.

Behavioral Decision Model An approach to decision making that views managers as having cognitive limitations and acting only in terms of what they perceive in a given situation.

Bounded Rationality The idea that people's limited mental abilities, combined with external influences over which they have little or no control, prevent them from making entirely rational decisions.

Bureaucracy A rational, systematic, and precise form of organization in which rules, regulations, and techniques of control are precisely defined.

Burnout A pattern of emotional, physical, and mental exhaustion in response to chronic job stressors.

Casual Time Orientation The perception of time as an unlimited and unending resource, leading to patience.

Centralization The extent to which executives delegate authority to lower organizational units.

Charisma The ability to lead others based on personal charm, magnetism, inspiration, and emotion.

Classical Decision Model An approach to decision making that views the manager's environment as certain and stable and the manager as rational.

Coercive Power Controlling others through fear of punishment or the threat of punishment.

Cognitive Dissonance The situation in which the pieces of knowledge, information, attitudes, or beliefs held by an individual are contradictory.

Cognitive Learning Theory A theory emphasizing that learning takes place in a complicated manner involving much more than acquiring habits and small skills.

Cognitive Skills Mental ability and knowledge.

Cognitive Style The mental processes used to perceive and make judgments from information.

Collectivism A value emphasizing that the group and society receive top priority.

Communication (or Information) Overload A situation that occurs when people are so overloaded with information that they cannot respond effectively to messages, resulting in stress.

Glossary

Complexity The number of different job titles and units within an organization.

Concern for Others An emphasis on personal relations and a concern for the welfare of others. Usually measured along a continuum, with materialism at the opposite end.

Conflict The opposition of persons or forces that gives rise to some tension.

Conflict Frame The lens through which disputants view a conflict situation.

Confrontation and Problem Solving A method of identifying the true source of conflict and resolving it systematically.

Consideration The degree to which the leader creates an environment of emotional support, warmth, friendliness, and trust.

Contingency Approach to Management The viewpoint that there is no one best way to manage people or work but that the best way depends on certain situational factors.

Contingency Theory of Leadership The position that the best style of leadership depends on factors relating to group members and the work setting.

Coupling The extent to which the parts of an organization are interdependent.

Creativity The process of developing good ideas that can be put into action.

Cross-functional Team A work group, composed of workers with different specialties but from about the same organizational level, who come together to accomplish a task.

C-Type Conflict Conflict that focuses on substantive, issue-related differences.

Cultural Sensitivity An awareness of and a willingness to investigate the reasons why people of another culture act as they do.

Cultural Training Training that attempts to help workers understand people from another culture.

Culture Shock A group of physical and psychological symptoms that can develop when a person is abruptly placed in a foreign culture.

Customer Departmentalization An organizational structure based on customer needs.

Cybernetic Theory of Stress, Coping, and Well-Being in Organizations The view that stress is a discrepancy between an employee's perceived state and desired state.

Decision The act of choosing among two or more alternatives in order to solve a problem.

Decision Criteria The standards of judgment used to evaluate alternatives.

Delphi Technique A group decision-making technique designed to provide group members with one another's ideas and feedback, while avoiding some of the problems associated with interacting groups.

Demographic diversity Differences in background factors about the workforce that help shape worker attitudes and behavior.

Departmentalization The process of subdividing work into departments.

Disability A physical or mental condition that substantially limits an individual's major life activities.

Disruptive Technology A new technology or start-up that blindsides a large successful company.

Diversity Training Training that attempts to bring about workplace harmony by teaching people how to get along better with diverse work associates.

Double-loop Learning A change in behavior that occurs when people use feedback to confront the validity of the goal or the values implicit in the situation.

Downsizing The laying off of workers to reduce costs and increase efficiency.

Dysfunctional Conflict A situation that occurs when a dispute or disagreement harms the organization.

Emotional Intelligence Qualities such as understanding one's own feelings, empathy for others, and the regulation of emotion to enhance living.

Emotional Labor A contributor to stress and burnout, emotional labor is having to modify and fake emotions and facial expressions when dealing with customers.

Empowerment The process of sharing power with group members, thereby enhancing their feelings of self-efficacy.

Equity Theory The motivation theory that employee satisfaction and motivation depend on how fairly the employees believe that they are treated in comparison to peers.

Ethics An individual's beliefs about what is right and wrong or good and bad.

Ethnocentrism The assumption that the ways of one's culture are the best ways of doing things.

Expectancy A person's subjective estimate of the probability that a given level of performance will occur.

Expectancy Theory The theory that motivation results from deliberate choices to engage in activities in order to achieve worthwhile outcomes.

Experience of Flow Being in the zone; total absorption in one's work.

Expert Power The ability to influence others because of one's specialized knowledge, skills, or abilities.

Extinction The weakening or decreasing of the frequency of undesirable behavior by removing the reward for such behavior.

Feedback Information about how well someone is doing in achieving goals. Also, messages sent back from the receiver to the sender of information.

Feeling-type Individual A type of person who in evaluating information has the need to conform and adapt to others.

Filtering The coloring and altering of information to make it more acceptable to the receiver.

Flat Organization Structure An organization structure with relatively few layers.

Force-field Theory The theory contending that an organization simultaneously faces forces for change (the driving forces) and forces for maintaining the status quo (the restraining forces).

Formal Communication Channels The official pathways for sending information inside and outside an organization.

Formal Group A group deliberately formed by the organization to accomplish specific tasks and achieve goals.

Formal Organization Structure An official statement of reporting relationships, rules, and regulations.

Formality Attaching considerable importance to tradition, ceremony, social rules, and rank.

Formalization The degree to which expectations regarding the methods of work are specified, committed to writing, and enforced.

Frame of Reference A perspective and vantage point based on past experience.

Functional Conflict A situation that occurs when the interests of the organization are served as a result of a dispute or disagreement.

Functional Departmentalization The grouping of people according to their expertise.

***g* (general) factor** A major component of intelligence that contributes to problem-solving ability.

Gainsharing A formal program of allowing employees to participate financially in the productivity gains they have achieved.

Goal What a person is trying to accomplish.

Grapevine The major informal communication channel in organizations.

Group A collection of people who interact with one another, are working toward some common purpose, and perceive themselves to be a group.

Group Polarization A situation in which postdiscussion attitudes tend to be more extreme than prediscussion attitudes.

Groupthink A deterioration of mental efficiency, reality testing, and moral judgment in the interest of group cohesiveness.

Growth Curve Model A model that traces the inevitability of change through a firm's life cycle.

Hawthorne Effect The tendency of people to behave differently when they receive attention because they respond to the demands of the situation.

Heuristics Simplified strategies that become rules of thumb in decision making.

High-context Culture A culture that makes more extensive use of body language.

Horizontal Structure The arrangement of work by teams that are responsible for accomplishing a process.

Human Relations Movement An approach to dealing with workers based on the belief that there is an important link among managerial practices, morale, and productivity.

Hybrid (or Mixed) Organization Structure An organization structure that combines two or more types of organization forms into one structure.

Individual differences Variations in how people respond to the same situation based on personal characteristics.

Individualism A mental set in which people see themselves first as individuals and believe that their own interests take priority.

Informal Communication Channels The unofficial network of channels that supplements the formal channels.

Informal Group A group that emerges over time through the interaction of workers, typically to satisfy a social or recreational purpose.

Informal Learning A planned learning that occurs in a setting without a formal classroom, lesson plan, instructor, or examination.

Informal Organization Structure A set of unofficial working relationships that emerges to take care of the events and transactions not covered by the formal structure.

Informality A casual attitude toward tradition, ceremony, social rules, and rank.

Initiating Structure The degree to which a leader establishes structure for group members.

Instrumentality The individual's subjective estimate of the probability that performance will lead to certain outcomes.

Intelligence The capacity to acquire and apply knowledge, including solving problems.

Intrinsic Motivation A person's beliefs about the extent to which an activity can satisfy his or her needs for competence and self-determination.

Intuition An experience-based way of knowing or reasoning in which weighing and balancing evidence are done automatically.

Intuitive-type Individual A type of person whose style of gathering information is based on a preference for the overall perspective, or the big picture.

Job Characteristics Model A method of job design that focuses on the task and interpersonal demands of a job.

Job Demands-Job Control Model An explanation of job stress contending that workers experience the most stress when the demands of the job are high yet they have little control over the activity.

Job Enrichment The process of making a job more motivational and satisfying by adding variety, responsibility, and managerial decision making.

Job Satisfaction The amount of pleasure or contentment associated with a job.

Knowledge Management (KM) The systematic sharing of information to achieve advances in innovation, efficiency, and competitive advantage.

Large-Scale Organizational Change The method used to accomplish a major change in the firm's strategy and culture.

Leader-member Exchange Model The model that recognizes that leaders develop unique working relationships with each group member.

Leadership The ability to inspire confidence and support among the people on whose competence and commitment performance depends.

Leadership Grid® A framework for classifying leadership styles that simultaneously examines a leader's concerns for task accomplishment and people.

Leadership Style The relatively consistent pattern of behavior that characterizes a leader.

Learning A relatively permanent change in behavior based on practice or experience.

Learning Organization An organization that is skilled at creating, acquiring, and transferring knowledge and at modifying behavior to reflect new knowledge and insights.

Learning Style A person's particular way of learning, reflecting the fact that people learn best in different ways.

Legitimate Power Power based on one's formal position within the hierarchy of the organization.

Linguistic Style A person's characteristic speaking pattern, involving amount of directness, pacing and pausing, word choice, and the use of jokes, figures of speech, questions, and apologies.

Locus of Control The way in which people look at causation in their lives.

Long-term Orientation In describing national culture, taking a long-range perspective.

Low-context Culture A culture that makes less use of body language.

Machiavellianism A tendency to manipulate others for personal gain.

Machine Bureaucracy An ideal organization that standardizes work processes and is efficient.

Management by Walking Around The process of managers intermingling freely with workers on the shop floor, in the office, and with customers.

Maslow's Hierarchy of Needs A classical theory of motivation that arranges human needs into a pyramid-shaped model with basic physiological needs at the bottom and self-actualization needs at the top.

Materialism An emphasis on assertiveness and the acquisition of money and material objects. Usually measured along a continuum, with concern for others at the opposite end.

Matrix Organization An organization consisting of a project structure imposed on a functional structure.

Mechanistic Organization A primarily hierarchical organization with an emphasis on specialization and control, vertical communication, and heavy reliance on rules, policies, and procedures.

Message A purpose or an idea to be conveyed in a communication event.

Meta-analysis A quantitative or statistical review of the literature on a particular subject; an examination of a range of studies for the purpose of reaching a combined result or best estimate.

Micromanagement Supervising group members too closely and second-guessing their decision.

Mixed Signals Communication breakdown resulting from the sending of different messages about the same topic to different audiences.

Modeling Learning a skill by observing another person performing that skill.

Motivation In a work setting, the process by which behavior is mobilized and sustained in the interest of achieving organizational goals.

Multicultural Manager A manager with the skills and attitudes to relate effectively to and motivate people across race, gender, age, social attitudes, and lifestyles, and to conduct business in a diverse, international environment.

Multicultural Organization An organization that values cultural diversity and is willing to encourage and even capitalize on such diversity.

Multiple Intelligences A theory that proposes that people know and understand the world in distinctly different ways according to the varying degrees to which they possess eight faculties: linguistic, logical-mathematical, musical, spatial, bodily/kinesthetic, intrapersonal, interpersonal, and naturalist.

Need for Achievement The desire to accomplish something difficult for its own sake.

Need for Affiliation The desire to establish and maintain friendly and warm relationships with others.

Need for Power The desire to control other people, to influence their behavior, and to be responsible for them.

Negative Lifestyle Factors A behavior pattern predisposing a person to job stress, including poor exercise and eating habits and heavy consumption of caffeine, alcohol, tobacco, and other drugs.

Network Organization A spherical structure that can rotate self-managing teams and other resources around a common knowledge base.

Network Structure (or Virtual Organization) A temporary association of otherwise independent firms linked by technology to share expenses, employee talents, and access to one another's markets.

Noise Anything that disrupts communication, including the attitude and emotions of the receiver.

Nominal Group Technique (NGT) An approach to developing creative alternatives that requires group members to generate alternative solutions independently.

Nonprogrammed (or Nonroutine) Decision A unique response to a complex problem.

Nonverbal Communication The transmission of messages by means other than words.

Normative Decision Model A contingency viewpoint of leadership that views leadership as a decision-making process in which the leader examines certain situational factors to determine which decision-making style will be most effective.

Open-Door Policy An understanding in which any employee can bring a gripe to the attention of upper-level management without checking with his or her immediate manager.

Operant Conditioning Learning that takes place as a consequence of behavior.

Organic Structure An organization laid out like a network, emphasizing horizontal specialization, extensive use of personal coordination, extensive communication among members, and loose rules, policies, and procedures.

Organigraph A map that provides an overview of a company's functions and the way people organize themselves.

Organization A collection of people working together to achieve a common purpose (or simply a big group).

Organization Development (OD) Any strategy, method, or technique for making organizations more effective by bringing about constructive, planned change.

Organization Structure The arrangement of people and tasks to accomplish organizational goals.

Organizational Behavior The study of human behavior in the workplace, the interaction between people and the organization, and the organization itself.

Organizational Behavior Modification (OB Mod) The application of reinforcement theory for motivating people in work settings.

Organizational Citizenship Behavior Behaviors that express a willingness to work for the good of an organization even without the promise of a specific reward.

Organizational Culture A system of shared values and beliefs that influence worker behavior.

Organizational Design The process of creating a structure that best fits a purpose, strategy, and environment.

Organizational Effectiveness The extent to which an organization is productive and satisfies the demands of its interested parties.

Organizational Politics Informal approaches to gaining power through means other than merit or luck.

Outsource The practice of having work performed by groups outside the organization.

Paradigm A model, framework, viewpoint, or perspective.

Parochialism The assumption that the ways of one's culture are the only way of doing things.

Path-goal Theory of Leadership An explanation of leadership that specifies what the leader must do to achieve high morale and productivity in a given situation.

Perception The various ways in which people interpret things in the outside world and how they act on the basis of these interpretations.

Personality The persistent and enduring behavior patterns of an individual that are expressed in a wide variety of situations.

Personality Clash An antagonistic relationship between two people based on differences in personal attributes, preferences, interests, values, and styles.

Personalized Power The use of power primarily for the sake of personal aggrandizement and gain.

Person-Role Conflict A condition that occurs when the demands made by the organization or a manager clash with the basic values of the individual.

Positive Reinforcement The application of a pleasurable or valued consequence when a person exhibits the desired response.

Power The potential or ability to influence decisions and control resources.

Power Distance The extent to which employees accept the idea that members of an organization have different levels of power.

Problem A discrepancy between the ideal and the real.

Process Consultation An intervention in which the organization development specialist examines the pattern of a work unit's communications.

Procrastinate Delaying to take action without a valid reason.

Product-Service Departmentalization The arrangement of departments according to the products or services they provide.

Professional Bureaucracy An organization that standardizes skills for coordination and is composed of a core of highly trained professionals.

Programmed (or Routine) Decision A standard response to an uncomplicated problem.

Project A temporary group of specialists working together under one manager to accomplish a fixed objective.

Punishment The presentation of an undesirable consequence for a specific behavior.

Racioethnicity A term referring to the variety of racial and ethnic differences.

Readiness The extend to which a group member has the ability and willingness or confidence to accomplish a special task.

Reengineering The radical redesign of work to achieve substantial improvements in performance.

Referent Power The ability to influence others that stems from one's desirable traits and characteristics; it is the basis for charisma.

Reinforcement Theory The contention that behavior is determined by its consequences.

Relaxation Response A general-purpose method of learning to relax by oneself, which includes making oneself quiet and comfortable.

Resource Dependence Perspective The need of the organization for a continuing flow of human resources, money, customers, technological inputs, and material to continue to function.

Reward Power Controlling others through rewards or the promise of rewards.

Role Ambiguity A condition in which the job holder receives confused or poorly defined role expectations.

Role Conflict Having to choose between competing demands or expectations.

s **(special) factors** Components of intelligence that contribute to problem-solving ability.

Satisficing Decision A decision that provides a minimum standard of satisfaction.

Self-determination Theory The idea that people are motivated when they experience a sense of choice in initiating and regulating their actions.

Self-efficacy The feeling of being an effective and competent person with respect to a task.

Self-managed Work Team A formally recognized group of employees responsible for an entire work process or segment that delivers a product or service to an internal or external customer.

Semantics The varying meanings people attach to words.

Sensation-type Individual A type of person whose style of gathering information is based on a preference for routine and order.

Sexual Harassment Unwanted sexually oriented behavior in the workplace that results in discomfort and/or interference with the job.

Shaping Learning through the reinforcement or rewarding of small steps to build to the final or desired behavior.

Short-term Orientation In describing a national culture, a demand for immediate results.

Situational Control The degree to which the leader can control and influence the outcomes of group effort.

Situational Leadership Model The model that matches leadership style to the readiness of group members.

Social Learning The process of observing the behavior of others, recognizing its consequences, and altering behavior as a result.

Social Loafing Freeloading, or shirking individual responsibility when placed in a group setting and removed from individual accountability.

Socialization The process of coming to understand the values, norms, and customs essential for adapting to an organization.

Socialized Power The use of power to achieve constructive ends.

Stock Option A financial incentive that gives the option owner the future right to purchase a certain number of company shares at a specified price, generally the market price of the stock on the day the option is granted.

Strain An adverse impact on employee health and well-being.

Stress The mental and physical condition that results from a perceived threat that cannot be dealt with readily.

Stressor Any force creating the stress reaction.

Subculture A pocket in which the organizational culture differs from that of other pockets and the dominant culture.

Substitutes for Leadership Factors in the work environment that provide guidance and incentives to perform, making the leader's role almost superfluous.

Team A special type of group in which the members have complementary skills and are committed to a common purpose.

Teamwork A situation in which there is understanding and commitment to group goals on the part of all team members.

Telecommuting Working at home and sending output electronically to the office.

Territorial Departmentalization An organizational structure in which those responsible for all the activities of a firm in a given geographic area report to one manager.

Territorial Games Also known as turf wars, territorial games refer to behaviors involving the hoarding of information and other resources.

Thinking-type Individual A type of person who in evaluating information relies on reason and intellect to deal with problems.

Total Quality Management (TQM) A management system for improving performance throughout an organization by maximizing customer satisfaction, making continual improvements, and relying heavily on employee involvement.

Transformational Leader One who helps organizations and people make positive changes in the way they conduct their activities.

Triarchic Theory of Intelligence The theory that intelligence is composed of three different types of intelligence: componential, experiential, and contextual.

Two-factor Theory of Work Motivation Herzberg's theory contending that there are two different sets of job factors. One set can satisfy and motivate people (motivators); the other set can only prevent dissatisfaction (dissatisfiers).

Uncertainty Avoidance The extent to which people accept the unknown and tolerate risk and unconventional behavior.

Urgent Time Orientation The perception of time as a scarce resource, therefore leading to impatience.

Valence The value a person places on a particular outcome.

Value The importance a person attaches to something that serves as a guide to action.

Value Judgment An overall opinion of something based on a quick perception of its merit.

Virtual Team A group that conducts almost all its collaborative work via electronic communication rather than in face-to-face meetings.

Voice-Recognition System An electronic device that can be commanded by human voice.

Wellness Program A formal organization-sponsored activity to help employees stay well and avoid illness.

Win-Win The belief that, after conflict has been resolved, both sides should gain something of value.

Work-Family Conflict Conflict that ensues when the individual has to perform multiple roles: worker, spouse, and, often, parent.

Ability, affecting job satisfaction, 21
Accommodative conflict resolution, 141, 141e
Achievement-oriented leadership, 218, 218e, 219e
Action learning, 309
Active listening, 172–173, 174e, 175. *See also* Listener role
Acxicom Corp., 282
Adjourning stage, 189e, 190
Adler, Nancy J., 99
Adler, Paul S., 260
Affective component of attitude, 49
Affinity groups, 187
Affirmative defense, 136
AFL-CIO, 135
African Americans: high context trait, 331; as managers, 25, 102–103, 244; marketing to, 326, 327, 330
Age, 23, 25, 51e, 326. *See also* Generational differences
Aha! Experience, 75
Alexrod, Richard H., 295
AlliedSignal/Honeywell, 296
Allstate Insurance Co., 326, 328, 329–330
Alphas Development Group, Inc., 24
Alternative workplace, 162–163
Amabile, Teresa M., 79
Amazon.com, 65–66, 79, 260, 291, 312
American Association of Retired Persons, 23
American Can, 15
American culture. *See* U.S. culture
American Express, 102–103
Americans with Disabilities Act (ADA) of 1991, 25, 26
America Online, 234
Analysis paralysis, 72
Analytical intelligence, 28, 28e, 71
Anderson, Paul, 61
Anger, handling employees', 143
Apple Computers, 167, 186, 225, 270, 344
ARC, 39
Architecture, 82, 188, 201, 318. *See also* Environment
Armstrong, Michael, 282
Arthur Anderson, 313
Ashley, Laura, 258

Ashoka: Innovators for the Public, 58
Asians, motivation, 99. *See also individual countries*
Assertiveness, 248
Associated General Contractors, 24
AT&T, 8, 266, 282, 320, 323
Attitudes. *See also* Perception: affecting values, 51; cross-cultural, 325; influencing organizations, 48–50, 282; in Leadership Grid®, 213–214, 215e; self-assessment, 200
Attribution theory, 47–48
A-type conflict, 140
Australian culture, values and ethics, 330, 331, 337
Austrian culture, values, 331
Autonomy, 112, 191, 241
Avoidance learning, 96–97
Avoidance motivation, 96–97
Avoidant style of conflict resolution, 141e, 142
Axelrod, Herbert, 75

Baby boomers, 23, 50–51, 51e, 76
Backstabbing, 246, 250
Badaracco, Joseph L., Jr., 57
Baggio, Rodrigo, 58, 72
Ballmer, Steve, 260
Bankers Trust, 333
BarnesandNoble.com, 312
Baumann, Jim, 164
Behavior, as function of reaction to environment, 20
Behavioral approach to leadership, 211
Behavioral approach to management, 6
Behavioral component of attitude, 49
Behavioral decision model, 67–70
Behaviorism, 96
Behavior modification. *See* Organizational Behavior Modification (OB Mod)
Justin Bell's Viper Driving School, 183
Benchmarking, 312
Bending the frame. *See* Large-scale organizational change
Ben & Jerry's, 344
Berger, Arlene, 24
Bezos, Jeff, 65–66, 79
Big Five personality theory, 30
Bilingual employees, 333, 341

Bing, Stanley, 253
Blair, Tony, 58
Blanchard, Kenneth H., 218
Blatt, Randolph, 107
Blockbuster Video, 85
City of Boca Raton, Florida, Faragher vs., 136
Bodek, Norman, 241
Bolas, Kristi, 151
Border's Book Stores, 80
Boston Group, 156
Bounded rationality, 70–74, 71*e*
Boynton, Richard L., 16
Brainstorming, 81, 111, 187, 195
Branden, Nathaniel, 22
BrandEra.com, 320
Brazilian culture, values, 58, 331
British culture: etiquette, 176*e*, 334*e*; rumors in, 168; values, 330
Broadcast.com, 233
Brooks Brothers, 310
Brown, Pat, 19
Buckman, Bob, 318
Buckman Laboratories, 305, 318
Bureaucracy. *See also* Organization structure: characteristics, 259–260, 259*e*; contributions by, 260; departmentalization, 262–264, 263*e*; hybrid, 264, 264*e*; line versus staff units, 264–265; modifications, 265–268, 265*e*; potential dysfunctions, 262
Bureaucratic orientation scale, 261
Burlington Industries, Inc. vs. Ellerth, 136
Burnout, 146
Bursch, Jeanne, 109
Bush, George W., 227
Butler, Daniel, 114
Butler, Mike, 123
Byrnes, John, 140

Canadian culture, values, 330, 331
Carpal tunnel syndrome, 150
Casual time orientation, 331
Center for Organizational and Leadership Effectiveness, 1
Centralization, 258
Century 21 People Services Realty, 323, 324
Cerent Corp., 226

Challenger role, 190
Chambers, John, 225, 226–227, 239, 278
Change: from challenging status quo, 312; coping with, 115, 296–298; downsizing/restructuring strategy, 287–292; managing organizational, 282–285, 284*e*, 285*e*; organizational development strategy, 292–296, 292*e*, 293*e*; people resisting, 285–287, 286*e*, 288
Charisma, 224, 225*e*, 228, 245
Charismatic leadership, 225, 227
Charles Schwab, 202, 290
Chase Bank of Texas, 87, 89
CheckFree Corp., 291
Check Point Software Technologies, Inc., 71
Chenault, Ken, 102–103
Chief knowledge officers, 316
Child care, as motivation, 87, 88, 92
Chinese culture: home buying, 341; management style, 332; negotiation process, 338; organizational citizenship, 50; values, 332
Christensen, Clayton M., 290
Christian, Rod, 39
Chrysler, 281–282, 315. *See also* Daimler/Benz; DaimlerChrysler
Cisco Systems, 226–227, 239, 278, 281, 290
Citibank, 107
Classical decision model, 67–70
Coca-Cola, Co., 344
Code of conduct, 279. *See also* Organizational culture
Codification strategy, 315–316
Coercive power, 239
Cognitive component of attitude, 49
Cognitive dissonance, 49
Cognitive intelligence, 71*e*, 72
Cognitive learning theory, 43
Cognitive skills, and leadership effectiveness, 209–210
Cognitive style, 33–34, 34*e*
Cohesiveness, groups achieving, 194
Coleman Co., 16
Colgate-Palmolive, 223
Collaborative conflict resolution, 141–142, 141*e*
Collaborative workplace, 185
Collard, John H., 295
Collectivism, 330

Collier, Stephanie, 24

Commitment, 21–22, 230, 314

Committee for the Democratization of Information Technology (CDI), 58

Committees. *See* Cross-functional teams

Common sense, sharpening, 6

Communication. *See also* Information sharing; Interpersonal communication; Knowledge management (KM): bilingual employees, 333, 341; case studies, 159, 277; and change, 286–287, 286*e*, 295; charismatic leaders, 225; in conflict, 140; for diversity success, 328; facilitating group effectiveness, 194; gossip, 240; impacting political behavior, 250; in job enrichment, 111; and social network analysis, 257; team-building vocabulary, 200, 201; of women versus men, 23

Communication overload, 170–171, 170*e*

Communication style, 170*e*, 172, 173–176

Competence, in effective followers, 230

Competition, benefiting from diversity, 325–327, 329–330, 330*e*

Competitive conflict resolution, 141, 141*e*

Competitive intelligence, 315

Complexity, 258

CompuServe, 305

Concern for others, 331

Conflict, 134. *See also* Stress; consequences, 139–143, 139*e*, 141*e*; contributing to bounded rationality, 71*e*, 73; cross-cultural resolution, 338–339; fostering creativity, 80; sources and antecedents, 135–139, 137*e*; in values, 53

Conflict frame, 134–135

Confrontation and problem solving, 142–143

Conger, Jay A., 225

Consensus, in attribution theory, 47

Consensus decision making, 195, 200

Consideration, 211–212, 213*e*, 219

Consistency, in attribution theory, 48

Consultative decision making, 195

Continental Airlines, 295

Contingency approach to management, 9–10

Contingency theories of leadership, 216. *See also* Leadership; Fiedler's, 216–217, 217*e*; normative decision model, 220–223, 222*e*; path-goal, 217–218, 218*e*, 219*e*; situational, 218–220, 220*e*

Cooperation, 134, 194

Corporate spirituality, 280

Cotsakos, Christos, 281

Coupling, 258–259

Courage, in effective followers, 230

Courtesy, 50, 245

Creative intelligence, 28, 28*e*

Creativity, 74; characteristics, 76–79; conditions necessary for, 79–80; conflict influencing, 140; in decision making, 68*e*, 69; enhancing, 80–82, 327; process steps, 74–76, 75*e*; right-brain/left-brain dominance, 71

Credibility, 169–170, 170*e*. *See also* Trust

Crisis, contributing to bounded rationality, 71*e*, 73

Crockett, Joan, 329

Crossan, Mary M., 308

Cross-cultural behavior. *See also* Diversity; International organizational behavior: communication, 174–176, 176*e*; processes, 335–339; values, 328, 330–333

Cross-functional teams, 139, 185, 193

Crown Zellerbach, 15

Crystallized intelligence, 76

CSX Railroad, 140

C-type conflict, 140–141

Cultural diversity. *See also* Cross-cultural behavior; Diversity; International organizational behavior; Race: among managers, 333–334, 334*e*; case studies, 323, 329–330; causing stress, 150; competitive advantage, 325–327, 329–330, 330*e*; and expectancy theory, 99; influencing mergers, 281–282; multicultural organizations, 334–335, 335*e*; scope, 324–325, 326*e*; success factors, 327–328; training, 339–341

Cultural sensitivity, 333

Culture shock, 340

Cummins, Susan, 107

Customer departmentalization, 263–264

Cybernetic theory of stress, coping, and well-being in organizations, 144

Daimler/Benz, 281–282. *See also* Chrysler

DaimlerChrysler, 324. *See also* Chrysler

Dana Corporation, 81

Data collection, 3, 125, 327

Datovech, Jim, 157

Davenport, Tom O., 314

Davis, Dick, 283

Davis, Linda, 151

Day, Dennis, 24

Dayton Hudson, 156–157, 290

Decentralization, 11*e,* 258

Decisions, 66

Decision criteria, 69

Decision making: bounded rationality in, 70–74, 71*e;* classical/behavioral model, 67–70, 68*e;* decentralized, 11*e;* ethical, 54–58; group styles, 195–196, 197*e;* normative decision model, 220–223, 222*e;* risk in, 66–67

Defense Industry Initiative on Business Ethics and Conduct, 61

Defining moments, 57

DeFrank, Richard S., 150

Dell, Michael, 67, 186, 315

Dell Computer, 67, 186, 315

Delphi technique, 196, 197*e*

Democratic decision making, 195

Demographic diversity, 22–26. *See also* Diversity

Denial, distorting perception, 46

Deontological approach, 55

Departmentalization, 262–264, 263*e*

Deutsch, Francine M., 138

Deutsche Bank, 333

Differentiation, 258

DiMonti, Jerry, 323, 324

Directive leadership, 218, 218*e,* 219*e*

Disabilities, 25–26, 39

Discrimination, 326

Disempowerment, 243*e*

Disney, 110

Disruptive technology, 290, 291. *See also* Information technology

Distinctiveness, in attribution theory, 47

Diversity. *See also* Cross-cultural behavior; Cultural diversity; Gender; Generational differences; Race: demographic, 22–26; enhancing creativity, 81–82; and group effectiveness, 193; sampling of ways people differ, 326*e*

Diversity training, 329, 339–340

Domain, 210

Domino's Pizza, 258

Dortch, R. Neil, 164

Double-loop learning, 309

Downsizing: causing conflict, 135, 140; as change strategy, 287–289; creating flat organization structures, 266, 267

Drayton, William, 58

Dual-executive teams, 208, 260

Dunlap, Al, 15–16, 30, 211

Dysfunctional conflict, 139–140

Eastern Air Lines, 210

Eastman Kodak Company, 39, 53, 114

Edwards, Jeffrey R., 144

Einstein, Albert, 19

Electrocomponents, 270

Electronic brainstorming, 187

Ellerth, Burlington Industries, Inc. vs., 136

Ellison, Larry, 208

E-mail, 162, 163, 196, 318. *See also* Information technology; Internet

Embrace-or-demolish strategy, 246–247

Emotional display, 248–249

Emotional intelligence, 34–36. *See also* Intelli-gence; and conflict, 134; contributing to bounded rationality, 71*e,* 72; and leadership effectiveness, 210–211; motivation in, 79

Emotional labor, 149

Empathy, 35, 173

Employee-centered managers, 212–213

Empowerment. *See also* Power: affecting job satisfaction, 21; in building team-work, 200; versus disempowerment, 243*e;* essence of, 240–242, 242*e;* and group effectiveness, 191–192, 193*e,* 196; in transformational leadership, 225*e*

Encouragement, fostering creativity, 80

Engineering New-Record, 24

Environment. *See also* Architecture: affect-ing intelligence, 26–27; in communi-cation process, 160*e,* 161; fostering creativity, 80; influencing behavior, 20; nonverbal communication, 165

Equal Employment Opportunity Commission (EEOC), 25–26, 38, 323
Equality, 23
Equity, 23
Equity theory, 99–100
Ernst & Ernst LLP, 257
Ernst & Young, 316
Esteem needs, 89
Ethics, 53–54. *See also* Values; cross-cultural, 337; in decision making, 55–58; and influence, 250; in learning from others, 312; philosophical basis, 54–55; of political tactics, 244–248; and sexual harassment, 137
Ethnicity. *See* Race; Racioethnicity
Ethnocentrism, 334, 336
E★Trade, 281
Evil charismatics, 225
Exchange, as influence tactic, 248
Excite, 234
Expectancies, 97
Expectancy theory, 97–99, 97*e*
Experience of flow, 79
Experimentation, 3–4, 44, 311. *See also* Risk taking
Expertise, 79, 310–311
Expert power, 239
Extinction, 97
Extrinsic motivation, 101, 103–104
Exxon, 187
Eysenck, Hans J., 26

Face time, 245
Familiarity, facilitating group effectiveness, 193*e*, 194–195
Family conflict. *See* Work-family conflict
Fannin, David, 16
Faragher vs. City of Boca Raton, Florida, 136
Federal Communications Commission (FCC), 54
Feedback, 95; changing organizational culture, 283; cross-cultural, 174; in goal-setting theory, 95, 96; interdependent, 193; in job characteristics model, 112; in job enrichment, 110; measuring diversity success, 329–330, 330*e*; and need for achievement, 92; in

OB Mod, 119; in organization development, 293*e*, 294; as part of recognition, 121; as political tactic, 245; as process step, 160*e*, 161, 170*e*, 172; 360-degree survey, 227–228, 229
Feeling-type individuals, 33–34
Feldman, Barbara J., 163
feng shui, 341
Fiedler, Fred E., 216, 217
Fiedler's contingency theory of leadership, 216–217, 217*e*
Filo, David, 233
Filtering, 169, 170*e*
Financial incentives. *See* Reward and recognition
Fiorina, Carly, 210
First Alert, 16
Flat organization structure, 266–267
Flattery, as political tactic, 245–246, 247
The Fletcher Companies, 199
Flexibility, 297
Fluid intelligence, 76
Focus, in effective followers, 230
Followership, 230
Food Corp., 241
Forced association technique, 79
Force-field theory, 284
Ford Motor Company, 159, 295, 296
Foreign Corrupt Practices Act, 337
Formal communication channels, 166–167, 167*e*
Formal groups, 184
Formality, 331
Formalization, 257–258
Formal organization structure, 257
Formative phase, 284, 284*e*
Forming stage, 189, 189*e*
Forquer, Greg, 85
Fortune, 253
4I framework, 306, 308–309. *See also* Learning organizations
42IS (information systems firm), 152
Frame of reference, 170, 170*e*, 171
French culture: etiquette, 176*e*, 334*e*; management style, 332; values, 331
Friedman, Tricia, 41
Functional conflict, 139–140
Functional departmentalization, 262, 263*e*
Fusaro, Bernadette, 7

Gage, John, 289
Gainsharing, 124–125
Gainsharing Inc., 124
Galloway, Tim, 107
Galusha, Sam, 301
Gardner, Howard, 29
Garrison, Terry, 333
Garvin, David A., 311
Gatekeeper role, 191
Gates, Bill, 260
Gateway Computer, 312
Geitner, Marisa, 39
GenCorp Inc., 85
Gender. *See also* Diversity; Sexual harassment; Women: affecting productivity and job behavior, 23, 26; building equality in, 24; communication differences, 173–174; discrimination based on, 326; and diversity training, 339; influencing organizational culture, 278; leadership differences, 228–229
Gender approach, to sexual harassment, 136
General Electric (GE), 116, 210, 226, 266, 289, 296
General Mills, 260
General Motors, 244, 256, 266, 327
Generational differences. *See also* Diversity: baby boomers, 23, 50–51, 51*e*, 76; causing conflict, 138–139; Generation X, 50–51, 51*e*, 76; Generation Y, 50–51, 51*e*
Genetics, affecting intelligence, 22
GeoCities, 233
George, Judy, 210
Gerhart, Pat, 129
German culture: conflict resolution model, 338–339; management style, 332; nonverbal communication, 175; values, 331
Gerstner, Louis V., Jr., 278, 284
g (general) factor, 27
Gilbert, Jacqueline A., 327
Glaser, Connie, 229
Goal interdependence, 192–193
Goals, 94
Goal setting, 92

Goal-setting theory, 94–96, 95*e*
Goleman, Daniel, 35
Golub, Harvey, 102
Gore, Bob, 198
W.L. Gore & Associates, 198
Gossip, 240. *See also* Rumors
Grandey, Alicia, 149
Grantham, Charles, 7
Grapevine, 167
Great person theory, 209
Greek culture, 330, 334*e*
Group decision making, 195. *See also* Decision making
Group polarization, 197–198
Groups. *See also* Teams: characteristics of effective, 191–195, 193*e*; developmental stages, 189–191, 189*e*, 192; potential problems within, 196–199; problem solving/decision making, 195–196, 197*e*; versus teams, 184; types of, 184–187
Groupthink, 199
Groupware, 187
Growth curve model, 283–284, 284*e*

Half, Robert, 245
Halo effect, 47
Halpern, Diane, 335
Hamel, Gary, 281
Haney, Jerry, 283
Harassment. *See* Sexual harassment
Hard skills, 5
Hawk, Tony, 19
Hawthorne effect, 8, 9
Hawthorne studies, 8–9
Hayes, Erika, 1
Helmsley, Leona, 210
Henderson, Cheryl, 1
Henderson, Postmaster General, 291
Heredity, affecting intelligence, 26–27
Heritage Christian Home, Inc., 39
Hersey, Paul, 218
Hershey, Milton, 282
Hershey Foods Corporation, 282
Herzberg, Frederick, 91, 110
Heterogeneous groups, 81–82
Heuristics, 70
Hewlett-Packard, 151, 210, 290

Hierarchy, 241, 242. *See also* Maslow's hierarchy of needs; Organization structure

High-context cultures, 331

High-impact learning, 312–313

Hirschberg, Jerry, 80

Hispanics. *See also individual countries*: ethnic harassment, 137; marketing to, 326; motivation, 99; values, 331

Historical Perspectives on Organizational Behavior, 15

Hodgson, Alda, 54

Hoenig, Jonathan, 19

Hofstede, Geert, 328, 331, 332

Home Depot, 156–157

Honda of America, 258–259

Honeywell, 61

Hong Kong, cultural values, 330

Horizontal structure, 268–269, 269*e*

Hostile working environment harassment, 136

Hotel Sofitel-Minnesota, 109

Howell, Andre, 330

HR Works, 163

Hubbard, Daniel, 202

Huff, Ron, 166

Human behavior, 6, 7

Human relations movement, 9

Humor, 76, 211, 249

Hybrid organization structure, 264, 264*e*

Hygiene factors, 91–92, 91*e*

IBM, 102–103, 167, 187, 226, 268, 278, 284, 295

IB Your Office, 107

Idea quotas, 81

Imagination Ltd., 185

Impression management, 225, 227, 245, 246

Incentives. *See* Reward and recognition

Indian culture, ethics, 337

Individual differences, 20–22. *See also* Personality

Individualism, 330

Influence, 238. *See also* Organizational Politics; Power; and ethics, 250; in network structure, 270; organizational tactics, 248–249

Informal communication channels, 167–168, 167*e*, 170*e*, 172

Informal groups, 184

Informality, 331, 338

Informal learning, 43–44

Informal organization structure, 257

Information overload, 170–171, 170*e*

Information sharing. *See also* Communication; Knowledge management (KM): contributing to bounded rationality, 71*e*, 72–73; controlled, as political tactic, 245; and empowerment, 241; methods, 316–318; and productivity, 11*e*

Information technology. *See also* E-mail; Internet: Committee for the Democratization of Information Technology, 58; in communication process, 161–165; disruptive, 290, 291; influencing organizational change, 289–290; substituting for leadership, 230, 289

InfoServ, 241

Infospace Inc., 260

Ingratiation, 248

Initiating structure, 211, 213*e*, 218, 219

Innovative thinking, 140, 225*e*, 281, 281*e*. *See also* Risk taking

Inspirational appeal, 248–249

Institutionalizing, in organizational learning, 309

Instrumentality, 98

Integrating, 141, 308

Integrative phase, 284, 284*e*

Integrity, in decision making, 55

Intel, 110

Intellectual abilities, 76, 134

Intelligence. *See also* Emotional intelligence: affecting job performance and behavior, 26–29, 27*e*, 28*e*; competitive, 315; and genetics, 22; influencing job satisfaction, 21; versus intuition, 71; triarchic theory of, 28–29

Interdependence, enhancing group effectiveness, 192–193, 193*e*

Interdependent feedback and rewards, 193

Intergroup relations, 336

International business, 324, 333

International Labor Organization, 144

International organizational behavior. *See also* Cultural diversity: cultural differences, 25; in framework of study, 12, 13*e*; values differences, 328, 330–332

Internet. *See also* E-mail; Information technology; Intranets: advocating, 226–227, 239; commerce, 41, 65; and customer departmentalization, 263–264; learning organizations using, 311; taking business from retailers, 156–157, 328

Interpersonal communication. *See also* Communication; Information sharing; Knowledge management (KM): barriers, 169–173, 170*e,* 174*e*; channels, 166–169, 167*e*; cross-cultural differences, 174–176, 176*e*; gender differences, 173–174; and information technology, 161–165; nonverbal communication, 165–166; power-oriented linguistic style, 176–177; process, 160–161, 160*e*

Interpersonal relations, 336

Interpersonal Skills, 15

Interpreting, in organizational learning, 308

Interrole conflict, 149

Intersender conflict, 149

Interviews, 3, 327

Intranets, 318

Intrasender conflict, 149

Intrinsic motivation, 101, 103–104

Intuition, 71–72, 71*e,* 308

Irish culture, values, 331

Israeli culture, values, 331

Italian culture, values and etiquette, 331, 334*e*

Ivancevich, John M., 150, 327

*i*Village.com, 163

Jackson, Jesse, 327

Jacques, Elliot, 260

Japanese culture: conflict resolution model, 338–339; ethics, 337; etiquette, 176*e,* 334*e*; home buying, 341; management style, 332; negotiation process, 338; rumors in, 168; values, 330, 331

Job characteristics model, 112–113, 112*e*

Job demands–job control model, 147, 149*e*

Job design, 191, 193*e*

Job enrichment, 110–111, 111*e*

Jobs, Steve, 186, 225

Job satisfaction. *See also* Motivation; Reward and recognition: attitudes influencing, 49–50, 50*e*; and demographic diversity, 26; individual differences affecting, 21; measuring group effectiveness, 193*e*; and organizational citizenship behavior, 50; sexual harassment affecting, 137

Johnson, Jennifer, 255

Johnson & Co., 255

Johnson & Johnson, 110

Juliber, Lois, 223

Jung, Carl, 33

Kansas City Area Transportation Authority, 283

Kansas City Harley, 194

Kansas City Star, 283

Kanungo, Rabindra N., 225

Katzenbach, Jon, 115, 184, 185

Kelleher, Herb, 278

Kelleher, Michael D., 140

Kelly, Robert E., 230

Kickul, Jill R., 50

Kimberly-Clark Corporation, 15

Kinko's, 107

C. R. Klewin Northeast, 24

Knowledge, 76, 311

Knowledge contributor role, 190

Knowledge management (KM), 305, 313–316. *See also* Information sharing; Learning organizations

Koch Industries, 291

Koehler, Fern, 283

Koestenbaum, Peter, 213

Komansky, David H., 244

Koogle, Tim, 233–234

Kopp, David, 41

Korean culture, etiquette, 176*e,* 341

Kotter, John, 168, 208

Koulopoulos, Thomas, 314

Kroc, Ray, 71

Kurzu, Laura, 85

Lane, Henry W., 308
Lane, Ray, 208
Large-scale organizational change, 294–295
Latin American culture, values and etiquette, 176e, 331
Laura Ashley stores, 258
Lawson, Phil, 329
Leader-member exchange model, 214–216
Leader-participation model. *See* Normative decision model
Leadership, 208. *See also* Management; accountable for diversity, 330; charismatic, 225, 227, 228; feedback improving, 227–228; gender differences in, 228–229; nature of, 208–209, 209e; self-assessment, 214; substitutes and followership, 229–230, 289; theories of (*see* Contingency theories of leadership); transformational, 223–225, 225e
Leadership Grid®, 213–214, 215e
Leadership style, 211; choosing, 230; differences in, 21, 332–333; self-assessment, 212
Leadership traits: cognitive skills, 209–210; leader-member exchange model, 214–216; Leadership Grid®, 213–214, 215e; personality, 210–211; research, 211–213, 213e; styles and behavior, 211
Leading by example, 248
Learning. *See also* Training: affecting organizational behavior, 42–45; avoidance, 96–97; characteristics and behaviors, 309–313; in job enrichment, 111; social, 100–101
Learning organizations, 306. *See also* Knowledge management (KM); assessing, 307–308; building blocks, 309–313; downsizing affecting, 288; framework, 306, 306e, 308–309
Learning style, 44–45
Least-preferred coworker (LPC) scale, 216
Legitimate power, 239
Leiter, Michael P., 146
Levi Strauss, 82, 323, 344
Lewin, Kurt, 282, 285

Lewis, Chadra, 301
Lidenauer, Alice, 188
Life-change units, 146–147, 147e
Lily Tulip, 15
Lincoln Electric, 124–125
Lincoln Electric Holdings, 267
Line groups, 135, 264–265
Linguistic style, 176–177
Listener role, 190. *See also* Active listening
Locus of control, 48, 147
Long-term orientation, 331
Lorenzo, Frank, 210
Lotus Development Corp., 344
Loughborough, David, 39
Love needs, 89
Low-context cultures, 331
Lucent Technologies, 210, 320
Luckman, Joyce, 129
Luthans, Fred, 120, 337
Lycos, 234

Machiavellianism, 243
Machine bureaucracy, 259
Mallett, Jeff, 234
Management. *See also* Leadership: versus leadership, 208, 209e; multicultural, 333–334, 334e
Management by walking around, 168
Managerial support: for diversity success, 327; favoring knowledge management, 313–314; influencing group effectiveness, 194, 196
Mannes, Tori, 87
Marcus, Richard, 225
Maslach, Christina, 146
Maslow, Abraham M., 88
Maslow's hierarchy of needs, 88–90, 89e
Massage therapy, 152
Mastery orientation, 44
Materialism, 331
Matrix organization, 265–266, 265e
Mausehund, Jean, 164
McClelland's achievement-power-affiliation triad, 92–93
McCoy, Millington F., 5
McDonald's, 69, 71, 278, 311, 327
McGill, Michael E., 224
McGregor, Douglas, 9

Mechanistic organization, 256. *See also* Bureaucracy
Mediator role, 190
Meeker, Mary G., 239
Meierding, Nina, 143
Melia Luxury Pet Products, 85
Mellon Bank, 258
Men. *See* Gender
Mental ability. *See* Intelligence
Mentoring, 340
Mergers, 2, 281–282
Merit pay, 123, 125
Merrill Lynch, 7, 187, 244, 290
Messages: in communication process, 160–161, 160*e*; improving transmission of, 170*e*, 171–173, 174*e*
Meta-analysis, 4
Mexican culture, values and ethics, 330, 331, 337
Meyer, Scherer & Rockcastle, Ltd., 188
University of Michigan, leadership style study, 211–213
Micromanagement, 201, 295
Microsoft, 110, 164, 260, 270
Middle Eastern culture, values and negotiations, 331, 338
Minorities. *See* Race
Mintzberg, Henry, 270
Mirroring, 166
Mixed organization structure, 264, 264*e*
Mixed signals, 170, 170*e*
Mobil, 187
Modeling, 42
Monocultural organizations, 335, 335*e*
Moorhead, Robert, 24
Moran, Charles D., 282
Morgan Stanley Dean Witter, 239
Morrow, Roy, 267
Motivating Potential Score (MPS), 112–113
Motivation, 88. *See also* Job satisfaction; Reward and recognition; affecting creativity, 79; in building teamwork, 200–201; choosing model for, 128–129; cross-cultural, 336–337; as emotional intelligence factor, 35; with financial incentives, 122–126, 122*e*, 124*e*; identifying needs for, 94; intrinsic versus extrinsic, 101, 103–104; job characteristics model, 112–113, 112*e*; job enrichment, 110–111, 111*e*; of

message receivers, 170*e*, 171; organizational behavior modification, 117–121, 118*e*; self-assessment, 90; self-managed work teams, 11*e*, 113–116, 115*e*
Motivation theories: equity, 99–100; expectancy, 97–99, 97*e*; goal-setting, 94–96, 95*e*; Herzberg's two-factor, 91–92, 91*e*, 110; Maslow's hierarchy of needs, 88–90, 89*e*; McClelland's achievement-power-affiliation triad, 92–93; reinforcement, 96–97; self-determination, 101, 103–104; social learning, 100–101, 102–103
Motivator factors, 91–92, 91*e*
Motorola Corp., 296, 309
Mount Bachelor Inc., 129–130
Mulcahy, Anne M., 207
Multicultural managers, 333–334
Multicultural organizations, 334–335, 335*e*
Multiple intelligence, 29
Myers-Briggs Type Indicator, 33–34

Napping, as stress reliever, 152, 153
National Association of Women in Construction, 24
National Center for Construction Education and Research, 24
National Urban League, 323
Need for achievement, 92, 93
Need for affiliation, 93
Need for power, 92–93
Needs theories of motivation, 88–93
Negative lifestyle factors, 147
Negative reinforcement. *See* Avoidance motivation
Negotiations, cross-cultural, 337–338
Neiman Marcus, 81, 225
Nelson, Katherine A., 55
Net Generation (Generation Y), 50. *See also* Generational differences
The Netherlands, values and management style, 330, 332
Network organization, 166
Network structure, 269–270
Neuman, George A., 33, 50
Nierenberg Group, 160
Nissan Design International, 80

Noise, in communication process, 160*e*, 161

Nokia, 278

Nominal group technique (NGT), 195–196

Nondiscriminatory organizations, 335, 335*e*

Nonprogrammed (nonroutine) decisions, 66, 74

Nonverbal communication, 165–166; conveying power, 177; cross-cultural, 175; in messages, 170*e*, 172, 173

Normative decision model, 220–223, 222*e*

Normative phase, 284, 284*e*

Norming stage, 189, 189*e*, 200

Northern Telecom, 335

Northwestern Mutual Life, 185

Nutt, Paul C., 66

OB. *See* Organizational behavior (OB)

OB Mod. *See* Organizational behavior modification (OB Mod)

OD. *See* Organization development (OD)

Office Depot, 107

Office Team, 163

Ohio State University, leadership style study, 211–212, 213

Ollila, Jorma, 278

Olson, Doug, 183

William Olsten Center for Workforce Strategies, 7

Oncale vs. Sundowner Offshore Services Inc., 136

O'Neal, Stanley, 244

Open-door policy, 143, 168

Operant conditioning, 96

Opportunity recognition, 75

Optimism, 72, 148

Oracle Corp., 208, 260

Orfalea, Paul, 107

Organic structure, 256

Organigraphs, 270–271, 271*e*

Organizations, 256

Organizational behavior modification (OB Mod): application rules, 119–121; steps, 117–119, 118*e*

Organizational behavior (OB), 2, 4; history, 6, 8–10; meaning and research methods, 2–4; productivity advantage, 10, 11*e*; skill development, 10–12; study benefits and framework, 4–6, 12, 13*e*

Organizational Behavior Research Methods, 15

Organizational citizenship behavior (OCB), 50

Organizational culture, 278; changing, 283 (*see also* Change); consequences and implications, 280–282, 281*e*; determinants, 278–279; dimensions, 279–280; diversity success philosophy, 328 (*see also* Cultural diversity); favoring knowledge management, 313; workers learning, 280

Organizational design, 256

Organizational effectiveness, 5–6, 7, 280–282. *See also* Productivity

Organizational politics, 238. *See also* Influence; Power; contributing to bounded rationality, 71*e*, 73; control of dysfunctional, 249–250; factors contributing to, 242–244, 242–248; tactics, 245–248

Organizational spirituality, 280

Organization development (OD): large-scale change, 294–295; process consultation, 294; process model, 291–294, 292*e*, 293*e*; Six Sigma in, 296; total quality management in, 295–296

Organization structure, 256. *See also* Bureaucracy; case study, 255; centralization and complexity, 258; degree of formalization, 257–258; e-mail affecting, 162; formal versus informal, 257; hierarchy, 241, 242; horizontal, 268–269, 269*e*; mechanistic versus organic, 256; network, 269–270; organigraphs of, 270–271, 271*e*; tight versus loose coupling, 258–259

Output Technology Solutions, 291

Outsourcing, 268

Overdorf, Michael, 290

Ownership culture, 279–280

Pacific Rim countries, values, 331
Pakistani culture, ethics, 337
Paradigms, 170*e,* 171–172
Parochialism, 334
Participant observations, 3
Participative leadership: empowering
    workers, 240; path-goal theory, 218,
    218*e,* 219*e*; women using, 229
Path-goal theory of leadership, 217–218,
    218*e,* 219*e*
Patterson, Brad, 85
Peetz, John, 316
Penn Racquet Sports, 84–85
Peoples, Cynthia, 87
People supporter role, 190
Perception, 45–48. *See also* Attitudes
Perceptual distortions, 45–47, 46*e*
Perceptual expectations, 335
Performance orientation, 44
Performing stage, 189, 189*e*
Perkins Williamson, Addie, 1
Personal growth, 5
Personality, 30. *See also* Individual differ-
    ences; and cognitive styles, 33–34;
    contributing to bounded rationality,
    71*e,* 72; in creative people, 78; emo-
    tional intelligence, 34–36; factors and
    traits of, 30–33; types A and B, 147
Personality clash, 138
Personalization strategy, 315–316
Personalized power, 238–239
Personnel, selection standards, 11*e,* 314
Person-role conflict, 53, 149
Pessimism, 72, 147, 148
Peters, Tom, 289
PetsMart Inc., 85
Pet Supplies Plus, 85
Pfeffer, Jeffrey, 10, 125, 238, 248, 316
Philip Morris, 323
Philippine culture, etiquette, 341
Physiological needs, 88
Piskurich, George, 7
Pixar Animation Studios, 225
Plaff, Lawrence A., 229
Pleasant, Shannon, 226
Polarities, 213

Politics. *See* Organizational politics
Porsche Driving Experience, 183
Position power, 239
Positive reinforcement, 96, 117
Power, 238. *See also* Empowerment;
    Influence; Organizational politics;
    contacts, 245; linguistic style, 176–177;
    need for, 92–93; in network organiza-
    tion, 270; sharing (*see* Dual-executive
    teams); sources of, 238–240
Power approach, to sexual harassment,
    136
Power distance, 330–331
Practical intelligence, 28, 28*e*
Presentation technology, 163–164
Prévost Car, Inc., 183
Problems, 66, 68, 75
Problem solving, 195, 311
Process consultation, 294
Process observer role, 190
Procrastination, 71*e,* 74
Production-centered managers, 212–213
Productivity. *See also* Organizational
    effectiveness: bureaucracy affecting,
    262; and individual differences, 21;
    measuring group effectiveness, 193*e*;
    OB studies influencing, 6, 7; from
    people-focused management, 10, 11*e*;
    of self-managed teams, 115; sexual
    harassment affecting, 137; and
    stress, 144
Product-service departmentalization, 263,
    263*e*
Professional bureaucracy, 259
Programmed decisions, 66
Projection, distorting perception, 47
Projects, 185, 265. *See also* Cross-
    functional teams
Punishment, 97, 117, 119–120

Questioning, 198
Quick, Gary, 92
Quick Solutions, Inc., 92
quid pro quo harassment, 136
Qwest Communications International
    Inc., 54

Race. *See also* Cross-cultural behavior; Diversity; *individual races*: discrimination based on, 326; and diversity training, 339–340; harassment based on, 137; influencing organizational culture, 278

Racioethnicity, 25, 326

Ralston Purina Company, 85

Randolph, W. Alan, 241

Rationality, 248

Readiness, in situational leadership, 219

Recruiting, 314, 326, 329

Reengineering, 268–269

Referent power, 239, 240

Reinforcement theory, 96–97, 118–119

Relaxation response, 153

Religion, influencing values, 52

Repetitive strain injuries (RSI), 150

Research methods, 3–4

Resource dependence perspective, 239–240

Restructuring, as change strategy, 287–289

Reward and recognition. *See also* Job satisfaction; Motivation; Reinforcement theory: affecting creativity, 82; in applying OB Mod, 119–120; case studies, 109, 267; in goal-setting theory, 95; influencing organizational culture, 279, 313; interdependent, 193; linked to organizational goals, 121; motivation through, 121–122; and need for change, 295; as part of knowledge management, 313

Reward power, 239

Rightsizing, 267

Risk taking. *See also* Innovative thinking: affecting behavior and performance, 31; and cautious people, 72; in decision making, 66–67; and experimentation, 311; and group polarization, 197–198; in handling change, 296–297; and need for achievement, 92; self-assessment, 32; and uncertainty avoidance, 331

Robbins, Tina L., 199

Role ambiguity, 149

Role approach, to sexual harassment, 136

Role conflict, 148–149. *See also* Work-family conflict

Routine decisions. *See* Programmed decisions

Rubin, Garret, 107

Rudeness, causing conflict, 138

Rumors, 167–168. *See also* Gossip

Runkle, Rebecca, 207

Russia, 337

Russo, Carl, 226

Ryobi Die Casting USA, 159

Safety needs, 88–89

Safeway Stores, Inc., 149

Sajkovic, Alexander D., 120

Salvatore, Kimberly, 24

SAP (software company), 289

SAS Institute, 125

Satisfaction. *See* Job satisfaction

Satisficing decisions, 70

Scandinavian culture, values, 331

Schilling, Steve, 7

Scientific management, 6

Scott Paper, 15

Sears Roebuck, 16

SEI Investments, 188

Selective perception, 47

Self-actualization needs, 89

Self-awareness, 35

Self-concept, 296–297

Self-confidence, 210

Self-determination theory, 101, 103–104

Self-efficacy, 72, 97–98, 240

Self-esteem, 22

Self-managed work teams, 11*e,* 113–116, 115*e*

Self-management, 2, 230

Self-regulation, 35

Semantics, creating communication problems, 169, 170*e. See also* Vocabulary

Senge, Peter, 306

Senkala, Bonnie, 39

Sex. *See* Gender; Women

Sexual harassment, 89, 135–137, 137*e*

Shadish, William R., 4

Shaping, 42–43

Shared vision, 310

Sharing style of conflict resolution, 141, 141*e*

D. E. Shaw & Co., 65
Short-term orientation, 331
Signature Brands, 16
Simon, Herbert A., 70
Singapore, values, 331
Single-loop learning, 309
Situational control, 217
Situational leadership model, 218–220, 220e
Six Sigma, 296
Skinner, B. F., 96
Slocum, John W., 224
Smith, Douglas K., 184
Smith, James C., 159
Social entrepreneurs, 58
Socialization, 280
Socialized power, 238
Social learning, 100–101, 102–103
Social loafing, 198–199
Social needs, 89
Social network analysis, 257
Social Security Administration, 260
Social skill, 35
Social support, 152, 194
Socio-independent leadership, 217
Soft skills, 5
Sommer, Steven M., 337
Sorenson, Lynde, 156–157
Southwest Airlines, 278, 281
South-Western, 30, 88, 189, 262, 282
Spanish culture, values, 331
Spencer Stuart, 133
s (special) factor, 27, 27e
Staff groups, 135, 264–265
Stahl, Jack, 344
Stamatis, D. H., 142
Stanford University Business School, 316
Staples, 107
Starbucks, 123, 260
State License Documentation, 61
Steelcase, 279
Steffens, John L. (Launny), 244
Steo, Elsa, 163
Stereotyping: affecting cross-cultural relations, 335, 336; by age/generation, 51e; distorting perception, 46; by gender, 173–174
Stewart, Martha, 31, 163
Stock options, 123–124, 124e

Stone, Mark T., 313
Storch, Gerald, 156
Storming stage, 189, 189e
Strain, 144
Strategic alliances, 166–167
Stress, 144. *See also* Conflict; case study, 151; cybernetic theory of stress, coping, and well-being in organizations, 144; factors contributing to, 146–150, 147e, 149e; managing, 150–154, 153e; symptoms and consequences, 144–146
Stressor, 144
Structural integration, 335
Stussman, Howard B., 24
Subcultures, 280
Subordinate power, 239
Substitutes for leadership, 229–230, 289
Sunbeam, 15–16
Sundowner Offshore Services Inc., Oncale vs., 136
Sunglass Hut, 266
Sun Microsystems, 289
Sunriver resort, 129–130
Supportive leadership, 218, 218e, 219e, 225e
Surveys, 3, 113, 125, 327
Sutton, Robert I., 316
Sutton vs. United Air Lines, 26
Swanson, 78
Swanson, Clark, 78
Swanson, Gilbert, 78
Sweeney, Jim, 85
Swiss culture, rumors in, 168
Systematic investigation, 311
Systematic observations, 3
Systems thinking, 309–310

Taiwanese culture, motivation, values, and etiquette, 99, 330, 341
Take-charge leader role, 191
Take no prisoners strategy, 246
Tannen, Deborah, 176
Target Stores, 156–157, 290
Task forces. *See* Cross-functional teams
Task interdependence, 192
Teachable point of view method, 318
Team learning, 310

Teams. *See also* Groups: dual-executive, 208, 260; enhancing organizational effectiveness, 5–6; versus groups, 184; self-managed, 11*e,* 113–116, 115*e*; setting goals, 95

Team skills, 186

Teamwork, 183, 184, 200–202. *See also* Groups

Technical and Computer Graphics, 166–167

Technology. *See* Disruptive technology; Information technology

TeleCommute Solutions, 7

Telecommuting, 7, 107, 162–163

Teleworkers, 162–163

Territorial departmentalization, 262

Territorial games, 247–248

Testimonial time, 7

Theory X, 9

Theory Y, 9

THF Publications, 75

Thinking outside the box, 80

Thinking-type individuals, 33–34

Thoman, G. Richard, 207

Thomas, Gerry, 78

Thomas, H. Roosevelt, Jr., 339

360-degree survey, 227–228, 229

Tichy, Noel, 318

Time-driven model, 221, 222*e,* 223. *See also* Urgent time orientation

Time Warner, 102, 234

Tinsley, Catherine, 338

Top management teams, 185–187

Toro, 156–157

Total quality management (TQM), 295–296

Traditional thinking, 80

Training. *See also* Learning: diversity, 329, 339–341; for downsized employees, 289; for empowerment, 241; and group effectiveness, 194, 196; off-site/outdoor, 183, 201–202; and productivity, 11*e*; of self-managed teams, 115

Transformational leaders, 223–225, 225*e*

Treviño, Linda K., 55

Triant, Deborah, 71

Triarchic theory of intelligence, 28–29, 28*e,* 76

Trump, Donald, 240

Trust. *See also* Credibility: in charismatic leaders, 225; and conflict, 140, 143; and empowerment, 242; and leadership effectiveness, 210

Turf wars, 247

Turnover, indicating need for change, 295

Twins, 26–27

Two-factor theory of work motivation, 91–92, 91*e,* 110

Tyler, David, 39

Type A personality, 147

Type B personality, 147

Uncertainty avoidance, 331

Unfreezing-changing-refreezing model, 285, 285*e*

UNISYS, 73

United Air Lines, Sutton vs., 26

United Parcel Service (UPS), 279

Urgent time orientation, 331. *See also* Time-driven model

U.S. Army, 89

U.S. culture: conflict resolution model, 338–339 (*see also* Conflict); cultural values, 330, 331 (*see also* Values); ethics in, 337 (*see also* Ethics); rumors in, 168; value of time in, 176*e,* 331

U.S. Office of Personnel Management, 277

U.S. Postal Service, 291, 311

Utilitarianism, 54

Valence, 98

Valeo SA, 301

Value judgments, 170, 170*e*

Values. *See also* Ethics: affecting organizational behavior, 50–53; contributing to bounded rationality, 71*e,* 74; cross-cultural, 328, 330–333; influencing organizational culture, 278, 279

Van der Heyden, Ludo, 270

Van Guilder, Dan, 114

Vecchio, Robert P., 5

Vergara, Gail H., 133

Vergara, Herman, 133

Videoconferencing, 187

Vietnamese culture, etiquette, 341

Index

Virtual organizations, 269–270
Virtual teams, 187
Virtue ethics, 55
Vocabulary, for team building, 200, 201. *See also* Semantics
Voice-recognition systems, 164–165
Volo, Chuck, 301
Volvo Commercial Finance Inc., 183
Vroom, Victor, 220, 222, 223

Wale, Barbara, 39
The Wall Street Journal, 289
Wal-Mart, 16, 31, 173
Walton, Sam, 173
Waterman, 310
Weber, Max, 259, 262
Weida, Gregg R., 85
Weimrach, Larry, 73
Welch, Jack, 210, 226
Well-being, 137, 144. *See also* Conflict; Stress
Wellness program, 152
Welsh, Dianne H. B., 337
West, Al, 188
West, Robert B., 62
Western Electric, 8
Western New York Computing, 189
"What's in it for me?" (WIIFM) principle, 88
White, Roderick E., 308
Wilson, James, 16, 23

Winfire.com, 41
Win-win philosophy, 141–142
Witt, L. A., 249–250
Women. *See also* Gender: in construction jobs, 24; cultural diversity attracting, 326; marketing cars to, 336; versus men as leaders, 228–229; mentors for, 340; personal-professional balance, 133; sexual harassment affecting, 137
Work-family conflict, 133, 137–138, 151. *See also* Role conflict
Workload sharing, 194
Workplace violence, 139–140
World Environmental Organization, 7
Wright, Julie, 33
Wright, Tom, 114
www.com (Internet company), 41

Xerox Corp., 207, 208, 209, 270, 310
X Games, 19

Yahoo!, 233–234, 270
Yang, Jerry, 233
Yearwood, Clinton, 329
YourAccounts.com, 291
Your Office USA, 107

Zemin, Jiang, 226